The Bahamas Cruising Guide

A DOLPHIN-NOMAD BOOK

Mathew Wilson

INTERNATIONAL MARINE
Camden, Maine

International Marine/
Ragged Mountain Press

A Division of The McGraw·Hill Companies

The name International Marine and the International Marine logo are trademarks
of The McGraw-Hill Companies. Printed in the United States of America.

ISBN 0-07-052693-1
Library of Congress Cataloging-in-Publication data available.

Questions regarding the ordering of this book should be addressed to:
The McGraw-Hill Companies
Customer Service Department
PO Box 547, Blacklick, OH 43004
Retail customers: 1-800-262-4729 • Bookstores: 1-800-722-4726

Additional Content and Research

Port Information: Janet Wilson
Photographs (unless otherwise credited): Mathew Wilson

Dolphin Voyaging, Inc., 1340 US Highway 1, Suite 102, Jupiter, Florida 33469
Tel: 561-745-0445; fax: 561-745-0650

Book Production and Advertising

Chief Executive: Alexander Kahan; Editor: Susan Hale; Design: Molly Allen;
Cartography: Joe Faucher and David Morin; Electronic photo enhancement: Chris Scott

Nomad Communications, Inc., PO Box 875, Norwich, Vermont 05055
Tel: 802-649-1995; fax: 802-649-2667

On the cover: The colors of the Bahamas are evident in this photographic impression of Pidgeon Cay, Abaco.

The maps "The Commonwealth of the Bahamas" and "Hydrographic Chart of the Commonwealth of the Bahamas" are
reproduced with permission of the Bahamas Government Department of Lands and Surveys.

Publication history: First Edition 1998
Imprint is last number shown: 9 8 7 6 5 4 3 2

Acknowledgements

THE production of this guide would not have been possible without the sponsorship of the Bahamian Government and a number of other agencies, particularly American Airlines. On the pure marine side, the assistance of Cetrek USA, KVH Instruments, Resolution Mapping, and Sea Recovery are gratefully acknowledged. Nobeltec helped us through two successive versions of NavTrek, the last of which promises to make our life much easier in the future.

We would like to record our thanks to a number of individuals, Captain Clarence Warden Morris, ex-Navy flyer and one time senior pilot of Delta Air Lines, contributed to Northers and Hurricanes, and left us with its final conclusion. Maxine Williamson and Shena Newton of the Bahamas Ministry of Tourism helped us greatly, as did Christopher Lloyd and the staff of BASRA. We thank Dwight Watkins of the Lands and Surveys Department in Nassau, and gratefully acknowledge Bahamian Government permission to reproduce in part the Hydrographic Chart of the Bahamas and the map of The Commonwealth of the Bahamas. Andrew Halkitis and Charles Kemp of the Bahamas Telecommunications Corporation helped us with Batelco towers and we thank them. Jonathan Ramsay of Balmain Antiques in Nassau was invaluable in guiding us through his unique collection of ancient maps, old postcards, magazines, and photographs. He provided the autographed photograph of the Duke and Duchess of Windsor in Nassau in 1940. Mike Klonaris of The Octopus Angle Company transposed Jon Ramsey's antique maps, back copies of the Illustrated London News, and old photographs into our slide images.

Blue Magruder of Earthwatch in Boston put us in touch with Diane Claridge and Ken Balcombe, whose welcome contribution on marine mammals appears in our Green Pages section. Our space shots are due to NASA, whom we thank for their willing assistance, and in this connection Mary Green of the Earth Observation Satellite Company and Laura Gleasner of the Earth Data Analysis Center at the University of New Mexico were vital in their help.

There is no place in the Bahamas where we've not sought and received local advice, and our data owes as much to our willing mentors as it does to our own eyes. Perhaps a broad sample brings this alive. In Black Point in the Exumas Walter Robinson, *Blue Marlin* on VHF 16, guided our hand on anchorages and storm refuges. In Salt Pond, Long Island, Basil and Roger Fox of the fishing vessel *Promocean* helped us in our search for the "North West" Passage over the Bank, and in Mayaguana Captain "Cap" Brown was our guide during two days of research. With regret fieldwork spanning two years generates a list too long to serve a useful purpose in print, so we conclude simply with a big "Thank You" to the boat captains, seamen, and fishermen of the Bahamas, as well as the countless people running every kind of business from laundries to fruit stalls who have taken the time to welcome us, talk to us, hold our hands, and tell us about their islands.

Finally, I record my appreciation and delight at Dolphin Voyaging's "marriage" with Nomad Communications in the production of this Guide. I use the word "delight" quite deliberately. Without the intuition, foresight, and talent of Molly Allen, the patient, gentle, but rightly challenging editing of Susan Hale, and the graphic wizardry of Joe Faucher and David Morin, this book could never have taken its final form. No other team I know could have stayed not only sane, but still able to laugh in the manic final period of putting it all together as seemingly impossible deadlines closed in.

Table of Contents

Table of Charts

Table of Charts (continued)

Table of Yellow Pages

Part I

A Survival Manual

Introduction

The Lessons of 500 Years of Voyaging in Bahamian Waters

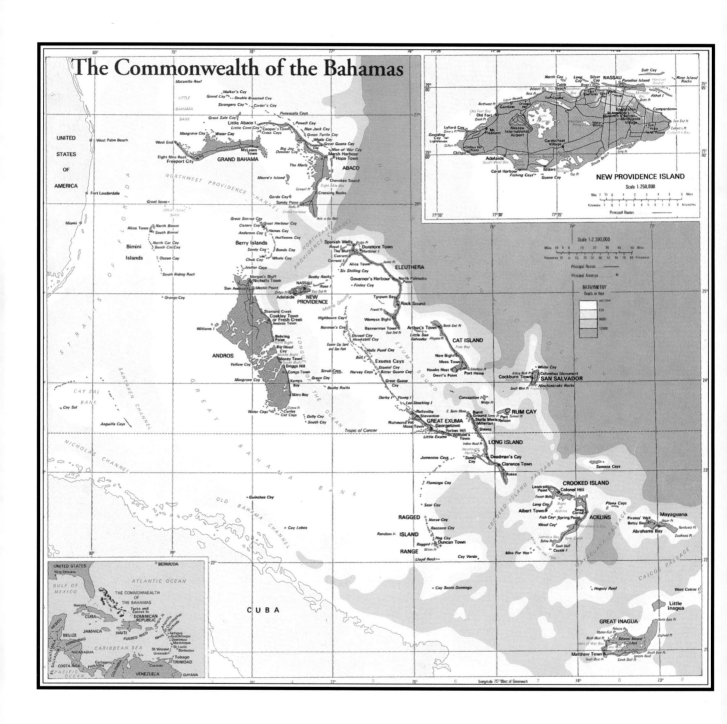

The Commonwealth of the Bahamas

Chapter 1
Introduction

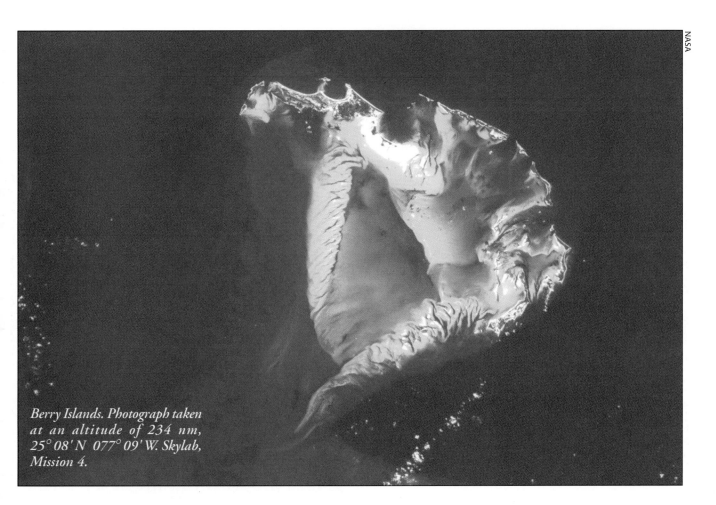

Berry Islands. Photograph taken at an altitude of 234 nm, 25° 08' N 077° 09' W. Skylab, Mission 4.

What Are These Islands?

LOOK down from space. Extending southeast from the east coast of Florida you'll see an ocean area of brilliant colors, turquoise seas, white sand, and specks of emerald, a scattering of islands and cays divided into contiguous groups by the dark sapphire blue tongues of deeper water. The larger islands stretch out for perhaps 100 miles in length but most of the cays are tiny, strung in chains like bracelets laid out under the spotlight of the sun.

Islands, Cays, and Keys

Let's get these Bahamian names right at the start. A *cay*, pronounced *key*, is a small, low-lying island, probably coral-fringed, mostly sand on a limestone-coral base. The word comes from the Spanish *cayo* (with the same meaning), which the early Spanish explorers took from Taino, language of the Arawaks, the indigenous island people whose extinction they brought about. It joins many other words, like barbecue (*barbacoa*), canoe (*canoa*), and hammock (*hammaca*) with the same origins. In the United States the word cay still survives today (misspelled) in the name Key West (*Cayo Oeste*, the westernmost cay).

As for an island, well, that's an island. Something bigger. You could say so big that if you're on one of the cays, it seems like a continental shore. Indeed Great Abaco Island, in the cays, is often referred to as "the mainland."

All around this magic area, save for one side, there is the deep water of the southwestern North Atlantic Ocean. It is some of the deepest ocean water in the hemisphere. On one side a narrow strait, the Florida Strait, separates the area from the east coast of Florida. Just 65 miles wide, the Florida Strait is far more than the continuance of the ocean around the islands: it's the mainstream course of one of the greatest

Pigeon Cay, Abaco.

maritime rivers in the world, the Gulf Stream. Immensely powerful, 45 miles wide here, the Gulf Stream flows north at 2.5 knots with the dynamic and thermal energy to create nightmarish seas from contrary north winds and, distantly, give the fortunate shores of its European landfalls exotic plants and mild winters, a climatic imitation of lands a thousand miles to their south.

A Cruising Ground?

If you draw lines around the Bahamas, you'll find that you've drawn a box that looks square on the map. Try it. Place your first line at 072° 30' W in the East, and the second at 079° 20' W in the West. In the North your line runs along 27° 25' N. In the South it's 20° 50' N.

Inside your box the islands run catty-corner, from the northwest to the southeast. If you try to count them you'll lose count around the 700 mark. If you try to work out the area contained within your square you'll settle for something like 90,000 square miles. Most of it is water. Perhaps it's simpler to say the islands are spread over something like 700 miles of ocean and circled with 900 square miles of coral reefs. And that ocean is deep. Within sight of land it is 10,000 feet deep, and the land by contrast is no more than 206 feet at its highest point.

But is it all ocean? No way. The Spanish called the area the *gran bahamar,* the "great shallow seas." There's nothing like it. It's a great tableland of limestone, coral, and sand, a raised reef-fringed platform on the edge of the Atlantic Ocean. Depths average 10–30 feet over much of the Bahamas but on all sides the ocean dropoffs plunge to depths your depth sounder will never register. The waters of the great shallow seas are something else, offering both clear sailing and a maze of reefs, coral heads, isolated rocks, and sandbores often too complex, and too subject to seasonal changes in the case of the sand, to be recorded accurately on a chart. The islands, as we've said, are low lying and average no more than 100 feet in elevation. This can give you identification problems, although their vegetation makes them relatively easy to pick up.

In the Bahamas safe navigation depends vitally on the colors we saw from space: the deep blues, the turquoise, the white, and the browns of reef and sea grass, and it also depends on the no-less-vital illumination of the sun. The Spanish, after losing seventeen treasure ships off the coast of Abaco in 1595, wisely avoided the sea they had named. It was no place for lumbering galleons, for them it was no place to be during the Northers of the winter months, and certain death if they were caught there by the hurricanes of the summer and early fall.

It's no bad thing to carry a sense of history as you cruise in Bahamian waters, but for us it's very different from the horror area dreaded by the Spanish. The Bahamas rates with the Virgin Islands, the Aegean, and Polynesia as one of the top boating destinations in the world. What more could you add to your wish list than 82°F water so crystal clear you can count the starfish on the bottom 30 feet below your keel, more places to explore than you'll ever find time to visit, with conditions just demanding enough to hone and prove your nautical skills, be it in a sailboat or a power boat?

It's the stuff of holiday dreams, sun, white sand, and palms, with more stars in the soft black velvet of the night skies than you'll have ever seen. Something like 20,000 US boats cruise in the Bahamas each year. The figures tell the story of how it is now.

Where to Go?
A Cruising Ground Analysis

It's a truism to say that the geography of the Bahamas has a profound effect on the cruising grounds the Bahamas offers. Generally where you have strings of small islands (the Abacos, Berrys, Exumas) you have good cruising grounds with infinite possibilities, whatever the weather. You can find places to explore, anchorages to tuck yourself into, and landfalls where you can get around on foot, or explore further by dinghy.

The big islands (Grand Bahama, Nassau, Eleuthera) are very different. Generally you have straight runs of open coast, few (if any) hidey-holes to explore or to use for shelter in adverse weather, and too much territory (if you want to see the sights) to get around other than by taxi (at high cost) or by taking a rental car. Eleuthera is perhaps the archetypal example of the "big" island seen in cruising terms.

Long and thin as it is, Eleuthera presents two coasts, the east (Atlantic) coast and the west (Eleuthera Bight) coast. The Atlantic coast has no shelter, near continuous offshore reefs, and is not a cruising ground. The west coast has only

What Are You Looking For?

Closest to the USA
Abacos
Andros
Berry Islands
Bimini Islands
Grand Bahama

Bimini

Best for Air Services to the USA
Abacos (essentially Marsh Harbour and Treasure Cay)
Bimini Islands (Bimini and Cat Cay)
Grand Bahama (Freeport)
Nassau (Paradise Island and Nassau International)
George Town

Best for Many Islands and Short Cruise Legs
Abacos
Exumas

Atlantis Casino, Nassau

Best for High Life
Grand Bahama
Nassau

Best for Short Legs and Ports of Call
Abacos

Best for Pretty Towns and Settlements
Abacos
Eleuthera

Best for Diving
Andros
Bimini Islands
Out Islands

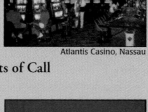
Hope Town, Elbow Cay, Abaco

Best for Sports Fishing
Abacos
Andros
Bimini Islands
Eleuthera

Best for Exploring
Abacos
Exumas
Out Islands

Bahamas Trophy

Best for Real Adventuring
Andros
Out Islands

Best for Getting Away from Everyone Else
Andros
Berry Islands
Out Islands

Palmetto Point, Eleuthera

three true, all-weather havens for the cruising boat, Hatchet Bay, Cape Eleuthera Marina, and Davis Harbour. In between there are places (Pelican Cay, Governor's Harbour, and Rock Sound) where you can find some kind of shelter, but overall you are fine travelling up and down the west coast of Eleuthera *if* the prevailing southeast winds are the weather of the day, and if this is so, you can safely anchor off most of the small villages; but in unsettled weather you have just those three options as your safety net.

Andros Island, the largest of the Bahamian islands (over 100 miles in length and 40 miles wide), favored with the third largest barrier reef in the world, would appear at first sight to be the most promising cruising ground you could imagine, but it's just not so. Much of Andros is a wilderness of mahogany and pine forest, scrub, marsh, tidal inlets, and flats. The barrier reef really is a barrier, and navigation inside the reef is hazardous.

Crew changes and the location of the nearest airport may well be a governing factor, and this, coupled with time available, often sets your limits. The decision of where to point your bow when you set off for the Bahamas is only yours to take. Your choice, as ever, must rest on what you want. Perhaps, if we give our assessment by categories, it may help your decision-making process.

What About the Time Factor?

Remember the meaning of time is entirely related to two factors, one under your control (at least in your initial choice of boat), and the other quite out of your control. The first is the passage speed and therefore the cruising range of your boat. The second is the weather. If you're unlucky, you might get holed up somewhere for eight days or so. It can happen. But let's assume that if time counts, you are not in a 30-knot express cruiser but a boat that will average somewhere between 5 and 8 knots on passage. Your time and space considerations (from the east coast of Florida) will come out to something like this:

One Week to 10 Days
Northern Abacos
Bimini Islands
Grand Bahama
Berry Islands

At Least Two Weeks
Abacos
Bimini Islands and the Berry Islands

One Month
Anywhere in the Northern or Central Cruising Grounds

Over a Month
You can reach the Far Horizons. But if the weather factor is not in your favor, you may find that just one month is not long enough.

About This Guide

This Guide is the First Edition of a series intended to be republished completely updated and improved every two years. Our aim has been to produce the best overall cruising guide to the Bahamas yet written, and the mission statement for Dolphin Voyaging, Inc., the parent company we set up to get the ball rolling, was simply "taking cruising guides into the 21st century." We hope we're getting there.

This is a guide for sail and power boat captains, it's not a tourist handbook. We deal with the land side, but only from a cruising boat angle. Even on the marine side we've had to be selective. With a target area spanning 7° of latitude and 7° of longitude, unless your guide is going to run into more than one volume, you can't go gunkholing up every creek. What we have done is to concentrate on a satellite view, to look down initially at each cruising area as it were from space, then make it comprehensible, and bring it to life covering the main routes, the main places, and placing hazard warning signs where necessary.

We're not just serving notice of a routine legal disclaimer when we say that this Guide is probably flawed in more than one place, and you should treat our advice with caution. We are still too close to the coal face to see the result of our shovel work. We recommend you study your charts, however outdated some of them may be, and take note of the utility of the excellent special-to-area guides now on the market. We all learn that safety lies in multiple references, and there are very few of us up there captaining a vessel who wouldn't agree that the more help we have at hand, the better.

This said, our purpose is to hold the hand of the first-timer and refresh the memory of the veteran, help you with

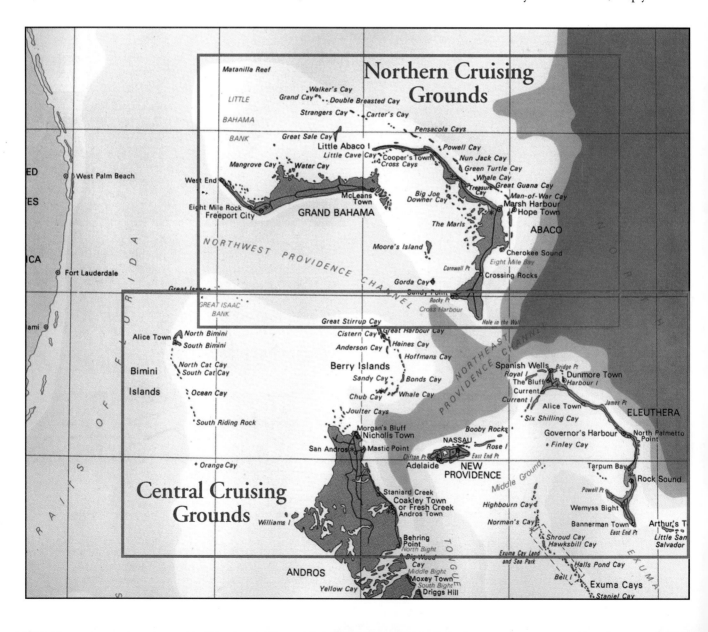

your planning and your day-to-day cruising in the Bahamas, and we hope you enjoy it. As the Contents show, the first part is devoted to general information designed to help take you safely to the Bahamas. The main part of the book deals with the Bahamas in three convenient parts:

- **The Northern Cruising Grounds**. The Little Bahama Bank passages, the Abacos, and Grand Bahama.

- **The Central Cruising Grounds**. The Bimini Islands, the passages across the Great Bahama Bank, the Berry Islands, Nassau, Spanish Wells, Harbour Island, Eleuthera, and Andros.

- **The Southern Cruising Grounds**. The passages across the Yellow Bank, the Exuma Cays and the Exuma Islands, and the Out Islands north of the Tropic of Cancer (23° 30' N).

More specialized areas, likely to be of interest only to those on passage to and from the Caribbean, and to the seasoned and dedicated explorer, are covered in one further part:

- **Far Horizons**. Under this we cover the Bahamas south of the Tropic of Cancer, the islands that are on your path to the Turks and Caicos (if you're incoming, the path that will lead you northwards), and included with this, the Unexplored Bahamas: South Andros and the Jumentos Cays.

Areas hazardous to navigation, which have never been regarded as cruising grounds, are not covered other than in passing reference. Immediately following each section are **Yellow Pages** that cover the shoreside in capsule form listing all the facilities you're likely to need, bars and restaurants, and shoreside accommodations, just in case you have shore-

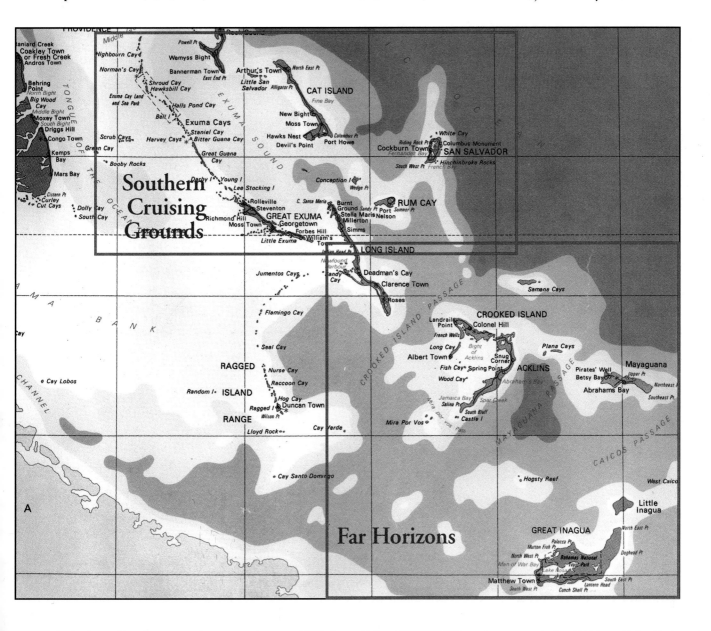

The Tropic of Cancer

The line of latitude running along 23° 30' N that marks the limit of the sun's summer migration into the Northern Hemisphere (it's the Tropic of Capricorn that sets the reverse limit in the South). Cross these lines and you're in the Tropics. In other words, coming from North America, you've got South. Real South. But more of this later under **The Far Horizons**.

based guests. Where there are annual local events, such as festivals and fishing competitions, we give the month in which they take place. The actual dates change from year to year. We conclude each **Yellow Pages** review with an entirely subjective list of **Things To Do**. We hope it's helpful.

We've taken great care to keep the Guide straightforward and easy to read and use, and we've not given unnecessary detail, nor endless reference to names that can well change. As for restaurants, we've made no attempt to grade them. A chef moves on, or a new owner takes over, and the standard of food can change dramatically. A refurbishment and new energy can alter a place almost beyond recognition. In the normal run of day-to-day life some days you get a good meal, and some days, for half a hundred reasons, it may be an "off" day. To judge a place on a single meal is unfair, and to run up flags for your favorites presumes that everyone else will feel the same way.

Three sections of colored reference pages follow the main sections of the Guide.

- The **Blue Pages** concentrate on Navigation, Seamanship, and Preparation.

- The **Green Pages** deal with the Environment, Recreation, and aspects of Bahamian life likely to be of General Interest to the cruising visitor.

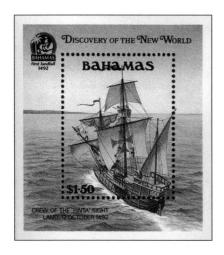

- The **Buff Pages** provide an "across the board" reference section on the Bahamian regulations and the Bahamian infrastructure, covering virtually all matters of concern to every captain flying a Bahamian courtesy flag, from Immigration and Customs, through Medical Facilities, to Duty Free Shopping.

This book will inevitably become dated from the time it goes to print. Other than geography and history, sooner or later almost everything will change, and it would be a miracle if we've not got some things wrong. This is a First Edition. Every subsequent edition will be followed by a later edition. We welcome your corrections and suggestions. For those who might have an interest in this kind of work, please see **A Recruitment Notice** in the final section of the Guidebook. As a point of interest, we settled on the two-year update span as being the only reasonable time frame for a cruising area the size of the Bahamas.

THIS IS A SERIOUS HEALTH WARNING!

Be warned that our maps and sketches are there to help you, but are NOT for navigation. Safe navigation is YOUR personal responsibility. Similarly our waypoints are there to show you how we played our voyaging, but your GPS and ours are unlikely to give identical readings. Therefore take care to build up a waypoint catalog you feel comfortable with, and don't take in blind trust the positions we selected. Please read what we have said under **GPS** in this Survival Manual on page 26.

Now you've had the real warning. We mean it. We've tried to hold out our hands to help you in every way we can, but take nothing on trust. All human beings are fallible. Do your own checking. Double check. Don't you always do it when you're navigating?

We wish you fair winds and raise our glasses to you in one toast that long before our time would bring any seaman to his feet. It was a toast to:

> The wind that blows
> The ship that goes
> And the lass that loved a sailor!

Your female crew may stay seated during the toast. Thank them for cruising with you!

With our best wishes,
Mathew Wilson

YELLOW PAGES

BAHAMAS GOVERNMENT TOURIST OFFICES

Area Code 242

Abaco Tourist Office, Marsh Harbour	367-3067
Bimini Tourist Office, Alice Town	347-3529
Eleuthera Tourist Office, Governor's Harbour	332-2142
Exuma Tourist Office, George Town	336-2430
Freeport, Grand Bahama, Ministry of Tourism	352-8044
Harbour Island Tourist Office, Harbour Island	333-2621
Nassau, Ministry of Tourism	322-7500
Nassau Tourist Information, Rawson Square, Nassau	326-9781

PORTS OF ENTRY

ABACOS
Walker's Cay, Green Turtle Cay, Marsh Harbour, Sandy Point, Spanish Cay (at weekends only), and Treasure Cay Marina

ANDROS
Fresh Creek

BERRY ISLANDS
Great Harbour Cay Marina and Chub Cay Club Marina

BIMINI
Brown's Marina, Sea Crest Marina, Bimini Big Game Club, and Bimini Blue Water Marina

CAT CAY
Cat Cay Club

CAT ISLAND
Smith Bay

ELEUTHERA, HARBOUR ISLAND, AND SPANISH WELLS
Governor's Harbour, Harbour Island, Rock Sound, and Spanish Wells

EXUMAS
George Town

GRAND BAHAMA
*Freeport Harbour, Bell Channel Marina, Port Lucaya Marina, Lucayan Village Marina, Running Mon Marina, Xanadu Beach Marina, and West End

GREAT INAGUA
Matthew Town

LONG ISLAND
Stella Maris Marina

MAYAGUANA
Abraham's Bay

NEW PROVIDENCE/NASSAU
Bayshore Marina, Brown's Boat Basin, *Clifton Pier, East Bay Yacht Basin, *John Alfred Dock, *Kelly's Dock, Lyford Cay Marina, *Nassau Harbour Dock West, Nassau Yacht Haven, and *Union Dock

PARADISE ISLAND
Hurricane Hole Marina

SAN SALVADOR
Cockburn Town

* denotes Ports of Entry primarily for commercial shipping

AIRLINE TOLL FREE NUMBERS

Air Canada	800-776-3000
American Eagle	800-433-7300
Bahamasair	800-222-4262
Carnival Airlines	800-437-2110
Delta	800-221-1212
Island Express	954-359-0380
Major Air	242-352-5778
Pan Am Air Bridge (formerly Chalk's International)	800-4-CHALKS
Paradise Island Airlines	800-432-8807
United Airlines (Gulfstream)	800-231-0856
US Air Express	800-622-1015

CHARTER AIRLINES

Cherokee Air	242-367-2089	Bahamas and Florida
Cleare Air	242-377-0431	Nassau only
Congo Air	242-377-8329	Nassau only
Dolphin Atlantic Airlines	800-353-8010	Florida
Island Air Charters	800-444-9904	Ft. Lauderdale only

AIRPORTS IN THE BAHAMAS

Airports shown in **bold type** are served by regular, scheduled airlines. Airports shown in normal type are used by Charter and Private aircraft.

ABACOS
Marsh Harbour
Spanish Cay
Treasure Cay
Walker's Cay

ANDROS
San Andros
Fresh Creek, Andros Town
Congo Town

BERRY ISLANDS
Chub Cay
Great Harbour Cay

BIMINI
Alice Town (sea plane only)
South Bimini
Cat Cay

CAT ISLAND
Arthur's Town
New Bight
Hawk's Nest

ELEUTHERA
Governor's Harbour
North Eleuthera for **Spanish Wells**
Rock Sound

EXUMAS
Norman's Cay
Sampson Cay
Staniel Cay
Black Point
Farmer's Cay
Moss Town, for **George Town**

GRAND BAHAMA
Freeport

INAGUA
Great Inagua

LONG ISLAND
Deadman's Cay
Stella Maris

MAYAGUANA
Mayaguana

NEW PROVIDENCE
Nassau International
Paradise Island

RUM CAY
Rum Cay

SAN SALVADOR
San Salvador

REFUELING IN THE BAHAMAS

NORTHERN CRUISING GROUNDS

ABACOS
Coopers Town
Elbow Cay Hope Town *Lighthouse Marina*
Elbow Cay White Sound *Sea Spray Marina*
Fox Town
Grand Cay
Green Turtle Cay Black Sound *The Other Shore Club*
Green Turtle Cay White Sound *Bluff House Marina, Green Turtle Club*
Man-O-War *Man-O-War Marina*
Marsh Harbour all the marinas except *Mangoes*
Spanish Cay *Spanish Cay Marina*
Treasure Cay *Treasure Cay Marina*
Walker's Cay *Walker's Cay Marina*

GRAND BAHAMA
Freeport *Running Mon Marina, Xanadu Beach Marina*
Port Lucaya *Lucayan Marina Village*, *Port Lucaya Marina*
West End *Harbour Hotel and Marina, Jack Tar Marina*

CENTRAL CRUISING GROUNDS

ANDROS
Fresh Creek *Lighthouse Yacht Club*
Morgan's Bluff contact *Willy's Water Lounge*

BERRY ISLANDS|
Chub Cay *Chub Cay Club*
Great Harbour Cay *Great Harbour Cay Marina*

BIMINI
Bimini Big Game Club, Bimini Blue Water

CAT CAY
Cat Cay Club Marina

ELEUTHERA
Harbour Island *Harbour Island Club* and *Valentine's Yacht Club*
Spanish Wells *Spanish Wells Marine and Hardware, Spanish Wells Yacht Haven*
South Eleuthera *Cape Eleuthera Marina* and *Davis Harbour Marina*

NASSAU NEW PROVIDENCE ISLAND
Bayshore Marina, Brown's Boat Basin, Claridge Marina, East Bay Marina, Harbour View Marina, Lyford Cay Club, Maura's Marine, Nassau Harbour Club, Nassau Yacht Haven

NASSAU PARADISE ISLAND
Hurricane Hole Marina, Paradise Harbour Club

SOUTHERN CRUISING GROUNDS

EXUMAS
Highborne Cay
Little Farmer's Cay *Farmers Cay Yacht Club*
Sampson Cay *Sampson Cay Club*
Staniel Cay *Staniel Cay Yacht Club*
George Town in **Great Exuma** *Exuma Docking Services*

CAT ISLAND
Smith Bay Government Dock, contact *New Bight Service Station* on VHF 16

RUM CAY
Sumner Point Marina

SAN SALVADOR
Riding Rock Inn Marina

LONG ISLAND NORTH
Stella Maris Marina

FAR HORIZONS

CROOKED ISLAND
Landrail Point
You can refuel can by can at the Government Dock if they have it available

GREAT INAGUA
Matthew Town (diesel fuel only)

LONG ISLAND SOUTH
Clarence Town Government Dock, contact *Henry Major*
Salt Pond, contact *Basil Fox*

MAYAGUANA
Betsy Bay Government Dock, contact *Batelco*

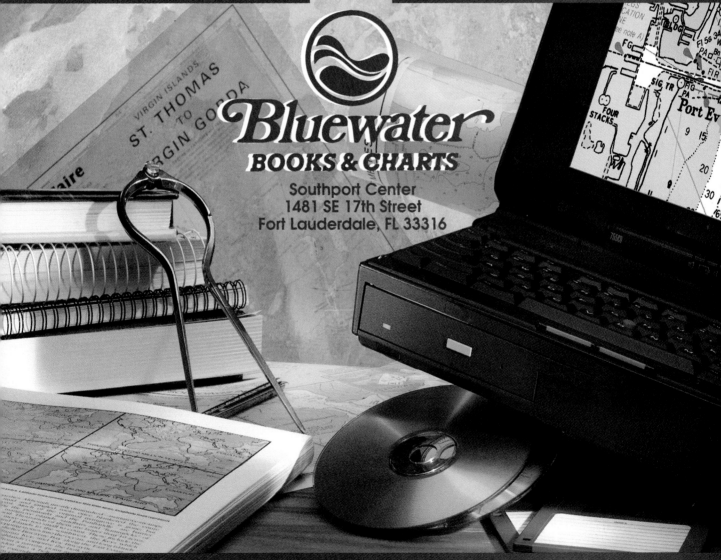

Chapter 2
The Lessons of 500 Years of
Voyaging in Bahamian Waters

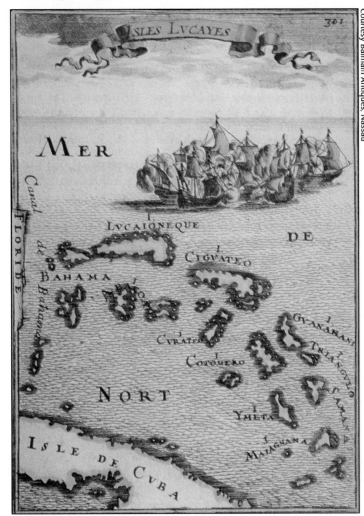

Ocean Approaches. One of the first charts of the Bahamas, drawn by the French map maker Alain Manesson Mallet (1630–1706). The shape of Cuba had been fairly accurately established by the Spanish by 1650, but the Bahamas were still unexplored, uncharted, and a high-risk area.

Ocean Approaches

Recommended Charts

INT 400/DMA 400	North Atlantic Ocean West Indies
DMA 27005	Key West to San Juan

For the ocean voyager there are as many routes into the Bahamas as there are navigable passes through the fringing reefs and gaps between the islands. On the shorter approaches from the Florida coast your departure port and route is decided when you've chosen your destination cruising ground, and your entry port options follow from this.

If you're coming from the south after a longer bluewater passage you may wish to make your entry port a place where most conventional commercial facilities are available, rather than fastening on a relatively isolated Out Island settlement,

but your options are always dictated by your eventual destination. Whatever you choose to do, it's sensible to keep your approach voyage into the Bahamas low stress.

- Don't arrive off your first landfall during the night. Use daylight to advantage.

- Keep the position of the sun in mind when you work out the time of your passing into shallow water. You want it behind you.

- Keep the navigation simple.

The routes we've chosen are the most common approaches. Those involving an initial Gulf Stream crossing will be covered in greater detail under **Crossing the Gulf Stream** on page 20.

From the West (Florida)

Recommended Charts

DMA 26300	Little Bahama Bank to Eleuthera Island
DMA 26320	Northern Part of Straits of Florida and Northwest Providence Channel

FOR THE ABACOS

Bound for the Abacos, the most popular approach is to head for West End in Grand Bahama, clear in there, and then enter the Little Bahama Bank the next day by way of Indian Cay Passage. This will take you to the Abacos by way of Mangrove and Great Sale Cays. As Indian Cay Passage carries no more than 5.5 feet at mean low water (MLW), if you have a deep keel you may have to discard this option and take the Memory Rock approach.

The way by Memory Rock is favored by those who wish to take their approach as a straight shot to the Abacos and clear in at their destination. You enter the Little Bahama Bank either just north or south of Memory Rock, and carry on to Great Sale Cay if you have to overnight on the way. Once you reach the Abacos, your entry ports could be Walker's Cay, Green Turtle Cay, or Marsh Harbour.

A popular alternative to these two routes is to head for Lucaya in Grand Bahama and take the Grand Lucayan Waterway to gain access to the Little Bahama Bank at Dover Sound, to the south of Mangrove Cay. Be warned that there is a fixed bridge with only 27-foot clearance on the canal, and the Dover Sound Channel carries only 4 feet of water at MLW. If you can make use of this shortcut, however, the saving in time is appreciable.

FOR GRAND BAHAMA

If you're making for Port Lucaya, the only way to go is to take it as a direct run from your Florida departure port.

FOR NASSAU AND THE EXUMAS

If you're bound for the Southern Berrys (Chub Cay), Nassau, the Exumas, or Eleuthera, the Bimini Islands are well placed to serve as your first staging point and entry port (your choices are either Alice Town on North Bimini, or Cat Cay). One way or another, your route will take you through Gun Cay Cut before you cross the Great Bahama Bank to the Northwest Channel Light. From there your route goes on to Chub Cay and, if you wish, straight on to Nassau.

WARNING

There's been shoaling on the Great Bahama Bank to the east of Gun Cay and Cat Cay. If you draw over 6 feet, you would be wise to make use of the tide on this first part of your Great Bahama Bank transit.

Alternatively you could set your course to pass north of the Bimini Islands to Great Isaac Light, and make Nassau your entry port. You'll have deep water all the way, plenty of sea room, and no navigational problems. All you have to decide is whether you want to stop in the Northern Berry Islands on the way, or take the Northwest Providence Channel down to Nassau.

Fort Lauderdale and Miami are the favored departure points for these routes.

The Gulf Stream Factor

Setting out for the Bahamas from Florida inevitably dictates a Gulf Stream crossing at the start of your voyage. For slower boats the further south (within reason!) you make your departure point the better. You'll want to gain the advantage of the push of the Stream. If you fight it, your crossing will become a tough crablike crawl across the Florida Strait.

From the South and the Southeast (the Caribbean and the Turks and Caicos)

Recommended Charts

DMA 26260	Passages between Acklins Island, Haiti, and Caicos Island
DMA 26240	Crooked Island Passage to Cabo Maisi
DMA 26280	Eleuthera Island to Crooked Island Passage
DMA 26282	Andros Island to San Salvador

Whatever your original start point, the Virgin Islands, Puerto Rico, or the Dominican Republic, the Turks and Caicos Islands lie squarely in your path to the Bahamas, and Providenciales makes an ideal stopping point if you want to break your journey. From then on the simplest and most straightforward plan is to select George Town on Great Exuma Island as your entry port. Your route will take you in deep water to the east of Acklins, Crooked, and Long Islands before you turn west toward George Town on your final leg.

There are two places of concern. The first is the passage between the Plana Cays and the northern end of Acklins Island. You have plenty of sea room there, but you must make sure that you are not being set closer to land than you'd wish. The second is to resist the temptation to round Cape Santa Maria on the northern tip of Long Island too closely. Stand well out before making your turn to the west. The Cape was previously supposed to mark the northern limit of the blind wanderings of Christopher Columbus immediately after his Bahamian landfall in October 1492. Now it is generally believed that he never got this far north, although he did reach Long Island. Had he continued northward, as he had been heading, he might well have discovered America. Instead he turned south, and found Cuba.

Terrapin *making a Bahamian landfall.*

From the Southwest (Havana and the Gulf of Mexico)

Recommended Charts

NOAA 11460	Cape Canaveral to Key West
DMA 26320	Northern Part of Straits of Florida and Northwest Providence Channel

Perhaps the southwestern approach is the easiest of them all. Just ride with the Gulf Stream as if you were a Spanish galleon and turn to the east when you reach the right latitude to make your chosen landfall.

Charts, Maps, and Books

You will find many of the charts, maps, and books mentioned in this Guide at your local marine store. Bluewater Books & Charts specializes in the Bahamas and Caribbean (1481 SE 17th Street, Fort Lauderdale, Florida 33316; Tel: 954-763-6533 or 800-942-2583, Fax: 954-522-2278). West Marine (PO Box 50050, Watsonville, California 95077-5050; Tel: 800-538-0775) is also a useful source.

At this stage of your planning you might also want to consider buying *The Bahamas Chart Kit* published by the Better Boating Association, Inc. (PO Box 404, 10 Commerce Road, Rockland, MA 02370; Tel: 617-982-4060). The kit is available from the Association, or from marine stores.

Northers and Hurricanes— Defining the Cruising Season

In any travel agency they'll tell you the Bahamian climate is near-perfect. In the winter (mid-December to mid-April) the temperature is 70–80°F (21–26°C). In the summer (mid-April to well into the fall) the daytime temperature is 80–90°F (26–32°C). A 12° difference. That's all. Humidity throughout the year runs 75–80 percent, but there's almost always a cooling breeze. Even in summer, heat and humidity rarely clamp down. Days and hours of per-day sunshine are high throughout the year with the summer index winning over winter. As for rainfall, the summer brings squalls and thunderstorms, which produce short bursts of torrential rain, but even in the gray weather produced by a Norther in winter, rainfall rarely lasts long.

What about hurricanes? The Bahamas, like the east coast of the US and the islands of the Caribbean from Barbados northward, lie in the hurricane zone. June to November is the hurricane season, and August, September, and October are the high-risk months. Does this count the Bahamas out for summer cruising? The answer is "no." You can expect maybe two bad storms a year, they'll tell you, but you'll get plenty of warning. This said, winter or summer, hurricane season or not, it makes sense to study Bahamian weather patterns before you set out.

The Bahamian Winter

The North American mainland is the primary driving force behind Bahamian winter weather. What happens in Canada and the continental US inevitably affects the Bahamas, sometimes a day or two later, sometimes sooner. If an Alberta Clipper brings sub-zero temperatures down across the Eastern States, you'll feel the cold as far south as George Town in the Exumas. If winter storms driving down from the northern quadrants blast Florida, the prevailing southeast Bahamian winds lose out and the North American "Norther" will take over, dominating what happens in the Abacos, Nassau, and as far south as the Out Islands. Sometimes the effects of a Norther will be felt as far south as Puerto Rico.

NORTHERS

This change to a winter weather pattern starts around mid-November. The wind cycle is largely predictable. In the Bahamas, as on the east coast of Florida, the wind first veers to the south and then to the southwest as a cold front starts driving down from the north. As the front comes closer the wind shifts to the northwest, then to the north, and then to the northeast. The strongest winds come just ahead of the cold front. During a Norther you can expect wild seas over the Gulf Stream and steep waves over the Banks. Wind strengths can reach Force 8 (34–40 knots), occasionally higher, and Force 6 (22–27 knots) is what you'll experience in the early period before the front arrives.

A Norther can last for days, or blow through within 24 hours. Sometimes a second Norther follows on the heels of the first so fast the wind shifts from northeast or east to northwest, and you get no break. Sometimes, just about when you think it's blown out, a Norther recharges itself and you get another two days.

As the Norther works itself out, the wind moves around to the east, and then stabilizes where it would like to be, in the southeast.

RAGES

You must also be aware that rough seas can build up within hours on the barrier reefs fringing the Atlantic Ocean, and normally navigable passages through the reefs become impassable. This is the deadly sea state the Bahamians call a "Rage." If there's any risk of Rage conditions you must take the threat seriously. It's always prudent to seek out local advice before setting out on a passage through the reefs at any time, winter or summer. Distant North Atlantic storms can create swells that will produce the same phenomenon. You will not survive to relate the experience if you attempt to force your way through a reef passage in a Rage.

KEEPING AN EYE ON THE WINTER WEATHER

Northers are never surprises. Just pay attention to North American weather. Eastern US weather forecasts and Nassau Radio give you ample warning of what is going to happen. In the Bahamas you'll note that wind shift, see the dark clouds build up, and then you'll get the wind and the rain.

What this cycle dictates is that you take careful note of the weather pattern before you cross the Gulf Stream, and in the Bahamas you work out where you'll go for shelter in the event of a Norther before you move on another stage in your cruising itinerary. Depending on the wind state, a Norther does not necessarily keep you penned in a harbor or captive in your anchorage. Sailboats can take advantage of the wind direction, and power boats, given the right sea state, can go largely where they will.

The Northers can make the winter sound like a no-no season for cruising in the Bahamas, but it's just not true. Normal winter conditions are your 70–80°F temperatures, Force 3–4 (7–16 knot) southeast winds, sun every day, and occasional squalls to wash the salt off your decks (you'll appreciate that, for fresh water is expensive in the islands). The famous colors of the water are there, the water temperature is around 73–75°F, and winter water visibility is 60–100 feet on average.

Northers can break this pattern and give you days when you're holed up, waiting to move on; but when they come, the Northers often bring exceptional clarity of air, a light that gives the Bahamas the intensity of a color slide, and a chill in the night air that's sometimes welcome. If you get cabin fever waiting out your first, second, or third Norther, work your way south. The further south you go, the less you'll be troubled by the tail-ends of the storms that plague the commuters of the Mid-Atlantic States and the citrus growers of Florida in the winter months.

Above, an approaching front, the clear sign of a marked imminent change. You are in for a complete reversal of the conditions you've been enjoying. Expect temperature change, an immediate increase in wind, the wind to veer, and low visibility. As the marked edge of the front passes through, the weather will settle into a new pattern (depending on whether it's a warm front or a cold front). If it's only a weak front, the disturbance in the more normal regular weather pattern may be brief, perhaps a matter of hours, or even less.

Below, the darkening weather of a rain squall. At best just rain, but never take it on trust. The front-like line of rain may carry high wind, sudden changes of wind direction, and gusts that are surprisingly strong. Be prepared to take it. Rain in sub-tropic and tropic waters is rarely just a gentle shower.

The Bahamian Summer

By May the Northers of winter will be history and the summer wind pattern settles to the influence of the southeast Trade Winds far to the south, giving wind from the southern quadrants for most of the time. The wind strength settles to an average 5–12 knots, enough to give you your sailing, and calms at night are more frequent than they are in the winter. Water temperatures rise in summer to around 85°F, and water visibility drops slightly to average 50–70 feet.

THUNDERSTORMS

Thunderstorms are a feature of the summer months. Anvil-headed cumulonimbus clouds build up over solar super-heated land and shallows, and you can expect everything that goes with a thunderstorm when they let loose, rain that seems as heavy as lead pellets, hail, lightning, thunder, and violent (60-knot) downdrafts. Microbursts with winds over 100 knots are, mercifully, rare events.

The towering summer anvil heads are one-off, one-cloud dramas. Isolated thunderstorms are always obvious, one-hour affairs for the most part, and normally develop and hit their point of discharge in the late afternoon. Out in the ocean, on a bluewater passage, you can expect a thunderstorm to

Towering, turbulent clouds, a highly visible danger signal. Expect thunder and lightning, heavy rain, visibility of less than 300 feet, a marked drop in temperature, and wind that at worst could hit gusts of between 40 and 60 knots. It will not last, but unless you are in safe, deep water, well clear of land and reefs, it is a threat to be taken seriously. Take precautionary action early (anchor somewhere safe, batten down). Your warning is the clouds. The accompanying fall in barometric pressure usually comes as it hits.

"go critical" during the night hours. If you're on passage, stay well clear of a developing thunderstorm. Radar, if you have it, is a great bonus for thunderstorm avoidance. If you are at risk, take your canvas down and batten down.

LIGHTNING STRIKES

How likely is it that you might be struck by lightning? Statistics published by the Marine Insurance division of BOAT/US give these figures (the base being any given year):

Auxiliary Sail	0.6%	6 out of 1,000
Multi-hull Sail	0.5%	5 out of 1,000
Trawlers	0.3%	3 out of 1,000
Sail only	0.2%	2 out of 1,000
Cruisers	0.1%	1 out of 1,000
Runabouts	0.02%	2 out of 10,000

Our research vessel, *Dolphin Voyager*, was one of the 0.3 percent. We had left her in the Central Exumas to fly back to the States for a week of meetings about this book. During that time a succession of unusually violent thunderstorms hit the Bahamas. The induced surge of a lightning strike, which found a target close to *Dolphin Voyager*, paralyzed the electronics, took out the battery charger, and fried the batteries. Don't be put off by this cautionary tale. Just look at the statistics. But pay those insurance premiums.

WATERSPOUTS

In the summer months you'll also see waterspouts that, although they may move erratically, can usually be avoided. Don't be tempted to sail through one. A waterspout is a marine tornado, short-lived normally, but still dangerous.

DON'T BE SURPRISED BY THE WEATHER

Bahamian weather never ceases to surprise. Yes, there are patterns to the winter months and patterns to the summer months, but we've crossed the Little Bahama Bank in early March in dead calm, literally counting starfish on the bottom as we passed. In late May, when the summer pattern should have been established, we've had 7 inches of rain in 24 hours at Man-O-War Cay together with 45-knot winds, and this "nasty" came as part of a three-day package of unrelenting grey skies, rainstorm after rainstorm, with winds flicking round the clock like a cow's tail in the black fly season.

Maybe we have changed the world's climate in the last century? But on the whole the Bahamas has a weather factor that still rates it as one of the best cruising areas you can find. Have faith. Bad weather never lasts forever, and the good days and the good weeks are magic.

Hurricane Season

The North Atlantic–Caribbean hurricane season runs June 1 to November 30. August, September, and October are the worst months. Seasonally, an average of ten depressions or tropical waves develop into tropical storms and reach "name" status. On average, eight of these will become severe storms and ultimately reach hurricane status.

No one would wish to risk being caught by a hurricane, but in many ways the hurricane months offer the best cruising in the Bahamas, and are not necessarily ruled out of your voyaging calendar as a high-risk period. Hurricane forecasting is accurate and will give you, from the first warnings of the development of a tropical wave, plenty of time to think ahead. When the warnings move up a notch into a tropical depression you should really focus on the weather and your planning moves into an active phase. It follows that to understand the dynamics of the hurricane development and learn the rules of hurricane avoidance, you must first be familiar with the language of the hurricane season.

TROPICAL WAVES

A tropical wave is a trough of low pressure. A wave shows itself with falling barometric pressure, overcast skies, and the arrival of a succession of mini-fronts, high wind, rain and thunderstorms, with periods of relative calm and rain in between. A tropical wave is born in the Atlantic and its movement is always westward and northward. The trough can pass through quickly, or may linger, nearly stationery, for days. You could say that a wave is an embryonic hurricane. If the pressure dropped dramatically and the winds started to revolve around the center of low pressure, that's exactly what you would have.

The forecast of a wave may persuade you to sit out its passing in comfort rather than set out on your next passage, and it will interrupt your sunbathing. If you're at sea, a wave is no severe threat to your safety but it does bring with it all the characteristics of a succession of line squalls, which means reefing if you're under sail, closing hatches, and concern for the dinghy you may be towing.

TROPICAL DEPRESSIONS

A tropical depression is the next stage. It's the development of the wave into a system of clouds and thunderstorms with a definite circulation, always counterclockwise in the Northern hemisphere. Top sustained winds are no more than Force 7 (28–33 knots) but gusts will be stronger.

TROPICAL STORMS

A tropical storm is the next step in the evolution of a hurricane. By now it's getting serious. At the outset sustained winds are up to Force 9 (41–47 knots), and gusts will be stronger. The counterclockwise rotation continues, and the storm will have a recognizable center. It's important to realize that the rotation of the storm is not simply circular but takes the form of a spiral, with the wind working inward toward the eye of the storm. This understanding plays a part in your storm evasion tactics if you're caught out at sea.

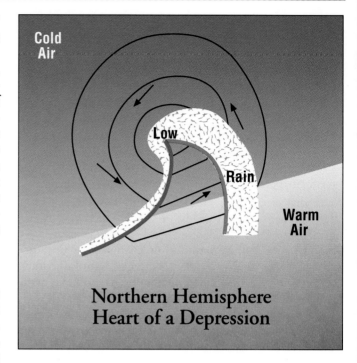

**Northern Hemisphere
Heart of a Depression**

A severe tropical storm moves into the Force 10 or Force 11 field with wind strength increasing to 63 knots.

The forward speed of a storm usually averages around 10 knots in its early days, and its course, which can be erratic, usually holds west and north. Warm water generally gives a tropical storm the energy burst it needs, and the Gulf Stream often becomes a hurricane interstate highway for this reason.

HURRICANES

When the sustained wind speed of a tropical storm exceeds 63 knots you are in the Force 12 bracket and you have a hurricane. From then on, although hurricanes are classed in order of magnitude as the wind speed goes up, from a cruiser's point-of-view it hardly matters. The highest recorded gusts have hit 175 knots, but the start point, 64-knot winds, is bad enough.

The forward speed of a hurricane, by record, is likely to average 20–25 knots. A speed of 40 knots has been known. The message is that you cannot outrun a hurricane at close quarters, and your evasion tactics (if you are caught in the danger area) hang totally on your careful plotting of its position and course. You must also plot its radius, in which broadly you'll find something like these figures as danger zones:

Distance from the Eye	Wind Speed
150 miles	Force 8 (34-40 knots)
100 miles	Force 11 (56-63 knots)
75 miles	Force 12 (over 64 knots)

Be aware that every hurricane develops its own unique intensity and footprint. These figures are no more than a generalization and must not be used for planning purposes.

STORM SURGE

Above high winds and waves, hurricanes carry with them a third agent of destruction, which is *storm surge*. A dome of water up to 20-feet high forms, if you like, the ocean pedestal of that spiral movement. This massive piling up, this mountain of water, may have as much as a 100-mile diameter. When it hits land, particularly if the hurricane coincides with high tide, storm surge is often the principal cause of hurricane deaths and damage.

STORM WARNINGS

The hurricane warning system is simple, will always give the area to which the forecast applies, and is based on one of two conditions, either tropical storm, or hurricane:

A **Watch** Alert   36 hours

A **Warning** Alert   24 hours

Long before you might find yourself listening to a Tropical Storm Watch (or even worse a Hurricane Watch) you should have anticipated the weather and be out of the danger area.

PLAYING IT SAFE IN THE HURRICANE SEASON

If you're cruising through the islands during the hurricane months, the rules you must follow are:

- Plot the location of every hurricane harbor or potential hurricane hole along your route.

- Set out with the extra ground tackle and extra dock lines on board to secure your boat against a severe storm, be it at anchor, in mangroves, or wherever.

Hurricane Categorization

Category	Pressure	Wind Speed	Surge	Damage Forecast
1	>980 mb (>28.94 in.)	64–83 knots (74–95 mph)	4–5 ft.	Not extensive
2	965–979 mb (28.50–28.91 in.)	84–96 knots (96–110 mph)	6–8 ft.	Getting worse
3	945–964 mb (27.91–28.47 in.)	97–113 knots (111–130 mph)	9–12 ft.	Extensive
4	920–944 mb (27.17–27.88 in.)	114–135 knots (131–155 mph)	13–18 ft.	Extreme
5	<920 mb (<27.17 in.)	>135 knots (>155 mph)	>18 ft.	Catastrophic

- Listen to a reliable weather forecast service at least once every day. Remote as it may seem, you must know what's happening in the North Atlantic Ocean between 07° and 20° N, and in the Southwest Caribbean Sea in much the same latitude. These are the hurricane breeding grounds.

- Use a plotting chart to record and follow the progress of all tropical systems.

- When a tropical storm or a hurricane is 250 miles away or so, and its track is projected into your area, you should think seriously about getting clear immediately. At this stage, depending on your speed, your location, and your distance to run to safety, you may be able to get right out of it.

- If you find yourself caught in the forecast path of an approaching tropical storm or a hurricane, take it very seriously. Take immediate action to seek the nearest hurricane hole or shelter. Don't try to outrun the storm.

SECURING YOUR BOAT

- Mangroves are ideal. Canals are good. Any landlocked water is better than open water. Try to get away from other boats. Their lines may not hold.

- Secure your boat. Use every line you have and all your ground tackle. Allow for storm surge.

- Reduce windage. No canvas or curtains of any kind should be above deck.

- Batten down, and leave the boat. Find shelter ashore. Don't stay on your boat. Your life counts. The boat can take care of itself; and you have insurance.

IN THE WORST CASE

If, in the worst case, you get caught at sea, it's vital to know your position in relation to the eye of the hurricane, and the predicted track of the hurricane at that time. If you don't know where the center of the hurricane is, if the wind is veering, you're in the *dangerous* semicircle. If the wind seems steady, or starts to back, you're in the *navigable* semicircle.

THE DANGEROUS SEMICIRCLE

The most dangerous half of the storm is the *northern* semicircle, the part that lies to the north of the path of the hurricane. It has this name because if you're caught in this area, you're in the path of the hurricane and its spiral rotation will take you deeper into its center. Your only hope is to try to break away to the north, and then get behind the worst of it.

Your immediate evasive action is get away with all the speed you can make, keeping the wind 10–45° on your starboard bow, and keep altering to starboard to take you above and eastward away from the storm.

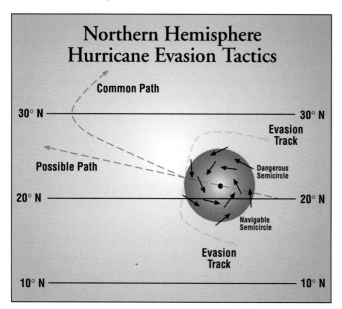

Northern Hemisphere Hurricane Evasion Tactics

THE NAVIGABLE SEMICIRCLE

The southern semicircle is known as the *navigable* semicircle, simply because your chances are better there. The hurricane will be moving away from you rather than toward you, and the direction of the wind will blow you away from the storm.

Your immediate evasive action is turn to bring the wind on your starboard quarter, make all possible speed, and keep turning to port to pass below and eastward away from the storm.

WEATHER BROADCASTS

Weather broadcasts are covered in the **Blue Pages** of this Guide on page 300.

A fishing vessel left high and dry by a hurricane.

Crossing the Gulf Stream

The Gulf Stream

For any vessel crossing to the Bahamas from the east coast of Florida or returning to Florida, the Gulf Stream is the dominant navigational consideration. Don't imagine it as a current. It's a 45-mile-wide river, more powerful than you think. You can't see the wash of its speed as you would if you were standing on a river bank, but it's always there, flowing northward at an average speed of 2.5 knots, day and night, in every season. It's hard to believe at first that it even exists when you look east from a Florida beach, out over the ocean.

In winter you can sometimes mark the Gulf Stream by the steam rising from its warm waters, degrees warmer than the colder coastal water. In winter too, and whenever a Norther is blowing, the sea horizon is often jagged, saw-toothed. That's when there are "elephants" out there, giant square waves, high seas kicked up by the Stream's determination to win its way north against the wind, come what may.

In summer you can identify the Gulf Stream by a color change to an ultramarine deep blue in which sometimes, if the sun is right, you will see light dancing in its depths. You can guess you're in the Stream when you see corn blond patches of Sargasso weed drifting north. You know you're there when the water temperature clicks up something like 2° above the shoreside ocean temperature, and your GPS shows you moving 2 to 5 knots faster to the north than your knotmaster indicates. Fishermen, tuned to the rhythm of ocean life, can fix the boundaries of the Gulf Stream by the run of pelagic game fish.

Passage Charts

Two good passage charts should be in your locker. DMA 26320 **Florida: The Bahamas, Northern Part of Straits of Florida and Northwest Providence Channel**, covers all routes crossing the Gulf Stream to Grand Bahama, the Bimini Islands, the Berry Islands, New Providence Island, and Nassau. DMA 26300 **West Indies: The Bahamas, Little Bahama Bank to Eleuthera Island**, covers routes continuing on to the Abacos and dropping south from the Abacos to Eleuthera.

Planning to Cross the Stream

Crossing the Gulf Stream in any kind of craft can best be compared to the progress of an ant crossing an airport moving walkway. The ant might well have wanted to make a direct crossing but, during its transit, inevitably the ant will be taken past its target. For every hour you are in the influence of the Stream you will be carried about 2.5 nautical miles (nm) to the north. Like it or not. Your first concern is to minimize the time you'll be in Gulf Stream water if you're crossing from a departure point more or less on the same latitude as your destination. If you're coming up from the south, then it's different. You want to stay on that walkway for as long as possible, getting a free ride to help you north before you turn off.

NOAA weather broadcasts give daily information about the Stream, its width, speed, distance offshore at different points, and its temperature, but for navigation it's sensible to assume that the entire distance you have to run from departure point to a destination lying anywhere along the 079° 15' W line of longitude will be subject to that 2.5-knot north-flowing current. Listen to NOAA's Gulf Stream information. Plot the edge of the Stream on your chart, its width, its speed, and record the temperature. Note when you're in the Stream, and when you leave it. If nothing else it will add interest to your passage across the Florida Strait, and you'll add to your store of knowledge.

The Gulf Stream Crossing Routes

The need to minimize the time you spend in the Stream, unless you're prepared to accept a long haul, effectively means you should set out from Florida no further north than Stuart (the St. Lucie Inlet). To set a southern limit, for in theory there are no problems in riding the Gulf Stream all the way north from its start, let's say no further south than Angelfish Creek at the north end of Key Largo. In this start zone area the hazards of most of the Florida East Coast inlets, Jupiter, Boynton, Boca Raton, and Hillsboro, dictate that unless you have up-to-date local knowledge, the right kind of craft, and a favorable tide, sea state, and wind, your departure ports come down to six options, of which the best (rated for simplicity of navigation, and pre-departure backup facilities) are marked with an asterisk (*):

- **Stuart** (St. Lucie Inlet)
- **The Port of Palm Beach*** (Lake Worth Inlet)
- **Fort Lauderdale*** (Port Everglades Entrance)
- **Miami*** (Miami Harbor Entrance)
- **Key Biscayne** (Key Biscayne Channel)
- **Key Largo** (Angelfish Creek)

In the Bahamas your landfalls and immediate ports of entry are:

- **West End, Grand Bahama** (for the Abacos).
- **Port Lucaya, Grand Bahama** (for Grand Bahama itself, the Abacos, and the Berry Islands).

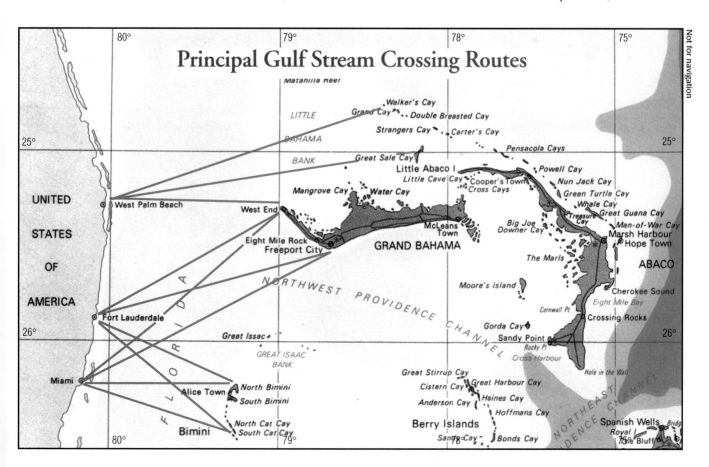

- **Alice Town in North Bimini** (for the Biminis, the Berry Islands, Nassau, and beyond).

- **North Cat Cay** (for the Biminis, the Berry Islands, Nassau, and beyond).

You can elect to continue on across the Little Bahama Bank or the Great Bahama Bank without staging or even clearing in at these first landfalls, but when you cross the West End–Bimini line you have crossed the Gulf Stream.

These are the best routes to minimize disadvantageous time in the Gulf Stream. You can make your own variations and there's no reason why a boat shouldn't leave Miami destined for West End, but to set out from Stuart or Palm Beach bound for Gun Cay Cut wouldn't make sense, especially for a slow boat.

You can make your own way to the Bahamas outside the area covered by these routes, but it might not be wise unless you're prepared for a voyage of exploration. In particular, south of South Riding Rock and Castle Rock Light (20 nm south of North Cat Cay) you're on your own. There are no navigational aids, and the accuracy of the charts is suspect. If you're approaching the Bahamas from anywhere further afield than the East Coast of Florida, the Gulf Stream is not your particular concern.

Weather

The Gulf Stream is a constant, reckonable force. The weather is not. Listen to the forecasts. Believe the bad ones. Don't trust the good ones! Go to the beach and look out over the ocean. What's it doing out there?

The most difficult and dangerous time for any vessel to cross the Gulf Stream is when the wind is from the north, and that includes the northeast and the northwest. Whether you are running a 180-foot motor yacht or an 18-foot sailboat doesn't matter—this is *definitely not* the time to cross. Remember that Gulf Stream flowing north at anything up to 5 knots. When the wind blows from the north it's like rubbing a cat the wrong way, all the fur kicks up and the result is the "elephants" we mentioned. High ugly waves as closely spaced as elephants in a circus parade. If it's like that, enjoy the chance to finish the job list you never completed. Take your crew to brunch, lunch, or dinner. See a movie. The Gulf Stream is *not* where you want to be.

Wait until the forecast is good and it *looks good*, too. Even then, be prepared to take unexpected weather. If it's uncertain, don't take a chance on the weather and try to grab what seems to be a window if you haven't got the speed to get there fast in safety. We all know the pressure of deadlines, you only have *x* days for your holiday, or you've got a flight to meet somewhere, but your safety comes first. The Florida Strait, because of the Gulf Stream, can become a very hazardous stretch of water if the weather turns against you. In the wrong weather it can be a killer.

Let's take a real life example of the way it can go in a worst-case scenario.

> **Extracts from *Terrapin*'s Log**
> [A 26-foot cutter-rigged catamaran]
> 14–15 March 1994
>
> 1700. Left Jib Club, Jupiter Island. Headed for Palm Beach [Waypoint 2]. Ideal evening cruise. Gentle wind. Sea state idle. Two-inch waves. Sunset off Juno.
>
> 1945. Palm Beach. On to Waypoint 3 [off Boynton]. Conditions roughened. Sea state kicked up and wind SW from 5 up to 20 knots. Sometimes higher. No problems.
>
> 2359. Sudden change. Waypoint 3 [On course for West End, Waypoint 4]. Wind everywhere. Horrid triangular seas and an evil swell from the North. A witches' cauldron. Terrapin thrown hither and thither.

Over the next eight hours conditions worsened with wild, jagged, confused seas, severe thunderstorms, and awesome displays of horizontal lightning. It was too rough and too dangerous to leave the security of safety harness and the protection of *Terrapin*'s center cockpit, the autopilot couldn't handle it, and it was too wet to keep even a DR (dead reckoning) log.

> 0915. Reached Waypoint 4. Worst-ever crossing. Worst possible combination of three opposing elements [Gulf Stream, wind, and swell]. Terrapin like an orange crate caught in a millrace. Sick as dogs all the way.
>
> 0940. Secured Jack Tar Marina. West End like paradise.

My scary tale is not meant to frighten but to caution. *Terrapin*'s ill luck came about from the unforecast coincidence of three Lows (one around St. Augustine, one around Marathon, and one east of the Abacos) that produced freak conditions in the Florida Strait over the night of March 14, 1994 and damaged five boats crossing that evening. The swell from a distant North Atlantic storm added to the chaos. As a matter of record the actual forecast for that night was:

High Pressure Monday, Tuesday, and Wednesday. No adverse systems. Dry. Good visibility. Wind NW 5 knots, maximum 12 knots. Seas maximum 2–3 feet. Slight N swell. West Edge of Gulf Stream 11 miles due East of Palm Beach. 45 miles wide. 75°F. 2.4 knots.

The lesson is simply this: a Gulf Stream crossing must be considered as serious as ocean passage making, and not as a "quick 50-mile run across to the Bahamas." Choose your weather. Prepare your craft well, even if you can see it's flat calm out there. And no deadlines!

Tactics

Terrapin's crossing was a night crossing, by deliberate choice, just as her route (down to a waypoint off Boynton) took her far south of her departure port (her home port, Jupiter Inlet) and added to the distance she had to run. The tactics of your crossing, whether it's day or night, and the route you select, depend entirely on your boat. When it comes to a Gulf Stream crossing, express or sedan cruisers and sport fishermen with a 30-knot capability share little in common with a displacement trawler or a sailboat, other than concern for the weather. Remember the ant on the moving walkway? A rattlesnake would fail to see that airport walkway as a problem area.

THE FASTER PASSAGE MAKER

If your cruising speed allows you to make the crossing in daylight, cross in daylight. Why lose a night's sleep and give yourself all the problems of identifying lights and tracking other ships only by radar or by their lights? Remember the Florida Strait is one of the world's busiest shipping lanes.

Leave early, to take advantage of the morning calm if there is one, and arrive on the Banks with the sun high overhead or behind you, for eyeball navigation. Your speed means that you have, perhaps, 3.5 to 4 hours actually in the Gulf Stream, which will take you 8–10 nm north of your track if you set a direct course and never alter course. The simplest approach in this case is to set that direct course. Using your GPS watch your cross track error (XTE) and keep altering, never allowing yourself to be taken over half a mile to the left or right of your course.

THE SLOWER CRAFT

Once you are down to a cruising speed of 8 knots or less, the effect of the Gulf Stream is magnified. Your XTE on a straight-line course, held and never altered, can build up from 15 nm or so to over 30 nm. It doesn't really work to take a straight line course and keep altering, for you are too close to the margins. If anything goes wrong, you're going to miss your target and crawling back down to the right latitude could be tough. There are two ways to work out how to play it.

For a trawler-type motor yacht, the simplest way is to predict your cruise speed, divide the distance to run by that figure, and find out how many hours you'll be on passage. Multiply that time by 2.5 (the speed of the Gulf Stream) and that'll give you the offset to the north, in nautical miles, that you would be taken off course. Draw a line parallel to a line of longitude *due south* from your destination waypoint and measure off that same offset. Lay off a new course to that point, wherever it is.

Take that as the course to set on your autopilot, and then let your XTE build up. Let the Gulf Stream bend your track back on to the course you originally wanted. If it works, your "false" course will coincide with the direct course at your final waypoint. Of course it won't work that precisely (unless you're lucky) but if you plot your position each hour you can fine tune your progress and make it come out as you wish.

Another way that works is to interface your GPS with your autopilot, and let your autopilot keep your XTE at or near zero. It's the KISS principle.

THE SAILBOAT

For the sailboat, whose cruising speed is much less predictable, it's sensible to work it out another way, using a bracket of the normal speed range or Speeds of Advance (SOAs) for your vessel. You know the straight line distance you would have to run on a direct course. Mark that course on your chart. Then draw a vertical line parallel to a line of longitude, *due north* from your desired starting waypoint and measure off 2.5 nms (which is the Gulf Stream factor, the average speed of the Stream as it flows north).

Set your dividers at selected distances representing your SOAs (4.5 knots, 5 knots, 5.5 knots, 6 knots or whatever) taking your nautical miles off the latitude scale. With one point on the 2.5 mark on the north line you drew, swing the dividers to cut the direct course line with the other point, marking each intersection in turn. Now measure the distances along your projected track of those intersections from your starting waypoint. Those new distances are your real achievable SOAs with the Gulf Stream vectored in.

Make up a crossing table under the headings *SOA* and *Achievable SOA*. Divide the straight-line distance to run by your achievable SOAs to get a third column in your crossing table, *Passage Time*. Now multiply your passage times

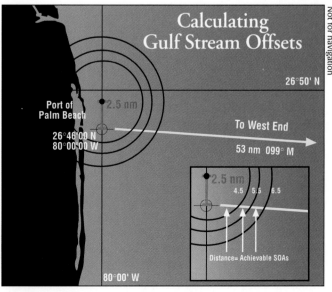

by 2.5 to obtain the offset south, in nautical miles, that you should set as your true start point at the outset to make your destination. This *Offset* becomes the fourth final column in your crossing table.

Crossing Table

Departure Waypoint	Port of Palm Beach	26° 46' 00 N	080° 00' 00 W
Destination Waypoint	West End	26° 42' 00 N	079° 01' 00 W
Straight-line distance to run		53 nm	
Straight-line course		099°M	

SOA	Achievable SOA	Passage Time	Offset
4.5 kts	3.5 kts	15.1 hrs	37.7 nm
5.5 kts	4.9 kts	10.8 hrs	27.0 nm
6.5 kts	6.1 kts	8.6 hrs	21.5 nm

For the boat reckoning a 4.5-knot SOA, this would dictate a start point on the 26° 11' 00 N line of latitude, off North Fort Lauderdale. For a 5.5 knot SOA you'd be better off with a start point just off Deerfield Beach, north of Boca Raton, on latitude 26° 19' 00 N. If you reckon on a 6.5 knot SOA, your Gulf Stream–crossing start point comes out on the 26° 24' 30 N line of latitude, which rounded off means that Boynton Beach or Delray would be fine. All you have to do now is guess your most probable SOA, and its matched offset starting point becomes the starting waypoint for the actual crossing. Mark your new course on the chart. From then on, as ever, plot your position and fine tune your progress as you go.

Most probably this seems far too complicated, with way too much fussing around, but what it does illustrate vividly is the power of the Gulf Stream. Translate those offsets to the south of your desired starting point into the nautical miles to the north of your destination waypoint that the Stream would take you, like it or not, and you can see that for a sailboat your initial offset is critical. Get that right, have a wind you can work with, and you're away. You hope your prudent offset, the boost of the Gulf Stream, and the wind on your best point of sailing will boost you to your destination over a beautiful parabolic curve, giving you one of the best runs you have ever had. It can happen. It does happen. It does work.

If you're sailing, your final consideration is the business of start time. It's set, quite simply, by your desired arrival time. You must make your landfall in daylight. You should have adequate daylight remaining in case something goes wrong. Early in the morning is fine, even if you're going in to one of the closer entry ports for, even with a rising sun, none of them present unusual problems. If you're going to cross the Banks it's better to have the sun high, particularly if you're going on to the Little Bahama Bank by way of Memory Rock or Indian Cay Passage because of the fring-ing reefs. Getting on to the Great Bahama Bank is fairly straightforward. For a sailboat these considerations almost inevitably dictate an overnight crossing.

Landfalls and Warnings

To the north of West End, the tall casuarina trees of Sandy Cay (9 nm south of Memory Rock and 7 nm north of West End) are a useful marker. West End's water tower is prominent, and its 150-foot Batelco tower has red lights at the top and its midpoint. There's a light on Indian Cay, immediately north of West End, but this is often hard to pick up. Freeport, on Grand Bahama Island, has approach buoys, as do the marinas between Freeport and Port Lucaya.

In the south, tiny uninhabited Great Isaac Island has a reliable 23-nm range light. In the Biminis, Gun Cay has a lighthouse that works some of the time. But it remains that your arrival in Bahamian waters, unless you're taking the Northwest Providence Channel route on to Nassau, should be timed for daylight. It's better for you, for lights can fail or be obscured in rain, it's less stressful, and it's safer. More detailed navigational advice is given for each island group in the appropriate section of this Guide.

Courses and Straight Line Distances (No Offsets)

Port of Palm Beach–Sandy Cay–Memory Rock	087°M	49.73 nm
Port of Palm Beach–West End	099°M	53.58 nm
Port of Palm Beach–Freeport (as a landfall)	108°M	67.34 nm
Fort Lauderdale–Bimini	122°M	46.70 nm
Fort Lauderdale–Gun Cay Cut	131°M	52.20 nm
Miami–Bimini	098°M	41.58 nm
Miami–Gun Cay Cut	109°M	42.59 nm

Returning to Florida

Navigation on the return passage to Florida poses no landfall problems. You'll pick up the loom of the lights of the East Coast anything up to 50 nm out at night, and condominium and office tower blocks around 10 nm out, depending on your height above the water. You can't miss Florida. There's 360 miles of it right in front of you.

Gulf Stream Rules

It remains to list the "rules" of making a successful Gulf Stream crossing:

- Never set out in adverse weather, or risk outrunning the onset of bad weather. Be especially wary of winds from the north. You want pussy cat conditions, not a wildcat!

- Always time your arrival in the Bahamas for daylight, preferably between dawn and noon.

- Don't single-hand. *If something happens to you, Murphy's Law will take over. Self-preservation is the name of the game, not macho image-making. The Florida Strait is no place to be when you're in real trouble.*

- If you're crossing in a small boat, go in convoy with similar boats or with another boat whose cruising speed matches your *achievable* speed, which, depending on the sea state, may be very different from the speed you can achieve in calm water.

- If you're making the crossing for the first time, or you're anxious about it (you may have reservations about the competence of your crew if something happened to you), team up and make your passage in company with another of your kind. Then get together for a celebration meal after your safe arrival!

- Always have enough fuel (even on a sailboat) to motor the full distance against head seas and arrive with not less than 20 percent of your fuel remaining.

- Always have a working VHF radio with a backup (hand held?) VHF.

- Ideally have GPS as your navigation system, for Loran becomes progressively inaccurate in the Bahamas.

- Check that you have a working depth sounder, working lights, a flashlight, an air horn, charts, binoculars, distress flares and smoke, and a Type I life jacket for every person on board.

- If you're on a sailboat or an open boat, have a safety harness or fitted tether for every person on board with a secure anchor point.

- If you can afford an EPIRB (Emergency Position-Indicating Radio Beacon), have one, preferably a 406 MHz EPIRB.

- Let a friend know when you are leaving. Call when you arrive. *If you don't call after your forecasted arrival within a time equal to one third of your anticipated passage time, the friend should contact the Coast Guard.* Make sure your friend knows the make, length, color, and call sign of your boat, your route, your time of departure, and how many people you had on board. Even better, leave them your Float Plan (see the **Blue Pages** under **Putting Out to Sea** on page 294).

The Return Passage

Add 180° to all courses for the reciprocal course to take you back to Florida. Again remember this is a straight-line direct course *with no offsets built in to it.*

Waypoints

See the **Waypoint Catalog** beginning on page 333, or the detailed island sections of this guide.

Navigation—*You* Are in Command

Conventional Navigation— From the Global Positioning System (GPS) to Basics

Conventional Navigation

As the captain of a Spanish galleon might have told you, in the Bahamas you need just about every aid to navigation you can get your hands on, as well as your own wits and skill. With the combination of bluewater ocean passages (however short) and coastal work in waters where reefs, rocks, and sandbanks are part of the tapestry of each leg you run, this is just about true.

The one navigational system we've never had to employ in the Bahamas is celestial, but we've carried a sextant for years and perhaps we should have kept in practice, just in case. Underpinning every aid to navigation is the most basic requirement of all: charts, even though these may be dated. With the charts you'll want your parallel rules, dividers, pencils, and so on. There's nothing very extraordinary in this, and of course you'll need a pair of binoculars and a hand-bearing compass (as well as a fixed compass on the boat). If you have this much, and your skills in eyeball navigation (see the next section on page 28), you're pretty well set and could go anywhere. But we live in an age of electronics, and why not take advantage of it? Top of our list comes the most accurate navigation system yet devised, GPS.

The Global Positioning System (GPS)

The Navstar/GPS system is a satellite-based US Government radio navigation system designed to provide global, all-weather, 24-hour position data. While intended for use by navigators worldwide, the GPS system was and is under the control of the US Department of Defense.

Claiming that national security was at stake, the Department of Defense superimposed a special mode known as Selective Availability (SA) on the satellite broadcast made available for civilian users (1575.42 MHz), which deliberately introduced timing errors to make the system less accurate than the broadcast available for the military. The Pentagon reserves the right to impose SA whenever they wish, and for safe navigation it must be taken that SA is in force, since it has been imposed almost continuously since 1991.

GPS without SA imposed will give position fixes accurate to +/− 15 meters (49.2 feet). With SA imposed you must reckon on accuracy of +/− 100 meters (328 feet), 95 percent of the time. In other words, you will know that you are within a football field's length of a known place on the surface of the world. Putting it yet another way, GPS draws a circle with a radius of 328 feet circle all around the position of your GPS antenna, and you are somewhere in-

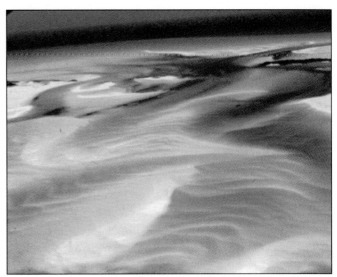

Constantly moving sand bars, Central Exumas.

side that circle. For the other 5 percent of the time you will be close but somewhere outside that circle.

At first your natural reaction is to conclude that SA puts the civilian user at risk, and that its imposition is unjustifiable in the context of national security. These conclusions are probably true, but the improved accuracy of the military system would not necessarily give the civilian user the ability to navigate by GPS alone through a narrow passage at night or with zero visibility. The reason is that most of the world's charts are based on hydrographic surveys carried out in the last century and the charts are only as accurate as the charting methods of the day could make them.

GPS Datum

The GPS Datum used in this Guide is WGS84. This is compatible with the National Oceanic and Atmospheric Administration (NOAA) NAD83 Chart Datum

Don't be surprised if your GPS and the chart you are using disagree on positioning, but remember the chart, in its depiction of coastline, offshore hazards, and depths will be good. Nonetheless, you are wise to take note of the dating and latest updating of the chart you're using, and look carefully for any warning notices about its accuracy.

Differential GPS

The US Coast Guard, in the interests of safe coastal navigation, have now introduced a supplemental radio broadcast system called Differential GPS, which removes the errors produced by SA and results, if you have a DGPS receiver, in a position accuracy between 5 and 8 meters (16–26 feet). In effect it is pinpoint accuracy. Before you come to rely absolutely on DGPS, you will want to be well aware that the DGPS beacons cover US coastal waters only. They do not, at this time, cover the Bahamas.

The introduction of DGPS does not itself solve the on-going problem caused by inaccuracies in charts, and the wise navigator will realize that DGPS accuracy can take him or her closer to known dangers than it's prudent to venture.

Units of Measurement

GPS on its first introduction was programed to work in the conventional navigation position fixing of degrees, minutes, and seconds. The wider use of GPS, particularly for land surveying, has led to a change in which seconds were replaced by hundreds (0.01) and thousands (0.001) of a nautical mile (nm). Some marine GPS instruments have followed this trend. Others continue to use seconds.

We have no wish to appear reactionary or to be fighting a rear-guard action against progress, but we've stayed with seconds. We feel that 1 second (101.33 feet), say two or three boat lengths, is as accurate a measurement as you can reasonably work with and achieve at sea. Perhaps the more overriding reason is that all our charts still carry latitude and longitude measured in degrees, minutes, and seconds. If you make use of charts (which you should!) it makes it easier to stay in the same system. We give a conversion table of seconds to thousands in **Appendix B** under **Conversion Tables and Useful Measurements** on page 340.

Charts

Like most of the world, the Bahamas were first charted, as we understand marine hydrography, in the 19th century. Since then the charts have been updated but it remains that the base charts were drawn using surveying methods, which although the most accurate means of their day, we now consider primitive. Many of the charts we use in the Bahamas today are based on surveys 50, maybe 100 years old, or even more. No chart should ever be considered perfect and this caveat applies to electronic charts, and all computer-driven chart displays, which are no more accurate than the paper chart upon which they are based.

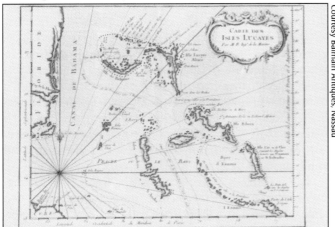

A chart of the Bahamas by Jacques Nicholas Bellin, 1751.

Courtesy Balmain Antiques, Nassau

You need your own eyes and sea sense as well as a chart. In the Bahamas the temptation is to ignore regular marine charts, which are unhandy for what are essentially short inter-island passages, and to rely on chart kits and sketch charts, sometimes supplemented by annotated color photographs, for approaches and harbor details. This is fine, but keep in mind that the chart kit itself also derives from the parent chart, the sketch map is only an illustration to help you find your way in to a harbor or anchorage, and the color photograph is dated from the time it was taken.

Navigation Marks

The nature of their world dictated that the Bahamians, born and brought up within sight of the sea, nurtured on a diet of conch, lobster tails, and fish, and more often than not "bused" to school by boat, would become highly competent seamen. The establishment of navigation marks has never been a high priority in the Bahamas. They know their reefs, channels, and cuts from childhood and can read their waters as if the colors were a map spread before them.

In the last century navigation marks set up by their British overlords were regarded with suspicion and at times destroyed or deliberately misplaced, for the only source of income for many islanders came from wrecking and the profits of salvage. There are navigation marks in the islands today, but their maintenance is not always the highest priority. Regard them as a bonus. Treat them with caution.

Natural Features

Coral is so slow growing that a reef will hardly gain visible height in a thousand years, but sand and sandbars move with currents and swells, and are moved in storms. Just as the bars and shoals of the Florida East Coast inlets are never constant, so the underwater profile of much of the Bahamas is always changing.

Be aware that no chart can serve as more than a warning that shoal waters exist in a general area and can never show you the passes that may exist through the shoals in the year that you are cruising there. Severe storms, such as Hurricane Andrew in 1992, can change the contours of the sea bed, obliterate navigation marks that may not be replaced for years, and uproot every tree, completely changing the profile and appearance of an island.

Batelco Towers

What you will find, more often than not, is that the essential similarity of the low-lying Bahamian cays and islands make identification difficult, and sometimes really confusing. There are few natural land features that are prominent enough to help you fix your position, and time and time again it's the man-made features that will count, like the silos around Hatchet Bay in Eleuthera, and the new water tanks that have been built in places like Grand Cay and

Batelco towers, George Town, Great Exuma.

Spanish Wells. Perhaps the greatest aid of them all are the radio towers erected by the Bahamas Telephone Company. These Batelco towers, faint against the sky at a distance, are the certain indicator of a settlement. Once you've picked up your Batelco tower, you've got it made.

Using GPS

We have already cautioned about the dangers of relying on GPS for coastal and inshore navigation. The problem, we repeat, is that your charts may not agree with the GPS. Okay, so the chart is wrong and the GPS is right, but you've got to live with it. In the Bahamas the greatest boon of GPS is to take you safely from waypoint to waypoint over waters that are clear of hazards. In other words use GPS for passage making, then forget it for coastal navigation other than noting latitude and longitude as a positioning grid. We often hold a line of latitude or longitude as a course for a stretch if it suits, or use the crossing of a certain line as a wake-up call that you are at a turning point. Other than this, go visual. It doesn't matter whether the GPS position of the entrance to Indian Cay Passage agrees with the chart, all that matters is that GPS delivers you safely to within a mile of it, and that you are not on the reef or the rocks!

It remains that GPS is a superb system for passage making. It enables you to make landfalls exactly where you want 100 percent of the time, regardless of the weather or time of day or night. Our plotting, like yours, is subject to the limitations of SA and inaccurate charts, and all you need to know is that we were somewhere near there, and that the position we have marked is the point at which we reckon basic navigation must take over.

Just remember: *In Bahamian waters* **you**, *not your navigational instruments, are in command!*

Back to Basic Navigation

What we really mean when we say "basic navigation must take over" is that your autopilot is switched to manual and you switch yourself on. It's essentially chart, compass, depth, and your eyesight that counts. Radar can help, particularly with landfall identification, but your own eyes are vital. In the Bahamas perhaps the best rule to follow is *if you can't see, don't move.* In other words, don't risk running inshore passages at night, or in bad weather (if you can help it) and particularly if all the Bahamian colors are lost and you can't read the water. At the end, it all comes down to "eyeball navigation."

Eyeball Navigation— the Myth, Fears, and Reality

Most of us have heard about "eyeball navigation." It's the magic art of reading depth contours by color "the way you've got to do it while you're there, otherwise you'll be on the reefs." As a first timer it sounds like the kind of skill that can only be acquired after three seasons, or maybe after you've left at least three keels lying on Bahamian reefs. The reality is very different.

Eyeball navigation is no more than using your eyes to pick your way forward, rather than taking a course off the chart and panicking when your depth sounder shows 4 feet of water. It's the same way you'd choose a route up a mountain side on land. You use your eyes and common sense to bend your route to suit the land, to take the easiest course, the best path, rather than blundering uphill on a set of compass bearings.

Navigating the Bahamas is eyeball stuff. You know where you want to go. Just use your eyes, steer your course looking ahead so that you can see the Bahamian equivalent of trees and rocks way ahead, rather than just two feet ahead of your bow pulpit. There's no magic about it. You could say it comes naturally. It's not difficult. Why? For one all-important reason. The dangers are color-coded. All you have to know is the color code.

For eyeball navigation we're talking about six colors: blue, green, yellow, brown, black, and white; and some shades in-between: turquoise and aquamarine. The last is the color that makes Bahamian waters seem like nowhere else on earth, a transparent green with a touch of blue in it that looks as if it's being floodlit from below. Estimating depth in ocean water with the clarity of a Florida spring seems impossible at first. Are you in five feet, or is that starfish eighteen feet down? But you soon learn that color is the give-away.

Before you start, you need polarized sun glasses. This brings two advantages. The first is that you cut surface reflection and you can see into the water. The second is that the colors are enhanced. Only polarized lenses will do this for you. You could add a third advantage, but any good pair of sunglasses will give you this: sunglasses cut glare, and prevent you being temporarily blinded if you swing around into the sun or, even worse, have to hold a course into the sun.

Sunlight

The position of the sun is the key to eyeball navigation. You need the sun to bring the colors of water alive, and you need the sun as a searchlight working to your advantage rather than as a blinding light in front of you. The optimum is to have the sun fairly high in the sky and behind you. The worst situation is to find yourself making your way through unknown waters into a rising or a setting sun. Don't take it on, unless you're certain that the depth, all the way, is more than safe for your boat draft.

Overcast days and rain make eyeball navigation difficult. If you have a tricky passage immediately ahead and you're caught by a rain squall, hold off until you can read the water. Even on sunny days the shadows of moving clouds can suddenly confuse the underwater map you're reading. But if those dark patches are in motion, you know they're clouds. Again you may have to hold back until you can see what the cloud shadow has been concealing.

The Colors

Now let's turn to the main colors. Let's take the sequence color by color showing the variations as they come, as you'll find them after crossing the Gulf Stream. First, deep blue water. Classic bluewater. Deep blue is absolute safety. Safe

A map of water colors that show you the way to go.

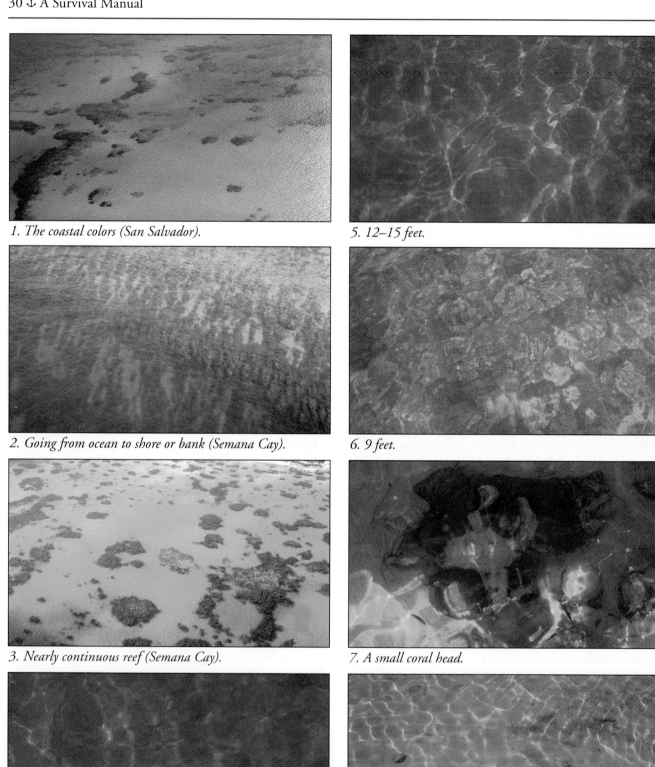

1. *The coastal colors (San Salvador).*

5. *12–15 feet.*

2. *Going from ocean to shore or bank (Semana Cay).*

6. *9 feet.*

3. *Nearly continuous reef (Semana Cay).*

7. *A small coral head.*

4. *30 feet or more.*

8. *5–6 feet (and a nurse shark).*

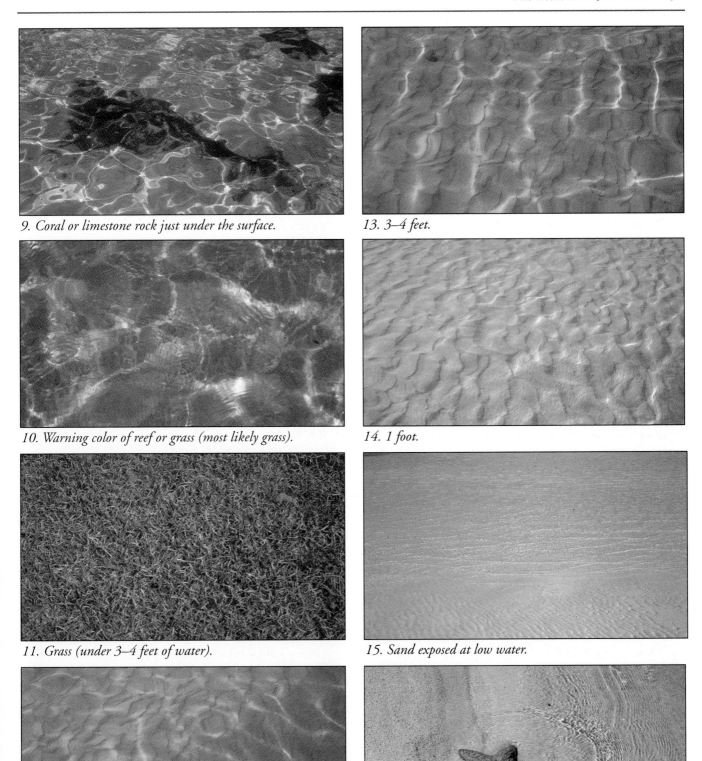

9. *Coral or limestone rock just under the surface.*

13. *3–4 feet.*

10. *Warning color of reef or grass (most likely grass).*

14. *1 foot.*

11. *Grass (under 3–4 feet of water).*

15. *Sand exposed at low water.*

12. *Upper left, 1–2 feet; lower right, 3–4 feet.*

16. *The very edge of the beach.*

deep ocean water. Light blue is the kind of depth, around 30 feet, you get at the edge of the Banks. You are safe, however surprised you may be to suddenly see everything on the bottom as clearly as if there were just three feet of water under your keel.

Green water is starting to become shallow, the color changing from dark to light as the depth decreases. Green is Banks water, going from 30 feet down to 15 or 12 feet. The paler the shade of green, the more shallow the water will be. Yellow, running into white, is shoal water. Reckon it to be 5 feet or less, and go slowly if you're running in deliberately to beach your boat. Otherwise avoid water that has taken on more yellow or white than green. Perhaps pale aquamarine could be a way to describe the warning color, the color that makes the prettiest photographs when it's set against a distant strip of darker blue deep water, or the sand and palms of a Bahamian beach.

Brown rings alarm bells. It could be grass, but it might well be a coral reef. Avoid it or slow down. Don't chance your luck. If it's grass, you'll learn that the edge of the brown is not as sharp as it will be if it's a coral reef. Grass, which shows dark on the bottom, can be your greatest confusion factor. Until you get used to it, and can second guess where grass should be, or could be, or will be, you can mistake grass for coral. The only way to learn is to get behind the wheel. Dark brown or black certainly rings an alarm bell. It's the color of a coral reef. Closer to the surface it will show sharp edges as you get nearer, but deeper features remain less distinct.

Dark brown or black is also the color of an isolated coral head. It's always a tough shot to guess whether it's two feet under the surface or ten feet down. It's best to reckon, unless you're in good deep water, that each coral head is a threat and avoid it. As you get closer to a coral head, if the surrounding bottom is grass, you may see a ring of sand around it where foraging fish have scoured the bottom.

Finally white comes in the alarm bell category. It's sand. Generally white will turn out to be a sand bore, but it can be a shelving beach. Sometimes in shoal water the aquamarine tint of the water makes it hard to see a sand bore that has built up close to the surface. If you're lucky a sand bore will show a dry white spine but, like an iceberg, there's more underwater than you can see on top. Stay well clear. White may also signal a "fish mud," an area of sand stirred up by a school of fish rooting around. But don't guess that it's a fish mud because no sand bores are shown on your chart in that area. Go cautiously.

Look at our pages of photographs. These give you an idea of the way it is.

Pulling the Navigation Package Together

Except for safe, deep-water passages, you don't sail at night in the Bahamas. You need your eyes, and you need your skill at reading the water. GPS is useful only for marking

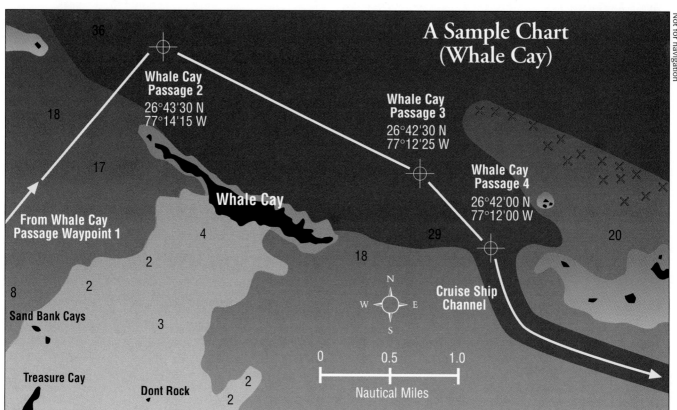

A Sample Chart
(Whale Cay)

Whale Cay
Passage 2
26°43'30 N
77°14'15 W

Whale Cay
Passage 3
26°42'30 N
77°12'25 W

Whale Cay
Passage 4
26°42'00 N
77°12'00 W

Whale Cay

From Whale Cay
Passage Waypoint 1

Sand Bank Cays

Treasure Cay

Dont Rock

Cruise Ship
Channel

Nautical Miles

the waypoints along your deep-water passages. Once you get into shallow water, or near shallow water, forget GPS.

What can help you? Essentially two things. The first we've already mentioned. It's your sun glasses. Polarized lenses. The second is height above water. You don't have to have a tuna tower, but the higher you are above the water, the better you'll be able to see. An aft cockpit sailboat is not necessarily disadvantaged. A lookout on the bow can take the con and pilot you through the shallows. We've done this with a lookout seated on the crosstrees, and it worked well.

Translating Reality into Charts

The color of the water is the key to all Bahamian navigation. Storms and currents may change the position of sand, but the water color will always reveal a sandbar. We've taken this critical factor of water color as the basis of our sketch charts. We show safe deep water as blue. Coastal waters, but still safe for navigation, are a paler blue. We show shallower water as green. We put the depths in feet on each chart, but these are average depths at MLW (mean low water) in that general area. They are not spot soundings. We show very shoal water that effectively forms a barrier to navigation as sand colored, and where it dries at MLW, we mark this. We show rocks and reef by red crosses to warn you off that area. To give contrast to our water colors, we show the land as black.

We show either latitude and longitude lines or alternatively selected waypoints, so that you can pick up your bearings. We show nautical miles in our scale. Main transit routes over deep water are shown in red or yellow. Our courses are shown in yellow. These indicate the general line of your course. They are not meant to be precise guidance, simply because you should be relying on eyeball navigation all the time, even if you are running on autopilot. Finally, we use symbols to mark marinas, anchorages, Batelco towers, and lights. On the latter, note the size difference in the symbols. The larger light symbol is a lighthouse. The smaller one might be no more than a light on a stick, sometimes almost impossible to identify from a distance. The typical common Bahamian marker light is a hurricane lamp on a pole with a stepped ladder giving the lightkeeper access to the lamp platform at the top.

Yes, use our sketch charts. But use conventional charts as well. Our sketch charts are designed to convey each sector of your cruising path as vividly as we can, to make it come alive, so you can understand what lies ahead at a glance. But they are only sketch charts. No navigator worth his salt sets out without conventional charts.

Follow the Mail Boats

Our final advice is the old Bahamian advice: "Follow the mail boats." Not only take note of their routes, but also their departure times, normally when the sun is high in the sky. Even a mail boat captain can't remember the location of every rock, reef, and coral head on his route.

The mail boat Eleuthera Express.

Final Notes and Reminders

Direction of Travel and Course Reversal

A guide necessarily has to be written sequentially from one direction, and in this case we chose to start in the north and work south, for most cruising visitors see the Bahamas this way, at least initially. When courses are given in the text we considered showing the reciprocal courses at the same time, but it was unnecessarily complicating. Almost all navigation systems now offer the facility of inverting or reversing any route entered or any track run, so you should have no problems. Alternatively just add 180° and do it the old way. Our close approaches and harbor entries hold good from all directions.

Latitude and Longitude

Our positions are shown in *degrees*, *minutes*, and *seconds*. Your GPS may show degrees, minutes, and seconds, or alternatively, either thousands or hundreds of a minute rather than seconds. We have stayed with seconds deliberately as every chart is based on the same system of measurement, and ideally you should plot your waypoints and your proposed courses on a chart for verification and reference before making any passage. If and when the charts change, we shall change. In the meantime we find no problems in using both systems of measurement side by side, and we have included conversion tables in this book.

Sketch Maps and Charts

The sketch maps and charts in this Guide are intended to illustrate the text and help bring it alive. They are *not* charts and they are *not* designed for navigation. We are not hydrographic surveyors, and our indications of routes, depths, and hazards are approximate. No more than that. We accept no responsibility for your safe navigation, which ultimately must always be the personal concern of the captain of any vessel. We therefore strongly recommend that you make full use of all the navigation aids available to you, not least of which are government charts, local notices to mariners, and your own eyes and skills.

Dolphins on the Little Bahama Bank.

Part II

The Northern Cruising Grounds

The Little Bahama Bank

The Northern Abacos

The Central Abacos

The Southern Abacos

Grand Bahama Island

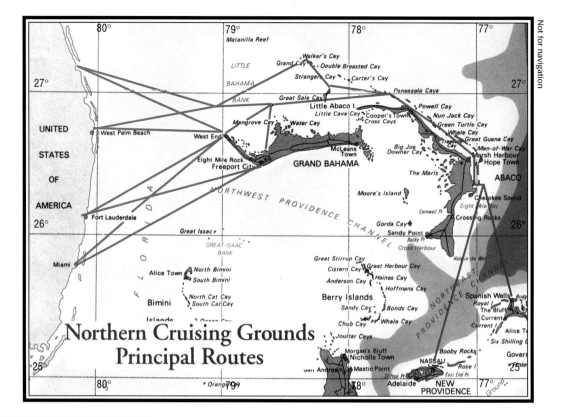

Northern Cruising Grounds
Principal Routes

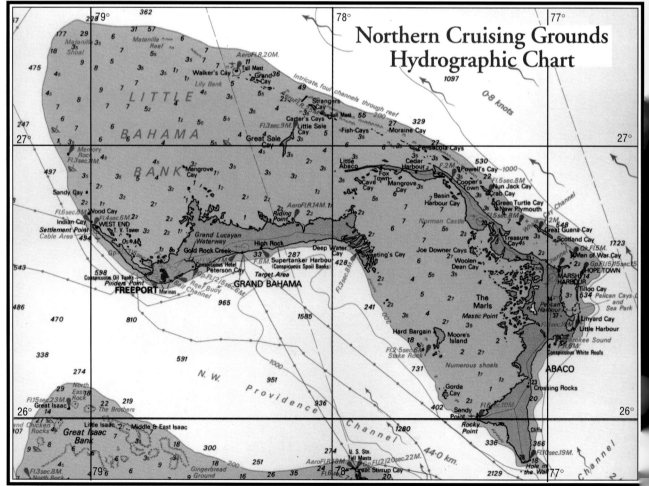

Northern Cruising Grounds
Hydrographic Chart

Chapter 3
The Little Bahama Bank

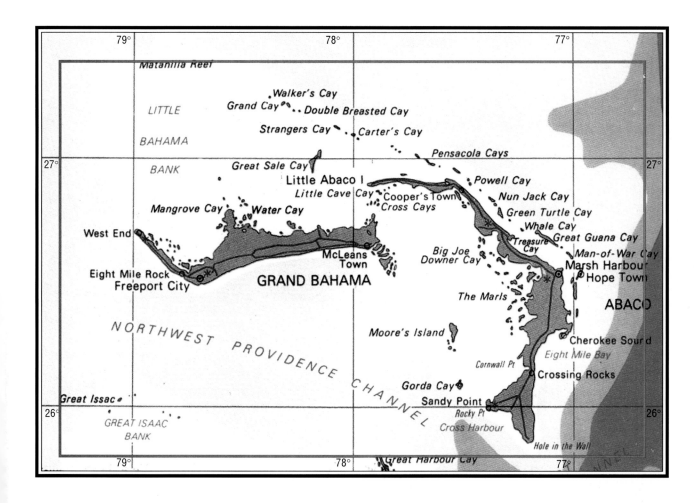

THE Little Bahama Bank is the northernmost of the shallow seas that give the Bahamas its unique character. Measured from west to east along latitude 27° (just north of Memory Rock to the barrier reef east of Allans-Pensacola Cay) it's roughly 85 nm. Measured from north to south, dropping down the line of 078° 30' W (just west of Walkers Cay to the shoals off the north coast of Grand Bahama) it is roughly 35 nm.

But these measurements are deceptive, for the Little Bahama Bank really encompasses a great sweeping area of shallow water that runs from the edge of the Florida Strait eastward across to the Abaco Cays fringing the Atlantic, and then, taking the Pensacola Cays as your pivot, swings southeast to form the Sea of Abaco, which runs between Great Abaco Island and the Abaco Cays for another 55 nm.

In the south the Little Bahama Bank is bounded by Grand Bahama, and properly speaking the shallows between the east end of Grand Bahama and Little Abaco Island, the area lying south of Little Abaco Island and west of the Marls, is also a part of the Little Bahama Bank. But this sector of the Bank, a mess of mud banks, sand ridges, and shoals is no cruising ground. Over the part you'll do your transits, the Little Bahama Bank offers depths that average around 15 feet and, provided you keep to the proven routes, no particular navigation problems. It's possible to transit the Little Bahama Bank at night, but the cays are low lying and have outlying reefs and shoals, there are many uncharted rocks and sandbars, the effects of tidal currents are guessable but not predictable, and there are few navigation lights. Unless you really want to get in touch with your insurance agent early in your cruise, we'd give night passage making over the Bank a miss.

The Particular Geography of the Little Bahama Bank

For the boat coming from Florida, unless you want to take a very long, circuitous ocean route, there's no way in which you can reach the Abacos other than by crossing the Little Bahama Bank. The obvious route is a straight shot across it from west to east, or the reverse if you're heading to, rather than coming from, Florida. An alternative approach, using the Grand Lucayan Waterway to cut through Grand Bahama Island shaves off part of a cross-Bank transit, but Mangrove Cay (see the map on page 41) acts as a focal point, a rotary, for both routes. There's still plenty of Bank to cross. For the slower craft the completion of a transit during daylight hours may be impossible (as it is with the Great Bahama Bank to the south) but unlike the drill crossing its southern cousin, you don't have to anchor out in the middle of nowhere. The Little Bahama Bank is saved, if you can put it that way, by the anchorage at Great Sale Cay, an uninhabited island (at which it's lawful to overnight if you haven't cleared in), located at just about the midpoint of the Bank.

West End is naturally the starting block and the finishing tape for your Little Bahama Bank transits (unless of course you opt for that Grand Lucayan Waterway alternative). For this reason we start with West End, which also, for Florida departure ports between Stuart and Palm Beach, is the closest arrival port in the Bahamas. If you don't want to stop there, you need not to clear in. You are perfectly lawful carrying on and clearing in later, when you reach the Abacos. We give you alternatives. First, let's look at West End itself.

From the Jack Tar Marina entry looking toward Indian Cay.

West End

West End (1 nm W)	WFSTW	26° 42' 00 N	079° 01' 00 W

West End is in Grand Bahama Island. On the face of it, we should include it in that section. We don't. Why? Look at the chart. West End occupies a strategic position, you could say that it's the Bahamian gateway on the Florida–Abaco route. Sure there's the alternative we mentioned, which is to go by way of one of the Freeport–Lucaya marinas in Grand Bahama and the Grand Lucayan Waterway, but this is not mainstream for most boaters. Not least anyone unable to accommodate a bridge clearance of 27 feet at high water midway up the waterway. So if you look at the West End route, primarily you have two simple choices: the first is to stage at West End before crossing the Little Bahama Bank, and the second is to carry straight on across the Bank.

So let's call West End the port of entry to the Little Bahama Bank, and we'll cover it here. First measure your distances and look at your courses, and you'll realize that West End (if nothing else) could be a vital refuge. For the sailboat, it's just right; at the end of your Gulf Stream crossing endurance, and a shot in the arm before you set off across the Bank. Many power boaters take the same kind of reasoning. The downside has been that West End (by this we mean the Jack Tar Marina complex) was going downhill, year by year, into dereliction. Much has changed and is changing. You now have two choices for a marina. The first is the long-standing but hitherto sadly rundown Jack Tar Marina, which has been there since the early 1950s, and is now about to undergo major redevelopment. The second is an entirely new (1996–97) marina that has been built in West End settlement, the Harbour Hotel and Marina, on the grounds of the old Harbour Hotel. This is a full-service Texaco StarPort, and we cover it in greater detail later in this section and in our **Yellow Pages**. As up to this time the name West End has meant the Jack Tar Marina, and as history is in the making there, we'll deal with it first.

The Jack Tar Story

A dream turned into nightmare, the Jack Tar Village Resort was the vision of the British holiday camp tycoon, Billy Butlin, and was one of the first serious vacation developments, geared to charter air travel, to be launched in the Bahamas. The date was 1951. The project included an airfield (now taken out of service), a marina (in worse shape as each year has passed), a complex of canals (never used), a commercial dock (used on occasion), a 424-room hotel complex (abandoned), 16 tennis courts, a 27-hole golf course (completely overgrown), and the largest freshwater swimming pool in the Western hemisphere. What went wrong? Blame it on the ending of the Freeport Initiative honeymoon (see the **Green Pages, History of the Bahamas** on page 303). The downhill slide started in the late '60s. By the 1980s Butlin was ready to cut his losses, and quit. It was tragic. The site he chose is unbeatable. It's the closest point to Florida in the Bahamas (other than Bimini), it has two good beaches so that whatever the wind direction you have shelter, there was plenty of land (2,000 acres) for expansion, it was on the doorstep of Freeport (with its casinos), and, of course, for the cruising visitor West End is right on the path to the Abacos.

When we paid our last visit to West End in late June 1997 the Jack Tar property was on the point of completion of sale to an Oregon-based developer, whose plans project a major marina refurbishment over 18 months. The deal was closed in mid-July. In the first phase a new 130-slip marina will be built while keeping one side of the existing marina in use, still as an entry port, until half the rebuild is in service and can take over. Further plans envisage the demolition of the Jack Tar hotel buildings and their replacement by a 50-room cottage-type hotel accommodation, the construction of private houses on the interior canal basins, the reopening of the airport, possibly reduced to just one 6,000-foot runway, and the taking up of an option to develop the remaining 2,000 acres of Jack Tar land. The superb mature trees and plantings laid down in the original development will be preserved. It may well be that the marina entry channels will be altered, and one proposal suggests keeping the entry to the commercial harbour as the sole channel and filling in the present marina approach channel.

The West End Resort (their trading name at the time of our writing) intends to have the new marina in service by May 1998, and the shoreside accommodations by the end of that year. We wish the project fair winds. West End is a strategic port-of-call and potential refuge for the sailor (we use the word in its narrow meaning), and the resurrection of the old Jack Tar Marina will be no less of a boon for the power boater: more so for those whose endurance calculations (both fuel and human) suggest that the one-shot run from Florida to the Abacos may be just too much to take in one day.

In our next edition the West End Resort will have full coverage under their own name, and we shall relegate the story of the Jack Tar Marina to history. In this Edition we continue to use the name Jack Tar Marina.

Approaches and Marinas

West End is an easy landfall. Its water tower (sited between the marina and the airfield) is prominent, and its radio mast also shows, perhaps more clearly at night with its red lights. To the north, Sandy Cay's tall casuarina trees will show up early on your horizon but don't be seduced by the landfall, for Sandy Cay lies 8 nm north of West End (too far north for the chart above right). It's a useful safety net, however,

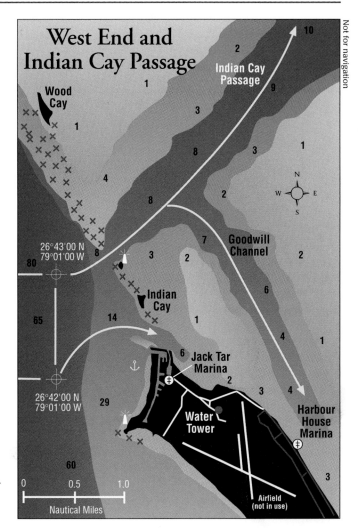

and we've been grateful for it more than once in bad weather. Remember that a barrier reef extends north from West End along the continuous western edge of the Little Bahama Bank. Abruptly that deep blue ocean color will change to green. Keep in the blue water. Our West End waypoint 26° 42' 00 N 079° 01' 00 W places you just off Settlement Point ready to turn in toward the Jack Tar Marina, perhaps anchor off the north bight (if the weather is right) or go on into the marina, or carry on through Indian Cay Passage. You will have to take the Indian Cay Passage if your destination is the second of West End's two marinas.

If you elect to anchor off, you are very exposed there. It is only viable as a short-term anchorage in settled weather. We reckon it has no utility as an arrival anchorage, and the only time we use it when we are sailing is to hold there for a matter of hours before setting off for Florida, so that the timing comes right and we reach Florida just after first light. In effect this means dropping your hook just before sunset, and leaving for Florida sometime during the night. It's easier (if the weather allows it) than making your way out of the

> ## WARNING
>
> The directions we now give are accurate for West End as we last saw it. Once development work is set in hand anything might change, and you would be sensible to check whether there have been any changes by calling the Jack Tar Marina on VHF 16 before making your approach.

Jack Tar Marina at night, and to attempt the Indian Cay Passage at night would be crazy.

West End as we said has two marinas. The Jack Tar Marina can be approached directly from the ocean if you come in from Florida or further down the Grand Bahama coast. If you want to stage in the Jack Tar Marina after an east-west crossing over the Little Bahama Bank, you must first gain ocean water through the Indian Cay Passage (or by one of the northern routes, Sandy Cay or Memory Rock).

The reverse process applies if you want the Harbour Hotel and Marina. Incoming from Florida you can only get there by taking the Indian Cay Passage and then the Goodwill Channel to lead you around and down the east coast of West End. If you're running out of daylight, have poor visibility, or are tired, this may not be a good idea. If you're coming in after a Bank transit, then you must still commit yourself to the Indian Cay Passage but branch off it into the Goodwill Channel to get to the Harbour Hotel and Marina. Here your primary consideration (other than depth, which always applies) is whether the sun is in your eyes. If it is, think twice.

THE JACK TAR MARINA

The entrance to Jack Tar Marina is straightforward. The first entry channel leads to the commercial dock and should be ignored, unless you've arranged to berth there. The second entrance comes up almost immediately. There's a shoal close inshore, so stand out between the two entry channels, and then you'll see two buoys marking your way in (leave the buoys on the starboard side) and you have good depth (6 feet MLW) all the way. The fuel dock is on your right, and the generally in-use and usable part of the marina is also on the starboard side.

At the time we were going to print the Jack Tar Marina was planning to position three new entry buoys (30-gallon drums) to mark the entry channel. Two red and one green. What is vital is to realize that a reef extends from the south of Indian Cay (which may still bear the hull of its last 1997 victim, a sailboat). Keep in the blue water until you are safely in the approach channel.

Sailboats are accommodated on the finger docks bow in, to the outside wall to starboard; the central dock is kept for power boats. It's prudent to let the marina staff direct you to your berth for the harbor has many rotten pilings, some broken off just below water level, and we ran on one entering one time using our own initiative. There is power and water, and the marina is well protected. The showers and toilets are in poor shape. There are washing machines and dryers, and the marina office will (if you ask) tune in NOAA weather from Florida (the advantage of that radio mast).

Local restaurants will seek your business and offer transport to the settlement, and there's a twice-daily local bus whose "word of mouth" schedule is rarely convenient but will occasionally time runs just to suit you. The staff in the marina office are friendly and deserve encouragement for having kept the Jack Tar Marina going through the years with no apparent backing. Think twice before fastening on West End with Freeport as your airport for crew changes, for your taxi fare there from West End will be $50 one way.

THE HARBOUR HOTEL AND MARINA

Harbour Marina (cent. dock)	HARBH	26° 41' 22 N	078° 57' 58 W

The approach to this marina lies through the Goodwill Channel, which branches south off the Indian Cay Passage. For vessels incoming from the Florida Strait your route must take the Indian Cay Passage directly as you complete your crossing. Since the Indian Cay Passage features as the start of one of the primary transit routes across the Little Bahama Bank, rather than repeat pilotage detail here, we cover it under its own heading. See page 42.

The Harbour Hotel and Marina has been built on and around the seawall extension of the old Harbour House Hotel, for those who know West End, in the center of the settlement. We give the position of the Harbour Hotel and Marina not for navigation but simply so that you can plot its position on your chart. The Goodwill Channel was unmarked at the time we were last there, but plans have been made to place stakes or buoys, and, one day, to dredge the channel. At present the depth is 4 feet at MLW, which dictates entry and exit at high water as a prudent precaution. Depth inside the marina is good, 8.5 feet at MLW by our reckoning.

This new marina is a welcome addition to West End and a definite plus for the settlement. Well set out, with every facility you would expect, the marina is attractive both in its pristine newness and for its facilities. A breakwater has been built that remains to be topped, but when this final work is completed the marina should be well protected from the north through to east and southeast, which is the vulnerable direction for the Bank coastline at West End. The entry through the breakwater is to be marked and lit at night.

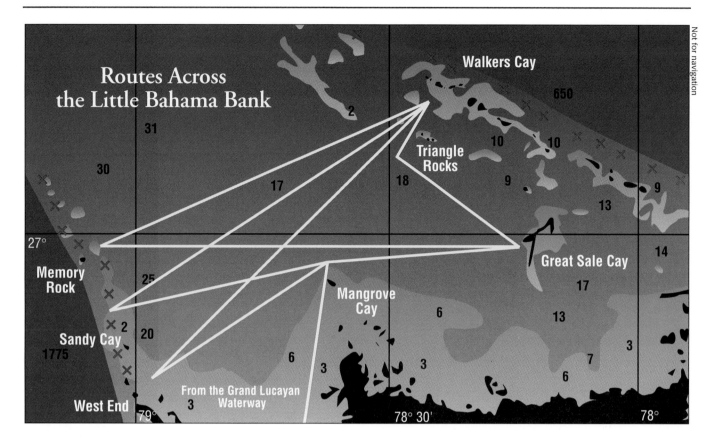

Routes Across the Little Bahama Bank

Walkers Cay

Triangle Rocks

Great Sale Cay

Mangrove Cay

Memory Rock

Sandy Cay

West End

From the Grand Lucayan Waterway

By-Passing West End— Clearing in Later in the Abacos

If you have put in to West End, obviously you'll clear in there for it's an entry port and you get the formalities over and done with right at the start of your cruise. There are other options open to you if you decide to bypass West End, however, and not having cleared in doesn't prevent you from anchoring at uninhabited cays, such as Great Sale, or indeed anchoring off anywhere—so long as you don't start

hitting the local bars and restaurants, or go shopping. Just remember to keep that Q Flag flying until you've cleared in. The Abaco ports of entry are shown on our map.

Crossing the Little Bahama Bank

Essentially you have a choice of three places to gain access to the Bank. The first is West End, the second is Sandy Cay a few miles to the north, and the third is Memory Rock. Great Sale Cay serves as a staging point on all routes, but you can also make it to Walkers Cay in one straight shot from West End, Sandy Cay, or Memory Rock.

Let's assume that you're bound for either Walkers Cay or Green Turtle Cay, the two main start points for cruising in the Abacos. Let's look at distances:

West End–Mangrove Cay–Great Sale Cay	46 nm
West End–Walkers Cay	43 nm
Memory Rock–Mangrove Cay–Great Sale Cay	47 nm
Memory Rock–Walkers Cay	41 nm
Great Sale Cay–Walkers Cay	19 nm
Great Sale Cay to Green Turtle Cay	57 nm

As for your choice of route, once distance, your speed of advance, and available daylight are worked out, everything falls into place. The best direct route from Florida to Walkers Cay is by way of Memory Rock. Bound for

Abaco Entry Ports

Walker's Cay
Grand Cay • • Double Breasted Cay
Strangers Cay • • Carter's Cay
Pensacola Cays
Great Sale Cay
Little Abaco I
Little Cave Cay
Cooper's Town
Cross Cays
Powell Cay
Nun Jack Cay
Green Turtle Cay
Water Cay
Whale Cay
Great Guana Cay
McLeans Town
Big Joe
Downer Cay
Treasure Cay
Man-of-War Cay
Marsh Harbour
GRAND BAHAMA
Hope Town
The Marls
ABACO
Moore's Island
Cherokee Sound
Eight Mile Bay
PROVIDENCE
Cornwall Pt
Crossing Rocks
Gorda Cay

Great Sale you can choose either West End or Memory Rock. The approach routes on to the Bank decide that one for you. You have three options.

- **Indian Cay Passage**, just north of West End, carries 5.5 feet at low water. It's a marked channel, but its marks have disappeared in the past, and strong cross currents can take you aground if you allow yourself to get pushed out of the channel.

- **Sandy Cay** is an alternative to Indian Cay Passage. The best route we've found lies around 4–5 nm north of Sandy Cay. It carries 6 feet at low water and requires eyeball navigation. Taking this entrance on to the Bank will add about 10 nm to your run to Mangrove Cay.

- **Memory Rock**. If you require greater depth than the two passages we've mentioned, you must gain access to the Little Bahama Bank by way of the deeper passages north of Memory Rock where you can normally find 6 feet or more without difficulty.

West End–Indian Cay Passage–Mangrove Cay–Great Sale Cay

West End (1 nm W)	WESTW	26° 42' 00 N 079° 01' 00 W
Ocean side (just W)	INDCW	26° 43' 00 N 079° 01' 00 W
Pass between piles	INDCP	26° 43' 25 N 079° 00' 15 W
2nd mark (50 ft N)	INDC2	26° 43' 45 N 078° 59' 50 W
3rd mark (50 ft N)	INDC3	26° 44' 45 N 078° 59' 10 W
Barracuda Shoal mark (SE)	INDCB	26° 45' 45 N 078° 58' 05 W
Mangrove Cay (1.5 nm N)	MANGR	26° 57' 00 N 078° 37' 00 W
Great Sale Cay (1 nm W)	GSALE	26° 59' 00 N 078° 14' 30 W
Great Sale Anchorage	GSANC	26° 59' 52 N 078° 12' 54 W

INDIAN CAY PASSAGE

We've listed waypoints, but recommend strongly that you do *not* use them to negotiate Indian Cay Passage. The only way is to go visual. If you fool around trying to navigate by GPS you may well run aground. Leave West End and turn west into the ocean. When you have good depth and are well clear of West End, turn northwest parallel to the Bank on a heading of something like 325°M to pass outside Indian Cay. After Indian Cay you'll see Indian Cay Rock with a tall mark (a light) on it, and to its immediate northwest, a piling standing in the channel, which has a board like an arrow indication pointing north.

This piling is the first of three similar pilings marking the south side of the channel. Leave it to starboard as you enter on to the Bank. At your entry point there's a reef (which is often hard to see) extending south from Wood Cay for well over 1 nm, so don't assume you have all the distance between that first piling and Wood Cay as your channel. As it is, the shallowest water in the area is around

Abandoned boat and conch shell mound, West End Settlement.

Wood Cay. Keep close to the marks all the way, and it's better to steer by them, taking them one by one, rather than setting courses. The tidal flow runs across this channel. At mid-tide you'll probably find yourself being carried to the right or left of the channel, so navigate by keeping your eyes on the marker astern as well as the marker ahead. This last piece of advice is for real. There's no way you can stay in a channel unless you check your direction both by the markers ahead of you and the markers astern.

Leave all three Indian Cay Passage channel markers (that first entry mark by Indian Cay Rock and the two more) to starboard. Then one final marker comes up, which is on Barracuda Shoal. Keep this marker about 0.5 nm to port as you're making your way on to the Bank. If you're in doubt, steer 048°M from the third Indian Cay Passage mark for 1.4 nm and this will keep you in the channel and safely off that shoal. When you pass the Barracuda Shoal marker you can alter course for Mangrove Cay and use your GPS then. You'll have some 21.99 nm to run to our Mangrove Cay waypoint.

As we write this, two markers have disappeared: one near Indian Cay and one midway to the Barracuda Shoal marker. They should have been replaced by the time you read this, but it may not happen. Or others may have disappeared. It is not a rare event.

THE GOODWILL CHANNEL

The Goodwill Channel, your approach to West End settlement and the Harbour Hotel and Marina, comes up to starboard on entry from the Gulf Stream after you've passed the fairly obvious bank lying to the north of the Jack Tar property. Some grassy patches come up on your course, and then you should see an inlet deeper than the surrounding bank running to the southeast, which will eventually lead to off West End settlement. We hesitate to place reliance on markers (the key one is missing now) and GPS, because sand can shift. Until such time as the Goodwill Channel is properly marked, search for it, and feel your way in. As we've said before, go in and out with the tide.

West End–Sandy Cay–Mangrove Cay–Great Sale Cay

Sandy Cay (3 nm W)	SANDC	26° 49' 00 N	079° 07' 00 W
Mangrove Cay (1.5 nm N)	MANGR	26° 57' 00 N	078° 37' 00 W
Great Sale Cay (1 nm W)	GSALE	26° 59' 00 N	078° 14' 30 W
Great Sale Anchorage	GSANC	26° 59' 52 N	078° 12' 54 W

The Sandy Cay route on to the Little Bahama Bank is not a marked passage. It can carry about 5.5 feet at low water and is more challenging for the navigator than Indian Cay Passage for you have no marks, and you must rely on your ability to read the water by its color, choosing your own route. Sandy Cay itself is a private island and visitors, if you had thought of taking a break there, are not welcome.

Set out from West End as if you were going to take Indian Cay Passage and then run northwest to Sandy Cay in deep water. You have about 6 nm to go. Don't try to go south of Sandy Cay. There's only one break in the reef there and the area is shoal. Better to go north and make your turn to the east some 4–5 nm north of Sandy Cay. Look at your chart and get an idea of what's ahead of you, and then go in slowly using your eyes. When you are safely past Sandy Cay and have a comfortable 12 feet of water under you, alter for Mangrove Cay or Walkers Cay.

Memory Rock–Mangrove Cay–Great Sale Cay

Memory Rock Light	MEMRK	26° 57' 00 N	079° 07' 00 W
Memory Rock (2 nm S)	MEMRS	26° 55' 00 N	079° 07' 00 W
Memory Rock (3 nm N)	MEMRN	26° 59' 15 N	079° 08' 00 W
Mangrove Cay (1.5 nm N)	MANGR	26° 57' 00 N	078° 37' 00 W
Great Sale Cay (1 nm W)	GSALE	26° 59' 00 N	078° 14' 30 W
Great Sale Anchorage	GSANC	26° 59' 52 N	078° 12' 54 W

We give the approximate waypoints that will place you in a favorable position to make a turn on to the Bank. Again, like the Sandy Cay route, there are no marks and you're on your own, relying on your eyes. We favor going north of Memory Rock, but we've taken the southern route in a 49-foot boat with a 4-foot draft on a high tide. There are shoal areas lying 2.5 nm east of Memory Rock across both approaches, but the chart shows these and you should have no problems. Once you've passed the shoals, you can alter for Mangrove Cay.

Memory Rock–Triangle Rocks–Walkers Cay

Memory Rock (3 nm N)	MEMRN	26° 59' 15 N	079° 08' 00 W
Triangle Rocks (0.75 nm N)	TRIRK	27° 11' 00 N	078° 25' 00 W
Walkers Cay (end of channel)	WLKRS	27° 14' 00 N	078° 24' 00 W

Cross on to the Bank north of Memory Rock. Then head straight for our Triangle Rocks waypoint on a bearing of 081°M, which you hold for 41.2 nm. At Triangle Rocks you then alter for the Walkers Cay approach waypoint, just 5.3 nm away, on a bearing of 346°M. Go visual when you get to that last waypoint. Forget the GPS. For the approaches to Walkers Cay see the next chapter **The Northern Abacos, Walkers Cay to Allans-Pensacola Cay** on page 47.

MANGROVE CAY

Mangrove Cay, which runs north–south just 20 nm east of West End, is low lying, uninhabited, and barely 0.75 nm in length. A shoal area extends south of the cay for more than twice the length of the visible land. The cay has a light. Mangrove is no more than a passage waypoint between West End (or Memory Rock) and Great Sale Cay, and a useful reverse course waypoint. It can provide a lee if you are caught out and must anchor before you can make Great Sale Cay.

Mangrove Cay is also where the Grand Lucayan Waterway route links up with our Little Bahama Bank transit routes, and of course it's the start point from which you'll turn south to join the Grand Lucayan Waterway if you've elected to head for Port Lucaya or return to Florida that way. See **Grand Bahama Island, The Great Lucayan Waterway** under **Going on to Mangrove Cay** on page 113.

GREAT SALE CAY

Great Sale Cay runs north–south for 7 nm (counting in its southern reef) and is barely a mile broad at its widest point. The long tongue of reef and coral heads extending 2 nm south from the southern tip of Great Sale Cay is a definite hazard to navigation and is difficult to see until it's too late. Stay well clear. Great Sale Cay is low lying, covered in scrub,

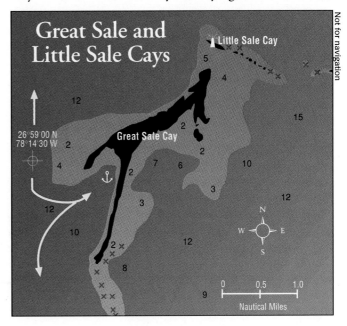

and is not particularly attractive, although it has a sand beach and the swimming in the anchorage is fine.

The anchorage, nearly a mile wide at its entrance, runs northward for nearly a mile. It carries 7–8 feet of water along its eastern side over sand and grass. The holding is adequate, but not good in some parts. You should dive to check your anchor. The anchorage shoals to the north and to the west, where you can find mostly grass and 4 feet of water. On shore, the east side is low coral and the west is mangrove fringed. Insects mean sunset barbecues are not a good idea. Great Sale Cay is uninhabited.

Great Sale anchorage is open to the south and west, and exposed to wind from every direction as the land is so low lying. While Great Sale offers protection from high seas from all directions other than the southwest quadrant, in high winds you can expect to find yourself in quite a chop, and dragging anchors are not unknown. During the sailing season you may find fifteen or more boats there, but we have, on occasion, found ourselves the sole occupants and then wondered what we'd missed that was going on in the outside world!

North of Great Sale Cay is Little Sale Cay, marked with a light, and Sale Cay Rocks, all of which are obvious.

Options After Great Sale Cay

After Great Sale Cay you're free to head in any direction. We offer Green Turtle Cay and Walkers Cay as the two most popular destinations for Abaco cruise start-points.

Great Sale Cay–Crab Cay–Green Turtle Cay

Great Sale Anchorage	GSANC	26° 59' 52 N	078° 12' 54 W
Great Sale Cay (1 nm W)	GSALE	26° 59' 00 N	078° 14' 30 W
South Sale Cay (3.5 nm S)	SSALE	26° 53' 00 N	078° 14' 00 W
Veteran Rock (0.5 nm S)	VETRK	26° 55' 30 N	077° 52' 30 W
Hawksbill Cays (0.75 nm NW)	HAWKB	26° 57' 00 N	077° 48' 00 W
Center of World Rock (0.5 nm S)	CENWD	26° 55' 30 N	077° 42' 00 W
Crab Cay (0.5 nm N)	CRABC	26° 56' 00 N	077° 36' 00 W
Angel Fish Point (0.5 nm NE)	ANGEL	26° 55' 30 N	077° 35' 00 W
Coopers Town (1 nm NE)	CPSTN	26° 53' 00 N	077° 30' 00 W
Green Turtle N (3.5 nm NW)	GTNTH	26° 47' 00 N	077° 23' 00 W
Green Turtle Cay (1 nm W)	GTRTL	26° 46' 00 M	077° 21' 00 W

There are no problems on this route, which, of all the longer Abaco Passages, remains one of our favorites. All you *must* do at the start is to make that straight run south to the waypoint we call South Sale Cay on a bearing of 185°M for 5.5 nm. Even if you can't see that reef extending south from Great Sale Cay, don't be tempted to cut corners and turn early for West End Rocks (or the reverse if you are heading west). We have, and were scared stiff, and in those days we drew just 2 feet 6 inches fully laden.

Thereafter it's all straightforward. After South Sale there's a 19.3 nm leg to Veteran Rock on 075°M. You may not see Veteran Rock. Don't edge toward it thinking you need it as a mark. It's awash at high tide. Stay well clear. It's 4.2 nm to Hawksbill on 075°M. When you get to the Hawksbill Cays don't be tempted to run too close, for rocks and shoals lie to the north of them. The next leg, 5.5 nm on 111°M, to Center of the World Rock (which is highly

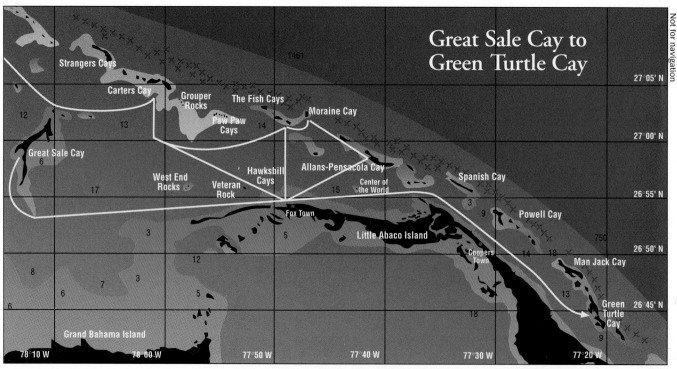

Great Sale Cay to Green Turtle Cay

Not for navigation

visible as a great doughball of a rock in the middle of no-where) should keep you clear of the outlying Hawksbill reefs. After Center of the World (which you should leave to port) it's 5.3 nm on 090°M to pass Crab Cay point (with its marker) on your starboard side.

At Crab Cay you turn southeast. It's just over 1 nm on 125°M to bring you off Angel Fish Point. Don't even think of cutting between Angel Fish Point and the south tip of Crab Cay. It could spoil your day. You stay on the same heading, 125°M for 5.1 nm to arrive off Coopers Town. Your course favors the west side of the Sea of Abaco because shoal areas lie between Spanish, Powell, Ambergris, and Nunjack Cays to the east. Visiting these cays you take an inshore passage, closer to the cays themselves.

After Coopers Town it's a change to 139°M for 8.6 nm to place you 3.5 nm northwest of Green Turtle Cay, and then you close the distance, altering to 125°M to place you ready to choose your landfall, either White Sound, Black Sound, or the anchorage off New Plymouth. For details on Green Turtle Cay see **The Central Abaco Cays, Allans-Pensacola Cay to Green Turtle Cay** on page 62.

Great Sale Cay–Triangle Rocks–Walkers Cay

Great Sale Anchorage	GSANC	26° 59' 52 N	078° 12' 54 W
Great Sale Cay (1 nm W)	GSALE	26° 59' 00 N	078° 14' 30 W
Triangle Rocks (0.75 nm N)	TRIRK	27° 11' 00 N	078° 25' 00 W
Walkers Cay (end of channel)	WLKRS	27° 14' 00 N	078° 24' 00 W

This is a straightforward, relatively short passage. From your Great Sale start point it's 12.5 nm on 328°M to take you safely off Triangle Rocks (see the chart on page 41). Then you alter to 346°M and hold it for 5.3 nm until you have placed yourself ready to go visual into Walkers Cay Marina. For details on Walkers Cay see **The Northern Abaco Cays, Walkers Cay to Allans-Pensacola Cay** on page 47.

YELLOW PAGES

WEST END

So much is changing in West End. The new *Harbour Hotel and Marina* has been built, almost within a year, at West End itself, and the long-standing *Jack Tar Marina* is on the verge of a total transformation, to be renamed the *West End Resort*. We've heard this promise many times in the past, but this time it seems to be for real. Our descriptions are based on what was there in June 1997, and the plans and aspirations revealed to us. West End, the oldest settlement on Grand Bahama, is useful only if you need a staging port or a Port of Entry for clearing in on arrival from the US, or somewhere to wait for weather before returning to Florida. But this will change as the new *West End Resort* development takes over, starting in late 1997. The current *Jack Tar Marina* is about two miles from West End Settlement, but there are nearly always taxis waiting at the marina that will take you there for $2, and some local restaurants that will send complimentary transport to collect you. There is an annual street festival in the settlement on Saturdays during June. **Customs** and **Immigration** are open from 8 am to 5 pm or on request, in the *Jack Tar Marina*.

MARINAS

JACK TAR MARINA (as it was in June 1997)
Tel: 242-346-6211 • Fax: 346-6546 • VHF 16

This old marina is badly in need of restoration. It is a safe haven after a turbulent Gulf Stream crossing, but will be a delight once the new 200-slip marina is completed, with new hotel facilities, swimming pool, airport, bar, and small cottages. At that point the entry channel will have been changed.

Slips	80
Max LOA	Up to 100 ft.
MLW at dock	8 ft.
Dockage	75¢ per foot per day, 30 ft. minimum
Power	50A and 30A available, $10 per day
Fuel	Diesel and gasoline at the fuel dock
Propane	From *RF Grant Electronics* in West End
Water	15¢ per gallon
Telephone	Outside the marina office; US 25¢ for calls
Showers	Free, no hot water, many not working
Laundry	$1 in quarters to use a washer or dryer
Ice	$3 per bag
Credit Cards	Major cards accepted with a 4% surcharge.

HARBOUR HOTEL AND MARINA
Tel: 242-346-6432 • VHF 16

This new marina, in the settlement at West End, fronts the original *Harbour Hotel*, which is itself due to be totally refurbished in 1998. A new sea wall will protect from the northeast on this exposed coast. Plans are for a dive boat and dive shop, as well as a marina shop to sell bait and tackle and a few groceries.

Slips	14 boats up to 60 ft., 30 boats up to 30 ft.
MLW at Dock	8 ft., but only 4 ft. in the approach channel at low water, 9 ft. at high water
Dockage	$20 per day up to 30 ft., 50¢ per foot per day over 30 ft.
Power	50A and 30A available
Fuel	Diesel and gasoline
Water	$5 per day
Telephone & TV	$10 per day for services and utilities
Showers	Yes, very clean
Laundry	Yes
Restaurant	*Harbour Hotel Rest.*, open 7 am to 11 pm
Swimming	Pool for hotel and marina guests
Accommodations	*Harbour Hotel and Marina*

SERVICES

Churches
St. Michael's Catholic Church Sunday Mass
Church of God of Prophecy
St. Mary Magdalene Church

Clinic
Open 8 am to 5 pm, Monday to Friday; doctor in attendance.

Police
In the turquoise painted building next to *Batelco*.

Post Office
Open from 9 am to 5 pm, Monday to Friday.

Telephone
Outside the *Batelco* office, next to the radio mast.

SHOPPING

Groceries
J & M Grocery On the waterfront, with limited supplies.

Hardware
R F Grant Electronics Tel: 346-6207
24-hour service; repairs, plumbing, and propane.

Liquors
T & J Liquor Store

Marine Supplies
Billie's Tel: 346-6057

RESTAURANTS

Baby Grants Bar Local sports bar
The Buccaneer's Club Tel: 349-3794
Serves Swiss and Bahamian food, and offers free transportation.
Harbour Hotel Bar and Restaurant Tel: 346-6432
Open for breakfast, lunch, and dinner.
The New Harry's American Bar and Restaurant at Deadman's Reef Tel: 349-2610 Open 12 noon to 11 pm with a complimentary drink and free transportation. They can cater for parties.
Paradise Cove at Deadman's Reef Tel: 349-2677 Serves hamburgers, hot dogs, and snacks, and offers a secluded beach, snorkel rental for $10, and beachfront accommodations.
The Star Tel: 346-6207 Local flavor, a 1940s time capsule.
Yvonne's Cafe Open all day, eat in or take out.

GETTING AROUND

Airport
The nearest operational airport is Freeport, a $50 taxi ride; the West End airport may be reopened to commercial traffic.

Taxis
Small buses usually wait within the *Jack Tar Marina*, or ask at the marina office, or pick one up in the settlement.

ACCOMMODATIONS

Harbour Hotel and Restaurant on the waterfront in West End Tel: 242-346-6432 They will have 33 rooms from $65 per night, suites from $85.

THINGS TO DO IN WEST END
- Take the dinghy across to Indian Cay and enjoy a little beach all to yourself.
- Go for a swim or dinner at Deadman's Reef, which will show you more of Grand Bahama Island.
- Dance the night away in the *Harbour Hotel* disco until 4 am.

Chapter 4
The Northern Abacos
Walkers Cay to Allans-Pensacola Cay

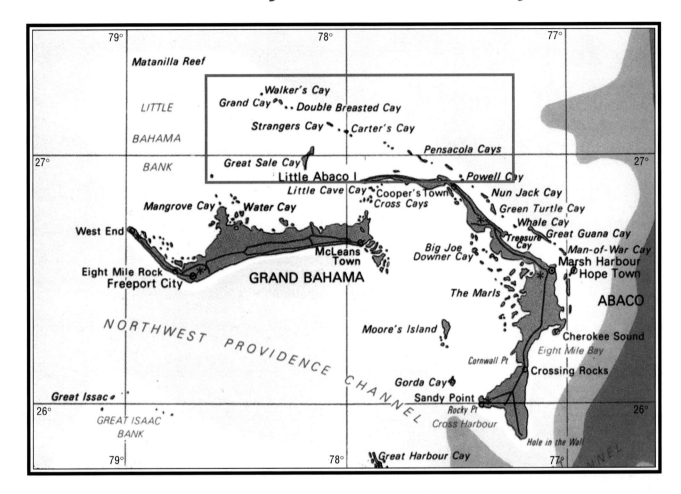

Ocean Passes

GOOD passes out into the Atlantic Ocean are rare between Walkers Cay and Allans-Pensacola, but we recommend two of them, one of which has an alternative.

- From Walkers Cay you have one route with two options. Head southeast paralleling **Walkers Cay** after leaving the marina and then turn out into the ocean between Walkers Cay and Gully Rocks on a heading of 060°M, or alternatively delay your turn until you can pass between Tom Brown's Cay and Seal Cay on a heading of 010°M.

- The **Moraine Cay Pass** out into the Atlantic is fine. Run about 1 nm southeast from Moraine Cay and then turn out to the ocean on a heading between 000° and 005°M.

Walkers Cay

Approaches
One of the Walkers Cay landmarks is its radio tower. This tower is now dwarfed by a much larger (275 feet) Batelco tower, almost a mini-Eiffel Tower, on Grand Cay to the south. Don't be fooled and take this tower as your heading. Remember Walkers Cay, with its cluster of rocks, is the "Land's End" land in the chain of islands that have opened up in front of you. You should see the gleam of white hulls in the marina long before you notice the Walkers Cay radio tower. A little later you'll pick up the first of the stakes marking the marina entry channel. The stakes are not the grand passageway that you might expect. There are only a handful of them, set far apart and single. If you're entering on a low tide, just go slowly and carefully. You gain deeper water after the last stake.

A SPORTS FISHING CENTER

If you're into sports fishing, Walkers Cay is the place to be. Along with Bimini, Treasure Cay, and Boat Harbour Marina in Marsh Harbour, Walkers Cay rates as one of the world centers for the sport and everything there takes its pattern from the life-style of the sports fishing fraternity. If you're cruising and searching for peace and quiet, you're unlikely to stay here long. This said, Walkers Cay may serve you well as a place to clear in, as a start point for your Abaco cruise, or as a well-found waystation to wait for favorable Gulf Stream weather on your return. It's a full-service marina.

Moving on from Walkers Cay

From Walkers Cay you're well poised to start a leisurely cruise southeastward, visiting each cay in turn. Your distances from potential anchorage to potential anchorage are short, your navigation is going to be a combination of eyeball and GPS (for you have to make some doglegs to avoid shoals and reefs), and you'll see little of civilization as we know it.

For your planning, first let's list the places where you can get fuel or provisions:

Walkers Cay	fuel and provisions (marina)
Fox Town	fuel (but depth at dock is less then 4 feet)
Spanish Cay	fuel and some provisions (marina)
Coopers Town	fuel and some provisions (open to weather)
Green Turtle Cay	fuel and provisions (well served with options)

Your primary concern should be the weather, for as it is over all the Bahamas, there are few anchorages that are good under all conditions. Against this, if the weather does start to change, the distances are so short you can run for a safer place within a few hours. There's no need to get paranoid about being caught out.

Walkers Cay to the Grand Cays

Walkers Cay (end of channel)	WLKRS	27° 14' 00 N	078° 24' 00 W
Triangle Rocks (0.75 nm N)	TRIRK	27° 11' 00 N	078° 25' 00 W
Grand Cays (1 nm S)	GRAND	27° 11' 00 N	078° 25' 00 W
Deep Water off Grand Cays	DWOGC	27° 12' 00 N	078° 19' 30 W
Grand Cays Anchorage	GCANC	27° 13' 10 N	078° 19' 18 W

The High Tide Short Cut

This is a simple, short run to be taken at high water. We reckon you can carry 6–8 feet if you get the tide right. You don't have to take the marked channel out of Walkers Cay. On leaving the marina turn southeast on an initial heading of around 130°M, aiming to leave Elephant Rock, lying just southwest of 27° 14' N 078° 22' W, on your starboard side.

Pass between Elephant Rock and Burying Piece Rocks, which will be on your port side. You'll be running on a line offshore of Burying Piece Rocks, aiming now to leave Sandy Cay (just southwest of 27° 13' N 078° 20' W) on your port side. Don't be tempted to pass between Sandy Cay and Little Grand Cay. Even at high tide you'll probably find only 4 feet there.

You'll see that just level with the north end of Sandy Cay there's an opening between Grand Cay and Little Grand Cay (the 275-foot Batelco tower is there and a prominent blue water tank with a white top that looks like a silo). Ignore the opening. Continue your heading, watching for the rocks south of Sandy Cay, until you pass the 078° 19' W line. At that time you'll see two more openings lying between Little Grand Cay and Felix Cay. Don't take the first. Go for the second. You'll see that it has a marker on the starboard side, and there's a prominent white house on Big Grand Cay behind it. Richard Nixon used to stay there to unwind while he was President.

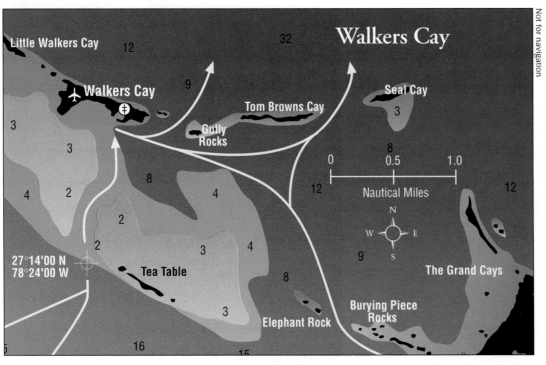

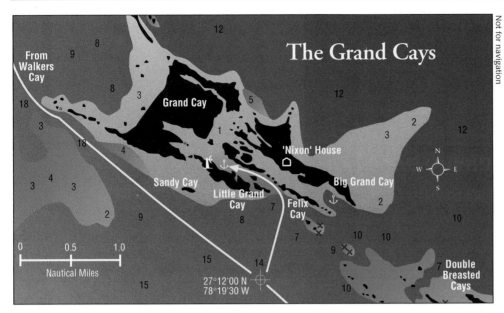

The Grand Cays

The Regular Route

Take the marked channel out of Walkers Cay. When you reach the Walkers Cay waypoint set a course of 165° M for our Triangle Rocks waypoint. From there head for Grand Cays on a bearing of 051°M. Your distance to run will be 5.3 nm on Leg 1, and 4.3 nm on Leg 2. When you reach the Grand Cays waypoint head for the center of Felix Cay, which lies in front of you, and take the second opening that opens up off your port bow. For the final stages of your approach, follow the guidelines we've given in the **High Tide Short Cut.**

Grand Cays

THE GRAND CAY ANCHORAGE

Go slowly in to the Little Grand Cay anchorage, favoring the starboard side of the approach channel. Off the settlement you'll find 6–7 feet of water with patches of 8 feet over sand and grass. Don't be tempted to work your way further inshore without checking it out first in your dinghy. Your distance run from Walkers Cay to get to Grand Cay will be about 8 nm, depending on the route chosen.

It's a good anchorage but open to wind and fetch from the northwest and southeast, and wind and current can chase you around 360 degrees. Make sure you have plenty of space to swing, and don't be surprised if you drag when the tide changes. Use two anchors if your primary doesn't reset all that well, or if you're not sure that it has set properly. Stay clear of the fairway in to the settlement (the deeper water on the starboard side as you enter), despite its attractive depths, for the cowboys come home from Walkers Cay too fast to avoid you at night. Use your anchor light, *at or near deck level,* so that it can be seen by someone at sea level. An incidental note: We've never seen so many rays cruising around an anchorage.

THE GRAND CAY GROUP

The Grand Cay group consists of five main islands (Grand, Big Grand, Little Grand, Rat, and Felix Cays) with a settlement on Little Grand marked with the prominent Batelco tower. About 200 people live there. The waters around the cays are shallow, a mix of bonefish flats, mangrove channels, and ocean beach. It's dinghy country, with good water colors, but the cays are not particularly beautiful and we've been plagued by flies there.

Other than going to the Grand Cays out of curiosity, we feel there's little that you'll find rewarding. It may have been a bad day the last time we landed, but our entrance into the bar at Rosie's passed ignored and unacknowledged. Nevertheless, Rosie's cracked conch is reputed to be "the best ever." As we left Grand Cay the Bahamian PR machine cut in and a little boy, struggling along over the uneven pavement at his mother's knees, turned to blow us kisses time and time again, until he was dragged around a bend and out of sight.

Grand Cays to the Double Breasted Cays

Deep Water off Grand Cays	DWOGC	27° 12' 00 N	078° 19' 30 W
Double Breasted Cays	DBRST	27° 11' 00 N	078° 16' 45 W
Double Breasted Approach	DBAPP	27° 11' 17 N	078° 16' 35 W

Choose a time close to high tide. On leaving the Grand Cays anchorage head straight out (steering something like 198°M) to get into deeper water, then steer around 154°M to run the 8.1 nm to the anchorage area off Double Breasted Cays.

Double Breasted Cays

We have friends who have long said that Double Breasted is one of their favorite stops in all the Bahamas. If you want a place to go gunkholing in the time-honored fashion of the true cruising boat, beachcomb, swim, snorkel, fish a little, and be amazed at the colors and clarity of the water, we join them in placing Double Breasted high on our list. We'd promised ourselves a full 24 hours there on our final Abacos research trip, just for the delight of it. When we got there the weather was against us. Sadly we had to move on.

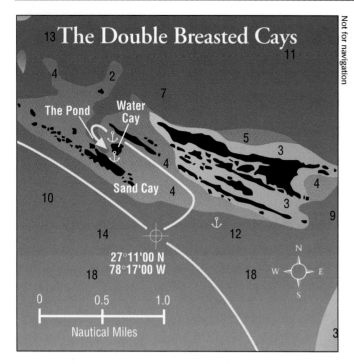

The Double Breasted Cays

Not for navigation

THE DOUBLE BREASTED CAYS ANCHORAGES

We've been wary of working in too close into the Double Breasted Cays and prefer to anchor off, using our dinghy to explore. The best place to anchor close in, if you want to simplify your life on the navigation side, is to make for our approach waypoint. Pass about 100 yards to the east of the reef (covered by 2 feet of water at MLW) on your port side. Once you're past the reef, take a northerly heading until you're 200 yards off the rocky islets ahead. That's your anchorage. Beware: there's a submerged rock at 27° 22' 39 N 078° 16' 59 W. Don't circle out too far finding your ideal spot. If you drop your hook there you'll have protection from the west through the north. The downside is that you're not protected from the prevailing winds, and it can be rolly. The holding is fair, gravelly sand with some grass and rock, and you don't want to get too close in to the land, for the water depth gets down to around 5 feet at MLW.

INNER ANCHORAGES
(WATER CAY AND THE POND)

Getting in and out of the Water Cay–Pond area is not difficult, but it's potentially hazardous. Once you're there, you'll be in a kind of private marine paradise. If you elect to work your way in, anchor off first, wait for the tide, and while you're waiting, check the route in your dinghy. Don't make your move until you've done this, and you've got good light so that you can get the eyeballing right.

From the rocky islets bear around to the west and follow the dark water (6–7 feet at MLW) all the way in. Pass midway between the first sandbar on your port side and the rocky islet to starboard. Then continue on to pass midway

between Water Cay to port and another rocky islet to starboard. After Water Cay you'll come to a second sandbar on your port side. If you reckon you've had enough inshore work at this point, you can anchor either on the north side of Water Cay or the north side of this second sandbank in 6–6.5 feet of water.

If you want to get in to the Pond, it becomes testing from this point on. Ahead of you to port you have the sandbar, and to starboard an opening in the line of rocky islands you've been passing. You want to round the sandbar turning to port, but must first pass a boat length away from the gap, squeezed between the opening itself and the sandbar. This gap carries a strong tidal flow. It's fine at slack water. At any other time you're either going to be sucked out to sea by an ebb tide, or pushed right on the sand by a flood tide. Hence the desirability of slack water. Once you've met this challenge, just make your way around Water Cay into the Pond to the south of Water Cay. Set two anchors. The current runs fast through the whole Water Cay–Pond anchorage area.

BIG ROMERS CAY, RHODA ROCKS, STRANGERS CAY, AND JOE CAYS

Big Romers Cay, Rhoda Rocks, Strangers Cay, and Joe Cays form, by any standard, a difficult area of banks, shoals, rocks, and reefs. It could well be a gunkhole fanatic's idea of heaven, but for the cruising yachtsman it could be unrewarding, and possibly prematurely aging, to choose it as a playground.

After visiting Double Breasted, even if we're intent on cruising the Abaco chain cay by cay, we leave this stretch to the locals. Of course you can make your way around these cays and Rhoda Rocks if you set your mind to it, but we

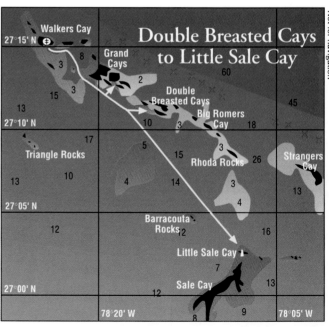

Double Breasted Cays to Little Sale Cay

Not for navigation

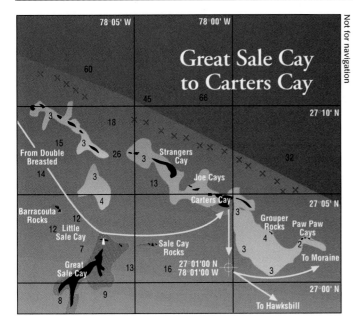

Great Sale Cay to Carters Cay

take a diversion and go on to Carters Cay by way of Little Sale Cay. The reverse applies running south to north.

Double Breasted Cays–Little Sale Cay–Carters Cay

Double Breasted Cays	DBRST	27° 11' 00 N	078° 16' 45 W
Little Sale Cay	LSALE	27° 04' 00 N	078° 12' 00 W
Mid-Carters (1 nm off)	MCRTR	27° 03' 00 N	078° 01' 00 W
Carters Cay (just off)	CRTRS	27° 04' 00 N	078° 01' 00 W
Carters Anchorage	CTANC	27° 05' 03 N	078° 00' 07 W

From Double Breasted Cays head 154°M for Little Sale Cay, which will take you on a run of 8.1 nm safely past Barracouta Rocks (you'll see them on your starboard side) to a point off Little Sale Cay. You then turn on to 101°M to run 9.8 nm to a point 1 nm south of Carters Cay, which we've called Mid-Carters. From then on you go visual.

LITTLE SALE CAY
Little Sale Cay, together with Sale Cay Rocks, runs east–west just 0.75 nm off the north tip of Great Sale Cay and spreads out along Latitude 27° 02' N for 4 nm. Little Sale itself, standing rocky and sturdy with a light on its west headland is an unmistakable landmark. It's one of the best Little Bahama Bank waypoints, but don't forget those four miles of rocks and shoals extending to the east.

Carters Cay

Feel your way in past the very obvious sandbars, leaving them to port. Head for the center of Gully Cay, and then turn to port to head toward the mark on the little rock, which will be on your bow. Keep about 1–2 boat lengths off

Gully Cay. Then round the end of Gully Cay, not too close inshore, and anchor between Gully Cay and what is plainly the remains of some kind of military camp on Big Carters Cay. You'll have the luxury of 20 feet of water there. Don't go in too far to the east for it shoals. Don't opt for mid-channel, for the tide rips through it. You are safe where you are. Only a Norther will give you a rough time.

But if you do go there, time your arrival for as close to high tide as you can, and that goes for your departure too. Despite all our concern for depths, we grounded at mid-tide as we left. The sandbanks and the shoal areas change. No air photograph, no chart, and no guide book can really help you. As ever in the Bahamas, you're on your own in many places. It's character building.

If you like offbeat, forgotten places, Carters Cay hits the spot. Once a US missile tracking station, Carters Cay has nothing in terms of civilization but its ruins. No one lives there, but Bahamian fishermen come to camp, with generators to give them light and charcoal grills as their kitchen, using the abandoned main barrack block and a set of shacks as their base. Over two or three days they will fill their boats with lobster and conch for sale as far away as Freeport. If you find them there, they keep much to themselves but will be happy to talk if you take the time to greet them.

Wander around Carters Cay. You may get the feeling that you've found the site of Dr. No's bid for World Domination in a James Bond movie. But above that, Carters has a magic that's captivating. It's partly that fantastic deep-water anchorage, partly the ease of access by tender to the ocean reefs on one side and the Banks rocks on the other, partly the colors of the water, partly the sense of peace and isolation. If this kind of thing appeals, go there.

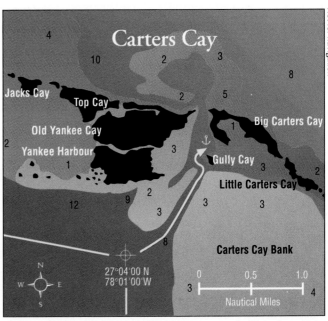

Carters Cay

GROUPER ROCKS, PAWPAW CAYS, AND PAWPAW ROCKS

The area to the southeast of Carters Cay is not unlike the confusion of shoals, small cays, and reefs around Rhoda Rocks. Here Grouper Rocks and the Paw Paw Cays effectively dictate that you must drop south from Carters Cay to gain deeper water before you can continue on your travels.

Assuming Allans-Pensacola is on your route plan, you have two options. One is to head for Hawksbill Cay and Fox Town and the other is to go to Moraine Cay for a daylight stop. Take your lunch there and go beachcombing. And then go on to Allans-Pensacola. Whichever way you go, you must first drop south to our Carters Cay south waypoint.

Carters Cay to Hawksbill Cay

Carters Cay (just off)	CRTRS	27° 04' 00 N	078° 01' 00 W
South Carters Cay (3 nm S)	SCRTR	27° 01' 00 N	078° 01' 00 W
Hawksbill Cay (3.75 nm NW)	HWKBL	26° 57' 00 N	077° 48' 00 W

First gain your offing from Carters Cay by getting 3 nm south on 185°M, and then take it to Hawksbill in one straight run of 12.3 nm on a heading of 115°M.

THE HAWKSBILL CAYS

Your landfall should be safely off the west end of Hawksbill Cay. When you get there, swing westward in a lazy half-circle to pass well away from the rock with the marker on it, and come in to the anchorage on the 26° 56' N line to anchor wherever you fancy under the westernmost end of Hawksbill Cay. You'll have around 8–9 feet of water, and relatively good holding. You are open to the east and west, but if the wind stays below 15 knots you'll be OK.

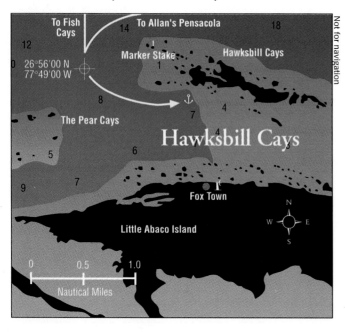

Cracking conch in Carters Cay.

FOX TOWN

Fox Town, landmarked by its 200-foot Batelco tower, does have fuel and some provisions, but is hardly likely to feature on your list as a provisioning stop. For a start it carries barely 4 feet at the local docks, and the approach, through a second chain of islets and rocks that parallel the Hawksbill chain but run close inshore, is likely to deter you taking your boat in.

If you settle for exploring in your dinghy, coming over from the Hawksbill anchorage, you'll find a surprisingly smart little settlement in many respects, better houses than average strung out along a deserted paved road, and two gas stations, one at each end of town (both ready to dispense marine fuel from their own docks) but both of them as deserted as the road, no sign of any kind of business. There's a mini-supermarket, which inexplicably lacked both bread and water while we were there, one restaurant, and two unnamed bars. There's a post office (open three days a week only), a police station that must boast some of the least-stressed members of the Force, and a clinic, which was closed. Life is taken slowly there, by all appearances.

A flashy low-slung red car with black tinted windows drives slowly through Fox Town as if seeking admiration but draws no response. The dogs bark but soon give up and relax into boredom. The flashy red car drives slowly back and disappears. The sponge fishermen spread the sponges they've pulled from the beds of the Little Bahama Bank out on the grass in front of one of the gas stations, and leave them to dry in the heat of the noon sun. It's late morning by then. Nothing moves. Even the dogs are asleep in the shade.

Hawksbill Cay to Moraine Cay

Hawksbill Cay (3.75 nm NW)	HWKBL	26° 57' 00 N	077° 48' 00 W
Fish Cays (safely off)	FISHC	27° 01' 30 N	077° 48' 30 W
Moraine Cay Approach (1 nm S)	MORAP	27° 01' 30 N	077° 46' 15 W
Moraine Cay (0.5 nm S)	MORAI	27° 02' 15 N	077° 46' 15 W

If you went south to Hawksbill Cay from Carters and then decide at that point you want to see Moraine Cay, it's an easy run. A course of 000°M will take you 4.5 nm to the Fish Cays waypoint, and then take your two short legs (094°M held for 2 nm and 005°M for 0.5 nm) to place you just south of the Moraine Cay anchorage. Go visual on these legs!

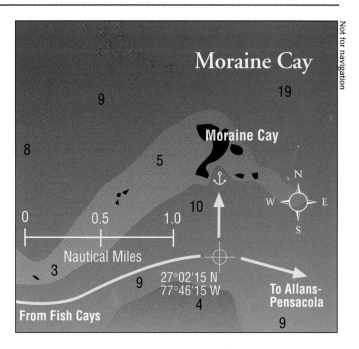

Carters Cay–Fish Cays–Moraine Cay

Carters Cay (just off)	CRTRS	27° 04' 00 N	078° 01' 00 W
South Carters Cay (3 nm S)	SCRTR	27° 01' 00 N	078° 01' 00 W
Grouper Rocks (3 nm S)	GRPRR	27° 00' 00 N	077° 57' 15 W
Fish Cays (safely off)	FISHC	27° 01' 30 N	077° 48' 30 W
Moraine Cay approach (1 nm S)	MORAP	27° 01' 30 N	077° 46' 15 W
Moraine Cay (0.5 nm S)	MORAI	27° 02' 15 N	077° 46' 15 W

Once again, first gain your offing from Carters Cay. Then for 3.5 nm you run on 115°M (the same course you would take for Hawksbill) until you are safely south of the Grouper Rocks area. From that waypoint you can turn directly for the Fish Cays on a course of 085°M with 7.9 nm to run. From there you have to get past the rocks of the most southerly Fish Cay on your port side and the Fish Cay banks on your starboard side. A course of 094°M held for 2 nm will achieve this, and place you due south of Moraine Cay.

FISH CAYS

The Fish Cays are nothing to write home about. Like almost all the Abaco Cays they have beaches on the ocean side, but otherwise offer neither good anchorages nor anything particularly exciting to explore.

MORAINE CAY

From your landfall due south of Moraine Cay turn north on 005°M for 0.5 nm, going visual, and anchor off the beach in about 8 feet of water. This anchorage is not an all-night stop unless you're very certain of your weather, for it's exposed and would be no fun in winds from southeast through southwest. As for exposure to the north, protected though it may be, you wouldn't want to go there in a Norther.

Moraine Cay, privately owned but open to visitors, is a daytime *must see* in this part of the Abacos. The beach on the west side, which you reach from your anchorage by dinghy,

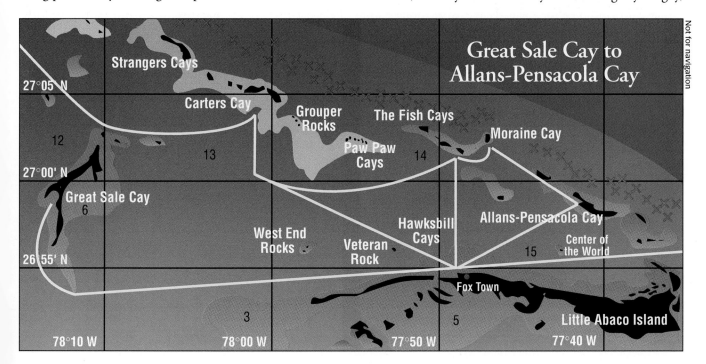

Beach at Moraine Cay (and Sophie Bell, working).

has a sweep of good sand, despite a ledge of rock close in-shore, and a 180° panorama that encompasses ocean reef, every color of Bahamian water, and a horizon that sometimes just merges limitless into the sky. Behind you there's nothing but one small island, white sand, and some palms. This place you would write home about.

Moraine Cay to Allans-Pensacola Cay

Moraine Cay (0.5 nm S)	MORAI	27° 02' 15 N	077° 46' 15 W
Allans-Pensacola Cay (0.5 nm NW)	ALPEN	26° 59' 15 N	077° 42' 15 W

This is a simple run of 4.6 nm on a course of 136°M. After leaving Umbrella Cay to port you'll see little Guineaman's Cay to port, and then the Allans-Pensacola anchorage will open up to you.

Allans-Pensacola Cay

THE ALLANS-PENSACOLA ANCHORAGE

The bay that forms the Allans-Pensacola anchorage, entered from the northwest, is nearly a mile in length. Only the first half of this is usable as an anchorage, for the southeast end shoals. Favor the inshore side to avoid Allans Cay Rocks. You don't want to take your boat further south than the headland by Allans Cay Rocks, unless you have shoal draft. It's a good anchorage, protected from everything but the west and through northwest to north, with around 6–8 feet of water and fairly good holding (but dive to check that anchor). It's popular for all these reasons, and because it falls into place as a convenient stopping point. It can be crowded in the cruising season.

Lying northwest–southeast across Latitude 26° 59' Allans-Pensacola is located at the very point where, having crossed the Little Bahama Bank from Florida, you may well wish to spend a night before heading further south, or alternatively pause before setting off westward to return home. At one time two separate cays, Allans Cay and Pensacola Cay (long known as the Pensacola Cays) were forcibly linked by a hurricane to the later advantage of cruising sailors, for the end result has provided an anchorage that, as we've said, is ever popular.

The unified cay is some 3 nm long. Other than the ruins of yet another US missile tracking station there's nothing on the island, but the beaches on the ocean side are good, and the cuts between Allans-Pensacola and little Guineaman's Cay to its north are one of our favorite areas for gunkholing and fishing.

Finally, be warned. On the southeastern tip of Allans-Pensacola there's a narrow creek-like entrance to a rocky channel that leads in to a landlocked basin surrounded by mangroves. It appears to be an ideal hurricane hole, and you may well be able to creep into it on a high tide if you don't draw too much. We grounded there once in our shoal draft days trying to get in with 2 feet 6 inches of draft. We'll come clean and admit that it was within two hours of low water, but be warned. And the bugs there may drive you mad.

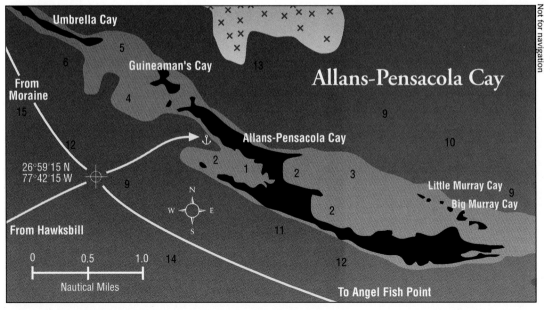

WALKERS CAY

Walkers Cay is the home of sports fishing. As the northernmost island in the Bahamas, with its good facilities and airport, it also offers a northern Port of Entry and jumping off place for Abaco. All facilities are found in and around the marina and hotel complex. **Customs** and **Immigration** (353-1211) are at the airport and can be called from the marina on arrival. They are open from 9 am to 5 pm, or on request.

MARINA

WALKERS CAY HOTEL AND MARINA
Tel: 242-352-1252 • Fax: 353-1339 • VHF 16 and 68

Slips	73
Max LOA	Over 100 ft.
MLW at Dock	5 ft.
Dockage	$1.25 per foot per day, including power
Fuel	Diesel and gasoline
Water	30¢ per gallon
Telephone	Outside the liquor store
Showers	Yes
Laundry	Yes, ask at the hotel
Credit Cards	All types accepted

SHOPPING

Groceries
Sea Chest Grocery

Gift shops
Sea Below Dive and Gift Shop

Treasure Chest Gift Shop

Liquors
Walkers Spirit

RESTAURANTS & BARS

Conch Pearl Dining Room   Open daily from 7:30 am for breakfast, and 7:30 pm for dinner.

Lobster Trap Restaurant & Lounge   Open from 11 am to 3 pm for lunch in the winter season, and for dinner during the summer. Indoor or outdoor dining, and a lounge with pool table.

Marlin Bar   Open from noon to closing.

GETTING AROUND

Airport
Pan Am Air Bridge
Flights daily, except Tuesdays, from Fort Lauderdale.

SPORTS

Charter Boats
Bonefishing: 18-foot Hewes Skiff, $300 per day; reef fishing: a 23-foot Hoog, $300 per day, $200 for a half day; deep-sea fishing: 50-foot Hatteras $700 per day, $400 for a half day.

Diving
Walkers Cay Undersea Adventures   Tel: 352-1252   Two-tank dive $75, resort course $125, snorkelers $20; rental equipment available. Bonefishing, deep sea fishing, secluded island picnics, tours of a tropical fish hatchery, and cookouts for dive groups.

Dive Sites
Daily dive trips to *Pirate's Cathedral*, *Flower Garden*, and *Spanish Cannon Reef*. Other dive sites are *Spiral Cavern*, *Barracuda Alley*, and the *Shark Rodeo* that usually attracts more than 100 sharks and groupers.

Fishing
Offshore, reef, or bonefishing.

Shuffleboard

Swimming
Salt- and freshwater pools with Jacuzzi.

Tennis
Two all-weather tennis courts.

ACCOMMODATIONS

Walkers Cay Hotel   Tel: 242-352-1252   62 rooms from $100 per night, suites and villas from $200, MAP $37.50 per person. Special package deals for small boaters, divers, and private pilots. Call 1-800-WALKERS.

THINGS TO DO IN WALKERS CAY

- Join in the action—charter a boat or find a friend with a sports fisher, and go deep sea fishing.
- Take your tender and spend a day gunkholing around Grand Cay.
- Go diving—there are some fantastic dive sites.

GRAND CAY

When you have anchored off and come in with your dinghy to the pier in front of *Rosie's Place*, you will find a small settlement, with just about 200 inhabitants, many of whom work at Walkers Cay. Apart from *Rosie's Place*, there is little ashore to attract the cruising visitor, but the gunkholing and fishing around Grand Cay is great.

SERVICES & SHOPPING

Accommodations
Rosie's Place Island Bay Motel   VHF 68 "Love Train"

Beauty Parlor
Rachel's Hair and Nails

Church
Shilo Baptist

Clinic
Grand Cay Community Clinic
Open 9 am to 1 pm, Monday through Friday, closed Wednesdays and weekends.

Fuel dock
Diesel and gasoline.

Groceries
Father and Son Grocery and Drug Store
Open 7 am to 9 pm Monday to Saturday, to 7 pm on Sunday.
L & S Restaurant and Grocery
Open daily for fresh bread, cakes, and canned food. Let them know in advance if you want to eat there.
Rosie's Place and Grocery   A small selection of groceries.

Restaurant
Rosie's Place and Grocery   A bar, pool table, and television, but you must order meals ahead of time.

Telephones
Outside the Clinic and outside *Rosie's Place.*

THINGS TO DO IN GRAND CAY

- Go bonefishing on the flats.
- Try Rosie's cracked conch.
- Count the sting rays and the starfish in the anchorage.

FOX TOWN

If you anchor off and take your dinghy in, friendly people and some surprising, almost Spanish-style villas welcome you to Fox Town. There is only 3.5 feet at MLW off the Shell fuel dock.

The settlement is strung out along the waterfront; sponge harvesting is still the main industry, and you can see sponges lying out to dry in the sun.

SERVICES & SHOPPING

Barber Shop
Fresh Cuts

Church
St. Chad's Anglican Church

Clinic
No posted opening hours.

Fuel
Fox Town Shell   Tel: 365-2046 • VHF 16
Diesel and gasoline, water and ice.

Groceries
M & M Grocery Store   Frozen meats, sodas, shoes, saucepans, toys, some fruit, but no bread or water the day we were there.
G & J Drugs & Snack Shop

Police
Next door to the post office.

Post Office
Open 9 am to 5:30 pm Monday, Tuesday, Thursday, and Friday.

Restaurant
Valley Restaurant   Serves fish, chicken, pizza, and burgers. Clean and cool with a pool table.

Telephone
Outside the *Valley Restaurant.*

Sponges drying in the sun.

Chapter 5
The Central Abacos
Allans-Pensacola Cay to Treasure Cay

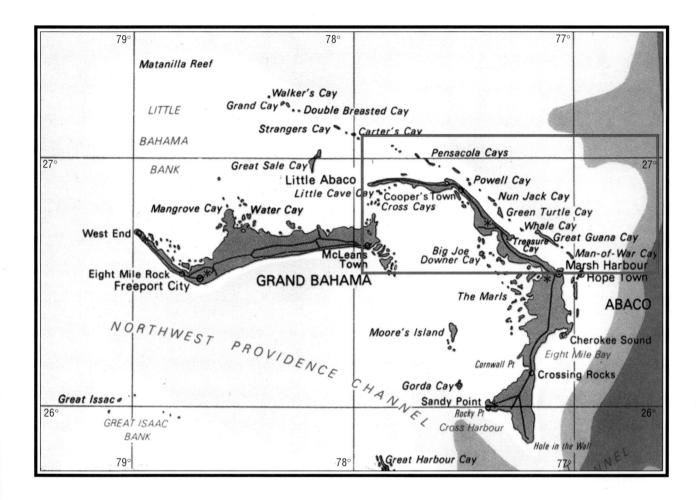

Ocean Passes

THERE are four passes out into the Atlantic Ocean in this sector. We're not entirely happy about the two Spanish Cay passes and would always take the Manjack route in preference.

- **Spanish Cay** offers two passes out into the ocean. North of Spanish Cay, and north of its tiny sibling Squances Cay, you can head out into the Atlantic on 060°M. You are aiming for a 1 nm gap in the reef whose center point is 26° 59' 15 N 077° 34' 20 W.

- An alternative route out of Spanish Cay takes you south of Spanish Cay around Goat Cay, heading on 085°M for 26° 56' 15 N 077° 28' 45 W.

- The gap in the reef north of **Manjack Cay** offers a good pass out into the ocean. About 1 nm southeast of Ambergris Cay there's one lone rock, easily avoidable in what otherwise is a wide channel between Ambergris Cay and Manjack Cay. Take the halfway point between this rock and the northwest point of Manjack Cay, and head out on about 030°M. Keep watching how you're going and watch the reefs on each side, but you should have 15–20 feet of water and will get safely clear.

- The most important pass is **Whale Cay Passage** to the south of Green Turtle Cay, which is a brief, obligatory detour out into the Atlantic if you are continuing south down the line of the Abaco Cays. We cover this in detail on page 65.

Moving on after Allans-Pensacola Cay

Allans-Pensacola Cay is fully covered in the previous section of this Guide, **The Northern Abacos, Walkers Cay to Allans-Pensacola Cay** on page 54.

If you look at the chart, you'll note that a series of shallow banks lie in the Sea of Abaco off the southwest tip of Spanish Cay, the Ambergris Cays, and the north end of Manjack Cay, all of which combine to dictate two primary options as you head south. The first is to stay on the western side of the Sea of Abaco, and run along the coast of Great Abaco Island. The second is to stay on the eastern side, paralleling the cays.

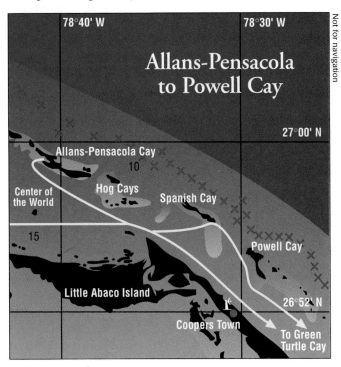

We covered the route from Crab Cay to Green Turtle Cay in our section titled **The Little Bahama Bank, Options After Great Sale Cay** on page 44, a route that takes you down the western side of the Sea of Abaco before you eventually alter your heading for Green Turtle Cay. Putting it in US East Coast highway terms, you could call this the I-95 of the Abacos. Its drawback is that it sweeps you right past the cays you may want to visit.

The alternative route, staying on the eastern side of the Sea of Abaco, could be called the A1A. It's the beach route. Slower, maybe. But you can stop everywhere. This sounds absolute, but it's not quite like that. Of course you can switch from one side to the other as you wish, but it's useful to look at it this way in passage-making terms. For ease of reference we'll repeat part of the western route. Initially both routes running south from Allans-Pensacola Cay are the same up to Angel Fish Point.

Allans-Pensacola Cay to Angel Fish Point

Allans-Pensacola (0.5 nm NW)	ALPEN	26° 59' 15 N	077° 42' 15 W
Crab Cay (0.5 nm N)	CRABC	26° 56' 00 N	077° 36' 00 W
Angel Fish Point (0.5 nm NE)	ANGEL	26° 55' 30 N	077° 35' 00 W

From Allans-Pensacola Cay a straight run of 6.4 nm on 126°M takes you to Crab Cay, and Angel Fish Point comes up almost immediately after that, just over a mile further on 125°M. This is your decision point. Head for Spanish Cay, or stay off the coast of Great Abaco Island?

THE HOG CAYS

The Hog Cays, which you pass on your way from Allans-Pensacola to Spanish Cay, are another ground for dinghy expeditions and picnics, but not an area where you are likely to want to anchor for any length of time. This said, Big Hog Cay has some tempting beaches. At this time a well-protected pond on the southernmost Hog Cay has a Department of Fisheries sign prohibiting entry.

Angel Fish Point to Green Turtle Cay (the I-95 Route)

Angel Fish Point (0.5 nm NE)	ANGEL	26° 55' 30 N	077° 35' 00 W
Coopers Town (1 nm NE)	CPSTN	26° 53' 00 N	077° 30' 00 W
Green Turtle N (3.5 nm NW)	GTNTH	26° 47' 00 N	077° 23' 00 W
Green Turtle Cay (1 nm W)	GTRTL	26° 46' 00 M	077° 21' 00 W

From Angel Fish Point hold 125°M for 5.1 nm to Coopers Town. After Coopers Town change to 139°M for 8.6 nm to place you 3.5 nm northwest of Green Turtle Cay, and then close the distance, altering to around 125°M to place you

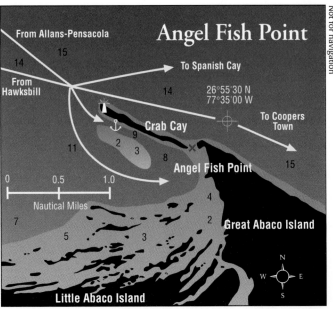

ready to choose your landfall, either White Sound, Black Sound, or the anchorage off New Plymouth.

Great Abaco Island

COOPERS TOWN

Coopers Town (1 nm NE)	CPSTN	26° 53' 00 N	077° 30' 00 W

If you're on the I-95 route through the Sea of Abaco, you'll have no problems stopping off at Coopers Town. Low lying though it is, as always its Batelco tower (200 feet here) is the giveaway. Simply slow down, make your way closer inshore, and anchor off. If you need fuel, then go in to the fuel dock there.

If you're on the A1A route, getting to Coopers Town from Spanish Cay requires a kind of dogleg because of the bank off the southwest tip of Spanish Cay. On leaving the Spanish Cay Marina, head about 219°M straight across toward the Great Abaco shoreline. You'll see a strip of sand beach, if you want to keep a landmark, slightly south of where your heading is taking you. You'll end up a comfortable distance offshore after running for 2.48 nm and your position then will be 26° 54' 43 N 077° 32' 47 W. Turn to run southeast parallel to the coast until you reach Coopers Town. The total distance is some 6 nm.

Coopers Town anchorage, if you can call it that, (for there's no anchorage at all in the proper sense), is bad news when the wind is from the north, east, and southeast. Forget it then. It also shoals close to the shore (what coastal waters do not?) but you are really limited by this. If you doubt it, note the length of the Coopers Town docks.

There's a Shell dock in Coopers Town, but very little else that you're likely to require. For an idea of the way it is there, see the story on page 60.

Angel Fish Point to Spanish Cay (the A1A Route)

Angel Fish Point (0.5 nm NE)	ANGEL	26° 55' 30 N	077° 35' 00 W
Spanish Cay (0.5 nm NW)	SPNSH	26° 56' 30 N	077° 32' 15 W

From Angel Fish Point you have 2.6 nm to run on 073°M to reach Spanish Cay.

SPANISH CAY

The entry to the Spanish Cay Marina is marked by two pilings painted red (on your starboard side) and green (for your port side). The marina is large, has good depth, and is accommodating and well run. A marina slip brings the dividend of good showers, the bars and restaurants, freedom to make use of the excellent beaches, and an exceptionally friendly and welcoming staff. Useful backup facilities include a separate fuel dock, and will include (but it's still on the plans) a Customs and Immigration office at

Flame trees in Spanish Cay.

the airstrip. We understand there is a visiting weekend service at this time.

Spanish Cay, 3 miles in length, is the property of a development consortium and is in its third incarnation. The resort and marina, once known as The Club at Spanish Cay, now flies its colors as The Inn at Spanish Cay. It is, we believe, on the market again. The complex as a whole boasts a 5,000-foot airstrip at the northwest end, and its club house, hotel-type rooms, two restaurants, and 65-berth full-service marina at the southwest end. The island is divided into lots, some with houses built, most still for sale. The most outstanding feature of Spanish Cay is its plantings. It has

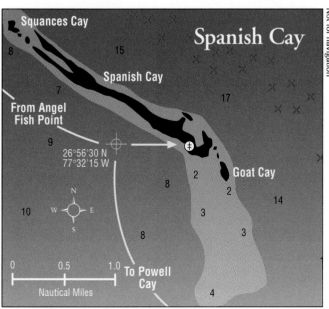

The Old Man and the Snapper

IT was a beautiful fish. A Lane Snapper very near its maximum size, certainly over 12 inches, silver with thin yellow stripes. We'd been going north around Whale Passage in the Abacos, and we'd started trolling then, when we were in the ocean. I'd kept the lines out when we came in the northern entrance, back to the Sea of Abaco, because the fish often hang out in the gaps.

"That's dinner tonight. It'll do us perfectly. I'll clean it when we stop." We'd thought of somewhere north of Coopers Town, for I had to return there. Allans-Pensacola, perhaps.

"It's kicking up a bit, isn't it?"

We hadn't noticed the weather much outside in the ocean, nor turning in with the wind behind us, but it was about 15 knots out of the east over the Sea of Abaco and kind of brisk.

"Not so hot for Coopers Town."

We were going to the Shell dock, just briefly, to check out a couple of things in the town. We headed on north. By then we'd stopped fishing and had the dock lines out. Fenders would come later, once we were alongside.

As we got closer I called Coopers Town Shell on the radio. The Fuel Dock answered on the second call.

"Come in at the end, round the north side. Go right round. Don't face the land, and don't come too close to the beach."

It was rolly there with the wind straight on the end of the dock and the full width of the Sea of Abaco with it to pile up the water. Two boats at anchor nearby were dancing like crazy. Maybe we should give it a miss?

"I'll try one pass. If it's a no-no, then that's it."

As I calculated my turn to the north of the dock and eyed the restricted sea room I had, an Old Man walked out along the boards and stood at the very end by a piling, just waiting, watching.

"He knows that bow line is going to be critical. Give him that first, and then lasso a stern line on to a post as fast as you can. We'll be OK then."

The turn was tight and we were bouncing as we straightened out with wind and wave right on the snout. I thought "It's too much. Abort now." But we were so close. "One try. Just this one pass'.

Janet, hanging to the foredeck rails, got the bow line to the Old Man and he had it round the post within seconds. "Good man, good man." Mole, in the cockpit, missed the first cast and took too long to get her act together for a second attempt. We were blowing off (there must have been a touch of south in that wind) and with a single screw boat there's no quick way you can kick the stern in if you're already tied at the head. By then Janet was at the stern and the Old Man was there, and we had it, a line ashore and he'd got it and cinched it tight. I went into neutral but left the engine running. Then we did the fenders.

"Fifteen minutes. Half an hour at the most," I told the Team. "I'll stay with the boat."

They made ready to go ashore. We'd thanked the Old Man and he went off down the dock to a small house at the end. A Shell flag on a mast was standing out like a board in the wind. By then I'd fixed a head spring. We were OK.

I took the fish out of its bucket and put it in a gallon Ziplock bag.

"We couldn't have done it without him. Will you give him the fish? Tell him where we caught it, just half an hour ago? It's the least we can do. He was great."

They went off.

About fifteen minutes later, when I was sure the boat was OK, I jumped from the coachroof on to the dock just in time to see a Whaler with four people on board heading toward us, having a rough passage. They tried to get alongside, missed, tried to swing round again, broached, took a lot of water, and didn't look too happy. Two men and two women. They seemed to have a lot of gear with them. One overloaded boat and getting very wet. By then I'd got their bow line and the Old Man had joined me, and took a second line.

We were handed two suitcases and two soft bags, and then one by one they climbed ashore. It wasn't easy.

"We're on a boat anchored off Powell" one of the men said. "We've got these people who've been with us who have to fly out of Treasure Cay today. We thought we'd come here to get a taxi for them. Treasure's too far to go in the Whaler in this."

He paused, and looked at the Old Man. "Can we get a cab here?"

Obviously there were no taxis in Coopers Town, or at least not that afternoon.

"Maybe you walk into town and somebody help you. Or maybe you call the airport. They have plenty of taxis there. They come and pick you up."

None of the Powell Cay people looked particularly happy. The would-be fliers had that kind of "I know it, we're going to miss this flight" look on their faces.

"Have you got a telephone?"

"In the town. You see it."

The Powell Cay boat party set off along the dock, each carrying a piece of luggage. I walked back to shore end after them with the Old Man. He stopped in the door of his fuel dock office. In the room beyond I could see what looked like his living quarters.

"You must have known I was bachelor and I live all alone," he said. "Now you give me that fish I got something to eat tonight. How you know that I don't know, but I'm going to enjoy that fish."

"You helped me get in here. I couldn't have done it without you."

He looked at the sea state. "There's going to be nobody getting in here now. Don't know how those people are going to get back across to Powell Cay there. You be OK. Just take her straight out. Now I'm going to fix that fish."

About ten minutes later Janet and Mole came back to the boat. "We've got a present for you. Close your eyes and hold out your hands." Obedient, I did so. Something soft, cloth was placed in them. It was a white T-shirt. Coopers Town? Surely not? I unfolded it.

SHELL HELIX MOTOR OILS

"The Old Man stopped us when we got back. He said it was to thank you for the fish."

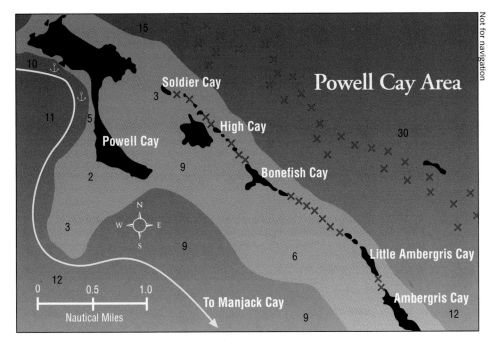

benefitted from being in private hands and the island is a mini subtropical paradise of native and not-so-native trees, palms, and flowering shrubs.

Spanish Cay–Powell Cay–Ambergris Cays–Manjack Cay–Green Turtle Cay (the A1A Route)

To take A1A south, turn to port when you leave Spanish Cay Marina and run parallel to the breakwater. Keep going, eyeball it between the little island on the south tip of Spanish Cay and the bank that will be on your starboard side, and cross the first gap opening up to the ocean. Watch out for the rocks on the northwest tip of Powell Cay, ignore the little beach on the northwest, and your first option in potential anchorages comes up along the run of Powell Cay's sweep of beaches facing the Sea of Abaco. The distance run from Spanish Cay Marina is roughly 4 nm, and if you want a rough position for reassurance, take 26° 54' 19 N 077° 29' 05 W or something like that. You'll find you have 6–8 feet of water.

You'll note that we are not giving courses or waypoints on this route. Navigation here must be done in the old way, using your eyes and common sense.

POWELL CAY

Powell Cay, about 1.5 nm in length, has fine beaches and unusually, its northern stretch of beach is divided by the first real elevation in land height that you'll have seen in the Abaco Cays, a seemingly great rock headland. Powell is uninhabited, but far from unfrequented for it's a popular stop with cruising visitors. It's also within easy reach of Coopers Town, just 2.5 nm away across the Sea of Abaco. If there are a number of boats anchored off Powell Cay, your congrega-

tion may well attract an opportunistic mobile snack bar from Coopers Town, which will set itself up near the pier.

To reinforce the popularity of Powell Cay with cruising visitors, the plus side is the good holding (penetrable sand and some grass), protection from the north through southeast, the Powell Cay beaches, and the snorkeling on the Atlantic-side reef. Cap this with the space of the Powell Cay anchorage ground, where it never feels crowded, and you have a winner. The shelling is reputed to be good on the southern beaches, but if you want to go down there, take your dinghy. A considerable area of shoal lies off the south end of Powell Cay, which extends to and includes Bonefish Cay. What's the downside? Wind from the west. Don't stay under those conditions (you won't want to, as soon as the wind shifts). Anything more? Yes. Anchor far enough offshore to escape the mosquitos.

Moving on from Powell Cay head southwest at the start to avoid the shoal area we've mentioned, and give yourself some offing from the two Ambergris cays, unless of course you want to anchor off and take your dinghy in to explore. From the south of Powell to the isolated rock 0.75 nm southeast of the southern tip of Ambergris Cay, the whole area is a mess of rock and reef. It's dinghy territory, not a playground for big boats.

BONEFISH CAY

Bonefish Cay has a crashed airplane to its southwest in some 5 feet of water, part of which just shows.

THE AMBERGRIS CAYS

When you reach Little Ambergris Cay you'll have run something like 8.6 nm from Spanish Cay. Both Ambergris cays have good beaches, but there are beaches just as good that offer a more user-friendly approach. As it is, Ambergris Cay is privately owned, so that counts it out. Watch out for the shoal area between the two cays, and look particularly for the shoal and rocks that run out for nearly half a mile southwest from the southern end of Ambergris Cay. There's a warning stake on one of the outermost rocks. Its position is approximately 26° 51' 35 N 077° 25' 50 W. After Ambergris you cross a 2 nm gap giving on to the ocean (of which the first half mile is unusable because of one outlying rock) before you reach Manjack Cay.

MANJACK CAY AND CRAB CAY

Manjack Cay has reasonable anchorages at its northern end, although there are shoal areas there. The best anchorage is in the bight formed by Manjack and Crab Cays where you'll fine good protection from the northeast through to the south and around 8 feet of water. Your position here will be around 26° 49' 03 N 077° 21' 47 W, and by then you'll have run some 14 or 15 nm southeast from Spanish Cay.

Green Turtle Cay

Approaches

Some 3 nm southeast of the Manjack–Crab Cay anchorage you'll find yourself positioned off the entrance to White Sound in Green Turtle Cay, with the entrance to Black Sound a tad further on and the anchorage off New Plymouth dead ahead on your bow. As you approach White Sound you'll notice the Bluff House Resort to port as you come from the north, and a dock for both fuel and where day trippers may secure. The main purpose of this dock was to accommodate the fuel tanker, and the Bluff House Marina, with what you might call its regular fuel dock (linked to the seaward one by pipeline), lies inside White Sound.

WHITE SOUND

There are no problems in entering White Sound. There's a marker at the entrance to the dredged channel leading into the Sound, and you'll have little problem recognizing the channel for it is well dredged, has a clean sand bottom, and is well marked. It offers 5 feet of water at MLW, is about a boat length in width (say around 30 feet), and leads you to the Green Turtle Club Marina, to starboard, or the Bluff House Marina, to port. Between the two docks there's an anchorage, with moorings also available. Don't be tempted to poke your way into the east extension of White Sound when you see it open up to starboard about halfway up the entrance channel, despite the mooring buoys you'll see there. Although there is perhaps 6 feet of water inside, the threshold carries barely 3 feet. More about this later.

BLACK SOUND

Entering Black Sound you'll see a marker post with a red light and a sign on the reef to your starboard side, and the end of a dock to port. Don't confuse that marker with a second larger sign that is slightly further to starboard, still on the reef, but closer to the tip of the point. The entrance channel is narrow, little more than your beam. As a guide, if you can't see the reef to starboard as you enter the channel, you have 5 feet. If the reef is exposed, you'll be down to 3 feet at MLW. You'll pick up a line of marker buoys inside, then stay in the center of the Sound until you reach either Abaco Yacht Services to port or The Other Shore Club and the Black Sound Marina, further on, both to starboard.

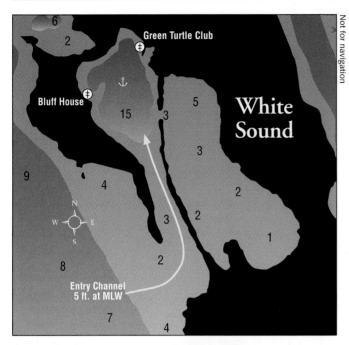

NEW PLYMOUTH SETTLEMENT CREEK

New Plymouth, as we've said, lies directly ahead and you can see where those who've anchored off have chosen to lie.

COMING FROM THE SOUTH OR GOING ON SOUTH

If you are approaching from the south, or heading that way for Whale Cay Passage, take note that there is a shoal area immediately south of the point on which New Plymouth sits. Stand out to get well clear of this.

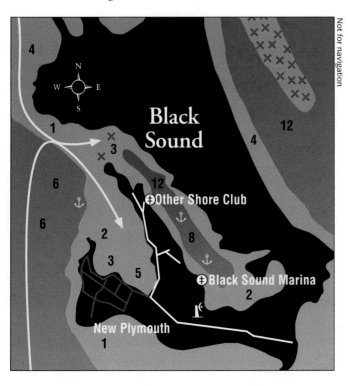

Anchorages and Marinas

Your choices of anchorages lie principally in the choice between the two Sounds and New Plymouth. White Sound has moorings and is normally fairly full. The buoys in the inner pond (some 15 in total) were placed there by the Green Turtle Club. We have reservations about them, concerned as we are about the depth of water over that access sill and the nature of the mooring itself, a concrete block, which we do not believe would hold in bad weather. There are also moorings in Black Sound. See our **Yellow Pages** for contact details.

If you choose to anchor off New Plymouth there are no problems in settled weather from the east. You'll see the Settlement Creek entrance markers to the town dock area and you must stay clear of the approach channel to the New Plymouth waterfront and clear of the routes that the Bolo ferries, operating from New Plymouth, will take from the adjacent ferry dock on their runs to Black and White Sounds and their crossings to mainland Abaco. Anchoring off New Plymouth you're exposed to the north and the west. The government dock, used by commercial shipping, lies on the west side of New Plymouth, and you wouldn't want to anchor in this area. The flow of traffic would not be good for you, nor would your anchoring be good for the commercial carriers. And if the weather changes from the prevailing winds, you're exposed to the south, west, and north.

Going to New Plymouth by dinghy you use the town dock to the right (as you approach it) of the Bolo Ferry dock. There's a small shed on the dock (it's the Green Turtle Cay Fire Station), a Batelco telephone kiosk, a trash dumpster, and a "Welcome to New Plymouth" sign. To run in, use the Settlement Creek entrance markers, going in on the Bolo ferry route. Your dinghy dock is on the right side of the town dock, behind the T.

Your choices in marina rest on the broad option of the two Sounds. In White Sound it's the Green Turtle Club Marina, or the Bluff House Marina, in the process of considerable expansion as we write. Both are good and have everything you will want, but you are remote from New Plymouth by land. The water route there, by dinghy, is the best way to go. Black Sound has the Other Shore Club, and the new Black Sound Marina. The Other Shore Club has fuel. Abaco Yacht Services are a repair and storage yard.

A Magic Island

Green Turtle Cay runs for 3 nm from northwest to southeast, parallel to Great Abaco Island and 3 nm out in the Sea of Abaco. The Atlantic side of Green Turtle presents an almost straight, unindented coast to the ocean, fringed with reefs and coral heads. The Abaco side has two bays in the north, and those two deeply indented sounds, White Sound in the north and Black Sound in the south, which we've already mentioned. The southeast corner of the island has a fine shallow bay, Gillam Bay, perfect for beachcombing. New

Northern Cruising Grounds

Atlantic Beach, Green Turtle Cay.

risk of drawing the world into an island that has largely held its unique inheritance, character, and integrity intact, we must admit that Green Turtle Cay has always been one of our favorite destinations, and rather than be accused of escapism, we'll keep secret the length of time we've spent there in the last few years.

NO NAME CAY

No Name Cay, immediately southeast of Green Turtle Cay, is uninhabited, has a good offshore reef, but otherwise has nothing to offer. You might land on its beach out of curiosity during your Green Turtle gunkholing, for No Name is barely a stone's throw off Gillam Point. However, if you want to bring a deeper draft boat closer to No Name Cay, beware of the shoals extending southeast from Green Turtle Cay. There are also shoals running southwest from the southern tip of No Name Cay, and a further shoal area between these two shoal areas.

Plymouth, the main settlement, is on the southwest tip of the island.

For many of those who know it, Green Turtle Cay is rated the number-one destination if you want a laid-back, relaxed island with everything you dream about. A pretty little settlement town in New Plymouth, plenty of choice in restaurants and bars from the high priced to basic, two small resorts in Bluff House and the Green Turtle Club, apartments and houses to rent, great beaches, and the safest anchorages in the Abacos. All of this is packed into three miles. How has it kept its magic? Like many of the best places, you can only get there by boat. At

The old jail, New Plymouth.

Green Turtle Cay to Great Guana Cay

Green Turtle Cay SW (Settlement Pt)	GTCSW	26° 45' 30 N	077° 20' 30 W
Whale Cay Passage 1 (2.8 nm SW)	WHLP1	26° 42' 00 N	077° 17' 00 W
Whale Cay Passage 2 (offshore N)	WHLP2	26° 43' 30 N	077° 14' 15 W
Whale Cay Passage 3 (offshore S)	WHLP3	26° 42' 30 N	077° 12' 25 W
Whale Cay Passage 4 (inshore S)	WHLP4	26° 42' 00 N	077° 12' 00 W
First Deep Channel Marker	DMKR1	26° 42' 15 N	077° 12' 10 W
Second Pair of Markers	DMKR2	26° 41' 52 N	077° 11' 53 W
Baker's Bay 1 (deepwater slot)	BKRS1	26° 41' 25 N	077° 10' 15 W
Baker's Bay 2 (deepwater slot)	BKRS2	26° 41' 05 N	077° 10' 05 W
Great Guana Cay (Delia's Cay Rk)	GGANA	26° 39' 45 N	077° 07' 00 W

First of all, check the weather the day you intend to do the Whale Cay Passage. Call anyone in the area on Channel 16 and ask what Whale Cay conditions are like. If everything's OK, go for it. The first leg from Green Turtle down to Whale Cay, 4.69 nm on a heading of 144°M from just off Settlement Point, is easy. Just remember that there's a considerable area of shallow water to the south of Green Turtle Cay. Get some distance out before you turn south toward Whale Cay.

Whale Cay and the Whale Cay Passage

Whale Cay, 2 nm south of No Name Cay, is famous for its passage out into the ocean rather than the island itself. This uninhabited cay runs for 1.5 nm and occupies a strategic position in navigational terms, for it lies at the very point that the Sea of Abaco becomes too shallow, due to sandbanks, for most cruising boats to negotiate. If you're heading for Hope Town or Marsh Harbour, the only route (albeit a fair-weather route) is to dogleg out into the Atlantic around Whale Cay and then continue your passage down the Sea of Abaco. Your brief excursion into the Atlantic will add another eight waypoints to your catalog and 5 nm or so to your distance run, all legs counted.

To the north the passage is wide enough to cause no anxiety, but there are rocks to be spotted and it's relatively shallow (more on this later), some 12 feet deep. To the south the passage is shallow but has a deep entrance channel dredged for cruise ships in a failed venture to develop Baker's Bay at the northwest end of Great Guana Cay into a tropical island adventure stop. While this dredged deep-water passage remains and will be used by you, the spoil banks, now mini-cays as regeneration has taken place, as well as the run of the channel itself make accurate navigation essential.

Your GPS comes into its own on the Whale Cay Passage, but use your eyes and your depth gauge as well, for successive winter storms will surely alter the bottom contours in this area.

Whale Cay Passage

The Whale Cay Passage is a simple three-sided box around Whale Cay, followed by two further legs that take you up the disused cruise ship channel to Baker's Bay on the northwest tip of Great Guana Cay.

- At Waypoint 1 turn on to 064°M to head out through Whale Cay Channel for 2.88 nm. To port you'll have Two Rocks and Whale Cay Channel Rocks. To starboard you'll pass the north tip of Whale Cay. Ahead, as a marker, you'll see Chub Rocks.

- At Waypoint 2 turn on to 127°M for 1.92 nm, running offshore and parallel to Whale Cay.

- At Waypoint 3 turn inshore on 149°M for 0.062 nm until you reach the approach to Loggerhead Channel (the southern Whale Cay pass, named for the bars in that area).

- At Waypoint 4 you're at the entrance to the dredged channel. The first deep-water channel marker comes up at 26° 42' 15 N 077° 12' 10 W, and the second pair of markers is at 26° 41' 52 N 077° 11' 53 W. At this point you hardly need your GPS. You can see the line of markers along the deep-water channel (don't get fooled by some markers that will be off to starboard), you can see the sand of Baker's Bay on your port bow and the main spoil island on your starboard bow.

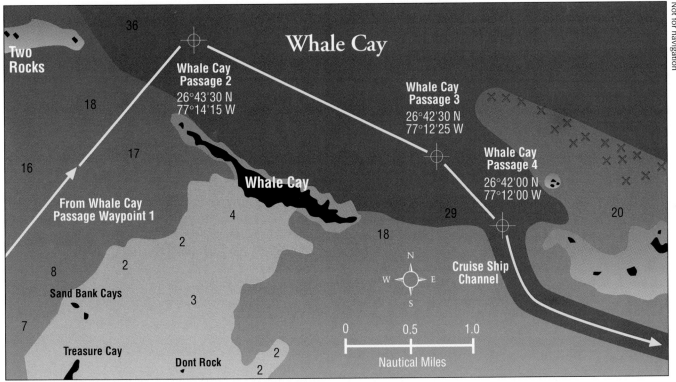

Two Rocks · 36 · Whale Cay · Whale Cay Passage 2 · 26°43'30 N 77°14'15 W · Whale Cay Passage 3 · 26°42'30 N 77°12'25 W · Whale Cay Passage 4 · 26°42'00 N 77°12'00 W · 18 · 17 · 16 · Whale Cay · From Whale Cay Passage Waypoint 1 · 4 · 2 · 2 · 8 · Sand Bank Cays · 18 · 29 · 20 · Cruise Ship Channel · 3 · 7 · Treasure Cay · Dont Rock · 2 · 2 · N W E S · 0 · 0.5 · 1.0 · Nautical Miles

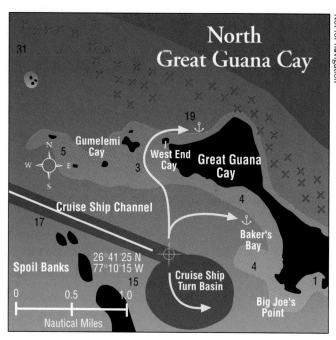

North Great Guana Cay

- On a heading of 116°M you'll reach the first Baker's Bay waypoint. The distance on this leg is 1.67 nm. Check your heading, but use the channel markers.

- Our two Baker's Bay waypoints serve to direct you between the Baker's Bay spoil banks, which will come up on your starboard side, and Baker's Bay to port. At the first waypoint turn on to 162°M and hold it for just 0.37 nm to reach the second waypoint. Here you're at the end of the deep-water channel with the mooring buoys intended for the cruise ships. At this point you're free to move about as you wish.

RAGES

The greatest knock-on effect of the shallowness of the Whale Cay Passes is that in high seas, particularly Northeasters, and whenever distant Atlantic storms have generated heavy swells, the water piles up on the Whale Cay shoals producing dangerously rough conditions, known locally as a "Rage." These are powerful, turbulent, and lethal seas.

In unfavorable weather under *no* circumstances should you even *think* of poking your nose out to check what it might be like out there. If someone has a deadline, a flight to catch from Marsh Harbour or something like that, change it to Treasure Cay, or take the Bolo Ferry to Treasure Cay and a taxi on to Marsh Harbour. The reverse applies, of course, if you're the other side of Whale Cay heading north.

Great Guana Cay

You've made it to Great Guana Cay. Rather than go on at once there are three places where you might well wish to stop and beachcomb for a while, or maybe even anchor.

DAY ANCHORAGE OFF THE NORTHWEST BEACH

From the cruise ship channel just south of Gumelemi Cay pick a northerly course that will allow you to pass midway between Gumelemi Cay and West End Cay. You'll have a minimum of 8 feet MLW all the way. Once you pass about 200 yards off West End Cay, turn to starboard and parallel the beach. One-half mile up the beach you'll find a good anchorage in 12 feet over fine sand, just 200 feet off the beach. This day anchorage, best when the wind is southeast, is one of the loveliest beaches in the Bahamas.

BAKER'S BAY

Baker's Bay, on the southwest side of the north end of Great Guana Cay, is the site of the failed commercial development. Why not anchor there, enjoy the beach, and the swimming? At last count four dolphins, two mothers and two calves, once part of the circus trained to entertain cruise ship passengers, are still in the area. The dolphin pens, where they were once held, remain. The best anchorage is the southeast corner of the bay in the lee of the point, where you'll have 6 feet or more. The holding is adequate, in sand and some grass. This is a much-favored stop for those who have completed the Whale Cay Passage heading south, and those who are waiting to pass through it on their way north.

THE SPOIL BANKS

The Spoil Banks are a popular stop, known for their shelling. If nothing else, it's an encouraging example of how nature, once given a free hand, can reclaim and make good the waste of mankind. The best anchorage is in the lee of the main spoil bank, 1 nm west of Baker's Bay. This is a fair-weather stop.

Baker's Bay to Great Guana Cay Settlement

The straight-line course to take you from Baker's Bay to the entrance to Great Guana Cay's settlement bay with its public dock and the Great Guana Beach Resort's dock is 122°M. The distance to run is just 3 nm. On your way you'll pass the new Guana Seaside Village resort with its dock. Although no marina facilities are offered, nor moorings, you are welcome to stop there for a drink or a meal. The dock carries just 4 feet at MLW, so you may wish to anchor off and dinghy in. Its exact position, for your chart, is 26° 40' 47 N 077° 08' W.

Great Guana Cay Anchorage and Marina

The best anchorage is just off the Great Guana Beach Resort in the bay behind Delia's Cay and the small point that

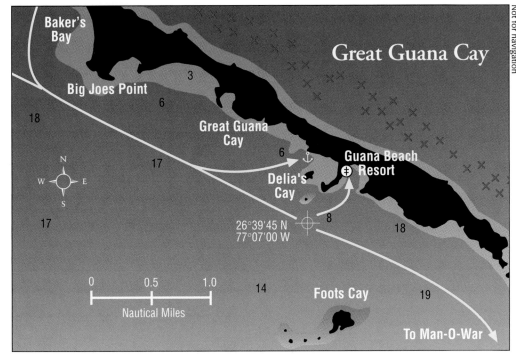

Not for navigation

GREAT GUANA CAY

Great Guana Cay is higher than the average Abaco cay, a rolling island, 5.5 nm in length with a nearly continuous Atlantic beach. Its settlement is tiny, just a handful of people, and in truth there's nothing in Great Guana Cay that would register in the tourist stakes other than the Guana Beach Resort, Nipper's Beach Bar on the ocean side, and the new Guana Seaside Village. Great Guana's superb beaches, and its distinction of being the last of the large Abaco Cays to suffer development, make it one attractive destination. We're left with the feeling that the whole of Great Guana Cay is up for grabs right now and that given a cash injection the island may change significantly over the next decade. If this is so, let's hope that it's handled well. The Guana Beach Resort in particular, which starts with the advantage of a superb site, has ambitious development plans.

Near the southeast of Great Guana Cay there's a private harbor that reportedly was carved out by a landowner hoping to sell waterfront lots with their own docks. As yet

shields the Great Guana settlement area and the docks from view as you come down from the north. On your approach look out for the submerged rock at 26° 40' 05 N 077° 07' 20 W, which is marked by a stake, but don't rely on the stake being there. Don't cut between the rock with a stake and Delia's Cay, for a submerged reef connects them. In the anchorage you'll find good holding in 8–10 feet of water. You're well protected from the east and southeast, although you may get some surge, but it would be untenable in a Norther. You can dinghy in from here to the Great Guana Beach Resort's dinghy dock.

The Great Guana Beach Resort marina, together with the public dock, are inside the bay to port as you enter, with the Guana Beach Resort dock coming up first. It is a dock, rather than a marina, for no facilities other than shore power are available. It has 6 feet at MLW, is exposed to the south, and the surge we've suffered there has made sleep impossible. This alone should cross it off your list as an overnight stop, but it's well protected from the north. No shore-side facilities, such as showers, are available unless you can negotiate the use of a room at the resort (and pay for its casual use). If you have just called in for a meal, you are asked to deposit $10.00 as a fee for securing there, but this is later credited against your restaurant bill.

Seven Mile Beach, Great Guana Cay.

it's undeveloped. One captain who by invitation was allowed to ride out Hurricane Bertha there in 1996 said that it offered superb protection. Add it to your panic list of potential hurricane refuges.

Treasure Cay

Treasure Cay (the "sounds good" name came with tourist development) is not a cay at all, but very much a part of mainland Great Abaco Island. It's both a resort community, served by a local airport with Customs and Immigration, and a full-service marina, primarily devoted to sports fishing.

The Treasure Cay Triangle

The Treasure Cay Triangle is the name we've given the area of the Sea of Abaco that has Treasure Cay as its apex and the full span of the Whale Cay Passage as its baseline. The heart of the triangle is the no-go part of the Sea of Abaco, the barrier of shallows around Treasure Cay Bank, the Sand Bank Cays, and Dont Rock, which makes the Whale Cay diversion a necessary way to continue your cruise, both north and south, on your all-Abaco itinerary. This barrier across the Sea of Abaco between Treasure Cay and Whale Cay at once dictates your approach routes to Treasure Cay.

Approaches

Whale Cay Passage 4 (inshore S)	WHLP4	26° 42' 00 N	077° 12' 00 W
Fish Cays S (1 nm S)	FISHS	26° 40' 00 N	077° 08' 00 W
Treasure Cay Entrance (1 nm SE)	TREAS	26° 39' 30 N	077° 15' 45 W

From the North. The safest route from Green Turtle Cay or the north, although it seems a diversion, is to take Whale Cay Passage to our Waypoint 4. From there head toward the Great Abaco shoreline on a course of 239°M, which will bring you to our Treasure Cay approach waypoint, just 1 nm southeast of the entrance to Treasure Cay Marina. This course takes you safely southeast of Dont Rock, which is easy to see, and northwest of a shallow bank that lies less than a mile southeast of Dont Rock. Your distance to run on this leg from the Whale Cay Passage waypoint is 4.18 nm. When you get close to the Treasure Cay entrance you'll see the Treasure Cay welcome sign.

From the South. Approaching Treasure Cay from the south, our Fish Cay waypoint is the focal point on all routes to Treasure Cay, unless you elect to go by way of Great Guana Cay and our Whale Passage waypoint. From our Fish Cay waypoint it's 7.48 nm on a heading of 298°M to our Treasure Cay approach waypoint. From Marsh Harbour it's 4.83 nm on 318°M. From North Point Set Rock it's 7.10 nm on 295°M. From Man-O-War it's 5.41 nm on 283°M.

After the Treasure Cay welcome sign you'll pick up a series of white pilings marking a sandbar on your starboard side and another sandbar, which may or may not show, to port. Stay between the markers and you'll have 7 feet of water all the way into the marina. On your way in you'll pass the Treasure Cay fuel dock to port, which is separate from the marina.

WARNING. THE DONT ROCK PASSAGE

There is an inshore route to Treasure Cay from the north that takes you past the Sand Bank Cays and around Dont Rock. The temptation to go this way, rather than going around Whale Cay Passage is irresistible at first sight, particularly if Whale Cay Passage is impassable due to weather. Forget it. Yes, it can be done. We've done it. But it's shoal draft, even at high water. The sands continually move in this area, and there's no "safe" course. The probability of your grounding is so high we'd count it as a certainty. In short, if it's calm, it's a hazardous passage. If there's any kind of sea running, it's dangerous.

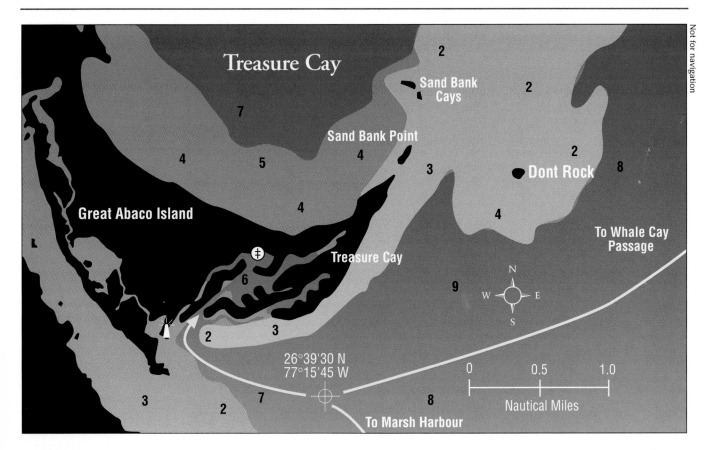

While You're There

If you're into fishing, you'll certainly have Treasure Cay on your visit list but it's highly likely to feature there for other reasons, as well. It's a good place to change crew or pick up guests, for the airport is almost on your doorstep. Treasure Cay has a great beach (some say it's world class), and for beach lovers it's well worth a lazy morning or an afternoon in the sun. What else? We hope you never have to head for Treasure Cay purely for this last reason, but think seriously about going there if you're in the area and a severe storm is coming your way. We have friends who moored their 42-foot trawler to two Treasure Cay moorings when Hurricane Bertha roared up the Abacos in 1996. The moorings held and the boat came through it, undamaged, in over 60 knots of wind. The network of Treasure Cay canals are another "hurricane hole" option you might want to keep on your "What If?" panic list.

YELLOW PAGES

SPANISH CAY

Spanish Cay is a privately owned island with all the makings of a tropical paradise. A pristine marina, coupled with the best in resort services, provides cruising boats with an ideal setting in which to relax and enjoy the welcome and hospitality that is found here. All the facilities are centered around the marina and hotel complex. **Customs** and **Immigration** can be called if you need to clear in, but only on weekends.

MARINA

SPANISH CAY MARINA
Tel: 242-365-0083 • Fax: 365-0466 • VHF 16

Slips	60
Max LOA	Over 100 ft.
MLW at dock	8 ft.
Dockage	85¢ per foot per day
Power	$15 per day for 50A, $10 per day for 30A
Fuel	Diesel and gasoline are available outside the marina on a separate fuel dock.
Water	24¢ per gallon
Telephone	No public telephone
Showers	Very clean, located by the restaurant
Laundry	Can be taken away and returned later in the day, washed and ironed
Ice	Available from the bar
Office	Open from 7:30 am to 6:30 pm
Credit cards	Major cards except American Express

SERVICES

Airport
Only private or chartered aircraft use the 5,000-foot runway.

Accommodations
The Inn at Spanish Cay Tel: 365-0083 or 359-6622 Fax: 365-0466 A small luxury resort with villa suites and seven apartments from $180 per night.

Boat Rental
$150 per day

Cart Rental
$10 per hour, $25 per day

Restaurant and Bar
The Point House Tel: 359-6622 • VHF 16 Overlooking the marina and the Sea of Abaco. Open for breakfast, lunch, and dinner. Excellent food served in a tropical garden setting. Dinner reservations preferred.

The Wreckers Light Bar An imaginative building on stilts set out over the water on the ocean side of the island, just a few minutes walk from the marina. Serves light snacks and drinks.

Liquors
The Ship's Store Liquor, gifts, and a few snacks.

SPORTS

Diving
Some reefs are only half a mile from shore, with waters virtually unseen by sport divers. *Meghan's Reef* has magnificent coral structures coming up from 40 feet, almost to the surface, while *Wrecker's Reef*, the site of ancient shipwrecks, has huge Elkhorn and Staghorn coral.

Tennis
There are four tennis courts available.

THINGS TO DO IN SPANISH CAY

- Take a golf cart ride around the island and try to decide on which lot you would build your dream house.
- Count the number of different trees and shrubs that have been planted on the island. How many can you name?
- Swim off one of the five Spanish Cay beaches or walk part of the seven miles of glorious coastline.
- Enjoy a romantic dinner under the stars in the tropical garden overlooking the Sea of Abaco.

GREEN TURTLE CAY

BASRA in Green Turtle Cay, Bluff House
Tel: 365-4247 • VHF 16

Perhaps the most-loved Abaco cay, and certainly a favorite cruising destination, Green Turtle remains a joy and a delight. The early settlement of New Plymouth has a timelessness and charm that has much to offer, with good restaurants, well-stocked stores and a thriving community of friendly people used to visiting boaters. Both White Sound and Black Sound provide sheltered moorings and marinas, while many boats of deeper draft prefer to anchor off New Plymouth. Good beaches, good friends, and a town jail with the doors falling off due to lack of use, complete the idyll. Green Turtle Cay is a Port of Entry for the Bahamas; the **Customs** and **Immigration** office (tel: 365-4077) is on Parliament Street in New Plymouth. It is closed on weekends unless specially requested. To find them, tie up your dinghy at the town pier, and walk up the street past *Laura's Kitchen* and the *Shell Hut* to the Albert Lowe Museum, take a left and walk a few yards to their office, up the steps next to the post office.

MARINAS IN WHITE SOUND

GREEN TURTLE CLUB AND MARINA
Tel: 242-365-4271 • Fax: 365-4272 • VHF 16

This is a well-maintained marina, in a lovely, sheltered position at the head of White Sound, with all the facilities that a good resort offers. With its own fishing tournaments, yacht club, and outstanding beaches within walking distance, it is one of the most popular marinas in the Abaco Islands.

Slips	35
Moorings	3 moorings, $8 per night; no live-aboards
Max LOA	100 ft.
MLW at Dock	7 ft.; only 5 ft. in the channel at low water
Dockage	70¢ per foot, $20 minimum charge
Power	$18 per day for 50A, $11 per day for 30A
Fuel	Diesel and gasoline
Water	22¢ per gallon
Telephone	Card phone outside the store on the dock, and in the clubhouse, where there is a fax machine and copier for use during office hours, from 8 am to 4 pm.
TV Hookup	$5 per day, $25 deposit for the connector
Showers	Complimentary to marina guests
Laundry	Tokens at Reception; $3.50 per machine
Restaurants	Two within club; dinner reservations by 5 pm
Provisions	Marina store open from 8 am to 5 pm daily, selling ice, beverages, snacks, and a few marine supplies.

Mail	The Club will send and hold mail for you.
Swimming	Freshwater pool, solar heated in winter
Gift Shop	There is a small boutique in the clubhouse.
Rentals	Bicycles, sailboats, and windsurfers
Dive Shop	*Brendal's Dive Shop* Tel: 242-365-4411 or 954-467-1133 Two dive boats, a sailboat, windsurfers, and a glass-bottom boat. Scuba instruction from beginner courses to advanced open-water certification, underwater photography, night dives, CPR and first aid course; dive and snorkel equipment to rent; all-day trips with seafood beach picnics and rum punch. One-tank dive from $45. Dive packages available with accommodation at the *Green Turtle Club*.
Boat Rental	*Donny's Boat Rentals* Tel: 365-4271
Cart Rental	*D and P* have carts and scooters available.
Bicycles	From *Brendal's Dive Shop*
Accommodations	At the *Green Turtle Club*, rooms from $125 per night, villas from $140
Credit Cards	Visa, MasterCard, and Amex accepted.

BLUFF HOUSE CLUB AND MARINA
Tel: 242-365-4247 • Fax: 365-4248 • VHF 16

At the time of writing, the *Bluff House Club and Marina* was only just beginning its reconstruction. But Louie Louie, the dockmaster, assured us that all we describe below will be achieved during 1998. Their fuel docks on both White Sound and the Sea of Abaco are open from 8 am to 5 pm daily, and accept Visa, MasterCard, and American Express.

Slips	50
Moorings	4 at $8 per night
MLW at Dock	8 ft., but only 5 ft. in the approach channel into White Sound at low water
Power	50A and 30A
Fuel	Fuel docks on White Sound and the Sea of Abaco
Water	20¢ per gallon
Telephone	On the dock
Showers	Yes
Restaurants	There will be three when the new *Bluff House Marina Village Pub* is completed down by the marina. At the time of writing, there is the main restaurant up in the hotel building serving excellent dinners. Reservations, with choice of menu, are required by 5 pm. Lunch is served daily at the new *Palms Beach Bar* where Kevin and the Gully Roosters play for the Thursday night barbecue.
Ice	Yes
Swimming	Pools at the marina and hotel, with a beach below *Bluff House.*
Boat Rental	Can easily be arranged
Cart Rental	Golf carts are available for $40 per day.
Accommodation	*Bluff House Club*, rooms from $90, villas from $175 per night.
Credit Cards	Visa, MasterCard, and Amex accepted.

MARINAS IN BLACK SOUND

THE OTHER SHORE CLUB
Tel: 242-365-4195 • VHF 16

Alan and Trudy Andrews have been welcoming guests to *The Other Shore Club* for 30 years, now with their daughter Babs and son Cleeve, and dockmaster Kevin McIntosh of Gully Rooster fame. This is without doubt the friendliest small marina in the Out Islands. It is an easy walk through the garden around to New Plymouth or over to Gillam Bay.

Slips	15
Moorings	4 moorings, $7 per night
Max LOA	50 ft., but 100 ft. alongside the fuel dock
MLW at dock	6 ft.; only 3.5 ft. in the channel at low water
Dockage	50¢ per foot per day
Power	$17 per day for 50A, $10 for 30A
Fuel	Diesel and gasoline
Water	25¢ per gallon
Telephone	By request, in the dockmaster's office
Showers	$3 each
Ice	$3.50 a bag
Accommodations	There is a house and an apartment for rent at *The Other Shore Club*.
Credit Cards	Visa, MasterCard, and Amex accepted.

BLACK SOUND MARINA
Tel: 242-365-4221 • Fax: 365-4046 • VHF 16

This small, newly opened marina, past *The Other Shore Club*, *Roberts Marine*, and *Roberts Cottages* on the west side of Black Sound, has well-landscaped grounds, picnic tables, and barbecue grills for guests set out under the trees, with clean and tidy facilities. It is only a few minutes walk into New Plymouth from this side of Black Sound.

Slips	15
Max LOA	55 ft., with 65 ft. on the T-dock
MLW at Dock	7 ft.; only 3.5 ft. in the channel at low water
Dockage	70¢ per foot per day
Power	$18 per day for 50A, $12 for 30A
Water	25¢ per gallon
Showers	$3; only one shower, but very clean
Laundry	$4 for the washer or dryer
Ice	Yes
Storage	Monthly rates available. Dockmaster Andrew Pinder will look after your boat and fax a checklist to you.
Accommodations	Apartments available above the *Sand Dollar Shop* in New Plymouth.
Credit Cards	Visa, MasterCard, and Amex accepted.

SERVICE MARINAS

DOLPHIN MARINE **White Sound**
Tel: 242-365-4262 • VHF 16

Evinrude and Johnson sales, service, and parts. Boston Whalers in stock. OMC and DONZI, and Brownie's Third Lung diving equipment.

ABACO YACHT SERVICES **Black Sound**
Tel: 242-365-4033 • Fax 365-4216 • VHF 16

This is a full-service yard with good mechanics, a travel lift, fork lift, and small boat hoist, so you would choose this marina if you need repairs done on your boat, or if you are looking for long-term dry dockage while you are away from the Bahamas. Yamaha sales and repairs are on site, as is the only coin-operated laundromat on Green Turtle Cay. The yard is open from 7:30 am to noon and 1 pm to 4:30 pm, Monday to Friday.

Dockage	50¢ per foot per day
Power	$6 per day for 30A, $10 for 50A
Water	25¢ per gallon
Showers	$3
Laundry	$4 tokens from the office for the washing machines, and $3.50 for the dryers
Ice	$3 a bag
Dry Storage	$4 per foot per month
Labor	From $20 per hour, painting $35 per hour
Accommodations	There is a house for rent.

ROBERTS MARINE   Black Sound
Tel: 242-365-4249 • VHF 16

Workshop with complete engine service, inboards and outboards, and a diesel mechanic on site. They have a few slips available for transient boats, and three moorings for $5 a night, or monthly. Boat sales and rentals, marine accessories, batteries and ice. Johnson dealer. Their store, *Roberts Hardware* (Tel: 365-4122 and VHF 16), in New Plymouth is well stocked with marine supplies, household goods, building supplies, and paints.

NEW PLYMOUTH

SERVICES

Bank
Barclays Bank   Parliament Street   Tel: 365-4144
Open from 10 am to 1 pm on Tuesdays and Thursdays.

Churches
Methodist Church   Services at 11 am and 7:30 pm on Sundays.
Miracle of God Church   Sunday services at 10 am and 7 pm.
New Plymouth Gospel Chapel   Completed in 1995, winning top honors in the Institutional category from the Institute of Bahamian Architects. Services at 10 am and 8 pm on Sundays.
St. Peter's Anglican Church   Dates from 1786, and has Sunday services at 11 am and 8 pm.
Roman Catholic Mass at the *Green Turtle Club,* Thursdays at 11 am.

Clinic
Tel: 365-4028   The clinic is on the street running down opposite the *Sand Dollar Shop*. There is a nurse on duty 24 hours daily, and Dr. Wilson calls in weekly.

Couriers
Fedex deliveries can be arranged via ferry from Marsh Harbour.

Dentist
Call 367-4070 or 365-4548 to make an appointment.

Hairdresser
Hubert's Cuts 'n' Curls   Parliament Street   Tel: 365-4100

Museum
Albert Lowe Museum   Tel: 365-1494   Open 9 am to 11:45 am and 1 pm to 4 pm, Monday through Saturday. Admission $3, with a gift shop and Alton R. Lowe's paintings for sale.

Police
Parliament Street

Post Office
Tel: 365-4242   Between customs and the library on Parliament Street. Open from 9 am to 5 pm, Monday to Friday.

Rest Room
Next door to the Library.

Telephones
There is a card phone on the public dock, and direct dial phone outside the library, next to the post office on Parliament Street. There is also one outside the Batelco office at the top of the hill leading out of New Plymouth, and two more inside. The office is open from 9 am to 5 pm, Monday to Friday.

SHOPPING

Boutiques
Bluff House Boutique at *Bluff House Club*
Green Turtle Club Boutique, in the lobby of the Clubhouse

Galleries
Lowe's Art Gallery   Tel: 365-4624   Showing Alton Rowland Lowe Paintings, and carved Bahamian boat models by Ventrum Lowe, at the head of Black Sound. Call ahead for an appointment. They have their own dock, and a lovely garden.
Ocean Blue Gallery featuring many local and island artists, is open within the *Plymouth Rock Liquors and Cafe*.

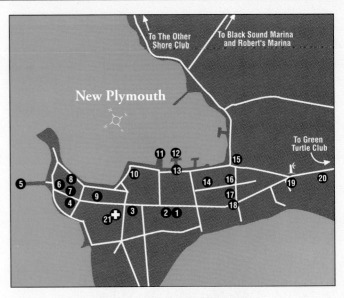

New Plymouth Directory

1 Post Office, Customs and Library
2 Albert Lowe Museum
3 New Plymouth Inn
4 Roberts Hardware and Marine Store
5 Commercial Dock
6 Liquor Store
7 Barclays Bank
8 Anglican Church
9 Sid's Grocery
10 Curry's Store

11 Public Dock
12 Ferry Dock
13 Bolo Ferry Office in house
14 B&M Seafood
15 The Wrecking Tree
16 Bert's Sea Garden
17 The Blue Bee Bar
18 Town Jail
19 Batelco
20 Rooster's Restaurant
21 ✚ Clinic

Gifts and Souvenirs
Loyalist Rose   Parliament Street
Shell Hut   On the street up from the public dock   Tel: 365-4188
Offers a selection of T-shirts, souvenirs, post cards, and more.
Sand Dollar Shop   Parliament Street   Tel: 365-4221
Original handcrafted jewelry, designed and manufactured by 9th-generation Abaco artists in New Plymouth, as well as souvenirs, T-shirts, gifts, and sportswear.
Vert's Model Ship Shoppe   Next to *Curry's Food Store*

Groceries
Curry's Food Store   Tel: 365-4171   Open 8 am to noon, and 1 pm to 5:30 pm, Monday to Friday; to 8 pm on Saturdays. Also T-shirts, wonderful fresh bread, and custom wood carvings. They have their own dinghy dock, and can also get propane for you.
Lowe's   Tel: 365-4243   Open 7:30 am to 6 pm, Monday to Friday, to 8 pm on Saturdays. Gifts as well as groceries.
Sid's Grocery   Tel: 365-4055   Open 7 am to 6 pm, Monday through Friday; to 7:30 pm on Saturdays. Well stocked with everything including fresh fruit and vegetables, pharmacy, and some hardware. Propane refills may take a couple of days.

Hardware
New Plymouth Hardware   Tel: 365-4305 • Fax: 365-4372 • VHF 16
Open 7:30 am to 4:30 pm, Monday to Friday; 8 am to 12 noon on Saturdays. Household goods and some marine hardware. No credit cards accepted, but they will let you use their fax machine.
Roberts Hardware & Marine   Tel: 365-4122 • VHF 16
Hardware and building supplies, paints, charts, rope, ice, and fishing and diving supplies.

Liquors

Plymouth Rock Liquors   Parliament Street   Tel: 365-4234
Open 9 am to 6 pm, Monday to Thursday; to 9 pm on Fridays and Saturdays. They stock more than 70 brands of rum, and will deliver to the town dock. The *Ocean Blue Gallery*, featuring many local and island artists, is located inside the liquor store.

Propane

Sid's Food Store   Tel: 365-4055 or
Curry's Food Store   Tel: 365-4171   Tanks may take a couple of days since they have to go to Marsh Harbour or Nassau.

Seafood

Abaco Seafoods   Tel: 365-4011

B & M Seafood   York Street   Tel: 365-4387
Excellent grouper, and lobster tails in season.

Sodas

Soda machine next to the *Red Door*, on Parliament Street, with Coke, Ginger Ale, Orange, Root Beer, Grape Juice and Goombay Punch for $1 in US quarters.

Videos

Porky's   Next to the *Sea Garden Club*

RESTAURANTS & BARS

Bluff House Club at White Sound   Tel: 365-4247 • VHF 16
The *Palms Beach Club* is open for lunch from 11:30 am to 3 pm, and for a barbecue on Thursday evenings. You are asked to make your dinner reservations for the restaurant with the choice of menu by 5 pm daily. Fantastic sunset views and great food.

Green Turtle Cay Club at White Sound   Tel: 365-4271 • VHF 16
Breakfast from 7:45 am to 10:30 am, lunch from 11:30 am to 3 pm on a beautiful terrace overlooking White Sound. Dinner is served in their elegant dining room at 7:30 pm. Please make your dinner reservations by 5 pm. Live music on the patio with Kevin and the Gully Roosters on Wednesday evenings.

Islands Restaurant and Grill   Tel: 365-4082   Above *Lowe's Grocery* on Parliament Street. Open daily, except Sundays, for lunch and dinner.

Laura's Kitchen in New Plymouth   Tel: 365-4287 • VHF 16
Open from 11 am to 3 pm and 6:30 pm to 9 pm daily. A favorite meeting place for boaters, with good home cooking, and daily menu changes; ice cream served all day. Complimentary transport is available for dinner.

McIntosh Take-away   Tel: 365-4625 • VHF 16
Lunch and dinner; delivery, take away, or dine right there. Also bread and cakes.

Mike's Bar 'n' Restaurant   Overlooking the anchorage
Tel: 365-4219 • VHF 16   Serving drinks all day, and home-cooked lunches and dinners to order from Josie Sawyer. A good place to watch the sunset, with their own dinghy dock.

Miss Emily's Blue Bee Bar   Tel: 365-4181   Famous! Since Miss Emily died in 1997, the *Blue Bee Bar* has been run by Violet Smith who knows Miss Emily's secret recipe for a Goombay Smash.

New Plymouth Inn   Tel: 365-4161 • VHF 16   Serving breakfast 8 to 9 am, lunch 11:30 am to 1:30 pm, and dinner at 7:30 pm, in the historic heart of town. An excellent Garden Brunch on Sundays 11 am to 2 pm. Dinner reservations required by 5 pm.

Ole B's Ice Cream and Sandwiches   Open 10 am to 5 pm Monday to Saturday; 7 to 9 pm Fridays and Saturdays. Delicious sandwiches, fried fish, chicken, and many varieties of ice cream.

Plymouth Rock Liquors & Cafe   Tel: 365-4234   Open 9 am to 6 pm Monday to Thursday; to 9 pm Fridays and Saturdays. Counter-style service for sandwiches and lunchtime snacks until 3 pm, in the liquor store.

Rooster's Rest Pub   At the top of the hill leading out of New Plymouth, on the road to Gillam Bay.   Tel: 365-4066   Open 10:30 am to 10 pm or later. Drinks and Bahamian food, with live music by the Gully Roosters on Friday and Saturday nights.

Sea Garden Club   Where Bert makes a brilliant Tipsy Turtle!

The Wrecking Tree   The corner of Bay Street, overlooking the waterfront.   Tel: 365-4263 • VHF 16   Serving home-baked bread, local seafood, and drinks all day. Their specialty house drink is a well-named Wrecker.

GETTING AROUND

Bicycle Rentals

Noel and Ivy Roberts, at the *Albert Lowe Museum*   Tel: 365-4089

Brendal's Dive Shop in White Sound   Tel: 365-4411

Boat Rentals

Donny's Boat Rentals in Black Sound   Tel: 365-4271 • VHF 16

Cart Rental

Cay Cart Rentals   Tel: 365-4406 • VHF 79
Golf carts $35 per day, Visa or MasterCard accepted.

Ferries

Green Turtle Ferry   Tel: 365-4151 • VHF 16   Bolo ferries leave from their own dock in New Plymouth, or will collect you from any dock in Black Sound or White Sound to go to Treasure Cay for the airport, or a taxi to Marsh Harbour. Ferries connect with most flights in and out of Treasure Cay airport and leave daily at 8 am, 1:30 pm, and 3 pm, with an additional service at 12:15 pm on request. Call for alternative timings, destinations, or where you need to be picked up, or inquire at the house opposite the end of their ferry dock in New Plymouth. The fare is $8 one way on a scheduled ferry. From Treasure Cay, the ferries leave for Green Turtle Cay at 1:30 pm, 3 pm, and 4:15 pm, with an additional one at 2:15 pm if enough people need it.

Taxi

McIntosh Taxi Service   Tel: 365-4309 • VHF 16 or 6
Cost between $5 and $10.

OMRI'S Taxi   VHF 16

Travel Agents

A and W Travel Service   Tel: 365-4140

SPORTS

Diving

Brendal's Dive Shop at the *Green Turtle Club* in White Sound
Tel: 365-4411 • VHF 16   Brendal and his wife Mary run an extensive dive operation. See our entry under *Green Turtle Club* for details. Two-tank dives from $70, snorkeling from $35. Guided reef trips including picnic lunches, sailboat cruises and rentals, windsurfers, and full scuba instruction courses up to advanced SSI qualification. Diving is year round, with water temperatures from 76°F in the winter months, to 89°F during the summer, and an average visibility of 100 feet.

Dive Sites

The Tarpon Dive   Dive with 11 Tarpon fish at 50 feet and feed a green moray eel.

Coral Caverns   Winding caverns with schools of silversides.

The Catacombs   Sun-filtered catacombs with fish and turtles at 40 feet, brilliant for photography.

The Wreck of the San Jacinto   The first US steamship; sank in 40 feet of water in 1865.

Fishing

Rick or Leigh Sawyer   Tel: 365-4261 • VHF 16 "Playmate" or VHF 71 "Spindrift"   Deep sea, reef, and bonefishing; snorkeling.

Lincoln Jones   VHF 16 "I Lost it"   Day trips, fish fry on the beach, snorkeling, and fishing.

THINGS TO DO IN GREEN TURTLE CAY

- Visit the Albert Lowe Museum for a fascinating look back at the history of Green Turtle Cay, and don't forget the Memorial Sculpture Garden.
- Walk over the hill to Gillam Bay and search for sand dollars at low tide.
- Enjoy an ice cream cone, and browse for souvenirs in New Plymouth.
- Shop for fresh food and provisions at the three excellent grocery stores.
- Have your boat hauled for a bottom job in Black Sound.
- Have your outboard motor fixed by the experts.
- Pamper yourself with a new hairdo at *Cuts 'n' Curls*.
- Enjoy a cool drink at *Miss Emily's Blue Bee Bar*, the *Sea Garden Club* or the *Wrecking Tree*, or watch the sun set over the anchorage from *Mike's Bar*.
- Jump up with Kevin and the Gully Roosters at the *Roosters Rest* on Friday or Saturday night.
- Take your dinghy around to Manjack Cay for some brilliant snorkeling and fishing.
- Make your dinner reservations at one of the restaurants by 5 pm, and enjoy some of the best food in the Islands.
- If you have books or magazines that you have finished, leave them at the library for others to enjoy.

ACCOMMODATIONS

Clubs and Inns
Bluff House Club   Tel: 242-365-4247   Single and double rooms from $90, suites and villas from $175, MAP $36.
Green Turtle Club   Tel: 242-365-4271   Single and double rooms from $125, suites and villas from $160, MAP $36.
New Plymouth Inn   Tel: 242-365-4161   Single rooms from $104, double rooms from $144, year round. Prices include taxes, breakfast, and an excellent dinner. Surcharge of 4 percent on credit card payments. Closed in September.

Cottages and Apartments
Coco Bay Club   On Coco Bay between two beaches Tel: 242-365-5464 $800/$1,000 per week for two-bedroom cottages.
Deck House   On White Sound   Tel: 513-821-9471 $1,150 per week for six people.
House on the Point   Gillam Bay   Tel: 242-365-4178 or 4225 $700 per week for four people.
Lintons Cottages   On Long Bay Beach   Tel: 242-365-4003 $1,300/$1,500 per week.
Long Bay House   Black Sound   Tel: 242-365-4294 $1,100 per week.
Osprey's Nest   Gillam Bay   Tel: 352-746-3500
Roberts Cottages   Tel: 242-365-4105 • VHF 16   Jean Roberts has three cottages available on Black Sound, including dockage for boats under 25 feet. There is an extra charge for boats over 25 feet, plus an electricity charge. The cottages rent from $600 per week. She also has two apartments above Barclays Bank, from $60 per night, with a dock for small boats on the creek shore.
Sand Dollar Apartments   Above the *Sand Dollar Shop* in New Plymouth   Tel: 242-365-4221
South Beach Apartments   Tel: 365-4283   Overlooking the Sea of Abaco, with dock facilities for small boats.

FISHING TOURNAMENTS & REGATTAS

May/June
Green Turtle Club Fishing Tournament and the *Bahamas Rendezvous* at the Green Turtle Club. Call *Green Turtle Club* at 242-365-4271 for more information.

July
Regatta Time in Abaco is held annually, the first week in July. Races form up in Green Turtle Cay, Man-O-War, Hope Town, and Marsh Harbour. Contact Dave or Kathy Ralph, Marsh Harbour, Abaco, Bahamas.   Tel: 242-367-2677, or Fax 242-367-3677.
Green Turtle Cay Regatta Week   The Bahama Cup, a race around Green Turtle Cay for visiting yachtsmen. Call *Green Turtle Club* at 242-365-4271 for information.

COOPERS TOWN

Coopers Town has little to offer the cruising boat, unless you need fuel or very simple provisions. It is a rolly anchorage, and there is nowhere to tie up other than alongside the fuel dock. Medious Edgecombe, who runs the Shell fuel dock, is most helpful and will assist you in any way possible. Coopers Town is not a Port of Entry for the Bahamas, so you cannot clear in through Customs or Immigration. It is an easy walk along the waterfront to find everything in town. A limited selection of marine stores, outboard engine spares, liquor, food, a laundromat, and ice are available at the Shell store on the fuel dock. *Murray's Service Center*, another fuel dock about a mile southeast of Coopers Town, has diesel, gasoline, ice, and groceries.

SERVICES & SHOPPING

Bakery
Eve's Restaurant and Bakery, specializing in souse.

Bank
Nova Scotia Bank   Open 9 am to 2 pm, Tuesdays & Thursdays.

Barber
Kool Cuts Barber

Church
Church of God's Cathedral

Clinic
Tel: 365-0019   There is a newly opened clinic in town.

Clothing
Shirley's Boutique

Drugstore
Edgecombs, also sells gifts.

Fuel
Shell Fuel Dock   Diesel and gasoline

Groceries
Wright Grocery Store, also has pies, bread and cakes.

Hardware
J & M Enterprises

Ice
Available from the fuel dock.

Museum
The Albert Doodle Museum

Police
There is a police station in town.

Post Office
Open 9 am to 5 pm daily, except Sundays.

Restaurant
The Conch Crawl, near the Shell dock. A bar serving lunch.

Taxi
Can be called by the fuel dock.

Telephones
There are two next to the government offices.

GREAT GUANA CAY

Most of the action in this long thin cay is centered around the resort and the tiny settlement on the bay's edge. Beaches on both coasts are great, long, and mostly empty; you can always find a sheltered spot. Great Guana is one of the last of the bigger Abaco cays to remain largely undeveloped, but change is in the wind. This island is well worth a visit. No Customs or Immigration.

MARINA

GUANA BEACH RESORT AND MARINA
Tel: 242-365-5133 • Fax: 365-5134 • VHF 16

A fuel dock is planned by the end of 1997; in 1998 the whole marina will be upgraded with power and water at every berth.

Slips	22
Max LOA	55 ft., with 70 ft. on the T-dock
MLW at Dock	5 ft.
Dockage	50¢ per foot per night. The dinghy tie-up fee is refunded if you have lunch at the resort.
Power	$12 per day for 30A, $22 for 50A
Restaurant	Pool-side and clubhouse dining, from 8 am to 9 pm. No in-between meal closings.
Ice	$3.50 a bag, from the hotel
Swimming	Marina guests may use the pool; beaches are within easy walking distance.
Boutique	A well-stocked gift shop at reception with T-shirts, swimsuits, beach towels, sunglasses, suntan lotion. Open 7:30 am to 5:30 pm.
Credit Cards	Visa and MasterCard accepted.

SERVICES & SHOPPING

Church
Sea Side Gospel Church
Clinic
Doctor visits monthly. Nearest medical facilities: Marsh Harbour.
Gift Shops
Bay View Gifts
The Bikini Hut, formerly *Milos Gift Shop*
P & J Variety Store
Tom's T Shirts
Groceries
Guana Harbour Grocery   Tel: 365-5067 • VHF 16   Open 8 am to 5:30 pm, Monday to Thursday; to 6:30 pm Fridays and Saturdays. Well-stocked: fresh fruit and vegetables, canned and dry goods, meat and dairy; some pharmacy, stationery, hardware.
Hardware
Guana Cay Hardware   Monday to Saturday, 8:30 am to 5 pm.
Liquor
My Two Sons Liquor Store   On the waterfront. Also has ice.
Post Office
Open from 9 am to 5 pm, Monday through Friday.
Telephones
One outside the post office, another outside *Tom's T-Shirts.*

GETTING AROUND

Bicycles and Cart Rental
Donna Sand   Tel: 365-5195 • VHF 16   Donna also rents cottages and sells real estate. Her husband builds houses.

Boat Rental
Edmund Pinder   Tel: 365-5046
Island tours, diving, fishing, and snorkeling.
Guana Cay Boat Rentals   Tel: 365-5148 • VHF 16
Ferries
AIT Ferries   **Great Guana Cay to Conch Inn Marina, Marsh Harbour,** leaves at 8 am, 11 am, 3 pm, and 5 pm daily; **Conch Inn Marina, Marsh Harbour to Great Guana Cay** leaves at 9 am, 12 noon, 4 pm, and 6 pm daily; $6 fare each way.
The Guana Grabber Ferry is now in use as a dive boat.

RESTAURANTS & BARS

Guana Beach Resort Restaurant   Tel: 365-5133 • VHF 16
Breakfast, lunch, and dinner by the pool and in the clubhouse. Famous for their Guana Grabbers, an exotic rum punch.
Guana Seaside Village   Tel: 365-5106 and 365-5107 • VHF 16
Breakfast 8 am to 9:45 am, lunch noon to 3 pm, and dinner 6 to 8:30 pm. Call ahead for dinner reservations. Menu changes nightly. Barbecue night on Saturdays with conch, fish, and pork. Coconut shrimp a specialty. Take your dinghy to their dock.
Nippers Bar and Grill   Bar opens at 10 am, lunch from 11 am to 3:30 pm, dinner 6 to 10 pm. Very casual! Fun Sunday pig roasts.

ACCOMMODATIONS

Dolphin Beach Resort   Tel: 242-365-5137   Brad and Robin Wilson will soon open a bed and breakfast with cottages, a gift shop, and swimming pool, so call them first to check progress.
Guana Beach Resort and Marina   Tel: 242-365-5133
Beachfront rooms from $125 per night, double occupancy, suites from $150 per night. MAP $35 per person. These prices will probably change after the rebuilding of the resort.
Guana Seaside Village   Tel: 242-365-5106   Roger and Katherine Abney have recently opened this 8-room resort, with all rooms facing on to an attractive pool and bar, a restaurant, a long dock leading out into the bay, and a short walk across to the beach on the northeast side of the island. Rooms from $120 per night, single or double occupancy. Boat rentals, golf carts, fishing guides available, with showers, water, and laundry for boaters.
Sea Fan Cottage   Tel: 603-659-8312
The Spencer Family Anchorage   Tel: 800-462-2426   Cottage.

REGATTA

Regatta Time in Abaco is held during the first week in July. Races form up in Green Turtle Cay, Guana Cay, Man-O-War, Hope Town and Marsh Harbour. Contact Dave or Kathy Ralph, Marsh Harbour, Abaco, Bahamas. Tel 242-367-2677 • Fax 367-3677.

THINGS TO DO IN GREAT GUANA CAY

- Walk on the seven-mile beach, and then snorkel the reef, which is close to shore and good for beginners.
- Take a picnic in the dinghy up to Baker's Bay, and have a fantastic time swimming without a crowd scene.
- Enjoy a Grabber by the pool at the *Guana Beach Resort*, as the sun goes down over the anchorage.
- Take the dinghy over to the *Guana Seaside Village* for lunch or dinner, and have a change of scene.
- Stroll over to *Nippers* for an island feast set among the sand dunes. What about the Pig Roast one Sunday?

TREASURE CAY

At this stage of your Bahamian cruise, if you've had enough primitive beauty and anchoring out and you're hankering after some amenities, Treasure Cay is worth a visit. It is also a good place for a crew change, with frequent flights in and out of Treasure Cay Airport. Almost all stores and facilities are within the resort, either in the long building behind the marina or within walking distance of it. Treasure Cay is a Port of Entry, and the dock staff can call **Customs** and **Immigration** for you.

MARINA

TREASURE CAY HOTEL RESORT AND MARINA
Tel: 242-365-8250 • VHF 16

Slips	150
Moorings	15 moorings on a first-come, first-serve basis for $10 per day.
Anchorage	$8 per day
Max LOA	110 ft., up to 130 ft. on the T-dock
MLW at Dock	5 ft.
Dockage	Under 70 ft., 80¢ per foot per day, $20 minimum per day. Over 70 ft., $1 per foot per day.
Long-term Dockage	From 50¢ per foot per day
Power	30A and 50A from $9 to $30 per day, according to boat length. Boats using two 50A shore power cords will be charged double.
Fuel	Diesel and gasoline at the fuel dock on the approach into the marina.
Water	$5 to $12 per day according to boat length. Reverse osmosis bottled water available in gallon bottles from *Abaco-pure* behind the *Spinnaker Restaurant*.
Showers	Yes
Telephones	Two by the *Treasure Cay Marina Shoppe*, and two for credit card or collect calls. Four more phones by *G & M Variety Store*.
TV	$5 per day, or $30 per week, $30 deposit required. Charges are included in dockage fees during March, April, and August.
Restaurants	*Spinnaker Restaurant and Bar* Tel: 365-8569 • VHF 19 Breakfast 7:30 to 10:30 am, lunch 11:30 am to 2:30 pm, and dinner 6:30 to 9:30 pm. Dinner reservations requested. Complimentary cocktail party Fridays at 6 pm. *Cafe La Florence,* in the long building, has home-baked cookies and ice cream. *Coco Bar* on the beach, serves lunch from 11 am to 5 pm daily.
Bar	*Tipsy Seagull Bar,* open 11 am to closing; live entertainment Fridays and Saturdays.
Barbecues	Barbecues provided for marina guest use.
Store	*Treasure Cay Marina Shoppe,* selling dive gear, T-shirts, gifts with a nautical flavor.
Credit Cards	All major credit cards accepted.

MARINE SERVICES

Edgecombe's Marine Services Tel: 242-365-8454 • VHF 16 Engine repairs and boat delivery service back to Florida.
Bill's Canvas Sail repair

SERVICES & SHOPPING

Bank
Royal Bank of Canada Open from 10:30 am to noon and 12:30 pm to 2 pm on Tuesdays and Thursdays.

Churches
Saints Mary and Andrew Catholic Church, on the road to the main highway. Mass at 5 pm on Sundays.

St. Simon's Anglican/Episcopalian Church, in the building behind *Abaco Ceramics.* Mass at 8 am on Sundays.

Treasure Cay Community Church Sunday service at 9 am.

Clinic
The Corbett Medical Centre Tel: 365-8288 Open 9 am to noon and 2 to 4 pm, Monday, Tuesday, and Friday; 8:30 to 11 am Saturdays. Dr. Ronald Wilson is there most days.

Dentist
Treasure Cay Dental Clinic By the Post Office Tel: 365-8425 or 365-8625 By appointment with Dr. Spencer for the first and third weekends each month. Open Fridays 11 am to 5 pm, Saturdays 9 am to 5 pm, Mondays 9 am to 2 pm.

Gifts & Souvenirs
Abaco Ceramics, by Treasure Cay Resort Tel or fax: 365-8489 Open 9 am to 3 pm, Monday to Friday. Bahamian handmade ceramic gifts and jewelry.

Bill's Canvas Bag Shop & Marine Upholstery Sells bags, repairs sails.

Little Switzerland

Seven Sister's Shop

Treasure Cay Marine Shoppe

Treasure Cay Directory

A Treasure Cay Marina

1 Fuel Dock
2 Batelco Tower
3 Golf Course
4 Shops, Post Office, Dentist, Bank
5 Marina Shop, Dockmaster's Office and Spinnaker Restaurant
6 Beach Bar
7 Abaco Ceramics
8 Church
9 ✚ Clinic

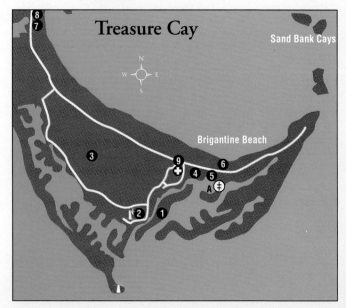

Groceries

Treasure Cay Mini Market   VHF 16   Open 8 am to 6 pm, Monday to Saturday. Well stocked with fresh fruit and vegetables, meat, pharmacy, stationery, household goods, gifts.

G & M Variety Store   Open from 7 am to 10 pm daily. Soft drinks, water, dairy products, toiletries, ice.

Laundry

Annie Wash & Press Laundry and Dry Cleaning

Liquor Store

Spikey's Duty Free Liquor Store
Open from 10 am to 6 pm, Monday to Saturday.

Post Office

Open from 9 am to 1 pm, and 2 to 5 pm, Monday to Friday.

Telephones

Many close to the marina, and the *Batelco* office is open for phone cards, faxes, etc. from 9 am to 5 pm, Monday to Friday.

GETTING AROUND

Airport

Treasure Cay International Airport is 7 miles away. Taxis are $14 for two people from the marina.

Airlines

Flights from Miami, Orlando, Nassau, Fort Lauderdale, and West Palm Beach.

Airways International	305-526-2000
American Eagle	800-433-7300
Bahamas Air	800-222-4262
Gulfstream International	800-992-8532
Island Express	305-359-0380
Twin Air	333-2444
US Air Express	800-428-4322

Bicycles

Wendell's Bicycle Shop   Open 8 am to 4 pm, bicycles to rent for $6 per day.

Boat Rental

C & C Boat Rentals   Tel: 365-8582 • VHF 16   8:30 am to 5 pm. Sunfish, Hobie Cats, windsurfers, scuba & snorkel gear, spear fishing, island tours.

JIC Boat Rentals   Tel: 365-8465 • VHF 16 or 79   20- to 28-foot boats, dive gear and fishing tackle rental, air fills, PADI instruction.

Car Rental

Cornish Car Rental   Tel: 365-8623

Triple J Car Rental & Gift Shop   VHF 06   Cars from $75 per day; carts and bicycles.

Cart Rental

JIC   Tel: 365-8465 • VHF 16   Golf carts; $20 half-day rental, $30 full day. MasterCard accepted.

Chris Carts   Tel: 365-8053   Golf carts $35 per day. Visa and MasterCard.

Ferries

Bolo Ferries run from the dock near the airport to Green Turtle Cay at 10:30 am, 1:30 pm, 3 pm, and 4:15 pm, coinciding with flight arrivals. Ferry fare is $8 to Green Turtle Cay.

Taxis

Call VHF 06. There are nearly always taxis waiting beyond the shops at the marina.

SPORTS

Cruises

Mermaid Boat Cruises   Tel: 365-8475
For scuba rental and entertaining evenings out!

Diving

Divers Down   Tel: 365-8465 • VHF 16 or 79
Dive equipment, snorkeling and reef trips, scuba diving, scuba instruction, and air fills. $75 for a two-tank dive, see John Cash.

Fishing

Fish for marlin, dolphin, wahoo, tuna, snapper, grouper, and amberjack from Treasure Cay or go bonefishing.

Golf

An 18-hole round of golf with a cart costs $40, special rates for marina guests.

Tennis

$12 per court per hour.

ACCOMMODATIONS

Brigantine Bay Villas   Tel: 770-993-7073   Two-bedroom villas on the waterfront, with a dock, from $150 per night.

Four Winds Cottages   Tel: 242-365-8568
Weekly, monthly, long-term rental.

GIF Enterprises Ltd   Tel: 242-365-8200 or 8620 (from 9 am to 5 pm) • VHF 16 or 77

Treasure Cay Hotel   Tel: 242-367-8538   Although the main hotel has been closed for several years, some of the marina view townhouses have been converted for hotel use. Rooms, suites, and houses from $85 per person per night, $130 per person per night during the winter season.

Treasure Cay Villas and Condos   Tel: 201-767-9393   Selection of villas and condos for rent. Packages with the major airlines.

FISHING TOURNAMENTS

May

The Treasure Cay Billfish Championship and the *Bahamas Billfish Tournament.*

THINGS TO DO IN TREASURE CAY

- Take a short walk over to the beach, where you'll find over three miles of powdery white sand set in a magnificent, horseshoe-shaped bay. The swimming is glorious. Enjoy lunch at the *Coco Bar* while you're there.
- Play 18 holes of golf on the 7,000 yard course.
- Explore the network of canals in your dinghy. These canals, incidentally, offer good hurricane protection.
- Shop for duty-free treasures at *Little Switzerland*.
- Explore New Plymouth and discover the charm of Green Turtle Cay, by taking a taxi to the Green Turtle Ferry dock and going across for lunch. The ferry leaves at 10:30 am, and returns to Treasure Cay at 1:30 pm and 3 pm. Or take your own boat across and stay for longer!
- Treat your crew to dinner ashore at the *Spinnaker Restaurant*.
- Enjoy world-class fishing within easy reach.

Chapter 6
The Southern Abacos
Great Guana Cay to Cherokee Sound
Including Hope Town and Marsh Harbour

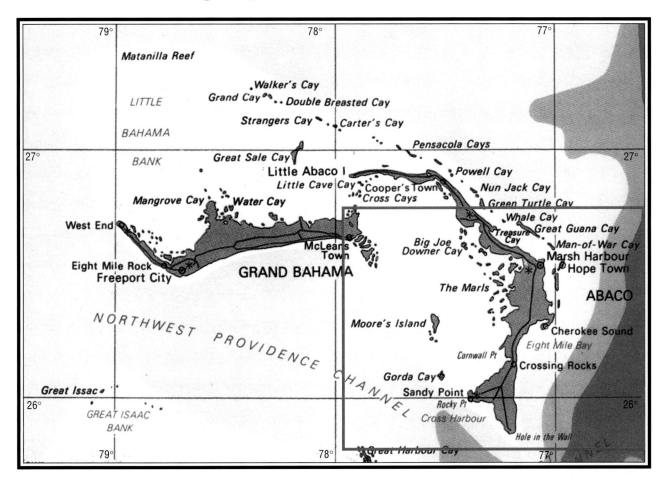

Ocean Passes

BETWEEN Great Guana Cay and Elbow Cay there are two gaps through the reef to the north and south of Man-O-War Cay. Neither of these is particularly good, and we favor either going north to Whale Cay or 21 nm further south to the North Bar Channel, just north of Lynyard Cay.

- From a start point about 0.5 nm northwest of **Man-O-War Cay** (26° 37' 00 N 077° 02' 00 W) you want to head on about 030°M for a gap in the barrier reef. It's not a wide gap and we don't recommend it.

- There's another way out into the Atlantic to the south of Man-O-War Cay, but this, like the first Man-O-

War option, is fine for those with the right boats and local knowledge, but why test your nerve? If you feel you must go this way, take your dinghy and a hand-held depth sounder and check it out first.

South of Elbow Cay the last stretch of the Sea of Abaco is fortunate in having two good ocean passes, North Bar Channel and Little Harbour Bar. Sometimes one of the two will be the better option as the result of wind and swell, but like all ocean passes neither should be attempted if there are strong inshore winds or a heavy ocean swell or, even worse, both. Just like Whale Cay, rage conditions make for lethal seas. We cover these passes in greater detail later in the chapter.

Great Guana Cay–Man-O-War Cay–Elbow Cay (Hope Town)

Great Guana Cay (Delia's Cay Rk)	GGANA	26° 39' 45 N	077° 07' 00 W
Man-O-War Cay (NW of)	NWMOW	26° 36' 00 N	077° 02' 00 W
Man-O-War Cay (harbor ent.)	MOWAP	26° 35' 15 N	077° 00' 25 W
Point Set Rock (E of)	EPTST	26° 34' 00 N	076° 59' 45 W
Hope Town (approach)	HPTAP	26° 33' 00 N	076° 58' 30 W

It's an easy run down to Man-O-War Cay or Hope Town and Elbow Cay from Great Guana. A heading of 136°M for 5.83 nm will take you off the northwest end of Man-O-War Cay, leaving Foots Cay and the Fish Cays (that's another set of Fish Cays) to starboard and Scotland Cay and the Fowl Cays with Fish Hawk Cay to port.

FOOTS CAY

Foots Cay is private.

FISH CAYS

The Fish Cays have little to offer.

SCOTLAND CAY

Scotland Cay is a private resort with an airstrip.

FOWL CAYS AND FISH HAWK CAY

The Fowl Cays and Fish Hawk Cay are a Land and Sea Preserve. You may visit the park area, but you must use the mooring buoys provided. You are not allowed to take anything from either land, beach, or water, and, hardly surprisingly, you're not allowed to fish there.

From the Man-O-War waypoint that placed you off the northwest tip of the cay, 1.6 nm on a heading of 124°M will take you to the entrance to Man-O-War harbor. As we talk of two cays, Man-O-War Cay and Dickie's Cay, you may need reassurance at this point, for it's impossible to identify two separate cays to port. Dickie's Cay lies so close to Man-O-War that it might be a part of it, and even when you reach the point of entering Man-O-War Harbour, it's still not apparent that a Dickie's Cay with a separate identity exists. At risk of offending local patriotism, treat them as one. To starboard you'll have no problems picking up Garden Cay and Sandy Cay.

Man-O-War Cay and Dickie's Cay

Man-O-War Cay Approaches and Anchorages

The northern entrance to Man-O-War harbor is for small boats or shoal draft boats only. The main entrance, which you will take, lies at the south tip of Dickie's Cay, and you go in between this point of land and the headland of the Man-O-War cove to the south. The entrance is narrow and hard to pick up from any distance away, but is marked by a

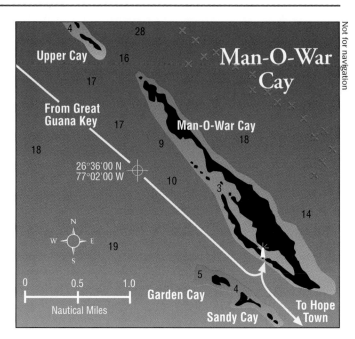

prominent marker light on Dickie's Cay. You'll have 5 feet at MLW there. Expect tidal flow. As soon as you clear the entrance you must decide whether you're turning to starboard to go on into the southern harbor area (to anchor), or turning to port to go into the main harbor (where you may anchor, or go on to the Man-O-War marina or boatyard of your choice). Be warned that Man-O-War harbor and its marina are always crowded, and if you want dock space, you should reserve it ahead of time.

Man-O-War Cay owes its double harbor to its hard-to-

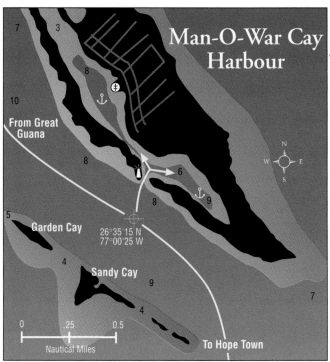

identify sibling. The west side of Man-O-War Cay is paralleled for a third of its length by Dickie's Cay, and this shielding produces the greater, northern part of Man-O-War harbor. The southern harbor lies wholly within Man-O-War territory.

Man-O-War Cay

Man-O-War Cay is famed for its boat building and a harbor that is reckoned to be one of the safest in the Abacos. The settlement itself, kept as clean as a new pin, reflects one of the most industrious communities in the Bahamas whose interests have always been primarily maritime: boat building, boat repairs, sail making, and ferry services. Inevitably Man-O-War has long featured on the tourist "must visit" lists, and has long been a port-of-call for every cruising boat passing that way, but somehow Man-O-War has maintained its integrity and kept its unique character. Part of the reason may lie in a strong religious sense of bonding that holds the little community somewhat apart from the ways of the outside world, not least of which is evidenced in a total ban on the sale of alcohol on the island.

Hope Town Harbour

Janet Wilson

Going on to Hope Town

To resume or stay on your course for Hope Town continue heading southeast on 160°M past and away from Sandy Cay for 1.38 nm, which will place you safely off Point Set Rock, on your starboard side, and well away from the shoal area that lies around Johnnie's Cay to port. From this last waypoint a heading of 138°M and 1.5 nm will place you ready to go visual and enter Hope Town harbor. The total distance run from Great Guana Cay will be around 13 nm.

We've given waypoints and courses but in truth we go visual running between Great Guana Cay and Hope Town. The navigation data is just a useful backup. We were caught once on the final part of this run down to Hope Town by a heavy rainstorm that wiped out all trace of land and inked out the radar with clutter for over 45 minutes. We crawled along, stalling for time, and when the storm passed we'd hit the spot and were right there, on the mark, ready for Hope Town. Thank you GPS!

GARDEN CAY AND SANDY CAY

Both Garden Cay and Sandy Cay are private.

JOHNNIE'S CAY

Johnnie's Cay is also private.

Hope Town and the North of Elbow Cay

The Approach to Hope Town Harbour

The approach to Hope Town isn't difficult, but you have to get it right from the start because you have a comparatively narrow entry channel to negotiate with a 90° turn to starboard. This channel carries some 5 feet at MLW. When you're just off the northernmost Parrot Cay, head roughly toward the famous lighthouse marking Hope Town but setting slightly north of it, aiming to clear the headland on which the lighthouse is built. The entrance channel to Hope Town harbor won't become immediately apparent, but aim to clear that headland by at least 100 yards at this stage.

You'll see a prominent yellow house with a reddish-brown roof on the rocky islet called Eagle Rock as you get closer. At first you can't even see that the yellow house is offshore rather than on the main shoreline. The house is your first approach marker, which will be on your port side, and the lighthouse headland will be to starboard. The entry channel is marked and becomes more apparent as you get closer, as will two leading marks.

As you line up for the channel you'll see a concrete road that ends abruptly at the water's edge. There's a white marker with a red reflector on the north side of the road at its ending, and a telephone pole, the bottom painted white, carries a second red mark a few yards further back down the road. Get the two marks in line and you're right in the channel.

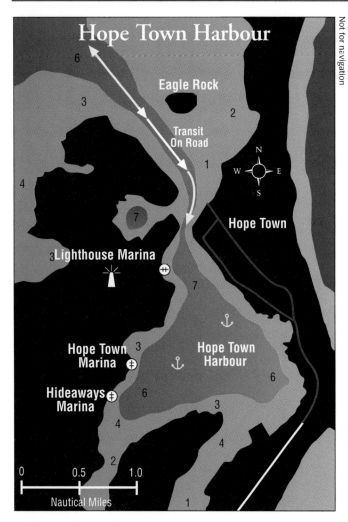

Hope Town Harbour

Not for navigation

Eagle Rock

Transit On Road

Hope Town

Lighthouse Marina

Hope Town Harbour

Hope Town Marina

Hideaways Marina

0   0.5   1.0

Nautical Miles

Elbow Cay, roughly on the same latitude as Hope Town. Just stay clear of the Albury ferry routes on their runs between Hope Town and Marsh Harbour, and up to Man-O-War. You have about 6 feet there and reasonably good holding, but you are completely exposed to the north and the south.

Hope Town

Hope Town is almost everyone's dream realized of how a place in the Abacos should look. A well-protected harbor, just big enough, watched over by the best-looking candy-striped lighthouse you ever did see, just how a lighthouse should look. The streets, other than the waterfront, are narrow concrete paths set between houses painted every color, in combinations your mother told you *never* to put together: pinks, greens, turquoise, salmon, yellows, blues, grey, and white are all there, together with gingerbread eaves and picket fences carved into hearts, whales, and pineapples. Flowers and flow-

ering shrubs grow as if they're bent on staking their claim to exotic colors, co-equal with the houses. Beyond and behind this quiet riot of colors lies the Atlantic, deep dark blue on its far horizon, brilliant green closer to the shore, marked with inshore reefs the color of well-worn boat shoes, and then as clear as sparkling spring water at its edge. What of the beach, the sand? It's Hope Town. It has to be pink. It very nearly is. It's wide, and goes on forever.

Here in Hope Town you can wander at will, drink and watch the sun go down, and dine as the lighthouse starts its nightly cycle. You'll share your Hope Town with many others, visiting yachts people like yourselves, the renters of holiday cottages and apartments, and those staying at the Hope Town Harbour Lodge, the Club Soleil, the Abaco Inn, and other places, as well as day trippers from Marsh Harbour. Somehow, despite its small size, Hope Town seems to absorb this alien influx. Sometimes there seems to be too many

Then you'll see your turn open up to starboard, and you're in Hope Town harbor. Keep your speed right down.

Hope Town Marinas and Anchorages

Lighthouse Marina comes up immediately to starboard, and further on, past a mini-headland of mangroves, is the Hope Town Marina and Club Soleil, and slightly further on is the Hope Town Hideaways Marina. The anchorage is to port as you enter, and most probably crowded. It's almost entirely taken up by moorings. See our **Yellow Pages** for your contacts.

There is a downside to most places, even Paradise probably has its problems, and Hope Town harbor is on our list of places where we never switch on our watermaker. The harbor, essentially landlocked as it is, has long passed its natural capacity to absorb pollution and cleanse itself with successive tides. There are too many boats there, one might question whether holding tanks are in use on every boat, and there is just too much boat traffic.

If you don't fancy a mooring in Hope Town Harbour you can anchor off outside between the Parrot Cays and of your own kind around, but it's rarely disturbing.

Hope Town has a pattern of life into which you'll fall, and soon, if you're anchored off, on a mooring, or at one of the three marinas, you'll realize that using your dinghy to get everywhere (for there's no other way to cross the harbor to get to the main town on the ocean side) is just a way of life. Go to the public dock at 7:30 in the morning to see the children gather to take the Albury ferry to get to school in Marsh Harbour. Many come in by small boat, just as you have. It's the way life goes in Hope Town. No stress. No tension. But the Happy Hours start at four in the afternoon, just in case it's all getting on top of you.

ANNA'S CAY
Anna's Cay is the tiny islet off the west side of the northern peninsula of Elbow Cay.

PARROT CAYS
The Parrot Cays are the chain of five cays running down the west coast of Elbow Cay from the latitude of your ap-

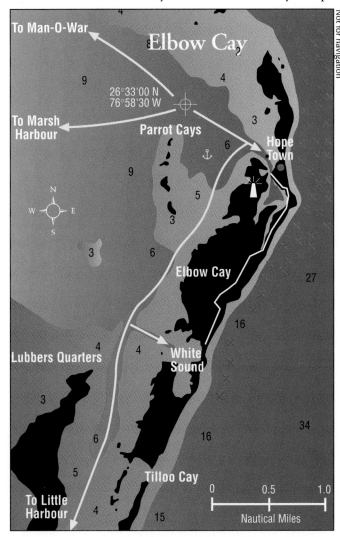

proach to Hope Town Harbour. North Parrot Cay, your initial landmark on your approach to Hope Town, has what appears to be an incomplete dock on it, six pilings with no decking and a light. The fourth cay (counting from north to south, and the largest one) is the base of the Gale family's Island Marine Boat Rentals. They will collect you from wherever you are, take you to Parrot Cay, rent you an Albury 20, Boston Whaler, or an Aquasport, and at the end of your rental period, deliver you back to wherever you started. Call them on Channel 16.

South of Elbow Cay and White Sound
Hope Town so dominates Elbow Cay that it's easy to forget that Elbow Cay itself continues for over 2.5 nm south-southwest from Hope Town Harbour. If you leave Hope Town Harbour and run offshore between Elbow Cay and the Parrot Cays, at just under the 2-nm point, the entrance to Elbow Cay's own White Sound will open up. You'll have to stand off about 0.5 nm out from the Elbow Cay shoreline after passing the last of the Parrot Cays, because shoal water extends this far offshore at the entrance to White Sound.

The White Sound entrance channel is marked. Don't cut inside the northern outer channel buoy for you'll hit shoal. Stay in the clearly marked channel. At the Abaco Inn end, directly ahead, there are red disk leading marks. Before you reach the end a second channel to starboard leads directly south to the Sea Spray Marina. Their dock, if you want to plot it, is 26° 30' 34 N 076° 58' 33 W. Again very clear marking and a well-defined channel will lead you in. You can take it that all the White Sound channels will give you 5 feet at MLW.

The Abaco Inn is sited at the end of the initial entry channel at the point where, but for its rocky spine, Elbow Cay might well have been carved by the ocean into two separate islands. The Abaco Inn dock has 6 feet and limited space. You must throw a stern anchor out as you come in and secure bow to (or come in astern, if you wish) but don't lie alongside. The Sea Spray Resort has the kind of space you'd expect at a marina, and is star quality. Attractive, and going places. But it is remote from Hope Town. There's no room for anchoring in Elbow Cay's White Sound, and the depths outside the channels are down to 2 feet in places. The best anchorage, if the wind is right for you, is just south of the White Sound entry point, well clear of the convergence zone if people are entering or leaving White Sound.

At the south end of Elbow Cay is Tahiti Beach (26° 30' 06 N 076° 59' 16 W), famed for its sandbar that virtually dries at low water, and a popular picnic spot for small craft. The apparent marina to the north of Tahiti Beach, part shielded by Baker's Rock, is private. South of Elbow Cay lies the Tilloo Cut with Tilloo Cay, and to the west is Lubbers Quarters with the shallows of the Lubbers Quarters Bank.

Marsh Harbour

Routes in the Marsh Harbour Triangle

Man-O-War Cay (NW of)	NWMOW	26° 36' 00 N	077° 02' 00 W
Man-O-War Cay (harbor ent.)	MOWAP	26° 35' 15 N	077° 00' 25 W
Point Set Rock (E of)	EPTST	26° 34' 00 N	076° 59' 45 W
Point Set Rock (N of)	NPTST	26° 34' 20 N	077° 00' 30 W
Hope Town (approach)	HPTAP	26° 33' 00 N	076° 58' 30 W
Marsh Harbour (off entrance)	NMRSH	26° 33' 25 N	077° 04' 00 W
Marsh Boat Harbour Marina	SMRSH	26° 32' 30 N	077° 02' 15 W

Providing that you stay clear of the shoals extending to the west from Johnnie's Cay and Lubbers Bank to the south, as well as the obvious inshore shoal areas, there are no navigational problem areas in the Marsh Harbour Triangle. We define this area by placing the apex of our triangle at the northwest approach to Man-O-War Cay, then drawing one line down to hit Great Abaco Island southwest of Marsh Harbour, and another line to hit Elbow Cay south of Hope Town. If both these points are on Latitude 26° 32' N that's about right. Join them and there's your triangle. Within this triangle you have a web of routes, all short runs of a few nautical miles, linking Marsh Harbour to Man-O-War Cay and to Hope Town, and Hope Town to Man-O-War Cay, Marsh Harbour, and the Boat Harbour Marina, and so it goes on. Your network has Point Set Rock has it hub, and you could hardly wish for a better landmark. Though you may wish to take note of bearings and distances, as well as the principal coordinates, you'll probably go visual for every trip in this area.

POINT SET ROCK

Point Set Rock has what appears to be a concrete shed on it that is very prominent. The shed is, in fact, the terminal for an underwater power cable that runs across to Elbow Cay. You can't miss it.

MATT LOWE'S CAY

Matt Lowe's Cay is private and was up for sale the last time we were in the area. If you want something like 5 acres of island with five beaches, a tiny harbor, and a house, you might wish to bid for it if no one else has snapped it up in the meantime. We never checked the asking price.

SUGAR LOAF CAY

Sugar Loaf Cay has houses on it. We've never stopped to explore it, reckoning it to be too much on the doorstep of Boat Harbour Marina and the Great Abaco Beach Resort.

Approach to Marsh Harbour's Harbor

There are no problems in entering Marsh Harbour, other than identifying your headlands and recognizing exactly where you are. From your arrival waypoint you'll first see a thin island, Outer Point Cay, taking the form of a headland, which you'll leave to port. Outer Point Cay has shoals extending out in a hook to the northeast so stay sensibly clear of it, about 200 yards or so. It also has a light, which may or may not work, but if nothing else the light stake helps your identification.

Continue on in a gentle curve to take you south until a small string of islets forming a second headland, known as Inner Point, comes up repeating the line of the first small cay. There's a light here too. Once you've cleared Inner Point, keeping about two boat lengths off, the harbor opens up to the east. Favor the north side as you go in, and a fairway (where you must not anchor) becomes obvious. You have plenty of water, good anchorages on both sides of the fairway, and a multiplicity of choices in marinas.

Approach to Boat Harbour Marina

Boat Harbour Marina is on the southwest side of the Marsh Harbour peninsula, and

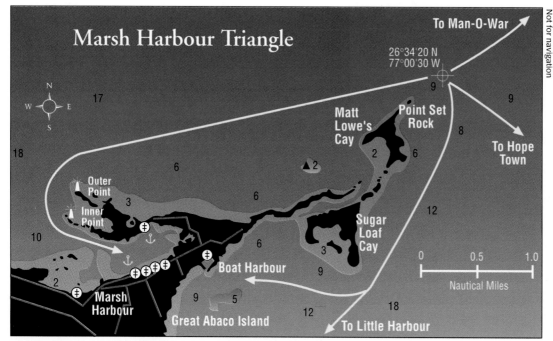

Marsh Harbour Triangle

To Man-O-War

26°34'20 N
77°00'30 W

Not for navigation

Matt Lowe's Cay

Point Set Rock

To Hope Town

Sugar Loaf Cay

Outer Point

Inner Point

Boat Harbour

Marsh Harbour

Great Abaco Island

To Little Harbour

0   0.5   1.0
Nautical Miles

Marsh Harbour

your access to it necessitates a totally different approach, which will take you to the east of Point Set Rock if you're coming from the north, then southeast of Matt Lowe's Cay and south of Sugar Loaf Cay. The marina is obvious and presents no difficulties. Its entrance is on the west side. Once you are there you're by no means marooned or separated from Marsh Harbour itself. A short walk to the main road and a turn to the left brings you right on the doorstep of the Conch Inn Marina.

Marsh Harbour Marinas and Anchorages

If we talk of marinas we'd put it simply. Boat Harbour Marina is the largest, arguably has the best facilities, but is also expensive. Conch Inn Marina is the most lively, has fuel, but its shoreside facilities still need a cash injection, despite recent upgrading. Mangoes is small, hangs its attraction on its restaurant and boutique, is perhaps the most attractive in its shoreside setting, but has no fuel dock. Harbour View Marina is as small as Mangoes, but other than a fuel dock, offers no particular pizzazz, although the floating Tiki Hut is on its doorstep. Triple J Marina is even smaller, but has a fuel dock. The Admiral's Yacht Haven is remote, but well run, and close by is a Pizza Hut that features conch pizza (the only conch pizza we've ever seen). If you want to distance yourself, the Marsh Harbour Marina on the north shore is the quietest, and wins a high score with its protection from Northers in winter and its exposure to the cooling southeast Trades in summer. It has a fuel dock, and a restau-

The Canary

JUST as the boat was rounding the Conch Inn Marina fuel dock I happened to look up and see her. She looked great. Not a trawler, hard to describe, a one-off fishing boat design that had good lines, stability, and a no-nonsense approach to weather written all over her, with a short mast and the real capability of carrying a foresail as well as a steadying sail. About 30 feet long.

I could have saved my quick appraisal for later, for she came into the next berth. She was single handed. A man who looked as if he'd sailed a bit, and a canary. The bird was right there, at the helm station, in a cage but looking alert. I helped him secure alongside.

Later, talking the way we all do when the sun is losing its heat and that first bottle of Kalik comes out of the cooler, I asked about the way he'd made the open cockpit helm station into an all-weather enclosure. I'd decided seven squalls back that it was the only way to go and I needed a role model.

"The canary likes it, too," he said. "He used to get pretty wet if I couldn't get him below in time."

I said I'd seen parrots, but never a sea-going canary.

"Got tired of sailing alone," he said. "One day I saw this canary. He seemed a nice bird, so I got him. He took to it well."

We had a slight intermission while we attended to some provisioning.

"After a while, I took him wherever I went. He seemed to like the dinghy, so whenever I had errands to do, he came with me. He didn't mind the bars. I put him down on the counter beside me. Sometimes he sings a bit. He always comes with me now."

"And what about on board?" I asked. "What do you feed him? And how does he take to long passages? Do you keep him in his cage the whole time?"

"Mostly. You wouldn't go bust feeding him. It's better than having a dog or a cat," he laughed. "You wouldn't believe it, but maybe he costs me five bucks a year. Just a packet of bird seed. And water. That's all he seems to want."

There was another lull while we attended to more urgent matters than reflecting on the cost of keeping crew in rations.

Then he continued, as it were in mid-sentence, "And you wouldn't believe it in rough weather. Couple of times when I haven't lashed his cage down, it's come down upside down and he's landed on his head. He was lying there once and I thought 'that's it.' Then he got back on his perch, hung on there for a while, and five minutes later was singing."

An hour or so later, back on *Dolphin Voyager*, I added three words:

Get a canary!

to my Florida shopping list.

rant serving lunchtime snacks, but only gets its restaurant in gear for Wednesdays and Sundays if you want to dine there. See our **Yellow Pages** for the fine detail.

As for anchoring, the fairway is clearly defined and outside of its lanes you are free to pick your spot. You should find at least 8 feet at MLW, and you're within a well-protected harbor. However, under threat of a severe storm you may want to find somewhere more snug with less craft around.

Marsh Harbour

We must admit to feeling schizophrenic about Marsh Harbour. Like it or not, sometimes you can't avoid it. You need that airport (unless you're set on using Treasure Cay) for crew changes. You may well be chartering a boat there from the Moorings fleet at the Conch Inn Marina, or from someone else. You may need its stores for re-provisioning. You may, if you're unlucky, need its backup services to fix faults, to put something right. But unless you fall into one of these categories, unless you've signed on for a fishing tournament or to take part in the annual Abaco Regatta, we feel you're unlikely to linger there for long.

The pluses are that Marsh Harbour has all these facilities, good restaurants, and even a traffic light in case you've forgotten what they look like. The minus side, simply put, is that it's not, we'd guess, what you had in mind when you set out for the Abacos. It's a hot, sprawling, disorganized town, noisy with road traffic, and the harbor is far from clean (we never use our watermaker there). Yet it seems to suit some cruisers who become semipermanent residents, bonded by the 8:15 a.m. Marsh Harbour Cruisers Net on Channel 68, which offers weather, advice, forthcoming attractions, and a kind of "Has Anyone Seen?" service if you've missed your friends somewhere up or down the line.

Heading North to Treasure Cay

Marsh Harbour (off entrance)	NMRSH	26° 33' 25 N	077° 04' 00 W
Point Set Rock (N of)	NPTST	26° 34' 20 N	077° 00' 30 W
Man-O-War Cay (NW of)	NWMOW	26° 36' 00 N	077° 02' 00 W
Fish Cays S (1 nm S)	FISHS	26° 40' 00 N	077° 08' 00 W
Treasure Cay Entrance (1 nm SE)	TREAS	26° 39' 30 N	077° 15' 45 W

Approaching Treasure Cay from the south, our Fish Cay south waypoint is the focal point on all routes, unless you elect to go by way of Great Guana Cay and our Whale Passage waypoint (see **The Central Abacos, Treasure Cay and the Treasure Cay Triangle** on page 68). From Marsh Harbour to our Fish Cay waypoint it's 4.83 nm on 318°M. From North Point Set Rock it's 7.10 nm on 295°M. From Man-O-War it's 5.41 nm on 283°M. From our Fish Cay waypoint it's 7.48 nm on a heading of 298°M to our Treasure Cay approach waypoint (1 nm southeast of the entrance to Treasure Cay marina).

Peter Johnson sculpture, Little Harbour.

The Last of the Abaco Cays

FOR many people the Marsh Harbour Triangle may be the turning point in cruising the Abacos, and if you started by crossing the Little Bahama Bank, you may well think of retracing your route when you get to Hope Town. For others, perhaps those who charter out of Marsh Harbour, the more immediate destinations, Hope Town, Man-O-War Cay, and perhaps Green Turtle Cay to the north, will satisfy a cruise itinerary.

If you decide to continue south from Hope Town, what's there? It's the last 10 miles of the Sea of Abaco (measured as a Brown Pelican might fly) but it comes out to more like 15 nm when you add up the legs of your courses down to Little Harbour. Great Abaco Island has another 30 miles to run before it ends, forbiddingly, in the unwelcoming South West Point with its lighthouse and Hole in the Wall, which sounds like a cruiser's refuge, but is no safe haven. Unless you have the curiosity to visit Cherokee, effectively your Abaco cruising grounds end, as does the Sea of Abaco, at Little Harbour.

If you're bent on leaving the Abacos and carrying on south across the North East Providence Channel, the North Bar Channel or the Little Harbour Bar will be your point of departure for Spanish Wells and Eleuthera, Nassau and the Exumas, or the Southern Berry Islands. If you're arriving from one of these cruising grounds, you're most likely to choose one of these ocean passes to gain the Sea of Abaco, rather than work your way offshore further north up the Abaco chain. These considerations apart, why head for Little Harbour? The answer is because of Little Harbour itself, the Pelican Cays Land and Sea Park to its north, and the anchorages of Lynyard Cay.

Just as the shoals off Spanish Cay and the Treasure Cay—

Whale Cay shallows dictated your options on courses in those areas, similarly here, south of Elbow Cay, Lubbers Bank and the Tilloo Bank dictate that you either set off south running about 1 nm off the coast of Great Abaco Island or you thread your way between Elbow Cay and Lubbers Quarters Cay, and then around Tilloo Bank. Whichever route you choose, tide will be much in your mind for these are waters where you want a rising tide for your passage making, and at least a half tide to enter Little Harbour.

Elbow Cay–Tilloo Cay–Lynyard Cay–Little Harbour

White Sound (just off)	WHSND	26° 31' 00 N	076° 59' 00 W
Lubbers Quarters N	LQNTH	26° 30' 20 N	076° 59' 05 W
Lubbers Quarters Mid Pt	LQMID	26° 29' 55 N	076° 59' 30 W
Lubbers Quarters S	LQSTH	26° 29' 05 N	076° 59' 45 W
Tilloo Bank W	WTILO	26° 25' 50 N	077° 01' 00 W
Tilloo Bank S	STILO	26° 25' 15 N	077° 00' 15 W
Tilloo Bank E	ETILO	26° 25' 15 N	076° 59' 15 W
North Bar E (0.75 nm SE)	NBARE	26° 23' 15 N	076° 58' 00 W
North Bar W	NBARW	26° 23' 40 N	076° 59' 15 W
Lynyard Mid Pt	LYNMD	26° 22' 00 N	076° 59' 40 W
Lynyard Anchorages	LYNAN	26° 21' 20 N	076° 59' 45 W
Little Harbour N	LHRBN	26° 20' 45 N	076° 59' 50 W
Little Harbour (just off)	LHRBO	26° 20' 00 N	076° 59' 45 W

Let's start at White Sound in Elbow Cay. From our waypoint there set an initial course of 192°M for 0.67 nm. This heading places Baker's Rock and Tahiti Beach on your bow. Look to port and a three-story house that has not been obvious as you set out from the White Sound waypoint appears around a little headland after you've run half a mile. You are close to your turn point, Lubbers Quarters north. It's here that we start jinking around Tilloo Bank.

Getting Around Tilloo Bank

Your route may sound complex, but it's simple and easy. See our circled inset map.

- At this first waypoint (call it Waypoint 1) turn on to 228°M, which you'll hold for 0.56 nm. Your heading will set you up aiming at the slight dip in the skyline profile of Lubbers Quarters Cay (not the "first" low part you'll see on the port bow, which is the dip formed between the trees of the south tip of Lubbers Quarters Cay and the low scrub that takes over where the trees gave up). If you're in doubt, just go by the bearing and you have the reassurance of a house with a triple roof line, which is almost on your heading. After your run of 0.56 nm you're at Waypoint 2.

- From Waypoint 2 head 201°M for 0.86 nm. Your heading takes you on a direct course for the tip of Tavern Cay, easily recognizable because it appears to have a white castle tower on it, and later you'll see a large blue-roofed house complex. In fact the castle tower (and its blue house) is on Tilloo Cay and Tavern Cay, undeveloped, is on the market at an astronomical asking price. It could be your chance to build a rival fortress. You'll get a better look at your new property on your next leg.

- At Waypoint 3 alter on to 205°M (no great change there) and at last you've got a chance to look at Tavern Cay. Hold 205°M for a relaxing 3.44 nm until you reach west Tilloo Bank, where you've got just two short runs to complete your Tilloo Bank circumnavigation.

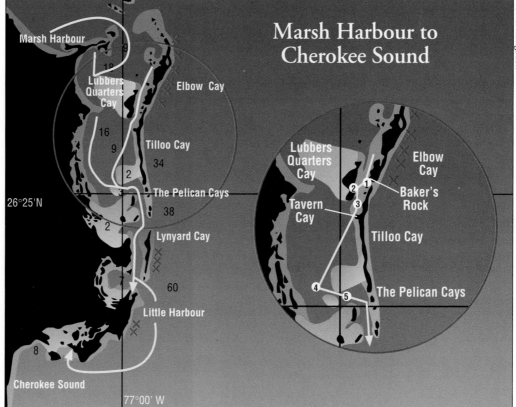

Marsh Harbour to Cherokee Sound

Not for navigation

- At Waypoint 4 turn on to 137°M for 0.89 nm, which places you south of Tilloo Bank. Pick up your landmarks as you go. The Pelican Cays will be coming off your port bow. Channel Cay will be ahead, just on your starboard bow. Now one slight alteration, another mile to run, and you've got around the Tilloo Bank.

- At Waypoint 5 head 096°M for 0.9 nm. This course leaves the north tip of Channel Cay to starboard and appears to take you straight to Pelican Cay. Maybe we should have called the waypoint there Pelican, but as we're really completing the business of getting around Tilloo Bank, we called it East Tilloo.

LUBBERS QUARTERS CAY

Lubbers Quarters Cay is useful to you navigationally but is unlikely to feature as a destination unless you're thinking of buying a lot there. Like many of the cays the land has long since been staked out and all the title holder now needs is your money and whatever site you fancy (when you've done with the lawyers) is yours. There is what might appear to be a public dock at 26° 29' 29 N 076° 59' 40 W, but this is private and a communal facility for the Lubbers Quarters Cay property owners.

TAVERN CAY

Tavern Cay, as we've said, is up for grabs.

TILLOO CAY

Tilloo Cay, which seems to stretch on forever (its length is just over 4 nm) has good beaches on its southwest tip, and you can work your way in there just north of Tilloo Bank. There's an inshore route south you can take over the bank if you hug the shore, but we reckon you're in little more than 2 feet of water, so it's dinghy territory unless you have real shoal draft or zero draft. Tilloo Pond is private.

The Pelican Cays and Dropping South toward Little Harbour

Once you've reached Pelican Cay it's plain sailing. You hardly need waypoints and courses to follow. At that east Tilloo waypoint a 90° turn and 186°M held for 1.58 nm will place you right by North Bar Channel. On this leg you'll see that Channel Cay, which at first sight looks uninhabited, has a house on it. Gaulding Cay becomes visible, and Cornish Cay with a house with a shiny roof. All of this is on your starboard side, as is Sandy Cay with its small boat moorings for snorkelers. To port you have the north–south run of the Pelican Cays and reefs, and the whole area you are transiting is the Pelican Cays Land and Sea Park. It would be a pity not to stop here and go snorkeling.

CHANNEL CAY

Channel Cay is private land.

THE PELICAN CAYS AND SANDY CAY

The Pelican Cays and Sandy Cay and the adjacent sea area form the Bahamian National Trust's Pelican Cays Land and Sea Park, which extends south to include the waters of North Bar Channel. You are allowed to anchor here, but *not* over coral and the holding on the east side of the Sandy Cay reef is not good. You must also be aware that swells coming in through North Bar Channel can make the Pelican Park sea area bumpy to say the least. If it's going to be rough there, forget it. The small boat moorings provided by the Bahamas National Trust may be used by you and if they're all taken, you must anchor independently over sand, not coral. It goes almost without saying that fishing, shell collecting, the taking of coral, or any predatory action is forbidden. Just snorkel and enjoy the reefs.

CORNISH CAY

Cornish Cay is private land.

NORTH BAR CHANNEL

North Bar Channel, just north of Lynyard Cay, has range marks set on Sandy Cay and Cornish Cay, and 16 feet of water. The range marks are not easy to see with the naked eye, but the lie of the cays themselves and the obviousness of North Bar Channel makes your navigation relatively easy. To your north is Channel Rock, and the only potential hazard are the rocks off the north tip of Lynyard Cay, but the

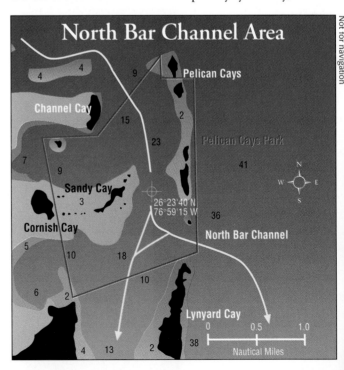

North Bar Channel Area

Not for navigation

range marks, the lie of the land, and your heading of 115°M will keep you clear. This pass is used by the mail boats.

From North Bar Channel to Little Harbour

Our North Bar Channel waypoint could be your departure point if you were setting out into the Atlantic. Bound for Little Harbour from there hold 199°M to run for 1.71 nm to the midpoint of Lynyard Cay to port. To starboard you have a strange axe-like headland protruding out from Great Abaco Island. This was the site of Wilson City, a one time mega-forestry concern, which is now derelict.

From this mid-Lynyard point if you alter slightly on to 192°M, a run of just under a mile (0.67 nm) brings you level with the best Lynyard Cay anchorages, which are fairly well protected from the ocean swell that you'd expect to come in through the Little Harbour Channel. Bridges Cay (with a white house) is now on your starboard bow, and the Little Harbour Channel is opening up to port. You may be tempted to stop here, or you may wish to carry on with your approach to Little Harbour.

Going for Little Harbour head 193°M for just 0.59 nm, which brings you to the waypoint we'd choose if we were using Little Harbour Channel to gain the ocean, or to come in from it. For Little Harbour turn on to 180°M for 0.75 nm, bringing you to our last waypoint in our Elbow Cay to Little Harbour list. From there you go visual.

LYNYARD AND GOOLE CAYS

Lynyard Cay, as we've hinted, has good anchorages on its southwest end, extending for the last third of its 2.5-nm length, which, at the south end, carry 15 feet of water surprisingly close to Lynyard Cay. There are houses on Lynyard that are private, but otherwise you can land there. Surprisingly the anchorages seem relatively well protected from the ocean swell. The reason for this may well be that Goole Cay to its south, and the extensive reef extending 0.75 nm further south from Goole Cay, act as a breakwater. This reef, which does not always show (other than by an upheaval in swell pattern), together with the reef extending north from Little Harbour's Lighthouse Point, set your limits for passing safely through Little Harbour Bar.

LITTLE HARBOUR BAR

Little Harbour Bar has 16 feet of water as well, and is fairly straightforward. Goole Cay, to the north, has that 0.75 nm reef running south from its southern tip, and Little Harbour Point has its reef running north for nearly 0.25 nm. If you set out from our Little Harbour north waypoint you should be fine, or position yourself so that a back bearing on the house on Bridges Cay reads 345°M, and you go out through the pass on 165°M.

When you reach our Little Harbour east waypoint you are set up either for going on to Cherokee, or setting out for

Spanish Wells (just under 50 nm on 170°M) or Egg Island (about the same distance on 359°). Nassau, either to Chub Rock on 075°M if you're bound straight for the Exumas, or to the harbor entrance on 200°M, is some 75 nm away. Whale Cay in the Southern Berry Islands (235°M) is just 40 nm over the horizon.

BRIDGES CAY

Bridges Cay is private property. The house on it is a useful landmark, particularly if you are entering Little Harbour Bar from the ocean.

Little Harbour

Approach and Anchorage

You can't miss the white beach to the east of the harbor entrance and Tom Curry Point is obvious on the port side. Just pause and check the state of the tide. The entry channel is shallow. If you need more than 3 feet of water, a half tide state is critical. If you're OK, swing easily to enter virtually in mid-channel and pick up the line of buoys marking the channel, four red and three green, to bring you curving gently east into the harbor. Either pick up a mooring buoy (painted red but now a faded reddish pink marked "Pete's $10") or anchor. You're there. 12 feet of water at high tide. A good 10 feet at low. The distance run from White Sound? 12.62 nm.

A Bahamian Dream

Little Harbour probably comes close to everyone's dream of a Bahamian hideaway, and it certainly met the critical demands of the extraordinary and dynamic Randolph Johnston, one of the great sculptors of this century. Johnston,

Pete's Pub, Little Harbour.

Sundowners at Pete's Pub.

who died in 1992 in his late 80s, spent the last forty years of his life in Little Harbour, pursuing his dream of living free to work in an unspoiled natural environment remote from the fetters, constraints, and pollution of 20th-century life in the developed world.

Today much of Little Harbour remains in the hands of his three sons, of whom only Pete maintains a relatively high profile with a gallery devoted to his father's work and his own, as well as that of other local artists, and Pete's Pub, a shack bar on the beach. The moorings marked as Pete's with their $10 tag are part of this enterprise. Little Harbour is almost completely enclosed, is protected from virtually all wind and surge, and has all the depth you need once you're in there. Don't forget that the entrance channel for most boats is a no-go until at least half tide.

The harbor itself has a good beach, there's another good beach on the north side of the island, a small reef that is worth snorkeling, the remains of the old lighthouse on Lighthouse Point (together with a modern light on the old rusty light tower), and the caves on the east side of the harbor where the Johnston family, when they first migrated to a nearly deserted Little Harbour, first found shelter while building their home. The waters in the harbor and around Little Harbour, as well as the reefs, are dedicated to the Bahamas National Trust. You'll find turtles swimming in the harbor.

Pete's Gallery is well worth a visit. Randolph Johnston's work is powerful and moving, and Pete's own work, marine sculptures (many of dolphins) and his gold jewelry may have you reaching for your credit card. Remember that the island remains in private hands, there are a number of houses around Little Harbour now (many belonging to winter resi-

dents) and there are no facilities for visiting boats other than the moorings. No stores, no fuel, no water, and no place to leave garbage. You are a guest there. Arrive quietly, enjoy your stay, and leave quietly.

THE BIGHT OF OLD ROBINSON

The Bight of Old Robinson to the west of Little Harbour, entered at any point between Bridges Cay and Tom Curry Point, has 7 feet of water in its central arc but otherwise is a maze of shallows with extraordinary blue holes with subterranean connections to the ocean, in which it's said that ocean fish like groupers may be found, far from their normal habitat. Sometime, we've promised ourselves, we'll devote a week to exploring this area but regret that to date the pressures of time have forced us to move on and stay with the main routes and main destinations.

The Alternative Great Abaco Side Route to Little Harbour

There's an alternative "inshore" route down to Little Harbour from Marsh Harbour. It's straightforward, and joins the Elbow Cay route at our West Tilloo Bank waypoint. If you're in the Marsh Harbour area, take our waypoint off Boat Harbour Marina as your start point.

Marsh Harbour–Witch Point–Tilloo Bank

Marsh Boat Harbour Marina	SMRSH	26° 32' 30 N	077° 02' 15 W
Long Cay (safely off)	LONGC	26° 31' 00 N	077° 02' 30 W
Witch Point (safely off)	WITCH	26° 29' 40 N	077° 01' 40 W
Tilloo Bank W	WTILO	26° 25' 50 N	077° 01' 00 W

All you have to do is complete two doglegs to get you clear of Lubbers Bank and safely off Witch Point, and then carry on as a straight run to West Tilloo Bank. Your initial course from the start waypoint is 194°M for 1.52 nm, and then off Witch Point change to 177°M and hold it for 3.88 nm, which will take you to West Tilloo. From then on, follow the route we've described running south from White Sound.

THE GREAT ABACO COAST BETWEEN MARSH HARBOUR AND SPENCER BIGHT

We've found nothing of interest on the Great Abaco coast between Marsh Harbour and Spencer Bight (just north of the Bight of Old Robinson) to tempt the cruising boat to stay awhile and explore, but the possibility remains that there may well be gunkholes worth visiting. Snake Cay in the middle of this stretch, whose rusting fuel tanks are conspicuous, is not worth considering and has poor holding.

Returning North Along the Great Abaco Coast

If you're heading north from Little Harbour inshore along the Great Abaco coast, simply reverse the route we gave south from Marsh Harbour Marina. If you're going on past Marsh Harbour to Man-O-War or further north, when you get to our original start point you have to dogleg part way to Hope Town before setting your course on for Point Set Rock. In this case, rather than going the whole way across the Marsh Harbour Triangle, we suggest you add a new waypoint to your catalog.

Marsh Triangle Mid	MARMD	26° 36' 50 N	077° 00' 10 W

Go to this new waypoint from the Marsh Harbour Marina waypoint. Then alter for our east Point Set waypoint. By then you'll probably know the area like the back of your hand and will be going visual. All this waypointing may seem unnecessary but, as we said some time back, rainstorms have wiped out all land while we've been in the Marsh Triangle.

Continuing on South– Little Harbour to Cherokee Sound

Little Harbour (just off)	LHRBO	26° 20' 00 N	076° 59' 45 W
Little Harbour N	LHRBN	26° 20' 45 N	076° 59' 50 W
Little Harbour Bar Pass	LHRBP	26° 19' 55 N	076° 59' 20 W
Little Harbour Bar E	LHRBE	26° 18' 55 N	076° 58' 50 W
Ocean Point (safely off)	OCNPT	26° 17' 45 N	076° 59' 20 W
Cherokee Point (off)	CHERP	26° 15' 40 N	077° 03' 15 W
Cherokee W	CHERW	26° 16' 00 N	077° 04' 15 W

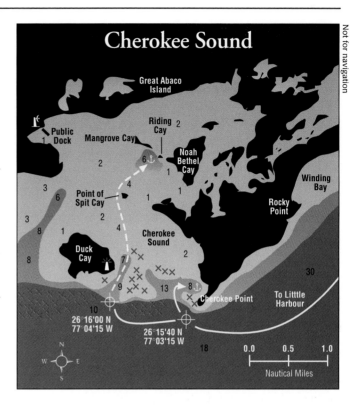

If you want to visit Cherokee, it's an easy 10-nm run from Little Harbour but not one that you should undertake if the ocean is kicking up. In short, if you don't fancy going out over Little Harbour Bar, Cherokee would be no fun trip. The first stages are simple. From just off Little Harbour go on 000°M for just 0.75 nm to get to our Little Harbour north waypoint, opposite the Little Harbour Bar. From there head 158°M for 0.95 nm to reach our Little Harbour Pass waypoint, which takes you safely out over Little Harbour Bar.

Then you need to gain some offing to get well out from the reef known as the Boilers, which lies off the Great Abaco coast between Little Harbour and Ocean Point, halfway to Cherokee. Head 162°M for 1.1 nm to gain this offing, and then turn to clear Ocean Point on 207°M for 1.25 nm. After this you can relax for a while, safely offshore, and run on 247°M for 4.28 nm to clear Cherokee Point, which is obvious.

Once you're around Cherokee Point, steer initially for its 250-foot Batelco tower. You can't miss it. You'll see water breaking on the reef and shallows to port. To starboard a beach will open up behind Cherokee Point with a small but precipitous cliff behind it. The water just off that beach is your anchorage, where you'll find a clean sand bottom that holds well and 8–10 feet of water. The anchorage is open to the south and southwest, and will take surge around the point if swells are running. This said, if the weather is right, it's one of the most pleasant places we've found. The beach is great. The water is fabulous.

Cherokee Sound and Cherokee in the distance. Approaching storm.

Cherokee and Cherokee Sound

The Cherokee Point anchorage is, for all practical purposes, the *only* anchorage worth considering in Cherokee Sound. Though the Sound may appear inviting when looking at a map, it's far too shallow for anything other than shoal draft craft, and from Cherokee Point the only way you can reach the settlement is by dinghy. If you're hell bent on getting your own boat into Cherokee Sound, then there's one way you might do it. Go on to our Cherokee west waypoint, which places you off Duck Cay. There's a narrow, partly dredged passage starting there that will take you into an anchorage between Mangrove Cay and Noah Bethel Cays where you may find 7 feet; *but* there could be as little as 3 feet in this approach channel at MLW and 5 feet at the maximum. When you reach this haven, you're still 1 nm from the settlement and have to get there by dinghy. Is it worth it? If you think it is, we suggest you wait off Duck Cay, call Cherokee radio, which keeps a listening watch on Channel 16, and ask for someone to come out and serve as your pilot.

CHEROKEE SOUND TO HOLE IN THE WALL

We can see no reason to parallel the last thirty miles of Great Abaco Island from Cherokee down to South West Point and Hole in the Wall. It's a hostile coast with tide sets that are incalculable, and has no place where you can take refuge. Hole in the Wall's so-called anchorage offers protection from the northeast and east, but that's it.

If you're setting off for Spanish Wells and Eleuthera, Nassau, or the Southern Berry Islands from the Sea of Abaco, your departure point should be either North Bar Channel or Little Harbour Bar, and your course set direct to your destination. Stay well clear of the southwest peninsula of Great Abaco Island.

One Final Snippet— Castaway

Back in our overview of the cruising potential of the Little Bahama Bank (see **Little Bahama Bank** on page 37) we dismissed the West Coast of Abaco as a viable cruising ground. We still believe our judgement holds. But if you were to make your way past Hole in the Wall, and turn northwest toward Sandy Point, you'd find yourself running along the northern bank of the Northwest Providence Channel. Once you've passed Sandy Point you'll have an isolated cay ahead, Gorda Cay. Fate has dictated that it lies right on the edge of the deep-water dropoff.

Want to play castaways on a desert island? Why not stop there. That's the island the Disney Corporation has leased from the Bahamian Government to develop into a cruise line stop. The work started in 1996, and the first ships will start calling there from April 1998. By then the desert island will have been landscaped, there'll be a 20-acre underwater park, and yes, just so that you can prove to your friends that you've been marooned, there'll be a post office with its own special cancellation stamp. Why special? Because Gorda Cay has been renamed. It's official. Amend your charts. It's now called Castaway Cay.

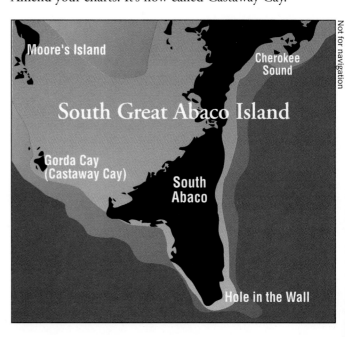

YELLOW PAGES

MAN-O-WAR CAY

BASRA in Man-O-War Cay
Denise McDonald Tel: 365-6048 or 6002 • VHF 16

This classic Abaco cay, steeped in the best boat-building and sail-making tradition, is well organized, self contained, and alcohol free. Man-O-War has much to offer cruising boats, with its good sheltered harbor and excellent marina and storage facilities where boats may be safely left for extended periods. The frequent ferry service to and from Marsh Harbor makes it readily accessible to an airport. Everything closes down promptly at 5 pm and all day Sundays, so this is not the place for bright lights and night clubs. The island population numbers around 275, increased by winter home owners and visiting boats.

MARINA

MAN-O-WAR MARINA
Tel: 242-365-6008 • Fax: 365-6151 • VHF 16

Slips	26
Moorings	10, cost $7 per night
Max LOA	70 ft.
MLW at Dock	8 ft., but only 5 ft. at low water in the harbor entrance.
Dockage	70¢ per foot per day, 40¢ per foot per day on a monthly basis.
Long-term Dockage	Boat checks are $15 per check; interior cleaning and basic supplies put on board can be arranged. Dry dinghy storage is $15 per month.
Power	40¢ per kWh for 30A and 50A
Fuel	Diesel and gasoline. Fuel dock is open 7 am to 6 pm, Monday to Saturday; 7:30 am to 4 pm on Sundays.
Propane	Refills the following day
Water	12¢ per gallon
Telephones	Two outside the *Dive Shop* at the marina.

TV	Free hookup. TBS, HBO, TNT, NBC, ABC.
Showers	In the office building, free to marina guests, otherwise $3. Open during office hours, key necessary in the evening.
Laundry	Washer and dryer $3.50 each, open 24 hrs. Tokens from the marina office.
Boat Cleaning	Bright work, varnishing, painting $20 per hr.
Restaurant	*Man-o-War Pavilion*, open for lunch and dinner daily except Sundays.
Coffee	Complimentary morning coffee for guests.
Barbecue	Gas grill at the gazebo
Ice	$3.50 per 10-lb. bag, block or cube
Trash	Free to marina guests, otherwise $1/ bag
Library & Videos	Book and video exchange in the office.
Mail	Mail can be held for you, and sent out.
Fedex and UPS	Can be arranged with the marina office.
Fax and Copy	In the marina office. Free to receive a fax, appropriate charge per page to send one. 50¢ per page for copies.
Office	Open 7 am to 6 pm, Monday to Saturday; 7:30 am to 4 pm on Sundays.
Dive Shop	*The Dive Shop* is open from 9 am to 5 pm, Monday to Saturday.
Credit Cards	Visa, MasterCard, and American Express
Dockmaster	Scott Eldon
Owner/Manager	Tommy Albury

MARINE SERVICES

Boat Builders and Storage
Albury Brothers Boat Yard   Tel: 242-365-6086   Open 7:30 am to 5:30 pm, Monday to Friday, and 8 to 9 am on Saturdays. Storage facilities can accommodate boats up to 100 ft.

Boat Rental
David Albury at the *Albury Boat Yard*   Tel: 242-365-6059   Open 7 am to 5 pm, Monday to Friday; 8 to 9 am Saturdays. Wide variety of boats to rent, as well as fishing guides and charters.

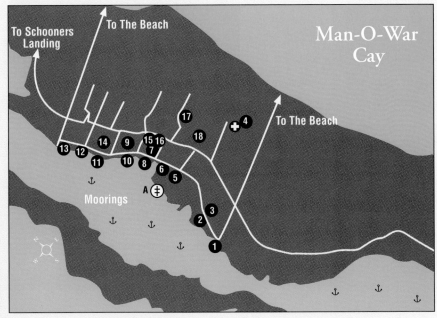

Man-O-War Cay

To Schooners Landing
To The Beach
To The Beach
Moorings

Man-O-War Cay Directory

A Man-O-War Marina

1 Bethel's Fiberglass
2 Albury's Ferry
3 Ena's Place
4 ✪ Clinic
5 Dive Shop
6 CIBC
7 Man-O-War Hardware
8 Edwin's Boat Yard II
9 Royal Bank of Canada
10 Albury Boat Builders
11 Albury's Harbour Store
12 Edwin's Boat Yard I
13 The Sail Shop
14 Tamarind Restaurant
15 Island Treasures
16 Man-O-War Grocery
17 Batelco
18 Post Office
19 Clinic

Boat Yard
Edwin's Boat Yard   Tel: 242-365-6006 and 365-6007   Full-service boat yard with hauling up to 65 ft. or 50 tons. Painting, welding, carpentry, and mechanical work; sailmaker on site.

Fiberglass
Bethel's Fiberglass   By the ferry dock

Sail Maker
Jay Mann at *Edwin's Boat Yard*   Tel: 242-365-6171

SERVICES

Banks
Royal Bank of Canada   Open from 9:30 am to 2 pm on Fridays.
CIBC   Open from 10 am to 2 pm on Thursdays.

Beauty Salon
Bahama Waves   Tel: 365-6310

Churches
Gospel Chapel
Church of God
New Life Bible Church

Clinic
Tel: 365-6081   Open on the third Thursday of each month.

Dentist
There is a dental service at the beginning of every month.

Ferries
Albury's Ferry Service   Tel: 367-3147 or 365-6010 • VHF 16
Daily:
Leaves Man-O-War for Marsh Harbour at 8 am and 1:30 pm.
Leaves Marsh Harbour for Man-O-War at 10:30 am and 4 pm.
Fares $8 one way, $12 roundtrip. Charters available any time; one way to Marsh Harbour, $50 for 1 to 4 people, and $10 per person over that number. Special trips to Little Harbour, Guana Cay, Hope Town, Treasure Cay, and Green Turtle Cay.

Garbage
Can be left in the bins beyond the sail shop if you are not a marina guest.

Post Office
Open from 9 am to 12 pm and 2 pm to 5 pm, Monday to Friday.

Telephones
Two outside the *Dive Shop* at the marina, one on the public dock, one by the school, and two inside the *Batelco* office.

Travel Agent
A and W Travel Service   Tel: 365-6002

SHOPPING

Bakery
Albury's Bakery   Tel: 365-6031
Lola's Bakery   Tel: 365-6073
Run from Mr. and Mrs. Sawyer's own house on Cemetery Road.

Clothing, Gifts, & Souvenirs
Bella Ena, The Shirt Shop   Souvenirs, clothing, household items.
Caribbean Closet   Open 10 am to 12:30 pm, and 1:30 to 4:30 pm Monday to Friday; 9 am to 1 pm Saturdays. Island fashions & accessories.
The Dive Shop at *Man-O-War Marina*   Open 9 am to 5 pm, Monday to Saturday. Some marine repair and maintenance supplies, beach accessories, dive gear and rental, gifts, clothing.
Island Treasures   Open 9 am to 5 pm, Monday to Saturday. T-shirts, gifts, and jewelry, as well as bicycles and carts to rent.
Joe's Studio   Tel: 365-6082   Open 9 am to 5 pm, Monday to Saturday. Locally carved native woodcrafts, half models, books, hand-crafted gifts.
Mary's Corner Store   Tel: 365-6178   Open 9 am to 5 pm, Monday to Saturday. Books, hats, jackets, bags, and T-shirts.

The Sail Shop   Tel: 365-6014   Open 7 am to 5 pm, Monday to Friday. World-famous canvas bags and accessories made by the Albury family.
Sally's Seaside Boutique

Groceries
Albury's Harbour Store on the waterfront   Tel: 365-6006   Open 7 am to 5 pm, Monday to Friday; 8 am to 5 pm on Saturdays. Canned and frozen goods, a good selection neatly displayed.
Man-O-War Grocery   Queen's Highway   Tel: 365-6016 • VHF 16   Open 7 am to 5:30 pm, Monday to Friday; 7:30 am to 9 pm on Saturdays. Homemade bread, fresh fruit and vegetables, imported meats, fish, and groceries. Free delivery to the dock.

Hardware
Man-O-War Hardware   Tel: 365-6011   Open 7 am to 4 pm, Monday to Friday, and to noon on Saturdays. Building, plumbing, and marine supplies, fishing tackle. Inter-island delivery service.

RESTAURANTS

Restaurants post their daily menus on the pole at the T-junction where the street up from the marina meets Bay Street.

Ena's Place   Tel: 365-6187   Open daily except Sundays for dining on their shady porch, or take-away. Sandwiches, conch fritters, nachos, homemade pies, ice cream, and yogurt.
Man-O-War Pavilion at the Marina   Tel: 365-6185
Open 10:30 am to 2 pm, and 5:30 pm to 8:30 pm, Monday to Saturday. Serving sandwiches and hamburgers as well as local fish, chicken, and conch. Barbecue nights on Fridays and Saturdays, when it might be a good idea to make a reservation.
Sally's Take Away   Tel: 365-6240   Snacks and fast food.
Tamarind Tree Shoal   Tel: 365-6380   Open daily except Sundays for snacks outside and take-away food.

ACCOMMODATIONS

Schooner's Landing Resort   Tel: 242-365-6072 • Fax: 365-6285
Daily rates from $150, weekly from $850. Four two-bedroom, two-bathroom units with air conditioning on a white sand beach, with a tennis court nearby.
Cocobanana   Tel: 242-365-6009
Bill and Sherry Albury. Two-bedroom, two-bathroom cottage.

REGATTA

July
Regatta Time in Abaco is during the first week in July. Races form up at Green Turtle Cay, Guana Cay, Hope Town, Man-O-War, and Marsh Harbour. Contact Dave or Kathy Ralph, Marsh Harbour, Abaco, Bahamas. Tel: 242-367-2677 • Fax: 242-367-3677.

THINGS TO DO IN MAN-O-WAR CAY

- Have your boat repairs expertly and efficiently carried out.
- Stroll through town; go for a swim off the North Beach.
- Visit the *Sail Shop* and watch how beautifully the Albury family make their canvas bags. You could always make a start on your Christmas list?
- Stop for a take away from *Ena's Place*.
- Reprovision with groceries and baked goods
- Admire Joe Albury as he creates his handsome frame models of Abaco dinghies.
- Relax and enjoy this picturesque and hospitable island, where time stands still.
- Visit with friends in the marina, and cook your catch of the day at the Gazebo.

ELBOW CAY & HOPE TOWN

BASRA in Hope Town
Stafford Patterson   Tel: 366-0023 • VHF 16 Seahorse Marine
Dave Gale   Tel: 366-0280 • VHF 16 Island Marine
Truman Major   Tel: 366-0101 • VHF 16 Lucky Strike

With the famous red-and-white-striped lighthouse beckoning you into its sheltered harbor on Elbow Cay, Hope Town can justifiably claim to be the Jewel of Abaco, and the dream come true for every cruising boat. It is picturesque and has some of the best facilities in the Abaco Cays, combined with a proximity to Marsh Harbour that provides good communications and ensures well-stocked stores and excellent restaurants. The village atmosphere with wooden houses painted the colors of Neapolitan ice cream, the glorious long beaches with a wonderful reef to snorkel within easy reach of swimmers, and all the fishing and diving to enjoy in the surrounding waters will make you wish you could stay forever.

MARINAS IN HOPE TOWN HARBOUR

(As they appear on your starboard side, entering the harbor)

LIGHTHOUSE MARINA
Tel: 242-366-0154 • Fax: 366-0171 • VHF 16

Your welcome at the *Lighthouse Marina* by Craig and Linda Knowles will set the tone of your visit to Hope Town. Nothing is too much trouble for these two. You come in to this marina first on your starboard side; it has the only fuel dock in town. The accommodations are good and clean and you can walk to the famous lighthouse and have repairs done to your outboard at the same time.

Slips	5
Max LOA	55 ft.
MLW at Dock	6 ft.
Dockage	50¢ per foot per day
Power	$8 per day for 30A, $10 for 50A
Fuel	Diesel and gasoline
Water	15¢ per gallon
Showers	$3, and very clean

Laundry	$3.50 per machine, tokens at the office.
Ice	Yes
Agency	Yamaha Sales and Service
Haul Out	Up to 10 tons
Marine Store and Gift Shop	Open 7:30 am to 4:30 pm, Monday to Saturday, with a good selection of marine supplies, fishing tackle, bait, T-shirts, & gifts.
Charters	*Lighthouse Charters* Tel: 366-0172 • VHF 16 Michael Houghton has 32-ft. and 36-ft. PDQ catamarans. $150 per half day; $250 per full day. Weekly charters bareboat or with a captain.
Accommodations	Apartment, cottage, and two houses available from $100 per night.
Credit Cards	Visa and MasterCard

HOPE TOWN MARINA & CLUB SOLEIL RESORT
Tel: 242-366-0003 • Fax: 366-0254 • VHF 16

With the resort facilities, and the excellent restaurant run by Margaret Malone, the *Hope Town Marina* is well placed for extended stays to explore the area. Its accommodations and swimming pool make it suitable for crew changes and guests who can fly in to Marsh Harbour and come over on the ferry.

Slips	12–14
Moorings	Numbered red cylindrical buoys, marked HT Marina. Call ahead.
Max LOA	Up to 110 ft.
MLW at Dock	6 ft.
Dockage	50¢ per foot per day
Power	$8 per day for 30A, $15 per day for 50A
Water	20¢ per gallon
Telephone	Inside the restaurant.
Showers	$3 each
Restaurant	*Club Soleil Restaurant,* open for breakfast, lunch, and dinner.
Swimming	Pool available to marina guests.
Transfers	Complimentary ferry across harbor to town.
Boat Rental	*Club Soleil Boat Rentals*
Accommodation	*Club Soleil Resort:* rooms from $115, MAP $32
Credit cards	Visa and MasterCard

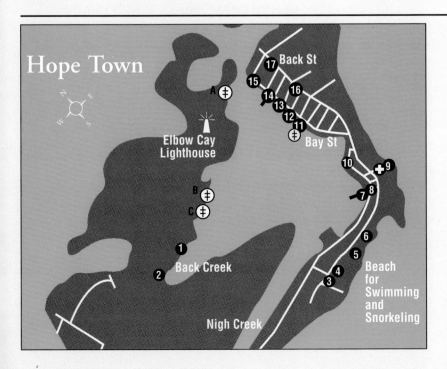

Hope Town

Back St

Elbow Cay Lighthouse

Bay St

Back Creek

Nigh Creek

Beach for Swimming and Snorkeling

Hope Town Directory

Marinas
  A Lighthouse Marina and Cottages
  B Hope Town Marina and Club Soleil
  C Hope Town Hideaways

  1 Sea Horse Marine
  2 Abaco Bahamas Charters
  3 School
  4 Batelco
  5 Hope Town Harbour Lodge
  6 Museum
  7 Public Dock
  8 Post Office
  9 Clinic
 10 Harbour's Edge
 11 Harbour View Grocery with dinghy dock
 12 Captain Jack's Restaurant
 13 Yacht Club
 14 Public dock
 15 Dave's Dive Shop & Boat Rentals
 16 Vernon's Grocery
 17 CIBC Bank

Sea Spray Resort and Marina, White Sound, Elbow Cay

HOPE TOWN HIDEAWAYS MARINA
Tel: 242-366-0224 • Fax: 366-0434 • VHF 16 and 63

The *Hideaway Villas* live up to their name, almost hidden amongst the lush plantings that run down to the pool and the marina. This is a pleasant, small marina on the edge of the harbor, and a good place to visit if you have friends who are more comfortable on land than on your boat.

Slips	12
Max LOA	74 ft.
MLW at Dock	4 to 5 ft.
Dockage	50¢ per foot per day
Power	$10 per day for $30A, $15 per day for 50A
Water	15¢ per gallon
Swimming	Pool overlooking the marina
Accommodation	*Hope Town Hideaway*
Dockmaster	Francis
Owners	Peggy and Chris Thompson

MARINA IN WHITE SOUND

This tranquil marina in the southernmost bay of White Sound on Elbow Cay has much to offer. Only a twenty-minute ride from Marsh Harbour on the ferry and three-and-a-half miles from Hope Town (with complimentary transport to town), you are close enough to enjoy all that Hope Town has to offer, without being in the center of town. *The Boat House Restaurant* serves some of the best food on the island.

SEA SPRAY RESORT, VILLAS AND MARINA
Tel: 242-366-0065 • Fax: 366-0383 • VHF 16

Slips	24
Max LOA	84 ft.
MLW at Dock	6 ft.
Dockage	85¢ per foot per day
Power	35¢ per kWh, for 30A or 50A
Fuel	Diesel and gasoline
Water	20¢ per gallon
Showers	$4
Laundry	45¢ per item
Restaurant	*The Boat House Restaurant* is open for breakfast, lunch, and dinner.
Ice	$4 per 10-lb. bag or block
Catering	Available to your boat
Bakery	*Belle's Oven*

Bicycles	$10 per day
Boat Rental	20-ft. Sea Spray for $85 per day, and a 22-ft. Sea Spray for $95 per day.
Fishing	Deep sea fishing for one to four people: $320 per half day, $500 per full day; bonefishing $100 in your boat.
Snorkeling	Trips; equipment $7.50 per day.
Transfers	Complimentary shuttle to and from town.
Accommodation	*Sea Spray* villas from $700 weekly.
Owners	Monty and Ruth Albury

SERVICES IN HOPE TOWN

Bank
CIBC   Tel: 367-0296   Open 10 am to 2 pm Wednesdays.

Churches
St. James Methodist Church on Back Street
Assembly of God on Cemetery Road

Clinic
Emergency: 366-0458 or 366-0087   Open 9 am to 1 pm Monday, Wednesday, Thursday, and Friday, in the low, single-story building next to the post office.

Museum
Wyannie Malone Historical Museum   Open 10:30 am to 12:30 pm on Monday, Wednesday, and Friday, and on Tuesday at 1:30 pm. There is no admission charge, but donations are much appreciated and memberships available.

Police
In the post office building.

Post Office
Open 9 am to 5 pm, Monday to Friday.

Telephones
One at the post office dock; one across from *Vernon's Grocery Store*; and one outside *Batelco,* up the hill, just past the *Hope Town Harbour Lodge.* The *Batelco* office is open 9 am to 5 pm Monday to Friday, closed weekends and holidays. There are two more phones inside.

Travel Agent
A and W Travel Service   Tel: 366-0100

SHOPPING IN HOPE TOWN

Clothing, Gifts, & Souvenirs
Island Gallery   Tel: 366-034   Open 9:30 am to 5 pm, Monday to Saturday.
Ebb Tide Gift Shop   Tel: 366-0088   Open 9 am to 4:30 pm, Monday to Saturday
Edith's Straw Shop
El Mercado Gifts
Fantasy Boutique
Kemp's Gift Shop
Waters Edge Studio   Tel: 366-0143   Original native wildlife carving.

Groceries
Vernon's Grocery & Upper Crust Bakery   Back Street
Tel: 366-0037 • VHF 16   Open 8 am to 6 pm, Monday to Saturday, closed Tuesday and Thursday afternoons. Well stocked with fresh bread, pies and rolls, fresh fruit and vegetables, imported meats and cheeses, and all the news daily.
Harbour View Grocery   Bay Street Tel: 366-0033
With their own dinghy dock. Open 8 am to 1 pm and 2 pm to 6 pm, Monday to Friday; to 7 pm on Saturdays. Propane tanks may have to go to Marsh Harbour to be filled.
Lorraine's Food Fair   Lover's Lane   Tel: 366-0031

Hardware
Village Hardware   Open from 8 am to 4 pm, Monday to Friday, and 8 am to 12 noon on Saturdays.

Liquor

Lighthouse Liquors Back Street Open 9:30 am to noon and 1 pm to 5:30 pm, Monday to Friday; to 6 pm Saturdays.

Propane

Harbour View Grocery Tel: 366-0033 See under groceries.

RESTAURANTS ON ELBOW CAY

Abaco Inn at White Sound Tel: 366-0133 Breakfast, lunch, and dinner is served in the dining room, or outside on their ocean-view terrace. Reservations required; complimentary transport available. They have their own dinghy dock.

Boat House Restaurant at *Sea Spray Resort* at White Sound Tel: 366-0065 • VHF 16 The new restaurant is open for breakfast, lunch, and dinner; complimentary transport available for dinner; reservations required. You can tie up at their dock.

Captain Jack's Overlooking the harbor Tel: 366-0247 Breakfast 8:30 to 10 am, lunch from 11 am, happy hour 5 to 6:30 pm, and dinner until 9 pm. Casual atmosphere with live music on Wednesdays and Fridays, and satellite sports TV. Ice for sale. Visa and MasterCard accepted.

Club Soleil Resort Tel: 366-0003 • VHF 16 Breakfast 8 to 10 am, lunch noon to 2, dinner 6:30 to 8 pm. Dinner reservations required.

Harbour's Edge Tel: 366-0292 Bar opens daily at 10 am. Lunch 11:30 to 3, dinner 6 to 9 pm. Happy hour 5 to 6 pm. Pizza and live music on Saturday nights; closed Tuesdays. Ice for sale, bicycle rental, pool table, and sports TV.

Hope Town Harbour Lodge Tel: 366-0095 • VHF 16 Sarah O'Connor and Peter Kline. Breakfast daily 8 to 10 am. Lunch and happy hour by the pool at the *Reef Bar*. Dinner 6:30 to 9 pm, Tuesday to Saturday. Dinner reservations are not required. Their Famous Sunday Brunch is served with Mimosas and a variety of Eggs Benedict; Tuesday is Barbecue Night by the pool.

Rudi's Place Tel: 366-0062 • VHF 16
A little way out of town, but they offer complimentary transport.

Munchies Back Street, next to *Kemp's Gift Shop* and opposite *Vernon's Grocery* Snacks, sandwiches, pizza, and ice cream.

GETTING AROUND

Bicycles

Harbour's Edge Tel: 366-0292

Hope Town Harbour Lodge Tel: 366-0095

Boat Rental

Club Soleil Boat Rental Tel: 366-0003 • VHF 16 22-ft. Scandia $80 daily; 19-ft. Mako $70 daily

Dave's Dive Shop and Boat Rentals
Tel: 366-0029 • Fax: 366-0420 • VHF 16 17-ft. Boston Whaler $65 daily; 22-ft. Paramount $90 daily. Complimentary delivery service to Hope Town, Marsh Harbour, or Man-O-War Cay. Dive trips and equipment. Visa and MasterCard accepted.

Island Marine Boat Rentals Tel: 366-0282 • Fax: 366-0281 • VHF 16 Dave and Phoebe Gale have the largest fleet in the Bahamas, and complimentary delivery service to your house, hotel, or yacht in Hope Town, Elbow Cay, Marsh Harbour, or Man-O-War Cay. 17-ft. Boston Whaler $80 per day; 20-ft. Boston Whaler $95 per day. Visa and MasterCard accepted.

Sea Horse Marine Boat Rentals Tel: 366-0024 • Fax: 366-0189 • VHF 16 In Hope Town Harbour and *Boat Harbour Marina* in Marsh Harbour. 18-ft. Boston Whaler $90 per day; 22-ft. Boston Whaler $120 per day. 21 boats available. Snorkeling gear and bicycles; complimentary delivery on request.

Sea Spray Resort Boat Rental at White Sound Tel: 366-0065 • VHF 16 20-ft. Sea Spray $90 per day; 22-ft. Sea Spray $105 per day. Deep sea fishing $320 per half day, $500 per full day, for one to four people. Reef & bonefishing $100 in your boat, snorkeling equipment $7.50.

Cart Rental

Golf carts are not allowed to drive through town.

Hope Town Cart Rentals Tel: 366-0064
$35 per day, $210 per week, cash or traveler's checks.

Island Golf Carts Tel: 366-0332 • VHF 16
$35 per day; Visa & MasterCard.

Ferries

Albury's Ferry Tel: 367-3147 or 365-6010 • VHF 16 The ferry from Marsh Harbour will drop you at any dock in the harbor on request, including in White Sound. Fares collected on board. Daily:
Hope Town to Marsh Harbour: 8 am, 11:30 am, 1:30 pm, 4 pm;
Marsh Harbour to Hope Town: 10:30 am, 12:15 pm, 4 pm.
Fares are $12 roundtrip same day, $8 one way. Children half price. Charters one way to Marsh Harbour are $50 for one to four passengers, $10 per additional passenger, during daylight hours. Special trips to Little Harbour, Man-O-War, Guana Cay, Green Turtle Cay, and Treasure Cay.

SPORTS

Boat Charters

Lighthouse Charters Tel: 242-366-0172 • VHF 16 PDQ Canadian catamarans, half-day sailing $150 for 1–4 people, full-day $275, includes snacks, light lunch, beverages. Snorkeling gear for rent. Ask Mike Houghton, the manager, for details.

Seagull Deep Sea Charters Tel: 242-366-0266 • VHF 16 Deep sea trolling for billfish, dolphin, wahoo, tuna. Half day $290; full day $490. Ask for Robert Lowe.

Wild Pigeon Charters Tel: 242-366-0266 • VHF 16 Maitland Lowe. Bone, reef, and bottom fishing: $190 half-day charter, $280 full-day in Mait's boat; $125 half-day or $200 full-day in your boat.

Diving

Dave's Dive Shop Tel: 366-0029 • Fax: 366-0420 • VHF 16 Daily dive and snorkel trips to Sandy and Fowl Cays. Two-tank dive $65, snorkelers can go for $30. Rental equipment available.

Fishing Tackle

Lighthouse Marina carry a good selection.

Village Hardware in town.

ACCOMMODATIONS

Abaco Inn Tel: 242-366-0133 Rooms from $105 per person, MAP $33 per day. Four beaches, swimming pool, complimentary snorkeling gear, bicycles, and transportation to town, rental boat dockage, and water sports.

Club Soleil Resort Tel: 242-366-0003 Rooms from $115 per night. Restaurant and bar, marina, swimming pool.

Elbow Cay Rentals Tel: 242-366-0033

Hope Town Harbour Lodge Tel: 242-366-0095 Single rooms from $100 per night with a harbor view, ocean front from $135, or *Butterfly House* from $300 a night for four people, $1,250 per week. Two restaurants and bars, fabulous beach with snorkeling on the reef, swimming pool, bicycles, golf cart rentals, diving and fishing, wild dolphin and kayak tours.

Hope Town Hideaways Tel: 242-366-0224 With their own 12-berth marina, and villas set in tropical gardens, from $1,099 per week, Chris and Peggy Thompson also handle rental accommodation all over Elbow Cay, and can help you with real estate.

Hope Town Villas Tel: 242-366-0030 Charmingly renovated 19th-century houses in town, from $150 per night for up to four people.

Lighthouse Marina Tel: 242-366-0154 Abaco Sound guest cottage from $900 weekly, house from $1,300 weekly; Lighthouse Point house from $1,300 weekly; Harbour apartment from $800 weekly. Rentals include 13- or 16-ft. skiff with outboard.

Malone Estates   Tel: 242-366-0100

Sea Spray Villas at White Sound   Tel: 242-366-0065
One-bedroom villas, harbor side from $700 per week, two-bedroom villas ocean side from $1,125 per week. Swimming pool, marina, boat rentals, clubhouse with cable TV, restaurant, yacht catering, free transport to and from Hope Town.

Turtle Hill Vacation Villas   Tel: 242-366-0557   Four new vacation villas to sleep six, with swimming pool, private beach access and golf carts; from $225 per night, $1,200 per week.

REGATTA

Regatta Time in Abaco is held during the first week in July. Races form at Green Turtle Cay, Guana Cay, Hope Town, Man-O-War and Marsh Harbour. Contact Dave or Kathy Ralph, Marsh Harbour, Abaco, Bahamas. Tel: 242-367-2677 • Fax: 367-3677

THINGS TO DO IN ELBOW CAY

- Climb to the top the lighthouse and admire the stunning view over the harbor and the neighboring islands.
- Swim and snorkel off the fabulous long beach running down the east side of Elbow Cay, or take your dinghy down to Tahiti Beach.
- Troll for sailfish, marlin, tuna, cobia, wahoo, and mackerel less than a mile offshore, or go bonefishing on the Tilloo Cay flats.
- Explore the town and admire the pastel-painted homes surrounded by bright flower gardens.
- Visit the *Wyannie Malone Museum* one morning to learn more about the history of this delightful town.
- Succumb to temptation at the *Island Gallery* and take home a memento of a happy visit.
- Indulge in Sunday Brunch at the *Hope Town Harbour Lodge* or the *Club Soleil*.
- Dive Johnny's Cay reef, Fowl Cay reef, and Sandy Cay reef. Sandy Cay is part of the *Pelican Cay Land and Sea Park*, and Fowl Cay is part of the *Fowl Cay Bahamas National Trust Preserve*. Do not take any shells or coral from them, and fishing is absolutely prohibited. You can pick up one of the moorings at Sandy Cay, the holding is not good there. There are also a few moorings at Fowl Cay. Don't ever anchor on any reef, you could damage the coral.

WATERS EDGE

MARSH HARBOUR

BASRA ABACO in Marsh Harbour
Victor Russell   Tel: 367-2226 • VHF 16 TAXI ONE

Not only the very heart of Great Abaco, but the center of commerce and government too, Marsh Harbour is the third largest town in the Bahamas with major roads leading through the island, and an international airport close by. With good communications to the smaller cays and settlements, it is perfectly suited to cruising boats needing stores or spare parts, with a wide variety of marinas, shopping, and medical facilities. Marsh Harbour is a Port of Entry, with **Customs** and **Immigration.** The customs dock is clearly marked with large pilings on the south side of the main harbor, and the customs office is in the house just east of the dock.

MARINAS IN MARSH HARBOUR

As you enter, to starboard:

ADMIRAL'S YACHT HAVEN
Tel: 242-367-4242 • VHF 16

A quiet, well-maintained marina, west of the customs dock, with few facilities but a *Pizza Hut* overlooking the marina, and a 10-minute walk into town.

Slips	26
MLW at Dock	6 ft.
Power	30A and 50A
Water	Yes
Fuel	Diesel and gasoline
Showers	Yes
Restaurant	*Pizza Hut*
Bar	*Promenade Deck Bar*

To port:

MARSH HARBOUR MARINA
Tel: 242-367-2700 • Fax: 367-2033 • VHF 16

This older marina, on the north side of the harbor, is under new management, but retains its original charm and a feeling of being slightly away from the rest of the busy world of Marsh Harbour. The *Jib Room Restaurant* has been newly redecorated and still offers the outstanding Steak Barbecue on Sunday nights and Pork Rib Barbecue on Wednesday nights, with music and dancing. Boat US members receive 25 percent off the first five days at the marina. Make time to snorkel the famous Mermaid Reef, right across the road from the marina.

Slips	52
Max LOA	70 ft.
MLW at Dock	6 ft.
Moorings	Yes
Dockage	60¢ per foot per day, less Boat US discount
Power	30¢ per kWh
Fuel	Diesel and gasoline
Propane	From *Corner Value* on Queen Elizabeth Drive
Water	Free to docked boats
Telephone	Yes
Showers	Yes
Laundry	$2 for each machine
Restaurant	*The Jib Room Bar & Restaurant* Open daily for lunch and dinner, with live music and barbecue on Wednesdays and Sundays.
Ice	Yes
Snorkeling	A five-minute walk to the beach to snorkel Mermaid's Reef.
Credit Cards	Visa and MasterCard

To starboard:

TRIPLE J MARINA
Tel: 242-367-2163 • Fax: 367-3388 • VHF 16

This small marina, with simple facilities, has plans for extension. They will add 150 feet of dock space in 1998, and improve their already well-stocked marine store.

Slips	24
Max LOA	55 ft.
MLW at Dock	5 ft.
Dockage	40¢ per foot per day, 35¢ per foot weekly
Power	35¢ per kWh, 30A and 50A available
Fuel	Diesel and gasoline
Propane	From *Corner Value* on Queen Elizabeth Drive.
Water	$5 per stay, or per month
Showers	Yes
Laundry	Behind the marine store
Ice	Yes
Marine Store	Marine supplies, fishing tackle, bait, diving gear, clothing, gifts, electronic parts and repairs, and a book exchange.
Credit Cards	Visa and MasterCard

To starboard:

HARBOUR VIEW MARINA
Tel: 242-367-2556 or 367-2217 • VHF 16

A very helpful and friendly marina, close to the amenities in town, with the *Tiki Hut, Sapodilly's,* and *Wally's* restaurants nearby and the newly redecorated *Lofty Fig Villas* just across the street.

Slips	36
Max LOA	60 ft.
MLW at dock	5 ft.
Dockage	40¢ per foot per day
Power	$7 per day for 30A, $14 for 50A
Fuel	Diesel and gasoline
Propane	From *Corner Value* on Queen Elizabeth Drive
Water	5¢ per gallon

Telephone	Yes
TV	Cable hookup, $2
Showers	Yes
Laundry	$2 per load in tokens to wash or to dry
Ice	Yes
Boat Rental	*D and E Boat Rentals* Tel: 367-2182 Charters and daily tours
Book exchange	In the marina office
Credit Cards	Visa and MasterCard

To starboard:

MANGOES MARINA
Tel: 242-367-4255 • Fax: 367-3336

A particularly pleasant marina, with well-landscaped shore facilities, an excellent restaurant, and beautifully clean showers. There is a Happy Hour for boaters under the cabana, from 5 to 7 pm on Tuesdays.

Slips	30
Max LOA	60 ft.
MLW at Dock	6 ft.
Dockage	50¢ per foot per day, 35¢ per foot monthly
Power	35¢ per kWh
Water	Free for stays of 2 days or more
Telephone	Yes
TV	Cable hookup, $2 per day
Showers	Yes, very clean.
Laundry	Yes, $2 for each machine.
Restaurant	*Mangoes Restaurant*, open for lunch and dinner, with outside terrace or inside air-conditioned dining. Serving snacks all day and a Caribbean night on Tuesdays. Complimentary dinghy dockage.
Bar	*Patio Bar*, with Hurricane Libby as the specialty drink.
Ice	$3.50 per bag
Barbecue	Grill available for use by marina guests.
Boutique	*Mangoes Boutique*, well stocked with island fashions and interesting gift ideas.
Credit Cards	Visa, MasterCard, and Amex

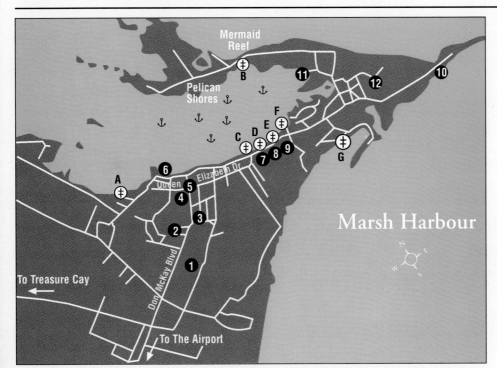

Marsh Harbour Directory

Marinas
  A Admiral's Yacht Haven
  B Marsh Harbour Marina
  C Triple J Marina
  D Harbour View Marina
  E Mangoes Marina
  F Conch Inn Marina
  G Boat Harbour Marina and
    Abaco Beach Resort

  1 Doctor's Office
  2 Abaco Market
  3 Dove Plaza and Post Office
  4 Barclay's Bank
  5 Traffic Light
  6 Customs House
  7 Wally's Restaurant
  8 Sapodilly's Restaurant
  9 Lofty Fig Villas
  10 Albury's Ferries
  11 Rich's Rentals
  12 Castle Café

To starboard:

CONCH INN MARINA
Tel: 242-367-4000 • Fax: 367-4004 • VHF 16

The largest of the marinas in the main harbour, the *Conch Inn Marina* plays host to the *Moorings* fleet and *Dive Abaco*, as well as the *AIT Ferry* running to Great Guana Cay. This combined with people on vacation staying at the *Conch Inn* makes it busier than all the others. The facilities are much improved recently, and its proximity to town and the airport makes it popular with bareboat charterers as well as visiting cruising boats.

Slips	75
Max LOA	Up to 100 ft.
MLW at Dock	5 ft. to 7 ft.
Dockage	60¢ per foot per day
Power	35¢ per kWh, 100A, 50A and 30A available.
Fuel	Diesel and gasoline
Propane	From *Corner Value* on Queen Elizabeth Drive
Water	$1.50 per day or $25 a month
Telephone	Yes
TV	Cable hookup for $25 per month
Showers	Yes
Laundry	$2 tokens per machine
Restaurant	*Conch Inn Bar and Café* Tel: 367-2319 Open for breakfast, lunch, and dinner.
Swimming	Pool by the hotel
Accommodations	*Conch Inn Hotel* Tel: 242-367-4000 Rooms from $90 per night
Bareboat Charters	*The Moorings Bareboat Charters* Tel: 800-535-7289 or 813-535-1446 Beneteau Oceanis and Jeanneau Lagoons from $2,310 per week.
Diving	*Dive Abaco* Tel: 242-367-2787 • VHF 16 Dive shop and daily dive trips; night dives. Two-tank dive $65, certification course $450, scuba introduction $100, snorkelers $35.
Rentals	Cars, scooters, and bicycles available.
Repairs	A *Moorings* technician will help you.
Sailboats	Charters from *The Moorings* in the marina.
Credit Cards	Visa and MasterCard

Marina facing Elbow Cay and the Sea of Abaco at Marsh Harbour:

BOAT HARBOUR MARINA
Tel: 242-367-2736 • Fax: 367-2819 • VHF 16

The largest of all the Marsh Harbour marinas, *Boat Harbour Marina* offers full resort facilities as well as proximity to town, without being in the busy main harbor. It has the added advantage of being closer to Elbow Cay, if you are headed to Hope Town or White Sound. There is considerable development and building going on in the area surrounding the *Abaco Beach Resort,* including many new private residences at the *Great Abaco Club.*

Slips	180
Max LOA	125 ft.
MLW at Dock	10 ft.
Dockage	$1.15 per foot per day
Power	30A $10 per day, 50A $17.50
Fuel	Diesel and gasoline
Propane	Same-day refill
Water	10¢ per gallon or daily rates
Telephone	Complimentary hookup. 50¢ service charge for local calls, $2.50 for long distance.
TV	$5 per day for cable hookup
Showers	Yes
Laundry	Yes
Restaurant	*Anglers Restaurant* open for breakfast, lunch, and dinner, overlooking the waterfront.
Bar	*Sand Bar* with a swim-up Tiki bar

Frangipani, Marsh Harbour.

Groceries	*Boat Harbour Mini Mart* open 8 am to 6 pm Monday to Saturday; to 10 am on Sundays.
Liquor	*A & K Liquor*
Gifts	*T-zers Gift Shop*
Diving	*Abaco Beach Dive Shop* Tel: 367-4646 Dive trips, equipment rental, and charters
Tennis	Courts are available.
Swimming	Pools at the hotel and marina
Golf	Can be arranged.
Rentals	*Sea Horse Rentals* Tel: 367-2513 Fleet of 24 boats, including Boston Whalers & Albury Brothers boats; bicycles and snorkeling gear.
Accommodations	*Abaco Beach Resort* Tel: 242-367-2158 Rooms, villas, and the Grand Villa from $145 per night.
Shopping	*Little Switzerland* and *Boat Harbour Marina Shop,* near the *Abaco Beach Resort* entrance.
Credit Cards	Visa, MasterCard, Amex, and Discover

MARINE SERVICES

Abaco Distributors   Tel: 367-2665 • VHF 72   "Abaco Stereo" Marine and personal electronics, service, sales, installation.

Abaco Outboard Engines   Tel: 367-2452   Yamaha agents, repairs, mobile service, boat hauling up to 30 ft. or 8 tons, marine store, tackle shop.

Asterix for Diesels   Tel: 367-3166 Gensets, marine, electrical troubleshooting.

B & D Marine   Tel: 367-2622 • VHF 16   Suzuki distributor, outboards, generators, marine hardware and supplies, fishing tackle, dive gear.

GETAFIX Ltd   Tel: 367-3166 John Heddon can help you with pumps, alternators, etc.

National Marine   Abaco Shopping Centre   Tel: 367-2326 Mercury & Mariner outboard sales, service, marine accessories.

The Outboard Shop   Tel: 367-2703 • VHF 16 Evinrude motors and parts.

SERVICES

Ambulance
Trauma One   Tel: 367-4082 • VHF 16 or 80

Banks
Most banks are on or near Don Mackay Boulevard, and open from 9:30 am to 3 pm Monday to Thursday; to 5 pm Fridays.

Barclays Bank   Tel: 367-2152
CIBC   Tel: 367-2166
Commonwealth Bank   Tel: 367-2370
Bank of Nova Scotia   Tel: 367-2142
Royal Bank of Canada   Tel: 367-2420

Churches
Church of Christ   Services at 11 am and 7 pm on Sundays.
Presbyterian Church of Abaco   Services at 9 am on Sundays.
St. John the Baptist Anglican/Episcopalian Church   Mass at 11 am on Sundays, other services during the week.
St. Francis de Sales Catholic Mission   Don Mackay Blvd.

Customs
Tel: 367-2522 or 367-2525   At the customs house by the government dock; and

Immigration
Tel: 367-2536 or 367-2675

Clinics
Blue Ridge Clinic at *Lowe's Shopping Centre*   Tel: 367-2295 or 367-3028   Two doctors, and a nurse, medical assistant, lab technician.
Marsh Harbour Clinic   Tel: 367-2510
One doctor, one nurse, open Monday, Wednesday, and Friday.

Couriers
UPS
Fedex at the *Abaco Shopping Centre*, Don Mackay Blvd.

Dentist
Dr J. Denise Archer, Agape Family Dental Centre   Tel: 367-4355
Open 9–5, Monday to Friday, and to 1 pm on Saturdays.

Doctors
Dr Frank Boyce, MD, Blue Ridge Clinic   Tel: 367-2295
Dr E Lundy, Abaco Medical Clinic   Tel: 367-4240
Dr BEA Rolle   Tel: 367-3390

Police
Tel: 376-2560 or 367-2594

Post Office
Don Mackay Boulevard   Tel: 367-2571
Open from 10 am to 5 pm, Monday to Friday.

Telephones
There are public telephones throughout Marsh Harbour.

SHOPPING

Bakery
Flour House Bakery and Catering Service   Tel: 367-4233
Open from 7 am to 5:30 pm, Monday to Saturday. A great variety of breads, cakes, pies, and pastries.

Drug Stores
Lowe's Pharmacy at *Lowe's Shopping Centre*   Tel: 367-2667
Chemist Shop Pharmacy   Tel: 367-3106

Dry Cleaners
Vans Dry Cleaners   Queen Elizabeth Drive   Tel: 367-2275
Open from 8:30 am to noon and 1 pm to 4 pm, Monday to Friday; from 9 am to noon on Saturdays.

Groceries
Abaco Wholesale   Don Mackay Blvd.   Tel: 242-367-2020/81
Fax: 367-2242   *Abaco Market, Golden Harvest, Boat Harbour Mini Mart and Abaco Wholesale* in Marsh Harbour, and *Treasure Cay Market* in Treasure Cay, are all part of *Abaco Wholesale* and offer galley stocking for boats with free dockside delivery. Talk to them, or fax them if you have special needs or delivery deadlines.
Bahamas Family Market   Queen Elizabeth Drive   Tel: 367-3714
Open from 7 am to 9 pm. Excellent, with a deli, bakery, and fresh produce; they will deliver to your boat dockside.
Boat Harbour Mini-Mart at *Abaco Beach Resort* and *Boat Harbour Marina*   Tel: 367-2020   Free delivery to docks.

Golden Harvest near the public dock   Tel: 367-2310   Open 8 am to 6 pm, Monday to Thursday; to 7 pm Fridays and Saturdays.
Solomon's   Tel: 367-2601   Wholesale food warehouse, offering full and half cases for boats.

Hardware
Abaco Hardware   Don Mackay Blvd.   Tel: 367-2170/2171
Open 7 am to 4 pm, Monday to Friday; to noon Saturdays. Marine & electrical, supplies, plumbing, hardware, paints, lumber.
Standard Hardware   Queen Elizabeth Drive   Tel: 367-2660 or 367-28ll   Open 7 am to 5 pm Monday to Friday; to 1 pm Saturdays.

Liquor
A & K Liquor   Queen Elizabeth Drive and *Boat Harbour Marina*
Tel: 367-2179   Duty free beer, liquor, wine, cordials; delivery.
Burns House Duty Free Liquor Store, Abaco Shopping Centre and Don Mackay Blvd.   Tel: 367-2135   Open 10 am to 8 pm, Monday to Saturday.

Optician
Abaco Optical Services at *Lowe's Shopping Centre*   Tel: 367-3546

Photographs
Snap Shop   Don Mackay Blvd.   Tel: 367-3020   One-hour service.

Seafood
Longs Landing Seafood   Bay and William Street   Tel: 367-3079

Sodas
Sawyer Soft Drinks   Sodas & canned drinks; delivery to dock.

RESTAURANTS

Anglers Restaurant at *Abaco Beach Hotel*   Tel: 367-2158   Open 7 am to 11 pm. Breakfast, lunch, dinner overlooking the marina.
The Castle Cafe and Seaview Gift Shop   Tel: 367-2315   Lunch from 11 am to 5 pm, Happy Hour 5 to 7 pm, Monday to Friday. The former home of Evans Cottman, the "Out Island Doctor."
Golden Grouper Restaurant   Dove Plaza   Tel: 367-2301
Serves American and Bahamian food, with nightly specials.
The Jib Room at *Marsh Harbour Marina*   Tel: 367-2700
Lunch 11 am to 3 pm, Happy Hour 5 to 7 pm and dinner from 7 pm. Closed Tuesdays, live music and barbecue Wednesdays & Sundays.
Mangoes   Tel: 367-2366 • VHF 16 "Mangoes"   Serving lunch 11:30 am to 2:30 pm, dinner 6:30 to 9 pm. Appetizers and snacks served all day. Good food and casual elegance overlooking the harbor, with live music Tuesday nights. Dinner reservations requested.
Sapodilly's Restaurant & Bar   Tel: 367-3478   At the harbor's edge, between *Harbour View Marina* and *Lofty Fig Villas*. Serving lunch 11:30 am to 3:30 pm, dinner 6:30 to 9:30 pm. Exotic drink selection, as well as salads, sandwiches, hamburgers, fresh fish, pies.
Sharkees Island Pizza   Tel: 367-3535
Delivery to your room or dock.
The Tiki Hut, a floating restaurant on the waterfront at *Harbour View Marina*   Tel: 367-2575   Open Thursday to Tuesday for lunch from 11:30 am to 2:30 pm and dinner 6:30 to 10 pm.
Pizza Hut at *Admiral's Yacht Haven*   Tel: 367-4488
Wally's   Bay Street   Lunch 11:30 am to 3 pm, dinner 6 to 9 pm. Bar open 11 am to closing with live music on Wednesdays and Saturdays.

GETTING AROUND

Airport
Two miles south of the harbor. Taxis charge $12 to the ferry dock or into town, for two people.

Airlines

Abaco Air	367-2266
Airways International	367-3193
American Eagle	367-2231 or 800-433-7300
Bahamas Air	367-2095/2039, or 800-222-4262
Cherokee Air	367-2089
Gulfstream	367-3415 or 800-992-8532
Island Express	367-3597 or 954-359-0380
Twin Air	333-2444 or 954-359-8271
US Air	367-3415 or 800-622-1015
Vintage Props & Jets	904-423-1773
Zig Zag	367-2889

Bicycles

R & L Rent-a-Ride Tel: 367-4289
Motorcycles $40 per day, bicycles $8 per day.
Sea Horse Rentals Tel: 367-2513

Boat Charters

The Moorings at *Conch Inn Marina* Tel: 242-367-4000, 800-535-7289, or 813-535-1446 Sailboats and catamarans.

Boat Rental

D and E Boat Rentals Tel: 367-2182
Daily tours and private rentals from the *Harbour View Marina.*
Laysue Rentals Tel: 367-4414 A 21-ft. Seacat for $90 per day.
Rich's Boat Rentals Tel: 367-2742 • VHF 16 19-ft. Paramount $75 per day; 21-ft. Paramount $90 per day; 26-ft. Paramount $135 per day. Also snorkeling gear, scuba and fishing tackle, bait, ice.
Sea Horse Rentals Tel: 367-2513 Boston whalers, bicycles, and water sports equipment.

Car Rental

H & L Rentals, one block south of the traffic light at the Shell station Tel: 367-2854 Cars from $70 per day, motorbikes from $35 per day; credit cards accepted.
Reliable Car Rentals at Abaco Towns Tel: 367-4234
Midsize cars and wagons with air conditioning for daily or weekly rental. Credit cards accepted.

Ferries

Albury's Ferry Tel: 367-3147 and 365-6010 • VHF 16
Albury ferries leave from the eastern shore. In addition to their regular ferry service listed below, they also run to Green Turtle Cay, Little Harbour, and Treasure Cay, and on request.
Daily:
To Hope Town: 10:30 am, 12:15 pm, 4 pm
To Man-O-War: 10:30 am, 4 pm, Monday, Wednesday, Friday
To Man-O-War: 10:30 am, 12:15 pm, 4 pm all other days
$12 round trip same day, $8 one way, children half price. Charters to Hope Town or Man-O-War cost $50 for up to four passengers, $10 per person after that. Charters to Great Guana Cay cost $80 for up to six passengers, $12 per person after that. *Extra charges apply for ferries leaving before 7 am or arriving home after 7 pm.*
AIT Ferries All AIT ferries leave from the Conch Inn Marina for **Great Guana Cay** at 9 am, noon, 4 pm, 6 pm; $6 one way.

Taxis

Available at the airport and in town. You can call one on VHF 06. Prices are high in Marsh Harbour because of union rules. Marsh Harbour to Treasure Cay Marina costs $55 for two people, and $65 to the Treasure Cay Ferry for Green Turtle Cay. Agree on the fare before you set off.

Tours

Papa Tango Island Tours Tel: 367-3753 • VHF 16
Day trips, fishing, diving, and snorkeling.
Sand Dollar Tours Tel: 367-2189
Daily tours all over Great Abaco from $20 per person.

Travel Agents

A & W Travel Tel: 367-2806
Travel Spot Dove Plaza Tel: 367-2817

SPORTS

Bonefishing
Capt. Justin Sands Tel: 367-3526 Fly fishing or light tackle.
Diving
Dive Abaco at the *Conch Inn Marina* Tel: 367-2787 • VHF 16
$65 for a two-tank dive, certification course $450, $35 for snorkelers. Dive shop, rental equipment including video camera with strobe, specializing in small groups.
Abaco Beach Dive Shop at *Boat Harbour Marina* Tel: 367-4646 or 367-2736 • VHF 16 Dive trips, equipment rental, charters.
Dive Sites
Favorite sites include *The Towers*, with 60-ft. tall coral pinnacles; *Grouper Alley*, with tunnels cutting through an enormous coral head; *Wayne's World* outside the barrier reef; and *The Cathedral*, a huge cavern where shafts of sunlight dance on the floor.
Fishing Charter
Seagull Deep Sea Charters Tel: 366-0266 • VHF 16 "Seagull"
31-ft. Stapleton, $290 for half day, $490 for a full day with Robert Lowe. Deep sea trolling for billfish, dolphin, wahoo, tuna.
Tennis
There are courts at the *Abaco Beach Resort.*

ACCOMMODATIONS

Abaco Beach Resort Tel: 242-367-2158
Rooms and villas from $145 per night.
Conch Inn Hotel Tel: 242-367-4000 Rooms from $90 per night.
Island Breezes Motel Tel: 242-367-3776
Lofty Fig Villas Tel: 242-367-2681 or 3372
Six villas from $80 per person per night, single or double.
Pelican Beach Villas Tel: 242-367-3600 Beachfront villas with dockage for small boats, from $145 per night.

FISHING TOURNAMENTS & REGATTAS

April
Boat Harbour All Fish Tournament
May
Bertram-Hatteras Shoot-Out Tournament
Penny Tuttle Billfish Tournament
June
Annual Bahamas Billfish Championship
July
Regatta Time in Abaco is held during the first week in July. Races form up in Green Turtle Cay, Guana Cay, Man-O-War Cay, Hope Town and Marsh Harbour. Contact Dave or Kathy Ralph, Marsh Harbour, Abaco, Bahamas. Call 242-367-2677 or fax 367-3677.

THINGS TO DO IN MARSH HARBOUR

- Take advantage of fresh produce to reprovision your boat.
- Rent a car and explore the length of Great Abaco Island. As you head further south, and the road becomes rough, look out for parrots between Hole in the Wall and Cross Harbour. The Abaco parrots have white heads and emerald green feathers, with a flash of red at their throats. They nest in rock crevices, while the Inagua parrots roost in trees. These are the only two islands with these rare birds, and their nesting ground in South Abaco is now a National Park. You will need a tough car with good clearance if you go down to Hole in the Wall; the road to Treasure Cay is good, but there are no signs.
- Take a ferry to explore another island that you may not have time to visit with your own boat.
- Enjoy one of the "special" evenings put on by local restaurants.

LITTLE HARBOUR

Little Harbour has great charm and a sense of being very much a special place. You feel like a guest from the moment you pick up one of Pete's moorings in the crystal clear waters of the tiny bay, surrounded on three sides by hills dotted with private homes, and the fine studio devoted as a museum and art gallery by the Johnston family.

It was here that the charismatic and dynamic sculptor Randolph Johnston and his artist wife Margot found their escape from the world and a place to work in peace. The Johnstons lived in a cave when they first came to Little Harbour, while they were building their house and studios. You can still visit the cave.

If you are interested in staying on shore in Little Harbour, call Peter Johnston at 242-367-2720 to ask about his studio apartment. There are no public telephones, fuel, water, groceries or showers/restrooms at Little Harbour.

Ferries
Albury's Ferry Tel: 365-6010 Will bring you to Little Harbour from Marsh Harbour if you don't have your own boat.

Gallery and Museum
Johnston Studios Art Gallery
Open from 10 am to 12 noon, and from 2 pm to 4 pm. A collection of Randolph Johnston's bronzes, together with his son Peter's current work, dolphin sculptures and jewelry, some of which is for sale, together with post cards and books.

Moorings
There are 12 moorings, and all buoys are marked **Pete's $10**. Pay the barman at *Pete's Pub*, or Kerry who lives on a boat in the anchorage.

Restaurant and Bar
Pete's Pub Open from 11 am to 2 pm, and again from around 4 pm. An attractive, open-sided, thatched beach bar overlooking the harbor. Serves burgers, hot dogs, and fritters for lunch. Their specialty drink is a lethal Blaster made with three types of rum and fruit juice.

Trash
Please take your trash away with you. Little Harbour has no facilities to dispose of it.

THINGS TO DO IN LITTLE HARBOUR

- Visit the Gallery and Museum, and the foundry if it's open.
- Walk over to the old lighthouse buildings overlooking the ocean.
- Explore the Johnston cave and imagine living in it.
- Take the dinghy around to explore the blue holes and shallow creeks in the Bight of Old Robinson.
- Snorkel the reef at the entrance to the harbor.
- Take a picnic across to Lynyard Cay for an exciting snorkeling day.
- Dive Sandy Cay Reef at Pelican Cays Land and Sea Park.
- Go to Cherokee Sound for the day.
- Enjoy good company and a Blaster at *Pete's Pub*.
- Sit back and enjoy the peace and beauty of Little Harbour.

CHEROKEE SOUND

Cherokee Sound has the most beautiful clear water in a sandy bay on the west side of Cherokee Point. The Sound once boasted a flourishing boat building yard, and the longest dock in Abaco. The dock is now rickety and not really safe to use, but the settlement is clean, neat, and tidy, with vegetables and fruit trees growing inside fenced gardens. We could find no restaurant or bar, but we were told there is a lady who will cook take-away meals. A 10-mph speed limit is posted in the town, and the road up to Marsh Harbour has recently been repaired.

Church
Epworth Methodist Church

Groceries
Cherokee Food Fair   Tel and Fax: 366-2022
Well stocked with fresh, frozen, and canned food, a card stand, some hardware, and a clothing corner.

Memorial
There is an obelisk overlooking the bay, commemorating the days of the old fishing sailing smacks.

Telephone
Next to the *Batelco* office.

THINGS TO DO IN CHEROKEE SOUND

- Swim in the glorious clear water.
- Take your dinghy and explore the narrow channel leading up to Mangrove Cay.
- Stroll through the settlement and admire the neat and tidy gardens with their mango trees.

Chapter 7
Grand Bahama Island
Grand Bahama
Grand Lucayan Waterway

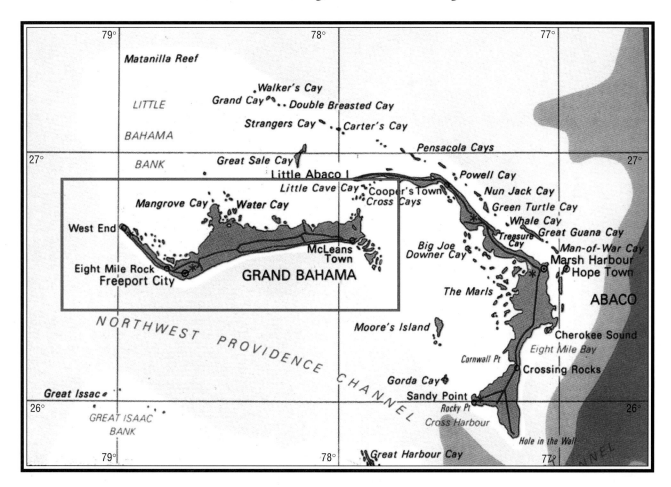

Grand Bahama

GRAND BAHAMA ISLAND, despite the fact that it seems to dominate any map of the Bahamas, is only the fourth largest Bahamian island (after Andros, Eleuthera, and Great Abaco). It runs east–west, sitting just above Latitude 26° 30' N for well over a degree of latitude. Put another way, it's something like 80 miles long and around 7 miles wide (16 at the widest point) for most of its length.

In the past, Grand Bahama has been unlikely to feature in any projected itinerary for the cruising sailor. West End is a port-of-call on one of the main routes to the Abacos. Freeport is a commercial port, available to you in an emergency, but is not a cruising destination. The marinas in the Freeport–Lucaya area (between Xanadu and the Bell Chan-

nel) are primarily power boat destinations, essentially geared to shoreside accommodation or intended for short visits, long weekends, club rendezvous, or the like. They are not really on the route to anywhere else, although the Grand Lucayan Waterway, just east of Port Lucaya, does offer a short cut through to the Little Bahama Bank, which those bound for the Abacos may find convenient.

Up to this time the entire energy and direction of Grand Bahama has rested in its Freeport commercial development and the lure of the Freeport–Lucaya area resort hotels with their casinos, and all the glitz that goes with a would-be Bahamian Las Vegas. Freeport Harbour, once virtually dedicated to BORCO (the Bahamas Oil Refining Company) has, with a decline in BORCO's fortunes, became a more general port with cruise ships calling in, container ships,

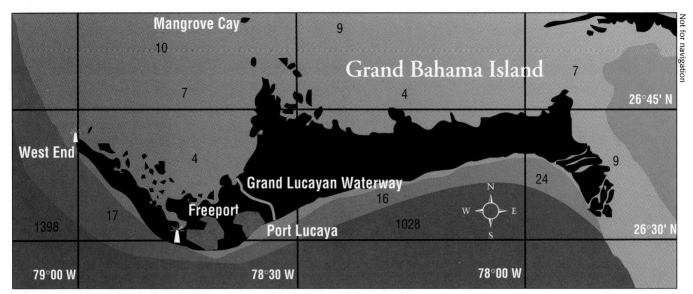

regular general freight runs from Florida, and hardly surprisingly, a regular port-of-call for a number of Bahamian mail boats. Customs and Immigration are there, as indeed they are at Freeport's International Airport, and between these offices offer an "on call" service to the Lucayan area marinas.

Now all this is changing. Shall we talk about cash injections? The one-time Hong Kong–based Hutchinson Whampoa Ltd. have as a new progeny the Freeport Harbour Company, a member of Hutchinson International Port Holdings Ltd. Add to this portfolio the Grand Bahama Port Authority and substantial real estate development interests in Grand Bahama, and the way ahead seems clear. What is projected? Let's look first at the Freeport–Lucaya area as it now, as we write this Guide, and then gaze into our crystal ball.

It's difficult to define the Freeport–Lucaya area in terms that are easily comprehensible. It's a vast track of almost flat territory paralleling the coast for almost 40 miles, some 7 miles deep. Development is sporadic, centering on oases that have some reason to exist, such as Freeport Harbour, the International Airport, and the main tourist-seeking resort complexes. In between there's little but yellow pine and scrub. The road system on the main tourist-oriented routes is good, well landscaped, and well kept. But there's nothing scenic there. Freeport International Airport, at this time still 1950s in vintage, offers reasonably good connections to the States but carries with it an $18 departure tax (as opposed to the all-Bahama standard rate of $15). The taxi fare in to the Bell Channel marina area is $10–15 one way.

We'll deal with the marinas separately. Inland the one major development is the vast complex built up by Princess Travel, which has culminated in a mini-city made up of the Princess Towers, the Princess Casino, the Princess Country Club, the International Bazaar, and the Castaways Resort.

Fly in or arrive by cruise ship, everything is here waiting for you. But nothing, other than the conch shells and the straw work, (even with kind judgment) could be considered Bahamian.

The marinas available to the cruising visitor offer a broader spectrum, from the comparative isolation of a virtually self-contained resort to what might be termed the high visibility end of the scale, the go-for-it resort with a Key West crowd scene, limbo dancers, shuffleboard, golden sand beaches, para-sailing, and Pusser's Painkillers thrown into the cocktail. As a measure of the current zenith of this density in tourist-targeted activity, in the Port Lucaya Marketplace complex (at our last count) there were 113 shops, restaurants, and bars.

Speaking with a narrow focus as cruising boaters, with all that this traditionally implies, we didn't cross the Gulf

Queen Victoria, International Bazaar, Freeport.

Stream to stay in places set on presenting a mirror image of the high-volume package deal resorts in the States. Yet we've found nowhere else in Grand Bahama Island we feel must be included in this guide other than the places we mention. Those we favor seem a small dividend from the fourth largest island in the Bahamas, but that's the way it is right now.

West End

For details about West End see **The Little Bahama Bank** on page 38. West End is a focal point for anyone setting out from Florida to cruise the Abacos, or returning to Florida from the Abacos. As such it's sensible to consider it not so much a part of Grand Bahama (which it is) but the entry port to the Little Bahama Bank, which is the sea area to the north of Grand Bahama Island.

One route to the Little Bahama Bank, which cuts out going around West End, is the already mentioned Grand Lucayan Waterway, which runs across Grand Bahama Island from a point just east of Port Lucaya. This is covered later in this section.

The Southern Coast
Freeport and Port Lucaya

Freeport

Freeport, located at the bottom corner of the boomerang-shaped form of Grand Bahama Island, is a major commercial port and is of no interest to the cruising skipper, other than as a possible refuge if you've been caught by lousy weather

crossing the Stream, have ended up off Freeport, and have to limp in somewhere. In case you wish to include it in your waypoint catalog, here it is, with our West End waypoint as a reminder:

Freeport (3 nm offshore)	FRPRT	26° 28' 30 N	078° 46' 00 W
West End (1 nm W)	WESTW	26° 42' 00 N	079° 01' 00 W

To add more specifics useful for navigation, from our Freeport waypoint West End is 19.03 nm away on a bearing of 320°M (or to reverse your course, our Freeport waypoint lies on a bearing of 140°M from West End). The coast in between the two waypoints is no-go territory, so keep well offshore (ideally 4 nm or more), particularly if you are being set toward the land.

You should have no trouble identifying where you are between these two waypoints at any time, other than at night, which could prove troublesome. We believe you should stay at least 4 nm offshore if you arrive off this coast during hours of darkness, get your visual fix at first light, and then carry on in daylight.

You'll see the West End water tower with the naked eye from 5 nm off Freeport, and Freeport's oil terminal, with its offshore tanker jetties and shoreside tanks and towers, is unmistakable. Aircraft approaching and leaving Freeport International Airport are also a sure indicator of where you are. There is a 200-foot Batelco tower (26° 31' 45 N 078° 41' 47 W) to the west of the oil terminal, and the entry to the harbor (should you need it) lies just west of those oil tanker jetties. The sea approaches around the jetties is a Restricted Area. You should not transit it, nor anchor there.

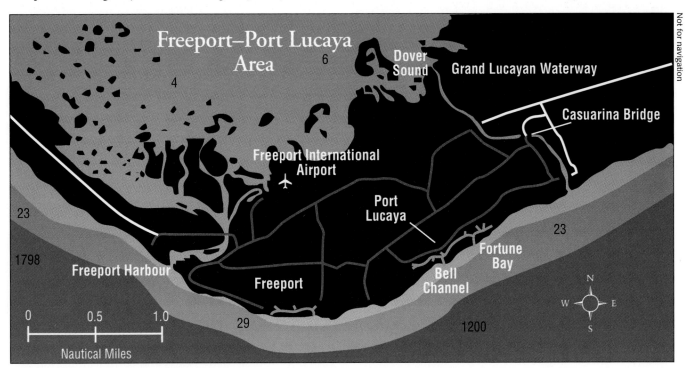

We would not enter Freeport Harbour without first contacting the Port Authority. Should you need them, there are (of course) Immigration and Customs facilities in Freeport.

Be aware that your charts are out of date. If you do have to enter Freeport Harbour at night your leading lights, under the original two fixed greens, are two vertical white pipe lights, both visible out to 5 nm. We have no sketch chart to offer you at the time of printing as Freeport Harbour is literally changing shape day by day, but the approaches (apart from the additional guidance of those two vertical pipe lights) haven't changed.

Signpost, International Bazaar, Freeport.

The Glitzy Coast

Between Freeport and the Bell Channel (which leads into the basin sheltering both the Port Lucaya Marina and the Lucayan Marina Village) there's a run of 7.5 nm on which four marina complexes, protected by their artificial entry channel breakwaters, are hidden from view as you make your way from west to east out at sea. These marinas, taken from west to east, are Xanadu, Running Mon, and Ocean Reef. After that you have Bell Channel with its marinas,

the Port Lucaya Marina and the Lucayan Marina Village.

Two governing factors apply on this stretch of coast. The first is that you should remain at least 2 nm offshore for absolute safety, until you actually turn to make an entry approach. The second is that you navigate primarily by the hotels (but we'll give you waypoints).

Xanadu

Xanadu (2 nm off)	XANDU	26° 28' 24 N	078° 42' 22 W

After a run of about 5 nm from Freeport you'll come to Xanadu. Your landmark is a squarish hotel block, which, from a distance, appears to have a Chinese-looking roof with a peak in the middle. Getting closer you'll see that the roof is flat, topped by a white pyramid. Get even closer, and you'll see colors. The sides of the hotel appear vertically striped black and white from the ocean (in fact it's dark green balconies and the backing of dark solar-tinted glass set against pink walls), and the roof line has two clearly pink bands supporting it.

Once you've got all this, the entry to the Xanadu channel is straightforward. Xanadu carries 6 feet at MLW. It's classed as an on-call entry port. If you elect to go there, you are remote from the International Bazaar heartland and certainly remote from the Lucaya end. Xanadu is a relatively quiet, self-contained resort with no overt push to it. We note that some sailboats have chosen Xanadu.

Running Mon

Running Mon (2 nm off)	RNMON	26° 28' 56 N	078° 39' 22 W

Running Mon Marina comes up 0.5 nm after Xanadu. Its identification is hardly difficult for the architecture here is very different. Rather than having a single tower like Xanadu, you pick up the Running Mon entry channel by a low-rise series of six white terraced apartment blocks, linked and all sloped back so that everyone's balcony gets some sun. A little further on, close to this terraced building, is what looks like a conventional (yellow) "clubhouse" type of building. The Running Mon beach looks good, and the whole scene is backed by casuarinas, which give it the appearance of seclusion and privacy.

Once you've taken all this in, the entrance into the marina is apparent. Running Mon, which is not recognized as an entry port, has only 4.5 feet at MLW. It's too close to the safety margin for most cruisers, and those who risk it may find the marina disappointing at closer sight. The sloping apartments on the beach are Time-Shares. The Running Mon resort, uninspiring and dull, faces its small dock area, built around pontoons. It's not, at this time, a place we feel you're likely to choose. Running Mon needs a massive cash injection, dredging, care, and considerable attention to put it in the league. We're not surprised to find it unfrequented save by local fishermen.

Ocean Reef Yacht Club

Ocean Reef (2 nm off)	OCNRF	26° 29' 22 N	078° 39' 50 W

After Running Mon there's a gap of about 0.5 nm or so, and you'll see what appears to be a huge white French chateau (complete with grey roof and turrets) come into view. As an aside, this is the home of Hayward Cooper, who built his fortune from a humble start running a small store on the road outside Freeport Harbour. A little later you'll pick up the breakwaters of the Ocean Reef Yacht Club marina. Again no problems here. This is not a Port of Entry.

The Ocean Reef Club is a gated Time-Share community that has an integral marina that is available to visitors. It's pleasant and clean, but seems totally remote and the fencing reinforces this sense of isolation. You may like it if you have coupled your visit with the use of Ocean Reef Club shoreside accommodations.

Bell Channel

Bell Channel (2 nm off)	BELCH	26° 29' 53 N	078° 37' 46 W

Your first landmark before the Bell Channel comes up is the 1950s slab-sided blue hotel (the Clarion Atlantik Beach) that dominates the coast between the Ocean Reef and the Bell Channel marinas. To the east of the Atlantik, from time to time lost in the trees until you get closer, you'll see the red and white "lighthouse" tower of the Lucayan Beach Resort and Casino, and further on, a cluster of pinkish townhouses, all huddled together (which are, in fact, on the east bank of the entrance channel to the marinas).

Bell Channel itself has a marker buoy with a light on it. The buoy (26° 29' 53 N 078° 37' 44 W) has no color but rust and from a distance is indistinguishable from six similarly rust-covered cruise ship mooring buoys that come up close to your track before you reach the Bell Channel. In reality your most accurate indication of the line of the Bell Channel entrance is:

1. The Lucayan Beach Resort striped tower (which will be to port), and

2. A low white building, part of the Lucayan Beach Resort (also to port), and

3. Para-sailing activity that is conducted from floating rafts (to port) and then

4. The pink town houses (to starboard).

But beware. As redevelopment kicks into gear (see the Crystal Ball section coming up later) much of this will change. The pink town houses will still be there; but everything else? Who can tell?

We can only write for the way it was when we were last there (the end of June 1997) and say that you'll have no problem getting your bearings. You'll have identified the two Bell Channel entry stakes, the line of the breakwater, and will probably be passing that rusty buoy with the light on it. The Port Lucaya Marina lies to port around the built-on peninsula that juts out into the Bell Channel lagoon. The Lucayan Marina Village is to starboard as you come in. Both marinas are recognized as on-call Ports of Entry.

PORT LUCAYA MARINA

If you like to be in the center of the action, the Port Lucaya Marina is the place to be. You can walk to the bars, restaurants, and shops that form their Marketplace area. There's live music there, on your doorstep. There are snorkel trips, beach parties, dive trips, submarines, and booze cruises all chasing your business, as well as the para-sailing we mentioned, the casinos, and the duty-free shopping, everything you might need from liquor stores to Colombian emeralds. Remember what we said earlier about the Key West crowd scene and everything from limbo dancers to Painkillers?

The Port Lucaya Marina is a large complex. It has two conventional docks (both to port, as you make your way in) with a fuel dock, and ahead lies a radius of secondary docks, on a separate peninsula, ringing a low-rise circle of rooms built around a central swimming pool. This Garden Wing carries with it the use of the showers and swimming pool, but no more than that. This means only one shower stall each for men and women, and one or three toilets (the fe-

Port Lucaya Marina.

males come out better there). We feel that some cruising visitors would prefer one of the quieter marinas.

THE LUCAYAN MARINA VILLAGE

If you want to remain detached from all this activity, go to the Lucayan Marina Village that lies to starboard after you've passed through Bell Channel. The "Village" part of the title hardly exists, other than as one run of completed townhouses, at the time of writing, but in essence a development is in hand that we can only compare in scale with something like Port Grimaud in Mediterranean France. Yes, it will be large one day, maybe too large, but at this time there's space, quiet, and none of the Key West hype and hoopla. The architecture and landscaping are first class, as are the facilities offered (a pool and bar, telephones, laundry machines, immaculate showers and toilets, all that you'd expect to find).

The Lucayan Marina, in its design, standard of construction, and state of maintenance is up to 5 Star international standards. It is the only place we've found in the Bahamas that merits this rating. It may count as downside that there are no restaurants yet, not even a breakfast coffee counter, nothing but that daytime pool bar. However there's a shuttle ferry that runs every half hour (8:00 AM TO 11:00 PM) from the dockmaster's office across to the Lucayan Beach Resort and Casino, adjacent to the Marketplace complex, so you don't need to put your dinghy in the water. We're not surprised that both power boats and sailboats are now using this marina in increasing numbers.

THE CRYSTAL BALL

So what's in the cards for the Freeport–Lucaya area? For Freeport, possibly one of the largest container ports in the Western hemisphere, which is being excavated now. This is not the stuff of dreams. With this development will come adjacent, vastly improved, cruise ship facilities, and hotels, shops, and restaurants. A mega-yacht hauling and repair facility is certain. Perhaps catering for smaller craft will follow. Link all this with Freeport International Airport, which Hutchinson Whampoa already own (together with the land between the airport and the harbor), hear talk of a connecting monorail, and you can catch the flow of the tide without opening your Tide Tables.

Let's move to Port Lucaya. Within two years the existing Port Lucaya hotels will have been demolished, to be replaced by one gigantic Flamingo Beach Hotel. Already the Lucayan Beach Resort has closed, with its Casino, and the Grand Bahama Beach Hotel has been reduced to marginal operation as we write. The Clarion Atlantik alone will survive Phase 1 to see the new development on its way, and then it too faces the hammer. The whole project, which includes a new 48-berth marina, is to be completed by 1999. We believe the Lucayan Beach Resort's mock-lighthouse may survive as a landmark, but this is not assured.

The Grand Lucayan Waterway

IF, say, you've set out from Florida either from Miami or Fort Lauderdale determined to cruise in the Abacos, your one alternative to going around West End is to stage in the Freeport–Lucaya area, and then use the Grand Lucayan Waterway as a shortcut to Mangrove Cay on the Little Bahama Bank. The reverse applies if you're on your way home. The largest engineering feat ever attempted in the Bahamas, the 1967 dream of opening the heartland of Grand Bahama to development as well as a direct route between Florida and the Abacos, cost $26 million. As a development it failed. As a canal, despite some shoaling and bank deterioration, it still serves.

The Grand Lucayan Waterway may not be what you expected. It's not so much a canal as a winding, 250-foot-wide dredged channel that heads mostly north almost aimlessly, it seems, with endless side basins, turning areas, and lesser canals opening off it. The banks are walled from the end of the south breakwater for much of the Waterway's length, though in some places the concrete embankment has given way to raw bank.

You may find company there but more normally the Grand Lucayan Waterway, although it is used, appears to carry no traffic, and there are few signs of life on its banks. Each side there's nothing but scrub, then a monolithic failed condominium (or was it a hotel?), and houses apparently abandoned during construction. As we've said, the Waterway was envisaged as the central artery of a whole new waterworld of development in the very heartland of Grand Bahama Island, a kind of Bahamian Venice. Later you'll come across some houses with evidence of human occupation.

PLUSES AND MINUSES—THE GRAND LUCAYAN WATERWAY

The Grand Lucayan Waterway is not a difficult route but we wouldn't attempt it, simply for prudence, in anything over the mid-40s in LOA, and we'd be happier at or below the 40-foot mark. We're talking now, in reality, about draft, beam, and maneuverability and the primary reason for this warning is that the Grand Lucayan Waterway is tide dependent in three respects. Let's take it straight out of our notebook:

- The state of the tide governs the depth throughout the waterway, that's obvious, but it's critical at the north end where at MLW you should not expect more than 4 feet. If there is more, that's a bonus. But who's going to risk it?

- To compound the situation, there's a tidal difference of 2 hours between the south end and the north end of the waterway.

• A further complicating factor is that strong tidal sets affect the choke points in the waterway (essentially Casuarina Bridge and the first spoil narrows in the north). This suggests that it's wise to avoid a transit of these points in hours 3 and 4 after a high or low, but because the Waterway is a complex water basin linking two entirely different sea areas, it's not quite that predictable.

You might well say "That's it. Let's go by West End," but read on. We'd take the Waterway every time in preference to heading for West End provided that our boat fit, and that wind and tide were pretty much in our favor. Now with the mention of wind we've introduced a further factor, but read on. Let's take the Grand Lucayan Waterway stage by stage, as you set out from Bell Channel for Mangrove Cay.

Approaches to the Grand Lucayan Waterway

Bell Channel (2 nm off)	BELCH	26° 29' 53 N	078° 37' 46 W
S Mark Lucayan Waterway	SLNWW	26° 31' 48 N	078° 33' 14 W
N Entry Posts Waterway	NLNWW	26° 36' 50 N	078° 38' 30 W
Waypoint off N Entry Posts	ONLNW	26° 37' 00 N	078° 38' 32 W
Cormorant Point (5 nm W)	CORPT	26° 41' 00 N	078° 42' 00 W
Mangrove Cay (1.5 nm N)	MANGR	26° 57' 00 N	078° 37' 00 W

Starting at Bell Channel

From the Bell Channel Entry buoy head 071°M to run parallel to the coast a safe 1.5 nm offshore for 4.5 nm. Keep in blue water, outside the line of white buoys you'll see running along the edge of the deeper water (the white floats are UNESCO mooring buoys set there to be used by dive boats and "submarine" tour boats, so that the reef along this stretch isn't ruined by random anchoring).

The buoy marking your turn-in point to access the Grand Lucayan Waterway carries red and white vertical stripes, has a red nose on top like a circus clown, and a white light. This is our waypoint SLNWW. At this point you can see the breakwaters backed by casuarinas very clearly. You'll be heading in on something like 000°M with just over 0.5 nm to run to the lights at the end of the breakwaters. As a fail-safe, just in case you miss that red-and-white striped buoy entirely, if you see Peterson's Cay come up on your port bow (a tiny islet with four wind-blown trees on it) you've gone too far. Turn back.

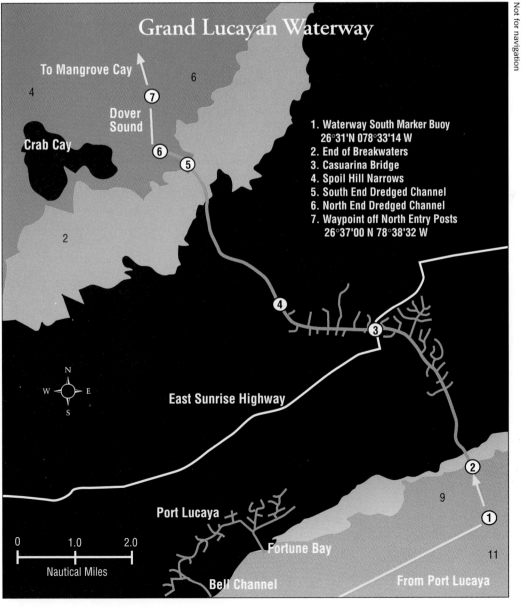

Grand Lucayan Waterway

To Mangrove Cay

Dover Sound

Crab Cay

1. **Waterway South Marker Buoy**
   26°31'N 078°33'14 W
2. **End of Breakwaters**
3. **Casuarina Bridge**
4. **Spoil Hill Narrows**
5. **South End Dredged Channel**
6. **North End Dredged Channel**
7. **Waypoint off North Entry Posts**
   26°37'00 N 78°38'32 W

East Sunrise Highway

Port Lucaya

Fortune Bay

Bell Channel

From Port Lucaya

0   1.0   2.0
Nautical Miles

The Southern Entry Breakwater to Spoil Hill Narrows (3.9 nm)

The major, southern part of the Grand Lucayan Waterway is straightforward. Once you're inside the breakwaters you're pretty well set. You've got maybe 14 feet there (if the tide is right) and you'll have 8–10 feet inside later. A warning sign, which you may not be able to read, tells you to stay at least 20 feet off the sides of the Waterway, and that if you're in trouble contact BASRA or the police on Channel 16.

You don't need a map or a chart of the Grand Lucayan Waterway, despite its many side alleys. Just follow your nose. You'll not get lost. Just 2.39 nm after entering the south breakwater you'll come to Casuarina Bridge, which carries the main and only road (the East Sunrise Highway) linking the east and west halves of Grand Bahama Island. This fixed bridge gives you 27-foot clearance above the water at high tide, but has no clearance gauges on its piers to tell you what's there at the time of your arrival. It's the first "choke" point you come to where you can expect to feel an appreciable tidal flow. Just keep motoring. Don't hang about.

The Waterway is much the same after Casuarina Bridge as it was before, but somewhat more straight in its course. After 1.51 nm you come to the second choke point. You'll find two conical mini-hills of spoil on each side of your bow flanking a narrow cut, and you won't be able to believe (at first sight) that you're supposed to go on and pass between them. At this point the Grand Lucayan Waterway changes character, and although there are no real problems lined up, you have to be a touch more alert in the northern part than the southern section requires.

Spoil Hill Narrows to Dover Sound (2.83 nm)

If there's a tidal set you'll really feel it at the Spoil Hill Narrows (the naming is ours). You have no room to maneuver and no room to pass oncoming traffic, for the width of the cut reduces the Waterway to something like 20 feet, if that, (albeit briefly) as you pass between the Spoil Hills.

At this point too you've lost your concrete embankments and the main course of the Grand Lucayan Waterway, now narrowed to 100 feet or less, becomes ditch-like in character. Stay in the center. You get a wall once again on the east side 1.28 nm after passing between the two Spoil Hills. When you reach this embankment favor the wall side, for the port bank deteriorates. Rocks and undredged ledges lie in the waterway itself on your left-hand side.

On this stretch, on the port side, a wetland wilderness opens up to the west with signs of distant human activity (a sand mound from some excavation, a radio mast) but none of this must take your eye off the canal. To starboard the scrub area will show further mounds of spoil, the concrete walls will open into another dead-end basin, and then on the port side, as that west bank falls away completely, you'll come level with the first of two concrete posts.

You can see you're close to gaining access to the Little Bahama Bank. There are two concrete posts that must be left to port, and then you're at the end of the Grand Lucayan Waterway and the beginning of a dredged channel leading you out onto the Little Bahama Bank. Your entry point, marked by two lighted posts (green to starboard and red to port as you're traveling, coming up from the south) are ahead of you. You'll have run 2.25 nm since passing between the two Spoil Hills, and will have another 0.58 nm to go before you gain the open water of the Bank.

Grand Lucayan Waterway, south entrance.

Casuarina bridge.

Dover Sound—
Getting out on the Little Bahama Bank

The Little Bahama Bank channel turns you sharply to port on a heading of 295°M passing between 5 pairs of pilings (note that Piling 4 to starboard has lost its port twin) and a final pair of lighted markers (again green to starboard and red to port as you're travelling from the south) with a prominent sandy spoil ledge to port.

This channel is narrow and open to wind from the north. It's also shallow (as little as 6 feet at best and maybe 4 feet at worst). You can't hammer through it at speed to counter a side wind for you may dig your stern in too deep and take the water you need right out of the channel. It's best to take the best compromise speed if you have a side wind, but keep going.

At the end pair of lighted poles your GPS position is NLNWW (26° 36' 50 N 078° 38' 30 W) but this is not the kind of position you should use as a waypoint. We plot the position simply as a matter of record. To proceed out on to the Little Bahama Bank, or for your incoming leg to the Grand Lucayan Waterway, your waypoint should be:

Waypoint off N Entry Posts	ONLNW	26° 37' 00 N	078° 38' 32 W

What's the total distance you'll have run from entering that south breakwater to passing out of the channel on to the Little Bahama Bank? 6.73 nm, or 7.41 nm from the south entry buoy. The time it will take you? You're asked to keep to a speed of 5 knots in the Grand Lucayan Waterway. Say 1 hour and 15 minutes, or about half the time it would take to get to West End from Port Lucaya.

Going on to Mangrove Cay

You'll probably be disoriented at this point for it's hard to pick up your bearings on first coming out of the Grand Lucayan Waterway. The shallows you are crossing are known as Dover Sound. The low-lying land to port is Crab Cay (the land mass is sort-of crab shaped). The island off your starboard bow is Sandy Cay. Look at your chart. North of Sandy Cay is the headland called Cormorant Point, and north of that is the cay that marks the extreme north tip of Grand Bahama Island, called Crishy Swash. North of that is Mangrove Cay.

A whole area of shallows runs along the west side of the Cormorant Point–Crishy Swash peninsula, the western edge of which is just over 4 nm offshore at its widest point. To get to Mangrove Cay you have to dogleg to the northwest to give Cormorant Point and the shallows a wide berth before you can head safely for Mangrove Cay, so a Cormorant Point waypoint comes into play here as well as Mangrove Cay.

Cormorant Point (5 nm W)	CORPT	26° 41' 00 N	078° 42' 00 W
Mangrove Cay (1.5 nm N)	MANGR	26° 57' 00 N	078° 37' 00 W

Your first leg will be 327°M for 5.06 nm, and your second 020°M for 16.61 nm, a total distance (after exiting the Dover Sound channel) of 21.67 nm.

Once you reach Mangrove Cay you're set fair for going on to Walkers Cay by way of Great Sale, or to Great Sale and points east. See our **Routes Across The Little Bahama Bank** on page 41 and our **Options After Great Sale Cay** on page 44.

Spoil Hill Narrows.

Entering Dover Sound.

YELLOW PAGES

FREEPORT & PORT LUCAYA

BASRA in GRAND BAHAMA
Tel: 352-2628 • VHF 16

Grand Bahama is changing so fast that no matter where you begin, you may never catch up. There is an air of calm along the wide, tree-lined boulevards of Freeport and Port Lucaya that belies the ongoing construction of well-planned and elegant new homes, and the massive dredging of the hugely expanding commercial harbor, with its state-of-the-art container port and vastly improved cruise ship facilities. The older, high-rise hotels are giving way to landscaped villas with every possible resort amenity, including golf courses, superb restaurants, and casinos. This said, it is still a happy island for visiting boats, with interesting places to visit on shore and some excellent diving and watersports. Freeport and Port Lucaya are Ports of Entry, and **Customs** can be called from any of the marinas to clear you in.

MARINAS

Marinas are listed west to east, from the commercial harbor:
XANADU BEACH RESORT & MARINA
Tel: 242-352-6782 • Fax: 352-5799 • VHF 16

A resort popular with honeymooners, the marina has good facilities and a friendly and helpful staff. The hotel has much to offer with its watersports, dive center, mile-long beach, tennis courts, beauty salon, and games room. Most people don't leave the resort, except to go shopping or check out the night life.

Slips	60
Max LOA	120 ft.
MLW at dock	6 to 7 ft.
Dockage	$40 per day up to 40 ft., $60 per day up to 60 ft., $100 per day over 91 ft.
Long-Term	Dockage available, 45¢ per foot per day, 3-month minimum, payable in advance.
Power	Included in dockage fee
Fuel	Diesel and gasoline

Water	Included in dockage fee
Showers	Hospitality room for showers and changing
Laundry	Yes
Restaurants	*Casuarina Cafe and Bar, Ocean Front Bar and Grill, Escoffier*, serving continental cuisine for dinner only.
Accommodations	*Xanadu Beach Hotel,* the pink hotel with the pyramid-shaped roof, a former hideaway of Howard Hughes. Rooms from $120 a night, MAP $35 a day.
Facilities	Freshwater pool, 3 tennis courts, beauty salon, games room. Mile-long beach with watersports, car and scooter rental, free transportation into Freeport.
Diving	*Xanadu Undersea Adventures* Tel: 352-3811 or 352-6782, ext. 1421
Deep Sea Fishing	*Paradise Marine* Tel: 352-4233 Also offers parasailing, reef and wreck snorkeling, glass-bottom boat cruises, jet skis; a few marine stores and fishing tackle in the shop.
Credits Cards	Major cards accepted.

RUNNING MON MARINA AND RESORT
Tel: 242-352-6834 • Fax: 352-6835 • VHF 16

A quiet marina with repair facilities, but a shallow approach channel with only 4 feet of water at low tide. This is the marina to come into if you need mechanics to work on your boat.

Slips	66
Max LOA	75 ft.
MLW at Dock	4 ft.
Dockage	From $27 per day up to 30 ft., $54 per day up to 60 ft., $72 per day over 71 ft.
Long Term	35¢ per foot per day, with power or water, 10 percent discount for annual contracts.
Power	Included in dockage fees
Fuel	Diesel and gasoline
Water	Included in dockage fees
Telephones	Two pay phones on the dock
TV	Cable TV hookup

Freeport and Port Lucaya Directory

Marinas
- A Xanadu Beach Marina
- B Running Mon Marina
- C Ocean Reef Yacht Club
- D Bell Channel Club & Marina
- E Port Lucaya Marina
- F Lucayan Marina Village

1. Grand Bahama Beach Hotel*
2. Clarion Atlantik Beach Resort*
3. Lucayan Beach Resort* with a lighthouse look-alike
4. Port Lucaya Marketplace
5. Rand Nature Centre
6. International Bazaar
7. Airport
8. Lucaya Shopping Centre & Winn Dixie
9. Sunrise Medical Centre
10. Rand Memorial Hospital
11. Lucayan Medical Centre West
12. Lucayan Medical Centre East

*scheduled for reconstruction in 1998/99

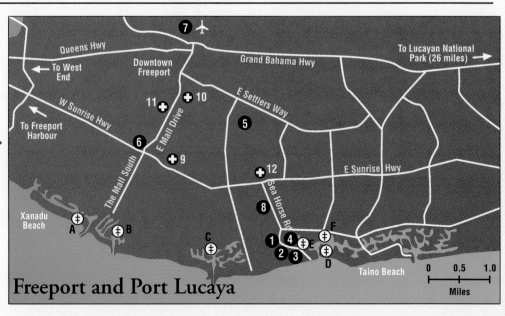

Freeport and Port Lucaya

Showers	Yes, and restrooms in the marina
Laundry	Laundromat on site, tokens from the front desk. $2.50 for washer and dryer.
Store	A few marine supplies and snacks
Restaurant	*Main Sail Restaurant* overlooking the marina, serves traditional Bahamian and popular American dishes. Open 7 am to 10 pm.
Accommodations	32 guest rooms overlooking the marina.
Facilities	Swimming pool, floating docks, yacht provisioning. A complimentary shuttle to the International Bazaar and Casino, Xanadu Beach and Port Lucaya.
Repairs	Experienced mechanics and repair facilities on site, with a 40-ton travel lift. Haul and launch $6 per ft. up to 25 ft.; $8 per ft. 26–35 ft.; $10 per ft. over 36 ft.
Fishing	*Deep Sea Fishing Charters* Tel: 352-6834 $60 per person half day, $720 per boat full day. Free transport from all Freeport Hotels.
Power Boats	*Grand Bahama Boat Rental* Tel: 373-9153 17-ft. Boston Whaler $90 for half day, $165 for a full day
Credit cards	All major cards except Diners/En route and Sun Card.

OCEAN REEF YACHT CLUB AND MARINA
Tel: 242-373-4661/2 • Fax: 373-8261 • VHF 16

This marina has excellent facilities, but is for members only. Inquire about membership. Rental or interval ownership can be arranged.

Slips	52
Max LOA	Up to 200 ft.
MLW at Dock	6 ft.
Dockage	$30 per day up to 42 ft., $60 per day over 62 ft.
Power	110v and 220v available
Telephone	Hookup available, fax from office
Cable TV	Satellite TV available
Showers	Yes
Laundry	Washers and dryers, $1.25 per machine
Restaurant	Snack bar for breakfast and lunches
Groceries	There is a small store at the marina.
Facilities	Swimming pool, Jacuzzi, tennis court, golf privileges, power boats, bicycles, shuttle service into town.
Accommodations	63 one-, two-, and three-bedroom villas and suites available.
Credit Cards	Visa, MasterCard, and Amex

BELL CHANNEL CLUB AND MARINA
Tel: 242-373-2673/3801 • Fax: 373-3802 • VHF 16

This marina belongs to the owners of the pink condominiums you can see on the east bank of the channel as you approach the Bell Channel to come in to the *Port Lucaya Marina* and the *Lucaya Marina Village*. Docks not in use are available to the public.

Slips	18
Max LOA	55 ft.
MLW at Dock	7 ft.

PORT LUCAYA MARINA AND YACHT CLUB
Tel: 242-373-9090 • Fax: 373-8632 • VHF 16

The well-established *Port Lucaya Marina* is the busiest of all the marinas in Freeport and Port Lucaya, with a wide range of activities and facilities. It is alongside the *Port Lucaya Marketplace* with its shopping crowds, many of whom wander around to look at the boats. Restaurants are open all day, booze cruises come and go, and everyone plays their music at full volume. If you want to live it up, this is the place for you! **Customs** and **Immigration** are on call in the marina. This is an official Port of Entry.

Slips	100
Max LOA	125 ft.
MLW at dock	7 ft.
Dockage	$1 per foot, $40 minimum per day. Long-term dockage by special arrangement.
Power	25¢ per kWh
Fuel	Diesel and gasoline dock open 7 am to 3 am daily.
Propane	Same-day refills
Water	$5 per day
Telephone	Hookup available
Cable TV	$2 daily
Showers	Next to the hotel restaurant by the pool, within the hotel's central garden.
Laundry	$1.25 washers, $1.25 dryers
Restaurants	*Tradewinds Cafe* at the *Port Lucaya Resort* Tel: 373-6618. All-you-can-eat breakfast and dinner buffets, 7 am to 11 pm, lunch from 11:30 am to 3 pm. *Pool Bar* at the *Port Lucaya Resort,* open daily 10–6. *The Brass Helmet* restaurant above *UNEXSO* is open from 7:30 am to 11 pm, with full-service dining, bar, and deli service. There are many restaurants in the Marketplace with a wide price range and choice. Some are open all day and late into the night.
Provisions	The marina office can arrange a bus that will take you to the *Winn Dixie* on Seahorse Avenue. Or you can take a cab, or a bus for 75¢ from the top of the main street outside the hotel and marina complex.
Yacht Club	Members-only yacht club, adjacent to the marina, open from 12 noon to 1 am.
Facilities	Domestic cleaning, laundry service, babysitting, and catering services are available through the marina office.
Accommodations	*Port Lucaya Resort and Yacht Club* Tel: 373-6618 Full-service resort hotel; 160 rooms overlooking either the pool or the marina. Rooms from $90 per night.
Deep Sea Fishing	*Reef Tours Ltd* Tel: 373-5880/5891/5892 *Night Hawk* Tel: 373-7726 or 373-3630
Diving	*Underwater Explorers Society* (*UNEXSO*) Tel: 373-1244 At the end of *Port Lucaya Marketplace* boardwalk. See **Diving** in our SPORTS section for details.
Parasailing	*Reef Tours Ltd* Tel: 373-5880/5891/5892 $30 a flight. Also snorkeling, beach parties, booze cruises, and glass-bottom boat tours.
Submarine	*Deepstar* at *Reef Tours Ltd* Tel: 373-8940
Transportation	Courtesy transport to Freeport International Airport and local grocery stores.
Credit Cards	All major credit cards accepted.

LUCAYAN MARINA VILLAGE
Tel: 242-373-7616 • Fax: 373-7630 • VHF 16

The *Lucayan Marina Village* is a new, state-of-the-art marina with excellent facilities and a very helpful staff. It surrounds an imaginatively designed village community where the colorful homes are still under construction; no two are alike. *Lucayan Marina Village* acts as host to several major Boat Owner's Rendezvous. There is a no tipping policy in the marina. **Customs** and **Immigration** are on call, and this is a Port of Entry.

Slips	125
Max LOA	130 ft.
MLW at dock	7 ft.
Dockage	$1 per ft. per day
Long Term	Rates are negotiable.
Power	25¢ per kWh, from 30A to 200A

Fuel	24-hour fuel dock
Propane	Same day refill on weekdays
Water	No charge for hookup
TV	No charge for satellite hookup
Telephone	No charge for hookup. Local and long distance calls billed at a nominal rate. Pay phones by the showers and laundry.
Laundry	$1.25 per load for washers and dryers
Showers	Excellent and very clean showers, with handicap-accessible toilets.
Restaurant	*The Pool Bar and Grill* serves lunch and snacks poolside during the day. For dinner *The Ferry Restaurant,* newly opened at the *Pelican Bay Hotel,* can be reached by the ferry from the marina dock.
Ice	$2 per bag
Accommodations	*Pelican Bay Hotel* offers a discount to visiting boats.
Fax	$4 to send a fax, $3 per page to receive
Maid services	Available
Office	Open from 7 am to 11 pm daily
Swimming	Two-level pool with Olympic-length lap area and separate children's pool
Barbecue Grills	There are grills set up for use in the grounds around the marina.
Fish Cleaning	Table available on the fuel dock
Marine mechanics and fishing guides	Can be contacted through the dockmaster
Pump Out	$20
Shuttle service	Complimentary ferry runs on the hour and half hour, 8 am to 11 pm, to *Port Lucaya Marketplace* and the *Pelican Bay Hotel.*
Credit Cards	Visa, MasterCard, and Amex
Security	This marina is in a gated community, with 24-hour security staff on duty

SERVICES

Ambulance
Tel: 352-2689

ATMs
Bank of Nova Scotia in the Bahamas, Princess Casino, Freeport, gives US currency.

Royal Bank of Canada, main branch on East Mall and Explorers Way gives Bahamian dollars.

All machines accept Visa, MasterCard, and cards connected to the Plus or Cirrus network.

The Royal Bank ATM accepts Honor cards.

The Scotiabank ATMs accept American Express as well as cards on the Honor and Novus network.

Banks
Most banks are open from 9:30 am to 3 pm, Monday to Thursday; to 5 pm on Fridays
Barclays Bank on Pioneers Way   Tel: 352-8391
Royal Bank of Canada   Port Lucaya Marketplace   Tel: 352-6631
CIBC on Queen's Highway   Tel: 352-6651
Bank of Nova Scotia at *Regent Centre*   Tel: 352-6774

Chamber of Commerce
Tel: 352-8329

Churches
There are 16 churches in the Freeport area, and only two of those are the same denomination, the Baptist churches of St. John's and the First Baptist. Every church has the times of services published in the Tourist Board's publication *"What to do"* in Freeport, or posted outside the church itself.

Clinics

Lucayan Medical Centre West   Tel: 352-7288
Lucayan Medical Centre East   Tel: 373-7400
Sunrise Medical Centre   Tel: 373-3333

Consulates
Are all in Nassau, these are a few:
  American Embassy   Tel: 242-322-1181
  British High Commission   Tel: 242-325-7471
  Canadian Consulate   Tel: 242-393-2123

Customs
Tel: 352-8500, and
Immigration
Tel: 352-5454

Dentist
Tel: 352-8492   Dr Larry Bain is at the *Sun Alliance Building,* Pioneers Way.

Fire Brigade
Tel: 352-8888

Hospital
Rand Memorial Hospital   East Atlantic Drive   Tel: 352-6735

Movies
Columbus Theatre   Tel: 352-7478

Performing Arts
Freeport Players Guild   Tel: 373-8400   Presents three or four plays between September and June at the Regency Theatre.
Grand Bahama Players   Tel: 352-7071 or 373-2299
Offers cultural productions featuring Bahamian, West Indian, and North American playwrights at the Regency Theatre.

Police
Dial 919

Post Office
Explorer's Way, Freeport   Tel: 352-9371
Open from 9 am to 5:30 pm, Monday to Friday.

Telephones
All the hotels and marinas have telephones; there are 10 in the *Port Lucaya Marketplace.* Use a Batelco phone card for better service. $20, $10, and $5 cards are available from the *Batelco* offices in the *International Bazaar* and downtown Freeport.

Tourist Information Booth
Open 9 am to 5 pm Monday to Friday, outside the *Marketplace* at Port Lucaya. Pick up a street map, leaflets, and a free comprehensive *"What to do"* booklet filled with descriptions of local places of interest, shopping, restaurants, sports, churches, etc.

SHOPPING

A wide selection of stores in the *International Bazaar* and *Port Lucaya Marketplace* offer something for everyone, and there are good shopping malls nearby.

Groceries
Winn Dixie at Lucaya Shopping Centre, Sea Horse Road
Tel: 373-5500

Winn Dixie at Freeport Shopping Centre, downtown
Tel: 353-7901

Winn Dixie at Eight Mile Rock   Tel: 348-2959   Free delivery to boats for orders over $100. All stores open 7:30 am to 9 pm.

Liquor Stores
Butler and Sands   Queens Highway   Tel: 352-6672
Open from 9 am to 6 pm, Monday to Friday.

Butler and Sands Duty Free Liquor Store at *Port Lucaya Marketplace.*
Open from 10 am to 7 pm, Monday to Saturday.

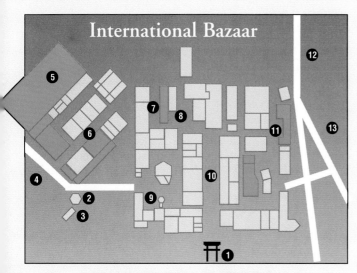

International Bazaar Directory

1 Torii Gate entrance
2 Tourist information
3 Police
4 Taxis
5 Bahamas Princess Resort and Casino
6 International Arcade
7 Scandinavian Section
8 French Section
9 Mideast Section
10 Oriental Section
11 South American Section
12 Buses
13 Parking

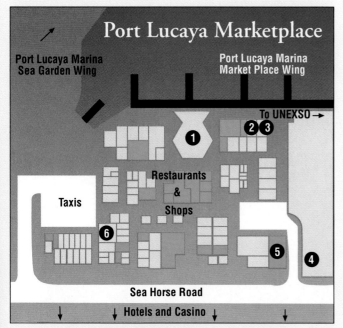

Port Lucaya Marketplace Directory

1 Count Basie Square. Open air meeting place and band-stand, with live music and dancing in the evenings.
2 Port Lucaya Yacht Club (upstairs)
3 Port Lucaya Marina Office (upstairs)
4 Tourist Information
5 Drug Store
6 Bank

RESTAURANTS

There are many, many excellent restaurants to suit all tastes. Try lots of different ones! Here are a few suggestions.

The Princess Resort and Casino   Sunrise Highway
Tel: 352-966l/6721/7811 A total of nine different restaurants.

Banana Bay   Fortune Beach, Lucaya   Tel: 373-2960   Chunky conch fritters and banana bread. Open 10 am to 6 pm; beachwear okay.

The Brass Helmet   Tel: 373-2032   Upstairs at *UNEXSO*, at the end of the *Port Lucaya Marketplace* boardwalk. Self-service and full-service dining, open 7:30 am to 10 pm; bar and deli open to midnight.

Cafe Michel's   Tel: 353-2191   A sidewalk cafe in the French section of the *International Bazaar* serving Bahamian and French cuisine. Reservations suggested for dinner.

Captain's Charthouse   East Sunrise Highway & Beachway Drive
Tel: 373-3900 or 373-3069   Tropical drinks, early bird specials, and a Bahamian Native Review feature at this unusual treetop level restaurant. Reservations suggested. Open 5 to 11 pm, dinner and show at 7 pm. Free transportation for dinner guests.

Clarion Atlantik Beach Resort across from *Port Lucaya Marketplace*   Tel: 373-1444   Four different restaurants including the *Arawak Dining Room* at the *Lucaya Golf and Country Club*. All serve very good food.

Pier One   Tel: 353-6674   Anchored on stilts in Freeport Harbour, with the best sunset on the island. Watch the cruise ships sail and the sharks being fed nightly. Reservations recommended for the Shark Pit sittings at 6:30 and 8:30 pm.

The Pub at Port Lucaya   Tel: 373-8450
Hearty pub fare, fresh seafood, and tropical drinks in a unique Victorian pub setting. Open from 11 am daily.

Ruby Swiss European Restaurant   Atlantic Way, opposite *Princess Towers*   Tel: 352-8507   Gourmet menu and seafood. Dinner special for two, $35 with gratuity. All-you-can-eat spaghetti bar for $9.75.

Silvano's Italian Restaurant   Opposite the *International Bazaar*, adjacent to *Silvano's Gelati*   Tel: 353-5111   These two establishments will make you feel like you are in Italy. *Gelati* is open for continental breakfast, ice cream, coffee, and desserts from 9 am to 11 pm; the *Restaurant* next door from 5:30 to 11 pm, serving homemade pasta. Reservations suggested.

The Stoned Crab on Taino Beach   Tel: 373-1442   Dine overlooking the ocean. The nautical theme restaurant serves seafood as well as other dishes. Open 5 to 10:30 pm. Reservations suggested.

Zorba's Greek Cuisine at *Port Lucaya Marketplace*   Tel: 373-6137   Freshly made authentic Greek dishes, as well as Ouzo and Retsina, accompanied by Greek music. Indoor and outdoor dining. Open from 8 am to 10 pm. No credit cards.

GETTING AROUND

Airlines
The departure tax from Freeport Airport is $18, not $15 as it is from every other airport in the Bahamas.

Air Canada (Nassau)	800-377-8411
American Eagle	700-433-7300
Bahamasair	352-8341
Delta/Comair	700-354-9822
Gulfstream	800-231-0856 or 352-6447
Laker Airways	242-352-3389

Bicycles and Scooters
Princess Country Club   Tel: 353-6721

Princess Tower   Tel: 352-9661   Bicycles about $10 a day, scooters from $40.

Buses
Cost 75¢ a journey around downtown Freeport or Port Lucaya, $1 between the two towns.

Car Rental
Don't forget! Drive on the left. Speed limit is 25 mph in town, 45 mph outside built-up areas.

Avis	352-7666 at the airport
	373-1102 in Port Lucaya
Hertz	352-3297
National Car Rental	352-9308

Taxis
Taxis charge $2 for first quarter mile and 30¢ for each additional mile. $2 per extra person.

Freeport Taxi Co	352-6666
Grand Bahama Taxi Union	352-7101

SPORTS

Diving
Caribbean Divers   Tel: 373-9111   Located at Bell Channel Inn, next to Port Lucaya. Rentals and specialty dives daily at 8 am, 10:30 am, and 1 pm. Two-tank dive $58; resort course daily at 9:15 am costs $79; snorkelers $20.

Underwater Explorers Society (UNEXSO) at the end of *Port Lucaya Marketplace* boardwalk   Tel: 373-1244   Reefs, wrecks, caverns, blue holes, night dives, underwater photography, marine identification, cavern diving, rescue diver courses, advanced open-water certification, medic first aid, dolphin dives, and a shark feeder program at Shark Junction. Two-tank dive $65; resort course $89; snorkelers $18. Certification course $360; underwater photography course $299 with your own equipment. *UNEXSO* also has an extensive dive shop, rental equipment, and a restaurant, *The Brass Helmet*, upstairs at their Port Lucaya base. *UNEXSO* was established in 1965, and administers diving access for the National Trust to the *Lucayan National Park* pre-Colombian underwater charted cave systems.

Xanadu Undersea Adventures at *Xanadu Beach Resort and Marina*, Freeport   Tel: 352-3811 or 352-6782   Night dives, rental equipment, repairs. Learn to dive classes every day at 8:30 am for $79. Two dives $55, snorkelers $18 on the 10:30 am boat.

Dive Sites
Theo's Wreck, a 230-ft. steel freighter sunk in 100 feet of water in 1982 as a dive attraction, is now cloaked in sponges and teeming with marine life. *Pygmy Caves* is a 65-ft. reef with caves and caverns within the coral, and *Ben's Caverns* makes an exciting dive trip though part of the Lucayan Cavern complex; one of the most extensive underwater cave systems in the world, with incredibly clear water and some amazing stalactites and stalagmites.

Fishing
Reef Tours Ltd   Tel: 373-5880 $60 per person for 4-hour fishing trips, leaving at 8:30 am and 1 pm. Four custom sport-fishing boats with tackle, bait, ice, and coolers provided.

Night Hawk   Tel: 373-7726 or 373-3630   Daily except Fridays at 9 am and 1:15 pm from the *Port Lucaya Marina*. $35 for a half day, bait and tackle provided. Shark fishing at 6 pm $40.

Golf
Fortune Hills Golf and Country Club   Tel: 373-4500 or 373-2222   A picturesque 9-hole course; $43 for non-members for 18 holes. The restaurant is closed on Mondays.

Bahamas Princess Resort   Tel: 352-9661   Two challenging 18-hole PGA courses, the Emerald and Ruby. $65 for 18 holes.

Lucaya Golf and Country Club   Tel: 373-1066 $80 for an 18-hole course. Designed by Dick Wilson with two lakes and the famous Balancing Boulders at the 18th hole. You can have lunch at the *Country Club*, or dinner in the *Arawak Dining Room*.

Horseback Riding
Pinetree Stables   Tel: 373-3600 $35 for an hour-and-a-half trail ride to the beach, accompanied by experienced guides. Dressage & jumping lessons; English saddles. Closed Mondays.

Parasailing
Reef Tours Ltd   Tel: 373-5880 $30 a flight.

Skydiving
Tandem Skydive Bahamas   Tel: 352-5995   Open 7 days a week at the airport. Jumps from 10,000 ft; professional instructors.

Sea Kayaking
Kayak Nature Tours   Tel: 373-2485   Trips to the Lucayan National Park or Grand Bahama's North Shore. Children must be over 10 years old. $75 per person.

Tennis
There are over 40 courts in the area, mostly at the hotels. Almost all are hard surface.

Waterskiing
Paradise Watersports at *Xanadu Beach Resort*   Tel: 352-4233 or 352-2887 $20 an hour, lessons cost $15 an hour.

ACCOMMODATIONS

There are so many good hotels in Freeport and Port Lucaya, including those surrounding the marinas, that we suggest that you look in the current edition of *"What to do"* or ask at the Tourist Information Booth at the *Port Lucaya Marketplace* if you need help finding accommodations.

BEACHES

Xanadu Beach, with a mile-long stretch of white sand.

William's Town, where occasionally you may meet riders from Pinetree Stables riding along the sand.

Taino Beach, where you can treat yourself to a seafood feast at the *Stoned Crab Restaurant*.

Smiths's Point, with island specialties like *Mama Flo's* cracked conch, or fresh fish at *Outrigger's* Wednesday night native fish fry.

Fortune Beach, and those chunky conch fritters from *Banana Bay*.

Gold Rock Beach, at the end of the trail from the Lucayan National Park, where you will find picnic tables but no rest rooms.

Flame trees, Grand Bahama

FISHING TOURNAMENTS & REGATTAS

February
Off Shore Deep Sea Fishing Tournament at *Xanadu Marina*

June/July/August
Bahamas Summer Boating Fling

June/ July
Annual Grand Bahama Sailing Regatta

Contact the Grand Bahama Tourist Board, 242-352-8044, for more information

PLACES OF INTEREST

Bahamas National Trust Parks
Rand Nature Centre   Tel: 352-5438
Two miles from downtown, with guided tours through the pine forest highlighting native plants and their medicinal uses, as well as migratory birds, reptiles, and a flock of flamingos. Open Monday to Friday, 9 am to 4 pm, Saturdays to 1 pm. Guided nature walks, Monday to Friday at 10 am and 2 pm; bird walks on the first Saturday of the month at 8 am; wildflower walk on the fourth Saturday at 8 am.

Lucayan National Park   Tel: 352-5438
Nature trails and one of the largest underwater cave systems in the world, 26 miles east of Freeport. *Ben's Cave* and *Burial Mound Cave* are habitats for rare underwater crustaceans and migratory bats in summer. Swimming is prohibited in the caves but you can dive them with *UNEXSO*.

Peterson Cay National Park   Tel: 352-5438 About 15 miles east of Freeport and a mile offshore, this is an inviting cay for picnics, with surrounding reefs for snorkeling and diving.

Botanical Gardens
Garden of the Groves at the intersection of Midshipman Road and Magellan Drive   Tel: 352-4045 Winding paths through 12 acres of mature tropical trees, waterfalls, fern gully, hanging gardens and a chapel designed after the original church at Pine Ridge. Open from 9 am to 4 pm daily.

Hydraflora Gardens on East Beach at Sunrise Highway Tel: 352-6052 With 154 native plant specimens and a special section devoted to bush medicine. Open daily except Sundays. Minimal charge for admission of guided tours.

THINGS TO DO IN FREEPORT

- Pick up your copy of the Bahamas *Trailblazer* map and *"What to do"* in Freeport and Port Lucaya, to give you suggestions and ideas of what is going on here.
- Shop till you drop. Explore the *Port Lucaya Marketplace* and the *International Bazaar* for designer bargains and treasures from all over the world.
- Take a voyage in a submarine.
- Improve your golf game at one of three excellent courses.
- Enjoy a guided bird walk through the *Rand Nature Centre*.
- Have your hair braided.
- Dive a pre-Colombian cave in the *Lucayan National Park* with *UNEXSO*.
- For a quick buzz, try skydiving or parasailing!
- Try your luck at the casinos.
- Rent a car for the day and explore the smaller settlements along the coast to West End. Or drive the other way out to the *Lucayan National Park* and *Barbary Beach*. Have a look at the *Grand Lucayan Waterway* as you pass and see whether you feel like taking your own boat through it.
- Join in the nightly dancing at the *Port Lucaya Marketplace*. All ages, lots of fun.

Part III

---◦—◦---

The Central Cruising Grounds

The Bimini Island Group

Crossing the Great Bahama Bank

The Berry Islands

Nassau and New Providence Island

Eleuthera

Andros

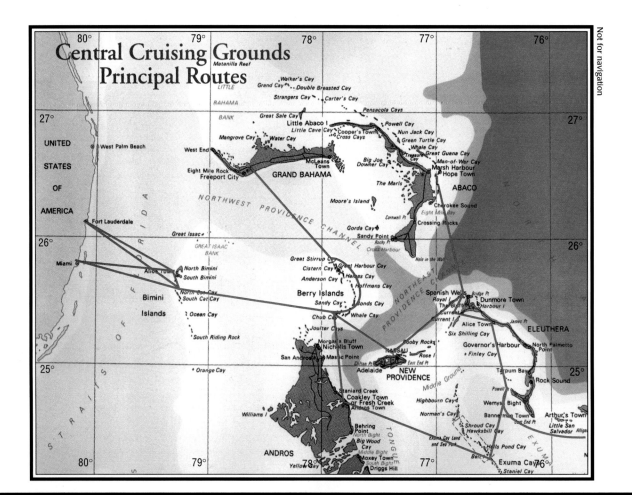

Central Cruising Grounds
Principal Routes

Central Cruising Grounds
Hydrographic Chart

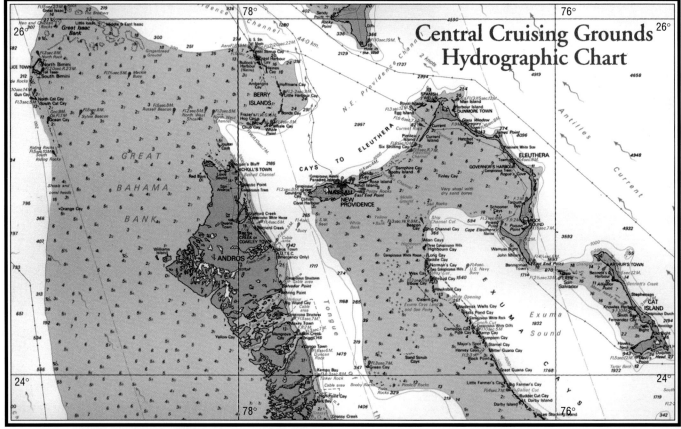

Chapter 8
The Bimini Island Group

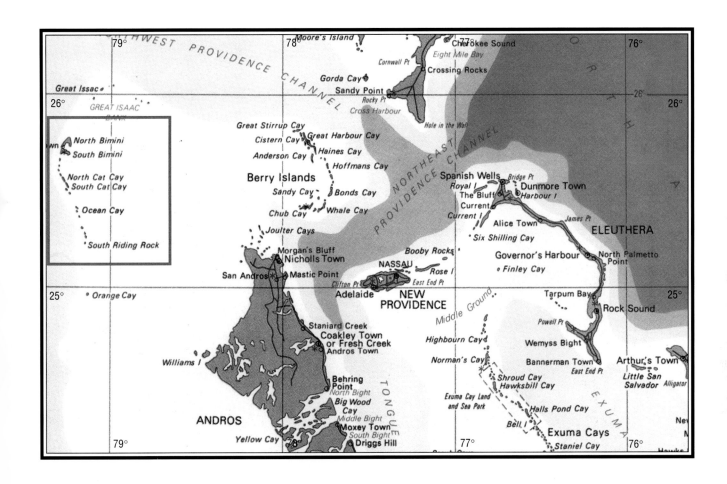

The Bimini Islands

BIMINI is a Bahamian name that rings a bell with most people. The immediate association is some kind of barefoot, laid-back island resort where anything goes, rum flows, deep sea fishing comes into it, together with the kind of weekends you wouldn't want your mother to know much about.

The name of the two small Bimini Islands (barely 9 square miles in land mass) serves as a convenient ID for the whole string of even smaller cays, rocks, and reefs that run south from North Bimini Island along the edge of the Gulf Stream for nearly 30 miles. However, when we talk of the Biminis, we really mean North and South Bimini Island, maybe with Gun Cay and Cat Cay thrown in. If we talk of Bimini, we mean North Bimini Island and Alice Town, but the town name is hardly ever mentioned. Bimini is the name that counts.

It wasn't always so. The Biminis did not have a promising beginning. Juan Ponce de León passed that way in 1513 looking for the Fountain of Youth, but left disappointed. You might say he was ahead of his time. Now, almost five hundred years later, he might well have found the rejuvenating shot he needed in a place whose bars outnumber any other kind of store.

Bimini got its head start in the 1600s in the high days of piracy, went on to wrecking as a business until lighthouses were built, spoiling that game, and then learned all the tricks of blockade running during the US Civil War. Their new skills hit the jackpot during Prohibition (1920–33) and Bimini became the center of the rum-running trade targeted at the East Coast. When the 18th Amendment forbidding alcohol was repealed, Bimini might have slumped, but the luck of these islands still held.

By 1935 Ernest Hemingway and others found that the Bimini Islands were at the edge of one of the best ocean fishing grounds in the world. Since then tiny North Bimini, shaped like a fish hook and just over 7 miles long (and barely the equivalent of a mega-yacht LOA measured across the shank of the hook from coast to coast), has dominated the scattering of islands that share its name as a group. Today Bimini (and the Biminis) win on all counts as a cruising destination. What are the star points?

- The Biminis are the closest Bahamian islands to Florida. Just 50 nm away. Only 2 hours if you can do 25 knots, and 10 hours if you can make 5 knots. Well within reach for weekend visits.

- Some of the best fishing you can find anywhere in the Islands. It's world class.

- Great diving and good snorkeling, with dive sites that eclipse Florida's best.

- A place that really is different. There's no mistaking, as you walk up North Bimini's one-car-wide King's Highway (the main street), you are *not* in the USA!

- That Bimini "naughty weekend" atmosphere, which makes most people let down their hair the moment they land, if not one drink later.

- North Bimini and its southern neighbor, Cat Cay, are *the* obvious places to stop after your Gulf Stream crossing, clear in, and spend a night before setting off again across the Great Bahama Bank. They're equally obvious places to wait for the weather on your return crossing across the Stream.

Although there are many places where you can anchor in the Biminis (always with a sensible regard to the weather), there are only two places where you can secure alongside in a marina. The first, top of the list, is North Bimini with six marinas. The second is Cat Cay, or North Cat Cay to be more accurate, with its Cat Cay Club.

If you're bound on bypassing the Biminis and carrying straight on across the Great Bahama Bank, North Rock (north of Bimini) and South Riding Rock (18 nm south of Cat Cay) may be your entry waypoints to Bank waters. Otherwise it'll be Gun Cay Cut, 9 nm south of Bimini and just north of Cat Cay, which will serve equally well as your access point to the Bank, whether you're staging in the Biminis, or riding past without touching land.

Heading For North Rock

Fort Lauderdale (1 nm due E)	LDALE	26° 05' 30 N	080° 05' 15 W
Miami (just off harbor channel entry)	MIAMI	25° 46' 00 N	080° 05' 00 W
N Rock (1 nm N of Moselle Bank)	NROCK	25° 51' 00 N	079° 16' 30 W

From Fort Lauderdale, North Rock is a run of 46.16 nm on 112°M.
From Miami, North Rock lies 43.95 nm on 087°M.

Heading For Bimini

Fort Lauderdale (1 nm due E)	LDALE	26° 05' 30 N	080° 05' 15 W
Miami (just off harbor channel entry)	MIAMI	25° 46' 00 N	080° 05' 00 W
Bimini (0.5 nm W offshore)	BMINI	25° 42' 30 N	079° 19' 00 W

From Fort Lauderdale, Bimini is 46.70 nm on 122°M.
From Miami, Bimini is 41.58 nm on 098°M.

Heading For Gun Cay Cut

Fort Lauderdale (1 nm due E)	LDALE	26° 05' 30 N	080° 05' 15 W
Miami (just off harbor channel entry)	MIAMI	25° 46' 00 N	080° 05' 00 W
Gun Cay (1.5 nm NW Gun Cay Point)	GUNCW	25° 34' 15 N	079° 19' 30 W

From Fort Lauderdale to Gun Cay Cut is 52.20 nm on 131°M.
From Miami it's 42.59 nm on 109°M.

Heading For South Riding Rock

Miami (just off harbor channel entry)	MIAMI	25° 46' 00 N	080° 05' 00 W
S Riding Rock W (2 nm SW Castle Rock)	SRDRW	25° 13' 30 N	079° 11' 00 W
S Riding Rock E (1 nm S Castle Rock)	SRDRE	25° 13' 30 N	079° 08' 30 W

From Fort Lauderdale to South Riding Rock is 71.38 nm.
From Miami it's 58.59 nm.

Approaches to the Biminis

The geographical position of the Bimini Island group (Latitude 25° 40' 00 N as a median line), the run of the Gulf Stream, and the relative position of the Florida East Coast ports tell you with just a glance at the chart that it would be foolish, if you're heading for Bimini, to choose a Florida departure point anywhere north of Fort Lauderdale. Even from Lauderdale it's necessary to buck the Gulf Stream for 50 nm to reach the islands, and our own choice is to use the shortest course (just under 42 nm), which runs from the Miami harbor entrance to Bimini, and build an offset for the Gulf Stream into our course. We reckon Miami is the best jumping-off point for the Biminis, but we give you the options as we see them.

In summary we conclude that South Riding Rock (71.38 nm from Fort Lauderdale and 58.58 nm from Miami) offers no advantages as a start point across the Great Bahama Bank. The Gun Cay Cut route is better and, even if you don't want to call in anywhere, this route takes you past two potential havens, just in case you're in trouble.

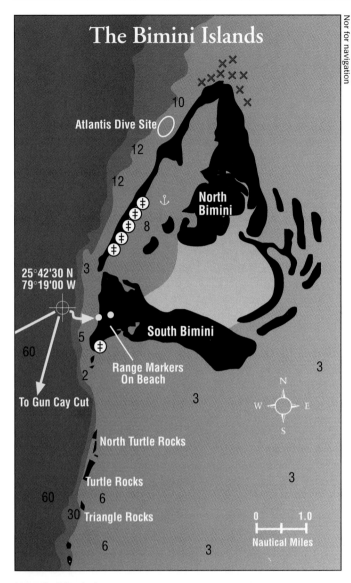

The Bimini Islands

Nor for navigation

Atlantis Dive Site

North Bimini

25°42'30 N
79°19'00 W

South Bimini

Range Markers
On Beach

To Gun Cay Cut

North Turtle Rocks

Turtle Rocks

Triangle Rocks

0   1.0
Nautical Miles

make your way up to the entrance to Bimini Harbour, which lies between North and South Bimini. You should have 5 feet at MLW, but go cautiously. We've found 4.5 feet at one spot and remember, this is not a dredged channel. It has shoal spots, and sand shifts in storms. If the wind is from the west and any kind of significant sea is running, this approach is not usable. Don't try it. Your immediate option is to divert to Gun Cay Cut and go to Cat Cay.

There are shoals extending out from both points of land at the entrance to the harbor. Choose your course carefully, staying mid-channel, and favor the mid-channel to port side of Bimini Harbour as you make you way up the fairway. The PanAm (formerly Chalk Airlines) seaplane ramp and the marinas come up on your port side, and to starboard you have the Buccaneer Point Canal leading into the heart of South Bimini Island (about 4 feet MLW at the entry point) but there's nothing there for you. The Bimini marinas are first Harcourt Brown's (derelict when we were last there), Weech's Bimini Dock, then the government dock (with the Customs but not Immigration, who are way down the street), Sea Crest Hotel and Marina, the Bimini Blue Water Resort, and then the Bimini Big Game Fishing Club. To starboard you have nothing after that canal entrance but a shoal area that virtually dries at low water.

Bimini Harbour is used by the Grumman Mallard seaplanes of the PanAm Air Bridge. You do *not* anchor in the main harbor freeway for this reason and also because local boats run fast through its length. The anchorage lies in the deeper water just past the Bimini Big Game Fishing Club. There's more than adequate depth there (8–10 feet) but take care that your anchor really sets, for the reversing tidal flow through Bimini Harbour is like a millrace. We mentioned speeding local boats. Don't swim too far away from your boat, or let a child stray too far, for the head of a swimmer would not be seen in time.

North Bimini

Bimini (0.5 nm W offshore)	BMINI	25° 42' 30 N	079° 19' 00 W
Bimini Approach Range	BIMAP	25° 42' 05 N	079° 18' 54 W

If you're bound for Bimini Harbour, our landfall waypoint places you off South Bimini, a tad northwest of the approach range leading into the approach channel, so that you have a chance to pick up your bearings before going close inshore.

Bimini Harbour
MARINA AND ANCHORAGES

The range markers (our approach range waypoint is where you want to be) lead you straight in toward the white sand beach on the west shore of South Bimini. Turn to port having safely passed a sandbar on your port side and rocks and shallows on the starboard side. By then you'll be close to the beach, but in deeper water. Keep parallel to the beach and

---

A WARNING: DOCK SPACE IN BIMINI

Bimini is crowded to capacity during its many fishing tournaments (see the **Buff Pages** under **Bahamian Holidays and Special Events** on page 330). It's crowded at Spring Break. It hits peak at any prime holiday weekend, particularly over the Fourth of July, and during the Summer Boating Flings. If you plan to visit Bimini at these times, book your marina space early.

ALICE TOWN

North Bimini's main settlement, Alice Town, is one place where you wouldn't even think of renting a bicycle. You can walk everywhere and cover the town in ten minutes. Alice Town is a strip of bars, shops, and market stalls that line the

King's Highway, the main street running behind the marinas. It's pure island life there with an 80-proof rating, with the Compleat Angler Hotel (the Hemingway haunt) as its epicenter. A parallel road, the Queen's Highway, runs along the Gulf Stream coast, and there the Anchorage Hotel (don't be fooled: there's no anchorage that side) is the focal point. The beach is good.

Atlantis or the Bimini Road Dive Site

The Atlantis Dive Site	ATLDS	25° 45' 44 N	079° 16' 44 W

You've heard that the Bahamas were the site of Atlantis? The evidence is right there. Want to dive it? There's a marker buoy there, waiting for you. Atlantis or the Bimini Road rock formation is on the sea bed in 15 feet of water off Paradise Point, North Bimini. We said "dive," but all you need is a mask and snorkel.

THE MARKER BUOYS

There are 16 mooring buoys in the Bimini area, all placed to mark dive sites by Bill and Nowdla Keefe who run Bimini Undersea Adventures. They welcome you to make use of these buoys when you go diving, but ask that you call them first on VHF 06 (Bimini Undersea) and check that the buoy you would like to use is not required by them that day.

What's at the Atlantis dive site? A relatively small area of roughly rectangular flat rocks lying almost totally buried in the sand, which look like the paving stones of a ramp or road, or perhaps the cap stones of an ancient harbor wall. Certainly the stones have the appearance of having been fashioned and placed by man rather than a geological freak of nature. If you go for the Atlantis theory you're into wish ful-

The Sand Bar in Bimini.

Atlantis

HAVING spent some time on another project researching the Atlantis legend over the last six years, we doubt it's Atlantis. OK, the stones do appear much the same as the stonework found in ancient Mediterranean sites dating around 3,000 BC, and we've seen ancient harbor walls now submerged in the Red Sea off the coast of Yemen that look similar. To throw in a wild card, Tiahuanaco, the ruined city on the ancient shore of Lake Titicaca in the Bolivian High Andes, joins the league with look-alike stonework that includes harbor walls. But geology discounts such fantasies. The "Bimini Road" is no more than naturally formed eroded beach limestone. In any event, the Atlantis of the legend, we'd say, was way too late in time to fit the Bimini site. But there's nothing worse than destroying a legend, is there?

Dive there anyway! We could be wrong. There's growing evidence of a global civilization that peaked and disappeared millenniums before our time, long before our civilization got its kick-start in Mesopotamia and Egypt. Dive it and see what you feel!

fillment, for it's impossible to divine any plan in the site and, were it prehistoric, too much (one guesses) lies buried to permit analysis. This site has also been linked with the Moselle Bank, to the northwest of Bimini, which was also wrapped up in the Atlantis theory, as were the "lemon shark" sand mounds discovered in 1977 in the mangroves to the east of Bimini. These might be termed Bimini's version of the Nazca Lines, both of which can only be seen from the air.

South Bimini

You can dinghy across to South Bimini or take the water taxi from the government dock. There's little to see there, though someone will always be willing to show you where Juan Ponce de León's Fountain of Youth once flowed, and there's a major new development, Bimini Sands, that promises townhouses with their own docks, but this has been a long time getting past the model house stage.

However, if you're virtually shoal draft, South Bimini offers a secluded alternative to the "Main Street" North Bimini marinas. Tucked inside the southern hook of south Bimini around Round Rock is the 22-slip Bimini Beach Club and Marina, a resurrection of a hurricane-shattered one-time much larger (70 berths) marina. It's disadvantage is a 4.5-foot depth and a shoal approach, that like the approach to its northern cousin, North Bimini, is a definite no-go in onshore weather, and an approach you wouldn't want to attempt in bad light or under any other adverse conditions. Its advantages are peace and quiet. Maybe you could send your mother a postcard from there? But see our **Yellow Pages** and make your decision. We'll watch its development.

South of the Biminis—
Gun Cay and Gun Cay Cut

Turning south from South Bimini, a run of 9 nm takes you to Gun Cay. You're in interesting waters. For snorkelers there's Turtle Rocks and the far more striking wreck of the *Sapona*, the victim of a 1929 hurricane, which is a good shallow dive, too. For divers there are two more shipwrecks to explore, the *Bimini Barge* in 65–100 feet, and the *Bimini Trader*. There's Picquet Rock and Holm Cay, and then, at the north end of Gun Cay, Honeymoon Harbour.

The rounded cove that forms Honeymoon Harbour is everyone's first dream of what a Bahamian anchorage should be like, with its sand beach and the Gulf Stream–side beach

Gun Cay Lighthouse.

Janet Wilson

just across a spit of land. The downside is that the cove is exposed to wind wherever it comes from, and at peak Bimini visit periods, if you get there first and are anchored in virtual isolation or even get in with the first wave of a holiday invasion, you'll soon feel that you're in a boat jam worse than being caught in Friday afternoon Beltway traffic.

On the south end of Gun Cay there's the famous landmark Gun Cay Light, and the passage between Gun Cay and Cat Cay to its south is the access channel to the Great Bahama Bank known as Gun Cay Cut.

You can make your way south from South Bimini on the Great Bahama Bank side, but you have to feel your way. There are shoals to the east of Turtle Rocks, and shoals to the east of Gun Cay, and in places you'll find little more than 6 feet at MLW. We don't favor it, and take the deep-water route on the Gulf Stream side every time.

Gun Cay Cut

Gun Cay (1.5 nm NW Gun Cay Pt)	GUNCW	25° 34' 15 N	079° 19' 30 W
Cat Cay (0.25 nm E of marina)	CATCE	25° 34' 00 N	079° 17' 00 W

Once you're at our Gun Cay west waypoint, turn to pass through Gun Cay Cut. The 2.5 nm or so you run through Gun Cay Cut must be taken visually, favoring Gun Cay Point and running in the deep water parallel to the shoreline (to avoid the shoal and reef extending north from Cat Cay) until you are through the Cut. Don't go too close in to Gun Cay as you go through the Cut, but there's plenty of water there and you can read the deeper water easily. Hold your course until, looking down the east coast of Cat Cay, you can see the entrance to Cat Cay Marina with its dwarf lighthouse.

Whether you're bound for a Bank crossing or for Cat Cay, turn to starboard at that point. Using the two lights, Gun Cay and Cat Cay as markers, one ahead and one astern, head south. This line will keep you clear of the shoal area close in to Cat Cay, and shoals that lie to the east of Gun Cay Cut. If you're going to Cat Cay, carry on into the marina.

If you're heading across the Great Bahama Bank, turn east to pick up your departure waypoint when you reach the line of Latitude 25° 34' 00 N. Your departure point is the waypoint we give. For routes across the Bank see **The Great Bahama Bank** on page 133.

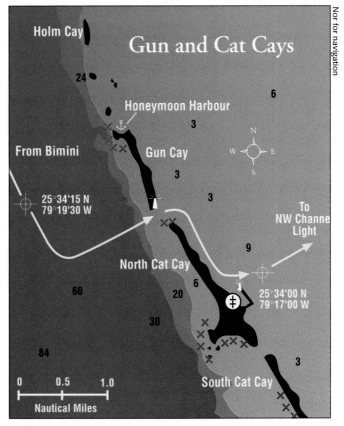

Not for navigation

Cat Cay

Cat Cay (0.25 nm E of marina) CATCE	25° 34' 00 N	079° 17' 00 W

Cat Cay is a private club situated on and wholly owning an island that is about 2.5 miles long and barely a mile wide. They welcome visitors (but not over the weekend of the Fourth of July) and you can clear in there, refuel, use all the marina facilities, and dine ashore in their restaurant. If you just call to clear Customs and Immigration into the Bahamas and then move on, you will be charged a $25.00 transient fee.

For some cruisers, Cat Cay is preferable to Bimini. If you're not interested in diving in Bimini waters, the Bimini crowd scene, and the Bimini bars, you'll find Cat Cay not only meets your requirements, but gives you a more peaceful time. It could just turn claustrophobic if you get held up there. The island, at least technically, is private turf and not a playground open to cruising visitors (unless they are members or guests). We spent nine days there once, holed up waiting for a chance to cross the Gulf Stream. Cat Cay was kind. We were allowed to walk around as we wished, but even then you can get to know one small island better than you ever intended. Have you heard of cabin fever?

South Of Cat Cay

There's little of interest (other than some good diving) in the remaining 18 nm run of the line of the small cays and reefs that form the "trailing end" of the Bimini chain. After Cat Cay is its uninhabited sibling, South Cat Cay, then the Victory Cays (a popular dive site), Sandy Cay, Ocean Cay (an aragonite sea mining operation that is a high-visibility landmark), Brown's Cay, Beak Cay, and the Riding Rocks leading to South Riding Rock.

AN INCIDENTAL NOTE

Do you know what aragonite is? We didn't. Aragonite, named after Aragon in Spain, is an orthorhombic mineral made up of calcium carbonate, $CaCO_3$. It resembles calcite, but is heavier and harder, has less cleavage, and occurs less frequently. Our source is Webster's *New World Dictionary*.

Any wiser? Apparently it's a pure limestone, used for cement and fertilizers.

To the south of South Riding Rock there's the lonely Orange Cay, another 18 nm further on, but we've never been there.

SOUTH RIDING ROCK

We deal with the South Riding Rock approach on to the Great Bahama Bank in our section **The Great Bahama Bank** on page 135.

Returning To Florida

Your destination waypoints on leaving Bimini to return to Florida are:

Stuart (St Lucie Entrance)	LUCIE	27° 10' 00 N	080° 08' 00 W
Jupiter Inlet (1.2 nm SE)	JUPTR	26° 56' 00 N	080° 03' 00 W
Palm Beach (1.5 nm E)	PPALM	26° 46' 00 N	080° 00' 00 W
Fort Lauderdale (1 nm due E)	LDALE	26° 05' 30 N	080° 05' 15 W
Miami (just off harbor entry)	MIAMI	25° 46' 00 N	080° 05' 00 W

For courses and straight-line distances see **Crossing the Gulf Stream** on page 20.

YELLOW PAGES

NORTH BIMINI

If this is your first taste of the Bahamas, just 48 miles due east of Miami, then you're off to a great start. Despite a heavy influx of visitors throughout the year, Bimini retains an air of calm and relaxation. With all the shops and restaurants located on the King's Highway in Alice Town, only a minute's walk away from the brilliant white sand beach off the Queen's Highway on the west side, nothing is hard to find or to reach. Once the sport fishing capital of Ernest Hemingway's world, the tradition is carried on with pride, as keen fishermen pour in to attend the major sporting events of the season.

Customs are open daily from 7 am to 7 pm. The customs office (347-3100) is located in a large pink and white building at the government dock. The **Immigration** office (347-3446) is located in the low pink administration building with police and the post office, a five-minute walk along King's Highway just north of the Big Game Fishing Club. You must walk up here after seeing Customs to fill out your Immigration cards and have your passports stamped.

MARINAS

As they appear on your port side coming into Bimini Harbour:

BROWN'S HOTEL AND MARINA

This property, at the time of writing, is near derelict and for sale. Although the outer docks are falling into the water, the docks that are still serviceable are used by Bill and Nowdla Keefe for their *Bimini Undersea Adventures* dive boats, as well as by a few local boats.

WEECH'S BIMINI DOCK
Tel: 242-347-3508 • VHF 68

Slips	15
Max LOA	135 ft.
MLW at Dock	5 ft.
Dockage	60¢ per ft. per day, $15 per day minimum
Power	$7.50 per day for 110V, $15 for 220V
Water	Wash-down water included in dockage fee
Showers	Yes
Laundry	Ask at reception
Ice	$2.50 per bag
Credit cards	Cash only

SEA CREST HOTEL AND MARINA
Tel: 242-347-3071 • VHF 68

Slips	14
Max LOA	105 ft.
MLW at Dock	5 ft.
Dockage	75¢ per ft. per day, $30 per day minimum
Power	$10 per day up to 40 ft., $15 per day to 50 ft., $20 per day to 60 ft., and $25 per day over 61 ft.
Water	40¢ a gallon
Showers	Yes
Laundry	Ask at Reception
Ice	Yes
Barbecue	Grill on the dock for use by marina guests
Boat Rentals	The dockmaster will help you.
Accommodations	*Sea Crest Hotel* Tel: 242-347-3071 Rooms and efficiencies from $80 per night.
Fax	$5 per page outgoing, $1 per page incoming
Credit cards	Visa, MasterCard, Amex

BIMINI BLUE WATER RESORT
Tel: 242-347-3166 or 3291 • Fax: 347-3293 • VHF 68

This small but very friendly marina has the added advantages of the *Anchorage Hotel* with a good restaurant, the *Compleat Angler* bar with its Hemingway charm, and easy access to the glorious white sand beach on the ocean side of the island, where you can swim and relax after your Gulf Stream crossing.

Slips	36
Max LOA	100 ft.
MLW at Dock	5 ft.
Dockage	75¢ per ft. per day, $30 minimum per day
Power	$10 per day up to 40 ft., $15 per day to 50 ft., $20 per day to 60 ft., $25 per day over 60 ft.
Water	40¢ a gallon
Fuel	Diesel and gasoline
Propane	Yes
Showers	Yes
Laundry	Ask at Reception
Ice	Yes
Restaurant	*The Anchorage Restaurant and Bar*, at the hotel, serves breakfast, lunch, and dinner.
Bar	*The Compleat Angler,* across the street from the marina, opens at 11 am.
Barbecue	Grill for marina guests on the dockside.
Swimming	Freshwater pool overlooking the harbor.
Accommodations	*The Anchorage, Bimini Blue Water Resort* Tel: 242-347-3166 Rooms, suites, cottages from $90 per night. Marlin Cottage, where Ernest Hemingway stayed, $285 per night.
Credit cards	All major credit cards accepted.

BIMINI BIG GAME FISHING CLUB
Tel: 242-347-3391 • Fax: 347-3392 • VHF 68

Slips	100
Max LOA	101 ft.
MLW at Dock	10 ft. to 12 ft.
Dockage	$1.25 per ft. per day
Dockage (small craft)	On floating dock, $25 per day up to 30 ft., no water or electricity
Power	$15 per day up to 39 ft., $20 per day to 49 ft., $30 per day to 59 ft., $37 per day to 80 ft., $50 per day over 80 ft.
Fuel	Diesel and gasoline
Propane	Yes
Water	45¢ a gallon
TV	Hookup to cable TV
Showers	Yes, very clean
Laundry	Yes, ask at the hotel
Ice	Can be delivered to boats
Restaurant	*Gulf Stream Restaurant* open 7:30–10:30 am for breakfast and 7–10 pm for dinner.
Bars	*Big Game Sports Bar* serves lunch from noon; Bacardi drinks and 4 televisions for watching sports. *Barefoot Bar*, open poolside from mid-morning to late afternoon. *Gulf Stream Bar* with calypso music in the evenings.
Barbecue	Grills for marina guests, near the cottages.
Box Lunches	Order from the restaurant for the next day.
Freezers	Limited freezer space for small boats to store bait. Ask the dockmaster, Don Smith.
Liquors	Liquor store near the front gate sells Bacardi rum products, beer, and soft drinks. Closed on Sundays. Deliveries to your boat.
Logo Shop	With many Bimini Big Game Fishing Club items; closed on Tuesdays.
Fishing	Sailfish, prize marlin, tuna, wahoo, kingfish, dolphin, and bonefishing available. Check with the dockmaster for recommendations.

Swimming	Pool in front of hotel building
Tennis	Court available; lit at night
Telephone	At the front office phone a small service charge applies, but there is a Batelco card phone outside the gate to the marina.
Credit cards	Visa, MasterCard, Amex. No personal checks.
Membership	Discount on charges for members.

SERVICES IN ALICE TOWN

Bank
Royal Bank of Canada On the King's Highway Open 9–3 on Monday & Friday, to 1 pm on Tuesday, Wednesday, & Thursday.

Churches
Community Church of God

Heavenly Vision Church of God

Holy Name Catholic Church

Mt. Zion Baptist Church

Our Lady and St. Stephen Anglican Church

Wesley Methodist Church

Clinic
North Bimini Medical Clinic Tel: 347-3210 Opposite Batelco on the King's Highway. Open 9 am to 2 pm, Monday to Friday.

Dentist
There is a dentist in Bailey Town.

Groceries
Brown's General Store in Bailey Town Tel: 347-2305 Open 7:30 am to 2 pm and 4 pm to 8 pm Monday to Saturday, and 7:30 am to 10 am on Sundays.

Jontra's Grocery Store on King's Highway, close to *The Big Game Fishing Club* Open from 7:30 am to 8:30 pm Monday to Saturday and from 7:30 am to 11 am on Sundays.

Roberts Supermarket Tel: 347-3251 On King's Highway, beyond the pink administration building.

Watson's Supermarket on King's Highway Open from 7 am to 7 pm, Monday to Saturday; to 10 am on Sundays.

Hardware and Marine Supplies
Bimini General Store At *Weech's Bimini Dock* Tel: 347-3359 Open from 10 am to 1 pm and 4 pm to 7 pm Monday to Saturday; closed Wednesday afternoons.

Laundry
Hinzey's, next to Hinzey's Apartments. Coin operated.

Porgy Bay Laundry in Vincent Ellis's apartment building has a pickup and delivery service.

Liquor Stores
Burns House Duty Free Liquors on King's Highway. Open 9 am to 5 pm Monday to Saturday, except Tuesdays 9 am to 2 pm.

Butler and Sands on King's Highway. Open from 9 am to 6 pm Monday to Saturday.

Sue and Joy Variety Store Open 8 am to 9 pm Monday to Saturday and 8–11 am on Sunday. Liquor, pharmacy, souvenirs.

Police
Emergency: Dial 919 or Tel: 347-3144 Located in the pink administration building with Immigration and the post office.

Post Office
Located in the police and administration building. Open 9–5:30, Monday to Friday. Separate mail-drop for US mail.

Shopping
There are many small shops and stalls selling everything from fresh-baked bread to T-shirts along the King's Highway, including a new straw market around the Customs House.

Telephones
In the marinas and along the King's Highway.

Videos
V Wee's Video Rental (in Bailey Town) Tel: 347-2249

RESTAURANTS

The Anchorage at the *Bimini Blue Water Resort* Tel: 347-3166 Well-cooked food in an old home setting, with large windows overlooking the ocean. Dinner reservations suggested.

Bimini Bay At the Island's north end. Call their taxi on VHF 68.

Captain Bob's Across from Sea Crest Marina.

CJ's Deli Opposite the Customs House.

Fisherman's Paradise Bar and restaurant on the south end of King's Highway facing the harbor.

Gulf Stream Restaurant at the *Bimini Big Game Fishing Club* Tel: 347-3391 Breakfast 7:30–10:30 am, dinner 7–10 pm. Live music; dinner reservations recommended. Good wine list; expensive.

Opal's Fish Restaurant Very relaxed: the menu is announced to the entire room and then orders are taken. Lunch from 12 noon, dinner from 7 pm.

Red Lion Pub On the waterfront with home-cooked food in a cheerful, friendly atmosphere. Bar opens at 5 pm.

BARS

There are many bars located in the marinas and attached to the restaurants. Everything is so accessible in Alice Town that it is fun to wander along and choose one that suits your mood.

Big Game Sports Bar at the *Bimini Big Game Fishing Club* Lunch from noon. Enjoy the best view in Bimini and a Big Game Conch Pizza. The *Gulfstream Bar* has calypso music in the evenings.

Compleat Angler Hemingway's favorite haunt, and a must visit. Open 11 am to 1 am, with live calypso music on weekends.

End of the World Bar, at the southern end of the King's Highway. Has autographed walls and sand floors.

Island House Bar opposite the *Red Lion Pub* Open 11 am to 3 am.

GETTING AROUND

Airlines
The Pan Am Air Bridge Formerly *Chalk's International Airlines* Tel: 242-347-3024 and 954-371-8628 Sea planes leave from the southern tip of North Bimini, using the harbor as a runway for the 25-minute daily flights to and from Watson Island, Miami, Walker's Terminal in Fort Lauderdale, and Paradise Island, Nassau.

Private pilots and charter flights use the 5,000-foot South Bimini airstrip; a taxi and ferry will take you to North Bimini.

BIA and *Island Air* to Fort Lauderdale Tel: 305-359-9942

Major's Air Service to Freeport Tel: 242-347-3230

Sky Unlimited to Nassau Tel: 242-347-2301 or 242-347-1540 Friday and Sunday service.

Bicycles
Bimini Undersea Adventures Tel: 347-3089 $5 per hour, $12 per half day, $20 per day

Boat rental
Weech's Bimini Dock Tel: 347-3028 or VHF 68

Buses
Frequent service up and down the length of North Bimini; hail a bumper sticker–covered bus on the street. Fare is $3.

Ferries
Leave from the government dock every few minutes for the 5-minute crossing to South Bimini. $5 one way, $10 round trip includes a tour of the island; taxis wait at both sides.

Golf Carts
Capt. Pat's at Sea Crest Marina Tel: 347-3477 $20 for the first hour, $10 per hour after that.

Compleat Angler Tel: 347-3122 $15 for the first hour, $10 per hour after that. They are all parked outside the entrance gate.

Mailboat
M/V Bimini Mack arrives in Bimini on Thursdays, and leaves for Nassau over the weekend. Office on the King's Highway open from 9 am to 4 pm Monday to Friday.

Scooters
Bimini Scooters at *Watson's Supermarket.* Tel: 347-2555 $10 per hour, $50 per day.

Sea Kayaks
Bimini Undersea Adventures Tel: 347-3089   Single: $7 per hour, $30 per day; double $10 per hour, $40 per day.

Taxis
Purple Cab Company Tel: 347-2379 & VHF 68 (not on Saturdays)

Windsurfers
Bimini Undersea Adventures Tel: 347-3089 $10 per hour, $40 per day

SPORTS

Diving
Bimini Undersea Adventures Tel: 347-3089 and VHF 06   Bill and Nowdla Keefe. $39 for a one-tank dive, $69 for a two-tank dive, introductory scuba lesson and reef dive, $99. Snorkelers $25, includes mask, fin, and snorkel. Wild dolphin excursions, rental equipment available, dive and hotel package options.

Dive Sites
Although there are more challenging sites around, the most famous site in the Bimini islands, or even in the Bahamas, is *Atlantis,* with its underwater pavement. *Rockwell Reef* and *Hawksbill* promise good marine life; the *Bimini Trader* and the *Bimini Barge,* sitting in 100 feet of water, are good wreck dives, as is the highly visible *Sapona.* The currents of the Gulf Stream guarantee excellent drift dives, particularly around *Victory Reef* and *Tuna Alley.* For a shallow-water dive, *Rainbow Reef* is hard to beat with just 25 to 35 feet of water. *Bimini Undersea Adventures* has marked a number of sites with its own buoys, that makes locating the dive site easier and also protects the reef. You are welcome to pick up one of their buoys for your dive if they are not using it themselves; call them first on VHF 06.

Fishing
Most marinas will arrange for charters or boat rentals. Expect to pay about $400 (half day) or $600 (full day) for deep sea fishing with a guide, tackle, and bait. Fishing guides for both deep sea and bonefishing are readily available.

FISHING TOURNAMENTS

Most of the fishing events are held at the *Big Game Fishing Club* and the *Bimini Blue Water Resort.* Contact the Bimini Progressive Sporting Club, PO Box 613, Bimini, Bahamas or call 242-347-3359 for additional information. See our Buff Pages under Bahamian Holidays on page 330 for a complete list of tournaments.

February
Annual Wahoo Tournament

March
Annual Bacardi Rum Billfish Tournament; Annual Bimini Regatta

April
Bimini Break Tournament

May
Annual Bimini Festival Fishing Tournament

June
Big 5 Fishing Tournament; Lauderdale Yacht Club Bimini Blast

July
Annual Latin Builders Tournament; Columbia-Kendall Fishing Tournament; South Florida Fishing Club Tournament; Bahamas Summer Boating Fling

August
Annual Bimini Family Tournament

September
Big Game Small B.O.A.T Tournament

November
Wahoo Tournament

ACCOMMODATIONS

The Anchorage at *Bimini Blue Water Resort* Tel: 242-347-3166 Rooms from $97.20 per day, Marlin Cottage $285 per day.
Bimini Big Game Fishing Club and Hotel Tel: 242-347-3391 Rooms from $149 per day, $298 for a penthouse.
Bimini Bay Tel: 242-347-2171 and VHF 68 Secluded, out-of-town resort.
Compleat Angler Tel: 242-347-3122   Rooms from $68 a night.
El Rancho Apartments $300 per month for a basic bedroom with bathroom, kitchen, and sitting room.
Sea Crest Hotel Tel: 242-347-3071 Rooms from $80 per day, suites from $180 per day.
Weech's Dock Apartments Tel: 242-347-3028 Rooms from $60 per day, apartments from $125.

SOUTH BIMINI

Although separated by only 150 yards of water from its northern neighbor, South Bimini has not shared in its prosperity. You can visit Juan Ponce de León's supposed Fountain of Youth on the island, though it is sadly overgrown. There are a few homes, a grocery store, and the airport with the police (347-3424) and a telephone, and the *Bimini Sands,* a new development under construction. These are the pink townhouses you see to the north of the two range markers that show your approach to Bimini from the Gulf Stream. They plan to have 100 slips available for residents, with a fuel dock, tennis courts, swimming pool, and **Customs** and **Immigration** clearance on site. There is also a marina at the southwestern tip of South Bimini, called the *Bimini Beach Club,* which has very shallow approaches.

MARINA

BIMINI BEACH CLUB AND MARINA
Tel: 954-257-0919 • 954-725-0918 • VHF 16

This marina was reopened in 1995 after extensive hurricane damage. They are still waiting to complete the dredging so that all 70 slips may be opened. Enter south of Round Rock, from the east side, where you will see the channel markers.

Slips	22 at the time of writing.
Max LOA	80 ft.
MLW at dock	4.5 ft.
Dockage	70¢ per ft. per day, minimum charge $21
Power	$15 per day up to 35 ft., $20 per day to 45 ft., $1 per ft. over 45 ft.
Fuel	Available in Alice Town on North Bimini
Water	45¢ per gallon from the marina, none available dockside.
Restaurant	*Bimini Beach Club Restaurant* is open for breakfast, lunch, and dinner, from short order to gourmet Bahamian and American.
Swimming	Saltwater pool at the resort
Diving	*Bahama Island Adventures* and *Scuba Bimini* offer dive trips and air fills, but no rental equipment. Diving should be arranged with the reservations office before arrival.

Fishing	Charters can be arranged.
Bicycles	$12 for half-day rental, $15 for a full day.
Kayaks	$25 for a half-day rental, $40 for a full day.
Snorkeling	Excellent snorkeling off the reef
Accommodations	*Bimini Beach Club Hotel,* harbor-view rooms from $90, ocean view from $95 per night.
Credit Cards	Visa and MasterCard

GETTING AROUND

Airport
Charter flights only use South Bimini.
Majors Air Service Tel: 242-347-3230   Fly to Freeport.

BIA Fly to Fort Lauderdale.

Island Air 305-359-9942   Four flights a week to and from Fort Lauderdale.

Sky Unlimited 242-347-2301 or 242-394-1540   Flights to and from Nassau on Fridays and Saturdays.

Taxi
TSL Taxis VHF 68

THINGS TO DO IN NORTH AND SOUTH BIMINI

- Take off your watch and get accustomed to Bahamian time.
- Go fishing!
- Follow the Hemingway Trail to the *Compleat Angler* for a drink and discover the difference between a Bahama Mama and a Goombay Smash. Enjoy the historic photographs on the walls and dance the night away to calypso music.
- Go even further back in time: dive the *Bimini Road* and discover *Atlantis!*
- Dine as you watch the sunset from the *Anchorage Hotel.*
- Take a photograph of the seaplane landing or taking off. You don't see many of them these days.
- Take your boat and your bride to Honeymoon Cove for the night.

CAT CAY

Cat Cay is an attractive island, privately owned by the members of the Cat Cay Club, with a good marina. Totally rebuilt after Hurricane Andrew, this marina welcomes visiting boats for a maximum of three nights, except over July 4th weekend when it is usually full of members and their friends. It makes a pleasant overnight stop after crossing the Gulf Stream from Florida, or having crossed the Banks from Chub Cay prior to returning to the States. You can clear in with **Customs** and **Immigration** at Cat Cay, but will be charged a $25 docking fee unless you stay overnight, when the fee is waived.

MARINA

CAT CAY YACHT CLUB
Tel and Fax: 242-347-3565 • VHF 16

Slips	110
Max LOA	140 ft.
MLW at dock	4 ft.
Dockage	$1.50 per ft. per day
Power	30A, 50A, 100A available, 25¢ per kWh
Fuel	Diesel and gasoline
Water	35¢ per gallon
Telephone	Batelco card phone on the dock
TV	Satellite hookup on the docks
Showers	Yes
Laundry	Yes
Ice	Yes
Clinic	A Cat Cay Club member who is a doctor runs the clinic when he is on the island.
Fax	The office will send or receive faxes for you.
Office	Open from 8 am to 5 pm
Provisions	There is a small commissary.
Restaurant	Open for lunch and dinner, with a pleasant veranda bar for drinks; collared shirt and long trousers required at dinner.
Shopping	The boutique has a good selection of clothes and some books.
Travel	STOL Islander aircraft fly daily to Fort Lauderdale using the 1,100-ft. landing strip.
Credit Cards	Major credit cards accepted.

Chapter 9
Crossing the Great Bahama Bank

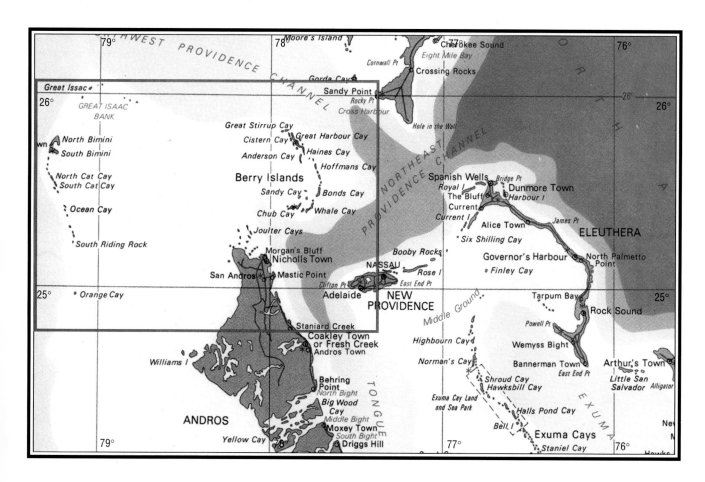

The Bimini Islands and Cat Cay

THE Biminis are prime cruising, fishing, and diving destinations in their own right. This apart, their proximity to Florida, together with the ongoing greater distances across the Great Bahama Bank, may well set them as the only possible Bahamian cruising ground within reach for those whose vacation time is short. In any event, these islands offer far more than simply serving as waypoints on the route to Chub Cay or Nassau, and it was for these reasons that we decided to treat them separately, rather than including them under the heading of **The Great Bahama Bank**, to which they are the entry port. This section links with the Biminis and continues the story across the Great Bahama Bank.

The Great Bahama Bank

The Great Bahama Bank is, by any standard, a significant sea area. It's a great tableland of shallow water that has a pervasive influence on the tides and currents, wave patterns,

navigable routes, and marine life of the Central Bahamas, just as the Little Bahama Bank influences the North. Let's mention size first. The Great Bahama Bank starts (if you can put it that way) at its northwest corner, pinned in position by Northeast Rock and Great Isaac Island almost at the junction of Latitude 26° N and Longitude 079° W. In fact the real start of the Bank is between 6 and 9 nm to the northwest and north, parallel to the 100 fathom line, but you can see that on your charts. If you take the Bimini Islands as your markers to make it easy, the Great Bahama Bank begins 29 nm north of North Bimini.

The Bank runs roughly west-east along the line of Latitude 26° N with a pronounced set to the southeast as it curves down to sweep up and claim the crescent of the Berry Islands. Then, having grabbed the Berrys, the line of the Great Bahama Bank backtracks to drop south along the east coast of Andros. On the west side the Great Bahama Bank falls almost due south from Bimini down a barrier chain of small cays, rocks, and reefs that mark the east edge of the Florida Strait. Around Latitude 23° N the Great Bahama

NASA

The Great Bahama Bank from Skylab, seen from the east.

Bank loses its geographic identity, and further south the Bahamian Out Islands are fragmented by a far more broken pattern of banks and shallows.

If you were to sum up the Great Bahama Bank, perhaps the easiest way is to say that it runs 50 nm across at its widest point and measures about 180 nm from north to south. Its waters are mostly 15–18 feet deep, but it spawns far shallower sandbars that are always changing, and for this reason the Bank is almost impossible to keep surveyed. There are navigation marks on the main routes across the Bank, but the constantly changing depth contours, as well as the loss of lights in storms or through human inattention, make these markers a bonus if they're in place, not signposts you should rely on.

For the cruising skipper the overriding factor comes with the size of the Great Bahama Bank and the consequent length of the three main navigational routes that cross it. Whichever way you play it, there's some 75 nm of Bank to cross heading out or heading back home. This means, if you're sailing from, say, Cat Cay to Chub Cay, the distance to run may be greater than your achievable daytime range. If this is so, and it's impossible to squeeze that Great Bahama Bank passage into every available minute of daylight and complete the course, there's only one answer and that's to anchor out during the night.

Anchoring out on the Bank is not difficult, it's done often, and it means that you don't risk sailing at night, for (as always) you needs your eyes to transit any area of shallow water. Just pick a spot well off the beaten track so that a Bahamian mailboat doesn't plough you down during the night, set two anchors, and have an anchor light that works.

In the way in which sea areas have their own characteristics, if you're going to get bounced by rough water crossing the Great Bahama Bank, it's highly likely that you'll meet this at the Northwest Channel Light and suffer it as you continue southeast. The Northeast Providence Channel particularly, which you cross to reach Nassau or Andros, is an area where confused seas are not unusual, a characteristic brought about by contrary tidal flows, the containment effect of two dead-ends of deep ocean that are trapped by shallow seas (the northwest salient of the Providence Channel and the Tongue of the Ocean), and wind, particularly Northers. Otherwise, like any shallow sea area, the Great Bahama Bank will kick up short, unpleasant seas when the wind hits 15 knots or so.

The tidal set across the Great Bahama Bank, like the set across its smaller twin to the north, is not the stuff of tidal atlases, but runs roughly northeast–southwest. Your autopilot may compensate for this or alternatively keep an eye on your cross track error and make continual adjustments, which will be needed both for tide and wind.

The Northwest Channel Light

The Northwest Channel Light is the focal point of all routes crossing the Great Bahama Bank. This buoy, 15 nm west of Chub Cay, marks the point at which you've crossed the Bank and have reached the inlet of deep water leading southeast directly into the Northeast Providence Channel. To be more accurate, the light is there to mark the start of a one-time more frequently used northwest Channel that crosses the Bank, but is now difficult to navigate and is not recommended as a cruising route. The Northwest Channel Light itself, at one time a handsome tower structure, suffered in an unfortunate dispute with a ship a few years ago. The remains of the tower can be plainly seen, and the present light is a red cone buoy to the immediate north of the original tower. Life isn't always fair, is it? The light, which got the worst of it, was in the right place.

As the Northwest Channel Light sets your exit point from the Great Bahama Bank, your options in route come at the start, and obviously where you choose to go once you've passed the Northwest Channel Light. Whether you choose to stop in Chub Cay or perhaps in Frazers Hog Cay, or go on to Nassau, or drop south to Andros is immaterial at the outset. Your route calculations hinge on the Northwest Channel Light waypoint.

Clearing In— Your Options in the Central Bahamas

If you didn't clear in at Bimini or Cat Cay, you still have plenty of options, some of them a long haul if you're prepared to stay away from land and keep your Q-flag flying. We'd guess that either Chub Cay or Nassau will be your choice.

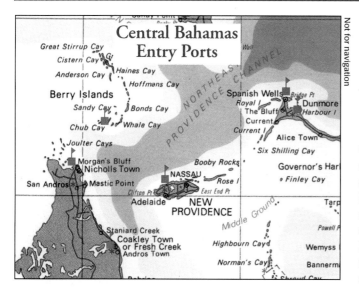

Not for navigation

Central Bahamas Entry Ports

This second shoal area lies north of the Northwest Channel Light and is marked by a buoy at its northwest corner. Your run brings you not far off the Northwest Channel Light.

- The third leg is a straight run due east to the Northwest Channel Light on 098°M for 3.84 nm.

Your total distance from North Rock to the Northwest Channel Light is 64.74 nm. You might find the thought of turning a Banks run, which could be achieved as a straight shot, into a three-leg passage (four legs or more if you add in going on after the Northwest Channel Light), a touch of navigational overkill. But if nothing else the changes in course relieve the monotony of a run across the Great Bahama Bank (there's nothing there, nothing to see) and might give you a sense of progress, other than just looking at your distance run or distance-to-run log.

The Routes Across the Great Bahama Bank

There are three major west–east routes to the Northwest Channel Light. We'll take these first, and cover the options that come after you pass the Northwest Channel Light later.

North Rock to the Northwest Channel Light

N Rock (1 nm N of Bank)	NROCK	25° 51' 00 N	079° 16' 30 W
Mackie Shoal (1 nm off Beacon)	MCKIE	25° 41' 30 N	078° 38' 30 W
NW Light Shoal	NWLSH	25° 29' 00 N	078° 14' 00 W
NW Channel Light (just NW)	NWCHL	25° 28' 45 N	078° 09' 45 W

If you want to bypass Bimini you can cross on to the Bank just north of North Rock, which lies to the north of North Bimini (your entry route here must also take you north of the Moselle Bank, which lies to the northwest of North Rock). There's nothing difficult in gaining the Bank this way, and you're set fair once you're in green water but you can't set a direct course for the Northwest Channel Light. Two shoal areas lie across what would be the straight-line track. There's also the wreck of a ship with just 3 feet of water, shown on the chart at 25° 47' 00 N 079° 06' 45 W, which lies to the south of our route by 0.75 nm. But watch and correct your XTE on the first leg. The first of the shoal areas, the Mackie Shoal, lies across your path at the 35-mile point, so you have to head a little more north than you might wish at the outset. Then you alter on to your second leg just northwest of the Mackie Shoal to aim off to clear the second shoal area.

- From North Rock to the Mackie Shoal area is 35.5 nm on a heading of 109°M.

- From Mackie Shoal to safely off the shoal by the Northwest Channel Light is 25.3 nm on 124°M.

Cat Cay to the Northwest Channel Light (through Gun Cay Cut)

Gun Cay (1.5 nm NW Cut)	GUNCW	25° 34' 15 N	079° 19' 30 W
Cat Cay (0.25 nm E of marina)	CATCE	25° 34' 00 N	079° 17' 00 W
NW Channel Light (just NW)	NWCHL	25° 28' 45 N	078° 09' 45 W

If you've come in through Bimini or Cat Cay, or just made these islands your Bahamian landfall, once you've passed through Gun Cay Cut on to the Bank you can set a straight course for the Northwest Channel Light. You can set a departure waypoint off Gun Cay but we believe Cat Cay (particularly when you reverse the course and are running east–west) makes the better departure and arrival waypoint, largely because of the shoals to the east of Gun Cay.

We give the Gulf Stream–side waypoint to the northwest of Gun Cay Cut as our landfall but this is for reference only. The 2.5 nm or so you run through Gun Cay Cut must be taken visually, favoring Gun Cay Point and running in the deep water parallel to the shoreline (to avoid the shoal and reef extending north from Cat Cay) until you are through the Cut and can see the entrance to Cat Cay Marina with its dwarf lighthouse. Using the two lights, Gun Cay and Cat Cay as markers, one ahead and one astern, head south until you are on the line of Latitude 25° 34' 00 N. Then turn east to pick up your departure waypoint. See **The Bimini Islands** under **Gun Cay Cut** on page 127 if you're in doubt about this passage on to the Bank. From Cat Cay to the Northwest Channel Light is 60.91 nm on a course of 099°M.

South Riding Rock to the Northwest Channel Light

S R Rock W (2 nm SW Castle Rk)	SRDRW	25° 13' 30 N	079° 11' 00 W
S R Rock E (1 nm S Castle Rk)	SRDRE	25° 13' 30 N	079° 08' 30 W
NW Channel Light (just NW)	NWCHL	25° 28' 45 N	078° 09' 45 W

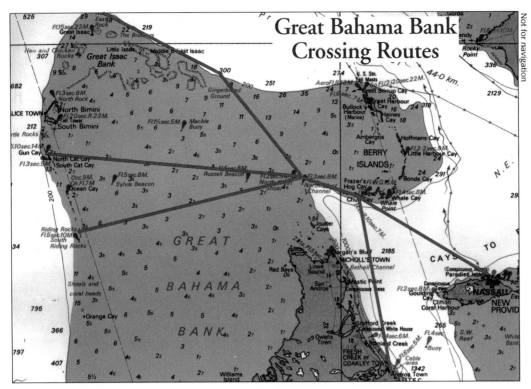

Great Bahama Bank Crossing Routes

have already cleared in, you may want to continue on a little way to Frazers Hog Cay, or to one of the Southern Berry Island anchorages. We give the waypoints to take you to Chub Cay here, and for the other Southern Berry options see page 144.

Nassau

The second option is to set a direct course for Nassau, which gives you a greater distance to run, but if you're heading for Spanish Wells and Eleuthera or the Exumas, and have the daylight in hand, going straight for Nassau may make sense.

Your first leg will be 47.44 nm on a heading of 123°M. Then a short run of 1.69 nm on a heading of 132°M lines you up with the entrance to Nassau Harbour. The distance to run from the Northwest Channel Light is 49.46 nm to the Nassau Harbour entrance.

Andros

If you're going to Andros, we suggest you go first to our waypoint 1 nm south of Chub Cay, and then set a course for your destination. It's a dogleg, but it's a safer route for it keeps you in deep water well away from the area of shoal, rocks, small cays, and reefs that lie to the north of Andros.

At the start you have 14.55 nm on a heading of 117°M to run to that Chub Cay waypoint. Then for Morgan's Bluff it's 12.82 nm on 202°M. For Bethel Channel and Nicholls Town it's 14.95 nm on 194°M. For Fresh Creek, to our mind the most likely destination, it's 40.25 nm on a heading of 172°M. Don't enter Andros waters at night unless you're set on calling your insurance agent the next morning.

Once again, if you have no interest in Cat Cay or Bimini you can pass on to the Bank just south of South Riding Rock. There are no problems gaining the Bank here, and you can set a direct course for the Northwest Channel Light, although we believe that you may find shallower-than-average water (perhaps as little as 6 feet in places) along this route. The 2.26 nm from the South Riding Rock west waypoint to the east waypoint must be taken visually, and the second waypoint is your departure point for the Great Bahama Bank crossing. The distance from this second waypoint to the Northwest Channel Light is 55.24 nm on a heading of 078°M.

Your Choice of Route

There's not a great deal of difference in the distance to run on all these routes, and your choice is bound to be set by your Florida departure port and whether or not you want to visit the Biminis, or overnight in Cat Cay. Don't forget too, if you've started calculating, that when you reach the Northwest Channel Light you still have at least 16 nm to run to get to Chub Cay, the closest of your destination options.

Options after the Northwest Channel Light

Chub Cay

Your first option and shortest leg (14.55 nm on a heading of 117°M) is to go to Chub Cay and clear in there. If you

NW Channel Light (just NW)	NWCHL	25° 28' 45 N	078° 09' 45 W
Chub Cay Entry Waypoint	CHUBC	25° 24' 15 N	077° 54' 50 W
Chub Cay (1 nm S)	CHUBS	25° 23' 15 N	077° 54' 50 W
Nassau Harbor NW (2 nm off)	NASNW	25° 06' 30 N	077° 23' 00 W
Nassau Harbor W (0.25 nm off)	NASHW	25° 05' 30 N	077° 21' 30 W
Morgans Bluff (2 nm E)	MRGNE	25° 11' 00 N	077° 59' 00 W
Bethel Channel (1.5 nm E)	BTHEL	25° 08' 30 N	077° 57' 30 W
Fresh Creek (1 nm E)	FRESH	24° 44' 00 N	077° 45' 00 W

Chapter 10
The Berry Islands
Great Stirrup Cay to Great Harbour Cay

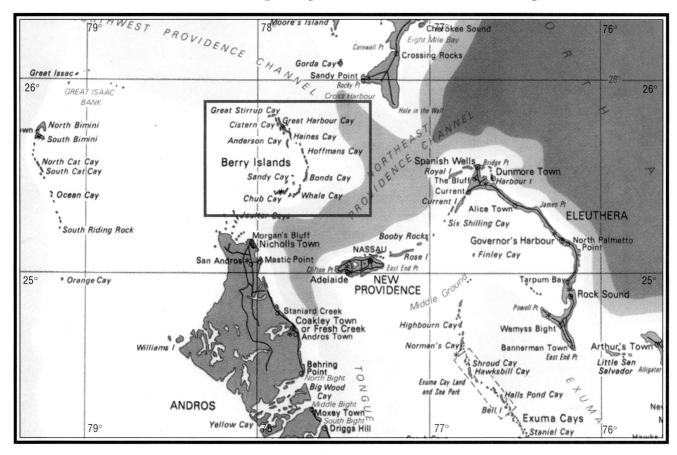

The Northern Berry Islands

WE'D suggest if you're bound for the Berry Islands from Palm Beach or anywhere north of Palm Beach that you head first for Grand Bahama, stage there, and cruise the Berrys starting in the north. If you're starting in Fort Lauderdale or Miami, go by way of Bimini or Cat Cay to Chub Cay, and do the Southern Berrys first. We reckon it's always sensible to keep your open-water passages as short as you can, and we always try to keep our passage making in daylight hours, if the distances work out. As we're covering the Bahamas from north to south, we'll deal with the route from Grand Bahama Island first. We'll cover the southern route to the Berry Islands later.

The Route from Grand Bahama Island

| Bell Channel (2 nm off) | BELCH | 26° 29' 53 N | 078° 37' 46 W |
| Little Stirrup Cay (0.5 nm off) | LSTRP | 25° 49' 30 N | 077° 57' 00 W |

Crossing the Northwest Providence Channel is a simple run of 54.56 nm on a heading of 142°M. Choose your weather, just as you do with every ocean crossing, and remember that you are passing through a major shipping lane. You'll have no problems in picking up both Great Stirrup Cay and Little Stirrup Cay from some 8 nm out. Once you are close to Little Stirrup Cay your navigation becomes, as it always is when making landfalls in the Bahamas, part GPS-dependent and part eyeball.

The Berry Island extension of the Great Bahama Bank, which lies to the west of the crescent of Berry Islands, is too shallow for anything other than shoal draft craft. If you're making for Great Harbour Cay Marina, you have to dogleg out to the west before turning in toward the harbor. If you are making for one of the Great Harbour anchorages you must work your way east around both Stirrup Cays, and enter the so-called "Great Harbour" between Great Stirrup Cay and the north tip of Great Harbour Cay.

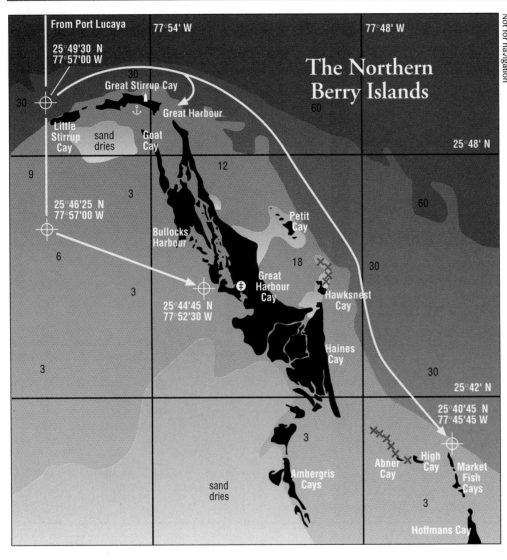

For the rest of the week the Royal Caribbean "Coco Cay" beach staff look after the island, its deserted bars and cafeteria, its water toys, and several hundred sun loungers. And yes, there were litter bins on that beach.

GREAT STIRRUP CAY

Great Stirrup Cay has also been claimed as private property, by the Norwegian Cruise Line, but you can go ashore and take the path that leads to the white painted Great Stirrup lighthouse in its grove of palm trees at the east end of the island. There's a small, not-very-good beach at Panton Cove, and we're sure no one would keep you from using it if you were anchored there. The cruise line recreation ground is Bertram Cove on the north coast, which would make a great anchorage as long as nothing was coming from the north or west, but it's small, a little tricky to enter, and has barely 6 feet in depth. Not being able to go there is no great loss to the cruising community.

At this point maybe we'd better make clear that Great Harbour (the sea area between Great Stirrup Cay and the north end of Great Harbour Cay) is no harbor at all. You can anchor there. It has some protection. But that's it. If you're after a real harbor in the Northern Berrys, there's only one, and that's Great Harbour Cay Marina on the west side of Great Harbour Cay (just about halfway down). Perhaps they should have cut down on the use of that name.

LITTLE STIRRUP CAY

Little Stirrup Cay, whose signs of habitation you may notice as you get closer to it (a white roof in the trees, and what appear to be litter bins on the west end beach as you round the point) is a Royal Caribbean Cruise Line playground. On Thursdays, Fridays, and Sundays the cruise ships deliver their passengers to Little Stirrup Cay for a day of swimming, volleyball, water sports, beach bar patronage, and buffet lunches. Everything is waiting for them, down to the glass-bottomed pedal boats and a First Aid station.

The Great Harbour Anchorages

PANTON COVE

Popularly there are reckoned to be three usable anchorages in the Great Harbour area. The first is Panton Cove, tucked up under the wing of the Great Stirrup lighthouse. It's shallow, 6 feet at best, and restricted by tiny little Snake Cay, which lies off the Great Stirrup Cay lighthouse dock. You can work your way in and lie there happily if you have shoal draft, otherwise you're forced to anchor further out, which can be rolly. You're protected from the north, but not much else. The holding around Panton Cove is not good, so check that anchor.

GOAT CAY

Goat Cay has good water, some 10 feet or more in places, off its east-facing side. This will shield you from the west, but otherwise you are in the open, exposed from all other directions.

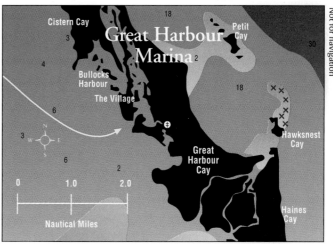

SLAUGHTER HARBOUR

Slaughter Harbour is the deeper pocket of water (some 6 feet) that lies immediately to the west of Great Stirrup Cay. We see no value in it as an anchorage. It's OK for a day visit, to snorkel and maybe gunkhole around a bit in your tender. The only valid approach is from the north, between the east end of Great Stirrup Cay and the west end of the rock wall that lies between the two Stirrup Cays. To try to approach from the south (the bank side) is shoal draft work at high tide and virtually impossible at low water.

Great Harbour Cay and Marina

Little Stirrup Cay (0.5 nm off)	LSTRP	25° 49' 30 N	077° 57' 00 W
West Marker Piling	WMARK	25° 46' 25 N	077° 57' 00 W
Great Harbour Approach	GHARB	25° 44' 45 N	077° 52' 30 W

If you are heading for Great Harbour Marina, once you're at our Little Stirrup Cay waypoint alter to a heading of 190°M

Wrecked fishing boat at 25° 48' 25 N 077° 55' 11 W, with only the pilot house showing.

and, watching the color of the water, run for about 3 nm to pick up what first appears to be a single piling, which is the outer mark of the approach in to Great Harbour Marina.

You may wonder what an apparently uncharted, isolated rock may be some 2 nm off on a bearing of around 115°M as you round Little Stirrup Cay. Closer it looks more like a swim platform, but you won't be going any nearer. It's the pilot house of a wrecked fishing boat lying in some 3 feet of water. The hull is mostly buried in sand. It's position, just in case you want to plot it, is 25° 48' 25 N 077° 55' 11 W.

Approach to Great Harbour Marina

When you get closer to the first Great Harbour Marina–approach piling, you'll see that it's not one but three pilings tied together with a flopped-over radar reflector (white and red, faded) fastened to them. You can just about forget GPS now. Change your heading to something like 115°M. This course points you toward the radio mast on Great Harbour Cay.

- You now have about 5.5 nm to run. In time you will start to pick up a well-spaced-out series of single piling marks. The first one (with no ID) comes up at 25° 45' 38 N 077° 54' 58 W (we haven't recorded this as a waypoint in our catalog for you shouldn't be using GPS on an approach like this, but in case you get a rainstorm blackout, here it is). Your course will adjust itself to around 125°M to fall in with the line of the posts, and the next one soon comes up, marked as red 4.

- There's a green 4, then a red/green BH marker, and always as a long-distance fail-safe, there's that radio mast. As you get closer to land you begin to realize that a headland must be masking the harbour entrance and that the houses you see off the port bow (with maybe an island trader there too) is the settlement with its government dock, which is *not* your destination. Next comes a red 8 and a red 10.

- Then you're at the point of turn into the cut leading to the harbor and you'll see that range markers have been set there, which you might have used if you could have seen them, red boards with white vertical stripes. Don't worry if you fail to pick them up on your approach. The vegetation conceals them, and their visibility, in terms of color, is zilch from any distance out.

Entering Great Harbour's real harbor is plain sailing, although we doubt you'll be sailing by then. It's a bit like going in to the fortifications the Spanish built to protect their treasure ships at Cartagena. First there's a narrow cut (where a swing bridge used to be) and then an inner harbor, where two Greens (14 and 15) and one Red (16) will swing you to starboard past the Fuel Dock (also to starboard).

You enter a second inner harbor. There's Red 18 with a "No Wake" caution and a post further ahead (no nav mark on it) again warning you "No Wake." There's no sign of a marina. Just past that second sign you turn to port into a third basin and the first docks are apparent, with town houses behind them. You're not there yet. Go on, and turn to starboard into a fourth final inner harbor where, with more town houses to port and the marina to starboard, you have reached Great Harbour Cay Marina.

Great Harbour Marina

The lineup of the Great Harbour Marina facilities sounds great, but the reality is that while the facilities there are adequate, they're hardly what you'd write home about. Showers and rest rooms (some locked and not available and some open) are adequate, the washing machines had been taken out of service when we were last there (apparently mortally sick) but may now have recovered, and there's shore power, water (and washdown water at a cheaper rate), a little store, and a liquor store (no wine).

A school in Bullocks Settlement.

One of the two restaurants (the Wharf) is open for breakfast and in the evenings (but not on Tuesdays). The circular restaurant you see as you enter the final harbor (the Tamboo) is open only on Wednesday and Saturday evenings, by reservation only, and serves as a kind of social club for the townhouse owners and visiting yacht people. There's a swimming pool by the marina, but its pool bar has been closed.

Long ago we decided that we had no desire to check out for real whether a harbor or an anchorage might be an adequate refuge come the *big* storm, and we don't intend to change that decision. It has occurred to us that Great Harbour Marina, given a spider's web of mooring lines and at least two anchors out as well, might be as good a hurricane hole as you could ever get. But what if you suffer a direct hit? Who can tell what might happen? I think if we were there at the wrong time we'd take all the precautions we've mentioned, check that we'd paid our last insurance premium, and fly out.

The near total protection of Great Harbour Marina does carry one disadvantage—there's almost no cooling breeze. By the time the sun has worked itself above the horizon, it's getting hot there. By noon, and in the afternoon, if you're hanging around your boat, you'll be close to heat stroke.

Great Harbour Cay and Cistern Cay

Nearly 6 nm long but hardly a mile wide, Great Harbour Cay is by geography and population (around the 1,000 mark) Top Dog in the Northern Berry Islands. It has an airstrip, regular service to Nassau, and the townhouses around the Marina plus a slowly growing number of vacation homes spell income for an island that has no resources other than conch taken from way out on the Great Bahama Bank.

The main settlement, "The Village" (sometimes identified incorrectly as Bullocks Harbour, which is to the south of Cistern Cay), lies just north of Great Harbour Marina and is a friendly, cheerful place with the Graveside Inn as its center of social entertainment. "You'll Come Alive at the Graveside Inn" the sign promises. The inn is, indeed, built at the very edge of the graveyard. Perhaps, if you're in Great Harbour Cay for Halloween you should try it.

Great Harbour Cay also bears the marks of a failed development, a hotel, and golf course on the spine of the island just to the east of the marina. The most attractive beaches lie on the east side (where all the new vacation home building is taking place), and Petit Cay offers an attractive anchorage if the wind is from the east, but otherwise is exposed. You can check it out from the Beach Club, a bar/restaurant built on the dunes due east from the marina (as the bird flies). The Beach Club itself, with a bar built around a massive cable drum, is rustic, showing signs of age, but attractive nonetheless and has good lunch snacks.

Getting around Great Harbour Cay is not easy. You can rent bicycles, dilapidated scooters, and maybe a jeep, but there are no taxis. There is a local bus, but you may never see it. We hitch hike. The walk from the marina to the beach bar, in the heat of the day, can make you wonder why you set out. If nothing else the necessary rehydration may double your bar bill.

Cistern Cay, which is almost a northwest extension of Great Harbour Cay, holds no particular attraction in cruising terms, nor does Lignum Vitae Cay to the north of Cistern Cay.

HAINES CAY, WATER CAY, AND MONEY CAY

Haines Cay (with a clutch of lesser islets, Anderson, Turner, and Kemp's Cays), as well as the slightly larger Water and Money Cays are fine for exploring in an inflatable or a Whaler, but are not a cruising ground.

THE AMBERGRIS CAYS, HIGH CAY, ABNER CAY, MARKET FISH CAYS

The Ambergris Cays, despite the attraction of their beaches, fall into the same category of being good for exploration with some good swimming, snorkeling, and maybe even fishing, but no place for a live-aboard boat. The sands and shallows around the Ambergris Cays, and Ambergris Rock to the south, are no-go territory if you need any kind of depth worth reckoning.

High Cay and Abner Cay offer nothing of interest, except maybe good fishing, and Market Fish Cays could be your start point for taking the west, Bank-side route down to Little Harbour Cay (which we cover under the next heading).

Moving on South from the Stirrup Cays

Moving on south down the Berry Islands (or coming north) there's only one safe route and that's to stand well out to the east of the Berry Island chain. From a start point off Great Stirrup Cay you want to gain and stay in deep water to clear Petit Cay, Hawksnest Cay, and Haine's Bluff as you head south. If you aim to keep about 1 nm offshore that's about right, or stay with the 30-foot depth contour.

Brenton Reef lies midway on a line from the south tip of Haines Cay to the north tip of Hoffmans Cay, so stand well clear of that. Watch out for a shoal that runs out from the north end of Hoffmans Cay, and there are offshore rocks halfway down it. There's a good anchorage behind White Cay, one of our favorites, which we'll cover in detail.

There is (as so often there is) a Bank-side route down (or up) the Berry Islands, but we're not attracted by it. These routes are rarely constant, for storms alter the lie of sandbanks and the nature of the cuts, and it would be misleading to pretend that we could offer useful guidance. If you want to try the inside route, either engage a local guide, or take it in stages, going ahead in your dinghy with a handheld GPS and a handheld depth sounder to prove each leg before you move.

This said, there's a "deep" water channel that will take you from the Market Fish Cays down the west, Bank-side of

Hoffmans, Devils, Little Harbour, and Comfort Cays. We bold that "and Comfort." There's no way you can pass, other than in your dinghy, between Little Harbour Cay and Comfort Cay. Your northern start point for the inside route, just above the northern Market Fish Cay, is 25° 40' 45 N 077° 45' 45 W. Then it's eyeball all the way, and stay in the blue water.

There's a point on this route (just to the north of Comfort Cay) where you can see the Darville settlement (with its skyline grove of tall tousle-headed palm trees) and beyond it, the abandoned house on the south point of Little Harbour Cay (also on the skyline, low and squat, like a fort) very clearly, and the temptation is to turn in between Comfort Cay and Little Harbour Cay. Don't do it. Keep to the west of Comfort Cay.

HOFFMANS CAY

Hoffmans Cay has a Blue Hole that you may wish to visit. It's easier to describe getting there from the south rather than the north, and if you use the White Cay an-

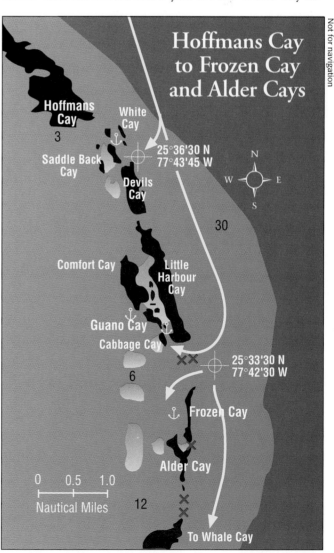

Not for navigation

chorage, that's how you'll be going.

Round the south tip of Hoffmans Cay and follow the west coast up. Miss the first beach you see, and go to the second, around a headland. Near the right end of the beach you'll find the start of a trail that takes you heading south into the bush. The trail climbs up over the spine of the headland and just about the time you're beginning to think you've volunteered for a jungle warfare course, the trail splits. The right fork goes to the first beach, the one you ignored. The left fork leads you almost immediately to the rim of the Blue Hole.

If you've been to Chichen Itza in Yucatan and seen the Sacred Well, the Hoffmans Cay Blue Hole carries much the same sense of shock when you first come on it. Suddenly you're right on the brim of this great sheer-sided hole, the water far below you, unfathomable but looking deep. At least in Hoffmans Cay there's no tradition of sacrificing living virgins, decked out in their best gold jewelry, by pushing them over the edge.

If you want to take the continuation of the trail that runs to your right along the rim of the hole, you'll find that within a few yards it takes you down under an overhang and you can reach the water there—and swim if you wish! Sacrificial virgins apart, it's said that someone once stocked the hole with just one grouper, but no one knows whether the fish found friends, died, or has survived in isolation. It could be, it just could be, that there's a world record giant grouper lurking there, if it found its new home agreeable!

THE WHITE CAY ANCHORAGE
Going down the outside route, after you pass the end of Hoffmans Cay you'll see a forbidding line of rock marking a low, pencil-like cay that fragments in rocks at its southern

tip. This is White Cay, and if you get in behind it, you'll find one of the most attractive anchorages in the Berrys.

First of all, ignore the gap north of White Cay. You want to go in the south gap, midway between the rocks at the south of White Cay and the north tip of Devils Cay (your turning point will be 25° 36' 30 N 077° 43' 45 W). As you turn you're on line for the south tip of Saddle Back Cay, which lies immediately behind White Cay. Beyond the south tip of Saddle Back, there's the south tip of another island lying behind Saddle Back. If you keep these two south tips in line as a rough transit, you won't go far wrong.

You'll have a good 18–24 feet of water, which will take you well inside. Once you come level with the sand of the beach on the north of Devils Cay, make a turn to starboard to head north between Saddle Back Cay and White Cay. The White Cay beach, roughly in the center of the cay, marks your anchorage. You'll find 12–18 feet of water there, and surprising depth close to the beach over sand. Otherwise it's grass all around. The beach itself, pure white sand backed with sea oats, is something to write home about. The anchorage is reasonably protected, but flanked as it is by two ocean passes, it can be rolly if the ocean is kicking up. Under those circumstances you wouldn't want to attempt running in there anyway. If wind and strong seas are running from the east, don't try it.

If you decide to travel on joining the inside route, you can do so here, or you can just pop round the corner to take in the Hoffmans Cay Blue Hole. In both cases go north around Saddle Back Cay. Don't even think of going around the south end—there's a reef running across there that acts like a doorstep. Not only is it too shallow for you to get over that sill, but the ocean water doesn't like it either. Any kind of sea running in results in tide race spoils and tide rips on the ocean side, and a powerful up-swelling over the reef that will vacuum the depth from under you one moment, and threaten you with a wall of water the next.

The cay beyond Saddle Back Cay whose south tip we suggested you might use as a transit has a pretty palm-backed beach in the middle. Obviously there are others who think so too, for we found a stone-built barbecue grill built in the little palm grove, and two crude deck chairs.

DEVILS CAY
We've found nothing of interest at Devils Cay.

COMFORT CAY AND LITTLE HARBOUR CAY
We take these two cays together as they are virtually joined at low water. The south end of Little Harbour Cay is shielded from the west by two further small cays, Guano in the north and Cabbage in the south. In the triangle formed by the Darville settlement on Little Harbour Cay, the north end of Cabbage Cay, and the southwest headland of Little

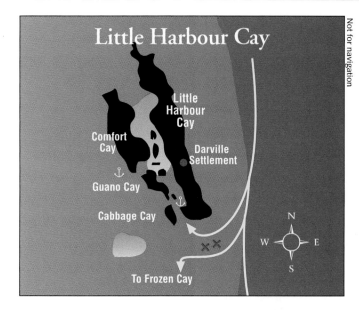

Harbour Cay lies the Little Harbour Cay anchorage.

If you are coming in from the ocean side, the cut between Little Harbour Cay and Frozen Cay is wide and deep, but there is one reef (which normally shows with breaking seas) mid-channel. Once you've got it, you can pass either side of it. We favor turning in on Latitude 25° 33' 30 N 077° 42' 30 W for this gives us the chance to check out the anchorage behind the north end of Frozen Cay as well as the Little Harbour Cay anchorage, and depending on the set of the swell, go for the better-protected one.

ANCHORAGES IN THE LITTLE HARBOUR CAY AREA

At first sight, particularly if you first see it at high water, the Little Harbour Cay anchorage looks the perfect place. Beware. Unless you are shoal draft there is only one place you can anchor and that is over the mid-channel sand patches level with the north end of Cabbage Cay. There's just room for two boats to anchor here, and you'll need to set two anchors because the tidal current is strong, runs north–south, and you will do a 180° swing every six hours. Dive your anchors and make sure they set, and if you're in doubt, dig them in by hand.

If you have shoal draft two further options are open to you. You can tuck yourself just under the tip of Guano Cay, or you can go on (but not at low water) and anchor off the Darville settlement, where you will have just enough depth to stay floating when the tide is out.

If all this is too daunting, you can anchor off the southwest tip of Comfort Cay. As there is a shoal area in your path as you come in from the ocean, two reassuring waypoints may help. These are first the narrow passage through the south Guano shoal area, which is 25° 34' 10 N 077° 44' 05 W, and second, the location of the anchorage,

which is 25° 34' 30 N 077° 44' 05 W. Of course if you're coming down the inside route you don't have to worry about that shoal area, at least until you head on south. Behind Comfort Cay you have plenty of sea room, and you can take your dinghy (which you would have had to do anyway) to get to Little Harbour Cay and the Darville settlement.

Although Frozen Cay falls in the Southern Berry Islands by our definition, it makes sense to note here that the anchorage lies on the east side behind the north tip of Frozen Cay (see chart on page 144). There are no problems getting there.

LITTLE HARBOUR CAY
AND THE DARVILLE SETTLEMENT

What's the attraction of Little Harbour? Well it's pretty much unfrequented, it's a good place to base yourself and go small-boat exploring, and Chester Darville's settlement, high on a spine of rock backed by the skyline of tousle-headed coconut palms we've already mentioned as a landmark, is worth visiting. You're welcome there for he runs a bar called Flo's Place (after his mother, Florence) and will serve meals too if you give him 3–4 hours warning.

There's nothing much unusual in this, but what is different is that the population of this settlement is just one family, with their hens and chickens, peacocks, sheep (some of whom must have had a goat or two in their ancestry), dogs, and cats. Talk to Chester about the hurricane that wiped everything off the island but the settlement his grandfather founded. Then sit outside, Kalik or one of his rum punches (regular or spicy) in hand, and watch the sunset.

Flo's Place, Chester Darville's settlement, Little Harbour Cay.

The Southern Berry Islands

HAVING started the Berry Islands as if you arrived there from Grand Bahama and ended the North ern Berrys with Little Harbour Cay, we start the Southern Berrys with Frozen and Alder Cays, which lie immediately to the south of Little Harbour Cay.

To the vessel arriving in Chub Cay directly from Florida, this may seem vexing, but a reverse treatment would equally disadvantage the cruising visitor arriving from the north. Patently to work in towards the center from each end of the Berry Island crescent would be absurd, so we continue the broad direction we set at the outset, to cover the Bahamas from north to south, and ensure that our approaches and fine detail, for want of a better word, are unisex.

The Southern Berrys have the distinction of being made up of some of the hottest property on the Bahamian market, and for this reason you could say that it's not the most hospitable cruising ground for the cruising yacht. Why? Out of the eight larger cays that form the major part of the Southern Berrys, six of them are private property. So unless you have island-owning friends, your "visit ashore program" may be limited. But on the plus side, yes, there are anchorages, the water colors are fantastic, the snorkeling is good, and, if you're fishing, the fish bite.

Frozen and Alder Cays

We treat Frozen and Alder Cays together for they are all but joined and share a near landlocked bight that might look, on the chart, like a great anchorage. It isn't. It's shallow inside, you may find 4 feet there at MLW if you're lucky, and it's mostly grass. There is one patch of sand. What's not so

Frozen and Alder Cays

Not for navigation

good is that the approach shoals rapidly the closer in you get, and if there's a swell running outside in the ocean, or strong wave action, it will be rolly inside there for you're exposed to surge over the barrier rocks linking the two cays, and exposed to wind from the east. We suggest you strike this off your possible anchorage list and settle for the anchorage we suggested in the last section, which lies on the Bank side behind the north tip of Frozen Cay. You have sea room there, and you can choose your depth. We've found 20 feet and 12 feet around 25° 32' 55 N 077° 43' 03 W. But check that anchor. The bottom is hard.

Both Frozen and Alder Cays are private. Frozen has undergone a major construction program, which if nothing else has given it two useful landmarks from the ocean side as you travel from north to south: a green-roofed building and then a blue-roofed building, both set in clumps of coconut palms.

Bond Cay and Little Whale Cay

Like Frozen and Alder, as well as Whale and Bird to come, these cays are in private hands, and this places quite a stretch of the Southern Berrys out of bounds on the land side. However there are two anchorages in the Bond Cay–Whale Cay gap area that you may want to use. We don't recommend taking the inside passage over the Bank, preferring (as we've said) to play safe on the ocean side. The ocean side does have hazards here, and you'll want to stay well out. Even if you are following the 30-foot depth contour, there are places where you may be caught short. Almost half way down Bond Cay a reef and shoal area suddenly reduce your depth to 16 feet around 25° 29' 12 N 077° 43' 04 W. Anticipate this and keep well offshore here. We reckon to stay out at least a mile, particularly if the set of wind and wave is pushing toward the shore.

The Bond Cay–Whale Cay Anchorages

If you're going to anchor in the Bond Cay–Little Whale Cay gap, you have the Sisters Rocks to take note of (they're easy to see) and a shoal area to the north of Little Whale Cay, which extends into the ocean. If you turn in at 25° 27' 15 N 077° 44' 15 W you should be well set for an anchorage that is more of a roadstead, in the old nautical sense, than a protected place. We wonder how such an open stretch of water gained the anchor symbol placed on the chart, for other than offering the right kind of depth and the sea room to accommodate a small armada, you're exposed to wind from every direction, as well as ocean swell.

But if the weather is kind, the Bond Cay–Whale Cay gap makes a good place to stop for a swim and lunch. Around 25° 27' 45 N 077° 46' 30 W we've found 12–18 feet of water, but you don't need coordinates to help you decide where to drop your hook. You have all the space you could wish for, and the depth, to settle anywhere you like.

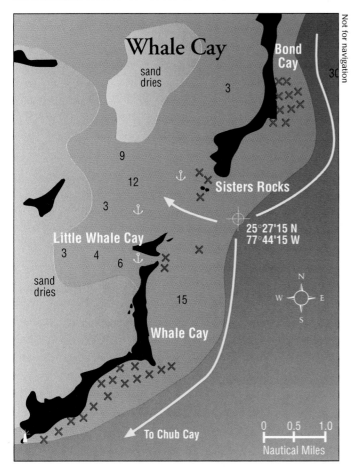

A second anchorage lies tucked between Little Whale Cay and the north tip of Whale Cay. This offers some protection from north and south, but little from the other directions, nothing from the east and southeast, and is still open to ocean surge. It has a measure of shoal ground and reef to negotiate whichever way you choose to approach it. The ocean way takes you between two reefs, keeping more north than south, holding closer to Little Whale Cay. If there's any kind of wave action or swell coming in from the ocean, you'll find breaking seas here and the approach, particularly at low water, is not attractive. Don't consider it. From the Bank you have 4 feet at the most in some areas, maybe less. Just go slow. Inside the anchorage you'll find 6–9 feet.

LITTLE WHALE CAY

Little Whale Cay, with virtually unlimited money lavished on it, looks good. A justifiable end, you might say, for the profits arising from the development of Freeport (for the developer of Freeport, Wallace Groves, took Little Whale Cay as his private kingdom). Just in case you need further identification, Little Whale Cay has a wind sock by its airstrip on the north end, and a truncated light house on the south end.

WHALE CAY

The ocean coast of Whale Cay is a potential nightmare with shoals and reefs extending off its two "elbows" where the lie of the island changes direction from north–south to southwest and then nearly west. The first elbow in particular has a singularly nasty shallow bight behind it. You're likely to run into it before you realize what's happening if you're not standing sufficiently far offshore. Your warning of the second elbow is a sand cliff fronting on the beach. Just stand well out at this point, keeping in 60 feet of water. When you reach the end of Whale Cay and Whale Cay light with Bird Cay ahead, your position will be something like 25° 23' 25 N 077° 48' 15 W.

BIRD CAY

Bird Cay is private. The ocean side has no particular horrors, so take a fairly straightforward run to clear its southwest tip, and then head for the southernmost point of Frazers Hog Cay. There's a potential anchorage just behind the southwest tip of Bird Cay (about 25° 23' 40 N 077° 50' 10 W places you there) with 10 feet of water, but from southeast to west it offers you no protection. If you have shoal draft you could creep further along the Bank-side coast of Bird Cay to escape the swells that can come around the corner, but Bird Cay doesn't rate on our list of anchorages. Like many other places, it's just somewhere you can drop your hook if the conditions that day are right.

Frazers Hog Cay and Chub Cay

The south headland of Frazers Hog Cay, known as Texaco Point, is a low-lying green whale of a mini-headland, which is hard to pick up from a distance. A waypoint of 25° 24' 05 N 077° 50' 50 W will place you just off it, ready to go up along the east coast of Frazers Hog Cay to anchor there, or to continue along the south coast of both Frazers Hog and Chub Cays if you're heading for Chub Cay Marina, or one of the two anchorages off Chub Cay.

Frazers Hog Cay Marina and Anchorage

If you want to anchor off Frazers Hog Cay, turn north at Texaco Point to parallel the east coast. You may not have anything more than 5 feet at the start, just off Texaco Point, but there is a channel there, and the popular anchorage has always been just off the shallow bight close to the north end of Frazers Hog Cay, which has 10 feet. We've never understood why this spot should carry any kind of fan club, for it has no protection from the northeast to southeast. Nonetheless it's been frequented for years now, certainly predating Chub Cay. Perhaps this alone fixed it on the charts as a stopping place. So many Bahamian anchorages are OK *if* the day you are there is right. Very few are all-weather havens.

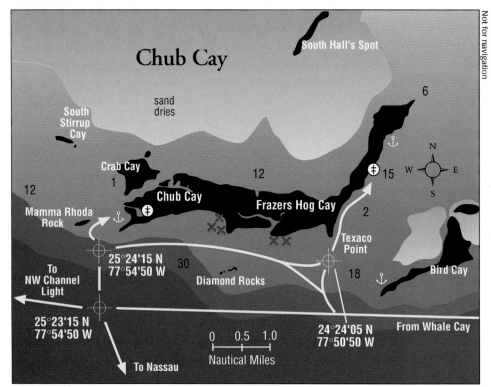

Cay begins, but it hardly matters. Watch for the very obvious Diamond Rocks to port. Ahead you'll have the barren Mamma Rhoda Rock and the Chub Cay light (like a black stake) on Chub Cay Point. The Chub Cay Marina masts and a water tower will be all too obvious. Your Chub Cay entry waypoint is 25° 24' 15 N 077° 54' 50 W, but you hardly need it because you should go visual. Go round Chub Point. An anchorage lies to starboard with 5–6 feet of water. Off your starboard bow you'll see the entry channel into the marina with its range marks. Be warned that we've found no more than 5 feet in patches in the approach channel and just 6 feet in the entry channel at low water. If you've failed to get hold of Chub Cay Marina on your way in, the reason is that they ignore Channel 16 and stay locked on Channel 68. Try it. The response time is rarely good, sometimes you draw a blank. If so, go ahead, enter, and see if you can attract attention.

If you want to anchor out away from the Chub Cay frontage, you have an alternative. Work your way past the Chub Cay entry into the channel between Crab Cay and Chub Cay. This is shallow, shoal draft stuff. We used to do this in our catamaran days when we were only drawing 2 feet 6 inches fully laden, but wouldn't think of it now with our 4-foot draft.

Chub Cay Marina

Chub Cay is at exactly the right geographic location to serve as a staging point for the Bahamas-bound boat coming from Florida to cruise in the Exumas, heading for Spanish Wells and Harbour Island, or content to remain in the Berry Islands. For the sports fisherman, intent on fishing the Northwest Providence Channel or the Tongue of the Ocean (between Andros and the Exumas Bank), Chub Cay couldn't be better placed. If you're sailing, Chub Cay comes at the limit of your daytime cruising range crossing the Great Bahama Bank. If you want to dive in the Bahamas, Chub Cay offers as wide a range of dive sites as the Bimini Islands. So Chub Cay, unusually, is one of the few places in the Bahamas where sailboats can sometimes outnumber visiting power boats, and the balance between trawlers and sports fishermen hangs on the season in the fishing calendar.

For all these reasons Chub Cay has modeled itself to serve

But all this said, a new boating facility called the Frazers Cay Club has opened just south of the Frazers Hog anchorage, based on a very handsome and well-restored old house that now welcomes you with an attractive bar and dining room, and rooms to let. The Frazers Club Marina boasts a single new T-dock with accommodation for ten boats, power and water, and by our count last time we were there, five mooring buoys. Both in 1996 and 1997 weather prevented us from getting in either to anchor off or use the new buoys or the dock, so our report is based on a visit by land. We have always heard that the channel off that coast is scoured and not good for anchoring, but now with the buoys and the new dock, we believe Frazers Hog Marina should be restored to your list as a valid option. Just think twice about the weather.

When we were last there the Frazers Cay Club was closed and the property apparently deserted. There were two boats on moorings, both local. No one appeared to be living on board.

We've been unable to contact the owner and get a definitive report on the status of the development, and the Chub Cay Bahamas Police detachment, who visit the property on their routine patrols, had no information. The owner was, they believed, in Florida.

Approaches to Chub Cay

Going along the south coast of Frazers Hog Cay and Chub Cay, it's hard to tell where Frazers Hog Cay ends and Chub

some four different communities. From an initial desire to be a club resort catering to those who would wish to build there and keep a private dock, Chub Cay has a membership, a member's side to the marina, and favored rates and some facilities to go along with their $1,500-a-year membership dues. The 130 or so members are primarily sports fishermen. Along with their members Chub Cay naturally attracts nonmember sports fishermen, and a stretch of dock space is reserved for them.

Chub Cay also caters to divers, who are accommodated in cabins on the non-member side of the marina, and it's this same side that has the berths for visiting boaters. The two transient docks extending out into the marina from the east side have no finger piers, so only the four slips alongside each T offer the facility of lying alongside. You have to come in having first figured out how you're going to get on and off your boat, over the bow or over the stern. Sailboats generally favor bow in and power boats, mostly, seem persuaded that stern first is best.

Chub Cay Marina has had its ups and downs, and like many places in the Bahamas, the attrition of climate alone, let alone severe storms, has made its effect felt. In 1992 Hurricane Andrew hit Chub Cay at the time when its material downslide was becoming critical, and providentially forced a reconstruction and modernization program that had become overdue. The recovery curve post-Andrew has been slow, but Chub Cay wins a Gold Star for what it has achieved to date. Dock power, once unstable and intermittent, is now working, as is cable TV. Shower and toilet facilities have been rebuilt (but we still consider the provision of just one toilet and one shower for the entire non-member side of the marina to be inadequate). The small

store is looking better than we've ever seen it, and the Harbor House restaurant, which you may use on your guest tab, has improved greatly in the last year.

Sadly, perhaps because of lax rules on holding tanks and a lack of shoreside facilities, the marina is polluted and urgently needs improved hydraulic engineering, perhaps a second channel, to help it self-cleanse and recover its natural state.

CRAB CAY AND SOUTH STIRRUP CAY

To the north and northwest of Chub Cay are Crab Cay and (to make the Berry Island crescent complete) a South Stirrup Cay. Neither of them hold particular interest.

THE MISSING CAYS

You'll note, checking your chart, that there are cays we've missed writing about. These are the mid-Bank cays in the Southern Berrys lying south of Latitude 25° 30′ N, the Fish and Samphire Cays, Cockroach Cay, and the Cormorant Cays. They're all there, accessible by tender or shoal draft boat with the right tide, but surrounded by barrier girdles of shoals and sand bores. They are not a cruising ground.

Approaches to the Southern Berrys

The Chub Cay Entry Route From Florida

NW Channel Light (just NW)	NWCHL	25° 28′ 45 N	078° 09′ 45 W
Chub Cay Entry Waypoint	CHUBC	25° 24′ 15 N	077° 54′ 50 W
Chub Cay (1 nm S)	CHUBS	25° 23′ 15 N	077° 54′ 50 W

Chub Cay is right on the Interstate connecting Florida with the Southern Berrys, Nassau, Spanish Wells and Harbour Island, and the Exumas as you swing past New Providence Island. Your route from Florida will first take you across the Gulf Stream to Bimini or Cat Cay, and then across the Great Bahama Bank to the Northwest Channel Light. As there may well be minor changes in your initial heading setting off across the Bank, we deal with these courses under **The Great Bahama Bank** on page 135. Here we'll just pick up the final legs.

From Northwest Channel Light, having stayed well clear (at least 200 feet) to the north of the new red buoy, you head 116°M for 14.47 nm, which will bring you 1 nm south of our Chubb Cay entry waypoint. You can identify Chub Cay some 8–7 nm out by its trees, golf ball water tower (on the left), and radio mast (on the right).

Once you've got to that Chub Cay south waypoint, go north on 005°M for that 1 nm, which brings you ready to enter Chub Cay Marina or ready to anchor off there. See **Frazers Hog Cay and Chub Cay** on page 145 for entry directions.

Sunset over Chub Cay.

Chub Cay To Nassau (New Providence Island)

Chub Cay Entry Waypoint	CHUBC	25° 24' 15 N	077° 54' 50 W
Chub Cay (1 nm S)	CHUBS	25° 23' 15 N	077° 54' 50 W
Nassau Harbour W (0.25 nm off)	NASHW	25° 05' 30 N	077° 21' 30 W

This is a simple route. At the outset run 1 nm south on a heading of 185°M to gain a reasonable offset from Chub Cay, and then turn to head 125°M for 34.99 nm, which will take you right to the entrance of Nassau Harbour.

At that point call Nassau Harbour Control on Channel 16 and request permission to enter the harbor area, giving them your destination.

Chub Cay To Andros

Chub Cay Entry Waypoint	CHUBC	25° 24' 15 N	077° 54' 50 W
Chub Cay (1 nm S)	CHUBS	25° 23' 15 N	077° 54' 50 W
Morgans Bluff (2 nm E)	MRGNE	25° 11' 00 N	077° 59' 00 W
Bethel Channel (1.5 nm E)	BTHEL	25° 08' 30 N	077° 57' 30 W
Fresh Creek (1 nm E)	FRESH	24° 44' 00 N	077° 45' 00 W

From Chub Cay down to Andros is a straightforward run from our waypoint 1 nm due south of Chub Cay. For Morgan's Bluff it's 12.82 nm on 202°M. For Bethel Channel and Nicholls Town it's 14.95 nm on 194°. For Fresh Creek, to our mind the most likely destination, it's 40.25 nm on a heading of 172°M.

Completing the Circuit—The West Side Route, Chub Cay to Great Harbour Cay

It remains to include one suggestion for those whose next destination after Chub Cay is Great Harbour Cay. Normally we would take the ocean route, going north outside the Berry Islands, to the east, and entering the Bank side by circling around Little Stirrup Cay. There's another way you can do it.

Essentially what you're doing is taking the Northwest Channel connecting the Northeast Providence Channel with the Northwest Providence Channel (look at your chart). You are circling around the west edge of the Berry Islands Bank to pick up the standard approach to Great Harbour Marina just southwest of Little Stirrup Cay. From Chub Cay you have six legs to complete before you are set to take the Great Harbour Cay Marina approach channel.

LEGS 1 AND 2

Chub Cay Entry Waypoint	CHUBC	25° 24' 15 N	077° 54' 50 W
Chub Cay (1 nm S)	CHUBS	25° 23' 15 N	077° 54' 50 W
NW Channel Light (just NW)	NWCHL	25° 28' 45 N	078° 09' 45 W

First, from your Chub Cay entry waypoint head 1 nm south on 185°M to gain an offing. Then turn for the Northwest Channel Light on a heading of 297°M, and you'll have 14.55 nm to run. Pass at least 200 feet north of Northwest Channel Light.

LEG 3

| NW Channel Light (just NW) | NWCHL | 25° 28' 45 N | 078° 09' 45 W |
| SW edge of the Berry Bank | SWEBB | 25° 30' 15 N | 078° 10' 30 W |

Your course will be 341°M and you'll have 1.65 nm to run.

LEG 4

| SW edge of the Berry Bank | SWEBB | 25° 30' 15 N | 078° 10' 30 W |
| NE edge of the Bahama Bank | NWBAB | 25° 40' 00 N | 078° 10' 30 W |

You are heading due north on 005°M with 9.75 nm to run.

LEGS 5 AND 6

NE edge of the Bahama Bank	NWBAB	25° 40' 00 N	078° 10' 30 W
1 nm W of W. Marker Piling	WMAW1	25° 46' 25 N	077° 58' 00 W
West Marker Piling	WMARK	25° 46' 25 N	077° 57' 00 W

You have a straight shot of 12.96 nm on a course of 065°M to get on the latitude of the first approach marker to Great Harbour Cay Marina. It should come up 1 nm to the east. Take that 1 nm to the marker (in fact it's 0.90 nm) on 095°M.

From then on go visual, following the directions we give in **The Northern Berry Islands** under **The Approach to Great Harbour Marina** on page 139. This route gives you a total of 40.91 nm to that first marker, where you have about 5.5 nm to run. A total of 46.41 nm in all. You may have saved perhaps 10 nm by not going up the east-coast ocean route of the Berrys.

WARNING

Be warned that this alternative over the Bahama Bank is a route that takes you over shallow and largely uncharted water, particularly in the sea area around the Northwest Channel Light. The only certain factor is that each year the nature of the depths will change as sands move. You should plan to negotiate the shallowest section around the Northwest Channel Light and the start of the Northwest Channel at High Tide. Our waypoints are there to help you set your courses, but are no guarantee of a safe route.

Good Samaritan? Think Twice Before You Act

THIS is a cautionary tale. Of course you've studied the navigation rules and know that the master or individual in charge of a vessel has a duty to provide assistance at sea to anyone requiring assistance in an emergency. None of us would fail to respond to a distress signal but, maybe unnecessarily, the law makes it quite clear that it's an offense under Section 2304 of the International Navigation Rules and Regulations not to do so.

We were on *Dolphin Voyager* on passage from Bimini to Chub Cay. By 1430 we were just 1 nm north of the Northwest Channel marker, and altered course for Chub Cay. The wind was northwest, 10–12 knots, with 2–3 foot waves. The wind had been increasing during the day, and the first white horses were beginning to speckle the green waters of the Great Bahama Bank. We'd overtaken a sailboat about an hour before and a sports fisherman had torn past us at something over 20 knots in the last half hour, but both vessels were out of sight. We were alone, but for a speck, probably an open boat, about a mile off on our port bow. Someone fishing, we guessed, on the edge of the Bank, maybe along the 3-fathom line. The deep water of the Northwest Channel, about 500 fathoms around there, plunging to twice that depth just 4 nm south of Chub Cay, makes for good fishing in that area.

As we drew closer to the boat we saw it was an open boat, apparently anchored, with two men in it. One of them started waving his arms up and down, then to make his signal more clear, took his white T-shirt off to use it as a distress flag. I altered to swing around toward the boat, which was about a quarter of a mile off, and called on Channel 16.

"White open boat waving. This is *Dolphin Voyager*, the blue-hulled power boat heading toward you. What's your problem? Over."

To my surprise we got an answer and also to my surprise it was "Will you go to 68?"

"*Dolphin Voyager* 68"

We made contact again. "This is *Dolphin Voyager*. OK what is it?"

"We've run out of fuel. Can you tow us in to Chub Cay?"

By then we were close enough to forget the radio contact and talk normally. The boat was a new-looking white Manta 28 with twin outboards, two men on board, both Bahamian. One of them was forward pulling up their anchor. Their anchor rode, if that was the proposed tow line, looked totally inadequate. I had no line capable of taking in tow a boat that was within eight feet of our own length. Clearly we weren't going to solve the problem within minutes, and circling the open boat at a safe distance was taking all my attention. The immediate answer was to anchor and drop back close to them. I did that.

Towing was out. No question of that. What about fuel? They had twin Yamaha 175s on the back. I had two 6 gallon tanks, pre-mixed 100:1, for my own outboard, coincidentally also a Yamaha. That should be more than enough for them with just 15 miles to run to Chub Cay.

"I'll pass you my tanks for my outboard. You give them back to me at Chub Cay, and pay for the fuel you've used. OK? And go easy getting there. I'll be on hand if you run out or anything goes wrong."

It was OK. They'd stay with me.

We pulled our hook up, I maneuvered alongside them, and Janet passed our tanks across. We stood off as they connected the tanks or transferred our fuel to theirs, and pulled up their anchor. Their engines started, we both swung round 180° out of the weather, and set off. They accelerated to 25 knots + and were away as if their tails were on fire. By the time we reached Chub Cay roughly an hour later they had long disappeared out of sight.

The dockmaster had not seen them, nor did he know who they might have been. Chub Cay office were unable to help. By nightfall there was no sign of them. We reported the incident to the police.

"You had no option. You had to do what you did. But I don't think we'll find them. They were not from here. Maybe Andros, maybe Nassau. I'll ask around. And I too don't think they were fishing."

We'd expressed the first of our doubts. The boat was too new, too snazzy, too well engined, too expensive, and too fast to be a fishing boat. And it had none of the confusion of marker buoys, line, pots, net, and rods on board that characterizes most Bahamian fishing craft.

More doubts crept in as we talked about it. No name on the boat that either of us could remember seeing, and no registration.

"Could we recognize the men if we saw them again?"

Oh yes. Janet could. Certainly one of them, with a cast in one eye and an earring. I'd been too preoccupied with station keeping to pay attention to either the men or their boat. Maybe, if we'd had calm seas it might have been different. I think then I'd have taken my fuel cans back while we were still out there. But there it was.

The moral of this cautionary tale? I'm not sure, for preaching is not in my line. Let me tell what I will do next time, if this kind of incident comes our way again.

(1) Stand off until I have a positive ID of the boat, size, color, make, engines, name, and registration. And photographs of the boat, and the crew on board.

(2) If it's a simple fuel situation, as this one was, and a source of fuel is only something like an hour away and the weather is not going to get significantly worse in the next two hours, tell them that I'll call for assistance; and that they are to stay where they are.

(3) If on the other hand the weather is worsening, and there is a real threat, then I'll do as I have done. But I'll take close-up photos too, ask for names and ID (which could be false, I know) and make sure, one way or another, that those who benefit from my Good Samaritan act have every reason to believe my boathook is firmly planted in their backs, trust is not a word that comes into it, and I'm not going to let go of that boathook handle.

YELLOW PAGES

GREAT HARBOUR CAY

BASRA in GREAT HARBOUR VHF 16

The Berry Islands are not well served in terms of marinas, and anchorages are the name of the game throughout the entire run of the islands. In the south, Chub Cay has long been recognized as a vital waypoint on the route between Bimini and Nassau. The only other Berry Island marina is *Great Harbour Cay Marina*. This is well located as a transit point between the northern and central cruising grounds, and is well placed as a base for boats wishing to cruise the Berry Islands. There is a superb, seven-mile long beach, with easy accessibility and glorious water colors, as well as some very good shelling. Great Harbour Cay is a Port of Entry, with **Customs** and **Immigration** located at the airport. The dockmaster, Rufus, will help you clear in.

MARINA

GREAT HARBOUR CAY MARINA
Tel: 242-367-8838 • Fax: 367-8115 • VHF 68

This is a friendly marina, well protected by the high ground around it. The glorious beaches and babysitting services offered make it a good choice for those traveling with young children. The neighboring settlement of Bullock's Harbour, with its small stores, a charming little school, and some unexpected sheep, is worth a visit.

Slips	80
Max LOA	110 ft.
MLW at dock	8 ft.
Dockage	$1 per ft. per day
Power	$9 per day up to 30 ft., boats over 30 ft. $15 per day for 110V, $20 per day for 220V.
Fuel	Diesel and gasoline at the fuel dock, open 8–12 am Monday to Saturday, 1:30–4:30 pm on Sundays.
Water	$10 per day for well water (not metered), 20¢ per gallon for reverse osmosis water, (metered).
Telephones	By the marina office, and next to *The Wharf.*
TV	Cable TV hookup available for $5 a day.
Showers	Yes, but in need of repair.
Laundry	Not working
Groceries	*Great Harbour Marina Store,* open from 8 am to 7 pm.
Ice	Yes
Mail	You can buy stamps from the marina store; the mailbox is outside.
Accommodations	*Great Harbour Cay Yacht Club* Beach villas and two-bedroom waterfront townhouses.
Restaurants	*The Wharf,* open for breakfast and dinner every day except Tuesdays. *The Tamboo,* open on Wednesday and Saturdays for dinner; reservations required.
Bar	*The Pool Bar* was closed when we were there.
Golf	The golf course has become overgrown since the closure of the adjacent hotel.
Rentals	Bicycles, cars, small boats, fishing charters, fishing and snorkel guides.
Services	Maid service and babysitting available.
Library	Books can be exchanged in the marina office.
Credit cards	Visa, MasterCard and Amex

SERVICES AROUND GREAT HARBOUR

Church
Church of God Prophecy
Clinic
Government Clinic   Tel: 367-8400   This clinic has a nurse.
Groceries
Great Harbour Marina Store Open 8 am to 7 pm. Water, bread, fresh fruit, vegetables, groceries, pharmacy, souvenirs, T-shirts.
Roberts Enterprises Open from 7:30 am to 5:30 pm, Monday to Saturday, and from 7:30 am to 10 am on Sundays.
Dean Enterprises Features a takeout restaurant called *Until Then,* as well as groceries and household supplies.
Police
Tel: 367-8344   In Bullock's Harbour, opposite the school.
Shopping
Lilly's Boutique at the airport   T-shirts and souvenirs, with silk-screening done on the premises.

RESTAURANTS AND BARS

Backside Lounge and Disco Enjoy the sunset, with cocktails and dancing, and a DJ on Thursdays, Fridays, and Saturdays.
Coolie Mae's Catering and Take A Way   Homemade foods, fresh-baked bread, and desserts.
Grace's Ice Cream Parlour Ice cream, hot dogs, coffee, and candy.
The Graveside Inn Tel: 367-8466   Open for dinner. This is the number-one spot in Bullocks Harbour, overlooking a cemetery, and serving good Bahamian food, especially conch.
Mama and Papa T's Beach Club Open for breakfast, lunch, and cocktails. Closed Sundays. Run by Mama and Papa T; snack foods and hamburgers on the beach, with a fantastic view.
The Tamboo Dinner Club at the *Great Harbour Cay Yacht Club* Open Wednesday & Saturday for dinner; reservations required.
Waterside Bar, Restaurant and Liquor Store Tel: 367-8244 In the village at Bullocks Harbour. This is a very friendly place, with dancing on weekends, and reasonable prices.
Wharf Restaurant and Bar, at the *Great Harbour Cay Yacht Club* Open for breakfast from 7 am to 12 pm, and for dinner from 4 pm to 11 pm. Closed on Tuesdays. Beautifully painted inside, with satellite TV and a good Bahamian/American menu.

ACCOMMODATIONS

Great Harbour Cay Yacht Club and Marina Tel: 242-367-8838 Marina townhouses from $180 per night; beach villas from $90 to $350 per night.

GETTING AROUND

Airlines
Falcon Air Flies to and from Nassau daily. Charter flights also use the airport.
Bicycles, Cars, and Motorcycles
Happy People Rentals Next to the marina. Will rent you a jeep, bicycles ($15 per day), a motorcycle, snorkel equipment, boat, dive and golf equipment, and can arrange fishing charters.
Ferry
Bahama Rama Mama at the Government dock.   VHF 16
Taxi
The Dockmaster will call one for you. An island tour costs about $20.

FISHING TOURNAMENTS

May
What's Out There? Great Harbour Cay Fishing Tournament

THINGS TO DO
IN GREAT HARBOUR CAY

- Fix a picnic on Petit Cay, but somehow you've got to get there!
- Take your dinghy north, up the Banks side of Great Harbour Cay, and visit Great Stirrup Cay Lighthouse.
- Head south and go fishing off the Market Fish Cays.
- If the Petit Cay picnic fails, just settle for a hamburger and a Kalik at the *Beach Club*.
- Or, you could swap ghost stories at the *Graveside Inn*?

BAHAMAS · 40c

Lace Short-Frond Murex · Murex brevifrons

LITTLE HARBOUR

Flo's Conch Bar and Restaurant welcomes you as you drop the hook in Little Harbour. Chester Darville and his family are the sole survivors of the Little Harbour settlement, which was devastated by Hurricane Andrew in 1992. The food is cooked and prepared by Chester's mother, Florence, after whom the restaurant is named. Dinner requests should be sent in on VHF 68 by 3 pm. Fresh bread is available to order for $3 a loaf.

Why have we chosen Little Harbour for one of our Yellow Pages when all that's there is just one house, one family, a bar, and a small restaurant? It's true. There is nothing else. We could have scooped it up in the main text and forgotten about a Little Harbour Yellow Page entry.

We do it as a way of highlighting just one small family venture out of the many in the Bahamas who have made countless cruising visitors welcome over the years. Of course they earn their living that way, but the greeting and hospitality are the same, whether you have come to pass the time of day, have just one drink, or an evening meal. It is people like the Darvilles who are the Bahamas, and who are the reality behind our Yellow Pages. This single entry is done deliberately as a reminder of this, and as a tribute to them all.

THINGS TO DO IN LITTLE HARBOUR

- Join up with anyone else anchored off Little Harbour, and enjoy a delicious Bahamian meal cooked by Florence.
- Get acquainted with some of their animals.

CHUB CAY

BASRA in CHUB CAY VHF 68

The whole island centers around the Chub Cay Club, which was badly damaged by Hurricane Andrew, but has been well restored and improved with many new facilities added. It makes a convenient overnight stop if you have just crossed the Great Bahama Bank from Bimini or Cat Cay, and are on your way to Nassau or Andros. There are lovely beaches within walking distance of the marina, and some wonderful ones you can visit with your dinghy on nearby Crab Cay.

At this time, charges differ greatly between members and non-members in both the resort and the marina, though the staff are equally friendly and helpful. Prices quoted are for non-members. **Customs** and **Immigration** are available 9 am to 5 pm, Monday to Saturday, located at the airport. Dockmaster Gerreth Roberts will help you contact them. There is a $25 charge if you take a slip in order to clear customs, but this will be credited to your bill if you stay overnight.

MARINAS

CHUB CAY CLUB MARINA
Tel: 242-325-1490 • Fax: 322-5199 • VHF 68

Slips	60
Max LOA	110 ft.
MLW at dock	7 ft.
Entry Channel	6 ft. at low water
Dockage	$1 per ft. per day, plus 8 percent tax
Long-term	Dockage from $620 to $1,000 per month
Power	35¢ per kWh, 50A and 30A available
Fuel	Diesel and gasoline
Water	35¢ per gallon
Telephones	Batelco card phones by the marina office, members' showers, the police station, and *The Island Shoppe*. There is also a pay phone outside the members' showers.
Showers	Separate facilities for members and non-members; only two toilets and showers for non-members.
Laundry	Washers and dryers, both sides of the marina; non-members $1.25 in quarters for each machine.
Ice	Yes
Restaurant & Bars	*Harbour House Restaurant* serves breakfast 7 to 9 am, lunch noon to 2 pm, and dinner 7 to 9 pm. The large, pleasant dining room is reserved for members, with a smaller section for non-members, though the food is excellent and the service is good in both. The bar is shared by everyone. *The Cay Bar* is a small, thatched palm bar by the marina swimming pool, open in the afternoons and early evenings.
Mail	Reception will send mail for you.
Fax	Reception will send and accept faxes for you. $7 to send one page within the Bahamas.
Accommodations	*Chub Cay Club* has Yacht Club rooms from $110 per day, and villas from $400 per day, with a special discount for members.
Credit Cards	Visa, MasterCard, and Amex
Dockmaster	Gerreth Roberts

SERVICES, SHOPPING, & SPORTS

Church
Chub Cay Chapel

Diving
Bahama Island Adventures Within the marina, but they have no rental equipment. $50 for a two-tank dive.

Fishing
This is the closest marina to the Tongue of the Ocean, and a very popular fishing center.

Groceries and Gifts
The Island Shoppe Open 9 am to 1 pm and 2:30 to 5:30 pm, Monday to Saturday. Small supply of groceries, liquor, and pharmacy goods, and a selection of gifts and logo items. They've had no bottled water when we've been there.

Police
The police station is behind *The Island Shoppe*.

Swimming
The pool by the marina is available to guests on visiting boats.

Tennis
There are tennis courts at the *Chub Cay Club*.

FRAZER'S CAY CLUB
VHF 16

This is a smaller, newer marina, with five mooring buoys on the northeast side of the island. When we visited *Frazer's Cay Club* the owner was absent coping with legal problems, the place was shut up and unoccupied, and we couldn't find out about future plans. There is no fuel dock, but it does have a recently restored charming clubhouse on a magnificent site, facing east toward Bird Cay. The anchorage would be exposed to anything other than a west wind, but if the weather is favorable it would certainly suit those who prefer to avoid the crowd scene of the *Chub Cay Club*. We suggest you call them on VHF 16 before going in, just to check that there is someone there.

Berths	10
Moorings	5
Max LOA	120 ft. on the T-dock
MLW at dock	7 ft.
Power	50A and 30A on the dock
Water	Available on the dock

GETTING AROUND

Airport
A 5,000 ft. runway, about a mile from the *Chub Cay Club*.

Airlines
Island Express Tel: 954-359-0380 Flights to Fort Lauderdale.
Miami Air Charter/Southern Pride Tel: 954-938-8991 Flights to Fort Lauderdale Executive Airport.

Bicycles
10 bicycles available to rent from *Chub Cay Club* for $15 per day.

Bus
The *Chub Cay Club* minibus will take you over to the airport, or within the Club area.

FISHING TOURNAMENTS

March and April
Member/Guest Billfish Tournament
Bahamas Billfish Championship

July
All Billfish Classic
Blue Marlin Tournament

THINGS TO DO IN CHUB CAY

- Go gunkholing looking for shells between Chub Cay and Crab Cay.
- Fish along the 100-fathom line up to Rum Cay (the Berry Islands' Rum Cay!), which lies halfway to the Northwest Channel light.
- Dive *Mamma Rhoda Rock* or *Chub Cay Wall*.
- Take your dinghy and explore South Stirrup Cay.
- Relax and enjoy the beaches before moving on to Nassau, the Exumas, or Spanish Wells, or as you wait for weather before crossing the Great Bahama Bank.

Chapter 11
Nassau and New Providence Island

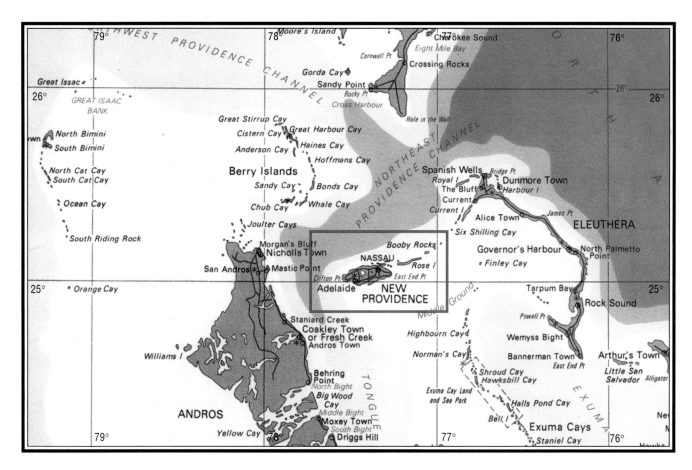

Nassau

NASSAU, capital and most highly populated city of the Bahamas as it is, dominates New Providence Island to the extent that New Providence Island has virtually lost its separate identity and its own name. Today when you speak of Nassau, you mean the whole island. If you mention New Providence, often you'll get blank stares. Nonetheless, we'll touch on New Providence Island, but only briefly, for Nassau (with Paradise Island included) is everything. For the cruising sailor, unless you're visiting friends living further afield in the island, it's going to be Nassau or nothing.

This is a cruising guide, not a travel guide. If we were to write about Nassau, like any city, let alone the capital of even a small nation, adequate coverage could run for pages, or form a book in its own right. We'll restrict ourselves to an overview. If you're going to spend time there, buy a set of guidebooks off the travel shelves.

New Providence Island is 27 miles long by 7 miles wide, taken as a rough measurement, and you can say that the eastern half, from Cable Beach to the quaintly named

McPherson's Bend in the Eastern Road, is the urban area we call Nassau. Some 162,000 people live there. They own 85,000 motor vehicles, and use this almost incredible number of cars on a road system inherited from the British, 90 percent of which is still 1950s in form and barely adequate for 20 percent of this traffic load. Be aware right at the outset that if you need to get around Nassau in a hurry, or get to the International Airport with any degree of urgency, you won't make it in the rush hours. Nassau becomes gridlocked.

You'll find most things you need in Nassau, sometimes after a lot of legwork, but there are extraordinary, unexpected stock deficiencies and temporary shortages. If you're in urgent need of some replacement part, Miami, Fort Lauderdale, and Palm Beach are only an hour away by air and served by almost hourly flights.

If you appreciate at the outset that Nassau is not your town, not there to serve you, the cruising sailor, you'll have made a sensible start. It's a tourist mecca both on the land side with its resort hotel complexes that are as close to being self-sufficient kingdoms as you can get, and it's the "Grand Central Station" for many cruise lines. When you're talking of cruise line days, with maybe ten cruise ships in port, and you know that the big ones carry close to 3,000 passengers and a crew of a thousand, you begin to understand Nassau, and quickly learn to live with (or rarely visit) Bay Street and the downtown area.

Where might you go? Well for a start don't choose a cruise ship day, but see the historic parts of Nassau if you've never been there before. Go to Paradise Island and see the Cloister and the Versailles Garden. See the Atlantis Resort simply for its artificial reef and interlocking pools and waterways. Don't wander around the back streets of Nassau at night. There is a high crime rate, and Nassau has endemic violent crime (which may be drug related), not just petty crime. Be sensible, street-smart as you would be in any city, and don't go around looking like a walking advertisement for Colombian emeralds.

Ocean Approaches

One look at the chart (below) will tell you that Nassau is well favored by its ocean approaches, and the reason it became the principal seaport and capital of the Bahamas is immediately obvious. Two great deep ocean marine highways meet off the north coast of New Providence Island, the Northwest Providence Channel connecting to the Florida Strait and the Northeast Providence Channel connecting to the open Atlantic. To the south the whole run of the Exumas and the Out Islands slanting down to the southeast serve as waypoints on the maritime highway to the Caribbean.

In approaching Nassau from the north, there are essentially no problems. From any other direction you have a Bank approach and that means you must choose your course. But that done, you'll have plenty of water all the way. The one less-than-hospitable area in terms of depth is the south, which is for the most part too shallow for coastal cruising. Just avoid it.

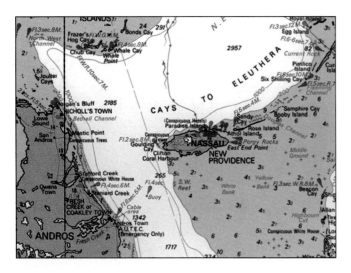

West Harbour Entrance Lighthouse.

Nassau Harbour (Western Entrance)

Nassau Harbour W (0.25 nm off) NASHW	25° 05' 30 N	077° 21' 30 W

This waypoint places you right off the entrance to Nassau Harbour, within sight of the first entry buoys. As you clear the entry breakwater you should call Nassau Harbour Control on Channel 16 and request permission to enter the harbor area, giving them your destination.

The waypoint we give is the start of the standard western approach into Nassau Harbour, between the west tip of Paradise Island (with its lighthouse) and the line of Long Cay, Silver Cay, and the Silver Cay breakwater, which will be on your starboard side. The entrance is well marked with entry buoys, and as you carry on into the harbor you'll see the massive cruise ship berths of Prince George Wharf ahead to starboard, and beyond, the unmistakable elliptical span of Paradise Island Bridge.

As you make your way into Nassau Harbour at first there's nothing for you to do but look at the sights until you've passed Potters Cay (where the local traders, fishermen, and mail boats tie up) and passed under Paradise Island bridge, with the roadway 70 feet over your head at high tide. Then you head for your marina or chosen anchorage.

AN ALTERNATIVE APPROACH FROM THE WEST

There is an alternative oddball approach into Nassau Harbour from the west. If you've hugged the north coast coming in from the west you'll arrive (on Longitude 077° 26' 00 W) off Delaporte Point. Ahead of you to starboard will be the towering lilac-pink extravagance of the massive Cable Bay hotels, and to port will be one small island, North Cay. On your bow you'll see the white Coral World underwater observation tower (a contradiction in terms there) with its flared base, and, yes, would you believe it, an elliptical bridge linking Coral Island (or Silver Cay) with Arawak Cay, the main commercial dock area.

The double-take is that the Arawak-Silver bridge is a mini look-alike of the Paradise Island bridge. Look hard. No, the white Coral World tower is **not** Paradise Island light. The bridge in front of you is **not** its big cousin, and Arawak Cay is **not** where the cruise ships tie up. But once you've got this all straightened out, you could go on into Nassau Harbour this way.

Nassau Marinas

Your choice of destination is likely to be one of three marinas:

HURRICANE HOLE

Hurricane Hole comes up first, to port, almost tucked under the bridge. Hurricane Hole has made its reputation meeting the needs of the mega-yacht fraternity, and hardly surprisingly its predilection (with somewhat limited space) lies with large white hulls and serious length. That's not to say you'll be turned from the door if they have room for you.

Once there you may find that Hurricane Hole is the heart's delight with the Atlantis Resort and its imitation reef, the white sand of Cabbage Beach, and the Versailles Garden all within walking distance, and there's no doubt that Paradise Island is a great deal more pleasant as a background setting than East Bay street on the other side of the harbor. Against this you are separated by that great span of bridge from mainland Nassau, its marine stores, the Bay Street heartland, and Nassau's historic sights.

NASSAU YACHT HAVEN

The Nassau Yacht Haven comes up almost as immediately to starboard. It has everything that you'd expect, including

> ## WARNING
> ### Charts and Nassau Harbour
>
> Most of the charts showing Nassau Harbour currently on the market are out of date. Harbor development that has taken place over the last ten years is not shown. In particular Potters Cay is still shown as an island with only the central portion "squared off" as dock (the whole is now developed), the bridge connecting Silver Cay and the commercial Arawak Cay is not shown, nor is the Coral World observation tower on Silver Cay (this is one of the most prominent landfall marks, which is far more obvious than Paradise Island lighthouse).
>
> Essentially this applies to DMA charts and all charts based on them. Check your charts carefully and check any new chart or chart kit you buy. You can still use them if they are outdated, but you should overwrite them with your own corrections while you are in Nassau.

an adjacent dive shop (we reckon the best), and the Poop Deck bar and restaurant on the second floor (by American counting). This has long been the epicenter of the boating world in Nassau. As for shoreside facilities, we'd class them as adequate.

Any disadvantages? As ever with the East Bay street marinas, as soon you as you step out into the street you wonder how long you need to spend in Nassau. It's busy, noisy, and not pedestrian friendly.

NASSAU HARBOUR CLUB

The third of our three primary choices is the Nassau Harbour Club, which is immediately recognizable, again to starboard, by its two open arms of main dock with a central heartland of club-like accommodation (but it's not a club) and a swim-

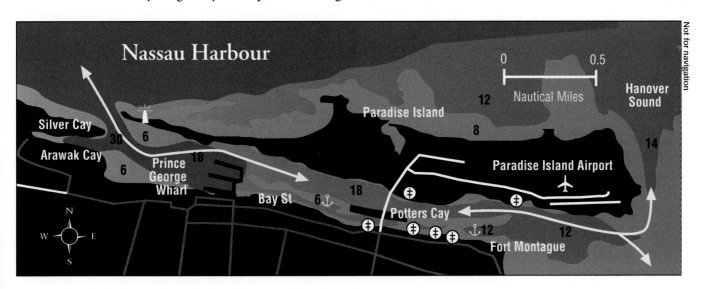

A cruise ship entering the West Harbour.

ming pool. Like the Nassau Yacht Haven it too has a second-floor bar and restaurant, and indeed a ground-floor bar as well. Shoreside facilities (shared with the swimming pool) are barely adequate, and overall the Nassau Harbour Club is showing its age.

The Nassau Harbour Club offers good package berth-plus-accommodation deals if you have crew changes in mind, and there's a major shopping center immediately across the street if you're in Nassau to provision, which is well worth taking into account.

OTHER DOCK SPACE

Between the Nassau Yacht Haven and the Nassau Harbour Club you'll find virtually all the marine facilities in Nassau devoted to cruising and sports boats, with Bayshore Marine/Maura's Marine, Lightborne Marine, Nautical Marine, and Brown's Boat Basin. Bayshore Marine have no transient berths, and the Texaco Harbour View Marina deal primarily with local long-term berths. Just west of the Paradise Island Bridge, but still on the same East Bay side, is the East Bay Yacht Basin, which is normally crowded, but may have space available.

Your list can be expanded by including the Paradise Harbour Club and Marina (Paradise Island side, east end) who may have space, and the Nassau Yacht Club, right by Fort Montague (East Bay side, also east end), who offer space, if they have it, to members of foreign yacht clubs offering reciprocal hospitality. On your entry into Nassau Harbour you may have noticed the Sugar Reef Harbourside Bar and Grill to starboard, built out on the water, half way between Prince George Wharf (the cruise ships) and Potters Cay. There's a small basin behind the restaurant with some slips. If you have nowhere else to go, you might find space there, but there are no facilities and no security.

ANCHORING

What about anchoring off? Nassau Harbour is busy. It has traffic running all night. It's crowded, particularly when the dive boats, sight-seeing expeditions, and booze cruises set out and return, let alone when the new PanAm seaplane link to Bimini and Miami comes in to land. The holding is not good.

If you do decide to anchor, check with Nassau Harbour Control and ensure that you are well clear of the fairways. More than one visiting yacht has been run down at night. You would be wise to arrange that someone remains on board the whole time, both for security and in case you drag.

ROCKING AND ROLLING

Some of the worst nights we've spent on board have been those when we've been secured alongside a marina berth in Nassau Harbour. Only Hurricane Hole and to a lesser extent, the Paradise Harbour Club and Marina have breakwaters. For the rest there's no protection. The endless traffic coming and going through Nassau Harbour, together with its prevailing east–west fetch, combine to set up a self-perpetuating never-calming crosshatch of waves and reflected waves, which will have you rocking and rolling this way and that, like a child's plastic duck in a Jacuzzi. When even at 4 a.m. you're still being thrown around by the wake of some passing cowboy, it can engender madness. We have experienced and enjoyed nights of surprising calm in Nassau Harbour, but come the first of the day's traffic, you're back to wake, waves, and continual motion.

Our advice is to get on with whatever you're doing in Nassau, and then move on. See our **Yellow Pages** for comprehensive coverage of Nassau, including a street plan.

Courtesy Balmain Antiques, Nassau.

Bathers at Hog Island (now Paradise Island), circa 1901.

Statue of Queen Victoria in front of the Parliament Building.

New Providence Island

AS the Lyford Cay Club just north of Lyford Cay on the east peninsula is the only facility open to visiting yachts in New Providence Island other than the marinas of Nassau Harbour, the south coastline of the island is likely to be of little interest to the cruising visitor. Coral Harbour, on the southwest end of the south coast, is the base of the Royal Bahamian Defence Force and is off limits, unless you have friends living further up the canals. Also marked out as off limits from time to time is the sea area boxed in by lines drawn 9 nm west and 8.5 nm south of Coral Harbour, which is used for gunnery practice. If you encounter any Defence Force vessel flying a red flag (or showing a red flashing light at night), live firing is taking place. It's best to stay clear of the area, period. This Danger Area is clearly shown on DMA Chart 26282 **Andros Island to San Salvador.**

Lyford Cay is a private club, but you may be able to take a berth there if they have space, or if you are visiting friends who are members.

Nassau Harbour (Eastern Entrance)

| Nassau Harbour E (0.75 nm off) | NASHE | 25° 04' 30 N | 077° 17' 30 W |
| Porgee Rocks | PRGEE | 25° 03' 45 N | 077° 15' 00 W |

Leaving Nassau Harbour (or entering it) at the east end presents no problems as long as you favor the north shore. Fort Montague masonry runs out into the water as does a shoal in that area, and the deepest water parallels Paradise Island Airport's runway. This deep-water channel is also the landing and takeoff run for the PanAm seaplane.

Porgee Rocks serve as a highly visual indicator of your departure point waypoint whichever direction you are bound

for, either northeast to Eleuthera or southeast to the Exumas. You may, if you are bound for the northeast, work your way out into ocean water between the east end of Paradise Island and the west end of Athol Island, but we see no particular advantage in taking a route that is shallow and requires careful eyeball navigation.

Once you've reached Porgee Rocks, if you're bound for Eleuthera, you still have four legs to go before you are in ocean water. If you're bound for the Exumas you can set a direct course to your Exuma waypoint from Porgee Rocks. For this reason we deal with each route separately.

Versailles Garden.

Moving to Eleuthera after Nassau

Nassau Harbour E (0.75 nm off)	NASHE	25° 04' 30 N	077° 17' 30 W
Porgee Rocks	PRGEE	25° 03' 45 N	077° 15' 00 W
Porgee Rocks N	PRGEN	25° 04' 45 N	077° 15' 00 W
Hanover Sound S	HNVRS	25° 05' 15 N	077° 15' 40 W
Hanover Sound N	HNVRN	25° 05' 50 N	077° 15' 45 W
Chub Rock	CHBRK	25° 06' 45 N	077° 15' 00 W
Little Egg Island (0.5 nm S)	LEGGI	25° 28' 00 N	076° 53' 15 W
Royal Island (1 nm S)	ROYLI	25° 29' 50 N	076° 50' 30 W
Meeks Patch (1 nm NW)	MEEKP	25° 31' 45 N	076° 48' 00 W

This is the route you are most likely to take if you want to see Spanish Wells, move on to Harbour Island, or start cruising south down Eleuthera. If you are heading for the Abacos from Nassau, this is the only direct route and we'd guess that you'll elect to stage in Spanish Wells on your way.

Our initial legs taking you away from Nassau may seem unnecessarily complicated, but we have worked it and proved it as a low-water route, taking the maximum advantage of the deeper water in Hanover Sound. Of course you can make changes. Anyway, the way we went is to take getting from Nassau Harbour to Chub Rock in 5 legs starting at our

Nassau Harbour east waypoint, north of Fort Montague. So it came out as:

• LEG 1	to Porgee Rock	114°M	2.31 nm
• LEG 2	Clearing the Porgee Reef area	010°M	1.00 nm
• LEG 3	Getting to Hanover Sound	315°M	0.78 nm
• LEG 4	Hanover Sound	358°M	0.59 nm
• LEG 5	Getting to Chub Rock	042°M	1.14 nm

After all this jinking around, the next leg is a straightforward 28.95 nm on a course of 048°M to take you (deep water all the way) to our entry waypoint to the Eleuthera Bank. You gain the Bank passing south of Little Egg Island, safely south of Barracouta Patch, and just south of the still-visible wreck (1970) of the *Arimora*, a 260-foot freighter.

The next leg (3.09 nm on 059°M) takes you past Royal Island and just north of the rocks that lie 1.25 nm south of Royal Island, and the final leg (3.75 nm on 076°M) places you north of Meeks Patch ready to go visual to enter Spanish Wells. See **North Eleuthera** under **The Western Approach to Spanish Wells** on page 168.

Moving to The Exumas after Nassau

Nassau Harbour E (0.75 nm off)	NASHE	25° 04' 30 N	077° 17' 30 W
Porgee Rocks	PRGEE	25° 03' 45 N	077° 15' 00 W

Once you're at our Porgee Rocks waypoint you can set a direct course for Allan's Cay, Highborne Cay, Normans Cay, or anywhere further south in the Exumas. As the choices are many, we don't list the waypoints here. See **The Exumas** under **From Nassau** on page 204.

Weather Reports in Nassau and New Providence Island

Nassau and New Providence are well served by additional weather reports that are not accessible in the other islands. These are:

0715 daily	VHF 72	Ranger broadcasts Florida and Bahamas weather
even hours	VHF 27	Nassau Marine operator broadcasts weather

The Nassau Marine operator forecast (VHF 27) is also available on request.

NASSAU

BASRA in Nassau
Tel: 322-3877 • SSB 2182 • SSB 4125 • VHF16

Nassau, the center of government, trade, and culture, is the most diverse and thriving town in the Bahamas. With cruise ships bringing visitors from all over the world, as well as hundreds of tourists staying at the hotels and playing the casinos, the relatively small islands of New Providence and Paradise Island host a large, cosmopolitan, transient population. There is the historical evidence of centuries of change and development in the islands to be found in Nassau's museums, rubbing shoulders with modern designer fashions and duty-free shops. As a tax haven, Nassau attracts international banks and an expatriate community, while young Bahamians are enjoying a high standard of living and vastly improved education and health care. The island of New Providence is well worth exploring: there is much to do and see, and local bus transport is inexpensive. As you approach on your boat, don't forget to call **Nassau Harbour Control** on VHF 16 for permission to enter the harbor. Even if you plan to anchor in the harbor, you must come into a dock to clear **Customs** if Nassau is your Port of Entry; the dock staff will help, or you can call Customs at 322-8791.

MARINAS

On New Providence
approaching from the west:

EAST BAY YACHT BASIN
Tel: 242-322-3754 • VHF 16

East Bay Marina is next to Potters Cay fish and fruit market, west of the Paradise Island bridge. The office and the few facilities are at the end of the dock. There is a *Burger King, Domino's Pizza,* and *Dunkin Donuts* across Bay Street from the marina.

Slips	25
Max LOA	70 ft.
MLW at Dock	Deep water slips
Power	$12 per day for 220v, $7 per day for 120v
Fuel	Shell fuel dock
Water	50¢ per gallon for 5–10 gallons, 40¢ per gallon for 11–25 gallons; 35¢ per gallon for 26–50 gallons, and 30¢ per gallon for over 51 gallons.
Ice	$2 per bag
Showers	Yes, but no toilets
Credit Cards	Major credit cards accepted.

NASSAU YACHT HAVEN
Tel: 242-393-8173 • Fax: 393-3429 • VHF 16

The *Yacht Haven* is a long-established, well-run marina in a good central position for visiting downtown Nassau and exploring New Providence. It is perfectly situated if you need any parts for, or small repairs to, your boat. The *Poop Deck* has long been a favorite watering hole for visiting boaters and local residents alike, with its upper-level bar and dining room overlooking the marina and the harbor. The dockmaster and all the staff are experienced, friendly, and very helpful.

Slips	120
Max LOA	150 ft.
MLW at dock	11 ft. inside marina, 18 ft. possible outside.
Dockage	$1 per ft. per day, $35 minimum.
Power	35¢ per kWh, $5 minimum
Fuel	Diesel and gasoline
Propane	Same-day refill
Water	Minimum $8 the first day, $6 per day after that. Includes washdown water, use of showers.
Telephone	Batelco card phone and USA direct phone by the office
TV	Hookup available
Showers	Yes
Laundry	$2 tokens for each machine from the office
Restaurant	*Poop Deck Restaurant and Bar,* serves lunch and dinner overlooking the marina. Bar opens at 11 am, lunch and meals from noon.
Ice	Yes
Library	Paperback book exchange in the office
Liquor store	On the dock
Marine Supplies	The marine supply stores (listed under **MARINE SERVICES**) are within walking distance of the *Yacht Haven.*
Repairs	Arrange with boat yards nearby. Brownie Third Lung repair and service on site.
Diving	*Bahamas Divers* Tel: 393-1466 PADI certification and resort classes, dive shop, rental equipment; two dive trips daily, to the *Lost Blue Hole,* or *Mahoney, Ana Lise* and *De la Salle* wrecks, and *Thunderball Reef,* one of the most filmed reefs in the world.
Snorkeling	Twice-daily three-hour trips for $20, wet suits and underwater cameras to rent; fins, masks and snorkels provided.
Fishing	Charters available
Taxis	Usually waiting outside the *Poop Deck*
Credit Cards	Major credit cards accepted.
Security	The marina entrance from Bay Street is locked and guarded at night.

BAYSHORE MARINA
Tel: 242-393-8232 • VHF 16

Bayshore Marina is a working boat yard. It has a few slips for transient boats, but not many facilities for visitors.

Slips	150
Max LOA	40–45 ft.
MLW at dock	6–7 ft.
Dockage	50¢ per ft. per day; long-term 22¢ per ft. per day up to 40 ft., 25¢ per ft. per day over 40 ft.
Power	$25 per month for 120v and 220v
Fuel	Yes
Water	Yes
Telephone	Pay phone on dock
Ice	Yes
Haul-out	For bottom painting, no repair facilities.
Marine Supplies	*Marlin Marine,* formerly *Maura's Marine* store on site.
Credit cards	Visa, MasterCard, and Amex

BROWN'S BOAT BASIN
Tel: 242-393-3331 • Fax: 393-3680 • VHF 16

This is a family-operated boat yard that sometimes has space available for visiting boats, but is primarily a working yard. *Brown's* marine supply store is opposite on East Bay Street.

Slips	60
Power	Yes
Fuel	Yes
Water	Yes

Repairs	Specialize in general boat and yacht repairs.
Travel Hoist	Up to 40 tons

HARBOUR VIEW MARINA

Harbour View Marina is a marina designed for smaller craft needing long-term dockage. It runs out from the Texaco Starport filling station, where you will find a telephone, fuel, ice, and provisions in the Starmart, and toilets at the garage.

NASSAU HARBOUR CLUB AND MARINA
Tel: 242-393-0771 • Fax: 393-5393 • VHF 16

This is a very pleasant marina, well-appointed and easily accessible to town. The *Nassau Harbour Shopping Centre* is directly behind it, with a large supermarket, hardware store, pharmacy, restaurant, and clothing store. It is a good place to book into if you want to meet up with friends who like to stay on shore. The accommodations are basic but clean, and they give a generous discount to marina guests.

Slips	65
Max LOA	Up to 200 ft. on the T-heads
MLW at Dock	5 ft.
Dockage	90¢ per ft. per day
Power	From $12 per day
Fuel	Diesel available
Water	From $6 per day
TV	Hookup available
Telephone	Hookup on docks
Laundry	Tokens $3 each
Restaurant	*Passin' Jacks* serves breakfast, lunch, and dinner upstairs on the balcony overlooking the harbor or in air-conditioned comfort, with piano music on Wednesday, Friday, and Saturday evenings. *Cuda Bay Bar and Grill* serves snacks, and has a pool table and live music.
Accommodations	*Nassau Harbour Club* Tel: 242-393-0771 Fax: 393-5393 50 rooms from $80 per night, with discounts for marina guests.
Facilities	Pool & sun deck; well stocked and comprehensive shopping mall across the street.
Credit cards	Major cards accepted
Security	The marina is only accessible from the street through the hotel from East Bay Street.

THE NASSAU YACHT CLUB and
THE ROYAL NASSAU SAILING CLUB

Both have small marinas near Fort Montague, but are not open for transient boats except by special arrangement.

On Paradise Island
approaching from the west:

HURRICANE HOLE MARINA
Tel: 242-363-3600 • Fax: 363-3604 • VHF 16

This protected marina adjoining the bridge onto Paradise Island offers excellent service and facilities equal to those in the US, with well-landscaped grounds and a high standard of maintenance. It is also much less rolly than some of the marinas on New Providence, but do book space in advance as Hurricane Hole is popular.

Slips	61
Max LOA	Up to 200 ft.
MLW at dock	15 ft. on the T-head, 9 ft. on inside slips. 8 ft. in the entrance channel at low tide.
Dockage	$1.15 per ft. per day, $1.25 per ft. on the T-head. Transient dockage $50.

Power	220v at 35¢ per kWh, 110v at $10 per day, 440v available.
Fuel	Diesel and gasoline
Water	10¢ per gallon
TV	Cable hookup is $6 daily.
Telephone	Hookup $3 daily, plus calls
Showers	Yes
Laundry	Yes
Restaurants	*The Pool Bar and Grill* is open for drinks and grilled snacks during the day within the marina. *The News Cafe* serves breakfast and a light lunch with a wide selection of coffee in the shopping mall next door, and *The Blue Marlin Restaurant* with its steel drums, flaming limbo, and cheerful barman who makes his own Ivan's Special drinks is only a minute's walk from Hurricane Hole at the end of the shops.
Groceries	An excellent shopping mall adjoins the marina with a good supermarket, deli, liquor store, bank, boutiques, and *Little Switzerland*.
Accommodations	The condominium apartments overlooking Hurricane Hole are usually booked at least a year ahead.
Facilities	Provisioning service for boats; proximity to the casinos, golf course, and hotels of Paradise Island; swimming pool and bar inside the marina.
Credit cards	Visa, MasterCard, Amex, no personal checks
Security	Security around the clock

PARADISE HARBOUR CLUB and MARINA
Tel: 242-363-2992 • Fax: 363-2840 • VHF 16

Slips	20
Max LOA	Up to 200 ft. on the outer dock
MLW at dock	5 to 6 ft.
Dockage	$45 per day minimum charge; 90¢ per ft. over 100 ft.
Power	30¢ per kWh
Fuel	Available nearby
Water	5¢ per gallon, $32 per 1000 gallons
Telephone	Hookup available on the dock.
TV	Satellite hookup
Showers	Yes
Laundry	Yes
Restaurant	*Columbus Tavern* overlooking Nassau Harbour, open for breakfast, lunch, and dinner; serves gourmet food and treats guests like members.
Accommodations	Timeshare condominiums
Facilities	Complimentary water taxi to the Straw Market; private beach club at the end of the island; car on Mondays to the *Nassau*

Harbour Shopping Center; swimming pool and whirlpool.

Credit cards	All major cards accepted.
Security	Gate house at the entrance

MARINAS OUTSIDE THE NASSAU HARBOUR AREA

CLARIDGE MARINA
Tel: 242-364-2218

This is the only marina on the southeast coast of New Providence, on an inlet near Yamacraw Road South. It offers limited facilities. The closest bus stop is about a mile away.

Dockage	$10 per night
Power	110v on a limited basis
Fuel	Yes
Water	Yes
Ice	Yes
Travel Hoist	Up to 40 tons
Storage	Long-term dry storage; bottom painting.

Nassau Directory

1 Cruise Ship Dock
2 British Colonial Beach Resort
3 US Embassy
4 Graycliff Hotel and Restaurant
5 Government House
6 Christ Church Cathedral
7 Cafe dell Opera
8 Pompey Museum
9 Straw Market

10 Ministry of Tourism
11 Barclays Bank
12 Bank of Nova Scotia
13 Surreys
14 Tourist Information
15 Rawson Square
16 The Cellar Restaurant
17 Cafe Matisse
18 Police

19 Batelco
20 British High Commission
21 Green Shutters Restaurant
22 Post Office
23 Bahamas Historical Society Museum
24 Gaylords Restaurant
25 Queen's Staircase
26 Water Tower
27 Fort Fincastle
✚ Princess Margaret Hospital

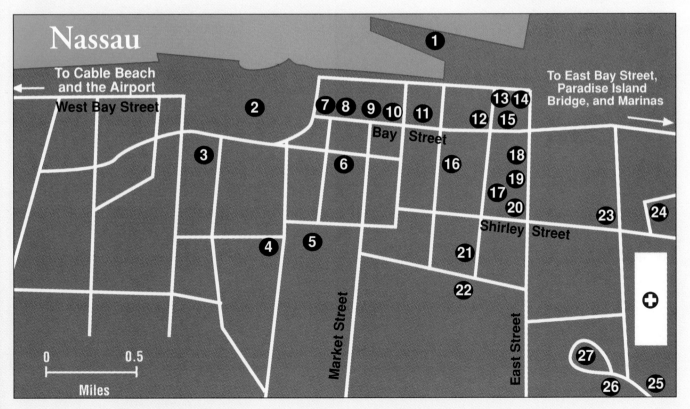

LYFORD CAY MARINA
Tel: 242-362-4131 • VHF 16

This is the most exclusive marina in the Caribbean, and is part of the privately owned Lyford Cay Club. The slips are reserved for members and their guests. They can occasionally take in transient boats for three or four days' maximum stay.

Slips	74
Max LOA	Over 100 ft.
MLW at dock	9.5 ft.
Dockage	$1.90 per ft. under 100 ft., $2.10 per ft. over 100 ft.
Power	100A, 50A, and 30A available; also 100A single and 3 phase; 35¢ per kWh.
Fuel	Diesel and gasoline
Water	$5 per day up to 50 ft., $7 per day to 100 ft., $10 per day over 100 ft.
TV	Cable hookup
Telephone	Hookup on docks
Showers	Yes
Laundry	Yes
Restaurant	*The Captain's Table* in the marina is open to non-Club members.
Shopping	Just outside the marina there is a shopping center with a *City Markets* supermarket, as well as a bank, hardware store, liquor store, boutique, public telephone, travel agent.
Credit cards	Visa, MasterCard, Amex, checks

MARINE SERVICES

Boat Yards, Marine Supplies, Agencies, and Repairs

All the agencies listed below are found on Bay Street and East Bay Street, within walking distance of most of the Nassau Harbour area marinas.

Brown's Boat Basin Tel: 393-3331/3680 • Fax: 393-1868
On East Bay Street, they have a small marine supply store across from their own boat yard.

Lightbourne Marine Tel: 393-5285 • Fax: 393-6236 On Bay Street; diesel engines and generators, Mercury outboards, agents for Perkins, Kohler and Mercury, and Quicksilver oils. Complete line of fishing tackle, some marine hardware and accessories in their well-stocked and friendly store across the street from the boat yard.

Marine Diesel Tel and Fax: 322-7135 On Bay Street; agents for Westerbeke, Yanmar, and Lugger.

Marlin Marine (formerly *Maura's Marine*) and *Bayshore Marina*
Tel: 393-7873 and 393-3874 • Fax: 393-0066 On East Bay Street; a well-stocked store, adjacent to their marina and working boat yard. Agents for Evinrude, Boston Whalers, and Sea-Do with a wide variety of equipment and fishing gear.

Nautical Marine Tel: 393-5713 and 393-3894. On East Bay Street; agents for Wellcraft, Mariner, Mercruiser, and Wahoo.

Sunpower Marine Tel: 332-2144 On Bay Street; agents for Johnson and Evinrude.

SERVICES IN NASSAU

Air Ambulance
Global Med-Tec   Tel: 394-2582 or 394-3388 • Cell: 359-2496

Ambulance
Med-Evac   Tel: 322-2881

ATMs
There are ATMs at the casinos on Cable Beach and Paradise Island, at the Tourist Information Booth in Rawson Square, and at most of the major banks.

ATMs operated by *Barclays Bank*, the *Royal Bank of Canada*, and *Scotia Bank* dispense US dollars for Visa, MasterCard, or cards connected to Plus and Cirrus networks.

ATMs at *Royal Bank* branches throughout the island and at Esso stations dispense Bahamian dollars.

The ATM at the *Bank of Nova Scotia* on Bay Street dispenses US dollars for Amex, Discover, MasterCard, Visa, and bank cards connected to Cirrus, Plus, and Honor networks.

Banks
As an international tax haven, the Bahamas are host to many banks, most of which have their offices in Nassau. For simple transactions, like cashing traveler's checks, we list the more convenient banks in downtown Nassau, which are mostly on Bay Street and open Monday to Thursday, 9:30 am to 3 pm, and Friday from 9:30 am to 5 pm.

Barclays Bank   Tel: 356-8000

CIBC on Shirley Street   Tel: 322-8455

Commonwealth Bank on East Bay Street   Tel: 322-1154

Lloyds Bank   Tel: 322-8711

Royal Bank of Canada   Tel: 322-8700

Scotia Bank   Tel: 356-1400

Churches
Nassau has 22 churches, representing 18 different religions. Most churches give their times of services outside the church, or you can look in the current edition of *"What To Do"* for information and times of services.

Customs
Departure Clearance: You are not required to clear out at an entry port in person when you leave the Bahamas. When you reach the US you must mail your Cruising Permit, Fishing Permit, and Immigration Card stubs to The Comptroller of Customs, PO Box 155, Nassau, NP, Bahamas.

Dentists
There are many dental practices in town, but it is best to go to Princess Margaret Hospital where they have a good dental department, and ask for their help and advice.

Embassies & Consulates
American Embassy   Tel: 322-1183

Canadian Consulate   Tel: 393-2123

British High Commission   Tel: 325-7471

For other consulates look in the yellow pages of the Bahamas telephone directory under *Diplomatic and Consular Representation*.

Fedex
Tel: 242-322-5656 or 322-1719   Has two offices; both offer to HOLD FOR PICK UP.

Fire or Emergency
Dial 919

Gaming
Paradise Island Casino   Open 10 am to 4 am.

Crystal Palace Casino   Open 10 am to 4 am; slot machines 24 hrs.

Hospitals
Princess Margaret Hospital, Shirley Street   Tel: 322-2861
Doctors Hospital, Shirley Street   Tel: 322-8411

Police
East Bay   Tel: 322-1275

Paradise Island   Tel: 363-3160
Cable Beach   Tel: 327-8800
Downtown   Tel: 322-3114

Post Office
On East Hill Street, a big yellow building. Open from 9 am to 5 pm, Monday to Friday.

Performing Arts
Dundas Centre   Tel: 393-3728

Shopping
The length of Bay Street, from Rawson Square to the *British Colonial Hotel,* is a shopper's paradise. From fancy designer stores, duty-free shops, and glamorously expensive jewelry, to *Straw Market* souvenirs and T-shirts, there is something for everybody. When there are several cruise ships in port, it can be crowded. The *Straw Market* has everything imaginable in straw, some of it beautifully made and very individual. You can try bargaining, it's all part of the fun.

If it's history you're interested in, browse through the fascinating collection of antique maps and prints upstairs at *Balmain Antiques* on Bay Street. For more practical needs, there are several shopping malls on the island with good *City Markets* grocery stores. The closest one to the main marinas on New Providence is the *Nassau Harbour Shopping Centre*.

Telephones
Located at all the marinas, hotels, and many locations downtown. Most now take Batelco phone cards, which are available in $5, $10, and $20 denominations from the Batelco offices and some stores. To dial the US direct, you will need either US or Bahamian 25 cents; dial 1-800-872-2881 from a pay phone.

RESTAURANTS

There are so many restaurants in Nassau that we suggest you look in the current issue of *"What To Do"* for ideas and inspiration. The variety is huge, and the standard generally good, though prices can be a little higher than stateside. All the big hotels and resorts have restaurants of their own; some, like *Atlantis,* have floor shows and casinos as well. Here are a few we have enjoyed, but there are many more to try.

Cafe dell Opera   Tel: 356-6118   Located upstairs in an old church near the *Straw Market* on Bay Street. Homemade pasta for lunch and dinner, to the music of the great operas.

Tercentenary plaque in Nassau.

Cafe Matisse Tel: 356-7012   On Bank Lane, behind Parliament Square, open daily from 10 am to 11 pm. Matisse prints and delicious Italian food served indoors, or outdoors in a delightful courtyard. Reservations suggested. Proper dress for dinner.

The Cellar Tel: 322-8877   Located on Charlotte Street for patio dining at lunch time; bar until closing time

Gaylords Tel: 356-3004   Located on Dowdeswell Street. Authentic Indian cooking in a 125-year-old Bahamian mansion. Open daily for lunch and dinner. Reservations requested.

Green Shutters Tel: 325-5702   An English pub on Parliament Street, offering fish and chips, shepherd's pie, and more.

The Poop Deck at *Nassau Yacht Haven* for well-cooked meals and a cheerful, busy atmosphere overlooking the marina, from noon onwards.

Sugar Reef Harbourside Bar and Grill   Tel: 356-3065   Located on Bay and Deveaux Streets. Moderately priced Bahamian and Caribbean food, open for lunch and dinner.

And a couple at the higher end of the scale, beyond our pocketbooks, though with a fabulous reputation:

Graycliff Tel: 322-2796/7   Located on West Hill Street; very special, and lovely with 14 guest rooms and a pool cottage.

The Sun and ... Tel: 393-1205   Located on Lakeview Street with traditional and inventive French cuisine.

GETTING AROUND

There are two main airports in Nassau, the big international airport at the western end of New Providence, and the smaller airport on the east end of Paradise Island. The latter is served mainly by *Paradise Island Airlines,* which brings people into the island resorts and casinos. Don't forget the $15 departure tax when you fly out from any airport in the Bahamas, except Freeport which adds an extra $3 in tax.

Airlines

Air Canada	1-800-776-3000
Air Jamaica	1-800-523-5585
American Airlines	1-800-433-7300
American Eagle	1-800-433-7300
Bahamasair	242-377-8222, 377-8504/5505
Carnival	242-377-6449 or 377-7971
Cleare Air	242-377-0341
Continental	242-377-2050 or 377-5486
Delta/Comair	1-800-221-1212
Gulfstream Intl.	242-377-7314
Pan Am Air Bridge	242-363-1687
Paradise Island Airlines	242-363-2845
US Air	1-800-622-1015

Seaplane Charter

Safari Seaplanes Tel: 393-2522 or 393-1179   Captain Paul Harding will fly you to the smaller islands.

Marcus and Rosie Mitchell Tel: 355-2034   They operate two planes, one of which is a sea plane, out of Sampson Cay.

Buses

Buses run throughout the island, charging 75¢ wherever you go. Most of them leave from and run to Bay Street, a couple of blocks either side of the *Straw Market*, but there are bus stops marked out of town. The drivers will stop anywhere to pick up a fare. It is good manners to greet your fellow travelers as you board the bus, and then sit back and enjoy the music, usually played at full blast. Pay the driver exact money as you leave, or just hand in $1 and don't expect change.

Car Rentals

Avis	377-7121
Budget	377-9000
Dollar	377-8300
Hertz	377-6321

Carriage tours

Surreys are based at Woodes Rogers Walk, by the cruise ship terminal and cost $5 per person for a 25-minute drive. The horses rest for two hours during the hottest part of the day.

Taxis

Meter Cab 323-5111

Bahamas Taxi Cab Union   323-5818

First quarter mile $2, each additional quarter mile 30¢, or agree on a price with the driver before you set off. The fare can mount more quickly than you expect.

SPORTS

Bowling

Village Lanes Bowling Club Tel: 323-2277   Located on Village Rd. $2.50 per game, 9 am to 5 pm, $2.75 after 5 pm. Shoe rental 75¢.

Cricket

At Haynes Oval on West Bay St. Saturdays & Sundays at 1 pm.

Deep Sea Fishing

Chubasco Charters Tel: 322-8148   Captain Mike Russell. Deep sea and shark fishing.

Born Free Charters Tel: 363-2003   Captain Philip Pinder. Deep sea fishing and snorkeling.

Brown's Charters Tel: 324-1215   Captain Michael Brown. Deep sea fishing and snorkeling.

King Fisher Tel: 363-2335   Captain Jessie Pinder. Deep sea and shark fishing.

No Limit Tel: 361-3527   Captain Arthur Moxey. Deep sea fishing, sight-seeing.

Diving

Bahama Divers at Nassau Yacht Haven   Tel: 393-5644   Two-tank dive $60.

Dive Dive Dive at Coral Harbour   Tel: 362-1143   Two-tank dive $65.

Dive Nassau on Bay and Devereux Streets   Tel: 356-5170   Two-tank dive $60.

Diver's Haven on Bay Street   Tel: 393-0869   Two-tank dive $60.

Nassau Scuba Centre at Coral Harbour   Tel: 362-1964

Stuart Cove's Dive South Ocean Tel: 362-4171   Two-tank dive $70.

Sun Divers at British Colonial Beach Resort   Tel: 325-8927   Two-tank dive $55.

Sunskiff Divers at Coral Harbour Tel: 361-4075   Two-tank dive $75

Dive Sites

If sharks and wrecks hold a fascination for you, the southwest side of New Providence Island is the place to go. At *Shark Wall*, you can position yourself in a sand patch among the coral heads in about 50 feet of water on the edge of the deep abyss known as the Tongue of the Ocean, as Caribbean reef sharks and maybe a bull or lemon shark cruise around. There is a shark-feeding program here. There is also the *Shark Buoy*, tethered in 6,000 feet of water, where silky sharks steal the show as they swim in groups of up to twenty at a time. Or go to the *Shark Runway*, only a mile offshore, which has about a dozen resident Caribbean reef sharks. As for wrecks, the Vulcan Bomber used in the James Bond movie, *Thunderball*, is now just a frame, but draped in colorful gorgonians and sponges. James Bond was busy here too, when he eluded the tiger shark in *Never Say Never Again*. The freighter called *The Tear of Allah*, where it was all filmed, lies in just 40 feet of water, with more and more marine life attracted to it as time goes on. And a new shipwreck, the *Bahama Mama*, has been sunk more recently as a dive attraction, sitting upright in less than 50 feet of water. *Southwest Reef* and *Goulding Cay* both offer magnificent, shallower dives with pristine Elkhorn and Staghorn formations. If you dive the Paradise Island side of Nassau, you must take in the famous *Lost Blue Hole*, which looks like a circular hole in the sand when seen from the air, but beginning at 45 feet down, the blue hole becomes a vast 100 feet in diameter. The *Barracuda Shoals* are one of the healthiest reefs in the area, in only 25 feet of water. And then there are four more wrecks to explore, the *Mahoney* being the most well-known as the steamer that went down at the turn of the century in a hurricane.

Golf

Cable Beach Golf Course Tel: 327-6000 The oldest golf course in the Bahamas, complete with clubhouse and pro-shop.

Paradise Island Golf Course Tel: 363-3925 18 oceanfront holes.

South Ocean Golf Course Tel: 362-4391 Driving range, chipping area, and two practice putting greens beside this 18-hole PGA course designed by Joe Lee.

Horseback riding

Happy Trails Tel: 362-1820 or 362-5613 Located at Coral Harbour. $50 for an hour's ride, maximum weight 200 lbs. From 2 to 10 people per trail ride with experienced guides, English saddles. Cost includes transportation to the stables; children must be over 8 years old.

Jet-Skiing

Nassau Marriott Resort and Crystal Palace Casino Tel: 327-6200

Atlantis Resort, Paradise Island Tel: 363-2000

Breezes Super Club at Cable Beach Tel: 327-5356 20 minutes for 1 person $35, 2 people $45; 30 minutes for 1 person $55, 2 people $60. 1 hour for 1 person $110, for 2 people $120.

Parasailing

Atlantis Resort, Paradise Island Tel: 363-2000

Forte Nassau Beach Hotel, Cable Beach Tel: 377-7711

Radisson Grand Hotel, Paradise Island Tel: 363-3900

Costs around $35 for a 5–7 minute "flight."

Squash

The Village Club Tel: 393-1580 Open 8 am to 11:30 pm. Racket rental; courts $8 per hour. Also sauna and swimming pool.

Cable Beach courts, across from *Radisson Cable Beach*

Tennis

There are courts at most of the major hotels.

Waterskiing

Radisson Cable Beach Resort Tel: 327-6200 On Cable Beach. $20 for 10 minutes.

Nassau Beach Hotel Tel: 327-7711 On Cable Beach. $20 for three miles.

Artificial reef at Atlantis Resort, Nassau.

Windsurfing

Atlantis Resort, Paradise Island Tel: 363-2000 $25 per hour.

Breezes Superclub on Cable Beach Tel: 327-5356 Free for guests.

Nassau Beach Hotel on Cable Beach Tel: 327-7711 $14 per hour.

REGATTAS

December/January
New Year's Day is the grand finale of a week of championship racing in Bahamian built sloops, off Montagu Bay.

September/October
Annual Bahamas Atlantis Superboat Challenge at Potters Cay

PLACES OF INTEREST

Ardastra Gardens and Zoo Five acres of lush, tropical gardens to wander through, and watch the marching flamingos perform at 11:10 am, 2:10 pm, and 4:10 pm. You can also see iguanas, monkeys, snakes, and rare Bahama parrots. Paths are signed, and many of the more interesting trees are labeled. Open daily from 9 am to 5 pm, admission $10.

Botanic Gardens With more than 600 species of tropical trees and plants. The curator can answer your questions. Open from 8 am to 4 pm, Monday to Friday, admission $1.

Canoeing at Lake Nancy Tel: 356-4283 An ecological adventure. Canoe rental available. You may see turtles, cranes, coots, ospreys, egrets, warblers, woodpeckers, and more! Open daily.

The Cloister and *Versailles Garden* on Paradise Island Features a 14th-century arched walkway built by monks and brought in by Huntington Hartford as part of his initial island development. Overlooking the harbor, this makes a popular wedding site.

Coral Island Silver Cay, off Arawak Cay. See turtles, stingrays, and sharks at the world's largest man-made coral reef in an underwater observatory, open 9 am to 6 pm daily. Admission charged.

Fort Montagu Built in 1741. It guards the eastern entrance to Nassau Harbour and was captured by the Americans during the American War of Independence in 1776.

Fort Charlotte Completed in 1789 to guard the western entrance to Nassau Harbour. Not a shot was ever fired against an invader by its 42 cannons, but there are still dungeons and a waxworks that you can visit free of charge.

Fort Fincastle Completed in 1793, built in the shape of a ship. Nearby is the 126-foot tall *Water Tower* with a dramatic view of the harbor.

The Retreat, Village Road The headquarters of the Bahamas National Trust, set in 11 acres of lush tropical gardens, with the world's third-largest collection of rare and exotic palm trees. Half-hour guided tours available, or self-guided tours with a map. Open from 9 am to 5 pm Monday to Friday, and from 9:30 am to 12:30 pm on Saturdays. Admission $2.

Museums

Bahamas Historical Society Museum, Shirley Street
Pre-Columbus, Lucayan, Taino, and Arawak artifacts. Open from 10 am to 4 pm, closed Sunday & Thursday. Admission $1.

Balcony House, Market Street The oldest wooden house in Nassau dating from the 18th century. Fully restored. Open 10 am to 4 pm on Monday, Wednesday and Friday, admission by donation.

Junkanoo Expo Located in an old customs warehouse on Prince George Wharf, Woodes Rogers Walk. You can relive Boxing Day (December 26th) and the Mardi Gras atmosphere of the carnival. Junkanoo paintings and handicrafts for sale. Open from 9 am to 5:30 pm daily.

Pompey Museum of Slavery and Emancipation, Bay Street
This was the old slave market until emancipation in 1834, and now has a post-emancipation exhibit. Open 10 am to 4:30 pm, Monday to Friday, and 10 am to 1 pm on Saturday. Admission $1.

BEACHES

There are many to choose from, but a few suggestions on New Providence are Cable Beach and Goodmans Bay, Orange Hill Beach, Saunders Beach, and South Ocean Beach. On Paradise Island try Paradise Beach and Hartford Beach.

THINGS TO DO IN NASSAU

- Pick up a copy of *"What To Do"* in Nassau, Cable Beach, and Paradise Island, and a Bahamas *Trailblazer* map, either from the Tourist Information office on Bay Street, many of the stores, or even from some of the marinas. It will give you current information as to what's going on, where and when.
- Buy yourself a hat in the *Straw Market*.
- Visit *Atlantis* with its water chutes, pools, lagoons, aquarium, and casino. It's the largest man-made, water-related, gambling resort in the Bahamas.
- Climb the 66 steps of the Queen's Staircase leading up to Fort Fincastle, and photograph Nassau from above.
- Stock up on groceries and fresh provisions before heading out to less well-stocked islands.
- Have any repairs to your boat seen to, and replace spare parts you have used on board.
- Watch the marching flamingos at the *Ardastra Gardens Zoo*.
- Go for a run with the Hash House Harriers. Call 325-2831 for times of runs.

Chapter 12
Eleuthera
Spanish Wells and Harbour Island
Hatchet Bay and Governors Harbour to Cape Eleuthera

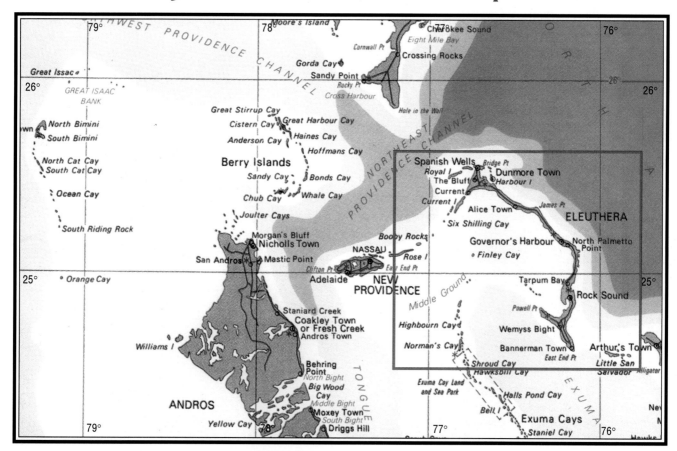

Approaches to Spanish Wells, Harbour Island, and North Eleuthera

THE north of Eleuthera is a distinct geographic area. You could say that it's an island in its own right, connected to "mainland" Eleuthera only by a bridge and this is true. But more important to the cruising visitor are the problems set by the unique geography of North Eleuthera. To the north and west it's surrounded by coral reefs. In the south the waters of the North Eleuthera Bight are shallow, and the coast itself is low lying, without any natural harbor or viable anchorage. To the east the seabed plunges to ocean depths within a mile of land, and your approach problems, for there are reefs there too and fierce tides, are compounded by the pressures of three thousand miles of North Atlantic fetch.

All this sounds far from encouraging. It remains that there are only three approach routes into the North Eleuthera

area. The first is from the west, taking advantage of a pass through the reefs lying to the south of Egg Island. The second is from the north through the reefs to the north of Bridge Point. The third is from the east, over a bar to the south of Harbour Island. There is only one approach that we recommend, and that's to go the Egg Island way. The north approach is not just difficult. It's dangerous. You need a pilot there. And we don't like the Harbour Island approach. If you ask "Is it worth going to North Eleuthera?," our answer is short and simple. You bet it is. We'll deal with the Egg Island approach first, as if we were coming in from Nassau, and we'll pick up the other two as we make our way around. Your initial destination, coming in this way, is bound to be Spanish Wells.

Your approach course coming from Nassau will be 048°M to reach the Little Egg Island waypoint (25° 28' 00 N 076° 53' 15 W) we listed under **Moving to Eleuthera after Nassau** on page 157. This waypoint, which places you 0.5 nm

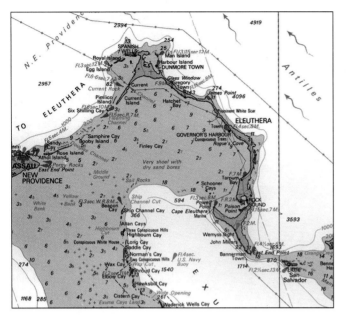

south of Little Egg Island and safely to the south of the still-visible wreck (1970) of the *Arimora*, a 260-foot freighter (whose captain didn't mean to set such a selfless and invaluable permanent marker on the northern limit of the Egg Island Pass). You have reef to the south as well, which is not marked, but the entry channel is wide. We'll take it in stages now. Rather than break the descriptive continuity of running from the pass directly to Spanish Wells, we'll deal with Spanish Wells first and then return, as it were, to cover Egg Island and Royal Island.

The Western (Little Egg Island) Approach to Spanish Wells (St. George's Cay)

Little Egg Island (0.5 nm S)	LEGGI	25° 28' 00 N	076° 53' 15 W
Royal Island (1 nm S)	ROYLI	25° 29' 50 N	076° 50' 30 W
Meeks Patch (1 nm NW)	MEEKP	25° 31' 45 N	076° 48' 00 W
Spanish Wells S entry (just off)	SPNWS	25° 32' 05 N	076° 48' 00 W
Spanish Wells E entry (just off)	SPNWE	25° 32' 38 N	076° 44' 20 W

From the Little Egg Island waypoint you have two straightforward legs to run setting you up ready to make your close approach to Spanish Wells. The first leg, 3.09 nm on 059°M, takes you just north of the rocks that lie 1.25 nm south of Royal Island. Here, if you're attracted by Royal Island's superb natural harbor and want an island to yourself (or possibly shared with others) opt out of this routing and turn north. If you're bound for Spanish Wells, a second leg, 3.75 nm on 076°M, places you north of Meeks Patch ready to turn directly for Spanish Wells harbor. Then take as your landfall mark the new Spanish Wells water tank, which is silo-like in appearance and on the skyline just behind the entrance to the harbor. Your heading will be around

080°M, you have about 1.5 nm to run before you're going to enter the harbor, and you'll have 6 feet under you at MLW. Other than this water tank there are no quick-and-easy ID points on this approach leg.

Spanish Wells

The Eastern Entry to Spanish Wells Harbour
By the time you've run 1 nm from that last waypoint you should have the water tower plainly in sight, and in the last half mile you'll be altering more directly for the water tank (which you'll now see is dark blue with a white top) on a northeast heading. As you get closer you'll see the narrow channel between Russel Island (with a lot of dredging showing on what will be your port side as you enter) and Charles Island (shaggy green vegetation). Your best lead marks are the water tank on the skyline and a second larger but more squat water tank (also dark blue) slightly to the right and below it at harborfront level, but these two water tanks do *not* set up a transit. Your other confirmation of your landfall (if they're in port, which is mostly April to July) are the fishing boats you'll see to the right of the second, lower-level water tank.

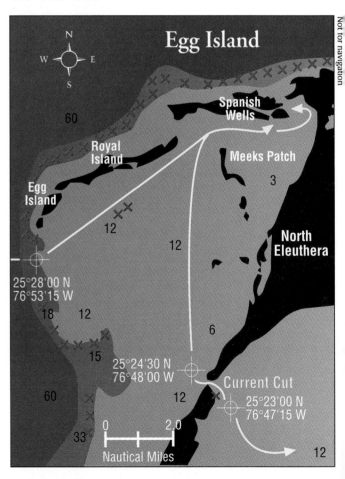

What about channel markers? We're talking now about two approach markers (both steel I-beams), hard to pick up from any distance out. The port marker has heeled over and the starboard marker (still upright) bears a faded trace of red paint—these are both right at the entrance to the channel. More obvious is the line of dredged sand and marl you'll have on the port side, which gives the line of the channel more clearly than the indefinite shoreline of Charles Island.

Once you're in the channel there's a further marker to starboard, and then you have two choices.

Fishing boats, Spanish Wells Harbour.

Turn to starboard if you wish to anchor behind Charles Island, or turn to port (note the channel you must stay in, it's obvious, and there's a marker piling to be left to starboard) if you wish to go to Spanish Wells Yacht Haven, recognizable at once by its large shed. You'll have good depth on your approach all the way. Well over 6 feet, and mostly 10 feet or more.

The Western Entry to Spanish Wells Harbour
There's an alternative route into Spanish Wells Harbour and that's to continue around Charles Island and pick up the channel that leads east–west directly into the cut between St. George's Cay and Charles Island. If you do this, beware of the shallows on both sides. Pick up the three channel marks (to be left to port), which will take you in a curve around the shallows to port. Then you'll see two channel entry markers with, as a companion to the starboard one, a leaning telephone pole. When you get close you may see that the starboard entry piling has a single red reflector on it, one of the kind you use to mark your driveway.

By now you're heading almost due west and there's a line of four single posts to be left to starboard leading you straight into Spanish Wells Harbour. You have good depth in this channel, but we see no reason to take this route into the harbor if you've come from the west. Don't be confused by a continuation of these markers leading east from the entry pair. This is the route used by the Spanish Wells boats bound for Gene's Bay ferry landing on Eleuthera, directly opposite the channel entrance.

Spanish Wells Harbour
Spanish Wells Harbour is, in fact, just one long cut running between St. George's Cay (Spanish Wells) to the north and two islands, little peanut-shaped Charles Island to the southeast, and Russel Island to the southwest. It's not a natural harbor in the sense of being a cove or a landlocked bay, but it serves well with adequate protection from virtually all weather other than wind funneling in from the east. The anchorage behind Charles Island has good deep water, at least 8 feet, but is swept by tidal currents and affected by the wash of every passing boat. In Spanish Wells Harbour they drive fast. There's no pussyfooting around at 5 knots or less if you live there. You should set two anchors, and make sure they're set. This apart, you're sheltered there, save at the extreme east end.

Spanish Wells Yacht Haven is your only marina, but it's well found and well kept, a pleasant, agreeable place with every facility you are likely to need, including a circular swimming pool, and rooms if you wish to put up shoreside guests. Inexplicably the shore power outlets are 50A so if you're running 30A, you'll need a pigtail. They may be able to lend you one. If you carry on up the cut, between Russel Island and St. George's Cay, to port there are two openings into the Mud Hole, the local hurricane shelter where, when a hurricane threatens, the local boats are laced with a spider's web of lines into the mangroves (a practice that saw its toughest test when Hurricane Andrew hit in 1992). The technique works.

Spanish Wells Harbour, which is entirely weighted in its

layout to favor the St. George's Cay side (the *'butment*, as it's called) is geared to supporting the fishing fleet. Counting from the east end, Ronald's Marine, the Anchor Snack Bar, Walton's Langousta Bar, Pinders Supermarket, Pool's Boatyard with its rail track into the harbor and its mini-drawbridge, the Texaco Service Center with Spanish Wells Marine and Hardware, and Jack's Outback (another snack bar restaurant) are the main shoreside facilities on the waterfront between that east tip of St. George's Cay and the Yacht Haven. The fishing boat services and docks continue right up the harbor to the St George's Cay-Russell Island bridge, where the two islands have a road link, at the west end.

You can take a small boat out under this bridge at half tide or better to gain the open water of the bank between Pierre Rock and St. George's Cay, and from there head east to reach the gap between Russel Island and Royal Island. At less than half tide the area to the east of the bridge dries. If you go this way, beware of the old bridge (brought down by Hurricane Andrew) that lies on the north side of the channel, to the east side of the bridge.

SPANISH WELLS SETTLEMENT (ST. GEORGE'S CAY AND CHARLES ISLAND)

St. George's Cay is so totally identified with and as being Spanish Wells that we deal with the island and the settlement (as well as little uninhabited Charles Island, which has no role to play other than in helping to form Spanish Wells Harbour) under the heading of Spanish Wells.

The name Spanish Wells sounds romantic. The legend that the Spanish filled their water casks from the sweet wells of the island now called St. George's Cay before setting off on the long haul to Spain sounds good, but is it credible? Look at the charts. Look at the reefs. Study the wreck his-

Small boat, Spanish Wells.

tory of the area. If you were a Spanish admiral with your pension coming up in six months time, would you lead your Treasure Fleet to Spanish Wells? But even if you doubt the legend, if you want to see the real Bahamas, Spanish Wells should be on your list. Go to its tiny museum. There's not much there but there's everything, from the house itself to the story the exhibits tell with unaccented simplicity. In Spanish Wells, if you wander around and talk to people, you begin to get a feel for the history and the making of a place, rather as low tide reveals the inshore reef that made the beach.

Spanish Wells is no tourist resort. Hurricane Andrew in 1992 ended the modest attempt that had been made up to that date to encourage tourism as an income earner. Spanish Wells is fishing, serious fishing, with ocean-going craft and the whole infrastructure to support them. It is self-reliance taken as far as you can reasonably take it, that goes straight back to 1648 and the Eleutherian Adventurers, who were tough, ornery, independent of mind, and not prepared to live by the rules of the day just because that was the way it had always been. Spanish Wells *is* Bahamian lobster fishing with something like 75 percent of its annual production and exports that have long found markets worldwide. You can see the end result in new houses, new cars, and the reassurance that they got it right.

If you're looking for tourist attractions, bars to sit in watching the sunset, and gourmet restaurants, you'll find nothing there. What you will find is a settlement of sturdy, well-built, well-cared-for houses in Abaco colors (but then weren't they much the same people?) in which real grass, flower beds, and trees are tended with an un-Bahamian care. You'll find cultivation taken seriously, land taken into use for fruit trees and bananas, and young flowering trees started, ready for the future, in cans and buckets. You'll see the evidence now of the lobster fishing prosperity in new houses, and a gradual expansion into Russel Island.

You may conclude that isolation lasted perhaps a tad too long in this settlement. Certainly old customs endure and the division between the sexes, what the men do, and what the women do, reflects a simple, pragmatic way of going about the business of living, albeit a life-style that would be reckoned by today's torchbearers of individual emancipation to be hopelessly sexist. You'll find an island with far too many cars for its population, but the fishing brings money and what other status symbol would you choose if you already have a house? In the evening the cars are driven around the few streets in something like a Spanish paseo, endlessly and aimlessly it seems, round and round the circuit. Perhaps the Spanish really were there.

Above all, what you'll find is kindness, a readiness to talk, and one very attractive, small close-knit community that has every appearance of having known where it was going since that magic date in its history, 1648, when they decided that Bermuda was too close to the British Crown politically and geographically to engender confidence in the future. They wanted freedom, and the right to determine how their own lives would shape. The story sounds familiar.

LITTLE EGG ISLAND AND EGG ISLAND

Little Egg Island is totally barren and Egg Island, despite a fishing shack that gives the appearance of habitation, has little to offer but a light that may, or may not, be working. You might find yourself drawn to the Egg Islands because the North Eleuthera reef, to which Egg Island has given its name, is easily accessible there, has good snorkeling, good diving, and there's good fishing, too.

ROYAL ISLAND

Royal Island (as you pass it) seems to go on forever, 4.5 nm long and 0.5 nm wide at its widest point. Its central, near-land-locked harbor, with the ruins of a house above it, is as perfect a natural haven as you could ever expect to find. On its north shore there are beaches and the protection (plus its attraction for snorkeling, diving, and fishing) of the Egg Reef, with little Goulding Cay as a playground to the north. Read Christopher Columbus's account of his first landing in the Americas. The physical description of the island of his landing fits Royal Island more perfectly than any other place, but the navigation side, when you try to figure out his Log, doesn't work out so well.

There was one abortive attempt made to develop a Yacht Club on the site of the house but it was never supported by the owner. Nevertheless, the one step forward taken (the placing of eighteen moorings in the harbor in 1992) remains today. Twelve of these have been in use, one of which can take a large boat, 100–120 feet in length. However we hear reports that the mooring chains are now suspect, and it may be that you should anchor. If you want to take a

Spanish Wells, northern beach.

mooring, call A-1 Broadshad in Spanish Wells on Channel 16. The price is $10 a day (or call him on 809-333-4427). But check that safety angle first. The harbor is well protected from everything but the south and southwest, but you can tuck yourself up in the ends (beware the east end) even if you get it blowing straight in the entrance. You have 10–14 feet MLW in the harbor.

As for entering, you go in the central, obvious entrance favoring the west side between the little cay with its marker and the headland with its board. You have 8 feet there at low water. Don't take the other side, the east channel. There's a submerged rock there (which is marked). Further along the Royal Island coast there's another entrance to the east end of the harbor, but this is small boat stuff, and not for you. The east end is, in any event, shallow, far too shallow at low tide to serve anything drawing more than 12 inches.

Is Royal Island for sale? Yes, it is, according to local rumors. The asking price is $13 million. Someone once offered $7 million, or so the story goes, and was turned down. You could always try.

RUSSEL ISLAND

Russel Island, at 3 nm in length, dwarfs St George's Cay's 1.5 nm but might best be considered the country estate of Spanish Wells. It has a considerable wealth of citrus and other planting under cultivation, some very handsome houses, two good beaches on the north side, and some fishing shacks.

The End of a Dream

Why is Royal Island uninhabited? Why is it neglected? It's a sad story. It was once the home of a Florida man, who built the house and outbuildings you can see in ruins on the ridgeline above the remains of his dock. He kept a boat there, and another boat on the north side, at another dock. He planted citrus trees and exotic fruit such as mangoes, as well as coconut palms. By every account the place was perfect. After his death at first there were caretakers, although his wife had returned to Florida. After her death the daughter inheriting the property had no interest in maintaining it. The last caretaker left, leaving his chickens and goats to fend for themselves, and was never replaced. That was thirty years ago. Casual vandalism, arson, and ultimately Hurricane Andrew led to the desolation you will see if you land on Royal Island.

Spanish Wells to Harbour Island–
The Devil's Backbone Passage

The Devil's Backbone Passage through the reefs around the north coast of Eleuthera is an exercise in coastal navigation, which, rather like marriage, should not be lightly undertaken. It's potentially hazardous but not dangerous given the right conditions. Because the nature of the navigational problems presented change as you make your way around the coast, it makes sense to get a Spanish Wells pilot to take you around the first time you do it, and talk you through the course. His services will cost you $60 but it's money well spent.

This advice given, what other cautions have we?

- *Never* attempt this passage in bad weather, particularly with wind, or wave, or ocean swells coming onshore out of the north.

- *Never* attempt it if the light is not good. Any time after 10 am, when the sun has got reasonably high in the sky, is OK, and around noon is best.

- *Never* attempt the passage from Harbour Island to Spanish Wells in the late afternoon with the sun in your eyes.

- *High water* is always an extra safety dividend. You could make it at low water, but it makes sense to have the reassurance of two feet or so extra under your keel.

- *If* you're overtaken by weather on this passage use your best anchor and wait until it clears or alternatively call for a pilot.

Let's take the Devil's Backbone Passage in stages.

Spanish Wells Harbour to Ridley Head

Leave Spanish Wells Harbour by the Gene's Bay ferry route (the east) entrance. At the two entry marks (25° 32' 38 N 076° 44' 20 W) turn north toward Pierre Rock, staying in the deep water. You have 6 feet of water all the way (maybe 5 at the least when the moon isn't working with you) at MLW as you then turn round Gun Point, staying about 50 feet off, to head toward the stake off Ridley Head. On this course across the bight between Gun Point and Ridley Head the dark patches ahead and to starboard are grass, and the dark patches to port are reef. Avoid the ones to port. Pass the Ridley Head stake leaving it to starboard (25° 33' 30 N 076° 44' 24 W). You have 30 feet of water going around the stake.

Immediately after rounding Ridley Head if you look at the beach you'll see two concrete vehicle tracks ending at the sand. If you were to turn out toward the ocean keeping these tracks directly astern (on a heading of something be-

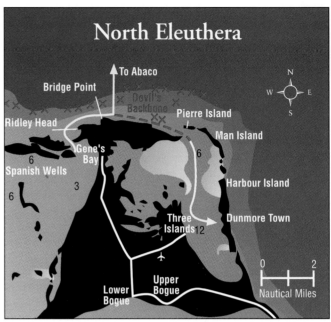

North Eleuthera

Not for navigation

tween 330 and 340°M) you would be set to make your way out through the reefs and make a course for the Abacos. You still need eyeball navigation until you're in deep water, and the channel through the reefs this way is narrow. There's another better route, the one we mentioned at the start of the North Eleuthera section. However we give this one as an option because it's there. If we were to go this way, we'd want to be piloted the first time we did it.

The Devil's Backbone—
A Cautionary Tale

We were caught at the critical stage of a Devil's Backbone passage by what we thought was a rain squall. It proved to be the leading edge of a 40-by-70 mile depression with wind, blinding rain, and wave coming straight out of the north. Within minutes visibility was less than a boat's length, the sea state was evil, and we were about to lose the battle to stay where we were between reef and rocks. We let the anchor go, but couldn't trust it. Any normal scope would have us wrecked. Two hours passed. Violent motion. Holding the head to weather. You get to understand the meaning of hanging on in there. There was no sign of it easing. If there was a lull, we'd have to move, but with no sun and zero water visibility we were blindfolded. We called for a pilot. Conditions were too bad for him to get around Ridley Head. Another hour passed. Then we got our break.

We heard later that a warning of sudden severe weather off North Eleuthera was broadcast, but not until well over an hour after we were hit. The freak storm was, in fact, the generation of Arthur, the first named storm of 1996. It was totally unforecast when we left Harbour Island. It had been clear skies, wind southeast around 10 knots, and the first indication of Arthur was just that rain squall on the sea horizon to the northeast.

RIDLEY HEAD TO BRIDGE POINT

Continuing on your way to Harbour Island, after Ridley Head set your course toward the next headland, which is Bridge Point, and you'll find yourself running along just off a beach. The dark patches to port are all reef. Keep favoring the beach and stay over the sand. When you run out of actual beach to starboard you'll see four dark patches (which are all reef) coming up on your starboard bow. Point out to sea slightly to leave these reefs to starboard. In doing this you'll find yourself heading over other dark patches (which are also reef) but you have deeper water on this heading and can pass safely over the reefs that appear in front of you as you alter (25° 33' 50 N 076° 43' 26 W).

BRIDGE POINT

Off Bridge Point at 25° 33' 55 N 076° 43' 20 W you can turn out through the reef ready to set a course for the Abacos, turning out to port where ahead you'll see two dark areas of reef divided by a narrower band of sand (there is another small streak of sand bottom on roughly the same line further to port, but forget that). Your heading to get away to the Abacos comes after you've crossed these three bands of color, the dark reef, then the narrow sand, and then the reef again, more or less wherever you fancy. There's deep water there for the whole width of that thin sandwich of water colors. Also see our note on **Moving on to the Abacos** on page 175. If you're incoming from the Abacos and you don't know your way around the northern Eleuthera waters, your best answer is to stop there, off Bridge Point, and call for a Spanish Wells pilot on Channel 16.

The Devil's Backbone Passage, Ridley Head.

BRIDGE POINT TO HAWKS POINT

- After Bridge Point head toward the Blowhole Rock, dark and cave-like, which you'll see on your starboard bow. As soon as you get close to the Blowhole Rock keep in close to it to avoid a reef that will come up on your port side, and then head to what appears to be the next headland (actually it's the north tip of Pierre Island).

- As soon as you're on this heading you're level with the start of the Devil's Backbone Reef, which comes up dark on your port side. Make sure you stay in the lighter water, close in to the beach (about 150 feet from it). Just hug that beach and don't be scared of it, for the Devil's Backbone is going to curve round and hook in front of you just as the sand makes a move to swing out. Go slow, watch and read the water, and you'll reach a point (around 25° 33' 48 N 076° 42' 04 W) at which you'll find yourself heading north of the north tip of Pierre Island (as if you were going to run past Pierre Island leaving it to starboard). This is the point at which most people run into trouble for, fearing that they're running too close to the sand, they turn away and crunch on the Devil's Backbone.

- Once you've made it past this point, you can breathe. The dark patches ahead of you are grass, not reef, enjoy the sight of Preachers Cave in the cliff to starboard, and then watch out as you reach the end of the beach. Ahead of you there are two dark coral heads that you leave to starboard, staying with your grass all the way. You are at Hawks Point.

HAWKS POINT TO CURRENT POINT

After reaching Hawks Point alter to head for Current Point, which is now obvious, leaving the isolated stake called the Monument (25° 33' 33 N 076° 40' 52 W) to starboard. Don't run too close to the Monument. It marks a ledge, not an isolated rock. On this leg you'll be in the grass all the way. Pass Current Point (25° 32' 58 N 076° 39' 52 W) staying 200 feet off it.

Current Point to just off Dunmore Town (Harbour Island)

After rounding Current Point you'll see a marker stake to port. Head toward it to leave it on your port side, and pass 100 feet from it (25° 32' 41 N 076° 39' 32 W) for you have shallows to starboard, which you can see by the color of the water. Then head toward the north tip of the south beach on Man Island. Keep those shallow patches to starboard, and then when you're clear, head more directly to place yourself off Dunmore Town.

Girl's Bank

We were intrigued by the name Girl's Bank. Why was it called that?

"My father, who was born in Dunmore Town, told me that if it was low tide when school ended for the day, the teacher used to take the girls out there to play."

He paused, thinking about it or maybe just thinking back. Then with a grin "I always wished it was girls in bikinis, and I still keep looking."

"What about the boys?" we asked.

"Oh, they just used to get banana fronds and use them as sleds to slide down that sand bank at the back."

—Captain John Roberts, *Four Girls*, Spanish Wells

You have two final hazards to avoid, neither of them difficult. Look out for Eastmost Rock and Westmost Rock to starboard, and avoid them. Look out for Girl's Bank to port (which shows clearly) and skirt round that. Then you're all set to make your approach to either Valentine's or the Harbour Island Marina, or to anchor off wherever you wish.

Harbour Island

Marinas and Anchorages
For marinas in Harbour Island your choice is limited to either Valentine's Yacht Club (the northern one, closer to the public dock) or the Harbour Island Marina (the southern one). If you want to anchor off, the best place is somewhere south of the Harbour Island Marina, away from all the traffic. Ferries from Three Islands (and North Eleuthera Airport) are running all day.

Harbour Island Marina.

Valentine's Yacht Club and Inn is well established, well known, and has a bar and restaurant as well as a dive shop on the premises. The Harbour Island Marina, rebuilt after Hurricane Andrew, is still developing. If you are content to be on the outskirts of Dunmore Town (Harbour Island Marina has rental golf carts), and content to accept fewer of the conventional facilities (just one shower and two restrooms), Harbour Island Marina has the prettier setting and the better ambiance. Both marinas, while well sheltered from the northeast, east, and southeast, are completely exposed to wind from any other direction. In the event of a Norther or strong winds from the west the Harbour Island marinas are virtually untenable and shelter may well have to be sought at anchor off the east coast of North Eleuthera.

A SECLUDED HIDEAWAY
Harbour Island is one of the fabled Bahamian hideaways, famous for its seclusion, relaxed life-style, friendly atmosphere, pretty houses, and pink sands. You could well propose a theory that given the last four assets, the first one, seclusion, is vital. If it's not remote, if it's too easy to get to, no place will long endure as a mythical recreational Eldorado. Before the coming of air services Harbour Island won on the seclusion factor. It was three times removed from Florida, for you had to stage through Nassau and Spanish Wells to get there. But hold it a moment: in truth make that five times removed, for if you were sailing there the Biminis, the Southern Berrys, Nassau, and Spanish Wells all came into the distancing process.

Now you can fly into North Eleuthera Airport and take a ferry from Three Islands ferry dock straight to Harbour Island and the streets of Dunmore Town. Has it lost anything because of this? Yes, of course it has. Is it critical? No, not yet. But if you still want to feel the magic of that distancing, of getting there and being remote, take the old route around North Eleuthera, make your way over the Devil's Backbone, and get to Harbour Island that way. There's still a great advantage in the cruising life. You see the world as it should be seen, wide screen in a slow-moving film, rather than a set of unrelated isolated bites like TV travel commercials.

PIERRE, MAN, AND JACOBS ISLANDS
The three islands to the north of Harbour Island have no particular interest, though anchorages may be found off them all. Beware that there are shallows on the west of all three islands and that there are no navigable gaps between them out into the Atlantic.

The Harbour Mouth Ocean Pass
The ocean pass known as Harbour Mouth lies at the south end of Harbour Island. A very extensive area of shoal (similar in extent to Girl's Bank) extends to the west from the south peninsula of Harbour Island as far as 25° 27' 50 N. To gain the ocean you have to run favoring the shore of

The fishing boat dock, Harbour Island.

North Eleuthera until you have passed the gap between Harbour Island and Whale Point, and then turn to go out into the Atlantic.

The route through Harbour Mouth carries little more than 6 feet even with a favorable tide, maybe less, and is beset by moving sandbanks, tidal currents, and ocean swell. An additional complication in your reading of the water color scheme is that a newly laid underwater pipeline has left a somewhat irregular sand scar running diagonally across the shoal area from Eleuthera to Harbour Island. The Harbour Mouth pass is best left to the locals, or learned from someone who is there and uses it. What does it offer you? Ocean fishing, and a good departure point for the Abacos or Cat Island. We would not use it as an arrival point.

Moving on to the Abacos

We believe Bridge Point is your best departure mark if you're setting out for the Abacos, and that your departure waypoint should be at least 0.75 nm off Bridge Point (say 25° 34' 30 N 076° 43' 30 W) to get you well into deep water before you set a course and settle down. We'd not come in this way from the Abacos. You would be chancing your luck with weather and on the time of day, and it makes no sense to put yourselves at risk. Take the route we recommend at the start of this section, going south of Little Egg Island.

North Eleuthera

An Inland Tour

There are times when you should check your lines, or your ground tackle, and leave your boat to take a taxi tour of the hinterland, for otherwise you'll never get the feel of the place that has been your destination. North Eleuthera (and indeed the whole of Eleuthera, taken section by section) is one of them.

If you're in Spanish Wells, get to Gene's Bay ferry landing and take a taxi from there. If you're in Harbour Island, get to Three Islands ferry landing and do the same. Take Glass Window, the break point between North Eleuthera and Central Eleuthera as your far out destination and turn-round point. We're not writing a land tour guide, but we'll mention just three places you might feel worth your time. They don't come up precisely in the order we list them. Look at your road map. You'll see why.

UPPER AND LOWER BOGUE

The Bogues take their name from a corruption of the word "bog" or low-lying, nearly useless land. It was unclaimed, unwanted right from the start and it was there that the freed slaves staked out their tracts when they were turned loose after Emancipation. Drive through to see a part of the Bahamas that is far removed from either Spanish Wells or Harbour Island's Dunmore Town. Both Upper and Lower Bogue were hit hard by Hurricane Andrew, for they have no elevation, and no protection. You can still see the damage.

THE CURRENT

The tiny settlement of The Current, "Population 131, Established 1648" as its welcoming sign advertises, was hit harder by Hurricane Andrew than anywhere else, and the traces are all too evident. Go there to reinforce what you learned from the Bogues and take a postgraduate course in real life in the Bahamas. While you're down that way go to look at Current Cut. Get the feel of it before you make use of it on your onward path down the west coast of Eleuthera.

THE GLASS WINDOW

The Glass Window is the point in the rock spine of Eleuthera, once no more than a natural arch undermined by the ocean, which became a real break. It was named for the facility to "look through" the window formed by the arch. There, today, the road crosses a rock gorge on a new bridge, the last in a series of storm-damaged bridges. Stop, and while your taxi turns around, look about you.

To the east, and right up to the concrete bridge itself (though well below it) you have the deep blue water of the Atlantic. To the west it's the turquoise green, far-shallower water of the Bahama banks. When the Atlantic rollers come surging in or the powerful swells of a distant mega-storm, three thousand miles of ocean fetch hit that rock spine beneath the bridge and can throw walls of water 100–120 feet high that will carry away anything on the bridge, and indeed (as has happened more than once) the bridge itself. It's a dramatic photo viewpoint at any time, and to see it in bad weather can lead to incredible shots. It can also lead to involuntary suicide if you venture too far out on the bridge. The Glass Window, in rough weather, has claimed victims almost every year.

Moving on to Central and South Eleuthera

Spanish Wells E entry (just off)	SPNWE	25° 32' 38 N	076° 44' 20 W
Spanish Wells S entry (just off)	SPNWS	25° 32' 05 N	076° 48' 00 W
Meeks Patch (1 nm NW)	MEEKP	25° 31' 45 N	076° 48' 00 W
Current Cut W (0.75 nm NW)	CURCW	25° 24' 30 N	076° 48' 00 W
Current Cut E (1 nm S)	CURCE	25° 23' 00 N	076° 47' 15 W
Hatchet Bay (just off to N)	HATBN	25° 20' 45 N	076° 30' 00 W

SPANISH WELLS TO CURRENT CUT

This is a short, simple run of 7.29 nm on a heading of 192°M, which takes you safely to the west of Meeks Patch and the Lobster Cays. You'll have no problems picking up the houses of The Current as a landmark, and Current Cut comes up (although it's well hidden at the start) about 0.5 nm south of The Current.

CURRENT CUT

Current Cut is your Panama Canal to take you directly (or as directly as you can go) from Spanish Wells to Hatchet Bay. Current Cut looks rather like a canal when you first see it, broader than you thought it might be, and has dark blue water, which is always reassuring. It carries a tidal flow well-known in diving circles as giving you the greatest drift dive ever. As a diver you're rocketed totally out of control through

Current Cut

Not for navigation

the Cut at 6 knots or more, with an escort of fish who seem very much in control of their destinies.

Up on the surface you may have to contend with the full force of the tidal current and wind, and if you've not got the power to punch through it, you may regret taking Current Cut. The best time is slack water, and make it high tide, for you have shallows to cross on the east side. Other than taking these simple precautions, you'll have no problems in the Cut. We had 37 feet of water almost all the way. Just stay in the middle of the blue.

- Once you emerge from the Cut, favor the north side. Pass the concrete dock where *Current Pride*, the mailboat ties up, and look out for two low rocks at the edge of the water, and then a sand track leading due north. Once you've passed these markers you're ready to turn south to pass to the east of the chain of barren cays lying just offshore to the south of Current Cut.

- You're in shallows here, and you must read the water and choose your path, heading to our Current Cut east waypoint, which lies just north of the small bay that will open up to starboard. Then you're clear to set your course for Hatchet Bay.

It goes without saying that the Current Cut part of this passage from Spanish Wells to Hatchet Bay is visual. Our waypoints are useful for checking your position but *not* for navigation. One final note. As you pass through the Cut on a high tide you may see a fishing boat anchored on the east side, bow into the tidal flow, with its nets spread like welcoming arms. The fish, who to the diver seemed so certain that they had their environment checked out and under control, may yet meet their nemesis.

CURRENT CUT TO HATCHET BAY

A straightforward course of 105°M held for 16 nm will place you just north of the entrance to Hatchet Bay, ready to make your way down the line of the coast for a mile or so, picking up landmarks. For a long time you'll have seen the Glass Window bridge off to port, and you'll pick up Gregory Town with no difficulty, and a scattering of houses to the south of it.

Hatchet Bay hides itself behind its cliffs and its narrow entrance, but its Batelco tower is a giveaway. A more interesting "lead-in" mark are the strange grey concrete silos on the spine of the island that are some 3 miles north of Hatchet Bay by road. A souvenir of a failed cattle-raising venture, these towers, set above the limestone cliff on a plateau of verdant green, can't fail to catch your eye. First three pairs become apparent, then later, about 2 nm off the final waypoint we give, another three silos come into view. They look like the remains of some vast prehistoric center of wor-

Hurricane Andrew
Sunday, August 23, 1992

That morning no one in North Eleuthera realized that Hurricane Andrew was heading their way. Most people were dressed and on their way to church when it dawned that the feel of the day was wrong, the weather forecasters were changing their views, and North Eleuthera was right in the predicted line of Andrew's path. Sunday activity changed to the frantic boarding up of windows and doors, laying in emergency supplies, and no doubt prayers too.

At five in the afternoon Andrew struck with 80 mph wind from the northwest. Just two-and-a-half hours later it was all over. Andrew had moved on. The wind had peaked at 210 knots and there was an 18-inch tidal surge above the highest tide levels ever recorded. The Current was the worst hit. Of 70 homes, 52 were destroyed. Of the 18 still standing, only 6 were inhabitable. There was no power, no water, no telephone.

Astonishingly there were only two fatalities. In the Lower Bogue a woman and a young child drowned in the inundation of rain and tidal surge. She might have escaped had she taken refuge on the second floor of her house, but she was blind drunk on rum.

Palmetto Point, South Eleuthera.

ship, a Bahamian stonehenge. By the time you've come to this conclusion you are off the entrance to Hatchet Bay, a light on a mast to port, some scruffy casuarinas to starboard, and that Batelco tower briefly in your gunsights before you lose sight of it as you straighten up to pass into the harbor.

We'll cover Hatchet Bay in the next section under **Central and South Eleuthera.**

Hurricane Andrew's legacy in Lower Bogue.

Central and South Eleuthera

AS we said at the beginning of this Guide in **Where to Go? A Cruising Ground Analysis**, Eleuthera presents problems for the cruising visitor. Long and thin, Eleuthera has two coasts, the east (Atlantic) coast and the west (Eleuthera Bight) coast. The Atlantic coast has no shelter, near continuous offshore reefs, and, as we said in that analysis, isn't a cruising ground. As for the west coast, it has only three, true, all-weather havens: Hatchet Bay, Cape Eleuthera Marina, and Davis Harbour. In between there are places like Pelican Cay, Governor's Harbour, and Rock Sound where you can find some kind of shelter. If the prevailing southeast winds hold steady, you have no problems cruising along the west coast of Eleuthera, and you can safely anchor off most of the small villages. In unsettled weather you have just those three "safe" harbors as your safety net.

Eleuthera too presents real problems if you want to see the island. Unlike a small cay that can be covered in a day with some walking, Eleuthera's 110-mile length means that even if you carve it up into bite-sized chunks, you'll need wheels to get around. Renting a car for an entire day is one solution, and then doing the island from top to bottom. Having said this, we go for the bite-sized chunks, but this increases the cost. Whatever you decide, there are places to see and the Eleutheran landscape, and its small villages, have a character of their own.

We particularly like Unique Village at North Palmetto Point. The nearby hotel (which carries the same name) faces a pink beach that rivals Harbour Island's, and offers refreshment in a gazebo-like restaurant-bar set high over the Atlantic beach with a 180° view of ocean and reef. In all our travels we must admit we failed in one objective and that was to reach the lighthouse at Eleuthera Point, the south tip of the island. The road running south from Bannerman Town gets worse and worse and you soon find yourself driving over limestone ridges through a tunnel of scrub, barely as wide as the car. If we had no conscience we might have let the rental car take it, but after a realistic assessment of the car's tires, suspension, steering, and probable mechanical reliability, and the fun factor if we had to walk back miles to Bannerman Town, we quit.

In this way the big island geographic factor does suggest that Eleuthera is not what we'd call a cruising ground in its own right, a destination (like the Abacos) that's enough in itself to occupy your cruising time. But if you're making your way from the Abacos to the Exumas, or southward to Cat Island, don't neglect Eleuthera.

Hatchet Bay

Hatchet Bay (just off to N)	HATBN	25° 20' 45 N	076° 30' 00 W

Hatchet Bay Harbour

Hatchet Bay Harbour was man-made, formed by cutting through the limestone cliff to form an entrance into a hitherto landlocked pond, thus giving the developing Hatchet Bay cattle-raising project a harbor it could use. The entrance to Hatchet Bay, kept well concealed from you by the cliffs, looks forbidding at first sight, far too narrow, but has good width (90 feet) and good depth (10 feet). Once inside swing easily round to starboard and head toward the two silver-colored propane tanks, favoring that far side of the east half of the harbor rather than the little island you'll leave to port. The Alice Town dock to starboard is not for you, nor the commercial dock (where

Current Pride will secure), which lies on your starboard bow as you straighten to run up the harbor.

Your choices lie either with securing alongside the concrete wall of Marine Services of Eleuthera (if they have space), taking up one of their moorings, or anchoring. If you can get space alongside, they have shore power but little else. There's one shower. You may find, if you're secured there, that opportunist teenagers and young adults try to touch you for money ("to help with school" or "to feed my children"). This is the only place in the Bahamas where this has happened to us. Other cruising visitors have found it so too. The "feeding children" request was made at 11 pm one night when the Harbour View Restaurant disco was in full swing, and the credibility of the request was questionable, to say the least.

Being inside Hatchet Bay Harbour is rather like finding yourself inside the flooded rim of a volcano. It's a strange feeling and the sense of security that should come with 360° protection is somewhat mitigated by the Hurricane Andrew wrecks still visible on the foreshore. Like all enclosed harbors it becomes hot during the day, it does not cleanse itself (we wouldn't use a watermaker there), and, come the evening, we hit the highest marks we've ever achieved on insect attraction.

HATCHET BAY HINTERLAND

Hatchet Bay and Alice Town appear to have merged into a single Hatchet Bay identity. There's little in the village, in truth, to attract the particular interest of the cruising visitor. If you want to see something of Eleuthera, your choice is to take a taxi or rent a car. Perhaps it was the requests for money, but we suggest taking routine security precautions (just for your peace of mind) if you're leaving your boat unattended.

Taking the main Eleuthera highway, if you go north through the silo country you can see Gregory Town and the Glass Window. You are also in a region of caves. You see one cave as you enter Hatchet Bay, on the cliff wall near the propane tanks. There are other, extensive caves in the limestone spine of the island in this part of Eleuthera, and a local guide can take you to them.

Going south of Hatchet Bay you find yourself once again in silo country, more abandoned grey concrete silos, grassland run wild, and scrub vegetation. It doesn't seem Bahama-like at all, but

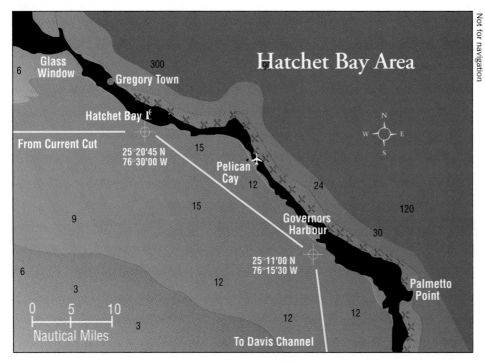

Not for navigation

Hatchet Bay Area

Glass Window
6
Gregory Town
300
Hatchet Bay
From Current Cut
25°20'45 N
76°30'00 W
15
Pelican Cay
12
15
9
24
120
Governors Harbour
30
25°11'00 N
76°15'30 W
6
3
12
12
Palmetto Point
0   5   10
Nautical Miles
3
12
12
To Davis Channel

A Pineapple Festival stall in Gregory Town.

Eleuthera is in many ways atypical of the Bahama Islands. Some three miles south of Hatchet Bay you come to the Rainbow Inn, sitting on the low cliffs overlooking a shallow bight and a little island called Rainbow Cay. It is, by reputation, the "only" place to eat in the area. While not strictly true, the Rainbow Inn attracts tourists in its own right and is far from being solely dependent on cruising visitors. Further south the road takes you into Governors Harbour, first going past its airport and Pelican Cay. Finally, if you want ocean beaches, the east coast, not a cruising ground as we know, has some beaches highly prized by surfers.

You might wonder at the lack of any development taking advantage of Hatchet Bay, which is arguably the only good "natural" harbor in Eleuthera. The reason seems to lie in that when the cattle-raising scheme failed in the 1970s, the land passed into the hands of the Bahamian Department of Agriculture. Wheels can turn slow in governments anywhere and, perhaps understandably, agriculture is rarely a torch bearer in promoting concrete development schemes. Despite proposals that cover the full range of options from resort hotels with golf courses to grand marinas, Hatchet Bay has remained locked in a time warp.

Hatchet Bay To Governors Harbour

Hatchet Bay (just off to S)	HATBS	25° 20' 30 N	076° 29' 30 W
Governors Har. (1.5 nm NW)	GOVHN	25° 12' 24 N	076° 16' 45 W

A run of about 14 nm (a tad less to the waypoint we chose) will take you in deep water all the way to just off the southwest tip of Levy Island, which offers your first choice in anchorages. Governors Harbour, despite its impressive name, is no harbor and has no facilities for visiting yachts. The holding off the main bay is poor to potentially disastrous, perhaps 2 feet of sand over hard rock, and no anchor will stay fixed there under stress. Levy Island offers two anchoring spots, one close to the island and one close to the mainland, but check the wind direction. What appears to be a third potential anchorage, tucking yourself under the southeast wing of Cupid Cay is not a valid option. It's shallow, the sea area is narrow, and Bird Cay offers little protection. In short, if the wind is from the southeast and is staying there, Governors Harbour is fine. If not, don't risk it. Go to Hatchet Bay and take a taxi to get to Governors Harbour.

PELICAN CAY

Pelican Cay, which you'll have passed on your way south, lies close to the coast just off Governors Harbour Airport. It offers usable shelter from the west if the wind turns against you, but is no place you would wish to stay. Go around the south tip of Pelican Cay to find deep water, for behind the north end it's shallow, and in the center Pelican is almost joined to the mainland. If you do make use of Pelican Cay, even if you dinghy in to the shore there's nowhere (other than the Airport) you can reach on foot.

Hatchet Bay or Governors Harbour to Cape Eleuthera

Hatchet Bay (just off to S)	HATBS	25° 20' 30 N	076° 29' 30 W
Governors Harbour (just S)	GOVHS	25° 11' 00 N	076° 15' 30 W
Tarpum Bay (8 nm due W)	TAPMW	24° 59' 50 N	076° 17' 55 W
Davis Channel (just E)	DAVCE	24° 53' 05 N	076° 16' 05 W
Cape Eleuthera (0.5 nm W)	CAPEW	24° 50' 20 N	076° 21' 05 W

The route from Hatchet Bay to Cape Eleuthera starts with a leg of 23.17 nm on a heading of 159°M to a point 8 nm due east of Tarpum Bay, taking you safely east of the shoals and sand bores that straddle the 25° N line of latitude forming a barrier right across the Eleuthera Bight. Once you get to this waypoint level with Tarpum Bay, you can alter course to a heading of 172°M for 6.95 nm, which takes you directly to the east entrance to the Davis Channel. If you're setting off from Governors Harbour you can do this run to the entrance of the Davis Channel as a straight shot, dropping due south, on a heading of 188°M for 17.92 nm.

Before you reach your Davis Channel entry waypoint you'll have entered isolated coral head country, and you're better off hand steering than staying on autopilot. You'll have plenty of depth, around 12–15 feet at the least, but it's better to be sure and avoid the coral rather than test the depth too late. You must have faith at this stage in that Davis Channel east waypoint. There's nothing there, it's just a place

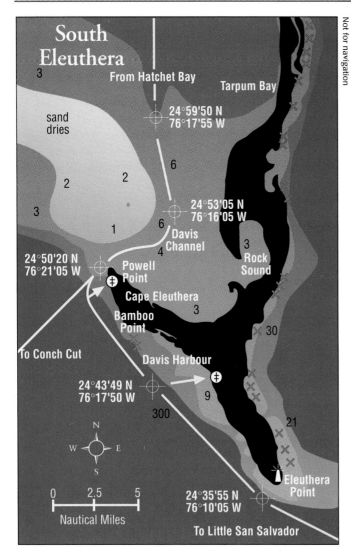

well clear to the north. Around this point the Davis Channel will have become even more certain in its course, deeper (some 15–18 feet) and darker, going on bluc rather than green. All the while the Schooner Cays are off your starboard side, and Cape Eleuthera shows plainly to port. (The obelisk marker, shown on the BBA charts, is incorrectly plotted and is some 0.75 nm southwest of the position shown.)

Keep in the luxury of your new deep water and round Cape Eleuthera when you feel ready to do so. Cape Eleuthera, and the Cape Eleuthera Marina, which has been usable but in a state of decaying suspended animation since the mid-80s, is ideally placed to be the jump-off point from Eleuthera to the Exumas. Our arrival waypoint is simply confirmation that you're there, off the entry channel. Alternatively go on to the Davis Harbour Marina, or continue on course for the Exumas.

TARPUM BAY

Tarpum Bay is very shallow and exposed to wind and weather over an arc of 180°. Tarpum itself has very little to offer the cruising visitor that cannot be more safely and easily achieved in a rental car. We don't recommend it as an anchorage, and the Tarpum Bay dock is totally off limits on depth alone.

ROCK SOUND

Rock Sound, which at first sight on a chart or a map looks as if it ought to be the ideal all-weather haven, other than in strong winds from the south, sadly fails to live up to its first promise. It's shallow, and your entry has to be made in a gentle curve in to the southeast favoring Poison Point (the south entry arm) rather than Sound Point (in the north) for there are coral heads that you must avoid. When you get closer in to Rock Sound itself, there's really nowhere to go. You can anchor off. The onetime choice spot used to be off Edwina Burrow's restaurant and bungalows to the north of the government dock (recognizable by a deteriorating concrete jetty) but Edwina's place, which has some shops and a bank nearby, has closed, and the main reason for going there no longer exists. It's shallow off that jetty, and we wouldn't feel easy lying there for any length of time or even through a night.

South of the government dock there's a wooden jetty (also deteriorating) right by the Harbour View restaurant, which nobody seems to claim. Tying up to the T of the jetty (the main run is too shallow on each side) brings no facilities and a depth that when we were there had a sailboat bumping the bottom at low water (5 feet perhaps, less at extreme tides), as well as bouncing to an unseasonable south wind. After looking at it in every way, and covering the shore side, we concluded that unless you have some compelling reason to visit Rock Sound, we saw little there that would persuade us to highlight it as a cruising destination.

in the sea, but go for it, for if you're there, right on that spot, the Davis Channel will go OK for you. There are no channel markers (just one reef marker, which you'll see way later on when you're nearly through).

THE DAVIS CHANNEL

At the entrance to the Davis Channel you must go visual, running for something like 6 nm, initially on a heading of 254°M but this will change gradually as you make your way west and pick up your bearings. The Davis Channel, at the east end, seems indeterminate at the start, hardly a channel but just 12–15 foot water with some coral, some weed, patches of sand, and not much to give you faith that you're on the way to anywhere. Just keep going, and stay on that heading. In time the sandbanks marking the north and south limits of the Davis Channel will become more apparent.

Then three blazes of exposed sand off your port bow resolves itself as a reef with a strange obelisk-like marker on it, a second dry area, and a low bar called Sandy Cay. Stay

Cape Eleuthera and the South

Cape Eleuthera Marina

Cape Eleuthera (0.5 nm W)	CAPEW	24° 50' 20 N	076° 21' 05 W

Cape Eleuthera Marina and its linked residential complex was allowed to go to ruin in the mid 1980s. It joins the list of the almost inexplicable Bahamian development failures. It could be one of the most attractive marinas in the Bahamas. Like West End, it has the twin benefits of a strategic geographic position (which in Cape Eleuthera's case would make it a natural port of call for virtually all traffic on the Exumas–Eleuthera–Abaco route), and a superb site. This apart, its design is outstanding, a well-protected circular harbor, well laid out, and with a tidal through-flow (aided by a well-placed canal) that keeps it as clean as ocean water.

The sadness is that other than shore power (50A sockets only), water, and fuel, there's nothing there. Jungle-like scrub and bush have overtaken everything built around the marina, and now even the docks (concrete finger piers) are deteriorating. Across the marina area are a small lineup of townhouse condos, all that remains inhabited, huddled together looking beleaguered, rather like the last soldiers to remain on their feet at Custer's Last Stand. The condo owners have cars. You, without a car, are miles from anywhere, even the nearest restaurant.

The entry channel has 12 feet at low water, and the fuel dock has just 6 feet, but otherwise Cape Eleuthera Marina is satisfactorily deep all over. On entering and leaving be careful of a ledge that extends out from the north entry arm and don't cut this turn too close. Line up well out and run straight in, and on leaving keep going straight until that ledge falls away.

Ocean Hole, Rock Sound, South Eleuthera (and Helen Platt).

Davis Harbour Marina

Davis Harbour (3 nm W))	DAVOF	24° 43' 49 N	076° 17' 50 W
Davis Harbour Entry Marker	DAVHM	24° 43' 49 N	076° 15' 05 W

Davis Harbour is hard to locate offshore. After you've gone around Cape Eleuthera stay out in deep water, and for safety pass perhaps 1.5–2 nm off Bamboo Point as you head south to avoid the rocks lying 1 nm south of Bamboo Point. After passing the line of Latitude 24° 45' 00 N you're OK to start closing toward the shore, aiming at the waypoint we show for the Davis Harbour Marina approach.

You won't see the outlying Davis Harbour marker until you're almost on top of it, and your first landmarks are the Deep Creek Batelco mast (some 2.5 nm north of Davis Harbour), a wrecked boat on a beach to the north of Davis Harbour, and a dense clump of casuarinas that masks Davis Harbour. The marker, when you pick it up, is a small red radar reflector on a white post planted on a large isolated coral head. By then you're going to be in 25 feet of water shoaling to 16 feet or less, and there are a number of isolated coral heads all around.

The Davis Harbour entrance, which bears 070°–075°M from the marker, should be obvious at this point. There's a double line of stakes marking the entrance and a Shell sign that shows against the trees, as well as a white painted signal mast. The entry channel is tide dependent, so if you draw something like 4 feet or more, you must check first with the dockmaster on Channel 16 before risking it.

Davis Harbour Marina is not attractive to the eye, and does not clean itself well. This said, as a place to berth your boat you have power, water, fuel, restrooms, and showers. On this account it beats Cape Eleuthera. The downside is that like Cape Eleuthera you really are in the boonies there, miles from anywhere, and there's no restaurant at the marina. But it's a good base for fishing Exuma Sound or taking off for the Exumas or the Out Islands.

Moving on from South Eleuthera

South Eleuthera to Cat Island

Cape Eleuthera (0.5 nm W)	CAPEW	24° 50' 20 N	076° 21' 05 W
Davis Harbour (3 nm W)	DAVOF	24° 43' 49 N	076° 17' 50 W
South Eleuthera (3 nm W)	SELEU	24° 40' 00 N	076° 15' 05 W
Eleuthera Point (1.5 nm SW)	ELEUP	24° 35' 55 N	076° 10' 05 W
Little San Salvador (2 nm SW)	LSSAL	24° 33' 00 N	075° 59' 00 W
The Bight (7 nm W)	BIGHT	24° 15' 00 N	075° 33' 00 W
Hawk's Nest (3 nm W)	HWKN1	24° 08' 45 N	075° 35' 00 W

Eleuthera is a good jumping-off point for Cat Island. You're closer there than you'll be anywhere else, and Little San Salvador makes a good stop on your way, either for a break or for a

The Moorings

We were in Hatchet Bay talking about most things and moorings came up. It wasn't that we wanted one for we were alongside the wall, but conversation moves like catspaws on water. You can never tell which way it's going to go.

"This man came in and anchored off. I shouldn't say it, but I didn't like him when he came ashore. You can tell, can't you? Anyway that night we had a bit of wind and he dragged. The next morning he came ashore again, and casually asked me how much we charged for the moorings."

She paused to pick a kitten off the desktop loudspeaker telephone-fax. "He always hits the speed dial and we get bills for calls coming in to places I've never heard of. Now I could have told him that I knew he'd already picked up one of our moorings because the boys had seen him do it, and told me first thing. But I thought I'd let him settle up."

In a kitten-free interval I made a call to catch up on home news while she was attending to other things.

"You know he stayed four days and never paid? He left early one morning, and obviously thought he'd got away with it. That we never checked the moorings? But he'd also let slip to someone that he was going to the Abacos by way of Royal Island. Well you know there's nothing there? But there are moorings. Do you know them?"

I did. We'd been bombed there by a white squall while we were doing a depth survey in our inflatable not three weeks back, and had clung to one of the moorings like half-drowned rats clinging to a ship's cask. You get to know your mooring well.

"Well I called A-1 who looks after them, as you know, and told him to look out. He'd got a real one coming."

We talked about A-1 for a while and the other Spanish Wells pilots we knew in common.

"You wouldn't believe it, but A-1 missed him. This man spent three or maybe four days in Royal Island, but A-1 had other jobs on and never got down to check the moorings. There's a sign, you know, asking people to check in on Channel 16. He'd never done that. But again he'd told someone that he was off to Abaco, and talked about making an early start. He was going out by Ridley Head. You know, the difficult way, through the reef? They told him not to try until the sun was high. Ten at the earliest."

Both kittens hit the speed dialer.

"That's it. No mackerel!" Neither animal seemed crestfallen. "All hell broke loose on Channel 16 at about 6:30 one morning. It was this man, he was shouting and screaming for help saying that he was on the reef, and would everyone come and help him, and he was going to lose his boat. It became clear that he wasn't sinking, but he was on the reef all right."

The kittens had been forgiven, or lost in the story she was in auto-feed, spooning something out of a can into two saucers.

"Mrs. A-1 called him. Said 'No-one's coming out to help you. It's too early. Too dangerous. You were told not to try that passage until 10:00. None of our men are going to risk themselves or their boats for you. And maybe anyway you owe some of them for some moorings? They went out to him later that morning, and took him and his boat back in to Spanish Wells."

"Did they get him?"

The saucers were put down on the concrete floor. "You bet they did."

---

more extended visit. But see our note under **Little San Salvador** in **The Out Islands North of the Tropic of Cancer** on page 242.

South Eleuthera to the Exumas

Cape Eleuthera (0.5 nm W)	CAPEW	24° 50' 20 N	076° 21' 05 W

Either Cape Eleuthera Marina or Davis Harbour Marina makes an ideal departure waypoint for the Exumas, giving you single-leg runs straight across the deep water of Exuma Sound. Your choices in landfall extend virtually the entire length of the Exuma chain. For most people the destination normally lies between the Ship Channel to the north of Ship Channel Cay (a distance of some 25 nm from Cape Eleuthera) to Conch Cut, just north of Staniel Cay (some 35 nm). There are three or four other cuts lying between these two passes, and as there are so many options open to you we cover landfall waypoints under **The Exuma Cays** on page 205.

An Alternative Route Back to Nassau

If you choose to return to Nassau from Eleuthera and for some reason you don't wish to take the Current Cut–Little Egg Island route to gain the deep water of the Northeast Providence Channel, there is an alternative route. From Governors Harbour or Hatchet Bay set a direct course for a point north of the south tip of Current Island. Get close to the shore of Current Island, in deep water, before you turn south to round the tip of the island, for there's a sand bar there, running out to the southeast from the end of Current Island.

Once you're around the island, if you want to anchor overnight, stay in deep water, turn north, and choose your spot between Current Island and the main Pimlico Island, just off the beach. Don't work too far to the north. There's a strong reversing tidal current there and you must set two anchors. If you don't want to stop, or when you're ready to move on, head toward the center of Little Pimlico Island, then parallel the coast of Little Pimlico running southwest until you've cleared its southern rock. Then head northeast into deep water and you're all set.

YELLOW PAGES

SPANISH WELLS

BASRA in SPANISH WELLS VHF 16

Originally settled in 1648, Eleuthera is considered the first democracy established in the western world. Early settlers, fleeing religious persecution, called themselves the Eleutheran Adventurers. Led by Captain William Sayle, they put ashore on North Eleuthera. Eleuthera has long been known for its agriculture, sometimes successful, some not. The great cattle-raising ventures, which failed, have left their traces around Hatchet's Bay. Pineapples remain Eleuthera's most famous crop, and fresh vegetables are highly prized.

The main centers of population in the North Eleuthera area are its two offshore settlements, Spanish Wells and Harbour Island, which are both served by North Eleuthera Airport. Because Spanish Wells is important as a fishing port, and Harbour Island (more properly called Dunmore Town) is a prime tourist destination, we have covered these two places in their own right.

Named for the Spanish galleons that were believed to have stopped here to take on fresh water, Spanish Wells has kept its association with the sea. Many descendants of the early loyalist settlers live among the nearly 1,500 people in this premier Bahamian fishing port, from where 70 percent of the annual Bahamian lobster harvest is caught. Colorful wooden houses are surrounded by immaculate gardens, and local people seem well content that Spanish Wells is not a tourist resort. There is an idyllic beach on the northeast side of the island that is easily accessible from any part of Central Road running through Spanish Wells. The beach has crystal-clear shallow water, is reasonably sheltered, and has good snorkeling further out off the reef. There are also beaches on the northern tip of Spanish Wells, and all along the north side of Russell Island. Spanish Wells is a Port of Entry. **Customs** and **Immigration** are located in the same building as the post office.

MARINA

SPANISH WELLS YACHT HAVEN
Tel: 242-333-4255 • Fax: 333-4649 • VHF 16

Slips	40
Max LOA	100 ft.
MLW at dock	5 ft.
Dockage	85¢ per ft. per day
Storage	Covered storage available
Power	35¢ per kWh for 220V
Water	25¢ per gallon
Fuel	Diesel and gasoline
TV	Hookup available for $5 per day.
Telephone	In the office
Showers	Yes
Laundry	Washer and dryer $3, tokens available from the office.
Ice	$3 for a small bag, $6 for a large bag.
Restaurant	Restaurant closed until further notice.
Bar	*The Lounge Bar*
Accommodations	Air-conditioned rooms and apartments available, with satellite TV.
Swimming	Pool for marina guests
Bicycles	$6 for a half day, $10 for a full day, available through the office.
Library	A small selection of nearly new books can be bought or exchanged.
Credit cards	Visa, MasterCard, Amex, and Esso

MOORINGS

Spanish Wells Pilot Service Tel: 333-4079 and VHF 16 "CINNA-BAR" or "DOLPHIN" Bradley Newbold and Edsel Roberts are experienced guides, and have moorings available.

MARINE SERVICES

Marine Supplies
Spanish Wells Marine and Hardware Store Tel: 333-4122
Fully stocked marine store, engine repairs on Mercury and Mariner engines as well as water, diesel, gasoline, ice, electricity, and hauling facilities for boats up to 30 feet.
Ronald's Service Center Tel: 333-4021 and VHF 16
Diving and marine supplies, Johnson outboards, apartments to rent on the beach, fresh fish and seafood dishes served.

Boat Yard
Pool's Boatyard Tel: 333-4462 Diesel and gasoline, electricity, showers, and boat storage, as well as a marine railway extending into the harbor that can haul very large boats.

SERVICES IN SPANISH WELLS

Bakery
Kathy's Bakery on Central Road
Wonderful baked goods and fresh bread.

Bank
Royal Bank of Canada Open 9:30–3 on Monday, to 1 pm on Tuesday, Wednesday, and Thursday. Fridays 9:30 am to 5 pm. Visa accepted for cash.

Churches
Gospel Chapel Services on Tuesday, Thursday, and Sunday.
Methodist Church
People's Church

Clinic
Tel: 333-4064 Located on Central Road. A general practice clinic with 24-hour emergency service. Open 9 am to 1 pm, and 2 to 5:30 pm, Monday to Friday, $30 for non-residents, cash payment only.

Customs
Tel: 333-4409 Located in the same building as the post office.

Dentist
Located at the Central Road clinic. Fillings and extractions only.

Doctor
Dr. JS Fifer Tel: 333-4854 Family practice next to the Water Tower. Open from 9 am to 12 noon, and 2 pm to 4 pm on Monday, Tuesday, Thursday, and Friday. Cash payment only.

Groceries
Pinder's Supermarket on the harbor front. Open 9 am to noon and 1:30 to 5 pm on Monday, Tuesday, Thursday, and Friday. Open 9 am to noon on Wednesday, and 9 am to 6 pm on Saturday. Free deliveries.
Spanish Wells Food Fair and Pharmacy Tel: 333-4677 • VHF 16
On the west side of the island. Open 8–5 Monday, Thursday, Friday, and Saturday, and 8 am to noon Wednesdays. The pharmacy closes at 1 pm on Tuesday. Good choice in the well-stocked grocery store with a pharmacy section and free delivery.

Liquor Stores
Langousta Bar Located at the *Yacht Haven*, and at Gene's Bay, when you cross over to North Eleuthera from Spanish Wells.

Museum
Spanish Wells Museum Next to the *Islander Shop* in a Spanish Wellsian house; dependent on them to open up. Fascinating insight into the life and history of this island. Admission $5.

Police
Tel: 333-4030   On Central Road, next to the All-Age school.

Post Office
Open Monday to Friday, 9 am to noon, and 1 to 5 pm.

Shopping
The Islander Store
Lynette's   Tel: 333-4205   Open 9 am to 5 pm, Monday to Friday, to 6 pm on Saturday. Jewelry, watches, clothing, and accessories.

Three Sisters Variety Store   Tel: 333-4618   Open 9 am to 5 pm Monday to Saturday. Clothes, jewelry, gifts, swimwear, and T-shirts.

Telephone
Outside Batelco on Central Road.

RESTAURANTS & BARS

Anchor Snack Bar   On the harbor front. Open daily from 9 am to 10 pm, closed during the afternoon, serving snacks and entrees. Busy on Saturday and Sunday, when everyone appears to know each other.

Captain's Diner   Open noon to 2 pm and 6:30 to 9 pm, Monday to Friday, noon to 2 pm and 6 pm to closing on Saturday, with very generous portions.

Jack's Outback   On the harbor front, east of the *Yacht Haven*. Open from 9 am to 4 pm and from 6 pm to closing. Reasonably priced and family run with a great location.

Generation Gap   Open 10 am to 2 pm and 7 to 11 pm. Imitation American diner where the young hang out for drinks and snacks.

Langousta Bar   Open from 9 am to 5 pm, and 7 pm to 10 pm.

The Lounge Bar at *Spanish Wells Yacht Haven*

GETTING AROUND

Airport
From North Eleuthera Airport, take a Pinder's taxi to the Gene's Bay ferry dock for Spanish Wells, and hop on the ferry to the island, which will cost you about $10 for two people. If you don't take a Pinder's taxi, you can figure on a $25 fare.

Bicycles
Spanish Wells Yacht Haven   Ask at the office, which is open from 8 am to 5 pm. $6 per half day, $10 for a full day.

Car Rental
M & M Car Rentals at *Spanish Wells Furniture Company*
Tel: 333-4595 or VHF 16   Open 9 am to 5 pm, six days a week. Golf carts, motor scooters, and car rentals.

Ferries
From Spanish Wells to North Eleuthera and Harbour Island, go to *Ronald's Marine Shop* where they call the ferry on VHF to take you over to Gene's Bay, North Eleuthera. At the landing you take a taxi across North Eleuthera (past the airport) to Three Islands on the East Coast. There you take a second ferry to Harbour Island.

Mailboat
Tel: 242-393-1064   Leaves Nassau on Thursdays for Spanish Wells, Eleuthera, Harbour Island, and The Bluff. Returns to Nassau on Sundays. Call the dockmaster's office in Nassau for more information.

Taxis
Pinders Transportation and Taxi Service   Tel: 333-4068/4041
Transportation from Eleuthera Airport to Spanish Wells.

SPORTS

Boat Charters
Ronald's Service Center   Tel: 333-4021
Boat charters and fishing trips.

Diving
Manuel's Dive Store   Carries basic diving equipment, but there is no dive center on Spanish Wells since Hurricane Andrew. Harbour Island is the nearest source.

Fishing
A-1 Broadshad   Tel: 333-4427 and VHF 16
Boat rentals, fishing guide, pilot, and snorkeling.

Captain John Roberts   Tel: 333-4171
Offers charters, pilotage, and deliveries.

Spanish Wells Marine and Hardware Store
Inquire about fishing trips.

ACCOMMODATIONS

Ronald's Service Center   Tel: 333-4021
Apartments to rent on the beach.

Spanish Wells Marine and Hardware Store   Four air-conditioned apartments above the store, from $55 per day and $330 per week.

Spanish Wells Yacht Haven   Tel: 333-4255
Air-conditioned rooms and apartments with TV.

THINGS TO DO IN SPANISH WELLS

- Go to the Museum; it's one of the best, maybe *the* best, settlement museum in the Bahamas.
- Take time to walk around the whole of Spanish Wells. The houses offer a photo opportunity at every corner.
- Find out about the Spanish Wells lobster industry. If they have time, maybe they will tell you how it works. Spanish Wells is a world leader in the lobster market.
- Ask a Spanish Wells pilot to teach you how to get around the Devil's Backbone passage.
- Go snorkeling along the northern reef, anywhere from Spanish Wells to Egg Island in the west. There is some of the best Elkhorn coral there you will ever see.
- Visit *Verenecia* at her *Patchwork Centre* on the Central Road. Although she may have none of her completed work on hand at the time, she has photographs of pieces that have been commissioned worldwide, and is delighted to chat with visitors.

HARBOUR ISLAND

Pronounced "Briland" by its residents, Harbour Island is one of the oldest settlements in the Bahamas. With tropical greenery stretching down to fabled pink sand beaches, narrow, flower-lined streets and islanders who are happy to greet you as you walk through their town, this place is everyone's idea of paradise. Even the fire truck, a genuine British antique fire engine from Nottingham, adds charm to an island that encourages you to relax and enjoy the fact that time here is not of the essence. This is a Port of Entry for the Bahamas, and you will find the large pink **Customs** house at the end of the town dock.

MARINAS

HARBOUR ISLAND CLUB AND MARINA
Tel and Fax: 242-333-2427 • VHF 16

This marina is slowly putting itself back together after the devastation of Hurricane Andrew. Situated on the southeast part of the island, it offers a calm and peaceful atmosphere just a short walk from Dunmore Town.

Slips	32
Max LOA	18 ft. to 22 ft. beam can be accommodated.
MLW at dock	10 ft., 12 ft. on outside slips.
Dockage	$1 per ft. per day
Power	30A and 50A at every slip
Water	Yes
Fuel	Fuel dock open daily from 8 am to 6 pm.
Propane	Yes
Showers	Two restrooms and one shower free to marina guests, located in the main building.
Laundry	Wash, dry, and fold service
Swimming	Pool in the marina
Telephone	Yes
Restaurant	*Devil's Backbone,* open from noon to 4 pm.
Credit cards	Visa, MasterCard, and Amex

VALENTINE'S YACHT CLUB
Tel: 242-333-2142 • Fax: 333-2135 • VHF 16

Slips	39
Max LOA	165 ft.
MLW at dock	13 ft.
Dockage	$1 per ft. per day
Fuel	Diesel and gasoline
Propane	Yes
Power	40¢ per kWh; minimum charge $15 up to 30 ft., $40 per day for boats over 80 ft.
Water	$10 per day
TV	Satellite hookup available, $5 a day.
Showers	Yes
Laundry	Yes
Ice	Yes
Telephone	On the dock
Restaurant	Open 8:30 to 10 am for breakfast, noon to 2 pm for lunch and 7:30 to 9 pm for dinner.
Bar	*The Reach Bar,* open daily, serving breakfast, lunch, and light dinners until 10 pm.
Swimming	Freshwater pool & Jacuzzi, and a shuttle to the pink sand beach.
Tennis	Championship courts
Bicycles	Can be rented
Diving	*Valentine's Dive Center* Tel: 333-2309 Resort dive $75, two-tank dive to sinkhole and bat cave $95, drift dive through *Current*

	Cut $75, *Eleuthera Wall* dive $195, rental equipment and Waverunners available from the dive shop.
Fishing	With *Bonefish Joe;* inquire at marina office.
Accommodations	*Valentine's Yacht Club and Inn* Tel: 242-333-2080 and 2142, fax 333-2135 Air-conditioned double rooms from $125 per night.
Credit Cards	Visa, MasterCard, and Amex

SERVICES IN DUNMORE TOWN

Bakery
Arthur's Bakery Tel: 333-2285 Open Monday to Saturday, from 8 am to 5:30 pm. Wonderful fresh bread and cakes with a cafe at the back of the store.

Bank
Royal Bank of Canada on Murray Street Tel: 333-2250 Open Monday to Thursday 9:30 am to 3 pm, Fridays to 5 pm.

Churches
on Dunmore Street:
Wesley Church, built in 1843
Gospel Chapel
St. John's Baptist Church

Clinic
Harbour Island Medical Clinic on Church Street Tel: 333-2225 A doctor is at the clinic Mondays and Wednesdays and a nurse on Tuesdays and Thursdays. Home visits on Fridays. $30 charge to non-Bahamian residents for all routine medical treatment.

Customs and Immigration
Tel: 333-2275 (Next to the town quay on Bay Street)
Tel: 335-1065 at the airport

Dentist
Located on Barracks Street

Family Eye Care Centre
Tel: 322-3393, or 332-2774

Gift Shops
Sugar Mill and *Doris' Dry Goods* on Bay Street
Daphne's Corner at *Romora Bay Club*
Island Treasures on Dunmore Street

There are also small stalls along Bay Street selling delicious fresh fish, straw hats, and conch shells.

Ruined mansion near Harbour Island Marina.

Groceries
on Dunmore Street:
Johnson's Grocery Tel: 333-2279 Open Monday to Saturday, 7:30 am to 1 pm and 3 to 7 pm, Sundays 8 am to 10 am.
Sawyer's Food Store Tel and Fax: 333-2358 Open Monday to Thursday 8–6, Friday and Saturday to 8 pm, Sunday to 10 pm. A good selection of groceries, boat provisions, fresh meat, vegetables, and videos; they will deliver to your boat.
Percentie's
Open from 9 am to 6 pm, with good fresh vegetables.

Laundry
Seaside Laundromat on Bay Street Open from 6 am to 6:30 pm daily.

Liquor
Bayside Liquor Store on Bay Street A large selection in stock.
Briland Booze Open daily except Sundays and holidays, from 9 am to 6:30 pm. Liquors, wines, beers, cigars. Free delivery to the dock.

Marine repairs
T & T Garage Tel: 333-2332 Outboard and engine repairs.

Museum
Sir George Robert Memorial Library Open 3:30 to 5 pm daily. A small, well-stocked library with changing photographic exhibitions that give a good idea of the history of the island.

Pharmacy
Harbour Pharmacy Tel: 333-2174 Located on the waterfront. Open Monday to Friday from 9 am to 5:30 pm, except 9 am to 1 pm on Wednesdays. Open 9 am to 6 pm on Saturdays.

Police
Tel: 333-3111 Open 24 hrs. on Gaol Lane.

Post Office
In same pink administration building on Gaol Lane as the police station. Open Monday to Friday, from 9 am to 5 pm.

Telephones
At the Batelco office on the corner of Gaol Lane and Colebrook Street. There is a phone card booth outside, and two booths inside for collect, cash, and international calls. You can send or receive faxes from this office. Batelco phone cards are for sale for $5, $10, and $20. Open Monday to Friday, 9 to 4:30.

Vegetables
Patricia's On Pitt Street, just north of the town center. Fresh fruits and vegetables, as well as homemade jams, bread, island spices, and hot sauce. Open Monday to Saturday, 7 am to 10 pm; Sunday 7 am to noon, and 1 to 4 pm. No credit cards.
Percenties (across the street from *Johnson's Grocery*) Open Monday to Saturday, 9–6. Fresh vegetables and a barber's shop.
Pineapple Fruit 'n Veg Tel: 333-2454 On Bay and Pitt Street. Open Monday to Saturday, 7 am to 9 pm; Sunday to noon.

RESTAURANTS

Most of the resort hotels have their own restaurants. There are snack bars and cafes throughout the island—try some of these:

Angela's Starfish Restaurant Tel: 333-2253 Located on Grant Street, at the north end of Dunmore Street. Open from 8:30 am to 10 pm. The bell signals last orders at 8:30 pm. The menu is written up on a blackboard and you order by writing down what you would like to eat. A good choice of dishes in a great atmosphere, with a garden area. No credit cards.
Bahama Bayside Cafe Tel: 333-2174 On Bay Street. Open daily from 7:30 am to 9 pm. No credit cards.
Dunmore Deli Open daily from 7:30 am to 4:00 pm. Tasty breakfasts and box lunches to go as well as delicious deli foods, with free delivery to your boat at the marinas.
Harbour Lounge Restaurant and Bar Open Tuesday to Sunday from 11 am to 11 pm for lunch and dinner. Varied menus and fabulous sunsets; live music Thursday nights.

The Landing Tel: 333-2707 Seafront location on Bay Street with an enthusiastic French chef. Open daily for breakfast, lunch, and dinner until 10:30 pm. Extensive Bahamian and Mediterranean menu. Happy Hour 5 to 6:30 pm daily, with live music on Fridays. Visa, MasterCard, and Amex accepted.
Runaway Hill Club Tel: 333-2150 On Colebrook Street. Open to the public for dinner only, Monday to Saturday at 8 pm. Reservations required, $40 fixed price menu. Visa, MasterCard, and Amex.
Sybil's Bakery Located on the corner of Dunmore and Duke Streets. Fresh-baked pastries, cake, or donuts under the Royal Poinciana tree during the morning, or fried shrimp with peas and rice, among other delicious dishes, from 3 pm.

Bars
Sea Grapes Club on Colebrook Street Open from 7 pm for music, dancing, snacks, cocktails, beer, and wine. Home of "The Funk Gang" band. Watch for the up-and-coming "Courage" band!
George's Bar on Colebrook Street Satellite TV and a pool table.
Gusty's on Grant Street Add your name to the vast collection of signatures on the walls, and try Gus's latest alcoholic concoction even if he doesn't know what goes into it . . .
Vic-Hum's or The Great Briland Forum on Barracks Street Bahamian license plates cover the yellow walls where Humphrey Percentie (street name Hitler) will show you the world's largest coconut. He runs his bar with the conviction that every visitor will want to write about it.

GETTING AROUND

Airport
North Eleuthera Airport Serves Harbour Island and Spanish Wells. Take a taxi from the airport to Three Islands Harbour for the ferry to Harbour Island, for about $4 per person. Then hop on the ferry (about $5 per person), and take a taxi in Dunmore Town to your destination.
Bahamasair Tel: 335-1152 Flies to Fort Lauderdale, Miami and Nassau. Also *Gulf Stream, USAir,* and charter flights.

Bicycles
Michael's Cycles On Bay Street Tel: 333-2384 and VHF 16 Open from 8 am to 6 pm daily with bicycles for $10 per day, motorbikes for $25 per day, and a 13-ft. boat for $70 per day. There are also golf carts, scooters, mini mokes, kayaks, and jet skis available, and you can pay with Visa or MasterCard.

Boat rental
Ivee Boating Tel: 333-2386

Car Rental
Johnson's Garage Tel: 333-2376 Contact Jeffrey Johnson.

Golf Carts
Big Red Tel: 333-2045 Golf carts, scooters, bikes, boat rentals.
Royal Palm Golf Carts Tel: 333-2728
Two, four, and six seaters, daily and weekly rentals.

Horse and Buggy Rides
Sunset Carriage Tours Tel: 333-2723 Robert and Susan Davis.

Mailboat
Harbour Island Town Dock Tel: 332-0186
M/V *Bahamas Daybreak* II Leaves on Sundays for Nassau. For more information call the dockmaster's office in Nassau at 242-393-1064.

Taxis
Can be picked up at the docks, or contact the following:

Wendell Bullard	Taxi 334	Tel: 335-1165
Abraham Johnson	Taxi 92	Tel: 335-1071
Jena	Taxi 8	Tel: 333-2116 • VHF 16
Big M	Taxi 20 or 174	Tel: 333-2043
Reggie	Taxi 24	Tel: 333-2116

Water Taxis
Big Bad Green Tel: 333-2102
Duke's Water Taxi Tel: 333-2337 • VHF 16
Ivee Boating Tel: 333-2386 Also has boat rentals
Keva Water Taxi Tel: 333-2287
Also day trips and island excursions.

ACCOMMODATIONS

Coral Sands Hotel Tel: 242-333-2320 $140 single room, $210 for two-room cottage, $40 per person MAP.
Dunmore Beach Club Tel: 242-333-2200 $290, double room.
The Landing Hotel Tel: 242-333-2707 From $80 for single rooms, cottage from $175, $50 per person MAP.
Pink Sands Hotel Tel: 242-333-2030
From $305 per person, including MAP.
Romora Bay Club Tel: 242-333-2325
From $180 per person, including breakfast and lunch.
Runaway Hill Club Tel: 242-333-2150 From $160 a night, single or double, in the main house, $50 per person MAP.
Royal Palm Motel Tel: 242-333-2528
Tingum Village Hotel Tel: 242-333-2161 $55, single room.
Valentine's Yacht Club and Inn Tel: 242-333-2080
From $80 per person, $35 per person MAP.

SPORTS

Diving
Valentine's Dive Center at *Valentine's Yacht Club* Tel: 333-2309
All diving facilities and rental gear available, as well as bonefishing, bottom, and deep sea fishing.
Romora Bay Dive Shop at the *Romora Bay Club* Tel: 333-2323
Individualized dive trips to suit special interests. They also have a resident diving dog! Rental gear and snorkel equipment available from the dive shop.

Dive and snorkeling sites
Man Island, where there seem to be octopus and sea cucumbers in every crevice.
Pink House, with its breathtaking elkhorn forest.
Devil's Backbone, nearly 3 miles of pristine reef, with three wrecks layered upon each other, representing various periods of history.
Current Cut is the most unusual dive in the Bahamas, a narrow opening between two islands that produces a 3- to 8-knot current to ride through schools of fish and Eagle Rays.
The Pinnacles, a pedestal for trees of Black Coral at 100 ft.
Potato and Onion Wreck is a spectacular 200-ft. ship, wrecked in 1895 in 15 ft. of water.
Eleuthera Train Wreck, a train that slid off a barge during the American Civil War in 25 to 35 ft. of water. You can still see the sets of railroad wheels and other parts of the train.
Cienfuegas Wreck, the wreckage of a passenger liner.
Carnavon Wreck, a 200-ft. freighter still intact since its sinking in 35 ft. of water in 1919.

BEACHES

The famous pink sand beach stretches for three miles along the eastern side of the island, the color produced by pink coral in the sand. It is ideal for children, as this beach is well protected by the reef, providing good snorkeling.

FESTIVALS, FISHING TOURNAMENTS, AND REGATTAS

June
Harbour Island Marina and *Valentine's Yacht Club* host the final rounds of the *Bahama Billfish Tournament.*
Harbour Island Fishing Championship

July and **August**
All Eleuthera Regatta and Homecoming

October
Harbour Island Regatta; North Eleuthera Sailing Regatta between Harbour Island and Three Islands Bay, North Eleuthera. Call 242-322-3549 for more information.

THINGS TO DO IN HARBOUR ISLAND

- Walk the town and take photographs; this is one of the prettiest places in the Bahamas.
- Go to the fabled pink beach for a walk or a swim.
- Choose a good day, and go offshore fishing along the east coast. Choose another good day and work your way back along the *Devil's Backbone* and learn all the secrets of that passage.
- Go to North Eleuthera. Take a cab and visit *Preacher's Cave* on the north coast. While you're there, why not make a day of it and head south to visit *Upper and Lower Bogue, Current,* and the *Glass Window*?
- Enjoy an evening drink as you watch the sunset from one of the bars and restaurants with a shady veranda.
- Dive a wreck! See if you can find the wheels of the Eleuthera train.

BAHAMAS · 45c Inflated Sea Biscuit • *Clypeaster rosaceus*

CENTRAL AND SOUTH ELEUTHERA

BASRA in Governor's Harbour VHF 16

This part of our Yellow Pages turns now to Central and South Eleuthera, which, because it is less frequented by visitors, still retains its early charm. Governors Harbor and Rock Sound both have **Customs** and **Immigration** services at their airports, and it is possible to arrange clearing in at Hatchet Bay, Governors Harbour, and Rock Sound (call 322-2250 for Governors Harbour Customs, or 334-2183 for Rock Sound).

The extreme length of Central and South Eleuthera and the relatively few safe harbors and good anchorages would make it confusing to cover the land survey of Eleuthera in isolated bites. So we have taken it in one sweep, as you would if you were renting a car and seeing it by road from north to south.

As you leave North Eleuthera to head south, over the Glass Window Bridge, (good photo opportunity!), the first place you will come to is **Gregory Town**, site of the June Pineapple Festival. Here the word "town" is misleading. *Mr. Bones,* across from the cemetery, has a good stock of wine, liquor, and beer, while the *Thompsons* head up a bakery, grocery, and gift shop. *Cartwright's Straw Market, Rebecca's Beach Shop,* and *Island Made* also tempt you with art, beachwear, T-shirts, and Androsia batik clothes. Or you can settle for a day's fishing with Captain Gregory Thompson (335-5369), who offers full- and half-day deep-sea fishing charters, snorkel trips, and coastal cruises. *The Cove Eleuthera* (242-335-5142) is enclosed by 28 acres of friendly hideaway, with 26 rooms scattered about the property, from $99 per room with $33 per day MAP. Their restaurants are open all year, serving American and Bahamian food; tennis, bicycles, snorkeling, and sea kayaks are all complimentary.

Heading further south you reach **Hatchet Bay** and **Alice Town**, officially two separate settlements, though the dividing line between them is distinctly blurred and the whole is now generally referred to as **Hatchet Bay**. Further confusion is also found in its frequent description as being one of the most popular harbors in Bahamian waters. It is true, the village has a peaceful air to it, and the local residents are incredibly welcoming, but there is no marina and limited docking facilities. Visit Hatchet Bay if you are looking for a quiet stopover point, but don't expect more than that.

SERVICES IN HATCHET BAY

Boat Charters
Charter Cats of the Bahamas   Tel: 335-0186 or 513-835-5829
Bare-boat yachts or a fully crewed Alden Schooner. They also have a 32-ft. sport fishing boat.

Car Rental
Larry Dean's Taxi Service & Car Rentals   Tel: 332-2568 or 335-0059

Marine Services
Marine Services of Eleuthera Tel: 335-0186 and VHF 16
Limited long-term and transient dockage or moorings, with electricity, water, fuel, and a 50-ton crane lift.

Post Office
Open from 9 am to 5:30 pm, Monday to Friday.

Provisions
Sawyer's Food Stores Tel: 334-2123

Restaurant
Harbour View Restaurant Tel: 335-0212 and VHF 16   Open 11 am to 2 am Monday to Friday, 10 am to 2 am on Saturday and Sunday. Specializing in cracked conch and grouper fingers.

Telephone
There is a pay phone outside the Batelco office.

Three miles after leaving Hatchet Bay, heading toward Governors Harbour, you'll come to **Rainbow Point**, where the *Rainbow Inn* (242-335-0294) hilltop restaurant has one of the largest dinner menus on the island. They offer Bahamian and continental dishes, with live entertainment on Wednesday and Friday nights. They are closed on Sundays and Mondays in the summer, and Sundays in the winter months. Oceanview rooms and villas from $105 per night, MAP $30.

As you pass the airport by James Cistern, you'll reach **Governors Harbour,** about halfway down this hundred-mile island. It is considered the main settlement in Eleuthera, but there is no good anchorage here. The old harborfront is still attractive, though *Club Med* has arguably selected the best site in the Governors Harbour area. The *All Eleuthera Sailing Regatta* is held here in August. Contact Jackie Gibson at 242-332-2142.

SERVICES IN GOVERNORS HARBOUR

Accommodations
The Buccaneer Club   Tel: 242-332-2000
Perched on a hill above Governors Harbour. A recently converted Bahamian farmhouse with six double rooms from $80 a night, and its own restaurant and swimming pool.
Laughing Bird Apartments Tel: 242-332-2012   Efficiency apartments overlooking the beach, from $65 per person.

Airport

American Eagle	800-433-7300	Flights to Miami
Bahamasair	800-222-4262	Flights to Nassau & Miami
USAir	800-662-1015	Flights to Fort Lauderdale

Bakery
Governor's Harbour Bakery Tel: 332-2071   Opposite the Blue Room Restaurant, with a wide assortment of cakes, breads, and pastries. Open 9–6 Monday to Friday, and 9–5 Saturdays.

Bank
Barclays Bank Open from 9 am to 1 pm Monday to Friday, also 3 pm to 5 pm on Friday.

Boutique
Brenda's Boutique Open Monday to Saturday, 9 am to 5:30 pm. Selection of clothes, shoes, children's wear, and souvenirs.

Car Rental
Edgar Gardiner Tel: 332-2665
Highway Service Station and Rental Cars Tel: 332-2077   Just south of Governors Harbour, with gasoline, a convenience store, and cars to rent.
Johnson's Car Rental Tel: 332-2226 or 332-2778   American and Japanese cars, for daily, weekly, or monthly rentals.

Clinic
Governor's Harbour Medical Clinic Tel: 332-2774

Liquor Store
Butler and Sands Liquor Store

Police
Tel: 333-2111

Provisions
Eleuthera Supply Shop Tel: 332-2026   A good selection of food, as well as a pharmacy section and hardware.
Sawyer's Food Stores Tel: 334-2123

Restaurants
The Blue Room Tel: 332-2736
The Buccaneer Club Tel: 332-2000   Open from 10:30 am to 2 pm for lunch, and 6 pm to 9 pm for dinner. Closed Wednesdays; poolside barbeque during high season.
Sunset Inn Tel: 332-2487

Taxis
Arthur H. Nixon Tel: 332-2568 or 332-1006
Tommy Pinder Tel: 332-2568 or 332-2216

Palmetto Point is three miles further southeast of Governor's Harbour. There the *Unique Village* has a restaurant on a superb site, perched on a cliff overlooking a fantastic beach and a stretch of ocean with coral reefs close to shore that are good for snorkeling. It's well worth visiting. The *Unique Village Restaurant and Lounge* (332-1830) has 10 rooms from $100 a night, MAP $35, and a restaurant that is open from 7:30 am to 10 pm, specializing in native dishes, steaks, and seafood. Palmetto Point is also home to *Unique Hardware,* a liquor store, and *Sands Enterprises Supermarket* (332-1662), which carries everything from food, gifts, and furniture to electrical fixtures and auto accessories. *Palmetto Shores Vacation Villas* (332-1305) with self-catering villas opening directly on to the beach, start from $90 a night. Sadly, they no longer have slips to offer for visiting boats.

About 15 miles from Palmetto Point, at **Tarpum Bay**, you come somewhat unexpectedly to two art galleries, the *MacMillan Hughes Art Gallery* and, two miles south of Tarpum Bay village, to the *Mal Flanders Art Gallery.* Tarpum Bay's most visible landmark is the remarkable castle-like tower built by artist-sculptor Peter MacMillan Hughes, whose work has long attracted attention. His studio is near his "castle." Here, too, is Mary Hilton's hotel, the *Hilton's Haven Motel* (334-4231), which has 10 suites from $65 year round and MAP $17, with its own restaurant.

From Tarpum Bay, the road drops due south to **Rock Sound**, past the airport. Rock Sound is a diverse settlement, closest to the two southern marinas. Here you will find vegetable fields and animal farms, and also the *Ocean Hole*, an inland Blue Hole, that is believed to be connected to the ocean. Rock Sound hosts the *Goombay Festival Season* in July, and in December continues the action with the *Eleuthera Junkanoo*. There is also the *South Eleuthera Sailing Regatta* held in April; call the Eleuthera Tourist Office (242-332-2142) for details.

SERVICES IN ROCK SOUND

Airport
Bahamasair Tel: 800-222-4262 Flights to Nassau and Miami.
Bank
Barclays Bank on the Queens Highway, adjacent to the Market Place. Open 9:30 am to 3 pm, Monday to Thursday, and 9:30 am to 5 pm on Friday.
Clinic
Rock Sound Medical Clinic Tel: 334-2226 or 336-2182
Fishing
Eleuthera Fish and Farm Supplies Tel: 334-2489
Gifts
Almond Tree Arts and Crafts
The store is sponsored by the Cotton Bay Foundation, with locally handmade gifts, souvenirs, native shell, and straw work.
Goombay Gifts
Groceries
Rock Sound Super Market in the Market Place.
Nat's Produce Store Fresh vegetables and fruit.
Sawyer's Food Stores Tel: 334-2123
Hardware
Rock Sound Hardware in the Market Place Tel: 334-2253
Liquor store
Duty Free Liquor Store Tel: 334-2250
Sturrup's Liquor Store in the Market Place.
Marine Supplies
Automotive and Industrial Distributors Tel: 334-2060
Automobile and marine supplies, with agencies in Nassau, Freeport, Marsh Harbour, and Nicholl's Town.
Police
Tel: 334-2052

Restaurants
Sammy's Place Tel: 334-2121 A casual restaurant with an extensive lunch and dinner menu, and a wide selection of beer.
Vita's Blue Diamond Restaurant Tel: 334-2425

MARINAS IN SOUTH ELEUTHERA
CAPE ELEUTHERA MARINA
Tel: 242-334-8311 • Fax: 334-8312 • VHF 16

This marina first opened in 1972. Its design and layout made it one of the most attractive marinas in the Bahamas, but sadly it went through a very bad time and had to close. It is now open for both visitors and more permanent residents; the US. Navy still keeps a tender, *Thunderstar*, secured at Cape Eleuthera to ferry people to and from their submarine testing ground. But nothing has been restored and no maintenance work has been carried out since 1993; there are no shoreside facilities here. You are a long way from anywhere if you are thinking of provisioning or dining out. There is a restaurant in Greencastle called the *Restaurant de Madelyn* (334-6412), which offers French cuisine with entrees from $20, but you will have to rent a car or find someone to drive you there.

Slips	25
MLW at dock	9 ft., with a 12-ft. entrance depth at low water
Dockage	45¢ per ft. per day
Power	50A only, 34¢ per kWh. No pigtails available.
Fuel	Diesel and gasoline
Water	Yes
Provisions	Stores in Green Castle and Deep Creek
Credit cards	Visa and MasterCard

DAVIS HARBOUR MARINA or HOBO YACHT CLUB
Tel: 242-334-6303 • Fax: 334-6396 • VHF 16

This marina is over 30 years old, but it is still well maintained and run, with friendly staff. Its southern location makes it remote in terms of getting to know Eleuthera, but is a good jumping-off point for Little San Salvador and Cat Island.

Slips	30
MLW at dock	7.5 ft., but a 4-ft. entrance at low water.
Dockage	$1 per ft. per day
Power	$15–20 per day for 110v, $20-25 per day for 220v.
Fuel	Diesel and gasoline
Water	$6 per day under 40 ft.; $12 per day over 40 ft.
Telephone	Yes
Showers	Yes, good ones
Laundry	Yes
Restaurant	No, but there is a grill for marina guests.
Provisions	In Green Castle and Deep Creek
Ice	Yes

THINGS TO DO IN ELEUTHERA
- Rent a car and drive the length of this attractive island.
- If you're there in June, check the date of the *Pineapple Festival*. If you're lucky and it's taking place, go and join in.
- Go snorkeling on the ocean side off the *Unique Village* beach.
- Take your photographs of the *Glass Window*, but not in bad weather. It can be dangerous there if heavy swells and high seas are coming in from the Atlantic.
- Stock up on art work in Tarpum Bay!
- You have a choice of restaurants over the two-hour drive all the way south. Pick your favorite.

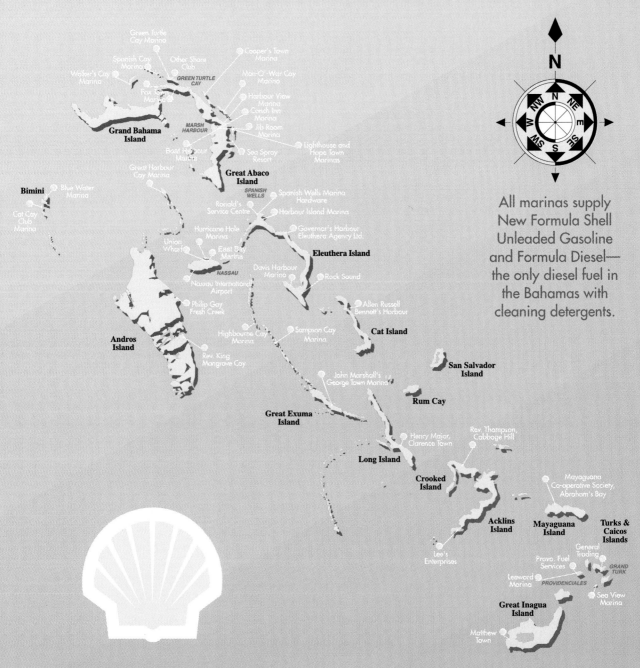

Chapter 13
Andros

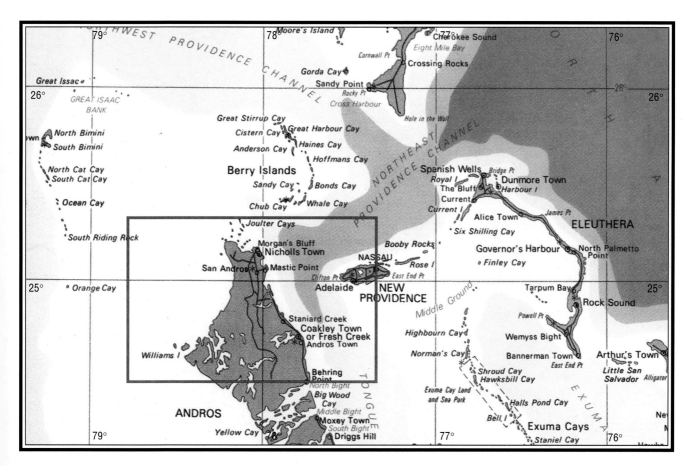

Andros Island

ANDROS ISLAND, over 100 miles in length and 40 miles wide (reckon it the size of Puerto Rico, but without the mountains) is the largest island in the Bahamas. It has about 5,000 inhabitants living in a scattering of isolated village clusters on the east coast, no road system to speak of, four small airfields, one marina, and about three (maybe five, depending on your classification) small resorts. The rest of the island is a wilderness of mahogany and pine forest, scrub, marsh, tidal inlets, and flats. Andros, the least favored (by its government) of all the big Bahamian islands has long been known as "The Sleeping Giant" or "The Big Yard." Why the sparse population and why just the east coast? The answer is that the west coast, a maze of wetland and mud flats, is uninhabitable. The interior, tangled, hot, and rife with insects, has no prevailing cooling winds and is almost uninhabitable. The east coast has the cooling wind, and it has the ocean, both as a means of communication (long before aircraft) and a means of sustenance, primarily by fishing.

If you look at the geography of Andros, you can see that three lateral physical divisions, where three bights of water cut right across the island from east to west, make Andros even less cohesive and less attractive as a ground for settlement. Effectively the land below the North Bight (from Behring Point to the south) is more remote than the fabled boondocks, and both Central Andros (Mangrove Cay) and South Andros can only be reached by boat and air.

All this said, it is water that has saved Andros. First the ocean. Running little more than a mile off the east coast, at well over 100 miles in length Andros has the third largest continuous barrier reef in the world (after Australia's Great Barrier Reef, and the Belize Reef). The extraordinary coral of this reef, and its marine life, has brought marine biologists and divers to Andros from all over the world. Long ago this reef should have been given the status of a World Heritage Site. Each year that the reef continues to lack the environmental protection of the world community highlights our continuing criminal failure to take elemental steps to preserve this frail water planet for our descendants.

Outside the reef, a singular and almost unique inlet of deep ocean water, known as the Tongue of the Ocean, divides Andros from the shallow bank to the east of the Exuma Cays (see chart below). The Tongue of the Ocean is abysmal (some 6,000 feet deep) and suddenly you're there, off the reef in water space, hanging off sheer walls that plummet into blackness. This ocean inlet has brought almost every kind of pelagic fish to the waters off Andros, and with them, the sports fishermen and the commercial fisherman. This phenomenal deep inlet has also brought the US Navy and the Royal Navy, jointly interested in undersea testing and evaluation programs, the purpose of which may be guessed, but is secret. This has also helped Andros survive.

Perhaps the third blessing that water has brought the island is abundant fresh water. Andros now supplies Nassau and New Providence Island with over 50 percent of the fresh water they require, shipped by tanker from North Andros. Now in Andros they'll tell you that both the naval testing and the export of fresh water have barely benefited their island directly, for the rent for the naval bases is paid into the accounts of the Bahamian Government, and the water is taken as a Bahamian birthright. Perhaps a greater annual dividend for Andros might have helped the Sleeping Giant attend to its yard.

Andros is, above all, a strange place. The reasons why Andros is as it is today are clear, and yet it puzzles. In a way it defeats logical explanation and falls, rather like Ireland, into the field of intuitive acceptance: that is how things are. An island where the ghosts of the Arawaks remain almost within touch (evidence of a mass suicide in an inland Blue Hole), a land the Spanish named but gave up as hopeless, a

Andros Reef, 30 feet down.

base for pirates like Henry Morgan whose treasure, so legend has it, remains buried in Andros, a refuge for the hard-pressed Florida Seminoles who were not enchanted by finding themselves and their territory included in the US (whose descendants allegedly survive in Red Bay to this day), a place in which tourist development has never taken root other than in remote fishing camps and latterly one or two dive resorts. Andros is a mystic, still largely unexplored place, fearsome in the remoteness of the interior, which is the home of the dreaded *chickcharnies*, a short-tempered feathered Androsian leprechaun with powerful psychic influence, whose habit it is to live hanging upside down from trees.

THE TONGUE OF THE OCEAN AND THE ANDROS BARRIER REEF

The Tongue of the Ocean, whether you approach it from the shallow green waters of the bank off the Exumas or directly from the Andros Coast is extraordinary, a color change that goes from green to ultramarine to ink blue almost instantly as your depth sounder goes ape and then gives up. If you're bent on fishing, there's nothing that can't be found in that deep blue water and you'll stop fishing for dolphin (not dolphin as in Flipper, but the fish the Spanish named *dorado*: we got it wrong in translation) for you'll catch too many. In the southern circlet of the Tongue of the Ocean they say that marlin, who somehow took a wrong turn off the Marlin Ocean Interstate Highway, are hanging out there and hungry.

As for the naval side, if you're around Andros Town you'll soon learn that AUTEC (the Atlantic Underwater Test and Evaluation Center) is everywhere you look, and manifests

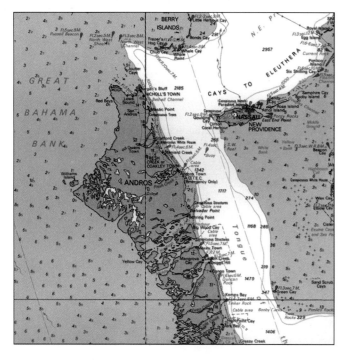

itself in an array of buoys (which attract the dolphin), strange towers, forbidden harbors, and communication masts. Other than using AUTEC facilities as landmarks, there's not much to be gained from their presence if you're a cruising visitor and you're likely to fall short of a welcome if you take an AUTEC harbor as a storm refuge. AUTEC is not for you.

The barrier reef is (the word comes up again and again) "awesome." We're talking about visibility (100 feet is minimal), coral formations, dropoffs and walls, blue holes, marine life, and the whole quintessence of the SCUBA world. You can dive the reef without guides, but you're wise to go guided. Your anchor depths off the reef are deep (45 feet or 50 feet), and your dive depths can be deep too (120 feet to even 185 feet if you wish). The blue holes can be hazardous, sucking in water and expelling water with the tide. You could be stuck in one for a tide change, which could spoil your day if you're on a single 80 cubic foot tank.

ANDROS AS A CRUISING GROUND

We're not surprised that Andros has remained a land apart in the Bahamas, and not surprised that the name Andros doesn't come forward often in cruising circle conversation. We've had a hard enough time trying to figure out the nature of the place and a newcomer to Andros might well be forgiven for believing that chickcharnies built the square offshore towers (as fishing shacks?) and strange creatures called autecs haunt the forests of the interior. Taking a cool dispassionate look at navigation in Andros is as difficult an exercise in comprehension.

Andros certainly falls into the big island category. It's Big Island magnified. What's the cruising analysis? There's just the one (east) coast that's approachable, (plus a shoal

Andros Reef, 30 feet down.

Ministry of Tourism

Bonefish.

draft trans-Andros passage through the South Bight). That one coastline, with its barrier reef, presents problems. There are very few places you can enter through the reef, and very few places where you can navigate with safety running inside the reef. There are too many coral heads, shallows, and the overall depth is mostly shoal draft at best. Support facilities for the cruising vessel are minimal in Andros. You could say virtually non-existent. Fresh Creek is the only place anywhere close to development and it's small (we were told "small is beautiful, and we want to keep it that way") and has little to offer in the support line.

We debated at length how best to handle Andros. We concluded that if we worked our way along the east coast, whichever way we took it, we'd end up writing a land guide to Andros, for there's almost no navigation advice we could give other than to say "once you're in Andros water, you're on your own—get someone local to guide you if this scares you." A negative approach, you might say, but there are plenty of straight travel guides out there if you want to read about the island. Think it through. The essence of cruising is safe, enjoyable navigation, not setting yourself the ultimate testing experience. Other factors come into the cruising "wish list," none of which are soft or decadent: airports for crew changes, marinas with telephones and shore power, fuel, and backup facilities (however minimal) coming up somewhere on your route every now and again. You might reasonably expect landfalls worth discovery trips ashore, and to be able to find transport to make your way around if you wish. Safe anchorages will be high on your list if you want to be alone, or away from telephones and shore power. Continue the analysis for yourself if you wish, but the greater part of Andros (while reachable by boat and often only by boat) is not, in our opinion, an area we would class as a cruising ground.

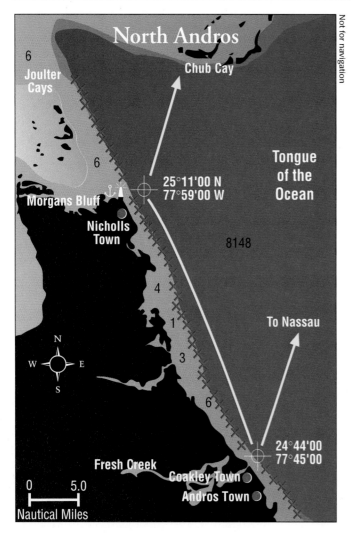

North Andros is the only part of the island that comes even remotely close to satisfying any of these parameters. We've concentrated on two areas that might feature on your visit list for one reason or another. The first is Fresh Creek, and the second (far less well-favored) is the north tip of Andros, Morgans Bluff and the Bethel Channel area (Conch Sound and Nicholls Town). In future editions, as Andros develops, we'll keep pace and we'll add more. Nothing we've said denies the fact that the whole east coast of Andros offers superb fishing (deep sea, reef, and flats) and superb diving. Central and South Andros offers tiny remote settlements where you can tuck yourself in (but carry insect repellent that works—you'll need it) and fish the flats. If this is your life, go for it; and if you're one of the small band who commute from Florida to the Exumas by way of the South Bight (where you may have 4 feet at high water) go for it. In our catamaran days, with a 2-foot-6-inch draft and no compelling requirement for shore power, we would never have hesitated to explore these unfrequented waterways. But for the reasons we've given, and as Fresh Creek is

the only place in Andros with the facilities to take cruising boats, we start there and work our way north to cover the other options.

Approach Routes to Andros

The Mid-Exumas to Fresh Creek

Staniel Cay (1.5 nm W)	STANW	24° 13' 00 N	076° 32' 00 W
Fresh Creek (1 nm E)	FRESH	24° 44' 00 N	077° 45' 00 W

The route from the mid-Exumas, just north of Staniel Cay, is an easy one (73.32 nm on a heading of 301°M) and one that avoids the worst of the coral head–cluttered areas lying on the western edge of the Exuma bank, just before you gain the deep water of the Tongue of the Ocean. We tried to find a course that could be taken as one straight run with the minimum of eyeball navigation on the way, and think we achieved it.

There are two areas where you should keep a particularly sharp lookout for coral heads. The first is around 24° 25' 00 N 077° 00' 00 W. There are a few there. The second area is just before you reach the Tongue of the Ocean. Around 24° 30' 22 N 077° 13' 00 W you'll find yourself in 12–13 feet of water with a minefield of coral heads all around you. Most of them are safely beneath the surface but don't trust any of them. Go slowly, and hand steer for a while. Within 2 nm you'll hit the 100-fathom line, and two miles later you'll have 500 fathoms under your keel.

Nassau to Morgans Bluff, Bethel Channel, or Fresh Creek

Nassau Harbour W (0.25 nm off)	NASHW	25° 05' 30 N	077° 21' 30 W
Nassau Harbour NW (2 nm off)	NASNW	25° 06' 30 N	077° 23' 00 W
Nassau Goulding Cay (1 nm W)	GLDNG	25° 01' 30 N	077° 35' 30 W
Morgans Bluff (2 nm E)	MRGNE	25° 11' 00 N	077° 59' 00 W
Morgans Bluff Entry Buoys	MRGNB	25° 11' 09 N	078° 01' 02 W
Bethel Channel (1.5 nm E)	BTHEL	25° 08' 30 N	077° 57' 30 W
Fresh Creek (1 nm E)	FRESH	24° 44' 00 N	077° 45' 00 W

From Nassau, immediately having cleared the west entrance to Nassau Harbour, you want to get offshore something like 2 nm before setting your course for Andros. If you're heading for Morgans Bluff, you'll have 32.9 nm to run on a heading of 283°M. If you're heading for Bethel Channel (Nicholls Town and Conch Sound), it's 31.3 nm on a heading of 279°M. If you're going to Fresh Creek, after leaving Nassau Harbour the best way is to go coastal, visual all the way, to just 1 nm west of Goulding Cay on the west tip of New Providence Island. Then set a direct course for Fresh Creek. You'll have 19.51 nm to run from Goulding Cay on a heading of 211°M.

Fresh Creek Harbour.

Chub Cay to Morgans Bluff, Bethel Channel, or Fresh Creek

Chub Cay Entry Waypoint	CHUBC	25° 24' 15 N	077° 54' 50 W
Chub Cay (1 nm S)	CHUBS	25° 23' 15 N	077° 54' 50 W
Morgans Bluff (2 nm E)	MRGNE	25° 11' 00 N	077° 59' 00 W
Morgans Bluff Entry Buoys	MRGNB	25° 11' 09 N	078° 01' 02 W
Bethel Channel (1.5 nm E)	BTHEL	25° 08' 30 N	077° 57' 30 W
Fresh Creek (1 nm E)	FRESH	24° 44' 00 N	077° 45' 00 W

From Chub Cay down to Andros is a straightforward run from our waypoint 1 nm due south of Chub Cay. For Morgan's Bluff it's 12.82 nm on 202°M. For the Bethel Channel (Nicholls Town and Conch Sound) it's 14.95 nm on 194°. For Fresh Creek, to our mind the most likely destination, it's 40.25 nm on a heading of 172°M.

Fresh Creek (Andros and Coakley Towns)

Approach to Fresh Creek

The approach to Fresh Creek is simple. There are two radio masts, one (AUTEC) some way south of Fresh Creek (and there's the AUTEC harbor there too, and an orange and white checkered water tower) and one radio mast (Batelco) north of Fresh Creek. There are two AUTEC towers (like square huts on stilts), one south of the entrance channel, and one north (right on the edge of it). To the north a string of some seven barren rocks (with a little green on some of them) run north-south, ending in a channel light marker. You pass out of deep water as you get closer to the channel light, and the rocks on your starboard side mark the line of the inshore reef. Of course that reef continues on your port

side too, but it's not so obvious. Favor the light side (the north), and favor that AUTEC tower to the north too (but don't get closer to it than 200 feet).

As you get closer to the entry to the Creek, you'll see a rock promontory running out a little way from the north point, and there's shallow water to the south (there's a ledge there, about 100 feet out in the narrows). Just swing around that rock promontory, which can be clearly seen, stay safely off the ledge, and make your way up Fresh Creek holding center channel.

ANCHORAGE AND MARINA

The Lighthouse Marina comes up almost immediately on your port side. If you want to anchor, go on past it, and find a place in the basin before the road bridge, and far enough off the government dock (which is to starboard, past the yellow Chickcharney Hotel) so that the mailboats have a turning circle. It's said that the holding there is not good, which comes as no surprise for dredging in the past and the swift-running tides must have scoured the bottom clean.

The tidal flow is formidable (over 6 knots at extreme tides) and making your way into the Lighthouse Yacht Club and Marina at any time other than slack tide demands well applied power and a degree of seamanship not normally called for at most marinas. It's worth holding off momen-

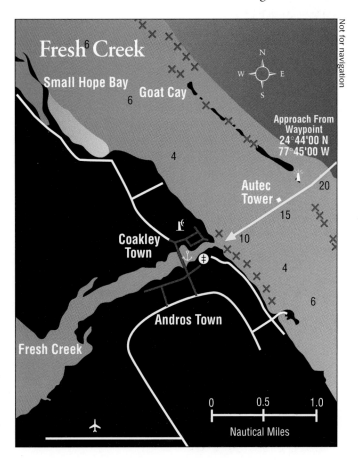

tarily to check the direction and force of the stream before committing yourself to an approach. Once you're there, and tied up, you're fine. You have hotel accommodation with its bar and restaurant, showers, laundry, fuel, and willing attention. There is no other place like it, no other marina, in Andros. If you are using your boat day by day, be aware that AUTEC broadcast warnings of areas they have declared off limits over Channel 16 each day.

Andros Town and Coakley Town

Andros Town and Coakley Town are Siamese-twin settlements linked by a bridge over Fresh Creek, and the whole settled area can be called Fresh Creek. Andros Town, to the south, has the Lighthouse Yacht Club and Marina, and the outlet for Androsian batik fabrics, tucked away behind in the trees. Other than the old lighthouse on the south entrance to the Creek which is in a sad state of neglect, that's Andros Town.

Across the bridge Coakley Town boasts two hotels, the Chickcharney and the Landmark, both with bars and restaurants and a kind of mid-Western rail town feel to them. There's a "supermarket" and there are a number of small shops, but Coakley Town is sprawling, perhaps awaiting better days, and has little to offer but the watering holes adopted by off-duty AUTEC personnel. Hank Roberts, the dockmaster at the Lighthouse Marina, has just opened a new watering hole with a small restaurant (which has clearly won AUTEC favor).

THE FRESH CREEK HINTERLAND

Explorers venturing out into the Fresh Creek hinterland will not find a multiplicity of excitements. In the south there's the AUTEC base. To the north, some 3 miles out of Coakley Town, you come to the mini-settlement of Small Hope Bay where, on a beach promontory, the Canadian Dick Birch opened his Small Hope Bay Club in the 1960s. Devoted primarily to SCUBA diving and the pursuit of a simple life that could be summed up as sarongs and bare feet, for over thirty years the charismatic Birch, with the assistance of three successive wives (who all stayed on with the team), built up a business that has a 60 percent repeat rate and gave birth to Androsian batik. Peter Birch has now taken over the reins on the death of his father, but the little resort continues unchanged. It's small, family, totally informal, communal in its life-style, and your welcome will be friendly.

Unbelievably, more so with all that barrier reef, Small Hope Bay is the only dive operation in business in Andros. There have been others, which have failed. If you're interested, sign on with the Small Hope Bay dive staff. They don't follow the PADI/NAUI/DAN rules for recreation diving and 185-foot dives are regularly on the program, but you're not compelled to go deeper than you wish. Nor are C-cards asked for or dive logs. All that's required before you dive with them is a simple checkout to ensure that you can remove and replace your mask and regulator under water.

Fresh Creek to the Bethel Channel and Morgans Bluff

Fresh Creek (1 nm E)	FRESH	24° 44' 00 N	077° 45' 00 W
Bethel Channel (1.5 nm E)	BTHEL	25° 08' 30 N	077° 57' 30 W
Morgans Bluff (2 nm E)	MRGNE	25° 11' 00 N	077° 59' 00 W
Morgans Bluff Entry Buoys	MRGNB	25° 11' 09 N	078° 01' 02 W

As a straight course from Fresh Creek, our Morgans Bluff waypoint is a run of 29.83 nm on a heading of 340°M. This course keeps you in deep water all the way. If you elect to try the Bethel Channel (for Conch Sound or Nicholls Town), your run on this heading stops short at 26.99 nm. We're not entirely happy with the Bethel Channel or with Conch Sound and Nicholls Town.

The Bethel Channel

Bethel Channel (1.5 nm E)	BTHEL	25° 08' 30 N	077° 57' 30 W

The Bethel Channel is the only viable boat channel through the Andros barrier reef between Fresh Creek and Morgans Bluff. It had importance in the past when the mailboat used the channel to serve Conch Sound settlement to the south of the Bethel Channel and Nicholls Town to the north. Now the Bethel Channel is a route for local, small-draft boats and is not an entryway to anchorages, docks, shoreside facilities, or any of the infrastructure of value to a visiting boat. Why do we mention it? Because the Bethel Channel is identified on the charts, and if we ignore it, you'll wonder why we missed it.

The Channel has an entry range (lighted, with white lights), which will bring you in through the passage (reckon 4 feet at MLW but the locals claim a greater depth) into inshore water. Keep going until you are about 100 feet from the shore, but use your eyes judging the water depth rather than measuring that distance off so precisely. Then turn north if you want Nicholls Town or turn south for Conch Sound, staying inshore (100–150 feet) all the while.

CONCH SOUND

Only the old Government concrete dock with a survey mark embedded in it remains to remind the straggling Conch Sound of its mailboat days, but even then the mailboat couldn't get in right up to the dock and passengers and goods had to be tendered ashore and embarked. They'll tell you that Conch Sound is a good anchorage, all along that coastline south of Bethel Channel, and has 7 feet of water if you don't get too far south and too close to Scotts Cays. Just off the cays, on the reef, you can see the 1926 wreck of the *Potomac*. Wrecks are always an encouraging sign when you're trying to work out routes through a reef, but the *Potomac* is a great dive site.

Deep water trophy.

The same reef that stranded the *Potomac* is the prime reason for local faith in the Conch Sound anchorage, in that the barrier reef gives protection even in onshore weather and (we quote) "it don't never get rough in here." The craft we found using Conch Sound were all Whaler-size local boats. As for Conch Sound as a place to visit, even though it has the somewhat surprising, newish, and upmarket Conch Sound Resort Inn (tucked away well inshore, in the village), we'd advise leaving it off your list of ports-of-call.

NICHOLLS TOWN

Nicholls Town is so spread out that it has no comprehensible cohesive identity. On the shore side, the very heart was taken out of Nicholls Town when the Andros Beach Hotel and its Dive Shop closed and the vandals started to take over. It has a great site on a pretty sand beach, and the hotel's docks (now deteriorating fast) were at least a place where you could secure alongside, although there was no power or water, you were open to the northeast and south, and exposed to surge. There's another small dock in Nicholls Town, immediately after you round the point after heading north from Bethel Channel and enter the shallow Nicholls Town Bay, but this is for local boats and you should not consider it. Until such time as the Andros Beach Hotel regains life and its docks are rebuilt, cross Nicholls Town off your list.

MORGANS BLUFF

You can't miss Morgans Bluff, a great 40-foot high spine of limestone that's the final marker of Andros Island. To its north there are small cays and shoals, but if nothing else Andros ends in style with its one long grey, jagged headland. The entry channel to Morgans Bluff is well marked with conventional buoys and you'll have no problems. The outer buoys lie at 25° 11' 09 N 078° 01' 02 W and are easy to pick up.

Around the corner behind the bluff, to port you have the long government dock, which is off limits to all but mail boats, traders, and the water tankers. The anchorage lies off the curve of sand beach, giving around 8 feet or more at MLW, and is completely exposed to the north. If you are there in a Norther, unless you have shoal draft and can work your way behind one of the cays to the north, or further round to the west into Lowe Sound, you're going to be uncomfortable if you stay. The anchorage is large, so you're unlikely to be crowded, but even if there's room to swing, you should set two anchors.

There's one small commercial harbor in Morgans Bluff, approached through an entry channel that carries a good 8 feet of water (as far as we could tell), and an interior depth greater than that. This has one concrete wharf, given to the mailboats and traders who are rejects from the major government dock outside, and the rest is a crude excavated basin, still unwalled but lined with old car tires with a surprising run of rustproof-painted iron bollards hammered into the bare soil. It is there that you'll find fuel. We hesitate to say a fuel dock, for you have to come alongside the car tires closest to the fuel pumps, and jump the gap to shore, but this is the only marine fuel in Andros until you reach Fresh Creek.

What of Morgans Bluff itself? There's Willie's bar by the fuel place which, if nothing else, has atmosphere. Further inland there are the derelict buildings of a failed wood pulp enterprise, whose smarter housing, high on the bluff, has now become the enclave of local government servants, police officers, schoolteachers, and the like. Apart from Henry Morgan's Cave (not very striking or believable), which lies off the main road in the limestone strata under the housing estate of the police officers and the schoolteachers, there's nothing more in Morgans Bluff.

Why go there? Go there if you need fuel. Go there for shelter (but not in a Norther). Go there to get a night's sleep at anchor, if your passage planning works out that way. Finally, if you're interested in Bahamian sailing regattas, go there for the Morgans Bluff Regatta in June. You'll be there with some 3,000 others, but if that's your scene, you'll find a place transformed. Like a sub-tropical Brigadoon, Morgans Bluff, which otherwise appears to have perhaps twenty visible inhabitants, takes off over one wild weekend and is jumping.

YELLOW PAGES

FRESH CREEK
(ANDROS AND COAKLEY TOWNS)

Little is known about Andros in the cruising world, due mainly to the lack of good anchorages or marinas. As the main harbor for the entire island, it is still a surprise to find Fresh Creek so quiet. It attracts those who have known of its hidden charms for many years, while cruising boats looking for excitement and glamour tend to ignore it. The largest island in the Bahamas, stretching some 100 miles from top to bottom, with some of the best scuba diving in the world together with superb fishing and more than 50 varieties of orchids growing here, Andros is still a mysterious and largely unexplored island.

There are two main settlements that border the Fresh Creek harbor entrance, so we will list their facilities together. Andros Town lies to the south, Coakley Town to the north, with a bridge linking the two. With the peaceful atmosphere that pervades Fresh Creek, you feel that visitors really can come here to relax. The few shops and restaurants are within easy walking distance of the marina. Fresh Creek is a Port of Entry for the Bahamas. The other two ports of entry on Andros are Mastic Point, near San Andros, and Congo Town in the south of the island. **Customs** and **Immigration** in Coakley Town are opposite the Landmark Hotel.

MARINA

LIGHTHOUSE YACHT CLUB AND MARINA
Tel: 242-368-2305 • Fax: 368-2300 • VHF 16

Owned and run by the Bahamian Government, the *Lighthouse Yacht Club and Marina* is the only marina on Andros. The hotel and the docks are both well maintained, and dockmaster Hank Roberts is extremely helpful.

Slips	17
MLW at dock	8 ft. to 10 ft.
Dockage	65¢ per ft. per day
Power	$12 per day for 50A power
Fuel	Open 7 am to 3 pm for diesel and gasoline.
Water	$5 per day
Telephone	Public telephone
Showers	Yes, very clean
Laundry	$2 per washer or dryer. Ask the Dockmaster how to start the machines.
Restaurant	*The Lighthouse Yacht Club Restaurant*, open from 7 am to 10 pm.
Ice	$5 a bag
Swimming	Pool with Tiki bar for marina guests
Bicycles	Yes
Tennis	Court available, free use of rackets.
Accommodations	*Andros Lighthouse Yacht Club*
Credit cards	Visa, MasterCard, and Amex
Dockmaster	Hank Roberts

SERVICES IN FRESH CREEK

Bank
Royal Bank of Canada (in Andros Town) Tel: 368-2071
Open Wednesdays 10:30 am to 4:30 pm.
Clinic
Health Centre in Fresh Creek Tel: 368-2038
One doctor, one nurse.

Laundromat
Tel: 368-2201. Open from 9 am to 5 pm Monday to Saturday.
Police
Tel: 368-2626
Post Office
In Coakley Town. Open from 9:30 am to 1 pm, and 2 pm to 4 pm, Monday to Friday.
Telephones
Batelco in Coakley Town. Open from 9:30 am to 4:30 pm, Monday to Friday. There are two phones inside the building and two for phone cards outside. Phone cards are for sale there.

SHOPPING IN FRESH CREEK

Boutiques
The Boutique at Small Hope Bay Lodge Tel: 368-2013
Open daily from 9 am to 5 pm. Androsia island fashions, jewelry, T-shirts, and film.
Clothing, Gifts & Souvenirs
Androsia Factory Outlet Store, at the Androsia Factory Tel: 368-2020
Open from 8 am to 4 pm, Monday to Friday, to 1 pm on Saturdays. Superb hand-screened batik that is exported worldwide; guided tours of the factory are available.
Straw Shop Locally made hats, baskets, and straw goods.
Groceries
General Store, in Coakley Town. Open from 8 am to 10 pm, Monday to Saturday, to 12:30 pm on Sundays.
Liquor
Skinny's Wholesale Liquor Open 9 am to 5 pm, Monday to Friday.

RESTAURANTS & BARS IN FRESH CREEK

The Lighthouse Yacht Club Restaurant Tel: 368-2305
Open from 7 am to 10 pm.

Landmark Hotel and Restaurant Also known as *Skinny's,* was undergoing renovation at the time of writing.

Small Hope Bay Lodge Tel: 368-2013 Located 3 miles north of Andros Town. Open for breakfast from 8 to 9:30 am, buffet lunch from noon to 1:30 pm, and from 7 to 9 pm for dinner. Dinner is $30 fixed price, including wine. Reservations required. Closed the last week of September and first week of October.

Hank's Place in Coakley Town Tel: 368-2447 Open for Bahamian food from 10 am to 10 pm, closed Sundays.

Chickcharnie Hotel Opening times depend on demand; it was closed when we were there.

GETTING AROUND

Airport
Andros Town Airport is three miles south of the town.
Bahamasair Fifteen-minute flights twice daily to and from Nassau. Some charter companies also fly in.
Small Hope Bay Lodge
Offers a one-hour flight to Andros Town from Fort Lauderdale.
Bicycle Rental
Small Hope Bay Lodge
Car Rental
Ellis Whymms Tel: 368-6224

Mailboat
Tel: 242-393-1064 Mailboats operate out of Potters Cay in Nassau. The *Lady D* leaves Fresh Creek at 7:30 am on Saturdays, and returns at 6 pm on Tuesdays. Call the dockmaster in Nassau for more details.

Taxi
Irwin Mackey Tel: 368-2333/4241 The fare from *Andros Lighthouse Yacht Club* to Andros Town is about $20 for two people.

SPORTS

Diving
Small Hope Bay Lodge Tel: 368-2014 The dive shop has clothing and Androsia Batik, as well as rental equipment. Specialty dives on *The Wall* and in *Blue Holes*. Weekly slide presentations and discovery snorkel with resident marine biologist.

Dive Sites
Over the Wall and *The Edge of the Wall* are classic barrier reef dives, while the *Coral Staircase* descends in steps down coral platforms. The *Marion* shipwreck lies in 70 feet of water; a barge, crane, and tractor await you.

Fishing
Andros Island Bonefishing Club (at Cargill Creek) Tel: 368-5167 Boats and guides available.

Cargill Creek Fishing Lodge Tel: 368-5129/5046 Skiffs and guides.

Charlie's Haven at Bellring Point Tel: 368-4087 Bonefishing.

Tennis
There are courts at *The Lighthouse Yacht Club*.

ACCOMMODATIONS

Andros Lighthouse Yacht Club Tel: 242-368-2305 Twenty rooms available from $130 per night, MAP $40.

Small Hope Bay Lodge Tel: 242-368-2013 Twenty beachfront cottages from $150 per night, including three meals daily. Custom-tailored specialty dives, bone, reef, and deep sea fishing, dive packages, hot tub, bicycles, sailboat, windsurfers, and nature walks. They offer flights into Andros from Florida.

Coakley House A three-bedroom house, set on two acres of land with a dock, available to rent through *Small Hope Bay Lodge*. Rates from $250 per person per day.

NICHOLLS TOWN

There is a Customs Office, a police station and the Andromed Medical Centre (329-2171 or 329-2055) on the Nicholls Town Highway, all housed in one smart new building on the outskirts of the settlement. The Batelco office has telephones inside and outside, and there is a CIBC bank (329-2382) and post office in Nicholls Town. Also you'll find *The Green Windows Inn* (329-2194), a supermarket, liquor stores, laundromats, and you can rent a car from *Tropical Car Rental* (329-2515). The two main resorts here, the *Andros Beach Hotel* and the *San Andros Hotel*, have been closed down for the last three years and show little sign of reopening, but other areas are prospering. You can buy diesel or gasoline at the commercial harbor.

MORGANS BLUFF

Willy's Water Lounge is a good starting point for information. For transport, Evan Rolle (329-7293) offers trips out to the reef in his whaler, as well as a taxi service. *Willy's Water Lounge* will direct you to the many grocery stores in the area, send you off in a taxi, and put you in touch with Philip, who takes dive trips to the reef. *Henry Morgan's Cave* is near Morgans Bluff, but take a flashlight with you. The settlement of Red Bay, home to the descendants of Seminole Indians, is 40 minutes away by car.

RESTAURANTS IN MORGANS BLUFF

Willy's Water Lounge at Morgans Bluff commercial harbor. Offers helpful advice, and good, simple food.

Rumours Restaurant and Disco on the road to Nicholls Town. A popular local restaurant.

Conch Sound Resort Inn Tel: 329-2060

Green Windows Hotel and Restaurant, Nicholls Town Tel: 329-2194 Restaurant, bar, hotel, liquor store, and rental cars

Big Josh Seafood and Restaurant at Lowe Sound

Joe's Seafood Grill at Lowe Sound. A new venture by a young local Androsian, the liveliest place to go with music every night, except Sundays.

FISHING TOURNAMENTS AND REGATTAS

June
North Andros Regatta, at Morgans Bluff, with a fishing tournament and a wild boar hunt. For more information, contact the commissioner's office at 242-368-2340.

July
Mangrove Cay Independence Regatta For information, contact the commissioner's office at 242-369-0494.

August
Annual Regatta at Lisbon Creek

Mangrove Cay Emancipation Day Regatta For information, contact the commissioner's office at 242-369-0494.

September
Annual Bahamas Free Diving Championship at Nicholls Town.

November
North Andros Thanksgiving Bonefish Tournament

THINGS TO DO IN ANDROS

- Dive and snorkel the third largest barrier reef in the world.
- Explore the creeks and lakes on this unspoiled island.
- Fish to your heart's content.
- Watch out for the chickcharnies; special elves with three fingers, three toes, red eyes, and feathers. Oh yes, and beards too. If you laugh at them, you may find your head is turned backwards.

Part IV

The Southern Cruising Grounds

The Northern Exuma Cays

The Southern Exuma Cays and Great Exuma Island

The Out Islands North of the Tropic of Cancer

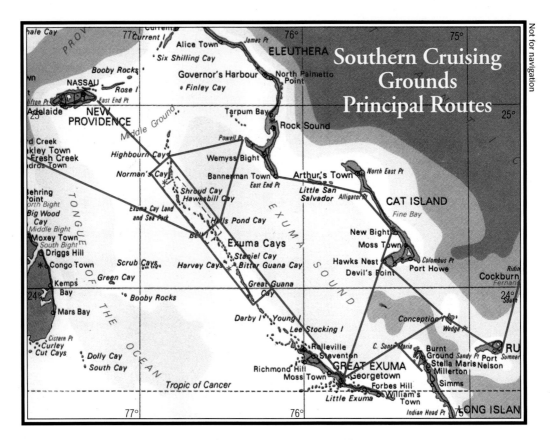

Southern Cruising
Grounds
Principal Routes

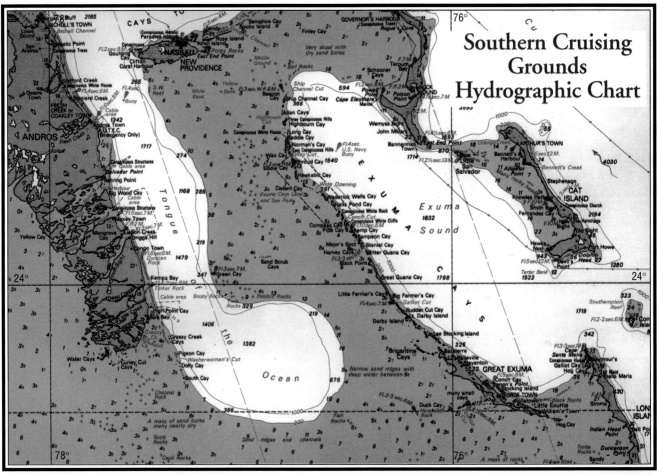

Southern Cruising
Grounds
Hydrographic Chart

Chapter 14
The Northern Exuma Cays
Allan's Cay to Little Farmers Cay

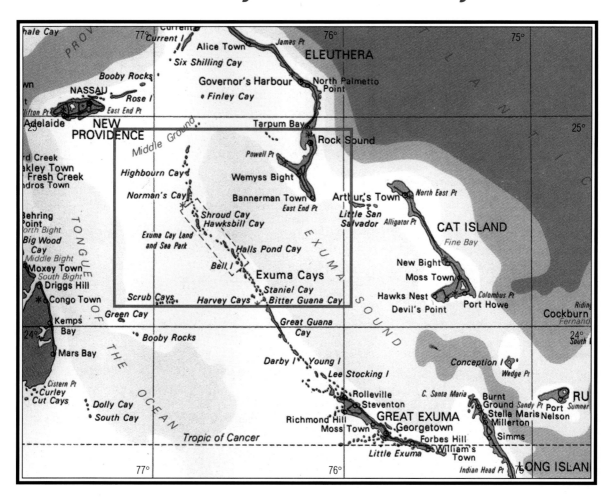

The Exumas

THE Exuma Cays and Great Exuma Island rate, with the Abacos, as one of the two most popular cruising destinations in the Bahamas. Both, as it happens, are roughly the same length measured as a chain of islands (the Exumas at some 95 nm are slightly longer) and both offer much the same attractions to the cruising boater: Bahamian water at its best, an apparently endless succession of small cays where if you feel escapist you can be on your own, and waystations where you can find fuel, food, and the rest of the cruising world if you've missed them.

It's a hard choice to say which cruising ground is the most attractive. The Abacos are easier to reach from Florida, for the Gulf Stream and the Little Bahama Bank are your only positioning passages. To reach the Exumas you have the Gulf Stream, the far greater extent of the Great Bahama Bank, the Northwest Providence Channel, and the Yellow Bank transit southeast from Nassau before you reach the top of the chain. There are differences when you reach your destination. The Abacos are more settled and have many more "pit" stops where you can find all the trappings of stateside life. In the Exumas, apart from Great Exuma Island with George Town, a three-figure population is exceptional and you could say that the facilities you'll find pretty much match the needs of the population.

The Exumas run northwest to southeast from 25° N to 23° 25' N, the chain starting some 35 nm southeast from Nassau and New Providence Island, and ending at the point where the Out Islands (the truly remote southern Out Islands) start. In some ways the Exumas are not dissimilar to the Florida Keys as a cruising ground, for you have two sides, an east coast and a west coast, both navigable, and a number of cuts between the islands that allow you to play the flexibility of switching sides to advantage in the light of the prevailing winds.

In the Exumas the east side is the deep-water side, Exuma Sound. Here you have no problems about coral heads, sand banks, and shoals, but you may have to face higher seas (for you are more open to the ocean) and the southeast prevailing wind may give you waves on top of those swells. To the west the Exuma Bank is protected from the prevailing wind, but it's the shallow side with every problem that Bahamian waters can give you, just to test your skills. You have to feel your way there. The difficult part of your decision making, if you can put it that way, is that the navigation is better on the Exuma Sound side, easier, simpler, no problem areas, and generally the cuts are easier to identify and enter from the east, *but* the prevailing weather is southeast and so much of the time the Exuma Bank offers you less wind, a gentler sea state, better conditions.

Our advice is simple. If you're in a hurry to reach George Town, go down Exuma Sound unless the weather is adverse. If you want to cruise the Exumas in the time-honored fashion, island by island, cay by cay, go the Banks route. Make your initial choice to fit the weather, and bear in mind you can switch from side to side, through the cuts, as you wish.

Just one glance at a map or a chart will tell you that the primary approach routes to the Exumas lie from Nassau and New Providence Island to the northwest, from Andros to the west, from South Eleuthera to the east, and in the south from the open ocean to the east of Long Island. We'll deal with each one in turn.

From Nassau

Nassau Harbor E (0.75 nm off)	NASHE	25° 04' 30 N	077° 17' 30 W
Porgee Rocks	PRGEE	25° 03' 45 N	077° 15' 00 W
Porgee Rocks SE	PRGSE	25° 03' 00 N	077° 12' 00 W
Junction White & Yellow Banks	WYBNK	24° 52' 00 N	077° 12' 00 W
Allan's Cay	ALLAN	24° 44' 45 N	076° 51' 00 W
Highborne W	HIGHW	24° 42' 30 N	076° 51' 00 W
Highborne E	HIGHE	24° 42' 00 N	076° 48' 00 W

As you leave Nassau for the Exumas, there are many choices open in choosing your landfall, but a waypoint off the Allan's Cays is probably a sound choice. This gives you the options of visiting Allan's Cay (where you can anchor, and see the iguanas), going on to Highborne Cay (for their anchorage, or the marina), going through Highborne Cut (to gain Exuma Sound), or continuing south along the Bank. Although just one landfall waypoint off the Allan's Cays would serve all these options, we list two waypoints, the first for Allan's Cay, and the second for Highborne Cay and Highborne Cut.

THE DIRECT ROUTE OVER THE YELLOW BANK

Porgee Rocks to Porgee SE	2.82 nm	110°M
Porgee SE to Allan's Cay	26.38 nm	139°M

On this approach your problem area is the Yellow Bank. There are many coral heads in this area, the shallowest of which lie some 3 feet below the surface at MLW. The average depth on the Yellow Bank at MLW will be around 6 feet. The bad news is that you cannot afford to run the Yellow Bank on autopilot. You must keep careful watch, you need the sun in the right position, you need favorable weather, and you must be prepared to thread your way around the coral heads as you cross the Yellow Bank.

Reckon that the tide on the Yellow Bank will be one hour behind Nassau. Your optimum time to gain the Yellow Bank is around 11 am, so that the sun is to your advantage. Finally, if the wind is going to be on your head and 20 knots

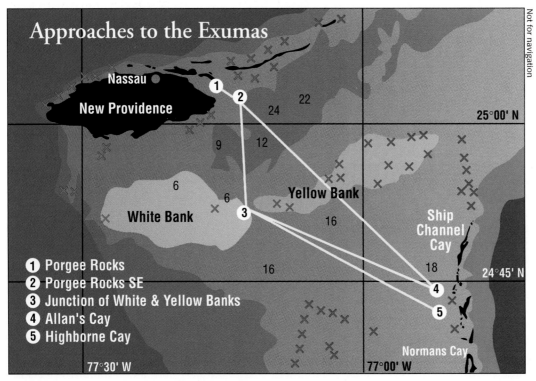

Approaches to the Exumas

Nassau
New Providence

Yellow Bank

White Bank

Ship Channel Cay

Normans Cay

Not for navigation

25°00' N

24°45' N

❶ Porgee Rocks
❷ Porgee Rocks SE
❸ Junction of White & Yellow Banks
❹ Allan's Cay
❺ Highborne Cay

77°30' W   77°00' W

or more, you'll get steep, nasty seas. You would be better off waiting for more favorable weather.

AVOIDING THE YELLOW BANK

If you are prepared to set a dogleg course directly south from our Porgee Rocks southeast waypoint, after 11 nm you'll reach a point midway between the Yellow and White Banks. From this waypoint you can alter course and head for your chosen landfall. Although this route is generally believed to be clear of keel-threatening coral heads and rock ledges, *don't* take it on trust. There are isolated coral heads there. From the time you pass on to the Bank (around 25° 55' 35 N 077° 12' 00 W) go slow and keep a lookout until you are well past the junction between the Yellow and White Banks on your new heading (116° for Allan's, 120° for Highborne) and safely southeast of the Yellow Bank. Read the chart, and use your eyes. The depth of water is a good indicator, perhaps 9–12 feet at MLW where you should take it slowly, and another 5 feet elsewhere. Take it slowly once again on your close approach to your final waypoint.

Porgee Rocks to Porgee SE	2.82 nm	110°M
Porgee SE to Yellow-White Junction	11.00 nm	185°M
Yellow-White Junction to Allan's Cay	20.39 nm	116°M
Yellow-White Junction to Highborne E	23.97 nm	120°M
Through Highborne Cut	Go Visual	

From Andros

Fresh Creek (1 nm E)	FRESH	24° 44' 00 N	077° 45' 00 W
Edge of Bank	EDBNK	24° 27' 30 N	077° 04' 00 W
Conch Cut W (6.5 nm W)	CONCW	24° 17' 00 N	076° 39' 00 W
Conch Cut E (0.5 nm E)	CONCE	24° 17' 30 N	076° 31' 00 W

From Andros we'd assume that Fresh Creek is your most likely departure point, and the most useful arrival waypoint you could choose is off Conch Cut, giving you the options of turning north for Warderick Wells or south for Sampson or Staniel Cays, turning north or south for other points, or going through Conch Cut to get into Exuma Sound.

On this approach route there's one area where you will find reefs and coral heads and *must* go slow, keeping a sharp lookout, and that's the point where you leave the deep water of the Tongue of the Ocean and come on to the Bank. We mark this as a waypoint to remind you. A second area where you must go carefully is after reaching our Conch Cut west waypoint, where you have sandbores to north and south as you go visual to Conch Cut itself. See our section on Conch Cut on page 213.

Fresh Creek to Edge of Bank	40.77 nm	119°M
Edge of Bank to Conch Cut W	25.08 nm	120°M
Through Conch Cut	Go Visual	

From Eleuthera

Cape Eleuthera (0.5 nm W)	CAPEW	24° 50' 20 N	076° 21' 05 W
Davis Harbour Entry Mark	DAVHM	24° 43' 49 N	076° 15' 05 W
Highborne E	HIGHE	24° 42' 00 N	076° 48' 00 W
Highborne W	HIGHW	24° 42' 30 N	076° 51' 00 W
Conch Cut E (0.5 nm E)	CONCE	24° 17' 30 N	076° 31' 00 W

From Eleuthera we reckon the best departure points are either just off Cape Eleuthera (which also suits Cape Eleuthera Marina if you use it) or just off Davis Harbour, taking either Highborne Cut or Conch Cut as your arrival waypoints. You then have the choice of staying in Exuma Sound, or making your way on to the Bank.

Cape Eleuthera to Highborne E	25.82 nm	257°M
Davis Harbour to Highborne E	29.96 nm	273°M
Cape Eleuthera to Conch Cut E	32.15 nm	203°M
Davis Harbour to Conch Cut E	28.37 nm	217°M
All passages through the Cuts	Go Visual	

From the South

| Cape Santa Maria (2 nm N) | SANTM | 23° 43' 00 N | 075° 20' 30 W |
| George Town Harbour (N entry) | GTHAR | 23° 34' 30 N | 075° 48' 00 W |

Making your way into the Central Bahamas from the south, all routes can be said to converge at Cape Santa Maria, the northernmost point of Long Island. Here you have to stand well out from land to avoid the reefs, and from here you can set a straight course for the entry point to George Town Harbour, which is almost bound to be your chosen entry point to the Exumas, if not to the Bahamas.

| Cape Santa Maria to George Town | 22.24 nm | 239°M |

A WARNING

Popularly, there is believed to be a route from North Eleuthera (Current Island), or Fleeming Channel to its southwest, which will take you to Exuma Sound or on to the Bank in the Beacon Cay area. We do not believe that this is a viable route.

The area of Bank to the immediate north of Exuma Sound in the Middle Ground–Finley Cay–Schooner Cays triangle is far more shoal, and far more hazardous, than the charts suggest.

We strongly recommend you do not attempt it.

The Principal Navigable Cuts Between the Exuma Cays

There are almost as many cuts or passes between the Exuma Bank and Exuma Sound as there are cays and islands in the Exumas. Some are navigable, in the fullest sense, given the right conditions. Others are more difficult passes, which you may explore in your dinghy, but are not transits between the Exuma Bank and Exuma Sound that we'd recommend. Even the navigable ones, as we've said, are subject to weather, and by that we mean the state of the tide, wind direction, wind strength, and the angle of the sun. Wind against tide will inevitably set up adverse seas, which at best will be uncomfortable, and at the worst, something approaching an Abaco Rage—meaning dangerous seas that could, particularly in some passes, be life threatening.

What we now list are the principal cuts we use. Other passes, which you may bring into use once you have gained the knowledge and confidence to negotiate them, are mentioned in our sections dealing with each geographic area. To help you in your route planning we give the approximate latitude of each cut.

The Northern Exumas

HIGHBORNE CUT 24° 42' N
At the south end of Highborne Cay. At least 6 feet at MLW and straightforward, but you need good light in your favor. As with almost all the Exuma cuts, it can develop a short chop with wind against tide.

WARDERICK WELLS CUT 24° 24' N
At the north end of Warderick Wells Cay. Apart from strong currents, it's a fine, wide pass.

CONCH CUT 24° 17' N
Between Cambridge Cay and Compass Cay. Again strong current, and in this case a rock awash in the middle, but there's plenty of room, no other hazards, and good depth. But stay north of that rock in the middle of the pass.

DOTHAM CUT 24° 07' N
At the north end of Great Guana Cay (named after Dotham Point). Sandbores on the Bank side dictate swinging north or south almost as soon as you are clear of the pass and the reef that extends west from the south tip of Gaulin Cay/Bitter Guana Cay.

FARMERS CUT 23° 57' N
Narrow but good depth. Used by the mailboats.

GALLIOTT CUT 23° 55' N
Again narrow, but good depth. Also a mailboat route.

The Southern Exumas

CAVE CAY CUT 23° 54' N
Deep (over 20 feet) but strong currents.

RUDDER CUT 23° 52' N
Straightforward. While a muddle of small cays and reef clutter the southeast on the Bank side, these present no problem.

RAT CAY CUT 23° 44' N
An unusual north–south pass between Rat Cay and Boysie Cay. If the wind gets up from the east, this is the best cut.

CONCH CAY CUT 23° 34' N
This pass is the west (and best) entrance into George Town Harbour.

The Most Popular Destinations

In the Northern Exumas there's enough to keep you happily gunkholing for months, if not years, and if you're bent on snorkeling and diving, as well as shoal-water exploration, you could go on almost forever without running out of new places to explore. Mindful that we are writing a cruising guide to the whole of the Bahamas, which necessarily implies a measure of selection, we put our money on four areas in this sector. All of them should feature high on your visit list. The first is the Allan's Cay–Highborne Cay area. The second is Normans Cay. The third is Warderick Wells and the Exuma Land and Sea Park, and the fourth is the Compass Cay–Staniel Cay area.

Sail Rocks to Allan's Cay

SAIL ROCKS, DOG ROCKS, BEACON CAY, BUSH CAY, AND SHIP CHANNEL CAY
Look at your chart. If you decided to cordon off an area of rocks, reefs, and coral heads where no one lived and few people visited, and said, "OK, let's call this a marine sanctuary and let the fish and lobsters get on with the business of regeneration," the sea area from the Sail Rocks down to and including Ship Channel Cay would be a good choice. De-

Conch shells.

spite the Ship Channel that passes through connecting the Exuma Bank with Exuma Sound south of Beacon Cay and north of Ship Channel Cay, we rate it as an area the prudent cruising navigator is better off avoiding. It's a maze of bare rock, reefs, coral heads, and tide rips that has never been charted accurately and, if you get into trouble there, it's uninhabited. We know of no anchorages there that we'd recommend.

So, on the face of it, you might well declare it as a sea reserve. It is unlikely to happen, for the only people who do frequent the area are Bahamian fishermen, and they might well object. More seriously, in settled weather if you want an area for exploring, snorkeling, and fishing that has little been touched by visiting boaters, you might decide to anchor off and dinghy in to look around.

SHIP CHANNEL

Ship Channel passage is a genuine pass, and the light on Beacon Cay (if it works) is there for guidance. But don't, even if the light is working, risk that passage at night. For the cruising yachtsman we see no utility in this cut through the Northern Exumas. It is, of course, the direct route from Nassau to Cape Eleuthera (or the reverse), but your track will take you through the worst part of the Yellow Bank. Even if we were going this way with no interest in visiting the Exumas, we'd elect to go through Highborne Cut and make use of the route we've already listed that avoids the Yellow Bank.

PIMLICO CAY AND ROBERTS CAY

Pimlico Cay is almost an extension of Ship Channel Cay. It has a house, sometimes used, at the southern end and there is a resident caretaker there. Roberts Cay, its tiny neighbor, also has a holiday house. Consider both cays as private property. There is a small potential anchorage between the two cays, only suitable for shoal draft (less than 3 feet) craft. Enter it from the south *only* at high tide and go in first by dinghy, checking the depth and noting rocks and reef as you go. This could serve as a refuge in bad weather, particularly in a Norther.

The Allan's Cay Group
(Allan's Cay, Southwest Allan's Cay, and Leaf Cay)

Allan's Cay	ALLAN	24° 44' 45 N	076° 51' 00 W
Highborne W	HIGHW	24° 42' 30 N	076° 51' 00 W
Highborne E	HIGHE	24° 42' 00 N	076° 48' 00 W

Allan's Cay is often the first destination of cruisers visiting the Exumas for two good reasons. It offers the first anchorage that can accommodate a number of boats in most weather, and it's the home of the iguanas, the prehistoric-looking large-size lizards that live here and in some of the more remote Out Islands, but nowhere else in the Bahamas.

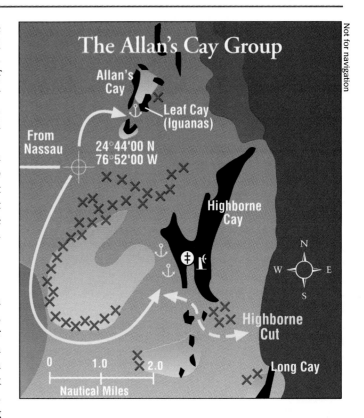

The Allan's Cay Group

In talking about Allan's Cay, in truth most people are referring to a group of three cays, Allan's Cay, Southwest Allan's Cay, and Leaf Cay, in which the sheltered water lies between them. Immediately south of the group there is a navigable cut between the Bank and Exuma Sound, but there are many reefs and coral heads in that pass.

Your approach to the Allan's Cay group, and your landfall recognition from either side, Bank or Sound, is not difficult, because when you're still some distance off the humpy higher ground of Highborne Cay to the south becomes visible, together with Highborne's 260-foot Batelco tower. If you are coming in from Exuma Sound our advice is to take Highborne Cut, swing out into the deeper water of the Bank to avoid the shoals and reefs to the northwest of Highborne Cay, and then make your way in to the Allan's cays from our Allan's waypoint. From the Bank side simply make for that Allan's waypoint. If there are other boats in the Allan's Cay anchorage you will see their masts showing above Allan's Cay.

Take the obvious way in between Allan's Cay and Southwest Allan's Cay, south of the little rock to the south of Allan's Cay. Then turn to anchor either in the bight of Southwest Allan's Cay to starboard or between Allan's Cay and Leaf Cay to port. Don't go further up the channel than the final part of Leaf Cay for it shoals rapidly. Check your anchor, as we have seen anchors drag there, and make sure it's well bedded. Then launch your dinghy and go to meet the iguanas. Do *not* take a pet on shore, and *no* garbage. The islands are a protected reserve.

Allan's Cay native iguana.

Allan's Cay to Normans Cay

Allan's Cay	ALLAN	24° 44' 45 N	076° 51' 00 W
Highborne W	HIGHW	24° 42' 30 N	076° 51' 00 W
Highborne E	HIGHE	24° 42' 00 N	076° 48' 00 W
Highborne Stake (0.5 nm due W)	HSTKW	24° 42' 30 N	076° 50' 00 W
Highborne (2 nm SW)	HIBSW	24° 42' 00 N	076° 52' 00 W
Normans Spit (W of)	NMSPT	24° 35' 30 N	076° 52' 30 W
Normans Cay (1 nm SW)	NRMNS	24° 34' 35 N	076° 49' 30 W

FROM ALLAN'S CAY TO HIGHBORNE CAY

To make for Highborne Cay from the Allan's group the safest way is to head out southwest on to the Bank and swing round to avoid the reefs and shoals that lie to the west of the Allan's Cay Cut. There is a direct route that shoal draft craft *could* take at high tide, but we see no point in trying to prove it. Save that for your exploration later on in your dinghy.

HIGHBORNE CAY

Lining up to enter Highborne Cay is not difficult. Highborne has a long white beach on the west side, the humpy high ground we've already mentioned, a white house and trees on one of the humps, and that 260-foot Batelco tower. The anchorage and the Highborne marina are to the south of the tower, and as you get closer you'll see boats at the dock. Ahead you'll see two rocks, one with a white stake on its north tip. You are going to leave that stake to starboard as you enter, and beyond these rocks, on the shore of Highborne itself, you'll see two orange range marks. Once you've got your bearings, there are no problems. Go in reading the water, particularly at low tide, and swing easily north toward the marina once you're safely past that stake. Keep in the deep water (there's a sand bar to port) and go on past the end of the concrete dock to where you plan to secure. The fuel dock is hard to starboard past the concrete dock, the slips themselves are ranged to port, and there are four moorings (white buoys) on your port bow as you make that final run in.

If you want to anchor off you have two choices. Just behind the southeastern tip of Highborne Cay on the west side, and along the line of the western coast of Highborne Cay (off that fine beach), remembering that at the north end there are reefs and shoals. Both anchorages are obviously weather dependent, but otherwise have good depth (about 12 feet MLW) and good holding.

Highborne Cay is private, but limited privileges and the use of the store are extended to visiting boaters. They have work in hand to extend the dock space by forty slips this year, and may decide to remove the moorings when this new berth space is available. For details see our **Yellow Pages** on page 221. If you are at anchor you may land on the

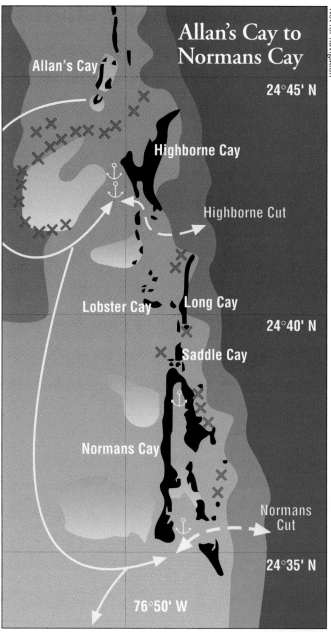

beaches, but respect the privacy of the island as a whole. With the Allan's Cay group, Highborne Cay rates as one of our favorite places in the Bahamas.

HIGHBORNE CUT

Highborne Cut, just to the south of Highborne Cay, is a relatively straightforward "read-the-water-as-you-go" pass between the Exuma Bank and Exuma Sound. Look at the chart, and then use your eyes. You should have no problems. Just remember that wind against tide produces turbulence, and that like all passes anywhere in the world, the current can run fast.

Highborne Cay to Normans Cay

If you are shoal draft, with the tide and the right light you can work your way south from Highborne Cay on the Bank side, past Oyster Cay, Long (sometimes called Spirit) Cay, Lobster Cay, and Saddle Cay to the north tip of Normans Cay. There the shoals to the west of Normans Cay will oblige you to detour to the west out into deeper water time and time again before you can work your way in to the Normans Cay anchorage around its south end.

As both Spirit Cay and Saddle Cay are private, unless you are particularly concerned with exploring this area, we suggest you take an easy loop out to the west to run from Highborne to Normans. All we would point out, just in case you need it, is that Long Cay (or Spirit Cay) offers an anchorage accessible from the Bank on its southwest tip (but open to the west) and Saddle Cay has an anchorage accessible from the Sound, but more difficult in its approach. You cannot mistake Saddle Cay. The name was well chosen.

The safe route from Highborne to Normans involves getting well out on to the Bank from a start point just off the Highborne Cay marina entrance, and staying out until you have cleared the shoal area known as Normans Spit, which runs out westward from the southeast tip of Normans Cay. Our courses work out as something like this:

From Highborne to gain that offing	1.88 nm	260°M
From this waypoint to off Normans Spit	6.52 nm	190°M
To a close approach waypoint	2.39 nm	114°M

This last point places you ready to go visual into Normans Cay's southern anchorage. It sounds like a lot of jinking around, but the plain truth is all you have to do is take one easy loop out on to the Bank to get to Normans from Highborne keeping about 3 nm offshore. And read the water!

NORMANS CAY

Normans Cay won fame, or rather infamy, as the base of the Colombian drug runner Carlos Leder during the bad days of Bahamian drug trading. The end result before the Leder barony was brought to an end was a tally of unproven

murders (when cruising boaters came too close to the Leder operation); a ruined development (once the heart of Lederland) on the south tip of Normans Cay with a dock falling into deterioration; the remains of a "Berlin" wall, which once guarded the northern boundary of Leder's territory (just north of the airstrip); a runway closed to traffic; a ditched aircraft in the southern anchorage; and an evil feel to the whole place. The Batelco-type mast you'll see on the southwest tip of Normans Cay is a disused radio mast, yet another souvenir of the Leder regime.

Ditched drug runner. (Not the original pilot.)

Today the visible signs of those days remain, but Normans Cay has a great deal to offer as a cruising destination. The approach to the southern anchorage is easy from either Exuma Sound or the Bank. On the Sound side the channel is narrow, carries about 7 feet, but is straightforward. Coming in from the west keep a touch to the south as you go in, following the obvious deep-water channel. Then you can follow a branch of this channel that runs roughly between the ruined dock and the ditched aircraft, or stay in the main stream (a pass through to Exuma Sound), which runs just north of a pretty little cay with white sand, a hillock, one teenage palm tree, and two baby palm trees. The depth overall in the anchorage is 6–8 feet at MLW. You are well protected there, other than from the southwest. If you are in the main tidal flow, expect a reversing current and 180° swings as the tide changes, but the holding is good. Don't go further up the apparent anchorage than the line running between the dock and the ditched aircraft, for it shoals.

The gunkholing around Normans Cay is good, the water is beautiful, and just north of the ruined dock (which is unsafe) there's a little beach. You are welcome to land, but the north end of six-mile long Normans Cay is private, and on the west of the airstrip (which is now open to charter traffic) there is a small development of vacation apartments (where you can buy ice). See our **Yellow Pages** on page 221.

Normans Cay has a second northern anchorage that is accessible only from Exuma Sound. Its approach is not easy. You would be foolish not to take your dinghy to reconnoiter the route in before you attempt it (we've seen two boats ground there at high water), and go in *only* with a high tide. Even then we've found only 4 feet 6 inches over the shallowest part of the entry passage, although there's a safe 15 feet inside. It's certainly well protected and even has a reputation as a hurricane hole. We'd go there to escape bad weather, but a hurricane? No. Not by deliberate choice.

NORTH HARBOUR OR NORMANS POND

If you want to try it, the entrance lies at the break in Normans Cay's east shore just north of Latitude 24° 37' 00 N. The entry channel lies between the two larger islets or rocks you'll see, each of which has a fallen marker on it, both looking rather like cannon facing inward at the pass, and on the far shore there's a conspicuous white house. The water is deep (you're going in on a high, remember?) and immediately you'll find a deep blue channel running straight and directly ahead of you. You may also note some range marks (if they're still there) encouraging you to go this way. Don't. Ignore the marks. The promising blue channel will end in a dead end.

The way you must go is to bear to starboard almost immediately after passing through the entry and feel your way over a shoal (that 4-feet-6-inch depth we wrote about), working your way closer to the shoreline to starboard. As you do this you'll enter deeper water and notice a pronounced shallow water contour running parallel to the shore. Stay in that deep water, keep going parallel to the shore, and you'll soon be in the basin of the North Harbour. The first of two caves that will come up to starboard is, if you like, the signal that you've made it. Thereafter you're free to roam.

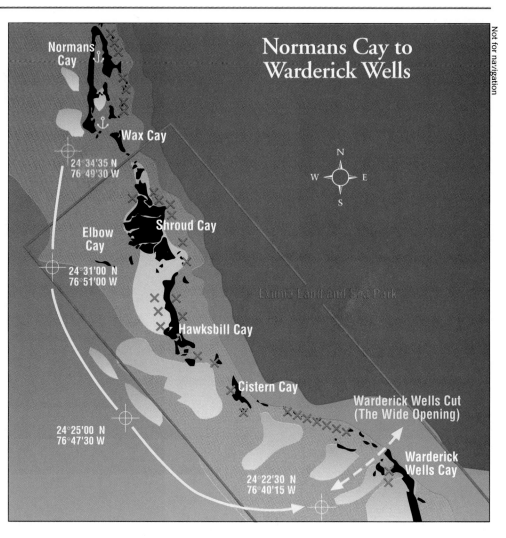

A third option in anchoring at Normans Cay is to make your way in north of Normans Spit to anchor off the airstrip beach, where you'll see the three houses of the MacDuff development, or further up the coast north of Skipjack Point.

Normans Cay to Warderick Wells

Normans Cay (1 nm SW)	NRMNS	24° 34' 35 N	076° 49' 30 W
Elbow Cay (1.5 nm W)	ELBOW	24° 31' 00 N	076° 51' 00 W
Cistern Cay (4 nm W)	CSTRN	24° 25' 00 N	076° 47' 30 W
Warderick Wells (5 nm W)	WWOFF	24° 21' 00 N	076° 42' 00 W
Warderick Wells (2.5 nm SW)	WELLS	24° 22' 30 N	076° 40' 15 W

The Wax Cays, Wax Cay Cut, Shroud Cay, Elbow Cay, Hawksbill Cay, the Cistern Cays, and the gap known as the Wide Opening lie on your route south from Normans Cay to Warderick Wells and the Exuma Land and Sea Park. Wax Cay, we reckon, falls into the Normans Cay gunkholing area. It has good rocks and reefs for exploring. Wax Cay Cut is not one we'd take to gain the Sound or come in from it. Little Wax Cay (part of Exuma Park) marks the northern boundary of the Exuma Land and Sea Park, and at that point you pack your fishing gear away. The first significant island in the Park area is Shroud Cay (part of Exuma Park), a curious three-mile long atoll surrounded by coral reefs with a heartland of mangrove swamp. No part of it is cruising boat ground, but you might want to poke your nose in somewhere in your dinghy to see what's there.

THE INSHORE BANK ROUTE FROM NORMANS CAY TO WARDERICK WELLS

If you elect to hug the coastline, what have you got there? We mentioned Shroud Cay. If you're there in March and April, that's the time Tropic birds nest there, recognizable by their white tails. Little Pigeon Cay, between Shroud and Elbow Cay, is private. Hawksbill Cay has great beaches and popular anchorages off the beaches on the east side from the center down to the south, but these are open to the southwest through to the north. Little Hawksbill Cay has been taken over by ospreys as their nesting territory. Cistern Cay is private. All of these cays are within Exuma Park. South from Cistern Cay the gaps out into Exuma Sound known as the Wide Opening (all of it part of Exuma Park) is a dream world for the experienced diver with drift dives and dives off Brad's Reef to the east of Long Rock, but tidal current dictates that this is no territory for the inexperienced. Hawk Fish Rocks, like Little Hawksbill Cay, have been claimed by the ospreys.

We have done this route in a shoal draft boat and even then sand bores, areas of shoal, and reefs oblige you to detour again and again, heading out to the west and coming back in again. Much of the shoreline, such as the Hawksbill Cay anchorages, are accessible to vessels with "normal" draft, but you are wise to take the state of the tide, as well as the angle of the sun, into your calculations before setting your general course.

THE WIDE OPENING

The Wide Opening is a viable route between the Bank and the Sound, and in many ways, the easiest approach route to Warderick Wells. The best cut lies at the north end of Warderick Wells Cay, and is wide, deep, and easily identifiable.

THE BANK ROUTE FROM NORMANS CAY TO WARDERICK WELLS

If you're bound southward on the Bank from Normans Cay to Warderick Wells, rather like the swing out on to the Bank from Highborne, you're much in the same game, particularly because Elbow Cay, a mile southwest of Shroud Cay, forces you out at that point. You'll note the prominent light stake on Elbow Cay. Your safe route on the Bank side will take you well off Shroud Cay, Hawksbill Cay, and the Cistern Cays to the south. The Cistern Cays have spawned sandbores that run far out to the west, and there's no point in attempting to work any closer to land than 3–4 nm along this route. The track we take is probably further out than you need to go, but we like the sea room and passage legs where you can relax to some extent. Our courses run something like this:

From Normans Cay to just off Elbow Cay	3.86 nm	199°M
From Elbow to off Cistern Cay	6.79 nm	158°M
Cistern to 5 nm off Warderick Wells	6.41 nm	134°M
And then to our final waypoint	2.19 nm	052°M

The approach into Warderick Wells anchorage from this waypoint is simple. You find you have a very obvious sandbore to starboard. Keep it that way. To port, in time, you'll realize you have another sandbore. Favor the first one. Your heading will be around 065°M, but more importantly, in the Wide Opening ahead of you will be two rocks, the left one looking flat like a table top and the right one rounded, a bit like an upturned salad bowl. Once

Warderick Wells northern anchorage.

you've got them identified, head toward the north tip of Warderick Wells just south of the salad bowl rock. You have deep water all the way, and don't go in the first entrances you see to starboard. Take the last one in, where you'll see a line of marker buoys start, white, red, blue, and then the line of white mooring buoys with maybe other boats already on them.

Call Exuma Park on VHF 16 and declare yourself as you enter. You should, by then, have already asked for and been allocated a mooring buoy by number. As you enter the Northern Harbour the darker, deep-water channel that curves ahead of you is as obvious as the Yellow Brick road leading to Oz. Just stay in the channel and pick up your allotted buoy (which are numbered from your entry point, the colored ones included). Then take your dinghy and check in at the Park HQ.

WARDERICK WELLS AND THE EXUMA LAND AND SEA PARK

The Exuma Park, a world-first in marine conservation, was set up in 1958 and covers 176 square miles of cays, rocks, and reefs running from Little Wax Cay in the north to Conch Cut in the south, and is bounded by Exuma Sound on one side and the Exuma Bank on the other.

Warderick Wells Cay is the site of the Park HQ and the principal visitor center with twenty-two moorings (anchoring is not allowed there). There are also four moorings in the southern anchorage. All these are reserved through Park HQ, and cost $15 for two nights (this may change in 1998). You may anchor wherever you wish in the Park area, but not, as we've said, in the north anchorage, and *not* on coral. For anchoring your dinghy when you go snorkeling or diving the same rule applies. You may anchor where you wish, but *not* on coral.

Nurse sharks.

It's a hard choice to decide whether to opt for the northern anchorage or the southern Warderick Wells anchorage, which lies between the southeast tip of the island and Hog Cay. Here the best approach is from the north, from Exuma Sound. The tip of Hog Cay is marked by a stone cairn, and you'll have deep water all the way in. Entering from the south, from the Bank, is better done at high tide with some judicious reading of the water, but it's possible. If you like relative isolation, this is the place for you and in slow periods of Park business you could well be alone here, with just the ospreys nearby on Little White Bay Cay for company. The Bank-side route between the two anchorages, inside Emerald Rock, London Gin Rock, and the Malabar Cays is shoal draft work, better explored in your dinghy.

We cover the Exuma Park in greater detail in our **Yellow Pages** on **The Exuma Land and Sea Park** on page 221. It is sufficient to say that a visit to Exuma Park is a must. We know of no anchorage more beautiful than Warderick Wells, and the stately crescent of boats in line on their moorings at sunset makes a mental photograph that will stay with you for life as the archetypal cruiser's dream. The swimming and snorkeling are superb.

WARNING

Sadly and almost unbelievably the Park is plagued by poachers, and its marine life, in most cases known reef by reef to the Park staff as familiar identifiable communities (a particular grouper lives in one place, so many lobster have been counted on the same reef, etc.), has suffered and continues to suffer. Undoubtedly Bahamian fishermen have been guilty, but the shocking fact is that visiting yachtsmen have been the greater predators, taking fish, lobster, and souvenirs. Do *not* do it. Apart from the mandatory $500 fine per person on board per incident (a single fish, lobster, or shell counts as one incident), your boat is liable to confiscation. *The Park Wardens have taken action against cruising visitors and will continue to patrol, make arrests, and impound vessels for violations regardless of the flag they fly.* The rules are absolute. Enjoy everything that is there. But leave it as you found it.

The Park authorities have recently completed a new Park Management Plan that is going to change a number of regulations, particularly relating to moorings, freedom to anchor, and possibly duration of visits from 1998 on. At the date of our writing this revision was not sufficiently advanced in execution for us to forecast its provisions. You should contact the Park Authority if the Park Area features in your cruising plans to learn of these changes.

Warderick Wells to Sampson and Staniel Cays

Warderick Wells (2.5 nm SW)	WELLS	24° 22' 30 N	076° 40' 15 W
Conch Cut W (6.5 nm W)	CONCW	24° 17' 00 N	076° 39' 00 W
Sampson Cay (off Twin Cays)	SAMSN	24° 12' 20 N	076° 31' 00 W
Sandy Cay (0.5 nm W)	SANDY	24° 11' 15 N	076° 30' 00 W
Staniel Cay (0.25 nm W)	STANL	24° 10' 15 N	076° 27' 15 W

Having left Warderick Wells we'd guess that your next stop is likely to be either Sampson Cay or Staniel Cay, both lying south of Conch Cut. It is at Conch Cut that you leave the Exuma Land and Sea Park area.

From Warderick Wells to Conch Cut	5.08 nm	175°M
From Conch Cut to Sampson Cay	8.66 nm	128°M
From Sampson Cay to Sandy Cay	1.24 nm	138°M

Our courses will take you well out on to the west, further offshore than you might think necessary. The reason for this is the sandbores that lie to the west of Bell Island and the Rocky Dundas–Fowl Cay area, which extend out as far as Longitude 076° 37' W.

THE HALLS POND CAYS, THE BELL ISLANDS, SOLDIERS AND O'BRIEN'S CAYS, CAMBRIDGE CAY

Halls Pond Cay (part of the Exuma Park) is marked by the derelict Exuma Cays Club that stands on a headland above its northwestern point. A beach there (with some mobile-type housing evident) offers an anchorage protected from northeast to southeast, but is open to surge from the Halls Pond Cay Cut. Better anchorages, but still shielded only from the east, can be found opposite the two sand beaches further down the west shore of Halls Pond Cay. However bear in mind that the cay is private, as is Little Halls Pond Cay, Soldier Cay, Bell Island, and Cambridge Cay (although they are all part of Exuma Park). O'Brien's Cay is the only one in this group to remain public land. Sadly but predictably it's the least attractive of the group lying south of Warderick Wells and north of Conch Cut, and few people go there. Anchorages can be found off Bell Island (on both the east and west side) and on the west of Cambridge Cay, if you work your way in behind a line of rocks running north–south down the west coast of the cay.

Conch Cut

Conch Cut W (6.5 nm W)	CONCW	24° 17' 00 N	076° 39' 00 W
Conch Cut E (0.5 nm E)	CONCE	24° 17' 30 N	076° 31' 00 W

Our Conch Cut west waypoint is unusually far offshore. The reason for this is the sandbores extending out to Longitude 076° 37' W from Bell Island to the north and Rocky Dundas–Fowl Cay to the south. A waypoint closer in would not usefully serve Conch Cut itself, Warderick Wells to the north, and Sampson or Staniel Cay to the south without doglegs. Once you are at Conch Cut west your route to and through the pass is direct and obvious.

Conch Cut is one of the best Exuma cuts, lying between Cambridge Cay and Compass Cay. It has, like all the Exuma cuts, strong tidal flows and its one hazard is a rock, barely awash, in the middle. But there are no other hazards, good depth, and plenty of room. Your course through the Cut must run to the north of that rock in mid-pass.

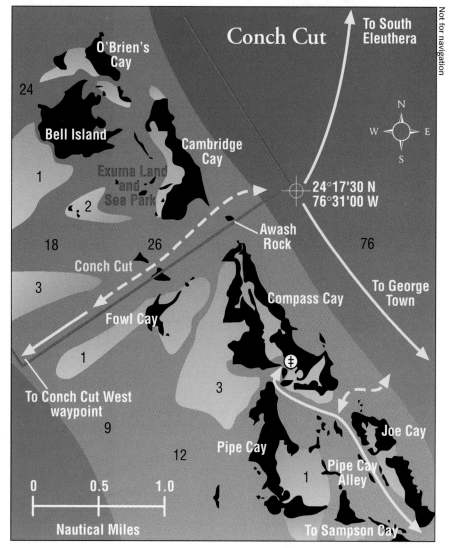

The Remaining Exuma Cuts

When you move south of Conch Cut, you must start to think seriously, if you are traveling on the Bank side, about the cut you will select to gain access to Exuma Sound if you are going on south to George Town. The most important of these from a routing point of view are Dotham, Farmers, and Rat Cay Cut. None of these cuts pose any particular navigation problems, but all the Exuma Cuts are subject to strong reversing tidal flows which, when running against wind, wave, and swell can kick up extremely turbulent, short, nasty, and potentially hazardous seas. The effect of this kick back can be felt as far as a mile or more off the cut, and if you're sensible, you won't force the issue and try to punch your way through. Hold off, wait for the slack, and then move.

These conditions affect the smaller cuts equally, and if anything make them even more hazardous under unfavorable conditions, for you have shallower, narrower passes, more rocks and shoals around your approaches, and at times sharp turns to hit the right deep-water channel at the right moment. Don't be put off by all this. Simply take it into account and pre-plan your cruising. Get the time of the tides, think of the wind, and study the geography of your chosen cut. If it's A-OK, go for it.

To save endless repetition we're not going to warn about tidal flows and the effects of tide against wind each time we list a cut. Take it as read that what we've said applies to them all. We have listed only one east waypoint (incoming from Exuma Sound) and one west (Bank-side) waypoint for each cut. A single waypoint works well in the Sound, but on the Bank side the channels threading between reef and sand often demand a succession of waypoints. But channels can change as the sand changes. Rather than list an endless stream of directions, as in any event you'll be eyeballing your way, we give you just one fix for reassurance. It should be enough.

Utility of the Exumas Cuts

The more we look at the geography of the Bank side and the real utility of the Exumas Cuts, the more we are led to three conclusions.

- The primary passage-making cuts we identified in our introduction on page 206 are vital to you whether you are on the Exuma Bank or in Exuma Sound. Other than the dubious importance of Rat Cay Cut, these passes are your best way of switching from one side to the other.

- The real utility of the secondary cuts is to open up anchorages on the Bank side if you're out in the Sound, or, if you've worked your way far enough south on the Bank, to give you your last opportunities to get out into the Sound. But the more

difficult eyeball navigation needed on the west side in many cases reduces their attractiveness for spur-of-the-moment changes in route.

- The Exuma Bank is no cruising ground south of Rudder Cut. In truth the practical limit to relatively straightforward Exuma Bank cruising comes at Cave Cay Cut. From then on making your way south is a slow business. It's fine if you want to take your time and poke around wherever you fancy, but it's time consuming if you have dates to keep.

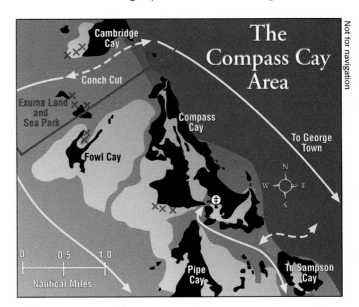

Conch Cut to Staniel Cay

Approaches from Conch Cut

Conch Cut E (0.5 nm E)	CONCE	24° 17' 30 N	076° 31' 00 W
Conch Cut W (6.5 nm W)	CONCW	24° 17' 00 N	076° 39' 00 W
Sampson Cay (off Twin Cays)	SAMSN	24° 12' 20 N	076° 31' 00 W
Sandy Cay (0.5 nm W)	SANDY	24° 11' 15 N	076° 30' 00 W
Staniel Cay (0.25 nm W)	STANL	24° 10' 15 N	076° 27' 15 W

Our Sampson Cay waypoint gives you access to the whole area lying between Compass Cay and Staniel Cay. In fact the waypoint might be better described as Twin Cays, for it is just west of these landmark cays. From our Conch Cut west waypoint (you're on the Bank side) you'll run 8.66 nm on a heading of 128° to get to the Twin Cays waypoint, and then if you're bound for Sampson Cay turn to a heading of 095°M to pass south of Twin Cays and the line of rocks and reef to their east. You'll see the Sampson Cay Club buildings ahead of you.

If you're going on to Staniel Cay, Sandy Cay serves as a waypoint in the same manner as Twin Cays. You have an-

Old sail boat, Sampson Cay.

marina and is in business, although the project is still in its early stages. See our **Yellow Pages**. And, if you stay there, you can use their beach on the Exuma Sound side, which is breathtaking. One of the best beaches in the Bahamas. It's world class.

From the Bank side the best approach into the area is north of Sampson Cay, taking the channel between Wild Tamarind and Overyonder Cays. There are three navigable cuts between Exuma Sound and Pipe Cay Alley, the first two north and south of Joe Cay, and the third between Thomas Cay and Overyonder Cay. The last is very narrow. Compass Cay Marina can be approached from the Sound through the cut north of Joe Cay but you run into shoal water soon after entry and the approach is not easy. Nor is it straightforward from the Bank side, which is a shoal draft route. We've been told that the Joe Cut route carries 8 feet and the Bank approach to Compass Cay carries 5 feet, but to our belief these are not MLW depths. We suggest you call Compass Cay Marina on VHF 16 if you wish to go alongside or pick up one of their moorings, and they'll be delighted to come out and lead you safely into the marina basin.

As Sampson Cay with its long-established marina and the Sampson Cay Club lies just to the south of this area, we suggest you use either Compass Cay or Sampson Cay as a base to first explore the area by dinghy if you are not familiar with it, and then venture in to drop your hook if

other 1.24 nm to run on a course of 138°M to get to the Sandy Cay waypoint from Twin Cays. Then around Sandy Cay to the west, and go visual for 3 nm towards Staniel Cay, with its 260-foot Batelco tower, on a heading of 118°M.

COMPASS CAY TO SAMPSON CAY

The cays between Compass Cay and Sampson Cay enclose a protected inner passage that we've always termed Pipe Cay Alley. Although much of the enclosed water is shoal draft or dries at low tide, there are deeper channels on both inner sides. It's an area of almost unbelievable water color, everything from white to turquoise to sapphire blue, with a clarity of water that can only be described as gin clear. However be aware that Compass Cay, Little Pipe Cay, Wild Tamarind Cay, and Overyonder Cay are private and your freedom to roam is not only limited by water depths. The good news is that the owner of Compass Cay has built a dock and laid three moorings as the start of a new

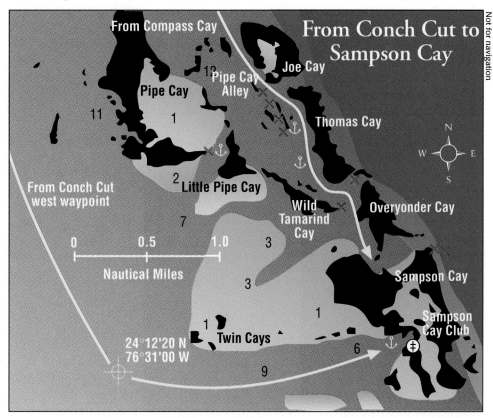

you decide to anchor there. The best area for anchoring, well shielded from the prevailing southeast winds, lies in the channel running along the west coast of Thomas Cay.

SAMPSON CAY

Sampson Cay is also private but has long been in business as a pocket-sized marina, and the Sampson Cay Club offers not only slips on an outer dock and moorings, but also a totally protected inner dock area where many people keep their boats on a long-term basis. In many ways Sampson Cay is a dream destination for the cruiser. Small enough to be a home, it has all the facilities you need: bar, restaurant, small store, accommodations ashore, and even a resident seaplane service. Read our **Yellow Pages**.

Compass Cay and Sampson Cay are the only places we know along this stretch of the Exumas with almost total protection. You might want to tuck this away in the back of your mind, just in case. That's not to say that you'd weather a direct hit from a hurricane in either place but in a severe storm you'd be better off there than anywhere else in the area.

FOWL AND NORTH GAULIN CAYS
AND THE MAJORS SPOTS

Between Sampson Cay and Staniel Cay you have a virtual repeat of Pipe Cay Alley with the protected channel between Big and Little Majors Spots offering yet another deep channel and shoal-water playground, culminating in the famous Thunderball Cave in the south, on the doorstep of Staniel Cay. In this alley between the two Majors Cays you have anchorages on either side, and can play these to advantage with the weather. However be aware that a strong reversing tidal flow courses down this conduit, and that heavy swell can bring in surge. The holding is not always good, and you'd be foolish to fail setting your anchor by hand if it hasn't taken satisfactorily, or quitting to find another place. To the west of Big Majors Spot there is good holding, and it's no bad place to anchor.

Staniel Cay

Sandy Cay (0.5 nm W)	SANDY	24° 11' 15 N	076° 30' 00 W
Staniel Cay (0.25 nm W)	STANL	24° 10' 15 N	076° 27' 15 W
Harvey Cay (0.75 nm W)	HARVY	24° 09' 15 N	076° 30' 00 W

Staniel Cay, with its landmark 260-foot Batelco tower, has long been the cruising mecca of the Central Bahamas because it's there, it is central, because it has a 3,000-foot paved airstrip, and because good facilities, two marinas, some moorings, sheltered anchorages, and adequate-though-simple stores are all at hand. It is also a very attractive settlement, neat, compact, and well planted with trees, not the least of which is a handsome breadfruit (remember the *Mutiny on the Bounty?*). Any more pluses? Well there's the legendary Thunderball Cave that would be a pity to miss. See our **Yellow Pages**.

Sampson Cay to Staniel Cay

Not for navigation

Twin Cays
15
Sampson Cay
3
15
5
Fowl Cay
Sandy Cay
5
Little Majors Spot
12
24°11'15 N
76°30'00 W
15
N
W E
S
Big Majors Spot
7
Thunderball Cave
2
Staniel Cay
Staniel Cay Yacht Club
7
Happy People Marina
6
To Great Guana Cay
0   0.5   1.0
Nautical Miles
6
4

Approaches to Staniel Cay

Either Sandy Cay (to the northwest) or Harvey Cay (to the southwest) are your lead marks to gaining Staniel Cay. From either of these you should be able to pick up that Batelco tower and steer for it. Once you pass Longitude 076° 27' 30 W go easy, and pay attention to the color of the water, particularly on your port side, for a sandbar bulges down from the north as you get closer in. Your heading now should be fixed on the larger of the low-lying rocks ahead, which has a hard-to-define stake on it. Short of this rock you'll become aware that deeper-water channels fork off to the north and south. The north channel leads you toward the Staniel Cay Yacht

Staniel Cay Yacht Club cottages (an...

Club and, if you go on "around...
ings of Club Thunderball. If you...
directly toward the Happy Peopl...

To gain Staniel Cay Yacht Clu...
of rocks heading up your deep-w...
a reef that extends north from t...
you go past the docks, and ther...
to them. If you're after the Clu...
carry on around the shoulder o...
the Happy People Marina is s...

If you wish to anchor off, t...
sandbank (on your port side...
Yacht Club) is good, as is ju...
little room here for mor...
Thunderball has eleven Sle...
If you're interested, contac...
off the northern of the thr...
temporary moorings for visitors...
is, in effect, the center of that island. The anchor...
and around the Majors Spots have already been covered.

The Marinas
The Happy People Marina has been a staple of Staniel Cay,
and with its hotel, restaurant, and bar has always been popular. Staniel Cay Yacht Club recently fell into disrepair and has
just been rescued in the nick of time. Now drive, energy, and
no small expenditure have effected a near-total transformation of the docks, the Club itself, its satellite cottages, and
even its landscaping. It's an ambitious undertaking, clearly
aiming for the upper strata of the market, and you'll see more
mini-mega yachts there than humble cruisers.

Around and About
We've already touched on Staniel Cay in capsule. At the
time of writing Staniel Cay has not had a central power

...planned and may be in operation in
...ake a significant difference to Staniel
...e high cost of running private genera-
...development. Already on the cards for
..., with air fills, to be set up at the Staniel
...We expect to see changes at both the
...arina and, perhaps, Club Thunderball.
...aniel as it is as we last found it, our **Yel-
...**he detail.

...say that Thunderball Cave is fun to dive,
...ut you need sunlight. Ideally strong, over-
...k its magic. The cave has two entrances, on
...he primary one) and on the east, and at high
...ls of both entries form sumps, and you have
...rwater to clear them. Inside you have surface
...gh dome above your head with shafts of sun-
...g down into the water. But it's what you see
...feet that counts. These shafts of sun reaching
...he depths, creating a blaze of neon blue in con-
...outer blackness, and the fish population, patient,
...t at all afraid of you.

...st time to dive it? At low water, and wait for the
...e tidal current is strong there. We say dive, but
...snorkel. All you need is a mask and fins. Take
...ad in a plastic bag to feed the fish, and an under-
...mera if you have one. At peak times you'll find
...rball Cave a forest of fins and snorkels, which can
...e magic. If all the world is there when you arrive in
...nghy, come back another time and try to see it with-
...e crowd scene.

...iel Cay to the Farmers Cays

...ey Cay (0.75 nm W)	HARVY	24° 09' 15 N	076° 30' 00 W
...k Point (0.25 nm W)	BLKPT	24° 05' 25 N	076° 25' 00 W
...ite Point (0.4 nm SW)	WHTPT	24° 02' 00 N	076° 23' 00 W

The entrance to Thunderball Cave, Staniel Cay.

Scuttlebutt
Nautical Books and Bounty

HARVEY CAY TO DOTHAM CUT
AND BLACK POINT SETTLEMENT

Harvey Cay, a short run of 3.46 nm on 170°M, is rather like Elbow Cay in the Northern Exumas, an outlying cay that makes staying out to the west necessary if you are passage making on the Bank side. From Harvey Cay to Dotham Cut west is a short run of 5.13 nm on a heading of 123°M.

BITTER GUANA AND GAULIN CAYS

Bitter Guana and Gaulin Cays are virtually one. Uninhabited, there's not much there other than a memory of disaster and sadness, for a boat carrying Haitian refugees was wrecked just off Bitter Guana Cay. Its crew and passengers, who all lost their lives, were buried there in a mass grave.

Dotham Cut

| Dotham Cut E | DTHME | 24° 07' 00 N | 076° 23' 00 W |
| Dotham Cut W | DTHMW | 24° 06' 30 N | 076° 25' 00 W |

Dotham Cut is recognizable as a wide clear opening as you run south on to this heading, which takes you to just off Dotham Point, a touch further south than you might think necessary at first. There's a sandbore running out to the west from the south point of Gaulin Cay, which you must avoid. With wind and tide fighting over this shoal, Dotham Cut can produce millrace conditions on the Bank side, but the Cut itself is fine, deep, and holds no other hazards. Your recognition of Dotham Cut is further aided by a light stake on Gaulin as well as white cliffs, rather like a mini-Table Mountain, further north up the cay. As with all passes, go through it visual.

DOTHAM CUT TO GEORGE TOWN

From Dotham Cut east to the northwest entrance to George Town Harbour is a straight offshore Exuma Sound run of 45.42 nm on 142°M. We reckon this is the most simple route to take to George Town from the Staniel Cay area. It presents no navigation problems and Dotham Cut is, as we've said, not a difficult pass.

DOTHAM CUT TO BLACK POINT SETTLEMENT

To go on to Black Point Settlement from the north, just go visual heading southeast on the Bank side to ease around Dotham Point and run parallel to the shore to anchor off the bay. Black Point's 100-foot Batelco tower is a good marker if you can't pick up buildings immediately. If you veer off toward Black Point you'll find yourself in another shoal area, and the best line to take is favor Dotham Point and then go straight for the government dock, which should then be visible.

BLACK POINT SETTLEMENT

Black Point Settlement, perhaps surprisingly, is the largest center of population in the Exumas after George Town. There seems to be no particular reason why this has come about, and the brief analysis put to us is probably right on the button: "It's good here. None of our children want to go to Nassau. We get bad stories of what it's like there. So they stay. There's not much here, but it's better than Nassau. And we fish a bit. We know the places, where to go."

The Black Point settlement area, on its wide east-facing bight formed by Dotham Point in the north and Black Point in the west, is attractive at first sight, and holds its attraction close in. You can anchor virtually

Small boats at Black Point settlement.

where you wish, best leaving a fairway open to the government dock, for that is used by the mail boat and by fishing craft. However, it is possible to come alongside there if you want. The depth is 6 feet at MLW around the outer half of the dock, shoaling to 3–4 feet closer to the shore. There is no fuel. If you elect to anchor off, as almost every visitor does, you'll find yourself over sand with 7 feet of water at MLW even quite close in, and it's good holding.

An alternative anchorage lies off the community dock, the smaller dock to the west tucked off a knob of land called Adam's Point. Here too, if you draw 4 feet or less, you could come alongside the dock but anchoring off in 12–15 feet of water is probably better. The little bay itself shoals past the dock. Again, other than an open shelter built for local partying, there are no facilities there, but it's a pleasant, well-shaded and quiet place, no further from the center of the settlement than the government dock.

Wherever you choose to go, you're exposed to the southwest through west to north in that bight, but in prevailing southeast winds, we reckon Black Point is a good place to call. If you were caught there by the onset of unfavorable weather, your choices are either to make a break for Little Farmers Cay or for Staniel Cay, if either look right to you, or do what the locals do. Go east around Dotham Point and enter Little Creek and hole up there. We were assured you have 4 feet at MLW but we've not tried it. What you do have there is total protection. The settlement, apart from its lack of fuel of any kind, has what you'd expect to find in any similar community. See our **Yellow Pages** for the detail.

Black Point to Little Farmers Cay

Black Point (0.25 nm W)	BLKPT	24° 05' 25 N	076° 25' 00 W
White Point (0.4 nm SW)	WHTPT	24° 02' 00 N	076° 23' 00 W
Farmers Cut W (0.75 nm NW)	FMRSW	23° 58' 05 N	076° 19' 40 W

GREAT GUANA CAY

At something over 10 nm in length, Great Guana Cay dominates the central Exumas. You expect more from it, but there's really nothing there for the cruising visitor. Black Point is the only settlement. You can anchor off the west coast at many places, and will be protected from northeast to southeast; there are beaches and places to explore, but go cautiously as you parallel the coast for there are reefs and coral heads that must be avoided. It's strange. There must be something in the name. Guana Cay in the Abacos at just over 5 nm can't quite rival its Exuma cousin in length but equally has a coastline that seems to go on forever.

Farmers Cay Cut

Farmers Cut E (0.25 nm E)	FMRSE	23° 57' 50 N	076° 18' 30 W
Farmers Cut W (0.75 nm NW)	FMRSW	23° 58' 05 N	076° 19' 40 W

The Little Farmers Cay 260-foot Batelco tower is a clear indicator of the proximity of Farmers Cay Cut. The entrance to the Cut from the east is well defined, and your entry route lies to the south of the small cay in the center of the Cut, aiming for the beach on Little Farmers Cay. Once you're in, you must avoid the patch of shoal and reef that lies immediately to the southwest of the little cay, and make your turn to starboard or port in the deeper water that is divided, a bit like a rotary, by that patch. From then on you have no problems. The water is clear and easy to read. Taking the Cut from west to east is relatively straightforward, for the deeper water shows clearly.

Little Farmers Cay

Little Farmers Cay could be the ideal, archetypal Bahamian settlement, or maybe it's just everyone's dream vision of just what a small Bahamian settlement should look like. It has a

A regatta racer built in Black Point.

Small Harbour, Little Farmers Cay.

superb site, the enhancement of two harbors (though both tend to shoal), enough land elevation to add interest, and attractive houses in a blaze of colors set among palms and flowering shrubs. It's something close to Polynesian. Unexpected. A surprise.

ANCHORAGES, MOORINGS, AND MARINA

Your choices there are to anchor off the southwest tip of Great Guana Cay, where a narrow tongue of deeper water places you just off the beach. The holding is not so good, but there are two moorings you can take up, and more are planned. See our **Yellow Pages** on page 225 for more information. Slightly better holding may be found to the west side of the sand bar enclosing that tongue of deeper water. You could drop south to the northwest cove of Big Farmers Cay, but this places you the full width of the cut away from the settlement, and in line for surge. Neither of the two harbors, Small Harbour and Big Harbour, are open to you as an option. Both shoal rapidly, and the good ground is already taken by local boats.

The government dock in Small Harbour is in use by fishing boats, and of course the mailboat.

Alternatively you can go alongside the Farmers Cay Yacht Club and Marina dock on the northeast tip of Little Farmers Cay. It's a big title for one comparatively small dock with just one building there and two fuel tanks, but read on. Here over the past few years the owner, Roosevelt Nixon, has patiently built the nucleus of what is intended to be a larger facility. His work to date has provided a good dock, albeit subject to the reversing current of the cut, with power (from his own generator) at night, water, fuel, a telephone, and a restaurant and bar, all well built and well run.

To get from there into the settlement you have two options. The first is to cross a bridge over the creek that runs behind the yacht club and take a beach walk along Big Harbour. The other is to walk along the sand road that runs to the north end of a 2,200-foot paved airstrip, and walk down the strip to the road running from its south end into the settlement. We go into this kind of detail because the plans for the future hinge on the geography of this site, the existing dock, almost half a mile of creek behind it, and the good fortune of the existing airstrip. In time the creek may well offer an all-weather harbor, a small colony of low-rise efficiencies may offer shoreside accommodations, a further bar may be built, and the airstrip is there. The plans are sympathetic to the environment, and the best in this regard we have seen in the Bahamas.

THE SETTLEMENT

We've already given an initial view of the settlement and our **Yellow Pages** give the detail. Perhaps the focal point of Little Farmers Cay from the visitor's point of view may well be the Ocean Cabin restaurant and bar, whose owner, Terry Bain, was the initiator of the First Friday in February festivals in 1986, and has been the driving force behind them since them. As often happens in the Bahamas, some two or three cruising boats have made Little Farmers Cay and the Ocean Cabin their winter home, and you'll find a small world there that may well attract you to join them.

YELLOW PAGES

HIGHBORNE CAY

This private island, with its small marina and welcoming hosts, Peter and Alison Albury, is a tiny Exuman paradise for your first stop after leaving the Nassau metropolis. There are only nine residences, four of which can be rented, and a grocery store. If you are tied up at the marina or are on one of their moorings, you are allowed to walk on the island; there are roads and trails to pristine beaches marked on the map you are given in your welcome pack when you sign in. Aloes can still be found on the cay, a legacy from an earlier aloe plantation, when watermelons flourished here as well. For visiting yachts at anchor, you can come into the dinghy dock, or fuel dock to refuel, but will be discouraged from visiting the island and charged $2 per bag to dispose of garbage. Reservations are important: call Peter and Alison ahead of time to make certain they have space for you.

MARINA

HIGHBORNE CAY
Tel: 242-355-1008 • Fax & Residence: 355-1003 • VHF 16

Slips	17, plans for 40 by mid-1997.
Max LOA	100 ft. or more alongside the piers
MLW at Dock	10 to 12 ft., less in the channel
Dockage	$1 per ft.
Moorings	Four at the time of writing, $15 per night on a first-come-first-served basis. When the new docks are completed they may be removed.
Power	50A is $25 per day.
Water	40¢ per gallon, or $1 in gallon jugs
Fuel	Fuel dock open from 8 am to noon and 2 pm to 5 pm, except Wednesday afternoons
Propane	Refills available on a two-hour turnaround.
Telephone	Public telephone with US-direct access, next to *Cheap Charlie's*
Laundry	Done by one of the island's housekeepers after 5 pm for $10. Contact Peter for details.
Bar	There are plans to build a bar and snack bar; *Cheap Charlie's* on the dock sells cold drinks, cigarettes, beer, and snacks.
Provisions	Leslie Blanche, whose husband Don is the assistant manager, runs the grocery store and will give you a ride there 9 am to noon, and 2 to 4 pm, Monday to Saturday, only 9 am to noon Wednesdays. Canned foods, produce, frozen meat, liquor, fish & lobster in season, T-shirts.
Ice	$5 for a 10-lb. bag
Sewerage	Please use holding tanks in the harbor.
Accommodations	Four houses available to rent from $200 per night, for four to six people.
Catering	*Janet's Catering Service* Call *Cool Runner* on VHF 16 for homemade bread and a delicious selection of appetizers, entrees, cakes, and other desserts.
Facilities	Every morning at 7:30 am Alison gives the weather report from NOAA, and from Nassau for the Bahamas. Listen on VHF 16 and switch to Channel 06 when she starts. Barbecue and outdoor dining area on shore; dogs are welcome on a leash provided you scoop the poop into the bushes. Marked trails and walking paths lead to fabulous beaches. Deep sea fishing only five minutes away.
Credit Cards	Visa, MasterCard, Discover, and checks

THINGS TO DO IN HIGHBORNE CAY

- Choose a new beach every day to visit.
- Snorkel staghorn and elkhorn reefs and the *Octopus's Garden*.
- Dive the *Highborne Cay Wall*, the *Basketstar* and *Filefish* reefs, and the 16th-century *Highborne Cay Wreck.*
- Take the dinghy up to Allan's Cay and introduce yourself to an iguana. Please don't feed them. They are prehistoric to look at, a protected species, and may nibble your ankles (which hurts) if you try to give them Cheerios for breakfast. And don't take your dog with you, either; they are banned on Allan's Cay, which is a Bahamas National Trust reserve, part of the Exumas Land and Sea Park. Why not snorkel *Barracuda Shoal* while you're up there?

NORMANS CAY

This is a favorite anchorage for yachts, where a partially submerged aircraft, a legacy from drug-running days, lies in four feet of water within the lagoon. There is a tumble-down dock and some deserted buildings at the south end of the six-mile long cay. Although it is a private island, you are allowed to walk on the southern end. There is ice available from *Mac Duff's of Norman's Cay*, a quarter of a mile north, who has oceanfront villas to rent (242-357-8846).

There is a designated area on the south end of Norman's Cay for trash. Please leave a $1 donation in the honesty box to help the residents with the cost of removing it to a landfill.

WARDERICK WELLS
EXUMA CAYS LAND AND SEA PARK

The Exuma Park covers 176-square miles of spectacular subtropical waters, coral reefs, and cays, from Wax Cay at the northern end to Conch Cut at the southern end, with a broad spectrum of natural vegetation and wildlife. It was established in 1958, and is supervised by the Bahamas National Trust. Some of the islands within the Park are privately owned so please respect their privacy. The Park Warden and his staff operate from the Headquarters building at the north end of Warderick Wells. You should check in at the headquarters building, where the staff can answer questions and provide information about the Park.

If you would like to take a mooring in the Park overnight, call *Exuma Park* on VHF 16 at least a day in advance so that when moorings are allocated at 9 am each morning, you can talk to them and ensure your mooring. At the time of this writing, you can stay for two nights for $15 or, better still, join their Support Fleet for $30 and enjoy the facilities provided through membership and donations, together with a newsletter and a chance to volunteer your time for them.

The island is covered with walking trails, and a huge diversity of wildlife, while the snorkeling within easy distance of the anchorage is breathtaking. The Park itself is the largest protected fish-breeding ground in the Caribbean, hence the problem with the two P's: Pollution and Poaching. Pollution is the responsibility of every visitor to the Park to keep to a minimum. Absolutely no trash, maximum use of holding tanks, minimum noise from jet-skis, radios, and rowdy parties (except at the Saturday evening happy hour at the headquarters with other visitors). Everything you bring with you take away with you. Be responsible and maintain and nurture this environmentally and ecologically superb site. And don't for one minute think that because you have made a $100 donation that you can go off and catch just *one* big fish. Or a lobster. Or a conch. You can't. Not only is it morally wrong, it's illegal too, and you can be fined. Big time. Your passport can be taken away. And your boat impounded. End of a happy vacation? You bet.

FACILITIES

Wardens	Ray and Evelyn Darville will do everything they can to help you. Evelyn allocates moorings for the day on the radio every morning, and Ray is a hard-working and knowledgeable warden with dedicated conservationist ideals.
Moorings	There are 22 in Warderick Wells near the headquarters, and 4 in the idyllic south anchorage on a first-come-first-served basis. $15 for two nights.
Booking	Call *Exuma Park* on VHF 16 at least 24 hrs. in advance. They announce mooring allocation at 9 am on VHF 16, switching to Channel 09, each morning.
Park Headquarters	Open 9 am to noon and 1 pm to 5 pm, Monday to Saturday; 9 am to 1 pm on Sundays. The headquarters has a communication center with VHF radio and cellular telephone (which is expensive), as well as maps and nature displays, but it is the Darville's home as well so please respect their privacy.
Library	In the headquarters; T-shirts and post cards also for sale. Ray's own book, written with Stephen Pavlidis about the Land and Sea Park, is for sale, giving an in-depth appreciation of what is in the Park and why it's so important to conserve it.
Lectures and Nature Walks	Given at the headquarters. Volunteers are encouraged to help with Park Management projects.
Credit Cards	Only cash, checks, traveler's checks

SUGGESTED SNORKELING SITES

Reefs equal land mass in the Bahamas, so treat them with respect. Don't touch, harm, or take anything you see. As visitors, we are privileged to enjoy the splendor of this underwater spectacle; leave it exactly as you find it for others to enjoy.

Off Hawksbill Cay, which also has good anchorages off the central west coast, and an excellent freshwater well near the anchorage. There are rare, white-tailed Tropic birds nesting here in March and April, providing spectacular flying displays.

Between *Little Cistern* and *Cistern Cay*.

Brad's Cay on the east side of *Long Cay*, with a cave on the northeast side.

Between *S. Hall's Pond*, *O'Brien's*, and *Pasture Cay* where there is a sunken drug-smuggling plane.

Cambridge and *Little Bell Cay*, which are private but have good reefs to the east and south.

Rocky Dundas, with dinghy moorings near the caves and reef.

And the Park's own *Sea Aquarium*, which you can locate by a sign on a small rock, with a dinghy mooring.

THINGS TO DO IN WARDERICK WELLS

- Swim off your own boat in some of the clearest water in the world.
- Snorkel the unbelievably beautiful and diverse reefs.
- See how many birds you can hear in the total peace and quiet of Warderick Wells, and spot them from the Bird Check List given out at the headquarters.
- Walk to the top of Boo Boo Hill and leave your boat's name as a memento. Keep to the marked "Shaggy Dog" trail to protect new indigenous plant growth, and wear sturdy shoes to protect your feet across the moonscape. Maybe you'll meet a Hutia on the way? Don't forget to take a camera; the views from the top are glorious, and you have to be photographed nailing your boat name to the great collection up there.
- Ask how you can help with volunteering in the Park.
- Listen for the ghosts of Warderick Wells on moonlit nights!

COMPASS CAY

At Compass Cay you will be welcomed by a friendly host, whom you may meet earlier if you are concerned about finding your way in and have asked for a pilot to help guide you to this enchanting private island. Tucker Rolle's family has owned land in this part of the Exumas for generations, and Tucker and Helen now run the *Compass Cay Marina*. They have plans to expand it by bringing in a larger generator so that more than three docks can connect to shore power, and by building two guest cottages overlooking the sheltered harbor. This tiny, almost landlocked harbor would certainly make a good hurricane hole. They proudly boast that theirs is the most beautiful beach in the Bahamas. We have to agree.

MARINA

COMPASS CAY MARINA
Tel and fax: 242-355-2064 • VHF 16

Slips	6
Moorings	3, cost $10 per night.
Max LOA	Up to 80 ft.
MLW at Dock	Shoal draft approaches, 8 ft. at the dock.
Dockage	50¢ per ft. per day, 40¢ per ft. per week, 30¢ per ft. per month.
Power	3 of the 6 docks have 110v shore power.
Fuel	No
Water	No
Telephone	There is no public telephone.
Trash	By arrangement
Accommodations	Tucker and Helen will occasionally take guests in their own house, until the guest cottages are built. Call ahead for details.
Facilities	Beach parties and potluck suppers on the beach with other guests. This beach is glorious, with good snorkeling on reefs that you can almost walk out to. Both Sampson and Staniel Cays are easy to reach in your dinghy if you need supplies or service.
Credit Cards	Cash or traveler's checks only

THINGS TO DO IN COMPASS CAY

- Enjoy lazy days on that gorgeous beach, and make new friends among the fish colonies on the reef.
- Take the dinghy to explore some of the little bays and inlets among the islands.

SAMPSON CAY

Sampson Cay is a tiny gem in the Exuma chain, privately owned by the Mitchell family. Marcus and Rosie Mitchell welcome you as friends to their *Sampson Cay Club and Marina*. The main dock and the fuel dock are easy to spot, as are the moorings on your port side as you come in. Through the narrow gap is a second, sheltered harbor where Rosie keeps her sea plane, and you can safely leave your boat for a while if you have to return home. This is a perfect center for exploring the central Exumas, with fantastic fishing and diving within easy reach, and snorkeling within dinghy reach.

MARINA

SAMPSON CAY CLUB AND MARINA
Tel: 242-355-2034 • VHF 16

Slips	30
Max LOA	100 ft.
MLW at Dock	8 ft., but less in the channel.
Dockage	85¢ per ft.
Moorings	4, cost $10 per night.
Power	50A and 30A for $10 per day
Fuel	Diesel and gasoline
Propane	Can be brought in from Staniel Cay.
Water	45¢ per gallon from the fuel dock.
Restaurant	An attractive bar with pennants flying, and a lounge and restaurant where you dine at a long table with other guests. See Jenny or Eulease and choose from a delicious menu before 3:30 pm to make your reservation. Dinner is at 7 pm; the restaurant is closed on Sundays.
Accommodations	Two cottages to rent overlooking the marina and seaplane beach; a charming two-story coral tower with air conditioning that looks like a lighthouse can sleep four people. From $125 a night.
Groceries	The marina store has a selection of canned and some frozen goods, as well as liquor and a few gifts and T-shirts. Paul, the dockmaster, will open it up for you.
Ice	$4 a bag
Laundry	$16 per load. Jenny or Eulease will do it for you if you give it to them early in the day.
Dive Rental	Dive equipment is available for rent.
Dive Tanks	Air refills are available.
Telephone	No public telephone
Trash	Only marina guests may leave trash.
Facilities	Marcus and Rosie Mitchell operate two planes, one a seaplane, and will meet airline flights arriving in Nassau or George Town. They will also fly you out in an emergency. There is a mechanic and some repairs are possible, as well as towing. Long-term storage and small-boat rentals are available.
Credit Cards	Cash or traveler's checks only

THINGS TO DO IN SAMPSON CAY

- Enjoy an excellent dinner with new friends.
- Snorkel and dive the many reefs within easy reach of Sampson Cay. Marcus or Paul will advise you where to go.
- Leave your boat in a safe harbor while you return home to complete some urgent business. Ask Rosie to collect you from Nassau when you come back.

STANIEL CAY

BASRA in STANIEL CAY VHF 16

With its good anchorages and moorings, two marinas, airfield, a central location in the Exumas, and its position in the middle of some of the most spectacular waters in the Exuma chain, Staniel Cay has long featured on most people's visit list. Brightly painted houses and the relaxed, informal feeling of Staniel Cay make it attractive for visitors who can only spend a few days, or for those with time to linger. The highlight of the year is the annual *Cruising Regatta* in January, which follows on from Junkanoo every New Year's Day.

MARINAS

STANIEL CAY YACHT CLUB
Tel: 242-355-2011 or 2024 • Fax: 355-2044 • VHF 16

Slips	10
Max LOA	150 ft.
MLW at Dock	7.5 ft.
Dockage	80¢ per ft. per day
Power	$25 per day for 50A, $15 per day for 30A.
Fuel	Diesel and gasoline
Propane	Yes
Water	50¢ per gallon
Telephones	Yes
Restaurant	Breakfast, lunch, and dinner in the clubhouse. Box lunches for picnics can be ordered the day before. Call ahead on VHF 16 if you are not staying at the Yacht Club.
Ice	Yes
Trash	$1.50 per bag, leave it behind the restaurant.
Boat Rental	SCYC has a 13-foot Boston Whaler to rent for $50 a day, excluding fuel.
Diving	*Oceanus Dive Society* specializes in taking small groups of divers of all levels.
Accommodations	Four air-conditioned cottages, a houseboat cottage, and a guest house from $125 per day, MAP $34.
Credit Cards	Visa, MasterCard, and Amex

HAPPY PEOPLE MARINA
Tel: 242-355-2008 • VHF 16

Slips	17
Max LOA	177 ft.
MLW at Dock	7 ft.
Dockage	80¢ per ft. per day
Power	$18 per day for 50A, $15 per day for 30A.
Water	50¢ a gallon
Propane	Yes
Showers	Yes
Telephone	Yes
Restaurant	*Happy People Restaurant* is open for breakfast, lunch, and dinner.
Ice	$3 for a 10-lb. bag
Accommodations	10 air-conditioned units, from $80 per day.
Credit Cards	Cash and traveler's checks only

MOORINGS

CLUB THUNDERBALL
VHF 16 "Thunderball"

Moorings	11, from $10 a day according to boat length.
Dock	There are two dinghy docks.
Restaurant	*Club Thunderball Restaurant and Bar*
Laundry	Three coin-operated machines

SERVICES & SHOPPING IN STANIEL CAY

Accommodations

Happy People Marina Tel: 242-355-2008 Eight double rooms, four with private bath, four with shared facilities; one cottage with two bedrooms and air conditioning. Rooms from $80 per day according to season, two weeks advance notice needed.

Staniel Cay Yacht Club Tel: 242-355-2024 Four waterfront cottages for two people from $800 per week, one cottage for four people from $1200 per week, one houseboat cottage for two people, plus two guests, from $800 per week. MAP $34 a day. Flights from Nassau or Fort Lauderdale can be arranged.

Airport

Island Express and private flights only.

John Chamberlain 355-2043

Solomon Robinson VHF 16 "Thunderball"

Marcus and Rosie Mitchell 242-355-2034 • VHF 16, on Sampson Cay   If you are meeting people from the airport you can tie up at the concrete dock by the *Isle General Store;* they can help arrange flights for you.

Beauty Parlor

Natajia's Unisex Salon Tel: 355-2005 • VHF 16 "Nikki" Call Nikki to make an appointment.

Bicycle Rental

Mr. Bob Chamberlain Located next to the *Staniel Cay Yacht Club.* Has six bicycles to rent, $5 for a half day, $8 for a full day.

Boutique

Lindsay's Boutique Tel: 355-2050
Next to *Happy People Marina.* T-shirts, bags, some clothes.

Church

Mt. Olivett Baptist Church

Clinic

St. Luke's Clinic Tel: 355-2010, and monitor VHF 16 out of hours   Open 9 am to 12 pm and 2:30 pm to 5 pm on Monday, Tuesday, Thursday, and Friday; from 9 am to 12 pm on Wednesday and Saturday.

Groceries

Burke's Blue Grocery Store Tel: 355-2014   Open 7:30 am to 7:30 pm Monday to Saturday. Burke Smith has groceries and limited household supplies, and can help with laundry and special mail boat orders if needed; fresh bread can be ordered.

Pink Pearl Supermarket Tel: 355-2040 and VHF 16 "Pink Pearl"   Proprietor Hugh Smith. Open 7:30 am to 7:30 pm Monday to Saturday, with bread, groceries, fruit and vegetables, household items, cold drinks, and beer; can help arrange for laundry.

Hardware

Isles General Store Tel: 355-2007 • VHF 16   Located just south of the settlement. Open 7:30 am to 12 pm, and 1:30 to 7 pm, Monday to Saturday. Has groceries, hardware, marine supplies, cleaning goods, ice, propane, and homemade bread and ice cream. There is a concrete dock inside the creek where you can tie up, and bagged garbage can be left for a small fee.

Library and Museum

Built in 1776, this is the oldest building on the island. Open on Tuesday and Friday from 11 am to 12 pm and 3 pm to 5 pm.

Propane

Refills available from the *Isles General Store.*

Post Office

Near the *Blue Grocery Store.*

Regatta and Fishing Tournament

Staniel Cay Cruising Regatta in January, headquarters at the *Happy People Marina.* Contact Kenneth Rolle, 242-355-2008 for information.

Annual Staniel Cay Bonefish Tournament in July.

Restaurants and Bars

Happy People Restaurant Tel: 355-2008 • VHF 16   Open 8 am to closing Monday to Saturday; 2 pm to closing on Sundays. Serves breakfast, lunch, and dinner, with last dinner at 9 pm. Live music on Saturdays. Call ahead for dinner reservations, and make arrangements the night before for breakfast. Famous for her "Theazel Burger;" Theazel Rolle was awarded the 1983 Bahamas National Tourism Achievement Award.

Staniel Cay Yacht Club Tel: 355-2024 • VHF 16   Open at the clubhouse from 10 am to closing Monday to Saturday, and for dinner on Sundays from 5 pm. Book ahead for dinner, and make arrangements the night before for breakfast and boxed picnic lunches. The bar, with a pool table and satellite TV, is open daily, but dinner only is served after 5 pm on Sundays.

Club Thunderball VHF 16 "Thunderball"   Open 11:30 am to closing Monday to Saturday, from 1 pm to closing on Sundays, dinner reservations requested before 4 pm. Serves Bahamian dishes with an emphasis on seafood, burgers, and sandwiches. Friday night barbecue, occasional pig roasts, and a Super Bowl party. The bar has a pool table, satellite TV, and dancing on weekends with local DJ. They have two dinghy docks.

Telephones

Batelco Tel: 355-2060 • Fax: 355-2063   Open Monday to Friday 9 am to 4:30 pm. They sell phone cards, will handle faxes. Phones also at the *Happy People Marina* and the *Staniel Cay Yacht Club.*

Inside Thunderball Cave, Staniel Cay.

THINGS TO DO IN STANIEL CAY

- Dive *Thunderball Cave*, a spectacular underwater cave with shafts of sunlight illuminating it, attracting schools of fish. It was made famous in the James Bond movie, *Thunderball.* Time your dive for slack tide, since the currents are strong here. Take a bag of bread crumbs left over from breakfast to feed some of the tiny, curious fish at the cave. You can tie up your dinghy to one of the two mooring buoys at the west end of the site.
- Have a Theazel Burger at the *Happy People Restaurant.*

BLACK POINT

BASRA in Black Point
Tucker Rolle 355-3014 or VHF 16

This friendly settlement has the second-largest population in the Exumas, after George Town. Anchor off, come in with your dinghy, and tie up to the government pier to explore Black Point. Highlights of the year are the *Black Point Homecoming* in April and the *Black Point Regattas* in August and October.

SERVICES & SHOPPING IN BLACK POINT

Accommodations
Scorpio's Cottages With the *Scorpio Inn*, serving Bahamian dishes for lunch and dinner, and snacks.
Ruby's Guest House Five cottages with full bath and air conditioning. Contact the *Scorpio Bar* for the managing agent two weeks in advance.

Churches
St. Luke's Baptist Church
Gethsemany Baptist Church

Clinic
Tel: 355-0007 For after-hours emergencies, call 355-3040. The Clinic is just across from the school, open Monday to Friday from 9 am to 1:30 pm. A nurse is on duty.

Groceries
Adderley's Friendly Store Tel: 355-3016 Where "a smile awaits you." Open from 9 am to 6 pm Monday to Saturday, and after church on Sunday, with groceries, fruit, and vegetables.
Darlene's Grocery Store Tel: 355-3026
Open most days; go to the house and ask her to open up.

Ice and Water
Available from Tucker Rolle and the community well. The water is free from the stand pipes by the curb, but you might want to boil it before drinking it.

Laundry
Beryl and Charlene Kemp

Mailboats
The *Etienne* and *Cephas* call in weekly from Nassau.

Post Office
Tel: 355-3043 Open from 9 am to 5 pm, Monday to Friday.

Restaurants
Lorene's Cafe Tel: 355-3012 • VHF 16
Opens at 8 am, serves breakfast, lunch, and dinner. Arrange breakfast the night before; no breakfast on Sundays.
Scorpio Inn Restaurant and Bar Tel: 355-3003 • VHF 16 Bar and restaurant serving Bahamian food. Open daily from 11 am, Sundays after church. This is where it all happens in Black Point.

Shopping
There is a straw market, a souvenir shop, and a sports shop.

Telephone
Batelco Tel: 242-355-3060 • Fax: 355-3063 Open Monday to Friday 9 am to 5:30 pm with a phone card telephone outside the office. Phone cards are for sale. The Batelco operator, Mr. Walter Rolle, can put you in touch with local guides for fishing and diving. Walter knows everything about Black Point.

LITTLE FARMERS CAY

Famous for its *Five F's Festival*, Little Farmers Cay boasts its own flag, too. Settled originally by freed slaves from Exuma, there are approximately fifty-five residents on the island today, some of whom of are descendants from those early days. This one-and-a-quarter-mile long island is the quintessential Bahamian cay.

MARINA
FARMERS CAY YACHT CLUB
Tel: 242-355-4017 • VHF 16

Slips	5
Moorings	There are two moorings between Little Farmers Cay and Great Guana Cay. Both cost $10 per day. The southern buoy off Great Guana Cay is owned by *Terry Bain* who can be called on VHF 16 "Ocean Cabin" or 355-4006. The northern float near Great Guana Cay is owned by *Hallan Rolle*. Call him on 355-4003 or VHF 16 "Little Jeff."
Max LOA	110 ft.
MLW at dock	8 ft.
Dockage	80¢ per ft. per day
Power	$22 per day for 50A, $15 per day for 30A
Fuel	Diesel and gasoline
Propane	From Hallan Rolle
Water	45¢ per gallon
Telephone	Yes
Showers	Yes
Laundry	Service available on request.
Restaurant	Serves breakfast, lunch, and dinner.
Ice	Yes
Mail	Will be held for your arrival.
Repairs	Small repairs.
Credit Cards	Visa, MasterCard, and Amex

SERVICES & SHOPPING IN LITTLE FARMERS CAY

Accommodations
Farmers Cay Yacht Club Tel: 242-355-4017 Three double rooms with twin beds & bath. Book at least two weeks in advance.
Ocean Cabin Tel and fax: 242-355-4006 Mooring for $10 a day, two cottages in the village, which you must book at least three weeks in advance. Library exchange.
Ocean Cabin Also hosts the rowdy and fun *Five F's* party annually, on the First Friday in February. Call 242-324-2093, or 242-355-4006 for more information.

Church
St. Mary's Baptist Church

Clinic
Tel: 355-4015 Call FCYC in an emergency. Located up the hill near the Batelco office. Open Monday to Friday, 9 am to 1 pm. Shirley Nixon, wife of Roosevelt Nixon at the *FCYC*, is the nurse at the Government Clinic.

Fresh Bread
Call ahead through *Ocean Cabin* to Earnestine Bain. Shirley Nixon will make cakes and desserts. Contact her through *FCYC*.

Groceries
Little Harbor Grocery Store Tel: 355-4019 Open 8 am to 7:30 pm.
Corene's Grocery Store In the village, by *Ocean Cabin*. Terry Bain will open up for you. Most islanders have supplies delivered by the mail boat, so the stores do not carry a large stock. If you need something specific contact the *FCYC* to order it.

Liquor Store
Little Harbour Liquor Store Tel: 355-4019 Open 9–5 Monday to Saturday. Ask Eugenia Nixon Percentie at *Little Harbour Grocery*.

Post Office
Near the Government Dock by *Corene's Grocery Store*. Open on Wednesday, handling incoming mail off the mailboat, and on Thursday, handling outgoing mail for the Friday mailboat.

Propane
Hallan Rolle Tel: 355-4003 or VHF 16 "Little Jeff" Take tanks in early for a same-day fill; available 9 am to 5 pm, Monday to Friday.

Restaurants
Farmers Cay Yacht Club Tel: 355-4017 or VHF 16 Call at least an hour ahead to make reservations; the restaurant serves breakfast, lunch, and dinner.
Ocean Cabin Tel: 355-4006 Call Terry Bain at least an hour ahead for lunch or dinner; make breakfast arrangements the night before.

Telephones
Tel: 355-4060 • Fax: 355-4063 Two telephones in the Batelco office, up the hill behind the village. Office open from 9 am to 5:30 pm, Monday to Friday; also sells Batelco phone cards.

Trash
Trash can be left at the dump near the airstrip or at the bins in the settlement.

GETTING AROUND

Airport
There is no scheduled airline service, but private aircraft can use the 2,300-foot paved airstrip.

Mailboats
MV Etienne and *MV Cephas* to and from Nassau.

Water Taxi
Hallan Rolle Tel: 355-4003 or VHF 16 "Little Jeff"
He will take you to Barreterre or to explore the surrounding islands, or on fishing or dive trips. There is no scuba gear to rent.

THINGS TO DO IN LITTLE FARMERS CAY

- Join the fun for *The First Friday in February Farmers Cay Festival*, also known as the Five Fs party, held the first weekend in February. Call 242-324-2093 or 242-355-4006 for more information.
- Take the Great Guana Cay cave tour with Hallan Rolle, and explore the 90-foot land cave.
- Visit JR's woodcarving shop up near the Batelco office, and take home a memento of Little Farmers Cay with one of his carvings from the *Ocean Cabin*.
- Just enjoy one small island that in many ways is as close to Polynesia in its feel, form, and flowers as you can get.

Chapter 15
The Southern Exuma Cays and Great Exuma Island
The Farmers Cays to Little Exuma Island

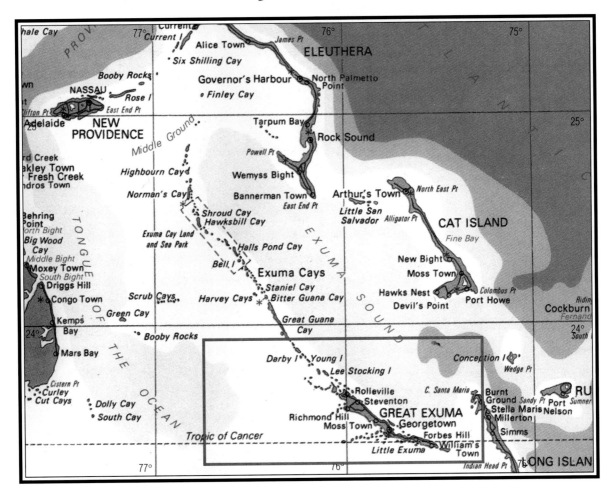

An Overview of the Southern Exumas

THE Southern Exumas continue the northwest to southeast line of the Exuma chain from Galliot Cut, just south of Farmers Cay, to Hog Cay and White Cay, just off the southeast tip of Little Exuma Island at 23° 23' 00 N 076° 25' 00 W. On the Bank side, south of Rat Cay Cut, sandbores and shoal water set limits on cruising territory, and in effect, on that side, you've gone as far as you can go. Rat Cay Cut is your last chance to switch to Exuma Sound to enter George Town. The cays and islands extending south from Rat Cay to Great Exuma Island on the Bank side offer a good area for shoal draft exploration, but if you carry any kind of draft it could turn into a nightmare ground of deceptive channels, shoals, sand, and reef. Leave it to the locals. The west coast of the two Exuma

Islands, masked by flats, mud, and mangroves, as we've said is no cruising territory, but it's good for bonefishing. This may seem a bleak report, but in the Southern Exumas everything pales into insignificance compared to George Town and Stocking Island, the Shangri-La of the Bahamas. Little Exuma Island itself is so diminished by its larger twin that it hardly features on the itinerary of most cruising boats.

George Town is, in itself, either the end stop and turnaround point on your cruise south from Florida, the launch pad for your voyage to the Caribbean, or a winter or summer haven. Whatever your plans, cruising in or passage making through the Bahamas takes on a fundamental change at George Town. Continuing south you're committed to serious blue-water passages with Atlantic swells and waves, a diminishing number of safe havens on your route, and few, if any, resources available until you reach the Turks and

Caicos. Cruising in the Bahamas north of George Town, as we all know it, has plenty of places to stop, shoal draft, and deep water–passage options, and very often a lee side and a windward side to your chosen route. Perhaps unfairly George Town has long been known as "Chicken Harbor," for many bound for the Caribbean find their first passage after George Town less than pleasant, and return to venture no further south. But as in all sailing, it's weather and timing that make the difference. There's nothing inherently dangerous about going on past George Town, and the span of Out Islands running south from Long Island to the Turks and Caicos form one of the least-spoiled tropic transits in the Western Hemisphere.

For all these reasons, George Town dominates the Southern Exumas and is all things to all people. Taking an opinion poll of the cruising community, some like it, some can't stand it for long, but almost every craft on passage between the Virgin Islands and the East Coast of the US will call in to George Town, Great Exuma Island, and no one cruising in the Exumas will miss it. The tide in the Southern Exumas runs about the same as Nassau times.

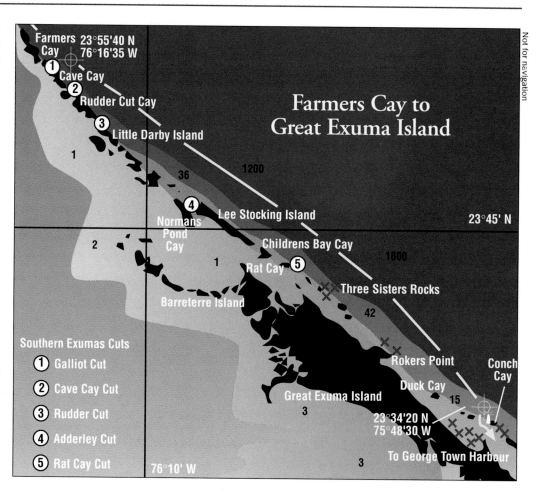

Not for navigation

Big Farmers Cay to Great Exuma Island

BIG FARMERS CAY AND THE GALLIOT CAYS
Big Farmers Cay, despite its size, holds nothing to excite the cruising visitor other than shoals and sand extending west into the Bank for over 1 nm. There are no anchorages in its 2.5 nm length other than the northwest-facing cove that opens into the Farmers Cut basin. If you choose to go in here, you are close enough to the Cut to suffer surge if any kind of sea is running outside. The Galliot Cays, which gave their name to the Cut, are largely unapproachable due to sand, reefs, and tidal flow, but an anchorage can be found by the edge of the sand off the northwest tip of Little Galliot Cay.

Galliot Cut

Galliot Cut E (0.4 nm NE)	GALLE	23° 55' 40 N	076° 16' 35 W
Galliot Cut W (0.25 nm W)	GALLW	23° 55' 10 N	076° 17' 15 W

Galliot Cut is not hard to pick out from the east with High Cay standing proud to its immediate north like an aircraft carrier, and a highly visible light on the north tip of Cave Cay. However, beware that this light is not at the extremity of the low-lying rock that runs north from this point, and a much smaller stake has been placed nearer the north tip of this reef. A continuing shoal area contours around the north tip of Cave Cay. Stay well clear of it. Once you're through the Cut, there's sand on both sides of the little unnamed cay that lies ahead, and more sand behind Little Galliot Cay off your starboard bow. You must turn fairly immediately either to starboard or port and pick your way from then on.

We don't like Galliot Cut. Ebb tide flows can build a wall of water there, rather like a standstill tsunami, and it's just too fast running for comfort. It seems to offer no particular advantage over its neighboring cuts. Why not use Farmers Cut?

CAVE CAY AND MUSHA CAY

Cave Cay is private, as is Musha Cay to the south. Both are being developed. There's an anchorage to the west of Cave Cay, which also has a shallow hurricane hole opening off the west coast. At one time this was an option open to you, but no longer. The hole is being set up as some kind of marina for private use. The area around Musha Cay, although visually attractive simply because of the contrasting colors of the water, is almost totally shoal save for the one north–south channel, which itself at any time other than high water, is a shallow-draft route. There are no anchorages there.

Cave Cay Cut

Cave Cut E (0.25 nm E)	CAVEE	23° 54' 10 N	076° 15' 10 W
Cave Cut W (0.25 nm W)	CAVEW	23° 53' 55 N	076° 16' 05 W

Cave Cay Cut looks narrow and appears unattractive for that reason, but it's deep and straightforward. The shore of Cave Cay is well-weathered and looks like a cave-breeding shore, if nothing else. To the south the demarcation of the Cut rests on the flank of the unnamed small cay lying to the north of the reef, rock, and shoal area to the north of Musha Cay. There was, and still might be, a Christian-type cross on the rock to the south, which was put there as a marker. It might well act as a deterrent rather than encouragement!

RUDDER CUT CAY

Rudder Cut Cay, another long one at over 2 nm in length, is private. Distinguished by the architecture of its guardian house set on a spine of rock, Rudder Cut Cay has a spawn of reefs off its southeast headland. See our notes on Rudder Cut. There are anchorages along the west coast of Rudder Cut Cay, and, rather like Cave Cay, Rudder Cut Cay also has its hurricane hole midway along its length, but this one is also no longer open to casual visitors.

Rudder Cut

Rudder Cut E (0.25 nm NE)	RUDRE	23° 52' 15 N	076° 13' 25 W
Rudder Cut W (0.1 nm SW)	RUDRW	23° 51' 50 N	076° 13' 40 W

A large prominent house on the north tip of Little Darby Island marks Rudder Cut, and for additional ID the beaches fronting east on this property show white sand backed by palm trees. The actual cut lies between Rudder Cut Cay in the north and the plug of a cay (no name) that sits in the apparent middle of the Cut. Go north of this cay. Deeper inside the Cut, on the Bank side, are a cluster of rocks anchored, as it were, by a massive rock whale look-a-like (the whale is swimming north). You can pass to either side of the whale and its chicks, but the south channel is narrow.

Entering Rudder Cut from the Sound, or exiting to the Sound, look out for the reefs around the southeast hammerhead of Rudder Cut Cay. Rudder Cut really is a pass to nowhere if you're in Exuma Sound, for every route accessing Rudder Cut on the Bank side is shoal draft, and tide becomes critical. It's at this point, south of Rudder Cut Cay, that the Exuma Bank side, unless you have the right draft and a passion for shoal-water exploration and bonefishing, really becomes a no-no as a cruising ground.

THE DARBY ISLANDS, GOAT, LIGNUM VITAE, PRIME CAY, MELVIN, AND BOCK CAYS

The Darby Islands, the onetime domain of an ardent Nazi who had plans for harboring U-Boats there, are still private and other than the anchorage between them, there is little for the cruising visitor there. Goat Cay and Lignum Vitae Cays are private. There's a neat little anchorage tucked up in the north mouth between the two Darby Islands, but it's shoal draft.

As you go further south, Prime Cay is private, as is Neighbor Cay and Melvin Cay. Bock Cay (the 100-foot radio mast is not a Batelco tower) is also private and under development. So the land is out of bounds, there are few anchorages worth marking as such, and the whole area is such a maze of shoal-draft channels that we can see little point in attempting to thread your way around the shallows. The next reasonable point at which you can access the Bank side from Exuma Sound with purpose is Adderley Cut.

Adderley Cut

Adderley Cut E (0.4 nm E)	ADDYE	23° 47' 25 N	076° 06' 25 W
Adderley Cut W (0.7 nm W)	ADDYW	23° 46' 45 N	076° 07' 25 W

Adderley Cut is primarily your access to Lee Stocking Island and the Caribbean Marine Research Center. Well marked with a stone beacon on Adderley Cay and a prominent house off the north headland of Lee Stocking Island, you can't miss the entrance. There's also a house almost at beach level on the north shore of Lee Stocking Island, which will become apparent as you get closer in. Your main hazards are the reefs extending north from Lee Stocking Island, which mercifully show awash in part, so you can take a line well to the north to avoid them. Beware too of the shoal area in the central part of the Cut as you gain the Bank.

NORMANS POND CAY, LEAF CAY, AND LEE STOCKING ISLAND

Normans Pond Cay, once worked for salt, has native iguanas. If you land there, pets are prohibited. Leaf Cay is shoal to the east, but has a useful anchorage to the west. Lee Stocking Island, running south from Normans Pond Cay, is important as the base of Caribbean Marine Research Center, one of NOAA's National Undersea Research agencies. Located on the northwest tip of the island, just under the anvil head of its northern promontory, the Research Center is open to visitors on request (call *Bahama Hunter* on VHF 16). You are asked not to go on shore without permission. Childrens Bay Cay, to the south of Lee Stocking Island, is private. Immediately south lies Rat Cay, and Rat Cay Cut, the only north–south cut in the Exumas.

THE BRIGANTINE CAYS

The Brigantine Cays, some forty in total, typify the Bank side at this point in the Exuma chain. A confusion of islets, banks, mangroves, and channels, which may well tempt the bonefisher and the explorer, are tidal to a degree and boat mobility ends with the start of an ebb tide.

Rat Cay Cut

Rat Cay Cut N (0.25 nm NNW)	RATCN	23° 44' 05 N	076° 02' 05 W
Rat Cay Cut S (0.1 nm S)	RATCS	23° 43' 45 N	076° 01' 55 W

Rat Cay Cut earns distinction as being your last option to switch between the Bank side and Exuma Sound. For this reason alone we listed it with our primary passage-making cuts, but in truth Rat Cay Cut is hardly on the main road to anywhere, for on the Bank side you are already deep into sand-maze territory. Nonetheless it offers access to good anchorages behind Childrens Bay Cay, Rat Cay, and Square Rock Cay to the south.

The Cut itself, unusual in that it runs almost north–south, has no approach problems. From Exuma Sound the bulk of Square Rock Cay looks like a detached bung held ready to close the passage if need be. Rat Cay and Boysie Cay both appear low lying and the entrance to the Cut seems diminished in importance through a lack of height on either side. Perhaps the distant Square Rock Cay is compensation.

CHILDRENS BAY CAY, RAT CAY, AND THE CAYS LEADING TO GREAT EXUMA ISLAND

As we've said, Childrens Bay Cay is private and Rat Cay offers anchorages but little more. Better anchorages in this area might be found behind Square Rock Cay. We would go no further toward Great Exuma Island on the Bank side than Square Rock Cay.

Heading South to George Town, Great Exuma

George Town Harbour Ent. (W)	GTAW1	23° 34' 30 N	075° 48' 30 W

Heading for George Town your arrival waypoint will be our George Town Harbour west entry waypoint. On your way south stand well offshore (at least 1 nm off the line of barrier cays and reef along the east coast of Barreterre and Great Exuma Island), and watch out for the Three Sisters Rocks (23° 43' N 076° 00' W). At Channel Cay you can close your offing to a third of a mile, and then pick up that waypoint.

Rat Cay Cut to Great Exuma Island

A scattered line of minor cays lead south from Rat Cay Cut to Rokers Point on Great Exuma Island. Inside these cays there is a shoal-draft channel, but it's primarily of interest only to local fishermen. Cruising boats bound for George Town are advised to stand off out in Exuma Sound and concentrate on heading for the west entry waypoint to George Town Harbour, between Channel Cay and Conch Cay.

At one time an island in its own right, Barreterre is now joined by a bridge to Great Exuma Island. The 150-foot Batelco tower, just north of Barreterre settlement, is a useful landmark at this point, as is the Farmers Hill 40-foot Batelco tower on Great Exuma Island, just south of Rokers Point.

George Town, Great Exuma Island

Approaches

George Town Harbour Ent. (W)	GTAW1	23° 34' 30 N	075° 48' 30 W
George Town Harbour Ent. (E)	GTAE1	23° 30' 00 N	075° 40' 00 W

George Town, despite being host to one of the highest annual cruising visitor totals in the Bahamas, strangely carries the reputation of a difficult, if not dangerous place to enter. It seems totally at odds with its popularity. Almost every sailing guide urges caution, and entry instructions can seem complex and daunting. Let's take a satellite view of George Town first. If you understand the way it is, the worries diminish.

An Introduction to George Town

George Town does not have a harbor. The "harbor" is a 9-by-1-nm-wide strip of water between the mainland of Great Exuma Island and, for the most part, Stocking and

The Government Building, George Town.

Elizabeth Islands and Great Exuma Island. Inside this strip you can find shelter, one side or the other, whatever the wind, but not all places are sheltered all the time, and in some you are even exposed to the prevailing southeast wind. In old-fashioned terms, it would be called a *roadstead*, a place where a large number of vessels can lie up and find better shelter than they would outside. Right from the start we have two harbor names, Stocking Harbour and Elizabeth Harbour, but they are essentially a continuance of each other. It's easier to think of George Town, or George Town Harbour. You'd think it would be one of the best-developed harbors in the

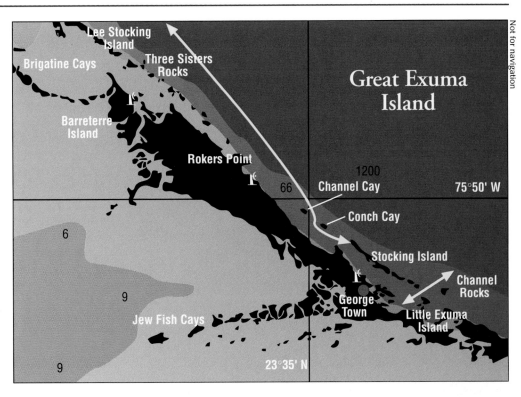

Bahamas, but with the failure of the early plantations in the Exumas, there never was the need to improve on what nature offered as a sheltered area.

Back in 1942, in the early days of the Second World War, the UK-US Lend-Lease agreement gave vital military hardware to Britain in exchange for bases for the US Navy in the British Atlantic and Caribbean colonies. George Town became a US naval patrol base, and the harbor was dredged to make it safe for seaplanes. Today that dredging has slowly infilled, and the bottom profile of George Town Harbour is much as it was at the start, shoal areas, rocks, and reefs scattered around, as well as dredged hollows.

What is inexplicable is that no project has been commissioned to set up navigation marks to take vessels safely in and out of George Town. Hurricanes are blamed, which can take out marks. Almost every year some attempt, often private initiative, is made to set up some marks, none of which endure for long. You are better off expecting none, and perhaps even ignoring those you do see, unless you're absolutely certain of their meaning. For guidance you have two easy-to-distinguish distant landmarks. The stone beacon on Stocking Island, looking like a shorn-off mini lighthouse, and the Batelco Tower, 180-feet tall with its two large satellite dishes, on the ridge to the south of George Town. However the harbor depth profile prevents you steering directly for either of these, except on certain legs.

The George Town Harbour area has two principal entrances. The west entrance serves if you are coming down the Exuma chain. The east entrance serves if you are coming from the

south or heading toward Long Island. Both have reefs and rocks, and in bad weather are not to be attempted. By bad weather we mean high winds, high seas, and bad visibility. To be safe you must be able to read your way in, and have absolute control over your boat. You would also be prudent, dependent on your draft, to take advantage of a favorable tide.

Because of the absence of marks, the only way to enter is by a series of legs from GPS waypoint to GPS waypoint, which will position you at or near each point where you should alter course. *Don't even think* of programming and setting an autopilot. This is eyeball navigation with GPS used as a helping hand rather than a set of old-fashioned position lines and fixes. Be mindful that your GPS and mine will never agree, your chart had its origins circa 1836, and its last serious update was in 1941. With this caveat, we'll take each entrance in turn and then deal with marinas and anchorages.

The West Entrance

George Town Harbour Ent. (W)	GTAW1	23° 34' 30 N	075° 48' 30 W
W approach Waypoint 2	GTAW2	23° 33' 40 N	075° 48' 40 W
W approach Waypoint 3	GTAW3	23° 33' 15 N	075° 48' 10 W
W approach Waypoint 4	GTAW4	23° 32' 45 N	075° 48' 00 W
W approach Waypoint 5	GTAW5	23° 32' 10 N	075° 47' 30 W
W approach Waypoint 6	GTAW6	23° 31' 55 N	075° 46' 30 W

With such a list of waypoints it looks like a potential nightmare, but it's not difficult. Just take it easily, in bite-sized chunks, and get your First Mate to call it out as you go. You'll have at least 6 feet on this route.

STAGE 1: GETTING THROUGH CONCH CAY CUT

Two simple half-mile legs will take you through Conch Cay Cut (don't confuse this with the Conch Cut already discussed further to the north). The first waypoint places you about 0.5 nm north of Conch Cay Cut. From there steer 199°M for 0.68 nm to clear the reef (on your port side), which runs northwest from Conch Cay.

At Waypoint 2 you'll be safely past that first reef. Turn to port on a heading of 138°M, which has you running parallel to Conch Cay and its reefs on the port side, and off the reefs that you'll see to starboard. Follow this course for 0.62 nm to Waypoint 3.

- Conch Cay (or rather its outlier) has a light on it.

- The Smith Cays, right on your nose on leg one, are to starboard and are easily identifiable. There are houses on the hill behind the Smith Cays.

- There may or may not be a marker on the reef you pass on your starboard side on Leg 2.

STAGE 2: THE SIMON'S POINT LEGS

Two easy legs around Simon's Point sets you up to enter the George Town Harbour area. From Waypoint 3 turn to starboard and head on 169°M for Simon's Point. Run for 0.52 nm on this leg to reach Waypoint 4 (standing safely off the point).

At Waypoint 4 turn to port on a heading of 148°M, and run parallel to the Great Exuma coast for 0.74 nm to reach Waypoint 5.

- Simon's Point has two highly visible pink houses.

STAGE 3: CROSSING TO STOCKING ISLAND

One further leg sets you up to continue on your own. At Waypoint 5 turn to port, and identify that Stocking Island beacon. Head for it. A run of just about 1 nm on this heading will take you across to the deep-water channel to our Waypoint 6, which is on the main fairway running parallel to Stocking Island. Once you're there, turn to starboard and follow its course (something like 140°M) to where you wish to go.

- You can't miss that Stocking Island beacon.

- Follow the boats. You can hardly go wrong. It's safe where everyone else has gone.

If you're bound for the George Town side, when you're just about level with the entrance to the Stocking Island basins, turn to starboard and head for the pink buildings of the Peace and Plenty Hotel if you want to anchor there. Head for the Batelco Tower to take you south of Regatta Point for Kidd Cove or the Exuma Docking Services.

There are other simpler ways of making this entry from Conch Cay Cut. It can be reduced to as little as three legs. In any event once you've done it once or twice you'll get

your bearings, so that you can go visual much of the next time, rather than taking note of GPS readouts and your distance log. We give what we've found to be a safe approach as a starter pack.

The East Entrance

Black Rocks (1 nm S)	BLKRS	23° 27' 00 N	075° 32' 00 W
George Town Harbour Ent. (E)	GTAE1	23° 30' 00 N	075° 40' 00 W
E approach Waypoint 2	GTAE2	23° 29' 10 N	075° 40' 15 W
E approach Waypoint 3	GTAE3	23° 29' 25 N	075° 42' 00 W
E approach Waypoint 4	GTAE4	23° 29' 25 N	075° 42' 35 W
E approach Waypoint 5	GTAE5	23° 30' 25 N	075° 44' 40 W

The east entrance also produces a list of waypoints, but once again these are not daunting if you take them in stages. Also, once again, do *not* attempt to go in or out on auto. What is important is that your are right on top with your eyeball navigation, for you are passing through reef country at the start. However, you should find at least 12 feet the whole way. Our Black Rocks waypoint applies *only* if you are incoming from or going out to Salt Pond or to the south of Long Island by the Neuvitas Rocks route. See **The Bahamas South of the Tropic of Cancer** on page 278.

STAGE 1: THE INITIAL ENTRY

As you approach our first waypoint you'll pick up the prominent isolated skyline house on Man-O-War Cay from some distance out, which will be off your starboard bow, and North Channel Rocks, off your port bow, show plainly and black.

- From our first waypoint, the initial East Harbour entrance, a course of 200°M held for 0.75 nm takes you safely in through a wide, deep, 20-foot cut to Waypoint 2.

STAGE 2: RUNNING UP TO RED SHANK CORNER

- At Waypoint 2 turn to starboard on 285°M for 1.5 nm to reach Waypoint 3, which lies just short of a coral reef to port and patches of isolated heads to starboard.

- At Waypoint 3 alter course just a tad to 280°M and eyeball your way for 0.5 nm to reach Waypoint 4, which we call Red Shank Corner. From this waypoint, if you want Red Shank Cays, you would work your way southwest around the coral to tuck yourself in behind the Red Shank Cays or Crab Cay.

STAGE 3: THE FINAL RUN IN

- From Waypoint 4 you have a comparatively long run of just over 2 nm on a heading of 305°M to reach Waypoint 5, which is between Stocking Island

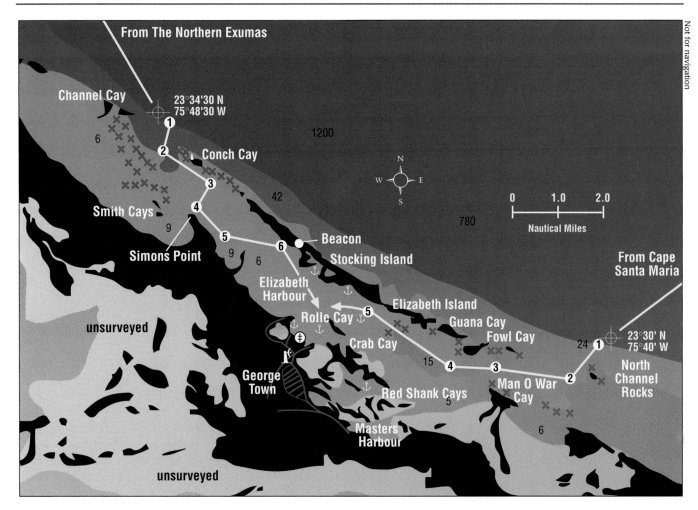

(to starboard) and Rolle Cay (to port). This run is *not* coral free, and you pass close between two reefs (approximately 23° 30' 05 N 075° 44' 00 W) that lie midway between Elizabeth Island and Crab Cay. Don't relax. You are *not* there yet.

- The passage between these reefs has been marked by two buoys (red/white to starboard, green/white to port **as you enter**) but these could be missing.

- A barrel marker has also been placed on the reef to the north of your route just short of our Waypoint 5.

From Waypoint 5 you can carry on, taking it visually to the Stocking Island anchorages, or swing around Rolle Cay and the little Moss Cays for Kidd Cove, the Exuma Docking Services, or the Peace and Plenty Anchorage.

Dock Space and Anchoring

At the time of writing, Exumas Docking Services, just past Regatta Point, is the only marina. A project to build a new marina in Masters Harbour (south of the Red Shank Cays) has been started. In 1998 haul-out and dry storage may be available, but the completion date of the envisioned full-service complex is a long way off.

Your choices for anchoring are almost unlimited but boil down to five broad options:

1. Anywhere off Stocking Island clear of the Harbour fairway.

2. One of the linked Stocking Island basins.

3. Off the Peace and Plenty Hotel.

4. In or just off Kidd Cove (south of Regatta Point).

5. Tucked in behind the Red Shank Cays or Crab Cay.

If you choose the remoter reaches of Stocking Island or the Red Shank area you are in for a longish dinghy ride to George Town to get your provisions or enjoy time ashore. In good weather this may be fine. In protracted bad weather, it may be too bumpy, too wet, and too uncomfortable to be worth attempting. Off Stocking Island take care not to anchor in the fairway. Off the Peace and Plenty you must keep clear of the government dock (on the north side of Regatta

Exuma Docking Services Marina (and Sophie Bell at work).

Point) and the turning basin. In the Kidd Cove area you must not obstruct the harbor fairway.

The three Stocking Island basins are well protected, but if you're lying off Stocking Island you'll feel anything from south through the western quadrants to north. It's almost exactly the reverse on the George Town side. To reach the distant but well-protected Red Shanks area remember that if you've come in through the west entrance, you must carry on and pick up the reverse course of our east entrance instructions to take you to Waypoint GTAE4, the place we call Red Shank Corner. From then on you are dependent on your eyeball navigation. You will find that there are other anchorages that may be found with careful reconnaissance, behind Rolle Cay, in the north bight of Crab Cay, and so on. Much depends on your curiosity, and skill.

The one long-established marina, Exuma Docking Services, is showing its age and, perhaps for too long now, it's been the only act in town. "Service is our thing" is advertised, but a working power hookup and constant voltage is not always certain, water is turned on only during the day and water pressure is often low, and the facilities on shore can best be described as just adequate. The marina as a whole is exposed from the northeast through to east, and you can expect discomfort, which can be acute, if you're unlucky and get these winds while you're there. Some recent seawall refurbishment has engendered a downside, for reflected waves in strong easterlies create an evil crosshatch for those secured closest to the shore. Under bad conditions the marina can become almost untenable, and your only hope, if you are on a small boat, is to find a slip in the lee of a megayacht and hope that your shielding big friend never moves.

These comments apart, Exuma Docking Services has the best site in George Town and the potential, more so

with its Top Deck Restaurant, to rival Nassau's Yacht Haven with its Poop Deck Restaurant and bar, if there were a mind to do so. Perhaps the threat of a potential rival will provide that spur.

George Town

There's no doubt that George Town is the best waystop in the Southern Bahamas, and if you're heading further south, little short of a compulsory stop, for after that you're in the Bahamian boondocks, on your own. As we've mentioned, George Town has both its *aficionados* and those who limit their time there to the minimum. It's a good harbor in prevailing winds, particularly on the Stocking Island side. It's a good place to restock, fill your tanks, get in touch with the world, and take a run ashore to stretch your legs, and you can dine well there. It has almost every facility you are likely to need other than the capability of hauling a boat and doing any kind of major work on it. The airport is well served and you can get crew out, friends in, and yourself home in a hurry if you need. See our **Yellow Pages** for details.

THE GEORGE TOWN MIGRATIONS

George Town is also an extraordinary place. Year after year Great Exuma and Stocking Island play host to a seasonal floating population equivalent to a small town. Each winter, in November, the first armada of George Town–bound winter residents sets out from Florida. They make their return passage in May. By midwinter some 300 visiting yachts are anchored off Stocking Island, in the Stocking Island basins, off the Peace and Plenty Hotel, and in Kidd's Cove off George Town itself. In Regatta weeks you can add another hundred boats to this total. The majority of the boats,

Exuma Markets dinghy dock, Lake Victoria.

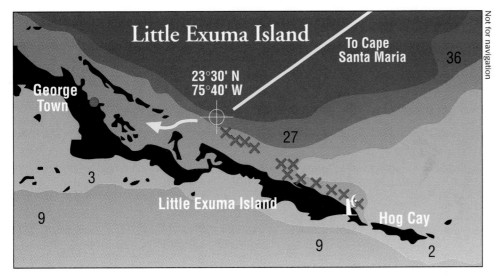

visitor. There are the ruins of abandoned plantations (notably on Crab Cay), early graves (Rolle Town), and good beaches (particularly on the doorstep, on Stocking Island). It's worth taking an island tour, but renting a car may seem wasteful at the end of the day.

LITTLE EXUMA ISLAND

Little Exuma, like Barreterre, is no longer an entity but is now joined by a road bridge to its larger sibling. The settlements, sparse and far apart, show a life-style close to subsistence living. George Town has it all. It is the magnet, the center of all that counts in the Southern Exumas, and the hinterland is abandoned.

THE REMAINING SOUTHERN EXUMA CAYS

Hog Cay and White Cay, lying south of Little Exuma Island, are the two last cays in the Exuma chain. Difficult to access either on the Exuma Sound or the Bank sides because of shoal water and coral, they are best left unvisited unless you elect to anchor off and take your dinghy in to explore. If you do decide to feel your way along the coast, the Williams Town 200-foot Batelco tower is a useful mark, but we would be very wary of going this way. Once we are clear of the east entrance to George Town Harbour, we are bound for the Out Islands.

THE FORGOTTEN CAYS

Not yet mentioned in the guide are the Jew Fish Cays that run west from Great Exuma Island roughly on the same latitude as George Town, and form a spur out into the Great Bahama Bank rather in the same manner as the Brigantine Cays. It's possible to access the ocean pocket north of the Columbus Bank through Jew Fish Cut (or alternatively gain the Bank from the south) or to achieve this by working out to the west around the extreme end of this chain at Hawksbill Rock, but we think you'd put yourself at risk and be crazy to attempt it.

George Town is the only place between Nassau and Providenciales in the Turks and Caicos Islands where you can touch base with the world by telephone, fax, e-mail, UPS, and air, buy provisions, and seek backup facilities you may well need. We see no value whatsoever in bypassing George Town. The Jew Fish route is difficult for navigation, which is an understatement, and this, if nothing else should persuade you that George Town would not have developed into the focal point it has become, were there not good reasons for it.

once they've dropped their anchors, never move until it's time to leave.

A permanent "transient" population of this size is bound to generate its own dynamic. If you're new to George Town, listen to the Cruisers Net that opens on VHF 16 (later switching to VHF 68) at 8:10 each morning. You'll discover a whole new world of boat people with a life-style that has evolved over the years into a community with its own social events, recreational programs, a safety net of mutual assistance, and what almost amounts to a territorial stake on the beaches of Stocking Island. Almost unnoticed, the cruising boats inbound from the Caribbean, or on their way there, come and go. To a lesser extent much the same migration takes place in the summer months, and there are those who reckon the summer there is the best season.

Is there a knock-on effect? Of course there is. In one word, pollution. The contamination problem that is ruining the marine ecology of the George Town area must be addressed *now*. Up to four hundred boats discharge raw sewage into a four-square-mile area (if that), part of which (the Stocking Island basins and Kidd Cove) is not well cleaned by the changing tides. Does it make sense? No. It's madness to let it continue. Would it be permitted by any community in the United States? No. Then why do we do it here? Even if the Bahamian Government fail to enact and enforce discharge legislation, we, the cruising visitors, ought to follow our own national code. Use your holding tank in harbor. When it is full, take a day trip out into the ocean. Three miles or more out, flush your tanks. If we, you and I, fail to take preventive action, George Town will become a marine Chernobyl within our lifetime. The bottom line is that it is not our land and not our sea to trash.

GREAT EXUMA ISLAND

For all its size, there is not a great deal in Great Exuma or Little Exuma Islands to draw the interest of the cruising

YELLOW PAGES

GEORGE TOWN

BASRA in George Town VHF 16

When you reach George Town you will feel you have arrived! From wherever you have been cruising, coming in to Elizabeth Harbour will feel like coming home. The reassurance of a forest of masts is a welcoming sight as you approach, and suddenly you feel you are not alone. You have found the rendezvous of the Bahamian cruising world. So, drop your anchor for a few days or several months of lotus eating within the protected harbor. After all, you can always pull up the hook and move to a more sheltered spot if the wind switches around. And there is a whole new world to be explored when you take your dinghy ashore. Useful things like water, propane, provisions, and telephones too, quite apart from restaurants, medical help, and those much-needed spare parts. Plan on taking time to enjoy this magical cruising destination to the full.

George Town is a Port of Entry. Incoming captains may clear **Customs** at the pink two-story administration building, between 9 am and 5 pm, Monday to Friday. If you arrive on a weekend, a public holiday, or outside office hours, you will be charged overtime. If the customs officer is at the airport, call for an appointment at 345-0071. The **Immigration** office is also in the administration building, open 9 to 5:30, Monday to Friday. Call the immigration officer at the airport (345-0073) to set up an appointment at any other time. There will be a $20 fee if the officer has to come into town outside business hours.

GUIDES AND PILOTS

If you are concerned about coming into George Town, don't worry. There are people out there who can help you.

Wendell Cooper	VHF 16 "Interlude"
Clifford Dean	VHF 16 "Gemini II"
Ed Haxby	VHF 16 "Exuma Fantasea"
Wendell McGregor	VHF 16 "Little Toot"

MARINA

EXUMA DOCKING SERVICES
Tel: 242-336-2578 and 2101 • Fax: 336-2023
VHF 16 "SUGAR ONE"

This marina is the only act in town, and can be unbelievably uncomfortable if the wind is from the northeast through east to southeast. A new dock wall was being constructed while we were there; we hope that the rest of the facilities will soon catch up. It is easy to walk out into town. If you are anchored off you can bring your dinghy here when you need to refuel with gasoline from their roadside pumps, otherwise you have to use one of the dinghy docks on Lake Victoria.

Slips	50
Max LOA	100 ft.
MLW at dock	8 ft.
Dockage	60¢ per ft. per day
Power	120v and 110v available
Fuel	Fuel dock has diesel, gas pumps on street.
Propane	Available from the filling station between *Marshall's Liquor Store* and the *Towne Cafe*.
Water	10¢ per gallon. Turned off at night, holidays, and weekends.
Telephones	Batelco card phone, and US-direct phone
Showers	Very primitive; only one was working when we were there. $20 deposit for the key.
Laundry	Laundromat under *Sam's Place*. There was a problem with rust in some of the machines, and many of them were not working.

Restaurant	*Sam's Place*, upstairs overlooking the docks, is open from 7:30 am for breakfast, lunch, and dinner.
Provisions	*Exuma Markets* is right across the street.
Ice	Yes
Liquors	*Sam's Liquor Store*
Marine Supplies	There is a limited selection of stores next to the marina office.
Car Rental	*Sam Gray's Car Rental*
Perfumes	*Scentuous Perfumes* has a small selection of perfumes and toiletries on the first floor of *Sam's Place*.
Credit Cards	Visa, MasterCard, and Exxon.

EXUMA FANTASEA
Tel: 242-336-3483 • VHF 16

A small boat marina on Lake Victoria, governed by the 8-foot width of the cut and the 8-foot clearance under the bridge. They have a dive shop, boat rentals, and are agents for Johnson outboard motors.

DINGHY DOCKS

Elizabeth Harbour at the government dock.

Lake Victoria, Exuma Fantasea, Exuma Markets, Harbour View Laundromat, and *The Two Turtles Inn* all have dinghy docks on the pond, reached by passing underneath the road bridge into town.

SERVICES & SHOPPING IN GEORGE TOWN

Bank
Scotia Bank Located opposite *Exuma Markets*, open 9 am to 3 pm, Monday to Thursday, and 9 am to 5 pm on Friday.

Beauty Salons
My T Fine and *Tranee's* Hair styling and beauty treatments.

Boutiques
The Sandpiper Opposite the *Club Peace and Plenty* with a wide selection of jewelry, post cards, and resort wear, much of it made on Andros.

Art and Nature At the *Two Turtles Inn*.

Churches
St. Andrew's Anglican Church The largest of the George Town churches, painted white and blue, and a landmark on the hill above the *Club Peace and Plenty*.

St. John's Baptist Church On the edge of Lake Victoria.

St. Theresa's Catholic Church Overlooking Lake Victoria.

The Church of God Prophecy

The Seventh Day Adventist Church

Times of services are posted outside the churches.

Clinic
George Town Medical Clinic Tel: 336-2088 Staffed by a doctor, a dentist, and nurses. General clinics from 9 am to 1 pm on Monday, Wednesday, Thursday, and Friday, and a children's clinic on Tuesday. As a non-resident, the standard consultation charge is $30. Out of clinic hours, you can call Dr. Reddy at 336-2606.

Couriers
UPS Tel: 336-2148 Daily deliveries and pickups from its office in town, in *Wally's Photography* building, opposite Regatta Park.

Faxes
Exuma Markets Fax: 242-336-2645 Will accept incoming faxes for boats. Sandy reads the list out on VHF 68 at around 8:10 am each morning, during the boaters' net. Faxes can be sent from *Exuma Markets* or *Batelco*.

Fresh Bread

Mom's Bakery Arrives daily from Williamstown with her van full of wonderful homemade breads, cakes, doughnuts, and pastries; parks right outside *Exuma Docking Services* at around 8:30 am. Listen out for her special of the day on the net on VHF 68. She will greet you with a big hug when you choose your "Bread of the Day."

Towne Cafe Located behind the filling station. Not only has very good homemade bread in the mornings, but also serves an excellent breakfast and lunch.

Fruit and Vegetables

A small selection of fresh local produce is available from the *Straw Market* ladies. Delicious fresh tomatoes, as well as red and green peppers, potatoes, grapefruit, and fruit and vegetables in season.

N and D Fruits and Vegetables Next to *Exuma Markets*, has fruit and vegetables, including fresh basil on request, as well as fantastic conch fritters and a selection of cold drinks and ice cream. You can sit at their picnic table and enjoy conch salad for lunch.

Groceries

Exuma Markets Tel: 242-336-2033 • Fax: 336-2645 With their own dinghy dock under the bridge and behind the store on Lake Victoria. This is the best-stocked store in the Exumas. Fresh fruit and vegetables, dairy and cheeses, imported meats, a great selection of canned and dried goods, bottled and canned juices and sodas, batteries, film, household cleaners, and more. They are generous to boaters in holding mail; they have a copier, and allow faxes to be sent and received on their number. Sandy reads out the list of faxes for boats on the boaters' net on VHF 68 at about 8:10 am. Open 8 am to 6 pm Monday to Friday, to 7 pm on Saturdays, and 8 to 10 am on Sundays.

Olgas's Variety Store Located just around the pond going south. Seems to be open almost continuously.

Smitty's Convenient Store Tel: 336-2144 On the Queen's Highway, a little way out of town toward the airport.

Hardware

Clarke's Hardware Across from Tino's Restaurant.

Darville Lumber Tel: 336-2114
At Hoopers Bay, about three miles out of town. Open from 9 am to 5 pm, Monday to Friday. Builders' supplies, with a good range of plumbing, hardware, garden, and marine supplies.

Exuma Supplies Tel: 336-2506 Hardware & household goods.

Laundry

Exuma Cleaners Will wash and fold your laundry for you. If you deliver it to them by 8:30 am, you can have it back the same day. Open 8 am to 5 pm.

Harbor View Laundromat
Located in the pink two-story building, with its own dinghy dock, across Lake Victoria from *Exuma Markets*. Has modern machines and large dryers. $1 per load, in quarters; open every day. *Crystal Springs* (336-2830) will meet you there and take your water containers to be filled, returning them later in the day. Listen for them on the morning boaters' net.

Liquor

Sam Grays at Exuma Docking Services.
John Marshall's by the gas station.
BGS past the Batelco office, on the road to Little Exuma.

Mail

Exuma Markets They will hold mail for you. Have it addressed to: your name, c/o your boat name, Exuma Markets, George Town, Exuma, Bahamas and mark it HOLD FOR ARRIVAL. There are boxes for incoming mail addressed to boaters inside the store. The post office is very good about holding mail not specifically addressed to Exuma Markets.

Marine Supplies

Exuma Docking Services Tel: 336-2578 A limited selection at their marine store next to the office.

Top II Bottom Tel: 336-2200 Open 8 am to 5 pm, Monday to Saturday. They have marine supplies, as well as household items.

Police

Tel: 336-2666, emergencies dial 919. Located in the pink administration building.

Post Office

Located in the pink administration building. Open from 8:30 am to 5:30 pm, Monday to Friday.

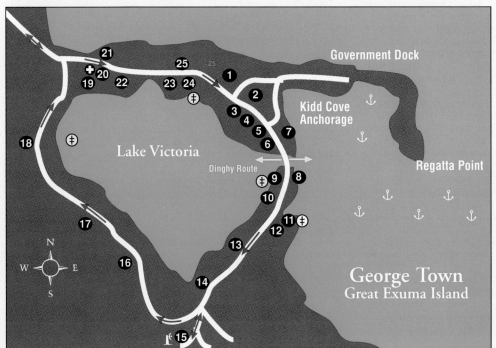

George Town Directory

1 Government Buildings (Customs, Immigration, Police, Post Office)
2 Regatta Park & Straw Market
3 School & Library
4 Two Turtles Inn
5 Towne Cafe
6 Liquor Store
7 Exuma Cleaners
8 Bank & Travel Agent
9 Exuma Markets
10 N & D Fruits and Vegetables
11 Exuma Docking Services
12 Mom's Bakery Van
13 Baptist Church
14 Tino's
15 Batelco
16 Eddie's Edgewater
17 Catholic Church
18 Harbour View Apartments and Laundromat
19 Clinic
20 Community Centre
21 Tourist Office
22 Anglican Church
23 Exuma Fantasea
24 Sandpiper
25 Club Peace and Plenty

Straw Market

T-shirts, locally woven baskets, shell jewelry, fresh vegetables & fruit, sold Monday to Saturday under the trees by Regatta Park.

Telephones

There are many telephones in town. Where there are two, one is usually a Batelco card phone, and the other a coin box where you can dial US direct, using an American or Bahamian quarter to connect you to an operator. There are three telephones outside the Batelco office, two outside the *Club Peace and Plenty*, two at *Exuma Docking Services*, two outside *Exuma Markets*, two in the Administration Building, two outside the *Two Turtles Inn*, and two at *Coconut Cove*.

Tourist Office

Tel: 336-2430   *The Ministry of Tourism* has a very helpful information center, opposite St. Andrew's Community Center. They are open from 9 am to 5:30 pm, Monday to Friday, and are well worth visiting to learn what is going on in the Exumas.

Trash

There are trash cans at *Exuma Markets*, and skips at *Exuma Docking Services*.

Travel Agent

HL Young   Tel: 336-2705   Located above the *Scotia Bank*.

Water

Coral Springs will refill drinking water containers if you take them to the *Harbour View Laundromat* dinghy dock early in the morning, and return them later in the day. Listen for their times on the boaters' net on VHF 68 at 8:10 am.

RESTAURANTS

There is something for everybody here, from a casual hot dog out of the back of the yellow bus, or a conch fritter at *N and D's*, to elegant dining at the hotels. Have fun trying them out!

Club Peace and Plenty   Tel: 336-2551   Serves breakfast, lunch, and dinner downtown, and at their *Beach Inn* and *Bonefish Lodge*. As a guest, you can ask for the free shuttle to take you for dinner at any of their restaurants. Snacks are also available at the Stocking Island *Beach Club*. Dinner reservations requested.

Coconut Cove Hotel   Tel: 336-2659   Serves elegant breakfasts, lunches, and dinners, and will make up picnic lunches on request. The chef creates some of the best dishes to be found in the Bahamas. Call ahead for dinner reservations and transport.

Eddie's Edgewater   Bahamian cuisine and local color on the edge of the pond, with a bar and restaurant. Open for breakfast, lunch, and dinner. Join in on Monday and Thursday evenings for hors d'oeuvres and Rake and Scrape live music.

Jean's Dog House   A social place to meet and enjoy hot dogs and daily specials from the back of the yellow bus, parked opposite the pink Administration Building from early morning.

Flamingo Bay   Tel: 336-2715 and VHF 16   Serves lunch and dinner, with seafood a specialty. Call ahead for a reservation.

Higgins Landing   Tel: 336-0008
On Stocking Island. Serves single-seating, fixed-menu, multi-course gourmet dinner for non-resident guests. Call before noon.

Kermits Airport Lounge   Tel: 345-0002
Open for breakfast, lunch, and dinner from 7:30 am to 8 pm. Bahamian cuisine, fast food, and takeout.

La Shante   Tel: 345-4136
Open for breakfast and lunch, and dinner by reservation.

N and D Fruits and Vegetables   Serves conch fritters, conch salad, hot dogs, and ice cream outside their store.

Ruth's Deli   Tel: 336-2596   Specializes in sandwiches, conch chowder, and guava duff. Open from 9 am to 5 pm.

Sam's Place   Tel: 336-2579
Located upstairs at *Exuma Docking Services*. Open from 7:30 am for breakfast, lunch, and dinner overlooking the marina.

Tino's   Tel: 336-2838   A small, friendly restaurant serving mainly Bahamian food on the edge of the pond. Open for breakfast, lunch, and dinner from 7 am to midnight, Monday to Saturday, and from 3 pm to midnight on Sundays.

Towne Cafe   Behind Marshall's store and the gas station. Open for breakfast & lunch from 7:30 am to 5 pm, serving their own bread, delicious sandwiches, salads, and Bahamian entrees.

The Two Turtles Inn   Tel: 336-2545
A great meeting place for casual dining, inside and outdoors with bar and satellite TV. Tuesday night is the fried fish buffet, and Friday night is their popular barbecue night.

Whale's Tail Restaurant and Bar   Tel: 336-2979   Located at Hooper's Bay. They have live music on Friday and Saturday nights, and they will bring you from town if you call ahead.

GETTING AROUND

Airport

George Town International Airport is 9 miles out of town, at Moss Town. Taxis will charge you $10 per person if you share with other people, or $21 if you go on your own. *Kermit's Airport Lounge* serves drinks and snacks at its International Bar, in a modern building opposite the main terminal.

Strachan's Aviation Service   Tel: 345-0641
Has an office at the airport, where they can be contacted for charter flights. They sell copies of the Bahamas Pilots Guide.

Airlines

Airways International   Tel: 305-887-2794
Flights to Nassau and Miami.

American Airlines for *American Eagle*   Tel: 345-0124/0125 or 800-433-7300. Daily flights to Miami.

Bahamas Air   Tel: 345-0035
Flights to Nassau, Miami, and Fort Lauderdale.

Island Express   Flights to Fort Lauderdale.

Bicycles

N & D Fruits and Vegetables   Next to Exuma Markets. They have some bicycles for $18 per day, $10 for a half day

Two Turtles Inn has bicycles and scooters.

Boat rental

Exuma Dive Centre   Tel: 336-2390
17-ft. Polar craft with bimini top for $75 per day, $375 per week.

Exuma Fantasea   Tel: 336-3483   17-ft. Boston Whaler with sun top and small dive platform, $200 per week; 18-ft. Boston Whaler with sun top and small dive platform, $300 per week.

Rev AA McKenzie   Tel: 355-5024   Located in Barreterre. Has a 17-ft. Boston Whaler, as well as a taxi service to get you there. He also offers fishing, shelling, snorkeling, and exploring.

Bus Service

A bus leaves George Town at 6 am, noon, and 5:20 pm for Williamstown and at 8 am, 2:45 pm, and 6:35 pm for Moss Town, returning from each place about 10 minutes after arrival. Fares are $3 for adults, and $2 for children, seats as available.

Car Rental

Don't forget to drive on the left! There is a one-way system around the pond. An average speed of 35 mph out of town is recommended. Valid driver's license required to rent a car. Average car rental is $60 per day.

Sam Gray   Tel: 336-210   Located at *Exuma Docking Services*.

Thompsons Rentals   Tel: 336-2442   Located above the *Scotia Bank* and has cars, scooters, and bicycles.

Mailboats

Frequent service from Nassau by the *M/V Captain Moxey*, *M/V Grand Master*, *M/V Lady Roslyn*, and the *M/V Sea Hauler*. The mail boats come into the government dock on Regatta Point.

Scooters

Exuma Dive Centre $40 per day, $240 per week.

Thompsons Rentals   Tel: 336-2442   Located above *Scotia Bank*.

Taxis

The minibus taxis all have numbers; call one on VHF 14. Several usually wait outside *Exuma Docking Services, Exuma Markets,* and *Club Peace and Plenty*. Several of the out-of-town restaurants run their own taxi service, so it is worth asking them for transport when you make a dinner reservation.

Towing

If you need assistance entering the harbor and some limited towing, contact *Wendell Cooper* on VHF 16 "Interlude."

SPORTS

Diving

Exuma Dive Centre   Tel: 336-2390
Dive trips start at $50, including tanks and weight belt. Basic and advanced scuba courses with certified instructors and dive masters. Snorkeling $25. You receive a 50 percent discount on any scuba rental equipment when you dive with them.

Exuma Fantasea   Tel: 336-3483 and VHF 16
Madeline and Ed Haxby. One-tank dive $55, two-tank dive $85, night dive $65. PADI instruction courses. Snorkeling $30 for groups of three or more. Rental equipment discount of 50 percent on a *Fantasea* rental boat or dive boat. Diving, fishing, and boating packages available with hotel accommodation. Dive shop at their small boat marina on Lake Victoria. Eco-dives by Ed Haxby, a marine biologist who has spent over 25 years in the Bahamas, provide insight into the specific habits and habitats of the various reef dwellers.

Dive Sites

Angelfish Blue Hole and *Crab Cay Crevasse* are two of the most exciting Blue Hole dives in the Exumas. *Pagoda Reef* has spectacular coral formations, while *Stingray Reef* is perfect for watching many different species of fish in less than 45 feet of water. *The Mystery Cave of Stocking Island* is part of an intricate cavern network extending beneath Stocking Island.

Deep Sea Fishing

Coopers Charter Services   Tel: 336-2711 and VHF 16 "Interlude"
Contact *Wendell Cooper* aboard the *Interlude*, or the *Peace and Plenty* on 336-2551. Half-day deep sea fishing for $300, full day for $500, fishing for grouper and snapper, half day for $250, full day for $400, including bait, fishing equipment, and your catch cleaned and filleted for you. Snorkeling from $20 per person, and sight-seeing to Crab Cay ruins and the Blue Holes for $35 per person. Shark fishing on request.

Fly Fishing

Trevor and *Marvin Bethel* and *Garth Thompson*   Tel: 336-2448
Club La Shante   Tel: 345-4136   Fly fishing, bonefishing, spin fishing, trolling.

Tennis

Courts at *The Palms* at *Three Sisters Resort* and at *Flamingo Bay*.

REGATTAS

George Town is famous for its two annual Regattas. In March each year the *George Town Cruising Regatta* attracts over 500 yachts for a week of racing and festivities. For information contact the Exuma Tourist Office (242-336-2430), Mr. Kermit Rolle (242-345-0002), Mrs. Mary Dames (242-336-2176), or Ms. Eulamae Knowles (242-336-2435).

In April the *Annual Family Island Regatta* hosts scores of locally built sloops, representing each of the major islands, for four days of fierce racing for the coveted *Best In The Bahamas* title. The carnival-like atmosphere in town includes a beauty pageant, fashion shows, volleyball, and weight lifting. Contact Mr. Stephen Hall (336-2685) or Christopher Kettel (336-2690).

The Bonefish Bonanza Tournaments are held at the *Club Peace and Plenty* in October and November.

ACCOMMODATIONS

Hotels

Club Peace and Plenty   Tel: 242-336-2551 • Fax: 336-2093
As well as a charming, historical downtown location, the *Peace and Plenty* also has its *Beach Inn*, one mile west of town, and the *Bonefish Lodge* (242-345-5555), three miles south of George Town. There is a shuttle service to and from both locations for dinner, and a regular ferry service to their private *Beach Club* on Stocking Island for swimming and snorkeling during the day. Swimming pool and bar at the hotel. Rooms from $140 per night, bonefishing packages from $914 per person.

Coconut Cove   Tel: 242-336-2659 • Fax: 336-2658
An idyllic setting, with gourmet meals that can be prepared to order if you have special dietary needs for your lunchtime picnic or evening dinner. Snorkeling, diving, bonefishing, deep-sea or bottom fishing, boat rentals, car & scooter rentals, and a shuttle service into George Town. Rooms from $120 a night.

Two Turtles Inn   Tel: 242-336-2545 • Fax: 336-2528   A small Inn with atmosphere in the heart of George Town. Rental jeeps available to explore Exuma, as well as snorkeling and scuba diving. The restaurant offers buffet-style dinners, with seafood and steaks on Tuesday and Friday. The bar is a meeting place for locals and visiting boaters alike. Rooms from $88 a night.

Hotel Higgins Landing   Tel: 242-336-2460   The only hotel on Stocking Island, between Silver Palms Beach and Turtle Lagoon. Accommodates ten guests in cottages with spacious verandas. Double rooms from $260 per person per night includes all meals.

The Palms at *Three Sisters Resort*   Tel: 242-358-4040 • Fax: 358-4043   Fourteen beach-front rooms from $105 per night, on Queen's Highway at Mount Thompson. Three miles from the airport, with its own restaurant and tennis court.

La Shante Beach Club and Resort   Tel: 242-345-4136
Rooms from $85 per night, at Forbes Hill, 12 miles east of George Town. This small hotel has its own private beach, open-air bar, and a restaurant serving three meals daily. Boat charters, deep sea fishing and bonefishing can be arranged with Trevor and Marvin Bethel, and Garth Thompson. There is a courtesy bus into town once a day.

Apartments

Ask at the Tourist Information Office for an up-to-date list of the many apartments in the area available to rent.

THINGS TO DO IN GEORGE TOWN

- Reprovision your boat with a wide selection of fresh island produce and imported stores.
- Dive the famous Stocking Island caves. Take care not to walk on the 4,000-year-old stromatolites on the island, or crush their fragile surface. They are the oldest evidence of life on Earth, the dominant reef-building structure for about 3 billion years.
- Race in one of the Regattas.
- Make new friends and share your boating experiences through the boater's net on VHF 68 in the mornings.
- Try a different restaurant for lunch or dinner each day.
- Rent a car for a day and explore Great Exuma, Little Exuma, and Barreterre. See the *Cotton House* at Williamstown and the ancient tombs at Rolletown. Have lunch at the *Fisherman's Inn* at Barreterre. Or go on tour with Christine Rolle and learn all about the herbal medicine of the islands.
- Read The Shark Lady's book, and then go and meet Gloria Patience in her own home at The Ferry, and see St. Christopher's Anglican Church nearby, the smallest church in the Bahamas.
- Go bonefishing in the flats on the south side.
- Relax and just enjoy this gorgeous island.

BARRETERRE

Although Barreterre is a separate island at the northwestern tip of Great Exuma, it is joined by two causeways. Despite this road link it has an identity of its own. There is another small community at Rolleville, with the *Hilltop Bar* and a couple of grocery stores, surrounded by pothole farms producing bananas, tomatoes, onions, and peppers. If you've driven up from George Town the term "pothole farming" may cause you to wonder if it doesn't apply to the road itself, rather than local agricultural methods. There is no marina here, but you can tie up a dinghy at the *Fisherman's Inn* and enjoy the friendly atmosphere and good food.

Clinic
Tel: 358-0053   There is a nurse at the government clinic. There is also a clinic at Steventon, just south of Rolleville if you need medical help before going down to George Town.

Fishing
Rev A. A. McKenzie Tel: 355-5024
He has a 17-ft. Boston Whaler and will take you fishing, shelling, snorkeling, to see iguanas, or just exploring.

Groceries
Mc Kenzie's Store   Groceries, liquors, and good fresh produce from local pothole farming, as well as gasoline.
Ray Ann's Variety Store   Canned goods, sodas, fresh vegetables.

Mail Boat
Comes in weekly from Nassau.

Regatta
Sailing regatta in Rolleville in August.

Restaurant
Fisherman's Inn   Tel: 255-5016   Two rooms to rent, as well as a bar and very pleasant restaurant overlooking the water. Taxi service to the airport and water and ice from Norman Lloyd.

Telephone
There are public phones by the Batelco station, and at the *Fisherman's Inn.*

LITTLE EXUMA

Little Exuma is a charming, smaller edition of its larger namesake, and well worth a visit. It is joined to Great Exuma by a narrow bridge at The Ferry, so named because for years that was the way you crossed between the two islands. Even now you can see the remains of the old haulover ferry alongside the new bridge.

The most famous inhabitant of The Ferry today is Gloria Patience, the Shark Lady. Do buy a copy of her book from Exuma Markets, and go visit this fascinating lady who has created a living museum at her house. Nearby is the smallest Anglican church in the Bahamas, St. Christopher's.

If you don't want to take your boat down to Little Exuma, one of the taxis will drive you or, if you are feeling energetic, you could make it a real adventure on a bicycle. Or include it on your day out with a rental car. But don't miss going on to Williamstown, where you can see the remains of an old Loyalist plantation, and the impressive, Greek-looking column that was built to guide the ships in as they picked up their cargoes of salt. There is a restaurant, *Kelson Point* (345-4043) at Williamstown, as well as another *Hilltop Bar*, a grocery store, and the very pretty St. Mary Magdelene Anglican church.

There is also excellent bonefishing along the flats on the south side of Little Exuma; the *Peace and Plenty* has its *Bonefish Lodge* there. Goats and slightly strange-looking sheep wander among what remains of stonewalled pastures as a reminder that this island has been farmed since the 1700s. Visit the *Cotton House* if you have time, and the ancient tombs at Rolletown on your way back to George Town.

Chapter 16
The Out Islands North of the Tropic of Cancer
Little San Salvador, Cat Island, Conception Island, Rum Cay, San Salvador Island, and The North Of Long Island

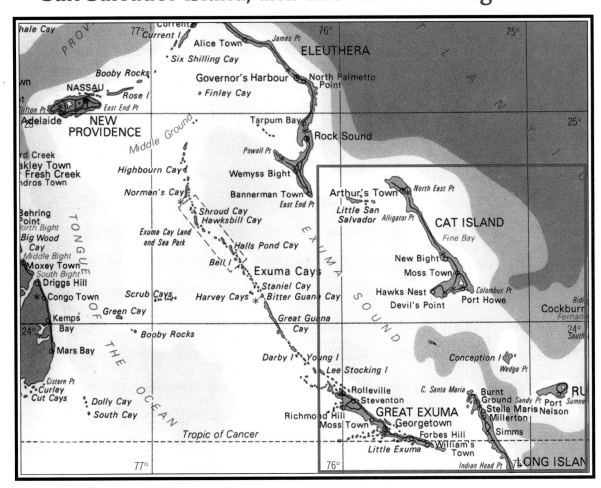

Approaches to the Out Islands from Eleuthera

YOUR waypoints on the route to Little San Salvador and Cat Island from Eleuthera (or the reverse) are shown below. From the north these two islands form a route that takes you into the center of the Out Islands lying north of the Tropic of Cancer (that magic line of latitude running 23° 30' N), and from the south of Cat Island you have decisions to make. We cover the broad options at the end of our entry on Cat Island. First, the waypoints. These are:

Davis Harbour (3 nm W))	DAVOF	24° 43' 49 N	076° 17' 50 W
South Eleuthera (3 nm W)	SELEU	24° 40' 00 N	076° 15' 05 W
Eleuthera Point (1.5 nm SW)	ELEUP	24° 35' 55 N	076° 10' 05 W
Little San Salvador (2 nm SW)	LSSAL	24° 33' 00 N	075° 59' 00 W
The Bight (7 nm W)	BIGHT	24° 15' 00 N	075° 33' 00 W
Hawk's Nest (3 nm W)	HWKN1	24° 08' 45 N	075° 35' 00 W

For planning purposes, so that you can start reckoning time and distance to wherever you want to go, if you were to take all our waypoints as the legs of a passage, it would work out something like this:

South Eleuthera to Eleuthera Point	139°M	6.01 nm
Eleuthera Point to Little San Salvador	113°M	11.0 nm
Little San Salvador to The Bight	134°M	30.0 nm
The Bight to Hawk's Nest	204°M	6. 5 nm

In reality in leaving Eleuthera for Cat Island you'll probably use the leg to Little San Salvador and will want to stop there (but read what we say about West Bay). Thereafter everything depends on what you're intent on doing. Making your way slowly down the coast of Cat Island, or taking a straight shot for Hawk's Nest? If the straight run south is your plan, then you've no need to go by way of The Bight and the two legs we show (simply to give an idea of the distance you have to cover) are invalid.

Little San Salvador Island

Little San Salvador (2 nm SW)	LSSAL	24° 33' 00 N	075° 59' 00 W

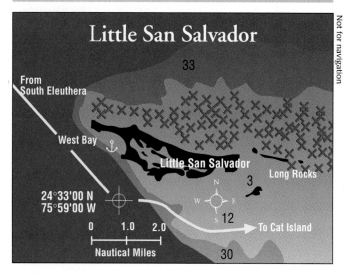

Little San Salvador, a onetime uninhabited 5-nm-long ridge of limestone, lagoon, and reefs, lies almost midway between Eleuthera and Cat Island, and for this reason alone was always reckoned to be a picnic stop if you passed that way. Ten nm southwest of Eleuthera Point and 14 nm west of Bennett's Harbour, Little San Salvador is a fair-weather destination, primarily because the whole sea area to the north and east of Little San Salvador is a maze of coral heads and reefs, and in weather in the less-than-gentle category you'd wish to keep well out in Exuma Sound. Long Rocks, a line of rocks and reef lying 4.5 nm east of Little San Salvador, is a good marker warning you to keep to the south on your passage to or from Cat Island.

The only attractive Little San Salvador anchorage is the bay on the west side, open from south through to northwest, which has a great beach, some good sand, and patches of coral that are easily avoided. The island's inside lagoon, despite a deep pond at its western end, has a shallow entrance so it remains dinghy territory, although it would make a superb hurricane hole. The island itself is nothing but tangled vegetation with matted secondary scrub and some ruins showing that at one time part of it had some kind of haircut and was inhabited. Though the island itself holds no temptation, the attraction of Little San Salvador is West Bay, and its reefs in good weather are well worth snorkeling or diving.

We write about Little San Salvador with hesitation, unsure at this time whether the island is about to be declared off limits. In any event it will no longer be a place where you can be alone. Holland America Line has acquired de-

velopment rights to Little San Salvador and in June 1997 moved a barge and temporary accommodations for a work force to the island. They plan to establish a day stop for their cruise ships there, for which permanent shoreside support facilities are to be built and manned by a resident staff. Popular belief has it that the staff will be home-based in Cat Island, and a ferry service set up to operate from Orange Creek to rotate staff and bring in supplies. Little Stirrup Cay in the Northern Berry Islands, the playground developed by the Royal Caribbean Line is, we would guess, the kind of model Holland America has in mind. As we write, excavation work has already started on the southwest point of West Bay.

Cat Island

The Bight (7 nm W)	BIGHT	24° 15' 00 N	075° 33' 00 W
Hawk's Nest (3 nm W)	HWKN1	24° 08' 45 N	075° 35' 00 W
Hawk's Nest (at the dropoff)	HWKN2	24° 08' 45 N	075° 32' 00 W

Cat Island, some 45 miles long with a width never exceeding 4 miles, fits the archetypal mold of the Bahamian Atlantic barrier island, like its kindred neighbors Eleuthera to the north and Long Island to the south. In essence its primary characteristics are identical: long and thin, a hostile east coast that is not cruising territory, and a west coast that is passable but almost completely devoid of good anchorages and with few natural harbors. On the face of it you could say that Cat Island doesn't rate high as a cruising destination, and the fact that only one marina has been established on the entire length of the island would perhaps support this judgement. But hold on. Let's look at it again.

Plantation House, New Bight.

First of all Cat Island is a stepping stone in the eastern route to the south, from the Abacos to Eleuthera, on to Cat Island, and then Conception, Rum Cay, and Long Island. It's your alternative to the Exumas, and Cat Island is also your bridge to San Salvador, the real outlier when it comes to Out Islands. But all this is geography. Is Cat Island itself worth a visit? The answer is "yes." Why? Because it has a mood and a feel of its own. There is almost no tourist development. It's an island of small settlements strung along its east coast, in which the ruins of abandoned houses often seem to outnumber those that are inhabited. Its length and the run of its limestone spines, which produce the highest land in the Bahamas, combine to divide the island into three parts, the north with Arthur's Town as its administrative center, the center, with New Bight furnishing the seat of government for the whole of the south, and the south itself, that low-lying hammer head running out to the west, which until comparatively recently was the back of beyond. As if to reinforce this division into three, Cat Island has three regularly used airfields, Arthur's Town, the Bight, and, although not used by commercial airlines but still carrying plenty of traffic, Hawk's Nest in the south.

The cruising geography of Cat Island is simple. Its western coastal waters are shallow, averaging 12 feet and barely half that close in. Further out, toward the dropoff, there's deeper water. Apart from the northern third it's largely free of reefs and coral heads. The holding generally is not good, the ground being hard sand over coral, and you should check and if necessary set your anchor by hand. Sandbores extend westward in the Orange Creek area, from Bennett's Harbour (Alligator Point), from just south of Fernandez Bay, and from the point just north of Hawk's Nest Creek. It's at that point that the dropoff comes within half a mile of the shore. The south coast is not navigable.

Like Eleuthera and Long Island, the only way to see Cat Island is by car. You need a rental car, or a new friend with wheels, and for this reason alone your landing place is critical. Gain your mobility and you'll find more than enough to keep you happy exploring for a day or more, and a friendliness that delights and surprises. However, weather is bound to dictate the length of your stay. Southwest through west to northwest and north rules Cat Island right out, except for one all-weather haven and that's Hawk's Nest. Choose your weather and you'll be fine, but maybe it's fortunate that you can, if need be, cover Cat Island in a day. If you're dreaming of weeks at anchor somewhere idyllic, perhaps with some regret you'll need to find a place other than Cat Island.

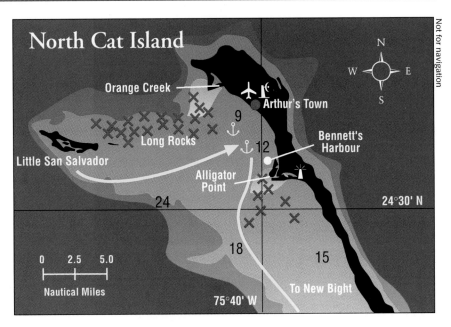

The North of Cat Island

As we've said the north of Cat Island has Arthur's Town as its center, and there you can find most of the basic support services you may require including an airport served by Bahamasair and a Batelco office, under its 200-foot tower. Your access to this area by boat is not easy, however.

ORANGE CREEK

Orange Creek (2 nm S)	ORNGS	24° 37' 00 N	075° 43' 00 W
Orange Creek (local dock)	ORNGE	24° 38' 48 N	075° 42' 45 W

Orange Creek, to the north of Arthur's Town, is the site proposed for a marina scheduled to be started in October 1997 under the hand of Nicholas Cripps, who at one time ran the Marsh Harbour Marina. The creek carries a reasonable depth of water in its final run, but an extensive sandbar that can be taken only by shoal draft craft, together with narrow width and shoaling inland, limit the utility of Orange Creek in its natural state. The plans, which call for a breakwater off the creek entrance and extensive dredging, have not met with universal approval and it may be that the concept is put on hold.

Should it proceed, it will be a courageous undertaking, one whose long-term viability is uncertain to our mind, for the sand spit lying off Orange Creek has changed its alignment and contours year by year with the weather. We wonder if, rather like the Florida East Coast inlets, Orange Creek may not suffer a continual shoaling problem, although good engineering may prevent this. Orange Creek already has an excellent general store that would be a windfall adjunct to a marina. In the final analysis we would welcome a northern haven, for one is sorely needed to complement Hawk's Nest in the south, and with both operative, Cat Island cruising would take on a new aspect.

BENNETT'S HARBOUR

Bennett's Har. (2.5 nm NW)	BNTNW	24° 34' 00 N	075° 41' 00 W
Bennett's Harbour (dock)	BNNTS	24° 33' 33 N	075° 38' 24 W

The only anchorage at this time giving direct access to northern Cat Island is Bennett's Harbour, on the north side of Alligator Point. The name is illusionary. We would not describe this cut into Bennett's Creek as a harbor. What you have there is a narrow cut, marked by a light, leading directly to a small dock used by the mailboat, the *North Cat Island Special*. Beyond this dock there's room for perhaps two boats and thereafter the creek shoals. The downside is the narrowness of this channel, barely 100 feet in width, and the tidal flow that sluices through it. If you try it, be aware of the sand and reef running out for some distance both from Alligator Point and the entry cut to Bennett's Harbour. It is not a straightforward approach. Go in at slack tide, preferably high, and secure yourself aligned with the channel with both a bow and stern anchor as well as lines taken across to each side, for there's no room to swing. Don't block the mailboat.

Bennett's Harbour may be hardly worth the effort. The restaurant by the dock is closed. There is no telephone. The settlement is half a mile up the sand road, and apart from one small "convenience" store, there's nothing there. The ultimate factor on the downside is that you are surrounded by mangroves, and that means bugs.

The Center and South of Cat Island

SMITH BAY

Smith Bay (1 nm W)	SMTHW	24° 20' 00 N	075° 30' 00 W
Smith Bay (government dock)	SMITH	24° 19' 58 N	075° 28' 32 W

Should you have to declare Cat Island as your Port of Entry, you are bound to land at only one place and that is Smith Bay. A cut opening into a creek, again marked by a light, serves a government dock built to accommodate mailboat services (in this case the *Sea Hauler*) and the exportation, though the adjacent Department of Agriculture warehouse, of Cat Island produce. At first sight Smith Bay seems a good harbor but its usable depth extends only from the entry channel to parallel the dock; the rest shoals rapidly, and you are not protected from surge or from the west.

Nonetheless it's here that Customs will clear you in, and it's only here (other than at Hawk's Nest) that you can obtain diesel and gasoline, which will be delivered by truck from the Shell service station in New Bight. To request clearance in, and to request fuel, call New Bight Service Station on VHF 16. They in turn will contact Customs at New Bight airport. However, other than securing these services, Smith Bay is no place we'd recommend and it's just too far

from New Bight. If you do elect to anchor there, the Shell station is also a car rental agency.

FERNANDEZ BAY

Fernandez Bay (1.5 nm W)	FNDEZ	24° 19' 30 N	075° 30' 00 W

To the south of Smith Bay, set in a cove-like hook of land, is the Fernandez Bay Resort. An upscale and attractive small resort, Fernandez Bay has been disappointed by its experiences with the boating community. For the boater, Fernandez Bay, given anything but the dreaded west weather, looks idyllic. Good depth, fair holding, a great beach, and of course the Fernandez Bay Resort itself, right on your doorstep. Seen from the beach, the view is somewhat different. It is a very small resort, and underline that word small. Sharing their hard-won retreat with boaters is not always appreciated by the paying guests, and when, as has happened, the honor bar system has been abused by non-residents and the one telephone is used as a boater's hotline, a sense-of-humor failure is almost inevitable.

Of course there's freedom of the seas and no one can stake out even one small bay as their private turf. What it really boils down to is the consideration to avoid intrusion in personal space, and the sensitivity to avoid swamping by numbers. Normal boating etiquette should serve, just plain good manners, but sadly it hasn't. Fernandez Bay may be a place where you can anchor but it's not a charted anchorage, nor is the resort in the business of hosting visiting boats. Perhaps they would welcome a cruising visitor if permission to anchor off were requested, and if the visitor made arrangements to use their facilities, bar, restaurant, dive shop, etc., and ran a credit

The Hermitage, Mount Alvernia.

Ministry of Tourism

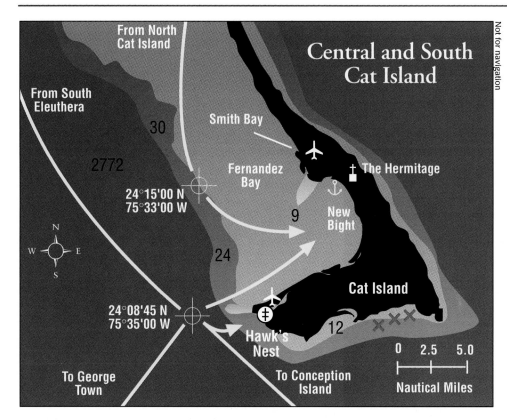

Not for navigation

Central and South
Cat Island

From North
Cat Island

From South
Eleuthera

30

2772

Smith Bay

Fernandez
Bay

24°15'00 N
75°33'00 W

9

New
Bight

✝ The Hermitage

⚓

24

Cat Island

24°08'45 N
75°35'00 W

12

X X X

Hawk's
Nest

0   2.5   5.0

To George
Town

To Conception
Island

Nautical Miles

indeed his chosen last resting place, is not in good shape. The stonework endures, but mortar crumbles. Much of the woodwork is rotten, shutters, windows, floorboards, even his bed. There's broken glass in some of the windows. Father Jerome's unique, simple but brilliant water catchment basin is overgrown with weeds, the cistern fouled, and the two outbuildings, kitchen and outhouse, are abandoned. If this deterioration continues the Bahamas will have lost not only a memorial to a great man, but also one of the few places that most people with any knowledge of the Islands has vowed to visit one day.

HAWK'S NEST RESORT AND MARINA

Like more than one Out Island resort originally built around an airstrip, Hawk's Nest has had a shady past. Now, refitted, remodelled, and with a marina in the process of complete revamping, Hawk's Nest has become Cat Island's only safe haven regardless of the weather. The plus side lies quite simply in a number of quantifiable advantages. First is that weather factor. You can class it as a hurricane hole, though no one ever would wish to test such a classification through a direct hit. The second is the availability of fuel and water, although fuel can run short. Following from this is the Hawk's Bay Resort itself with a 4,600-foot hard-surfaced airstrip if you need it, excellent shoreside accommodations if you are switching crews or have guests joining you, and its bar and restaurant. The third is the proximity of the outstanding deep-sea fishing grounds off the south coast of Cat Island, which are literally on your doorstep, and great bonefishing is right there too, also on your doorstep.

What are the disadvantages? For a start, if the wind is strong from the south through west to the north you'll not get in. The same applies to getting out. The entry point to Hawk's Nest Creek becomes a mess of wild water. Once you are safely in, you're way out in the Cat Island boondocks there. You're also going to be hot in that marina, for there's no wind in there, and if you have air conditioning, you'll need it. You'll need it too because of those bonefish flats and your securing screen of mangroves. The insects are there. In force. If this puts you off the marina, you can always anchor off the resort itself.

card. But just swinging in, dropping a hook, and running a dinghy on the beach with a sackful of garbage? That's a real social no-no. And there's another problem too. Do you use your holding tank? They swim off that beach.

NEW BIGHT AND MOUNT ALVERNIA

| The Bight (7 nm W) | BIGHT | 24° 15' 00 N | 075° 33' 00 W |
| New Bight (the dock) | NBGHT | 24° 17' 15 N | 075° 24' 54 W |

Your final option, and the only real option in central Cat Island is to anchor off the settlement of New Bight. Of course you're open there, wide open from south right through the west to north. But if you anchor off that 230-foot Batelco tower you're right in the heart of the settlement, with pretty much everything within walking range. Ignore the small concrete dock, which has rock around it, and run your dinghy right up on the beach. You can even walk from there to Mount Alvernia, the extraordinary hilltop (206 feet) hermitage of Father Jerome, the famed architect and builder of the two Clarence Town churches on Long Island. That hilltop is the highest point in the Bahamas, and that, whatever your religion and your interest in Jerome churches, should make Mount Alvernia (a.k.a. Comer Hill) a place of pilgrimage.

We cover Mount Alvernia more completely in our **Yellow Pages**, but we make one observation now in the hope that it may generate action. Father Jerome's Hermitage, and

APPROACHES TO HAWK'S NEST

Hawk's Nest (3 nm W)	HWKN1	24° 08' 45 N	075° 35' 00 W
Hawk's Nest (at the dropoff)	HWKN2	24° 08' 45 N	075° 32' 00 W
Hawk's Nest (marina entry)	HWKNM	24° 08' 46 N	075° 31' 36 W
Hawk's Nest Resort (beach)	HWKNB	24° 09' 19 N	075° 31' 25 W

Your approach to lie off Hawk's Nest Resort is simply to take its truncated radio mast and low buildings as your marker, and work your way in to anchor off the beach wherever you feel comfortable. The holding there is not good but you can get by well enough in light wind and light swell. You'll have some protection from the south and southwest, but it's not worth considering if you have anything strong from the west side through to the north and northeast.

If you want the marina, you are looking for the entry to Hawk's Nest Creek. To the north on a low point of land there are two houses. Immediately south of the two houses is one of the bonefish lagoons. Running out from the land is a line of stunted casuarinas on a raised bank that runs into a low breakwater of rocks, exposed only at low water. To starboard you have a prominent line of rock with an orange ball marker on a stake at the north end. There are two marker buoys just off the entrance that take you in slightly slantwise, heading southeast momentarily to clear a reef to starboard off the entrance, just before you turn into the creek on around 060–065°. The channel is obvious. You have 5.5 feet at MLW at the entry point and in the marina itself. The fuel dock comes up to port, and you turn to port almost immediately after into the marina basin. You are required to use your holding tank in the marina, and clean fish only on an outgoing tide.

This entry channel is not passable in westerly weather, not only because you may bottom in the troughs, but also because you turn broadside to the coastline briefly as you enter into the channel proper. If in doubt, particularly if seas are breaking at the entrance, turn away and call Hawk's Nest on VHF 16.

There is talk of removing the disused marina fuel tanks and using their site for a convenience store, enlarging the marina, improving its tidal flow, and taking action to counterattack the insect population. Having seen what has been achieved to date, we have every reason to believe that this will come about.

MOVING ON FROM CAT ISLAND

Hawk's Nest is well placed for moving on to the other Out Islands, or indeed making your way to George Town. It lies at the apex of a triangle whose base runs from George Town through Cape Santa Maria (the northern point of Long Island) to Conception Island, all of which are just about equidistant from Hawk's Nest. If you want to head directly for San Salvador from Hawk's Nest, we suggest you create a waypoint north of Conception Island to accommodate your turn to run east somewhere above the line of 24° N. Our "standard" route to San Salvador goes from Rum Cay, which we reach by way of Conception, but there's no reason why you should follow our tracks. Your distances and bearings in the triangle are:

Hawk's Nest (3 nm W) to George Town (W)	207°M	36.5 nm
Hawk's Nest (3 nm W) to Conception (NW)	133°M	30.9 nm
Hawk's Nest (3 nm W) to Cape Santa Maria	160°M	28.9 nm

Conception Island

Conception (NW anchorage)	CONNW	23° 50' 30 N	075° 07' 45 W
Conception (Wedge Point)	CONWG	23° 48' 00 N	075° 07' 00 W

Conception Island itself is barely 3 nm by 2 nm in land area, but sits in a surrounding shield of reefs that extend 4.5 nm to the north, 4 nm to the east, and just over 1 nm to the south. The island itself rises to 60 feet in part, which as you make your landfall can deceive you into thinking that this high land is your aiming point. It may be, but rather like the bull's eye being just the center of a target, you must be acutely conscious of those rings of surrounding reefs and go cautiously as you draw close to the island. The whole island, with its reefs, is a marine park, protected exactly under the same terms as the Exumas Land and Sea Park, and is uninhabited. You are welcome to visit Conception Island, may anchor and land there, and may dive its reefs. Take nothing from this pristine and beautiful site, and leave no footprints.

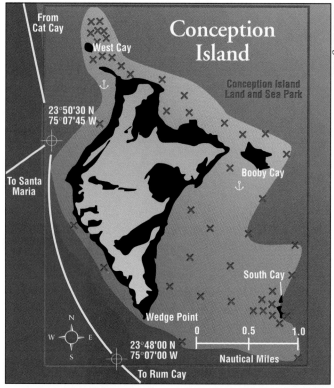

Approaches to Conception Island

George Town Harbour E to Cape Santa Maria	059°M	22.24 nm
Cape Santa Maria to Conception (NW)	063°M	13.87 nm
Cape Santa Maria to Conception (Wedge Point)	074°M	13.33 nm

THE NORTHERN ANCHORAGE

The most often-used anchorage lies on the northwest tip of the island proper, shielded in part by West Cay. You are exposed there from the northwest through west to the south, and you may find surge from easterly ocean swell, particularly if the set is from the northeast. The depth there is 30 feet running to shoal draft off the beach, and there are isolated reefs and coral heads in the area, which can be easily seen. Enter with the light in your favor. Just to the north of this anchorage there is the 4-mile run of Southampton Reef, which, for divers, is a prime destination. Snorkeling or diving on any reef or coral head will be equally rewarding. The creek halfway down the west coast of Conception Island is shoal draft and not a viable anchorage.

THE EASTERN ANCHORAGE

It is possible to work up along the east coast of the island, eyeballing around Wedge Point (you'll note the wedge-shaped rock formation that led to the name) and pick your way up toward Booby Cay. In calm weather, with nothing threatening, this presents no problems other than the need for careful navigation. We'd hesitate to select this east anchorage as our base for an extended stay unless we had confidence in stable conditions, with nothing changing in the middle of the night, simply because you can't cut and run from there.

Rum Cay

Rum Cay (Sandy Point)	RUMSP	23° 38' 45 N	074° 57' 30 W
Rum Cay (SE)	RUMSE	23° 37' 15 N	074° 47' 30 W
Rum Cay (Port Nelson)	RUMPN	23° 37' 15 N	074° 51' 00 W
Rum Cay (marina outer buoy)	RUMOB	23° 38' 10 N	074° 51' 00 W

Rum Cay, a solid 9-by-5-nm chunk of an island has a reassuringly solid appearance from the ocean. It too has surrounding reefs, but these are tucked close to its shoreline, and only one reef, extending 2 nm north from the northwest tip is a significant offshore hazard (and its last victim, a Haitian boat that foundered there two years back, is still visible as a warning). However, the inshore reefs have claimed many vessels over the years, and continue to do so. Our waypoints are chosen to set up two approaches to St. George Bay and the Port Nelson–Sumner Point area, which is your destination if you're visiting Rum Cay. We cover these approaches in detail but two factors are vital for a safe arrival or departure. The first is good weather, and the second is the sun, which must be in your favor. If it turns out

Conception Island and Rum Cay

Not for navigation

that you can add the advantage of a high tide to these two factors, you have a winning combination.

Rum Cay, with a head count of 52 Bahamians and 8–10 Americans (some of them part-time residents), is uninhabited for its greater part, has an airstrip (which may be extended soon) on the west side of Port Nelson, and no road system. The extended settlement of Port Nelson, with its dock, is the whole of Rum Cay in human terms. The one exception, ten minutes walk from Port Nelson, is a new marina, the only one on Rum Cay, at Sumner Point. We devote some time to Rum Cay, which up to this date has been largely avoided by cruising yachts because it's only anchorage was open to prevailing winds, the reefs had a bad reputation, and all in all, Rum Cay just seemed to be a detour that was not worth taking. In fact geographically Rum Cay is well placed as a waypoint on the route to and from the Caribbean, and our own feeling is that with the continuing development of the new marina, Rum Cay, suddenly, is on the map.

Approaches to and from Rum Cay

Conception (Wedge Point) to Rum Cay (Sandy Pt)	143°M	12.70 nm
Rum Cay (Sandy Point) to Conception (Wedge Point)	323°M	12.70 nm
San Salvador (Cockburn) to Rum Cay (SE)	214°M	28.60 nm
Rum Cay (SE) to San Salvador (Cockburn)	034°M	28.60 nm
Clarence Town to Rum Cay (Sandy Point)	006°M	30.75 nm
Rum Cay (Sandy Point) to Clarence Town	186°M	30.75 nm

FROM THE SOUTHWEST

The southwest point of Rum Cay, Sandy Point, can be rounded reasonably close in, between a quarter and half a mile offshore, and a course set from there to Sumner Point,

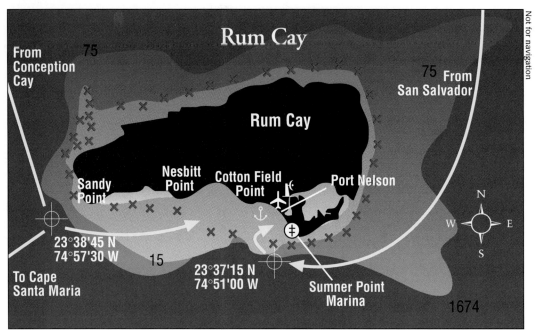

route we've outlined.

If you're bound for the Sumner Point Marina, you'll be led in by a succession of orange-red buoys, the next one bearing about 085°M from that first decision-making outer buoy. *Don't* set a compass course. From now on you are eyeballing as you go, using the buoys as markers, all of which you leave to starboard going in. There are, in effect, four legs to cover. The first around 085° as we've said, the second 135°M, and the third 112°M. By then you are so close to the marina you can see the last short leg clearly and the white PVC entry stake, which is also left to starboard.

You'll pass close to some coral. Just be conscious that a continuous reef lies to starboard the whole time, but isolated patches of reef come up on your port side as well. Pass reasonably close to the buoys, don't cut corners, and you'll be fine. Your depth will start at 20 feet, go to 10 feet, and then 8 feet. The entry channel has 8 feet at MLW. If you have any problems, or if the buoys are not there, call the marina and ask them to guide you in.

FROM THE SOUTHEAST

Coming into St. George Bay from the southeast you must avoid the reefs that run west for just over 1 nm from Sumner Point. The only safe approach is to run on an east–west line almost 1.5 nm south of Sumner Point straight to our Port Nelson waypoint. *Don't* be tempted to turn in sooner than Longitude 074° 51' 00 W, even if you see what you take to be the entry buoys leading you into the marina.

At our Port Nelson waypoint turn to run due north on Longitude 074° 51' 00 W and you'll soon pick up, to starboard and about 1 nm ahead, the first of the orange-red buoys marking the route in to the Sumner Point Marina. Don't run too close to this buoy, which you leave to starboard. Keep well to port. It marks the outer limit of the reef. Once you're at that mark, follow the instructions we've already given in the last section.

ANCHORAGE AND MARINA

The Port Nelson anchorage is the bight of St. George Bay running along the frontage of the settlement from the dock westward toward Cotton Field Point. You may

which will be the southernmost tip of land you see. You have deep water all the way until you cross Longitude 074° 51' 30 W, which brings you level with Cotton Field Point, with a prominent house on it. Ahead of you, at the most half a mile away, you'll see an orange-red buoy. This is the outer marker of the route into Sumner Point Marina, and it's also the point at which you can turn to port toward the anchorage. Adjust your heading to approach this outer buoy, as if to leave it to starboard. Your position at this time should be around 23° 38' 10 N 074° 51' 00 W, standing safely clear of the buoy in around 20 feet of water. Now you have a decision to make. Anchorage? Or marina?

Wherever you're bound, it's not a bad idea to check out your orientation at this stage. Cotton Field Point, with the prominent house, is 345°M. Summer Point bears 100°M. The marina is just north of it. You'll see the white sand from the dredging, the Texaco sign, and the oil tanks. Port Nelson hardly shows. A few houses, some palm trees, and its new (1997) 200-foot Batelco tower. The settlement dock is lost against its background.

If you want to anchor off, turn for Cotton Field Point, favoring the house to the east with the shiny tin roof bearing around 005°M. To the right of this house you'll see the ruined buildings of the Rum Cay Club. The anchorage lies between the house with the shiny roof and the dock at Port Nelson, which will become apparent as you get closer. Make your way in eyeballing as you go, and then turn to parallel the beach if you want to be closer to Port Nelson.

There's an inshore route from Sandy Point to the anchorage, but we see no point in it. There is coral on the way, Cotton Field Point is hard to identify right at the start, and you're making life unnecessarily difficult. Take the deep-water anchor virtually wherever you fancy in suitable depth anywhere along the beach. There are two pockets of slightly deeper water that will become apparent. Don't go west of Cotton Field Point. You're open from southeast through south to west in St. George Bay, and you can get thrown around if the wind comes from these quadrants in any strength. Don't be fooled by the name Port Nelson. There's no port there. In the past it was the risk of changing weather, let alone the openness of St. George Bay to prevailing winds, that put many cruising visitors off Rum Cay. This risk has now been negated by the new Sumner Point Marina.

Sumner Point Marina, small, still under construction, is a surprise and a delight. With fuel, water, and power it has all the basics, but the real delight is a clubhouse-like restaurant and bar, its friendly owners and their gourmet evening meals that win unreserved and well-deserved praise. By the end of 1997 the marina should boast eighteen slips, and the potential to accept perhaps twenty vessels, Mediterranean moored, without power and water. These services will be available in time, probably in 1998.

At the time of our last visit (April 1997) fourteen boats were accommodated in the marina basin (which is still being dredged), some alongside, some bow or stern in to a second dock, and some Mediterranean moored to a sand barge across the basin. The onset of strong southwest winds made this strange medley of options totally acceptable to a sudden influx of refugees bringing in a complete mix of craft, the largest a 107-foot motor yacht. It's worth noting that so far two hurricanes have hit this new marina. At the time of *Erin* in 1996 eleven boats sought shelter and survived. With *Lili* the marina sheltered eight boats. One of them, a delivery boat fitted out with just four 15-foot lines and one anchor, was driven ashore but refloated later, undamaged. The others went through it unharmed.

Longer-term plans for the Sumner Point Marina include a secluded megayacht dock with a private apartment ashore and a private beach, a number of residential homes with docks, some of them rentable, and stores offering fresh vegetables and provisions as well as lubricants and marine spares.

PORT NELSON

Port Nelson has spread itself along its loosely aligned grid of sand roads, and its two small stores, three bars, and two restaurants are distanced as if proximity were forbidden by local zoning. You can find most staples in Port Nelson, there's a Batelco office, and those bars and restaurants. Don't expect to find much, though. There's not much there. Rum Cay suffered when its salt pond operation became economically inviable, leading to a population drop from 5,000 to 60. It has suffered from its isolation and from hurricanes (the last, *Lili,* in 1996). What Rum Cay does have to offer is superb snorkeling, diving, and fishing. It has, in addition to its reefs, the wreck of the ill-fated HMS *Conqueror,* the Royal Navy's first propeller-driven warship, which came to an untimely end on the reef off Sumner Point. The onetime Rum Cay Club, an ambitious and well-set up diving resort to the west of Port Nelson, ran into a reversal of fortune, closed some years back, and its buildings were totally devastated by *Lili.* With this final blow the certainty of employment for every adult on the island came to an end.

HMS CONQUEROR

In 1860 HMS *Conqueror* was one of the Royal Navy's latest ships, and took pride of place in the line of battle in that day. She was a 101-gun battleship, capable of throwing a prodigious weight of metal from a broadside, still very much a three-decker with the masts and full rig of a ship of the 18th century, but with the incongruous addition of a smoke-

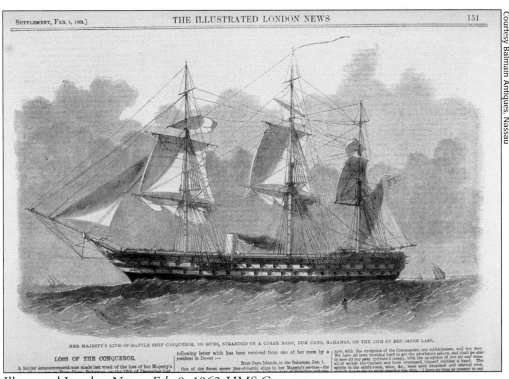

Courtesy Balmain Antiques, Nassau

Illustrated London News, *Feb. 8, 1862.* HMS Conqueror.

stack amidships and a vast, primitive, coal-burning engine driving one great screw. Still virtually on her maiden voyage, she was lost on Sumner Point Reef, Rum Cay, on December 13, 1861. Her crew of 1400 all survived.

She was 20 nm out in estimating her position and, after making her landfall, cut rounding the southeast point of Rum Cay too fine and went hard on the reef. Her captain, fearing that his crew (most of whom could not swim in those days) would drink themselves insensible when it became obvious the ship was lost, ordered all ale, wine, and spirit casks to be broken and their contents ditched. He then sent the two largest ship's boats, rigged with sail as well as oars, to Nassau and Jamaica requesting help. For the next two days the ship's company unloaded everything they could salvage, and set about making a camp on the island. The captain remained on board with one midshipman and ten seamen until the ship broke up. Then all of them, less the boat parties, were marooned on Rum Cay. They were rescued soon after the news of the disaster was known.

HMS *Conqueror* is still there. You can dive her, in some 30 feet of water.

San Salvador Island

San Salvador (Cockburn)	SNSAL	24° 02' 45 N	074° 33' 45 W

Approaches to and from San Salvador

Rum Cay (SE) to San Salvador (Cockburn)	034°M	28.60 nm
San Salvador (Cockburn) to Rum Cay (SE)	214°M	28.60 nm

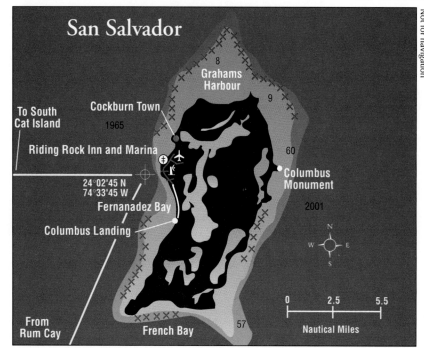

San Salvador

To South Cat Island
Cockburn Town
1965
Riding Rock Inn and Marina
24°02'45 N
74°33'45 W
Fernanadez Bay
Columbus Landing
From Rum Cay
French Bay
Grahams Harbour
8
9
60
Columbus Monument
2001
57
0   2.5   5.5
Nautical Miles

VHF

San Salvador, exceptionally, has always had an island VHF net on Channel 06. You may get no response on 16 if you use it. We suggest, while you're in San Salvador waters, using VHF 06 as your calling channel.

San Salvador, roughly 12 by 6 nm, is a strange mix of elevation, hills and bumps (140 feet at the highest) and creeks and lakes that take up most of the interior land area. It might well be just another Out Island clinging to subsistence but for two strokes of fortune. The first was the alleged First Landing of Christopher Columbus after his 1492 Atlantic voyage. Many now dispute this attribution (see the **Green Pages** under **The Columbus Controversy** on page 308) but long established official endorsement that San Salvador was indeed his first stop brought the island a star role in a set of Bahamian Quincentennial postage stamps. The second benefit dealt by fortune is simply the spin-off of fame. With the aura of being the "Columbus Island" has come four commemorative memorials (one of these to the landing of the *Santa Maria* replica in 1991), selection as the offshore transit site of the Olympic flame on its way from Greece to Mexico, two resorts, the Riding Rock Inn, and a Club Méditerranée, an airfield (being extended to take even larger jets), regular Bahamasair service, and cruise ship visits.

Comparatively tightly bound by its fringing reefs except in the north, where the coastal reefs extend out for 3 nm, San Salvador is famed in the diving world for its almost incredible dropoffs, where the bottom contour hits 600 feet within a handspan and 6,000 feet within a second handspan. Only 5 nm out from that fringing reef you'll have 24,000 feet under your keel. Its relative isolation and geographic location well off the beaten track between Florida and the Caribbean, however, has meant that San Salvador has never been a popular cruising destination. This is reinforced by the absence of natural harbors and the sole alternative of one small marina that is open to surge.

ANCHORAGES AND MARINA

The only anchorages are Grahams Harbour in the northeast, which is completely exposed to the north, an uneasy anchorage off Cockburn Town or Fernandez Bay on the west coast, and French Bay, not easy to enter and coral strewn, in the south, open from the southeast through south to the west. The

Not for navigation

Cockburn Town and the Riding Rock Marina.

only marina, part of the Riding Rock Inn complex to the north of Cockburn, has eight slips, and plans to build fourteen to eighteen new ones by the turn of the century. At present the marina can accommodate a 150-feet LOA with 6 feet in the entry channel at MLW and an inside depth of 8–9 feet. The marina right now consists of two basins, the entry channel being at the center. The north basin, finished and in operation, has all the facilities you expect to find but is subject to surge in all weather from north through west to south, and in rough weather can be wild inside. The south basin seems to be marginally less affected by surge, but this is hardly a dividend worth reckoning at this time. The south basin is unfinished, but it does provide additional space, and it's possible to anchor there, Mediterranean moor, or tie yourself right across the basin if your lines are long enough.

The marina's surge problems stem from a lack of a well-sited breakwater, and the extension of the north arm of the entry channel has done nothing to solve it. Not only does this raise the issue of the comfort factor in the marina as a serious consideration if you're thinking of going there, but also, if there's any significant swell, particularly from the west and southwest, your entry or exit through the 50-foot cut is perilous. The entry channel does have range markers and is not difficult in calm conditions.

Riding Rock Inn built its trade on diving, and in the past its marina served adequately for its three dive boats and the occasional visiting yacht. Now the attention of the sports fishing community has turned to San Salvador with the realization that San Salvador waters offer blue marlin, yellowfin tuna, and wahoo (the last record breakers) right on the doorstep, and the island is now a fishing destination. This may spur Riding Rock to put both money and energy

into solving the surge problem at the same time as their planned extension. There is a new government dock midway between the Riding Rock Marina and Cockburn Town, but although you could enter and secure here, and we doubt that anyone would turn you away, you'll find yourself with high walls, no pilings, some surge, and no shoreside facilities. This newly cut basin is where the mailboat comes in, and this alone suggests it's better not to use it. In an emergency, it's another alternative.

COCKBURN TOWN

Cockburn (pronounced "Coburn") Town is recognizable offshore by its Batelco Tower (200 feet) and large satellite dish, and the ruins of its old government dock. Cockburn is an entry port, has the range of facilities you expect to find in the main Out Islands, a Batelco office, a clinic, and food stores, but there's nothing of substance there. Even the little museum is run down and appears to have been abandoned. For the visitor arriving by air, the two largely self-contained resorts provide everything for their clientele.

It remains to say that the color of the water all around San Salvador is outstanding. The ocean dropoff runs so close to the land all around the island that it brings deep ultramarine blue water virtually within swimming distance of the beaches. You have three bands of vivid color almost wherever you look, the white sand, the aquamarine of the shallows, and then this deep, deep blue. But despite this gemlike brilliance, the cruising visitor, unless taken up with big game fishing or diving the walls, is unlikely to rate San Salvador high on their visit list.

New government dock, San Salvador.

The North of Long Island

Cape Santa Maria (2 nm N)	SANTM	23° 43' 00 N	075° 20' 30 W
Cape Santa Maria E (3 nm E)	SANTE	23° 43' 00 N	075° 17' 00 W
Calabash Bay (2 nm W)	CALAB	23° 39' 15 N	075° 22' 45 W
Stella Maris (off Dove Cay)	STELA	23° 33' 30 N	075° 21' 00 W

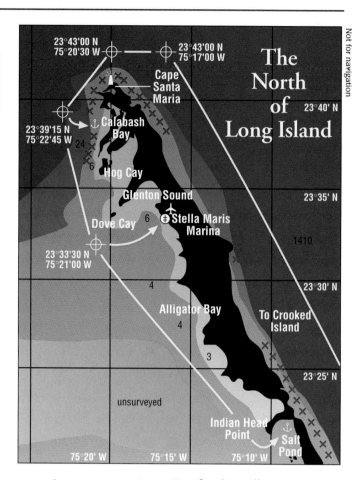

At near 80 nm north to south Long Island is aptly named, and its Slim Jim shape, rarely more than 4 nm in width, seems to accentuate that length. Rather like some stretches of I-95, Long Island seems to go on forever, more so if you're on your passage south (or north) when its eastern coastline drags on interminably. On the island itself, perhaps it's the constriction of that narrow width, but there's little there in terms of major settlement.

Geography has dictated that Long Island was not dealt a favorable hand in cruising terms. Your negotiation of Cape Santa Maria, the northern tip of Long Island, requires caution and understanding. The east coast is rocky, steep, and weather beaten, best held at arm's length well offshore. All along that coastline there are only two places, Clarence Town and Little Harbour, where you can seek shelter, and neither of them would be a cruising destination in its own right (both are covered later under **Far Horizons, The Bahamas South of the Tropic of Cancer** on pages 264 and 265). The west coast is the Bank side, with sandbores and shoals both in the north and building up south of Salt Pond, which effectively bars that side below Salt Pond as a cruising ground. In effect only the northwest quarter of Long Island is likely to feature in your cruising itinerary. Calabash Bay offers a good anchorage in the right weather, and the Stella Maris Resort and Marina, some 6 nm south of Calabash, is well worth visiting. Another 15 nm further on Salt Pond, host to the annual Long Island Regatta, will probably be as far south as you will wish to venture down the western shore. We also cover this later.

Approaches to and from Long Island

George Town Hrbr Ent. E to Cape Santa Maria	059°M	22.24 nm

CAPE SANTA MARIA

The north point of Long Island, Cape Santa Maria, is dangerous. Reefs surround the cape and run out for a mile north of it, and a bank with barely 50 feet of water extends a further two miles offshore. As the surrounding ocean has depths averaging 6,000 feet, you can understand that savage breaking seas can develop around this cape even under conditions of moderate swell. For this reason we set our Cape Santa Maria waypoint 1.5 nm north of the reefs, close to the north tip of this bank. In bad weather we'd add another mile north to this, and for a night passage, for prudence, add another mile of northing.

If you are turning south down the east coast of Long Island, it makes sense to take our Cape Santa Maria east waypoint as your turning point, for this will give you some 2 nm offing at the outset as you run down the Long Island coastline. Your actual course obviously depends on your destination. If you're coming up from the south and heading for George Town or the shelter of Calabash Bay, the natural temptation to round the cape within a mile or so is hard to resist, but don't do it. Stand well out. Our Cape Santa Maria East waypoint is a good one to choose to keep you well off the reefs and the Santa Maria shoal.

Cape Santa Maria itself is easily recognizable (it is, after all, the only land in sight) and a light stands on the top of a prominent white cliff. It is around this cape, if you're outward bound, that you'll meet ocean swells and waves for the first time. You will also experience a strong set to the northwest, particularly if you are heading for Conception Island or Rum Cay. Your XTE can build up rapidly unless you take this into account early in the passage.

The Long Island West Coast

CALABASH BAY

Calabash Bay, some 2 nm to the southwest of Cape Santa Maria, an attractive temporary haven from prevailing winds, has to be entered through its fringing reefs. The entry passage is not difficult, but requires care and attention. We suggest a Calabash Bay waypoint as a indicator, but don't make compass courses serve as rigid legs. From roughly the position we suggest, initially point toward the north end of Galliott Cay and settle to latitude sailing along 23° 39' 15 N, or thereabouts, on a heading of 090°M until you're through the reefs. But remember this is eyeballing, not a straight-line guaranteed safe course. Once through the reef you can anchor where you will. There's good depth, 9–15 feet, as you move in towards the beach.

STELLA MARIS

The Stella Maris Marina, an adjunct of the Stella Maris Resort, lies under a protective hook of shoal water just south of Dove Cay. After passing about 500 yards to the west of Dove Cay make sure you clear the shoal (known as White Sand Bank) to port, turn on to a heading of 090°M keeping the shoal on your port side. Our Stella Maris waypoint may be helpful as an indicator. About 1 nm after your turn you'll pick up the Stella Maris marks, and follow the deeper water channel into the marina. Stella Maris can take only twelve boats and much of this space may be taken up by Stella Maris regulars. Call ahead. Once you're there you are in the hands of a very competently run, slick, upscale resort organization, primarily centered on the Stella Maris Inn, which is 2.5 miles inland (they'll take you there). Unusually for such a small marina complex there is a haul-out facility, a machine shop, and some highly skilled engineering expertise on tap, in addition to all the normal facilities. See our **Yellow Pages**.

SALT POND

Salt Pond, the venue of the Long Island Regatta, is the best-protected anchorage on the west coast of Long Island, although it's open to the west. The clutch of small cays off the settlement offer shelter if there's wind from the west, but it could be crowded bunching up with the local boats. As Salt Pond lies on 23° 01' N, we cover it, and the route to it, in our section **Far Horizons, The Bahamas South of the Tropic of Cancer** on page 278.

The Long Island East Coast

Clarence Town is the only settlement of any size with anything approaching an all-weather anchorage on the east coast of Long Island. As Clarence Town lies on 23° 06' N, and is geographically more linked with passages to the Turks and Caicos than cruising to the north of Long Island, we cover it in **The Bahamas South of the Tropic of Cancer** on page 264.

YELLOW PAGES

CAT ISLAND

Like most of the Bahamian islands settled for many centuries, over the years the name has changed. Cat Island was originally called Guanahini by the Lucayan Indians, then San Salvador by the Spanish, and finally Cat Island by the British after noting the huge number of cats imported by the Spanish to rid the islands of its rat population. Or could it be named after Arthur Catt, one of Blackbeard's contemporary brigands? Plantation houses still stand as reminders of earlier prosperity on the island, when cotton, pineapple, and sisal grew here in such abundance that ships called in at the Cat Island ports from New England and Europe, and the railroad (the only one ever constructed in the Bahamas) at Old Bight was kept busy.

THE NORTH OF CAT ISLAND
From Orange Creek to Smith Bay

Orange Creek, the northernmost settlement on Cat Island, is home to the *Orange Creek Inn* (354-4110) with its opportunities for bonefishing, the *Sea Spray Hotel* (354-4116) where rooms are from $60 a night, a food store, and a laundromat. Nick Cripps, who many of us knew from Marsh Harbour, plans to build a new marina here.

Arthur's Town, the center of government for Cat Island, and briefly the boyhood home of Sidney Poitier, has an airstrip served by *Bahamasair* (354-2049 on days of flight) three times a week, a Batelco office (with a card phone outside), a clinic (354-4050), a police station (354-2046), restaurants, and grocery and liquor stores. Motor scooters can be rented from Pat Rolle, at *Cookie House Rentals.* (354-2027), who also runs the *Cookie House Restaurant,* and bakes homemade bread daily.

CENTRAL CAT ISLAND
From Smith Bay to New Bight

Way further south, at the **Smith Bay** settlement, you will find a good road to the eastern shore, as well as the main clinic (342-3026) for Cat Island with a resident doctor. There are a couple of stores, the *Little Bay Inn* (342-2004), and a government dock for the mailboats from Nassau and the Department of Agriculture to ship out island produce. To clear in here call *New Bight Service Station* on VHF 16, who will contact **Customs** and **Immigration** at New Bight airport for you and make arrangements for them to come to Smith Bay. *New Bight Service Station* will also truck fuel in for you. Look out for the massive African Cotton Tree, covered with scarlet flowers in early spring.

Fernandez Bay is home to the *Fernandez Bay Village,* (242-342-3043) a remote and low-key luxury resort with a heavenly crescent-shaped white sand beach and rooms starting at $185 a night; they are not too keen on having boats at anchor in "their" bay. The restaurant opens for breakfast, lunch, and dinner; dinner reservations are requested.

NEW BIGHT AND MOUNT ALVERNIA

If you plan to anchor in the Bight, your best bet is to position off **New Bight** where everything is within walking distance. If you have not cleared in, remember that Smith Bay is your Port of Entry, and you must go there first to have these formalities completed.

Mount Alvernia is particularly interesting because of its church. A young priest, Father Jerome, trained as an architect at the end of the last century, and then decided to become an Anglican missionary. Not too many years later, he switched to

the Roman Catholic faith, and in 1908 arrived in the Bahamas to rebuild local, but frail, wooden churches that could not withstand hurricane-force winds, reconstructing them in stone. When he was 62 years old he decided to build the Hermitage, modeled on scaled-down European monastic buildings, on the top of the highest hill in the Bahamas, Mt. Comer, a.k.a. Mount Alvernia, standing 206 feet above sea level. Here he lived out the rest of his life, until the late 1950s. There are fantastic views from the top of the hill, and it is well worth the short climb up to his chapel, the Bell Tower, and his own monastic quarters. You can see other examples of his work in the Catholic Church of St. Francis of Assissi at Old Bight, and in the two churches of different faiths at Clarence Town on Long Island.

Accommodations
Bridge Inn   Tel: 242-342-3013   Rooms from $70 per day.

Airlines
Bahamasair   Tel: 342-2017 on day of flights, which are from Nassau on Sunday, Monday, and Wednesday.
Air Sunshine   Tel: 342-3117
Flights from Ft. Lauderdale and Sarasota on Monday, Tuesday, Wednesday, and Thursday. Connecting flights to Turks and Caicos, Dominican Republic, San Juan, and USVI.

Aircraft
Tony Armbrister (342-3043) and Larry Meredith (342-3018) will fly you from Cat Island, or collect you in Nassau.

Bakery
McKinney Town Bakery in the pink house. Open from 8 am to 6 pm with fresh bread, coconut pies, Danish pastries, and on weekends, souse, chicken, and fries.

Car Rental
New Bight Service Station   Cars $80 per day.

Customs Officer
Bradley Dorsett   Tel: 342-2016

Fuel
New Bight Service Station   VHF 16   Call ahead if you need to clear in with customs, buy fuel for your boat, or rent a car. They will truck diesel for boats to Smith Bay, and have diesel and gasoline for cars. Propane tanks can be sent to Nassau.

Groceries
New Bight Food Market and Liquor Store   Open 8 am to 7 pm. Groceries, bread, fruit, vegetables, pasta, sodas, small pharmacy.
Romer's Mini Mart   Some groceries, meats, and sodas.

Liquor Store
Harry Bethel's Wholesale Liquor Store

Police
Tel: 342-3039   Office open from 8 am to 5:30 pm.

Post Office
In the same building as the police and Batelco

Restaurants and Bars
Blue Bird Restaurant and Bar   Tel: 342-3095 or 3023
A delightful, small restaurant by the water, run by three sisters, Neacker, Grace, and Jennie. Open from 7:30 am for breakfast, lunch, and dinner. Dinner reservations requested three hours ahead. Bahamian dishes and fish dinners, disco music to 2 am.
Bridge Inn Motel and Restaurant   Tel: 342-3013   Breakfast, lunch, and dinner daily, featuring fresh seafood, garden-picked vegetables, and tropical fruits. Barbecue night on Fridays.
Sailing Club Bar and Restaurant   Open from 9 am to 9 pm, serving Bahamian dishes. Dancing Friday and Saturday nights, closed Sundays.
Touch Me Not Bar

Telephone
Batelco   Tel: 342-3060   Card phone at the *Batelco* office, behind the police station.

SOUTHERN CAT ISLAND
New Bight to Hawk's Nest

In years gone by, **The Village** was the end of the railroad used to bring farm produce to the port for export. There is little to be seen of it now, since many miles of rail track were torn up and shipped to England to produce armaments during the WWII.

At **Old Bight** you will find St. Mary's Church, donated by Governor Balfour, who read the Emancipation Proclamation, standing as a monument to Emancipation. There are still ruins of former plantations to be seen east of the settlement.

HAWK'S NEST
BASRA in HAWK'S NEST VHF 16

Hawk's Nest is unique in that it joins the exclusive list of the small Bahamian resorts that offer both their own private airfield and a full marina for visiting boats.

MARINA

HAWK'S NEST RESORT AND MARINA
Tel: 242-357-7257 • VHF 16

This sheltered marina, far up the creek and cut out of man-groves, has hurricane-protection potential, although on still days it can be hot and airless. This minus factor is entirely offset by the benefit of the *Hawk's Nest Resort*, built near the site of a 17th-century settlement, only a short walk away, with its bar, good restaurant, friendly staff, and air-conditioned rooms if you want them. Water is always in short supply, so please use it sparingly, and use holding tanks. They have no pump-out facility, and the creek is slow to clean itself. Pets are welcome, so long as they are on a leash off your boat and, on their early morning walks, use the wooded area away from the marina.

Slips	8
Max LOA	80 ft.
MLW at Dock	5.5 ft.
Dockage	$1 per ft. per day includes power and water. Minimum $50.
Fuel	Diesel and gasoline
Propane	Tanks go to Nassau for refill
Showers	$5 at the Clubhouse
Laundry	$3 each for washers and dryers
Telephone	Office cell phone, $3 a minute
Provisions	Nearest store is *BJ's Payless* at Devil's Point
Restaurant	At the clubhouse
Ice	Yes
Credit Cards	Most major credit cards accepted.

SERVICES

Accommodations
Hawk's Nest Resort 10 ocean-view rooms from $135 year round.
Airfield
At *Hawk's Nest Resort*
4,600-foot hard-surfaced air strip for private and charter aircraft. The nearest public airport is at New Bight.
Boat Rental
26-foot fishing boat with tackle and a captain, $75 per hour, or $300 a day.
Diving
Wall dives, reef and wreck dives, snorkeling.
Doctor
Smith's Bay Clinic 342-3026
Restaurant and Bar
Hawk's Nest Resort Open for breakfast, lunch, and dinner, with a very good atmosphere and food. Catch of the day at dinner, or they will prepare your catch for you. Reservations requested for dinner.

SPORTS

Caving
With some 2,000 caves, blue holes, sink holes, and sea caves on Cat Island, ranging from Arawak and Lucayan caves to vast underground caverns, this is an area waiting to be explored. Bring your own equipment with you, and ask Nick Cripps at Orange Creek for more information.
Diving
Cat Island Dive Center at the *Greenwood Inn*   Tel: 342-3053
Three guided dives daily, shore diving from the beach.
Fernandez Bay Dive Shop   Tel: 342-3043
Two dives daily, specializing in small groups.
Hawk's Nest Resort   Tel: 357-7257
Dive Sites
First Basin Wall is a spectacular dropoff in 100–200 feet of water, while at *Third Basin Reef Wall,* between 110 feet and 130 feet you are surrounded by black coral, seafans, and colorful sponges. *The Tunnels* can be reached from the beach, starting very shallow and going down to a coral garden at 30 feet. There is a magnificent *Blue Hole* out on the bank with large groupers, schools of fish, and Caribbean reef sharks.
Fishing
Excellent bonefishing on the west side of Cat Island, and also in Little San Salvador. To the south there is good offshore fishing, and sailfish come to breed between Little San Salvador and Eleuthera.
Fishing Guides
All the resorts offer fishing, but there are also some guides:

Orange Creek	Lincoln & Willard Cleare	354-4052
The Cove	Jeffrey Smith	342-2029
Smith's Bay	Jeffrey Smith	342-2029
Devil's Point	Nathaniel Gilbert	342-7003
Port Howe	Charles Zonicle	342-5005 or 342-5011

THINGS TO DO IN CAT ISLAND

- Make time to climb the rough track leading out of **New Bight** up Comer Hill (Mount Alvernia) to see the Hermitage built by Father Jerome. There are steep steps as you approach, with hand-carved stations of the cross, but the 360-degree view from the top is well worth the short climb, especially at sunset.

- Attend the annual *Cat Island Regatta* in August, with sailboat races at The Bight, and lots of rake and scrape, festivities and fun.

- Go around to Port Howe and Bailey Town, the most historic area on the island. In pirate days it was ringed by fortresses against such infamous brigands as Augustino Black and Blackbeard, Black Caesar and Josephus, and American privateers. The Spanish were here in 1495, and much later the Deveaux plantation, the house of which still stands, sadly in ruins. (See our **History of the Bahamas** in the **Green Pages**). Now the *Greenwood Beach Resort* and *Cat Island Dive Centre* have rooms from $65 per night, MAP $40, located on an eight mile, pink and white sand beach.

- From **Orange Creek**, hike over to the Blue Hole, where local people still wash clothes in the fresh water. Continue on to visit Griffin Bat Cave, where slaves lived and made windows and walls at the entrance. Take a flashlight!

RUM CAY

At one time way off the beaten track, Rum Cay is now becoming an increasingly popular cruising destination. When you could only anchor off, exposed to weather, few boaters stopped here, but the new *Sumner Point Marina* has now made all the difference. Although there are only 52 residents, traces of an earlier prosperity can still be found dating from the days of salt production. It is believed that the name Rum Cay derives, of course, from a ship wrecked off the shore while carrying that precious cargo. The diving off the Rum Cay reefs, largely unexplored, places Rum Cay as one of the premier dive destinations in the Bahamas. But beware, you must be self-sufficient. There is no dive shop. For snorkelers, the inshore coral, with some superb coral heads and elkhorn, is some of the best we've seen. For sport fisherman, there are blue marlin, tuna, and record-size wahoo. *Sumner Point Marina*, where Bobby, Jeni, Jon, Bob, and Fran will give you a warm welcome, is very much in service, and still expanding.

MARINA

SUMNER POINT MARINA
Tel: 242-357-1000 and 357-1334 • VHF 16

Slips	25
Max LOA	140 ft.
MLW at Dock	7 ft.
Dockage	95¢ per foot per day
Moorings	No mooring buoys, but space for 20 boats inside the marina, Mediterranean moored. The charge is 50¢ per foot per day.
Power	$25 per day for 50A, $15 per day for 30A
Water	30¢ per gallon
Fuel	Diesel and gasoline
Laundry	Arrangements can be made
Restaurant	Yes
Repairs	Limited service available
Ice	Yes
Credit Cards	Visa, MasterCard, checks, and cash

SERVICES IN PORT NELSON

You can walk to **Port Nelson** from the marina in 10–15 minutes.
Aircraft
Manfred Roon   Cell phone: 242-357-9527
Will fly you from Rum Cay in a twin-engine five-passenger plane. Arrange through *Sumner Point Marina*.
Churches
St. Christopher's Anglican Church
St. John's Baptist Church
Both have 11 am services on Sundays.
Groceries
Last Chance Market Open 9 am to 4 pm daily. Canned and dry goods.
Restaurants and Bars
Kayes Restaurant Open daily, but call at least 2 hours ahead on VHF 16. Last meal served at 8 pm, but bar will stay open.
Ocean View Restaurant Open daily, but call 2 hours ahead on VHF 16 for dinner reservations.
Sumner Point Marina Restaurant Open daily for great food. Make reservations.
Toby's Bar Open daily, happy hour on Fridays at 7:30 pm.
Two Sister's Take Away Open from 8 am to 5 pm, but call ahead on VHF 16. Fresh bread, simple dishes.
Telephone
Batelco office at the foot of the Batelco tower (242-357-1000). Open from 9 am to noon and from 2 pm to 5 pm.

THINGS TO DO IN RUM CAY

- Dive or snorkel some of the best and least-known reefs.
- Go for a walk around the widespread settlement of Port Nelson. Its sand roads are attractive, and you are seeing the real Bahamas as every island once was.
- Explore the wreck of the Royal Navy's first steam-powered ship, *HMS Conqueror*. Take local advice to help you find it.
- Catch up on your telephone calls. Rum Cay is now the proud owner of a new 200-foot Batelco tower.
- Take your dinghy to the Salt Lake on a calm day. Improve your water-reading skills as you watch for spectacular corals heads, and go slowly when you are in the lake so as not to disturb the turtles or scare the bonefish.

SAN SALVADOR

San Salvador needs no introduction as the island that is widely believed to have been the first landfall of Columbus in the New World. With its deserted beaches and spectacular wall dives, it boasts some of the finest diving year round, with normal visibility between 100 and 200 feet, as well as museums and historic monuments to mark the 1492 arrival of the European Discoverer of the Americas. Cockburn Town (pronounced *Coburn* Town), is a Port of Entry. **Customs** (331-2131) and **Immigration** (331-2100) are here if you need to clear in, or you can call *Riding Rock Inn* on VHF 16 as you make your way into the marina.

MARINA

RIDING ROCK INN RESORT AND MARINA
Tel: 954-359-8353 or 242-331-2631 • VHF 16

Slips	24
MLW at dock	From 9 ft. to 13 ft., only 7 ft. in the entrance
Dockage	80¢ per ft. per day, or $4.80 per ft. per week
Water	$10 per day up to 40 ft., $15 per day to 50 ft., $18 per day over $51 ft.
Power	$10 per day up to 40 ft., $15 per day to 50 ft., $20 per day over 50 ft.
Fuel	Diesel and gasoline available
Showers	Yes
Laundry	Yes
Ice	$3 a bag
Restaurant	Yes
Accommodation	*Riding Rock Inn*
Bicycles	$6.50 for a half day, $10 for a full day
Rental Cars	$85 per day
Diving	*Guanahini Divers* Three dives daily, rental equipment, and dive shop.
Sport Fishing	Two boats with guides and tackle
Swimming	Freshwater pool
Tennis	Court available
Credit cards	US checks, drawn on US funds, payable to *Riding Rock Inn Resort and Marina*.

SERVICES & SHOPPING IN COCKBURN TOWN

Accommodations *Club Med Columbus Isle,* two miles north of town
Tel: 242-331-2000   From $1,050 to $1,700 per person per week; requires advance booking.
Riding Rock Inn Resort and Marina   Tel: 242-331-2631
42 single or double rooms and villas from $95 per night.

Bank
Bank of the Bahamas   Tel: 331-2237   Open from 9 am to 3 pm on Fridays.

Churches
Holy Saviour Catholic Church
Church of God Prophecy

Clinic
Tel: 331-2105   With a resident nurse, the clinic is open from 9 am to 1 pm, Monday to Friday. Outside clinic hours you can call the doctor on 331-2033.

Drug Store
J's Discount Drugs   Tel: 331-2570

General Store
Laramore's   Tel: 331-2282   Open Monday to Saturday from 9 am to 5:30 pm.

Museums
New World Museum, about 3 miles north of *Riding Rock Marina* at North Victoria Hill. A one-room museum with displays of Lucayan pottery; admission $1.

San Salvador Museum, next to the Catholic Church in Cockburn Town. This former jail was turned into a small, two-room museum a few years ago, devoted to a Columbus display and some Lucayan artifacts. Ask at *Batelco* to have it opened.

Police
Tel: 331-2010, or 331-2919 in an emergency. Office open from 9 am to 5:30 pm Monday to Friday.

Restaurants and Bars
Charlie's Sunset Lounge   Tel: 331-2012 and VHF 06   Serves breakfast, lunch, and dinner, but call ahead.
Club Med Columbus Isle   Tel: 331-2000   Just north of town, will take reservations for dinner if they have space available.
Harlem Square Club   Bar and wholesale liquor.
Riding Rock Inn Restaurant and *Driftwood Bar*   Tel: 331-2631   Open for breakfast, lunch, and dinner. Dinner from $25.25 includes a glass of wine, soup, salad, entree, and dessert.

The Three Ships Restaurant and Bar   Tel: 331-2787 and VHF 06   Breakfast, lunch, and dinner.

Telephones
Batelco   Tel: 331-2033   Open Monday to Sunday from 8 am to 5 pm. Card phone and pay phone outside, phone cards available at the office.

GETTING AROUND

Airport
North of Cockburn Town with a 4,500-foot runway that is being increased in length; not far from the *Club Med.*

Airlines
Air Sunshine   Tel: 331-2631 (in Florida: 1-800-435-8900)   Flights to Ft. Lauderdale, Tampa, and Sarasota.
Bahamasair   Tel: 331-2631   Daily flights to Nassau; Thursday and Sunday flights to Miami.
American Eagle   Tel: 331-2076   Charter service for the *Club Med,* so call ahead; flights on Saturdays and Sundays.

Bicycles
Riding Rock Inn   Tel: 331-2631
$6.50 for a half day, $10 for a full day.

Mailboat
M/V Maxine   To and from Nassau.

Rental Cars
D & W Rent a Car   Tel: 331-2184
Riding Rock Inn   Tel: 331-2631 $85 per day.

Scooters
Tel: 331-2125   At the Airport.

Taxis
Available at *Riding Rock Inn.*

DIVING

Club Med Columbus Isle   Tel: 331-2458   Three 45-foot catamarans and a decompression chamber, with kayak scuba diving.
Guanahini Divers Ltd. at the *Riding Rock Inn*   Tel: 331-2631   Three dives, full day $80; resort course $105; snorkelers $20.
Jean Michael Cousteau Snorkeling Adventure $240 equipment rental, underwater camera and video rental, and underwater photography course. Same day film processing.

Dive sites
Devil's Claw, Double Caves, Great Cut, Telephone Pole, and *Vicky's Reef* are all spectacular wall dives, while *The Hump* and *Snapshot Reef* are shallower dives, abounding with underwater life, with some great macro-photo opportunities.

THINGS TO DO IN SAN SALVADOR

- Walk the Long Bay beach that Columbus and his sailors are believed to have landed on five centuries ago.
- Dive, dive, and dive again!
- Photograph the Columbus Cross and Olympic Monument on Long Bay, only three miles out of Cockburn Town.
- Take your camera with you to the Chicago Herald Columbus Monument, on the east side of the island, near Crab Cay. This monument was placed to welcome other mariners sailing in across the Atlantic. Explore the eastern beach while you are there, with its six miles of pink sand.
- Visit the spectacular 160-foot *Dixon Hill Lighthouse,* built in 1856, which is still operated by a kerosene lamp. The lighthouse keeper will be pleased to show you up there; it is kind to leave him a few dollars to say thank you.

THE NORTH OF LONG ISLAND

Called Yuma by the Indians, and Fernandina by Columbus, this largely undeveloped island stretches for more than 60 miles, still looking very much as it did when the first European explorers reached the Bahamas. The beaches of Cape Santa Maria at the northern tip are among the prettiest anywhere in the Islands, perfect for beachcombing and exploration. It is such a very long island, that it is easier to explore it by renting a car, since so much of it is not visible from the water. *Stella Maris Resort* is a Port of Entry. **Customs** and **Immigration** at the airport can be called on 338-2012 and VHF 16.

MARINA

STELLA MARIS MARINA
Tel: 242-338-2055 • VHF 16

Slips	12
Max LOA	90 ft.
MLW at dock	4.5 ft.
Dockage	70¢ per foot per day.
Power	36¢ per kWh for 30A and 50A.
Water	Yes, but not drinking water.
Fuel	Diesel and gasoline.
Propane	Is available. Ask at the marina office.
Telephone	Only for emergencies and office use
Showers	One shower/restroom for marina guests
Restaurant	*Pot Cakes*, next door to the marina complex, open Monday to Friday from 7 pm.
Accommodations	*Stella Maris Resort*, which is about 2.5 miles from the marina.
Boat Repairs	Good repair facilities
Credit Cards	Visa, MasterCard, and Amex

SERVICES & SHOPPING

Accommodations
Stella Maris Resort Club   Tel: 242-338-2051
Rooms from $110, villas from $250, MAP $42.

Airport
Stella Maris airport has a 4,000-foot runway with regular flights via Nassau, as well as private charters through the *Stella Maris Resort*.
Island Flight Center at the Airport   Tel: 338-2006 and 2007
Can arrange charter flights with *Long Island Wings*.

Bank
Bank of Nova Scotia at the airport   Tel: 338-2000
Open from 9:30 am to 2 pm on Tuesdays and Thursdays.

Bicycles
Available free of charge for hotel guests.

Car Rental
From the *Stella Maris Resort*.

Clinic
Tel: 338-8488   The nearest clinic is at Simms and is open from 8:30 am to 4 pm on Monday to Friday. Out of hours phone or radio the *Stella Maris Resort*.

Groceries and Hardware
Stella Maris General Store on the road between the marina and the hotel.   Tel: 338-2020   Open from 8 am to 6 pm Monday to Saturday with groceries, hardware, plumbing and electrical goods, and pet food.

Liquor Store
The New Watering Hole

Mailboat
M/V Nay Dean and *M/V Windward Express* bring mail and passengers from Nassau.

Police
Tel: 337-0999 or 338-8555

Restaurants
Pot Cakes next to the marina
Stella Maris Resort Club Dining Room and Garden   Tel: 338-205
Full-menu breakfast, lunch, and dinner served, Bahamian and European cuisine. Cave parties, patio cookouts, moonlight dinner cruises, and beach barbecues.

Scooters
Three mopeds from *Stella Maris Resort*. $30 for a half day, $46 for a full-day rental.

Straw Works
About a mile south, Mrs. Birdie Knowles makes many different types of straw goods, hats, bags, place mats, etc.

Taxis
Available at the airport to take you to the *Stella Maris Resort* for $5. To and from Cape Santa Maria costs about $40.

SPORTS

Diving
Stella Maris Resort   Tel: 338-2050   Original shark dives, trips to Conception Island, slide presentations.

Dive Sites
Shark Reef 8 to 18 sharks, conditioned to the sound of a dropping anchor, will surge around a bait bucket at hyperspeed.
Barracuda Heads, rich in marine life, specially its namesake.
Flamingo Reef, and the intact wreck of the *MS Comberbach*, which sits in 90 feet of water with a shattered bus sitting in a forward hold.
Grouper Valley, a blue-water dive with especially large fish and schools of Nassau grouper.
Conception Island, where walls drop vertically from 40 feet to 6,000 feet, and nearby *Southampton Reef,* where at least 150 wrecks lie in shallow elkhorn and staghorn coral.

Regattas
The *Stella Maris Resort* hosts the *Bahamian Outer Islands International Gamefish Tournament* in March.

THINGS TO DO IN STELLA MARIS

- Take advantage of the repair facilities at Stella Maris.
- Explore the beaches of Cape Santa Maria.
- Rent a car and see the rest of Long Island.
- Enjoy some fabulous diving; do you feel brave enough to dive the *Shark Reef* and watch the sharks being fed?
- Visit Mrs. Birdie Knowles and take home some of her interesting straw goods.

CAPE SANTA MARIA

Cape Santa Maria Beach Resort and Fishing Center
Tel: 242-357-1006   Villas from $195, single or double occupancy. Call ahead for reservations if you are not staying at the resort. Deep-sea, reef, and bonefishing packages, Sunfish sailboats, bicycles. Restaurant open for breakfast, lunch, and dinner seven
days a week, from 7:30 am to 9 pm.

SIMMS

Simms is a small town outside Stella Maris, with a post office, Batelco office, and the clinic that serves Stella Maris as well.

Part V

Far Horizons

The Bahamas South of
the Tropic of Cancer

The Unexplored Bahamas

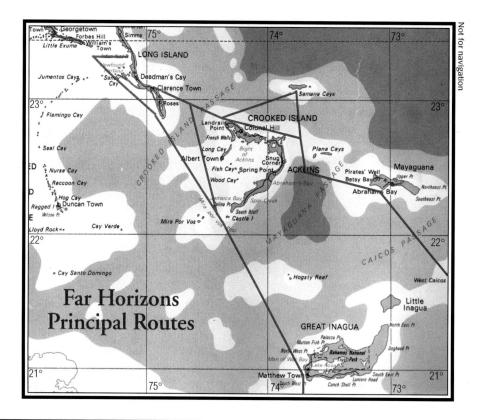

**Far Horizons
Principal Routes**

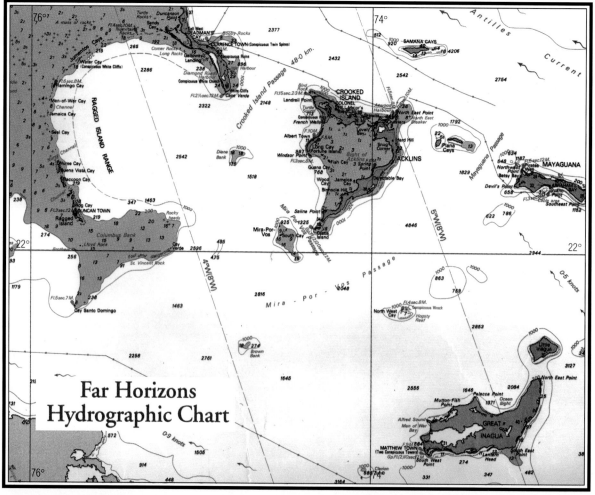

**Far Horizons
Hydrographic Chart**

Chapter 17
The Bahamas South of the Tropic of Cancer

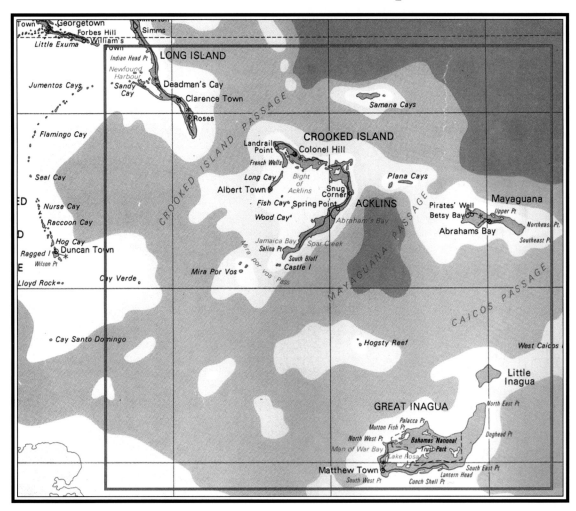

South of Latitude 23° 30' N

THE generally perceived wisdom that it's different south of George Town is true. For good reason we drew the bottom line of the Southern Cruising Grounds along the Tropic of Cancer, Latitude 23° 30' N. The Exumas and the north of Long Island, with Calabash Bay and Stella Maris, fell within the Southern Cruising Grounds, as we defined it, as did the Out Islands we've covered so far, Cat Island, both San Salvadors, Conception Island, and Rum Cay. In our experience that's about as far as most people want to roam.

So what about this line? Why is it so special? Well, we'll admit for a start that it's academic that it happens to be the Tropic of Cancer (that's as far north as the sun travels above the Equator during our summer). From this at once you realize that below the line you're in the tropics. The real tropics. Not the subtropics. The difference on the ground, as it were? Not much. Not immediately. But once you head

south of the 23° 30' N line you're in a different game. You're exposed to the Atlantic, you have legendary passages to negotiate, all of which carry a weather factor (rather like crossing the Gulf Stream), there are almost no all-weather anchorages, few settlements, and over much of the area, no sources of fuel. It goes without saying that you shouldn't venture into these waters in a craft that isn't well found and well equipped. The sailboat really comes into its own here, for it's not fuel dependent. The power boat must calculate fuel and endurance, and keep a 20 percent reserve in hand.

What it boils down to is this. This area lies across the direct path to and from the Caribbean. If you're going that way (or returning), then fine. Choose the best route suited to you, and do it. If you have no purpose other than poking around to see what it's like down there, maybe think twice about it. That is if passage making or cruising in an area like this lies outside your experience. But let's look at two basic considerations before you set out.

Fuel

Between George Town or Rum Cay and Providenciales in the Turks and Caicos Islands, your *only* sources of fuel are **Long Island** (Clarence Town), **Crooked Island** (Landrail Point), **Mayaguana** (the government dock), and **Great Inagua** (Matthew Town). The first three run out of fuel time and time again. You must check ahead if you hope to tap what they hold, for they may be waiting for resupply.

Air Links

There's another consideration above fuel that may be worth taking into account, and that's air links with the outside world. You're unlikely to schedule crew changes during your transit from George Town to Provo, but you might have to fly someone out in an emergency. Where can you do it? Bahamasair serves **Crooked Island**, **Acklins Island**, **Mayaguana**, and **Great Inagua**. Just keep it in the back of your mind.

The Bahamian Interstate Highways to the Caribbean

A quick glance at the chart will tell you that the obvious direct route, you could say the I-95 to the south, is to parallel Long Island's East Coast, leave Crooked and Acklins to starboard and Semana to port, leave the Plana Cays to port, maybe stop in Mayaguana, and go on to Providenciales. Of course if you're heading for the Windward Passage, you'd drop almost due south down the Crooked Island Passage and wouldn't want to fool around in the Turks and Caicos, and maybe you'd stop in Great Inagua. But every route has options at every waypoint.

AN ALTERNATIVE ROUTE?

For a long time now we've always had an idea that we could find a way to handle that 80 nm length of Long Island to better advantage, and play it for weather rather like going up or down the Sound side or the Bank side of the Exuma chain. Of course it's always been possible to cross the Bank on the west of Long Island, but the route has always been a series of doglegs that have doubled your distance to run.

Our rationale was simply this: *if* a better route could be found, you'd have a real option on leaving George Town that might obviate getting holed up by freak weather. But dream routes, like Columbus's short cut to China and the fabled North West Passage, rarely work out. Our West Passage route from George Town to the Caribbean still kicks off with six doglegs over the Bank, and these are daytime transits. We've got no brilliant option to offer.

We'll start with the traditional **Eastern Route**. However we'll cover the **Western Route**, which runs from George Town to Salt Pond, and on to the South Point of Long Island by way of Nuevitas Rocks, later on. Just in case someone fancies going that way.

The Eastern Route South

George Town to the Turks and Caicos Islands

These are the principal waypoints. Additional waypoints feature in the text. The waypoints on the two shortest routes to the Turks and Caicos Islands are highlighted.

George Town E–Sandbore Channel	(North Approach)	231.2 nm
George Town E–Providenciales North	(for Sellars Cut)	239.2 nm

George Town Harbour Ent. (E)	GTAE1	23° 30' 00 N	075° 40' 00 W
Cape Santa Maria (2 nm N)	SANTM	23° 43' 00 N	075° 20' 30 W
Cape Santa Maria E (3 nm E)	SANTE	23° 43' 00 N	075° 17' 00 W
Mid-Crooked Island Passage	MIDCP	23° 00' 00 N	074° 39' 30 W
Crooked Is. Bird Rk (2 nm NW)	BRDRK	22° 53' 00 N	074° 23' 00 W
Crooked Is. Landrail Pt (1 nm W)	LNDRL	22° 48' 30 N	074° 21' 15 W
Acklins Is. Atwood Har. (3 nm N)	ATWOD	22° 46' 00 N	073° 53' 00 W
Acklins Is. NE Pt (4 nm NE)	ACKNE	22° 46' 00 N	073° 43' 00 W
Semana Cay (2 nm S)	SMANA	23° 02' 00 N	073° 46' 00 W
Plana Cays W (5 nm W)	PLNAW	22° 37' 00 N	073° 43' 00 W
Plana Cays S (7 nm SW)	PLNAS	22° 30' 00 N	073° 43' 00 W
Mayaguana SW (S of Low Pt)	MAYAW	22° 18' 30 N	073° 04' 00 W

TURKS AND CAICOS ISLANDS

Providenciales N (7 nm NW)	PROVN	21° 55' 00 N	072° 15' 00 W
Sellars Cut (at the reef)	SLLRS	21° 48' 50 N	072° 12' 50 W
Sandbore Approach (2 nm NW)	SBORA	21° 46' 00 N	072° 28' 00 W
Sandbore Pass W (at the reef)	SBORW	21° 44' 55 N	072° 27' 30 W
Sapodilla Bay (1 nm SW)	SPDLA	21° 44' 00 N	072° 18' 00 W
Caicos Shipyard (1.75 nm S)	CAIYD	21° 43' 00 N	072° 10' 05 W

Headings °M and Straightline Distances

The direct courses we quote are not dreamworld. We know, if you're a sailor, you can't sail them, just like that. Even a power boat has to take account of the sea state and, yes, the wind too. But we show these courses as it's the only way in which you can indicate both direction and a ballpark distance to run. All your passage plans are based on these two primary factors. You vector in the weather, and all the rest, the business of choosing the route you actually take, together with the seamanship, is up to you.

George Town Harbour Ent. (E)	Cape Santa Maria	061°	22.0 nm
Cape Santa Maria	Santa Maria East	097°	3.2 nm
Santa Maria East	Bird Rock	142°	70.0 nm
Santa Maria East	Clarence Town	160°	39.0 nm
Clarence Town	Bird Rock	123°	35.0 nm
Santa Maria East	Mid-Crooked Pssg	149°	55.0 nm
Clarence Town	Mid-Crooked Pssg	124°	18.0 nm
Mid-Crooked Passage	Mira Por Vos Pssg	174°	55.0 nm
Bird Rock	Acklins NE	108°	38.0 nm
Bird Rock	Atwood	112°	29.0 nm
Bird Rock	Landrail Point	168°	4.8 nm

Landrail Point	French Wells	172°	7.8 nm
Bird Rock	Semana Cay	083°	35.0 nm
Atwood	Semana Cay	030°	17.0 nm
Semana Cay	Acklins NE	178°	16.0 nm
Acklins NE	Plana Cay W	188°	9.0 nm
Plana Cay W	Plana Cays S	188°	7.0 nm
Plana Cay S	Providenciales N	122°	90.0 nm
Plana Cay S	Sandbore N	130°	82.0 nm
Plana Cays S	Mayaguana W	116°	38.0 nm
Mayaguana W	Providenciales N	128°	52.0 nm
Mayaguana W	Sandbore N	143°	47.0 nm
Providenciales N	Sellars Cut	163°	4.6 nm
Sandbore Approach	Sandbore W	104°	0.9 nm
Sandbore W	Sandbore Mid-P	126°	3.1 nm
Sandbore Mid-Pass	Sandbore E	112°	2.2 nm
Sandbore E	Sapodilla Bay	099°	3.5 nm
Sandbore E	Sapodilla S Dock	109°	4.5 nm
Sapodilla South Dock	Caicos Shipyard	100°	6.4 nm

The East Coast of Long Island

CAPE SANTA MARIA

Cape Santa Maria (2 nm N)	SANTM	23° 43' 00 N	075° 20' 30 W
Cape Santa Maria E (3 nm E)	SANTE	23° 43' 00 N	075° 17' 00 W

As a warning, we repeat what we said in the last chapter about Cape Santa Maria: the north point of Long Island, Cape Santa Maria, is hazardous. Reefs surround it and run out for a mile north of it, and a bank with barely 50 feet of water extends a further two miles offshore. With surrounding ocean depths averaging 6,000 feet, you can understand that savage breaking seas can develop around this cape even under conditions of moderate swell. For this reason we set our Cape Santa Maria waypoint 1.5 nm north of the reefs, close to the north tip of this bank. We'd add another mile north each in bad weather and for a night passage.

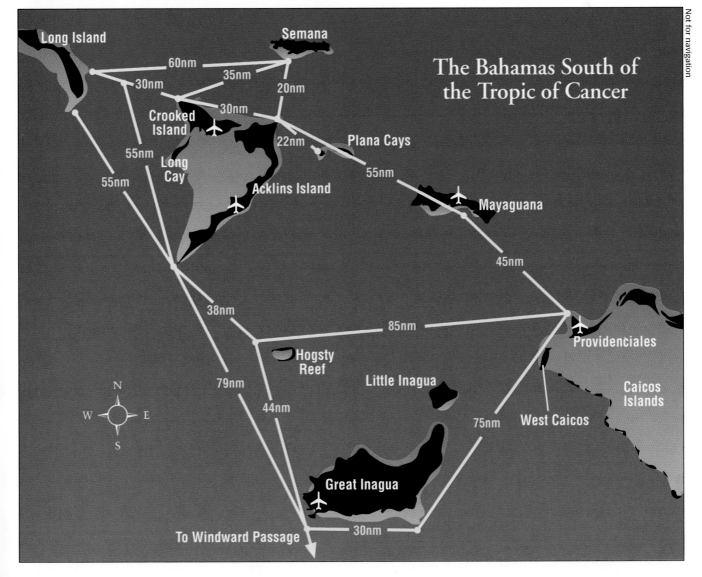

Not for navigation

The Bahamas South of the Tropic of Cancer

The east coast of Long Island.

Heading south down the east coast of Long Island, it makes sense to take our Cape Santa Maria east waypoint as your turning point, for this will give you some 2 nm offing at the outset as you run down the Long Island coastline. Your actual course obviously depends on your destination. If you're coming up from the south and heading for George Town or the shelter of Calabash Bay, the natural temptation to round the cape within a mile or so is hard to resist, but *don't* do it. Stand well out. Our Cape Santa Maria East waypoint is a good one to choose to keep you well off the reefs and the Santa Maria shoal. Cape Santa Maria itself is easily recognizable (it is, after all, the only land in sight) and a light stands on the top of a prominent white cliff. It is around this cape, if you're outward bound, that you'll meet ocean swells and waves for the first time. You will also experience a strong set to the northwest.

CLARENCE TOWN

Long Is. Clarence Town (2 nm N) CLART   23° 08' 00 N   074° 57' 00 W

Clarence Town was once reputed to be one of the best-kept settlements in the Bahamas, famous for its two spectacular Father Jerome (of Cat Island Hermitage fame) churches. The churches are still there, but sadly Clarence Town has lost its shine. Nonetheless it's worth a visit for the churches, for fuel if you want to top up (note the warning on page 262), and because it's really the last place where you're still within reach (by road and air) of backup resources in Salt Pond, Stella Maris, and George Town.

As you approach Clarence Town from a mile out it's almost impossible to pick up your bearings, and your orientation comes as you pass the outlying Booby Rock. The anchorage, an ill-defined area off the government dock, has an entrance to the north nearly a mile wide, which narrows between reefs to a quarter of this on the line between

Strachan Cay and Harbour Point. Initially head to leave Booby Rock well to port, and pick up your bearings when you draw level with Booby Rock (bearing 085°M). At this point you should be at about 23° 06' 50 N 074° 57' 30 W. You'll pick up two landmarks:

- A red-roofed prominent house bearing 195°M
- The white twin-spired (round towers) Catholic church bearing 220°M

Steer for the apparent middle of the open channel ahead of you on a course of about 180°M. Your approach line is simply to head for the center of this wide opening, spotting the breaking surf on your starboard bow, and tending to favor that side if you cannot see the reef to port, which runs out to the west from the north of Strachan Cay. Treat Harbour Point and Lark Point (the northwest tip of Strachan Cay) as the entry arms to a harbor and stay between them, mindful of their reefs. Just read the water and don't head for Clarence Town until you've cleared Harbour Point and have the government dock in plain view. That's all there is to it. To make your way out of Clarence Town steer for the house

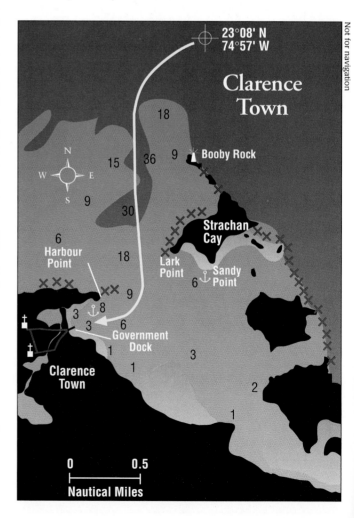

St. Peter's Church, Clarence Town.

with the palms (the only house) on Strachan Cay at the start, and then turn to port when you're in mid-channel. Steer due north watching out for those reefs. You should have no problems. It's an easy exit.

The anchorage owes its protection to this less-than-effective shielding in the north and the line of reef and cays to the east (Booby Rock in the north, with Strachan Cay and others unnamed on the charts), but there's scant shelter from wind other than from the west, and no real protection from wind and surge from northwest through to east. Even southeast weather will bring surge into the anchorage. It is perhaps a timely reminder, if you call in here, that you are now on an Atlantic coast and even distant Atlantic storms may bring heavy ground swell a day or two later into Clarence Town Harbour, with rollers carrying right through the anchorage on to the beach.

Nonetheless Clarence Town is not unvisited, and has an alternative anchorage across the way under the south tip of Strachan Cay, known as Sandy Point, which some prefer. Your depth in the anchorage will be around 8–15 feet, depending on how far you work your way in, and the ground

is mostly grass with a few sand hollows, which are the best places to go for. An anchor digs in well there with encouragement, and by that we mean diving. In anything approaching stronger winds (15 knots or more) keep a close check on your position. Many boats have found that they are dragging. When you select your spot, keep clear of the direct approach to the government dock, which is used by the mailboat.

Ashore you'll find fuel on request at the government dock, the Harbour Restaurant, Batelco, basic foodstuffs, and the two Father Jerome churches with their twin spires. Visit the churches. Their architecture is remarkable, and both carry their size (unusual in the Out Islands) dominating the settlement as if they were medieval cathedrals sited in a rural village. The Roman Catholic church, with its round towers, white paint, and blue windows, looks as if it had been lifted from the Greek Cycladic Islands. Inside it's plain, quite unadorned, and simple. In contrast the Anglican church is more ornate, and certainly shows the kind of decoration more normally associated with Catholicism. It's a strange reversal, and both churches, for those who have an interest in such matters, are fascinating.

LITTLE HARBOUR

Long Is. Little Harbour (1 nm NE) LLHBR	22° 59' 00 N	074° 50' 00 W

Little Harbour, some 11 nm south of Clarence Town, has been reported as an all-weather anchorage. Once isolated, Little Harbour has now been connected to the main Long Island highway by a rough dirt road, but it remains that the closest settlement, on the intersection of the dirt track with the main road, is twenty minutes away by car or truck, although there are two or three isolated houses on the way.

Government dock, Clarence Town.

Not only is Little Harbour disappointing in its remoteness but, attractive in terms of shelter as it might seem looking at the chart, it fails on most counts as a refuge.

There are three entrances to Little Harbour, of which the southernmost is usable if you favor the north side, but all these entrances break heavily in weather from northeast through to southeast and we wouldn't attempt an entrance (or an exit) in anything other than calm, high-visibility, good-light conditions. Inside Little Harbour shoals totally to the south, and about as far as you get tucked into the southern end is the raw blaze where the newly dozed track ends, but we're talking of 2–3 feet at MLW. Another alternative is to turn north and seek a deeper spot behind the island, but you are in the surge channel here. Bear in mind that even if you entered Little Harbour under ideal conditions, a change of weather could keep you there for anything up to two weeks.

Little Harbour appears to be home to two local fishing boats, both flat bottomed, whose traps are piled on the shore, and, when we were last there, a Performance 40 open-cock-pit, cigarette-look-alike with four 250-hp Yamaha outboards on the back, the whole outfit painted something approximate to a non-reflecting Navy grey camouflage. The owners of this remarkable boat take a close interest in visitors. We give Little Harbour as a listing because it is there. Only a dire emergency would lead us to use it.

Branching Off for the Windward Passage

Mid-Crooked Island Passage	MIDCP	23° 00' 00 N	074° 39' 30 W

After leaving Clarence Town and hitting the 23° N line of latitude you're just about lined up to turn into the Crooked Island Passage and head south if you want to aim for the Windward Passage. Alternatively you may want to run down to French Wells and explore the Crooked–Acklins–Long Cay archipelago going counterclockwise around it.

The Crooked–Acklins–Long Cay Triangle

Seen from space, the triangular atoll formed by Crooked Island, Acklins Island, and Long Cay is spectacular. All around is the deep blue of deep ocean. A thin line of break-ing white seas define the fringing barrier reefs, which are almost continuous around the archipelago. Then there's a narrow band of brilliant light blue shallow water, and the green of the land. Inside this frame, almost like a jewel in a setting, is the turquoise water of the Bight of Acklins form-ing a virtual lagoon.

The existence of these linked islands, roughly 50 nm north to south by 30 nm east to west, effectively forms a kind of rotary across your direct route to the Caribbean. At this point you meet the first of the West Indian Passages, all of which slant in from the Atlantic, ancient deep-water chan-nels, which can be a welcome change from shallow waters.

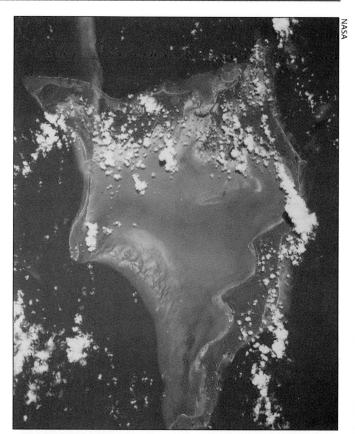

The Crooked–Acklins–Long Cay archipelago from Skylab.

But anticipate other changes. Ocean swells, together with high seas in unsettled weather, can produce surprising and less-than-welcome bumpy rides. Or it could be pussy cat.

Counting the passages as you go south, the Crooked Island Passage is the first. Then it's the Mayaguana Pas-sage. And then the Caicos Passage. Further to your south is the closest true entry point to the Caribbean, the Wind-ward Passage. Heading for Providenciales, one way or another, you are going to cut across the first three pas-sages. As for the land, watch out for the barrier reefs and stand well offshore everywhere unless you are definitely closing for a specific destination. Our advice is to stand 5 nm off any coastline, and add more miles to that if you are passing the southeast point of Great Inagua Island. Per-haps the last fact to add to your intelligence file, if you're a Campari drinker, is that these islands are the world source of cascarilla bark, the ingredient that gives Campari its bitter, astringent taste.

Nature, in a sense, has ill-served the passage maker. In a perfect world, the Crooked–Acklins–Long Cay archipelago should offer havens if you want to rest or wait out the onset of unfavorable weather. In reality your choices there are very limited and, as is true with most of the Bahamas, all-weather anchorages do not exist. The one exception lies with true shoal draft craft, who can play the Bight of Acklins to advantage.

Crooked Island

BIRD ROCK

Crooked Is. Bird Rk (2 nm NW)	BRDRK	22° 53' 00 N	074° 23' 00 W
Bird Rock (exact)	BRDRK	22° 50' 42 N	074° 21' 34 W

Bird Rock, the northern of the Crooked Island Passage light-houses, is dated 1876. It's not only a fine landmark but a triumph of construction built from Crooked Island stone quarried from nearby Gun Bluff. At one time its mechanism and lenses were a match to Hope Town lighthouse in the Abacos (which is still operating in its original state), but when the Bird Rock Lighthouse was electrified, its 19th-century machinery and museum-quality Fresnel lenses were trashed. Today the lighthouse, having survived over 100 years up to its modernization, is deteriorating rapidly and, despite its strategic position, is no longer working. Nonetheless, it's worth visiting.

PORTLAND HARBOUR AND PITTSTOWN POINT

Portland Harbour Entry	PTLNH	22° 50' 24 N	074° 21' 15 W
Portland anchorage	PTLNA	22° 50' 12 N	074° 20' 47 W
Pittstown Point (exact)	PITDN	22° 50' 00 N	074° 20' 50 W

Portland Harbour at the northwest tip of Crooked Island is, in truth, the perpetuation of mistaken identification. There's no harbor, just a ring of circling reef where, if the wind's from the south, you can find a pleasant anchorage off the beach just to the east of Pittstown Point. You'd be uneasy there at any other time, and crazy to think of it with either west or north wind. Your entry point lies to the south of Bird Rock. Working your way in, you have 20 feet of water, keeping the obvious coral to starboard, and then, when you're "inside" Bird Rock, turn to starboard toward the center of the first white sand beach. It's eyeball stuff, the coral easily seen and easily avoided, with the main reef lying on your starboard side. Anchor over sand as close in as you desire, comfortably off the beach about midway between Pittstown Point and the next mini-point to the east (22° 49' 59 N 074° 20' 32 W). There'll always be some motion in there, but with south winds and no significant ocean swell, it's fine.

Pittstown Point is the location of a small, relaxed, low-rise resort known as Pittstown Point Landings, just 2 miles north of Landrail Point, up a sand road that has the feel of Florida's A1A years back in time. The twelve-room hotel is centered on its 2,000-foot paved airstrip (to be extended to 4,000 feet), and guests arrive piloting their own aircraft or fly Bahamasair to Colonel Hill, the Crooked Island airport. Pittstown Point Landings (extraordinarily the site of the first post office in the Bahamas) has had a checkered past. Now, after more changes in ownership and management than you might believe, it has hit its stride. It's a delight, certainly on

our short list of the remoter places, which, for setting and ambiance, win instant stars as an island retreat. Not surprisingly over the years a small colony of some sixteen or seventeen houses, hardly noticeable at first sight, have tucked themselves under the wings of the small resort.

We had hoped that Crooked Island, with its strategic position, might one day offer better facilities for cruising boats and the Pittstown Point area would be our choice. Despite talk at one time that Salt Pond might be opened to the ocean and dredged to accommodate a marina, it seems that nothing is in the cards. The Salt Pond idea, to our mind, would prove an expensive mistake, and the best answer might be two sets of moorings, one in Portland Harbour and the other between Pittstown and Landrail Points, with a dingy dock at the hotel. But the accent lies on attracting the airplane rather than the boat, and we doubt that it will come

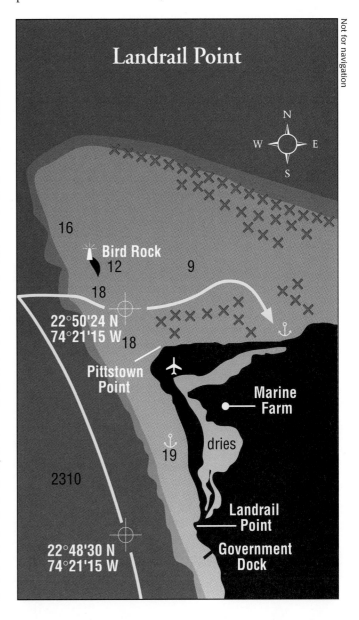

about. If you choose to visit you must find the weather to fit, and trust your own hook in one of these two anchorages.

LANDRAIL POINT

Crooked Is. Lndrail Pt (1 nm W)	LNDRL	22° 48' 30 N	074° 21' 15 W
Landrail anchorage	LNDGA	22° 49' 10 N	074° 20' 48 W
Landrail small boat harbor	LNDSB	22° 48' 18 N	074° 20' 29 W
Landrail Government Dock	LNDGD	22° 48' 07 N	074° 20' 22 W

Landrail Point, about 4 nm south of Bird Rock, appears the most unlikely place to construct a government dock to serve the mailboat (*Lady Mathilda*), but it's there with a small settlement behind it. The geography of this part of the coast is that the dropoff of the Crooked Island Passage runs close and parallel to the shore at Landrail, while further south the margin of offshore shallows gradually increases until you're held well off the coast by a shallow shelf. There's no protecting reef off Landrail, and both the mailboat (and you) can make your way in from deep water to virtually within a stone's throw of the shoreline.

The government dock is no real option for you (because of surge) except for a short visit to take on fuel. Your landmark for the dock, which doesn't stand out clearly from the shore and is not looking as good as it was before Hurricane *Lili*, are the fuel tanks (three large and one small) just to the north of the dock, and a yellow building with blue shutters just by the dock. If you want fuel, call *Early Bird* on VHF 16. If the quantity is small, you can fill your cans at the nearby gas station. If you need more than can be handled by can, they'll send the fuel truck (carrying both diesel and gasoline) to the dock to meet you.

Old cannon at Marine Farm, Crooked Island.

The best place to anchor lies to the north of Landrail Point, halfway to Pittsdown Point, off the white sand beach just opposite the only mid-beach stand of casuarinas. However, the absence of a reef doesn't mean there's no coral there, and you must read your way in. You'll anchor in 20–30 feet of water over good sand, and only one anchor should be necessary. Here you'll be OK in east to northeast winds, and wind from the south at no significant strength. Anything from the north is a real put-off. Don't be tempted to move closer to Landrail Point. The bottom there looks OK, sand in part, but it's thin sand over rock. A grapnel might eventually hold, but you're likely to drag.

There's a small-craft basin cut into the rock at the north end of the settlement, which you can enter in your dinghy, but you may prefer to run your dinghy right up on the beach. Landrail Point is a small, compact settlement spread around a short triangle of roads, one marked *Pittstown* and the other *Inland and Airport*. There's a clinic, a one-room school, the Seventh Day Adventist church, the gas station (smart and up to date) that we've already mentioned, and Gibson's Lunch Room (long-standing and well reputed), run by Marina Gibson, the BASRA representative. Thunderbird's can take you fishing and scuba diving, and there's a Batelco card phone by the government dock. The people of Landrail, mostly Seventh Day Adventist, are friendly and approachable. Just remember that their Saturday figures as your Sunday, and that alcohol is not part of their life-style.

FRENCH WELLS

French Wells (2 nm W)	FRWW1	22° 41' 00 N	074° 19' 00 W
French Wells (1 nm W)	FRWW2	22° 41' 05 N	074° 18' 00 W
French Wells anchorage	FRWAN	22° 41' 04 N	074° 16' 29 W

Although not directly on the Eastern Route, it may be that weather or the desire simply to take a break from passage making prompts you to divert briefly to French Wells at the south tip of Crooked Island. French Wells, despite its alluring name, has long ago lost its population. Nonetheless, it offers what is arguably the best all-weather anchorage in the Crooked–Acklins–Long Cay archipelago. Follow the deep water of the Crooked Island Passage dropoff and then, when you're off French Wells, turn in between Crooked Island and Rat and Goat Cays (to the immediate north of Long Cay) and head almost due east on 090°–095°M. To port and starboard you have sandbars reaching out toward the dropoff, and you have a shoal area to cross with perhaps just 12 feet at MLW. Then, passing the south point of Crooked Island you'll find yourself in a deeper channel bordered by shoal on both sides.

Work your way in and anchor in 15–20 feet over sand. The further in you go, within reason, the more protected you'll be and the better the sand underneath you. You're

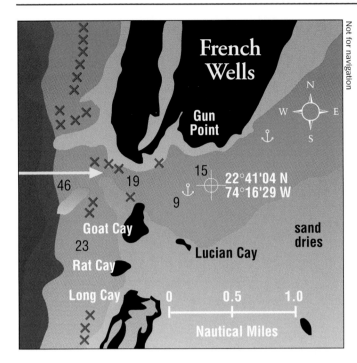

shielded by sand virtually on all sides, and only really vicious west weather could rock you. We're told it "never gets really bad in there." If you're lucky, flamingos will join you at dusk and at the turn of the tide, the bottom fishing is good. On the west side of Crooked Island, running north from its southern tip for just over 3 nm, is one of the most fabulous continuous runs of pure white sand beach facing pure white-sand-bottomed turquoise water we've seen in the Islands. Talk about perfect swimming beaches? That's it.

The Rest of Crooked Island

Colonel Hill, a strung-out settlement resting securely notched into its north coast spine of limestone, is (we were told by a proud schoolteacher) the capital of Crooked Island. The greater part of the island's population of 300 live spread along on the Colonel Hill–Cabbage Hill ridgeline. To the east, in the low ground, is the airport, and in the west, high on that spine, a Batelco tower with three great satellite-dish antennae. For Crooked Island, together with road improvement, centrally generated electricity is on its way, and by the time this guide is published, Crooked Island will have relegated to standby status every generator on the island.

LONG CAY

Logic would normally dictate that we cover Long Cay, running south from French Wells and the south tip of Crooked Island, at this point in our text. However as it's not part of the Eastern Route from George Town to Providenciales, we leave it until later. It remains that if you elect to take the Crooked Island Passage and are making directly for the

Windward Passage, you will continue on south, paralleling Long Cay. To see our comments on going this way, please turn to the **Western Route** on page 278. We now continue with the Eastern Route.

Acklins Island

The North of Acklins Island

Acklins Island, with a population of around 500 spread over 150 square miles, has a look of depopulation, if not almost total dereliction at first sight. The center of Acklins in terms of government, airport, clinic, communications, and police is Spring Point, sited on the Bight of Acklins, almost exactly halfway down the west coast. This at once places it out of reach of any cruising boat. Roads on the island are poor but are being improved now as centrally generated electricity is coming to the island; nonetheless getting around is not easy, and is difficult to say the least if you have no wheels. The east (ocean) coast has a virtually continuous inshore reef and there is no place into which you could, with safety, bring a boat.

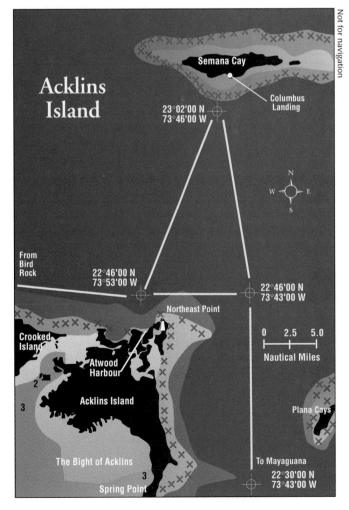

Semana Cay, most probably the true Columbus landfall.

to steer almost due south leaving Umbrella Rock and the white light on the headland to port. Look out for the coral inside the harbor area, and once inside the curve of the anchorage, turn to port and find your chosen place to drop your hook. There are two houses there, on the foreshore. There's a small settlement, Chesters, about two miles to the west, with little or nothing but one small store, a telephone, and sandflies. A second small settlement, Pinefield Point on the east coast some 4 miles south of Northeast Point, is primarily a fishing village. If you wish to find a local guide try Newton Williamson answering on VHF 16 as "Holiday Inn" or use Batelco and call 344-3210.

The reef known as the Northeast Breaker lies 4 nm east of Acklins Northeast Point. It's marked on the chart, and it shows as breaking seas. Stay well clear.

It remains that if you're taking the Eastern Route between George Town and Providenciales, the only place in the North of Acklins that has any utility to you is Atwood Harbour in the northeast. As the south of Acklins Island is only relevant to those taking the Western Route, we leave this to be covered under that heading.

ATWOOD HARBOUR AND NORTHEAST POINT

Atwood Harbour (3 nm N)	ATWOD	22° 46' 00 N	073° 53' 00 W
Atwood Harbour (inside reef)	ATWD2	22° 43' 40 N	073° 53' 05 W
Atwood Harbour (anchorage)	ATWD3	22° 43' 12 N	073° 52' 47 W
Acklins Is. NE Pt. (4 nm NE)	ACKNE	22° 46' 00 N	073° 43' 00 W

Atwood Harbour, an opening giving you entry into a cup-shaped bay behind the reef some 2 nm southwest of Acklin's Northeast Point, is just about the only anchorage worth that name in the Crooked–Acklins area. It has good protection once you get in there except from the north, when it should not be attempted, but the getting in requires care and attention. It's unfortunate that Atwood lies at the limit of a natural passage length in either direction, in other words, it's a good end-of-day run. This means that many people reach Atwood just too late to have good light and are, most probably, tired. In the last few years about a dozen boats have run into trouble entering Atwood. Be warned; but don't be put off.

The break in the reef is well-defined but you have no particular leading mark as you enter the harbor, other than

Semana Cay

Semana Cay (2 nm S)	SMANA	23° 02' 00 N	073° 46' 00 W

Semana Cay, some 35 nm from Bird Rock and 20 nm from Acklin's Northeast Point, is not on your route, but we include it for you may wish to divert there purely out of interest. Semana Cay, no longer populated, lies 30 nm northeast of Crooked Island, and is 9 by 2 nm in land area with a sibling mini-cay to its east. Its surrounding reefs extend the

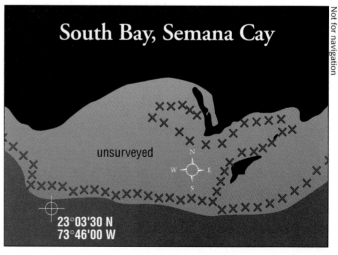

Not for navigation

sea area of the whole Semana Cay landmass to something like 16 by 4 nm. Semana Cay is well off your track, and despite the apparently protected bays on both the north and the south coasts, has no easy-to-enter anchorage. The problem is simply those surrounding reefs that have no breaks, no apparent cuts through the coral, and the weather factor. You need settled weather.

Why go there? Perhaps because you're a maritime history buff, interested in the Columbus Voyages, and a member of the "It Wasn't San Salvador" school. See **The Columbus Controversy** on page 308. There's a compelling case for believing that Semana Cay was where Columbus made his first trans-Atlantic landfall. Alternatively you might elect to go there simply because it's there, or because it's remote and largely unvisited, except occasionally by fishermen from Acklins Island.

If you're determined to go there, forget the bay in the north. The only place to attempt a landing is the bay in the south. The first point to register is that **you** have to find your way through the coral. Hopefully you can anchor off and scout the area by dinghy first, and hopefully too you'll have the dividend of the extra two feet that a high tide will give you. Mark your way in with temporary buoys. Even the Acklins fishermen do this, but if you find other people's markers there, be wary of using them. Check the whole thing out yourself. Once in, you'll be safe if the wind is from the north, if there is any kind of wind kicking up. Forget Semana Cay if the wind is northwest or southwest, and forget it whenever high seas are running.

The Plana Cays

| Plana Cays W (5 nm W) | PLNAW | 22° 37' 00 N | 073° 43' 00 W |
| Plana Cays S (7 nm SW) | PLNAS | 22° 30' 00 N | 073° 43' 00 W |

West Plana Cay offers a good anchorage on the west side in northeast to east winds, but you will feel swell there so expect to roll. Avoid it in northwest and southwest winds. In good weather West Plana's a good place for beachcombing, but you're unlikely to want to stay there long. It's twin, East Plana Cay, has poor anchoring, by repute, but we've not tried it. East Plana is the only undisturbed habitat of the hutia, a small native Bahamian cat-size rodent. One can only guess that one day, way back in time, the hutias

were great swimmers. Maybe they had to be, and their choice of East Plana Cay as a desirable property was no accident. The Arawaks reckoned hutia hot dogs, hutia hamburgers, and just plain roast hutia were gourmet fare.

Mayaguana

Betsy Bay (0.75 nm NW)	BETSY	22° 25' 00 N	073° 09' 00 W
Mayaguana SW (S of Low Pt)	MAYAW	22° 18' 30 N	073° 04' 00 W
Mayaguana SE (0.6 nm S of reef)	MAYAE	22° 20' 00 N	072° 58' 25 W

Mayaguana marks the midway point between Acklins Island and Providenciales. Sizeable though it is at some 24 nm in length and a good 6 nm in width at the fatter western end, the island is for the most part a low-lying tangle of scrub and trees and has very little to offer the cruising visitor, other than shelter. Its population of five hundred are spread between three settlements: Pirate's Well on the northwest coast; Betsy Bay on the west coast, just 2 miles south of a new government dock where *Lady Mathilda*, the weekly mailboat, calls; and Abraham's Bay, the largest settlement, in the center of the island on the south coast. Mayaguana was once part of the US missile tracking network, which left the dividend of an 11,000-foot runway (of which only 7,700 feet is now usable) located 5 miles west of Abraham's Bay, and a dock that serviced their fuel tank farm, on Start Bay, which was known locally as POL (port of landing? or petrol, oil, and lubricants?). Once used by the mailboat, the USAF dock is now in a state of advanced decay. Little else of this period remains. The four stripped-out aircraft—seized drug runners—on the apron at the airfield, are of a later date.

Were Mayaguana anywhere else other than right on the main cruising path to and from the Caribbean, it would probably remain almost totally unvisited, but it's there, right on your route, and you may wish to call in. Its isolation is also broken by the weekly mailboat calls, and twice weekly

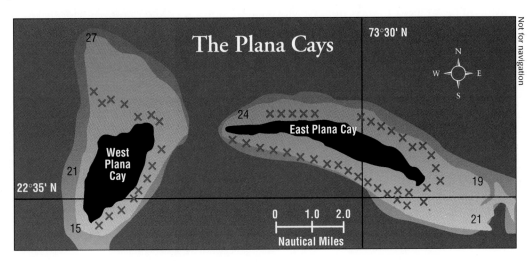

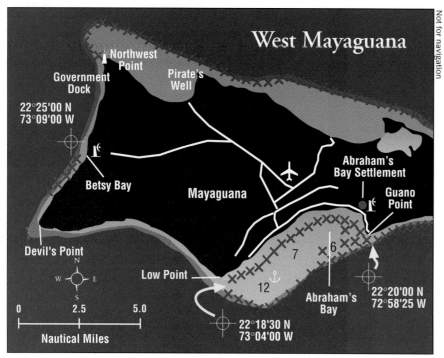

Not for navigation

Bahamasair visits (Mondays and Fridays), for Mayaguana has the good fortune to be a brief stop on the scheduled Nassau–Inagua service. Add these pluses, together with centrally generated power, regraded and surfaced roads, a Batelco station, a police post, and a government clinic, and Mayaguana wins status as a diversion refuge, if for no other reason. And for this reason we cover it in some detail.

Turning to navigation, the chart of Mayaguana can frighten at first sight. The island is surrounded by an almost continuous reef that forms great bights at the northwest tip, the east, and at Abraham's Bay in the south. Look at the chart and you'll see no less than eight shipwrecks marked on the reef, but the Mayaguana total is far higher than this. Your options boil down to two alternatives. The first is to anchor off the west coast, where from Northwest Point down to the first sand beach south of Betsy Bay there's no barrier reef. The depth is good, and you're protected from the prevailing winds, east and southeast, but it's a real no-no in northwest and southwest weather. The second option is to go into Abraham's Bay.

NORTHWEST POINT TO BETSY BAY

| Government Dock | GOVDK | 22° 26' 57 N | 073° 07' 45 W |
| Betsy Bay (0.75 nm NW) | BETSY | 22° 25' 00 N | 073° 09' 00 W |

Northwest Point is low lying, but is marked by a light pole close to its tip, and shows even more prominently by the breaking seas on its barrier reef. If you had shoal draft you could work your way inside the reef close to Northwest Point, and anchor somewhere off the foreshore running east to Pirate's

Well, but it's very shallow there and you're totally open to the north. Pirate's Well has nothing to offer, just one very small store and, a surprising choice of location, a small, low-rise beach hotel under construction which may, one day, be completed. We suggest you don't consider Pirate's Well as an option.

A new government dock 1 nm south of Northwest Point has been cut through the beach rock and coral to provide a square basin with one concrete wall for the mailboat. The beach reef on the north side of the dock was not completely cut away and remains a hazard, but there are range marks, two triangles on stakes on the land behind the dock. The depth at the dock is good, 6–8 feet at MLW by guess, and there is some surge. This is the best place where you can easily take on fuel, either diesel or gasoline, if you need it, *if* the island has fuel in stock. The fuel will be brought to the dock in drums. There's no filtration. You either come alongside, or bring your fuel cans ashore having anchored off (remember there's no offshore reef there). The government dock is untenable, even for the mailboat, in southwest and northwest winds of any strength, and under these conditions the mailboat will divert to Abraham's Bay where whatever can be easily offloaded is cross-decked into small boats.

The best way to call for fuel, or indeed for anything in Mayaguana, is to call Batelco on VHF 16, and they'll look after you. If for some reason you get no response, try the police, who also monitor Channel 16.

Betsy Bay is recognizable offshore by its shortish 104-foot Batelco tower with a dish antenna coupled to it. The settlement parallels the beach, which has an inshore reef about 100 feet off. Anchoring off is fine in prevailing southeast winds, but out of the question if the weather is southwest or northwest. There's plenty of depth, but check your holding. The settlement has nothing to offer, and lost its dock to a hurricane.

LOW POINT AND ABRAHAM'S BAY

Mayaguana SW (S of Low Pt)	MAYAW	22° 18' 30 N	073° 04' 00 W
Mayaguana SE (0.6 nm S of reef)	MAYAE	22° 20' 00 N	072° 58' 25 W
Abraham's Bay Batelco Tower	ABBAT	22° 20' 05 N	072° 58' 00 W

Abraham's Bay, at just over 5 nm in length with a width of nearly 2 nm is an all-weather anchorage, accessed by two gaps in the reef. Apart from its very obvious barrier reef, two landmarks are useful in defining each end of Abraham's Bay. In the west are what appears to be two towers, the high

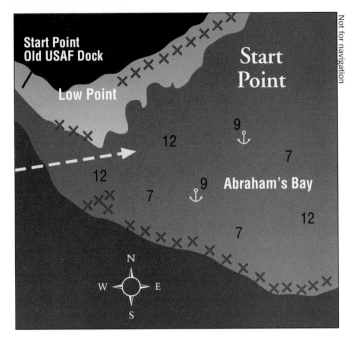

end remains of a larger ridgeline building once part of the USAF missile tracking complex, and the remains of two water tanks. In the east, there's the 175-foot Batelco tower in Abraham's Bay settlement.

The entry at the west end, just to the east of Low Point, places you furthest away from the settlement and is the easier of the two cuts to negotiate as it carries some 12 feet at MLW. The break in the reef is easily defined, and it is this entry that is used by the mailboat if it has to divert to Abraham's Bay. Your primary coastline landmark, just to the west of Low Point, is the remains of the US missile station dock (22° 20' 06 N 073° 03' 51 W) with a tank farm behind it. The range marks still stand, but the dock is unusable. Nonetheless, this docking facility, partly kept in use, is the island's source of fuel. The fuel tanker anchors off, runs its discharge hoses over the sea to the dock, where they are connected to working pipelines running back to two in-use fuel tanks in the farm.

This apart, once you've made your entry to Abraham's Bay to the east of Low Point you can anchor almost anywhere it suits, but avoid the shore for it shoals and dries at low tide over much of its span. There's little advantage in working your way closer to the Abraham's Bay dock at the east end of the Bight.

At the east end under Guano Point, which has a light stake, you have a better-defined break in the reef but less water, only 6 feet at MLW, and the opening is deceptive, for there's a middle bar (which is that 6-foot depth). Work your way in, and once inside the reef turn to port to anchor. Don't head toward the Abraham's Bay concrete dock that lies to starboard. The dock, despite a scar with the semblance of a channel carved by a local fishing boat, is only

approachable by dinghy, and don't even try it at low tide. You'll find barely a foot of water there. Don't be fooled by the fishing boat if it's at the dock. We have a concern about our entry waypoint, having got a latitude reading in this part of the island just over a quarter of a mile north of the chart's coordinates. Our GPS may have been acting up. The chart may be wrong. For safety we have set our southeast waypoint to the south by twice the error.

ABRAHAM'S BAY SETTLEMENT

A ten-minute walk from the Abraham's Bay dock will bring you into the settlement by the Batelco tower and the government offices. Customs and Immigration offices exist in Abraham's Bay, which are used on occasion by officers stationed in Inagua, but the Commissioner has vested powers to act in their absence, and so for all practical purposes Mayaguana can be taken as a Port of Entry. The Batelco office is open seven days a week, and further into the settlement you'll find the police station, the government clinic (staffed by a nurse—a doctor from Inagua visits once a month), two small stores, and two places where you can get food or a drink. The Batelco office will guide you.

ELSEWHERE IN MAYAGUANA

There are places where in settled conditions you can work your way in through cuts in the reef, around Northwest Point as we've already mentioned, or almost due south or

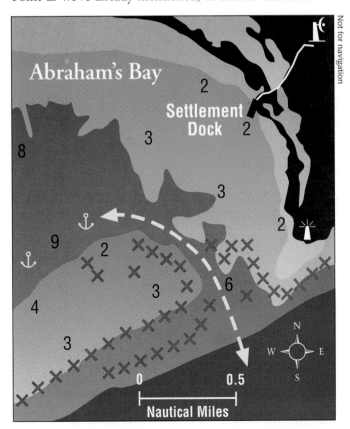

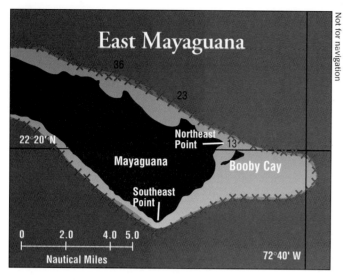

East Mayaguana

due north of Booby Cay in the eastern bight, but we think you'd be crazy to attempt it.

A stillborn US vacation housing development on North Beach (22° 24' 22 N 072° 58' 50 W), launched under the curious cover title of the Mayaguana Ecological Group, has yet to produce more than the frame of one half-completed Italianate house and some foundations. There was talk of a cut in the reef, some dredging, and a marina. The bight is shallow there.

TWO CAUTIONARY TALES

Two open boats from Acklins went to Semana fishing. Quite often Acklins boats go there for a week, camp out, and then return. On the passage back the engine of one boat failed. By the time the other realized something had gone wrong, the missing boat was over the horizon. They backtracked, but failed to sight the lost boat. They had no VHF. They searched, but failed. Five men were on board the missing boat. Over the next five days the weather worsened, with winds reaching 35–40 knots on two of those days. The missing boat was

given up for lost. On Day 5 a tanker sighted the boat off the Long Island coast. The five men were still alive.

❋

A small sailboat lies wrecked on the reef just south of Abraham's Bay dock. It was towed there, having gone on the reef by the Guano Point Pass, but by then it was past recovery. Her captain sailed late in the day for the Pass despite heavy surf breaking along the reef, and realized as he got close that the seas were too much for him. He turned back, but had lost his light by then and with it his ability to read the water. He hit an inner reef.

The Turks and Caicos Islands

Approaches To Providenciales

Providenciales N (7 nm NW)	PROVN	21° 55' 00 N	072° 15' 00 W
Sandbore Approach (2 nm NW)	SBORA	21° 46' 00 N	072° 28' 00 W
Sandbore Pass W (at the reef)	SBORW	21° 44' 55 N	072° 27' 30 W

Whether the Turks and Caicos Islands are your turnaround point or just a waypoint on an extended passage makes little difference to the geography of your approaches in the early stages, unless you are going to bypass the Turks and Caicos completely as some do, who don't want to transit the Caicos Bank. If you elect to stop in the Turks and Caicos, and experience the incredible sensation of crossing that Bank, you're

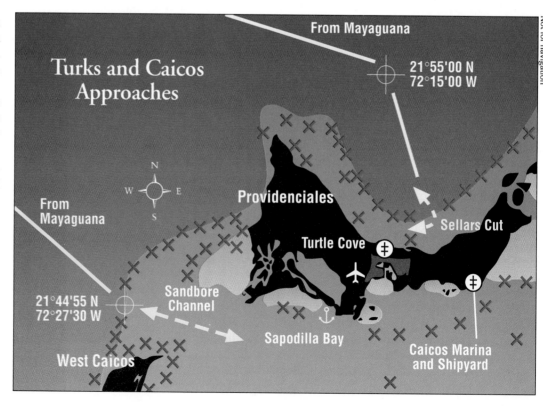

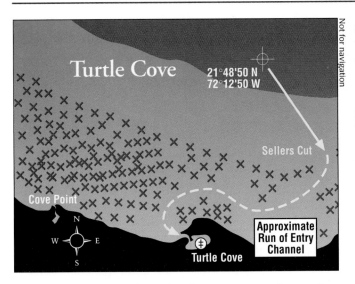

Turtle Cove

21°48'50 N
72°12'50 W

Not for navigation

Sellers Cut

Cove Point

N · W · E · S

Turtle Cove

Approximate Run of Entry Channel

bound to make Providenciales (known as Provo) your first stop and your port of entry. Why? Because it's there, right on your path. And Provo has everything. Nowhere else in the Turks and Caicos has much to offer the transient boater.

You have two options, as Provo is a barrier island, one of the circlet of islands bordering the Caicos Bank starting at West Caicos in the west and continuing around to South Caicos in the southeast. If you elect to stay outside the Caicos Bank initially, then you'll head for the north coast of Provo, making to pass through the barrier reef at Sellars Cut, with Turtle Cove Marina your destination.

If you want to get on the Bank at the outset, then you must pass between Provo and West Caicos, through a well-known cut called Sandbore Channel. After that you have the option of anchoring off the south coast of Provo in Sapodilla Bay, or going on to the Caicos Marina, which lies some distance outside the center of Provo.

Turtle Cove

Providenciales (7 nm NW)	PROVN	21° 55' 00 N	072° 15' 00 W
Sellars Cut (at the reef)	SLLRS	21° 48' 50 N	072° 12' 50 W

If you're heading for Turtle Cove, you want to make our Provo Approach north waypoint your landfall after crossing the Caicos Passage, and then run in the 7 nm to our second waypoint, which lies just outside the Sellars Cut pass through the reef. You're set to turn almost due south to pass through the reef, which is marked. However once you're inside the outer reef, you're still not in the clear and although buoys mark your approach channel into Turtle Cove Marina, you'd be foolish not to call them on VHF 16 while you are still outside the reef and ask for reassuring, up-to-date instructions (for the passage in has been changed in the past) or, even better, someone to guide you in.

Once there you are in a full-service marina, very much in the heart of a continuous tract of tourist development

and you may not even need to visit the center of Provo itself, which lies two miles away to the west, with the airport a mile or so further on. Turtle Cove Marina is a Port of Entry.

Sandbore Channel

Sandbore Approach (2 nm NW)	SBORA	21° 46' 00 N	072° 28' 00 W
Sandbore Pass W (at the reef)	SBORW	21° 44' 55 N	072° 27' 30 W
Sandbore Mid-Pass	SBORM	21° 44' 30 N	072° 24' 00 W
Sandbore Pass E (S Bluff shoal)	SBORE	21° 44' 00 N	072° 21' 45 W

Sandbore Channel has suffered from bad PR on occasion and wrongly been considered a difficult pass. The reverse is true. It's a good, relatively straight, 10–15-foot-deep half-mile-wide cut through the reef some 2 nm north of the northwest point of West Caicos. Your approach marker, which may not be so encouraging, is the wreck of a ship on the reef 1.5 nm north of Sandbore Channel. Hold on your course, keeping in deep ocean water (naturally using your eyes rather than GPS and autopilot) until you reach our Sandbore Pass west waypoint. Then turn for the pass.

You'll want to favor the north side, for there it is more easily defined. The seas break on the reef there, and the cutoff (shown vividly by the change in color of the water) between the pass itself and the shoals and reef to the north, is more clearly seen. Don't wander off toward the south side of Sandbore Channel, for it's harder to pick up your line. It should go without saying, but we'll say it, don't attempt the Sandbore Channel with the sun in your eyes. We tried it once. Never again.

We give a mid-pass waypoint for reassurance, which places you just south of a reef called Halfway Reef, and an east entry waypoint, which lies just south of the shoal extending south from Bluff Head. Although we've given headings as a general indication of line, take the Sandbore Pass visual. No autopilots! South of Bluff Head you gain the Caicos Bank, and your options are to cross the Bank without stopping, head for the anchorage at Sapodilla Bay, or go on to the Caicos Marina and Shipyard.

Sapodilla Bay

Sandbore Pass E (S Bluff shoal)	SBORE	21° 44' 00 N	072° 21' 45 W
Sapodilla Bay (1 nm SW)	SPDLA	21° 44' 00 N	072° 18' 00 W

If you're heading for Sapodilla from our Sandbore Pass east waypoint you have no problems. Go visual. Sapodilla Bay is ahead of you, clearly seen, with the Five Cays beyond it. The anchorage is virtually all-weather, carries some 5–10 feet of water, and has good holding. It's not so hot there with wind from the south, and you may wish to reconsider your destination if that's the way it is. Sapodilla Bay has most facilities, it is an entry port, but it's three miles outside the center of Provo.

Caicos Marina

Sandbore Pass E (S Bluff shoal)	SBORE	21° 44' 00 N	072° 21' 45 W
Sapodilla S. Dock Pt. (1 nm S)	SPDLP	21° 43' 10 N	072° 17' 00 W
Caicos Shipyard (1.75 nm S)	CAIYD	21° 43' 00 N	072° 10' 05 W

If you want to make for the Caicos Marina and Shipyard, the best track to take is to set a course to pass to the south of Sapodilla, and run on to our Caicos Shipyard waypoint. Then turn north to make your approach into the marina, and follow their channel marks, which may or may not be there. If the marks are missing, call them on VHF 16 rather than trying to find your own way in, which might prove a mistake. The Caicos Marina is a full-service yard, and it's a Port of Entry. It's also a seven-mile journey from the center of Provo itself, which, if you need provisions, a bank, and all the rest of the stops that most of us do need after our longer passages, could turn out to be less than convenient.

The Caicos Bank

We'll not deal in detail with crossing the Caicos Bank for it's not properly a part of this Guide, except to say that it's some 60 nm across, something like 6–12 feet in depth, and peppered with reefs and coral heads. For this reason you must cross in good daylight, and if you're going from west to east, don't start heading straight into a rising sun. It's a strange feeling to anchor for the night out of sight of land in water this depth. If you have no moon, the stars are fantastic.

For some strange reason many people refuse to consider making this crossing, but we count it as one of the most memorable legs of our passage making. If you want to preview what the Caicos Bank looks like, fly from Miami to San Juan in Puerto Rico. Most probably your track will pass directly over the Caicos Bank. Rather like the Bight of Acklins, it's jewel-like in its brilliance.

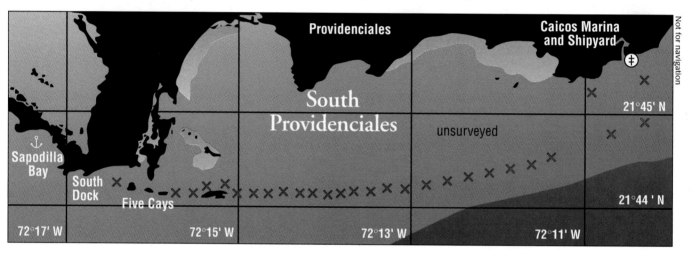

Clarence Town Thursday Night

IF YOU'VE been to Hope Town or around the Abacos, you might have heard or bought Gordon Wynne's recording *Island Country*, with its lead song *Hopetown Saturday Night*. If you haven't heard the track, no matter. That was about Hope Town. This is about Clarence Town Thursday night.

SSB reception wasn't too hot around 1700 when we were trying to listen to Herb (the weather prophet Herb Hilgenberg as *Southbound Two* on 12359.0 kHz). We could hear the questions, but not his responses. At least only in part. But we'd had it cutting up a bit during the day, southwest to west, 10–15 with some higher gusts, and it stood to reason that it was going to be northwest during the night, then maybe north by morning, clocking through to northeast during Friday morning. If you'd held a Town Meeting pretty much everyone would have

agreed, although it's hard to hold a Town Meeting with only two boats. But one thing was clear. The winds were increasing.

The realization was a bit like being encouraged with a sharp pointed stick. But I guess the pointed stick had really come into play that morning. Suddenly we were dragging and there was no doubt that the anchor was hopping like a kangaroo over the sea grass with no intention of resetting itself. With the mile-wide entrance of Clarence Town Harbour astern, it wouldn't have been a matter of active concern, but for that western reef running out from Harbour Point, which by then was just two boat length's away. I was alone. Mike was ashore, on a borrowed car run up to Deadman's Cay with Lawrence, from the other boat. That left Linda and their nine-year old on theirs.

Linda was quick. On the VHF, and within ten minutes, had rowed over to join me in her cockleshell of a dinghy in seas that made her look like an Olympic veteran in a white water event. It took us four attempts to get the hook holding. Then the wind cut by half. She had an easier passage back.

There was no need to guess what came up on the "to do" list. By the end of the afternoon Mike and I were lying to two anchors, well dug in by hand, with one precious Pony tank, saved for that kind of activity, exhausted. It was still southwest, but we were covered from southwest through northwest to north.

"In the morning, come first light," I said "we'll reset to face northeast and east. It'll clock around then."

Just in case it got rough during the night we took the outboard off the dinghy, and hoisted the dinghy itself on the davits. "One less thing," I added to my smug reassurance, "to think about."

But there's nothing worse than thinking you've got it all sewn up. We had a couple of Kaliks, listened to Herb, spoke to our neighbors. Thanked Linda again. We were all set. We'd all taken note too that the mailboat was coming in during the night. That meant proper anchor lights. No fooling around with a votive candle in a glass jar as a substitute.

Clock around? You bet it did. By midnight. Straight out of the east with whitecaps, and we were rolling like a pig taking it broadside on, suspended between 75 feet of chain on one end and 50 feet of chain plus some nylon on the other, with much of the nylon taut across the keel. It wasn't anywhere near the text book illustration of how you lie to two anchors. How long did we have before both anchors broke free? Maybe as many minutes as you've got fingers to count on, but . . . Could we fall back on one? No way. Not the way it was. Problem? Coral and a beach too close downwind. It seemed kind of urgent to get a third anchor out.

We had a third anchor, yes, but the two backup anchors were intended as alternatives to the Bruce, or alternative second anchors. Dumb. I don't know why I'd never envisaged lying to three anchors. We had no more chain. No more rode. Improvise. OK. Use power to place it? No. The moment we moved forward we'd break the tenuous hold of two existing anchors. And that nylon rode was probably hard against the prop. Use the dinghy? You bet. Where was it? High on the davits, snugged up tight. The rewards of sensible prudence!

By two in the morning we'd logged more night dives than I can remember. The Delta, at the end of two joined 60-foot half-inch braided dock lines, was dug in well upwind as best I could. Dock lines are not the best anchor rode I know, and it had been pulling way too high too soon at the start, but the catenary was fixed by a 30-foot leader of half-inch 3-strand nylon held flat to the sea bed by the dinghy's mini-Fortress with its short

length of chain. It seemed to be working out OK. We had the dinghy along with us, less than happy in a near-bathtub mode by then, but we'd bail it when we got the chance. All that remained was to dive for the dive light I'd dropped (switched off, naturally) on the seabed somewhere, double check the two original anchors, and rework one of them to complement the Delta. Behind Strachan Cay there was a blaze of light moving north, intense white deck lights, a red, a masthead, even more lights, another red close behind. The mailboat? Coming in now? Oh no. Not right then. Please. Anyway we'd long had the generator running, our masthead was on, and we looked like a Festival of Lights ourselves. We'd be OK. We were off her path. We'd got time, before she was close in, to fix a fender as an anchor buoy to the new anchor so that we could locate it easily, if we had to, in all that slop of wave and trough.

We were still in the water. Within ten minutes the blaze of lights was head-on. Maybe it was the perspective from dead sea level that made her seem enormous, more like a nuclear aircraft carrier, but even worse we had a red, green, and white with a whole load of other lights coming our way. We shot back to our boat. The nuclear aircraft carrier resolved itself into the mailboat towing a Bahamian fishing boat, around 40 feet in length. Both had their nav lights and deck lights on. They parted company about four mailboat lengths off our fender marker. The fisherman held out there, standing off, as the mailboat came on in to the government dock with a blinding searchlight flicking around Clarence Town Harbour like a serpent's tongue. At least we got three or four reassuring licks from that probing light. With some neat maneuvering (and no assistance whatsoever from Clarence Town) she made it in, and was secure within half an hour. The fishing boat strobed all her lights on and off four or five times, like a Christmas tree when you first hook up last year's lights, and just like last year's tree lights, that was it. The whole lot went out. There was blackness. Was she moving in? We waited. Nothing. OK. She must have anchored off. Back into the water.

It was 0315 when we had a mug of soup, divided the rest of the night into two watches, and settled down. By 1015 the next morning we had the two original anchors relocated and reset, the third anchor with its baby Fortress and our dock lines back in reserve, and could look around. The fishing boat, anchored off, was lifeless. Sleeping late? On the mailboat they'd started unloading around 0830. Just after midday she sailed, paused to pick up the fishing boat and take her in tow, and disappeared into weather that might have been nothing to them, but would have given us about as stable a ride as a boiled egg balanced on an armadillo's back.

We were kind of tired by then. But that was it. That's the way it can go. Clarence Town, Thursday Night.

The Western Route South

IN our introduction to this chapter we expressed some doubts about the viability of a Western Route down the west coast of Long Island and onward toward the Windward Passage. We'll reinforce those initial hesitations now. In short the route kicks off with too much fooling around on the Grand Bahama Bank as you work your way south to the deep water pocket contained in the circlet of the Ragged Islands–Jumentos Cays. Let's apply a harbor/anchorage factor to this route. Scorecard? Close to zero. After Salt Pond the West Coast of Long Island is bad news, Long Cay is no good, South Acklins is not so good, and your last Bahamian island, Great Inagua, has a harbor that barely wins a 3 on our 1-to-10 scale. What about the route itself? You have the Mira Por Vos Passage, Castle Island with its strong current sets, and Hogsty Reef in the offing before you reach Great Inagua, which is no haven. You could ask what's the point of going this way?

Well, it just may be that it'll suit you, sometime, for some reason. It just may be that, after making your way south down the east coast of Long Island, you elect to take the Crooked Island Passage bound for the Windward Passage. So that will take you down to Long Cay and the Mira Por Vos Passage and your route then becomes the lower part of our Western Route. So we'll deal with it.

George Town to the Windward Passage or the Turks and Caicos Islands

As we did for the Eastern Route, we highlight the principal waypoints on this route, and include additional waypoints in the text. These highlighted waypoints combine to produce the shortest direct routes:

George Town East–Windward Passage North Approach	248.4 nm
George Town East–Sandbore Approach	257.4 nm

George Town Harbour Ent. (E)	GTAE1	23° 30' 00 N	075° 40' 00 W
Exumas Black Rocks (1 nm S)	BLKRS	23° 27' 00 N	075° 32' 00 W
White Cay Bank N	WCB-N	23° 24' 55 N	075° 20' 30 W
Long Is. Salt Pond (2 nm W)	SALTP	23° 20' 20 N	075° 10' 00 W
White Cay Bank E	WCB-E	23° 19' 45 N	075° 18' 10 W
White Cay Bank W	WCB-W	23° 19' 55 N	075° 31' 05 W
Nuevitas Rocks (1 nm E)	NUEVR	23° 10' 00 N	075° 21' 30 W
Long Is. South Point (2 nm W)	STHPT	22° 52' 00 N	074° 54' 00 W
Long Cay (2 nm off Windsor Pt.)	LONGC	22° 32' 30 N	074° 25' 00 W
Acklins Is. Salina Pt. (1 nm NW)	SLINA	22° 14' 00 N	074° 18' 00 W
Mira Por Vos Passage	MIRAP	22° 06' 30 N	074° 25' 00 W
Hogsty Reef (3 nm W)	HGSTY	21° 41' 00 N	073° 54' 00 W
Gt Inagua (3 nm W Mtthw Twn)	INAGA	20° 57' 00 N	073° 44' 00 W
Sandbore Approach (2 nm NW)	SBORA	21° 46' 00 N	072° 28' 00 W
Windward Passage Approach N	WINDN	20° 30' 00 N	073° 50' 00 W

Headings °M and Straightline Distances

Once again we repeat our warning given under the Eastern Route. The direct courses we quote are not dreamworld. We know, if you're a sailor, you can't sail them, just like that. Even a power boat has to take account of the sea state and, yes, the wind too. But we show these courses as it's the only way in which you can indicate both direction and a ballpark distance to run. All your passage plans are based on these two primary factors. You vector in the weather, and all the rest, the business of choosing the route you actually take, together with the seamanship, is up to you.

George Town Harbour East	Black Rocks	119°	07.9 nm
Black Rocks	White Cay Bank N	108°	11.0 nm
White Cay Bank N	Salt Pond	123°	11.0 nm
Salt Pond	White Cay Bank E	273°	07.5 nm
White Cay Bank E	White Cay Bk W	278°	12.0 nm
White Cay Bank W	Nuevitas Rock	146°	13.0 nm
Nuevitas Rock	Long Is South Pt	282°	31.0 nm
Long Island South Point	Mira Por Vos Psg	157°	53.0 nm
Long Island South Point	Long Cay	133°	33.0 nm
Long Cay	Acklins Salina Pt	168°	20.0 nm
Acklins Island Salina Point	Mira Por Vos Psg	229°	09.9 nm
Long Cay	Mira Por Vos Psg	188°	26.0 nm
Mira Por Vos Passage	Sandbore Appr	108°	111.0 nm
Mira Por Vos Passage	Windward Psg N	169°	102.0 nm
Mira Por Vos Passage	Gt Ing (Mtthw Twn)	159°	79.0 nm
Mira Por Vos Passage	Hogsty Reef	139°	38.0 nm
Hogsty Reef	Gt Ing (Mtthw Twn)	176°	45.0 nm
Inagua (Matthew Town)	Windward Psg N	200°	27.0 nm

The West Coast of Long Island

George Town Harbour Ent. (E)	GTAE1	23° 30' 00 N	075° 40' 00 W
Exumas Black Rocks (1 nm S)	BLKRS	23° 27' 00 N	075° 32' 00 W
White Cay Bank N	WCB-N	23° 24' 55 N	075° 20' 30 W
Long Is. Salt Pond (2 nm W)	SALTP	23° 20' 20 N	075° 10' 00 W

After leaving George Town Harbour by the east entrance, you gain the Bank to the south of Black Rocks and the reefs to their east, and head for the waypoint we've identified as White Cay Bank north. This will keep you well clear of the shoals lying between Hog Cay and White Cay, and the shallow water to the east of White Cay. Don't contemplate getting on to the Bank between Little Exuma Island and Hog Cay. This is not a viable route. Sure, you could take it at high water with a 2-foot draft, but it's not a pass worth entering on your option list. From that White Cay Bank north waypoint you can head directly to our Salt Pond approach waypoint.

SALT POND

As we mentioned in our coverage of the north of Long Island under **The Out Islands North of the Tropic of Cancer** on page 252, Salt Pond is the best-protected anchorage on the west coast of Long Island, although it's open to the west. The small cays off the settlement are the Salt Pond ace-in-the-hole if it blows from the west, and all the Salt Pond boats not riding to all-weather moorings migrate from one part of the anchorage to another, playing the shelter of the small cays to advantage as the weather changes.

Salt Pond was hit hard by Hurricane *Lili* but is rebuilding and by the time this Guide is published should be back on line in all respects with fuel, water, and all the normal shore-side facilities, including an excellent marine store, that you expect to find in a settlement devoted to being the support base for a fishing fleet and the hosts of the annual Long Island Regatta. However, other than coming alongside to take on fuel or to take on supplies, there are no marina facilities in Salt Pond. You are unlikely to want to stay long there, although the proximity of Deadmans Cay airport with its Bahamasair service may be worth noting.

Deadmans Cay airport is not the Deadman Cay shown on the charts to the west of Long Island's Duncanson Point, but is on the Long Island mainland and on the main highway some six miles south of Salt Pond.

Crossing the Bank

Long Is. Salt Pond (2 nm W)	SALTP	23° 20' 20 N	075° 10' 00 W
White Cay Bank E	WCB-E	23° 19' 45 N	075° 18' 10 W
White Cay Bank W	WCB-W	23° 19' 55 N	075° 31' 05 W
Nuevitas Rocks (1 nm E)	NUEVR	23° 10' 00 N	075° 21' 30 W

We turn now to the business of crossing the Bank to gain access to the deep water to the south of Nuevitas Rocks and lying to the west of the southern tip of Long Island. This can't be achieved as a straight shot from Salt Pond. You must make three dogleg passages to avoid the shoals that make 95 percent of the Bank to the southwest of Salt Pond a no-go area. Your only possible route is to go from Salt Pond to our White Cay Bank east waypoint, then on to the west waypoint, and once there take up your heading to Nuevitas Rock.

The routes we give are general lines of courses to steer but not *safe-switch-on-the-autopilot and sit-back,-relax, or go-below-to-make-some-coffee* routes. You must use your eyes, and con the boat yourself. Nothing is constant, shoaling is ever changing. As you get close to Nuevitas Rock you are in coral head territory, and this at once dictates additional caution.

In our search for the perfect Western Passage we've come across the name "The Comer Channel," which appears to have been associated with this route at some time. The Comer rocks lie well to the south and clearly have no association with the Bank route. We all know Bahamian names repeat, but no one we spoke to in Salt Pond had any knowledge of a trans-Bank Comer Channel, and we've drawn a blank.

NUEVITAS ROCK

At Nuevitas Rock we reach the only point in this Guide (other than Hogsty Reef) where we must stand aside and have no advice to offer. Detailed exploration of the Nuevitas Rock area was on our research program agenda, and twice we failed to make it there. An unprecedented run of southwest weather prevented us attempting it from Salt Pond, and an unbelievable eight days of adverse weather ruined all plans of getting there around South Point of Long Island when we were on the east coast. In the end available time dictated priorities and we were obliged to move on elsewhere. It has not been our policy to write a guide based on second-hand information. This said, we have been told by Salt Pond fishing boat captains that the Nuevitas pass into deeper water is fine, and there are no problems.

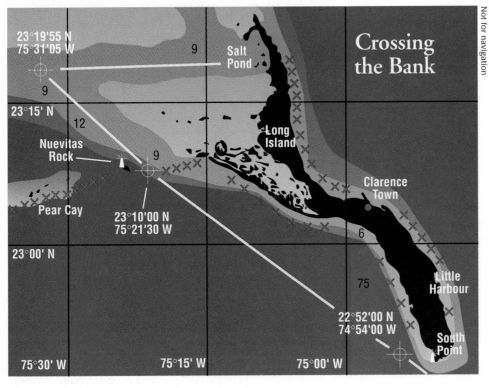

Not for navigation

Nuevitas Rock to the Mira Por Vos Passage

Nuevitas Rocks (1 nm E)	NUEVR	23° 10' 00 N	075° 21' 30 W
Long Is. South Point (2 nm W)	STHPT	22° 52' 00 N	074° 54' 00 W
Long Cay (2 nm off Windsor Pt.)	LONGC	22° 32' 30 N	074° 25' 00 W
Acklins Is. Salina Pt. (1 nm NW)	SLINA	22° 14' 00 N	074° 18' 00 W
Mira Por Vos Passage	MIRAP	22° 06' 30 N	074° 25' 00 W

Once you're in deep water you can set the first of two courses that will take you past the south tip of Long Island, on across the Crooked Island Passage past the southwest point of Long Cay, and through the Mira Por Vos Passage, leaving Castle Island and Acklins Island on your port side. The first leg keeps you well away (some 10 nm to the east) of Diana Reef, which is the only threatening area in this deep pocket of ocean water. If you've made your way down the east coast of Long Island and chosen to turn into the Crooked Island Passage, rather than continuing on to Mayaguana and the Turks and Caicos, your intersection with the Western Route comes at the Mira Por Vos Passage.

If you need to seek shelter, there are few options open to you. To anchor off the west coast of Long Island about 1 nm north of South Point is one possibility. French Wells (see page 268) is another. The east coast of Long Cay, about 1 nm north of Windsor Point, the southern point, has long been regarded as an anchorage, for you're protected from the west there and by shoal water from most other directions, but it doesn't quite work out so well. As one local fisherman put it, "the ocean is too close there." Jamaica Bay on the west side of the southern end of Acklins Island is an option, but it too is weather dependent. The last possibility is to tuck yourself inside the reefs under the south coast of Castle Island. That's fine if it's calm, full daylight with sun, and all is at peace with the world, but it's not a foul-weather refuge.

LONG CAY

Long Cay (2 nm off Windsor Pt.)	LONGC	22° 32' 30 N	074° 25' 00 W

Long Cay, with a population of around 25, is yet another once-prosperous Bahamian island that has fallen on hard times. Its now overly large church is sad evidence of this decline. In the past Long Cay was a pit-stop for sailing vessels taking the Crooked Island Passage, a sponging center, and, like so many islands, had a hand in salt production too. Albert Town's west coast, open to surge, has no anchorage. You can work up inside the bight but there's very little that Albert Town itself has to offer. We don't recommend it.

North Cay, Fish Cay, and Guana Cay

To the southeast of Long Cay on the edge of the Bight of Acklins lies North Cay, Fish Cay, and Guana Cay. These

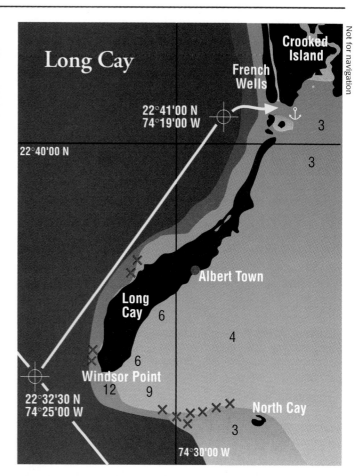

three cays are the last refuge of the local species of iguana, which for reasons yet unknown have suffered a devastating population drop in the last few years. The iguanas are the subject of a scientific study hoping to determine the cause for this reversal. If you call there, tread carefully. Land no animals. Leave no garbage.

THE BIGHT OF ACKLINS

Spectacular as it may be from space, unless you're hot on shoal draft exploration, the Bight of Acklins is not a cruising ground.

ACKLINS ISLAND

Acklins Is. Salina Pt. (1 nm NW)	SLINA	22° 14' 00 N	074° 18' 00 W

We covered the north of Acklins Island under the Eastern Route. The south of Acklins is not tourist territory and even in Spring Point they admit that they rarely ever venture down that way. This leaves, in near total isolation, the one southern settlement of Salina Point. Nearby Jamaica Bay, just past Salina Point on the northwest coast (the Bight coast), or alternatively, just under Salina Point if you can work your way close in, are about the only viable anchorages in the area. Although you may be tempted to try to probe further in, local advice is against it. The channel is not easy to find, and if the weather turns you may have a tough time getting out and away from there. If you anchor in Jamaica Bay you can make contact with the Salina settlement, but there's not much they can offer other than fresh bread and, yes, there is a telephone.

The east or ocean coast of Acklins is forbidden territory. It is a long run of nothing but near continuous reef and coral heads. Keep well clear of it.

The Mira Por Vos Passage and Castle Island

Mira Por Vos Passage	MIRAP	22° 06' 30 N	074° 25' 00 W
Castle Island (lighthouse)	CSTLE	22° 07' 30 N	074° 19' 00 W

Mira Por Vos! Look Out for Yourself! The Spanish must have been terrified by the Mira Por Vos area, a nightmare of coral and sand almost bang in the middle of the southern entrance to the Crooked Island Passage. If you couldn't slip between the Mira Por Vos Cays and Castle Island, a tough shot for the captain of a lumbering galleon to call, you had to go to the west of the Mira Por Vos Cays. But if the set, which runs that way, and the wind forced you too far west, you'd be on the Columbus Bank. If you clawed your way off that, but got taken too far to the northwest, you'd end up in the deep water trap ringed from the west to the northeast by the Jumentos Cays and Long Island. You could regret the day you got the captaincy of that galleon, or even worse, command of that fleet of treasure ships.

Small wonder that the Spanish decided to take the Gulf Stream route from Havana, settled on St. Augustine as a takeoff point into the Atlantic, and quit trying to cruise in the Bahamas.

The Castle Island lighthouse, the southern complement to Bird Rock in the north, marks the southern exit of the Crooked Island Passage. Sadly this lighthouse, in its conversion to power, suffered the same vandalism as the result of bureaucratic ignorance or disinterest as Bird Rock. Beware of the currents around Castle Island. As always at a place that is the focal point of a deep-water passage, here compounded by the shallows of the Mira Por Vos reefs, shoals, and cays, the

currents are strong and unpredictable. Expect anything from southwest to northeast.

The potential harbor we mentioned on the south coast of Castle Island has a break in the reef some 200 feet wide, and the reef shows plainly on both sides. Current may be your greatest problem, but if you work your way in, you'll find an adequate day anchorage with 8–12 feet of water.

Options South of the Mira Por Vos Passage

Mira Por Vos Passage	MIRAP	22° 06' 30 N	074° 25' 00 W
Hogsty Reef (3 nm W)	HGSTY	21° 41' 00 N	073° 54' 00 W
Gt Inagua (3 nm W Mtthw Twn)	INAGA	20° 57' 00 N	073° 44' 00 W
Sandbore Approach (2 nm NW)	SBORA	21° 46' 00 N	072° 28' 00 W
Windward Passage Approach N	WINDN	20° 30' 00 N	073° 50' 00 W

At this point on the Western Route your only sensible course, if you're heading south, is to make a straight run for the Windward Passage, standing well to the west of Hogsty Reef and well off Great Inagua. If you're bound for the Turks and Caicos, you've already gone out of your way but a straight run to Sandbore Channel passing well north of Hogsty Reef and, of course, well north of the two Inagua Islands, is also quite possible.

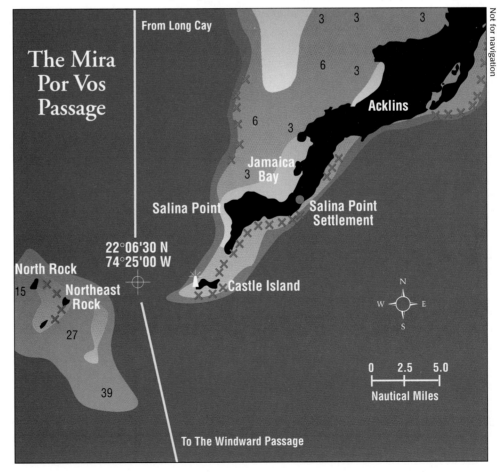

FOR PROVIDENCIALES

If you want to head for the Turks and Caicos, your course should be something in the order of 108°M and a run of 111 nm or so will place you at our Sandbore Approach waypoint. For your close approaches, turn to the description we gave under **The Eastern Route** on page 275. It's not an efficient way to reach Providenciales when you compare it to the Eastern Route, and we certainly wouldn't give it stars as a scenic route.

FOR THE WINDWARD PASSAGE

If you're heading for the Windward Passage you'll be setting off on something like 169°M with something plus of 100 nm to go, a run that can be broken with no great cost in diversionary miles at Great Inagua.

We'll conclude this section on the Western Route with brief coverage of the remaining two Bahamian territories that lie in this area of ocean but are not on your direct track, whichever heading you follow.

Hogsty Reef

Hogsty Reef (3 nm W)	HGSTY	21° 41' 00 N	073° 54' 00 W

About as remote as you can get in Bahamian waters, over 30 nm from land in any direction, Hogsty Reef is a one-off in the Western Hemisphere, a near perfect atoll. It has also, in its time, been a mean ship-cruncher and no one knows how many vessels have fixed the exact position of Hogsty Reef more accurately than they might have wished. It's one of the fabled remote Bahamian dive sites, visited occasionally by live-aboard dive boats, but otherwise you might wish to give it a miss. If you do elect to go there, it's entirely possible to make your way into the lagoon through a pass on the west side to the south of Northwest Cay and anchor

Hogsty Reef

21°42'00 N

6   9

21   12

Northwest
Cay   9

21   21

18   Southeast
Cay

0   1.0   2.0

Nautical Miles

73°48'00 W

Not for navigation

wherever the depth suits you. You'll find anything from around 18 feet down to 6 feet in there. What it might be like being caught there in bad weather is not the stuff of pleasant dreams. Hogsty is deadly in southwest and northwest weather. For a long time Hogsty Reef has been on our "dive destination list." We'll make it one day.

A trimaran with four on board ran on the reef attempting to enter the lagoon some time back. There was no one else there. Hogsty Reef was deserted. Five days later a small Bahamian fishing boat passed, and stopped. They could take no more than one person on board. Three of the trimaran crew were left to trust that their companion would reach some place where he could make contact with the outside world. It must have been an unnerving period. They were lucky. Eventually they were rescued by the US Coast Guard.

The Inagua Islands

Great Inagua, which dwarfs its smaller sibling to the northeast, Little Inagua Island, also dominates the Southern Bahamas by land mass alone, some 40 nm wide running east to west by 26 nm north to south. Its baby sibling, just 5 nm away across a strait, is a stout 10 nm wide by 8 nm running north to south. Despite the total land mass, perhaps it's a blessing that the two islands lie on no direct track, for there's nothing there, and both islands are surrounded by reefs.

LITTLE INAGUA

Other than one possible anchorage off its southwest point, there's absolutely nothing in Little Inagua to attract the cruising or passage-making visitor.

GREAT INAGUA

Gt. Inagua (3 nm W Mtthw Twn)	INAGA	20° 57' 00 N	073° 44' 00 W

Great Inagua has more to offer. Its one settlement, Matthew Town on the southwest tip, has an airstrip, a very small harbor, and more of substance to offer than the normal Out Island pit stops, for the island is the source of raw product for Morton Salt, over a million tons of it exported each year— 99.4–99.6 percent pure. This good fortune (which the ghosts of Rum Cay must envy) brings a salt-loading dock to Man of War Bay (on the west coast to the north of Matthew Town), the salt pans to go with the commercial activity, and has given Matthew Town the stamp of a company town, with better stores and company backup facilities, as well as a backdrop of stockpiles of salt that give the disorienting appearance of snow-covered peaks. Salt skiing may yet come in vogue.

Matthew Town

But for the visiting yachtsman there are few attractions. The reefs around the island are formidable, particularly at Southeast Point where they run out for 5 nm, and there are no

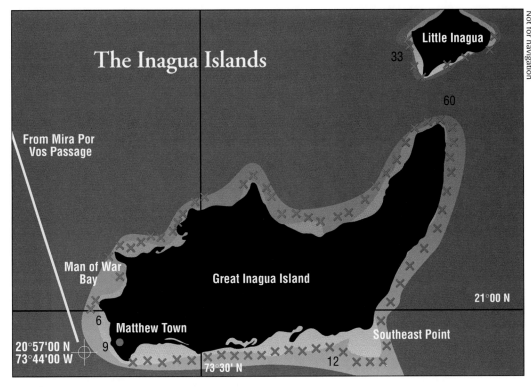

The Inagua Islands

Little Inagua

33

60

From Mira Por
Vos Passage

Man of War
Bay

Great Inagua Island

21°00 N

6
Matthew Town

20°57'00 N
73°44'00 W

9

Southeast Point

73°30' N

12

Not for navigation

MATTHEW TOWN HARBOUR

If you're going to enter the harbor, go carefully. The slanted entry into this small concrete and rock basin has a single leading mark at its southeast corner. Watch out for the reef to starboard that runs out from the shore as you approach. Once inside you have an advertised 10 feet at MLW. To starboard you have the concrete dock used by the mailboat, which has a short arm on the seaward side and a longer run on the land side. But apart from the fuel facility near the range marker in the southeast corner, there's

anchorages anywhere, save off Matthew Town where there are no reefs, but wind and ocean swell make any extended visit hellish. The small harbor offers little better shelter and is a death trap in winds from the south through west to north. What is there to draw you in? Perhaps fuel. Possibly backup engineering from the workshops of the Morton Salt Company, if you can persuade them to help you. Maybe medical help or even air evacuation if you have a casualty. That alone may be worth an entry in your "what if?" file.

nothing there other than the Bahamas Defence Force office and a Batelco telephone box. This is essentially a government dock used by the mailboat. It is not, and was never intended to be, a facility for cruising boats. You will also find the US Coast Guard in Matthew Town, but there by invitation only. If you run into trouble, the responsibility for monitoring Channel 16 lies in the hands of the Bahamas Defence Force.

INAGUA NATIONAL PARK

If none of this sounds particularly encouraging, perhaps, in settled weather, there's a good reason for visiting Great Inagua. The Inagua National Park, given a boost by the Audubon Society, is now home to the largest colony of West Indian flamingos in the world, narrowly saved from extinction. The pink birds share their habitat with a number of other birds now becoming rare in the Bahamas, not the least of which is the cute little Bahamian Parrot,

Ministry of Tourism

once reported to have circled their landings in flocks by an early visitor cruising in the Out Islands. His name? Columbus. Christopher Columbus. For all these reasons we have covered Great Inagua in our **Yellow Pages**.

Michael Sponable

Salt mountains, Great Inagua.

YELLOW PAGES

SOUTH LONG ISLAND

BASRA in SALT POND VHF 16 "SUNSEEKER"
BASRA Dockmaster in CLARENCE TOWN VHF 16

The south of Long Island is rarely visited by cruising visitors. The west coast waters are too shallow, and Salt Pond is as far as you can go on this side. But perhaps the Long Island Regatta, which is held there, will attract you? The east coast will be likely to feature in your plans if you are bound for the Turks and Caicos or the Caribbean, but there is only one place you can put into on this coast, and that is Clarence Town.

LONG ISLAND, WEST COAST

THOMPSON BAY

Thompson Bay is very quiet, with any activity centered around *Thompson Bay Inn*. It is about two miles north of Salt Pond, with a quiet anchorage outside Regatta time and bad weather.

Accommodations and Restaurant
Thompson Bay Inn Tel: 338-0052 • VHF 16 *"Aquarius"*
Open for breakfast, lunch, and dinner from 8 am daily. Accommodations for up to 12 people in single and double rooms. Also offers car rentals.

SALT POND

Church
First Assembly of God
Clinic
Deadman's Cay Health Centre Tel: 337-1222
The main clinic for southern Long Island, with a doctor and nurses. Out of hours you can call the doctor at 337-0555, or the nurses at 337-0666.
Fuel
Long Island Petroleum Tel: 338-0032 • VHF 16
Diesel and gasoline.
General store
Harding Supply Center Tel: 338-0333 and 0042 Open 8 am to 8 pm Monday to Saturday, and 10 am to 8 pm Sundays. Some groceries, cold drinks, lumber and marine supplies. They are also a Johnson and Evinrude/OMC outboard distributor.
Regatta
Long Island Regatta is held each May at Salt Pond, accompanied by a series of sports events, rake and scrape bands, junkanoo parades, and plaiting the Maypole. For more information contact Raphael Cartwright (242-393-3949), Mr. Henderson Burrows (242-394-1535), or Mr. Geoffrey Treco (242-328-2495).

LONG ISLAND, EAST COAST

CLARENCE TOWN

Clarence Town is noted for the twin-spired churches designed by Father Jerome. If you have already visited Cat Island this name will be familiar to you. Father Jerome was a young priest, trained as an architect at the end of the last century, who decided to become an Anglican missionary. In 1908 he arrived in the Bahamas to rebuild local, but frail, wooden churches that could not withstand hurricane winds and reconstructed them in stone. Here in Clarence Town you find two examples of his work, one Anglican, the other Roman Catholic, the faith he later adopted.

Going farther back in time, legend has it that the Arawak Indians once inhabited the caves north of Clarence Town, which were more recently used to mine bat guano for fertilizers. An authenticated Arawak chair from here resides in a Minnesota museum, thanks to a traveling clergyman who took it back to his home town. All this you will learn if you take the hour-long tour of the caves.

Bakery
Oasis Bakery, one mile north of town. Call on VHF 16 to ask what's baking; it could be fresh breads, pies, and buns.
Car Rental
Phil's Rent a Car VHF 16 At Turtle Cove, 3 miles out of town, but Phil will deliver to Clarence Town. 10 cars, assorted sizes.
Churches
St. Paul's Anglican Church, east of town.
St. Peter's Catholic Church, where it is possible to climb the narrow tower with caution.
Both have services at 11 am on Sundays.
Clinic
By the dock in Clarence Town, open 9 am to 3:30 pm, Monday to Friday. There is no phone, but you can call the Commissioner's office (337-3030) and they will put you in touch with the clinic.
Fuel
Clarence Town dock has diesel and gasoline.
Groceries
Harbour Grocery VHF 16 Open from 8:30 am to 7:30 pm Monday to Saturday, 8 to 10 am Sundays. Canned & dry goods, cold drinks, and insect repellent: a must in Clarence Town.
Marine Supplies and Repairs
Milander's Auto and Marine VHF 16 Open 8 am to 5 pm Monday to Saturday. Carlos Milander has limited spare parts in store, but can help with most repairs. He can also put you in touch with two diesel mechanics to come to your boat. One is Red Major, who can be contacted at *Oasis Bakery*; his wife runs the bakery. The other, Rudolph Pratt, lives in Cabbage Point, but will come to Clarence Town. He also runs a mobile diesel fuel operation if Clarence Town dock is out of diesel. Extra charge for delivery.
Police
No VHF radio, but the office is open 9 am to 5:30 pm Monday to Friday.
Post Office
Tel: 337-3030. Open from 9 am to 5:30 pm Monday to Friday.
Restaurant and Bars
Harbour Rest Restaurant and Bar VHF 16 for reservations
Open from 10:30 am to 8 pm for meals, later for the bar.
Skeeters
Sells beer and liquor to drink on his small patio, or to take away.
Telephones
At the Batelco office Tel: 357-1004 Open from 8:30 am to noon, and 1:30 pm to 5 pm, with phone cards for sale.
Vegetables
The Department of Agriculture runs a warehouse consolidation facility at the docks. You can find bananas, limes, peppers, pumpkins, and watermelons almost all year. In the spring you'll also find tomatoes, onions, and sweet peppers; in the summer, mangoes and pineapples too. This is open most days from 9:30 am to 5 pm, but you can call ahead on 357-1024 to check. The stocks are best when the mailboat arrives.

THINGS TO DO IN LONG ISLAND

- Visit *Hamilton's Cave*. If you call "Cave Man" on VHF 16 and arrange a time to go, Leonard Cartwright will take you. Or stop by his house, about 6 miles north of town, advertising CAVE TOURS, and find out his schedule. It is interesting, and kids will love the huge stalagmites and stalactites.
- Take part in the *Long Island Regatta*, held at Salt Pond each May.

Hamilton's Cave.

THE CROOKED–ACKLINS–LONG ISLAND ARCHIPELAGO

Crooked, Acklins, and Long Islands, for most of us, are not really cruising destinations. The islands are sparsely populated, with long stretches where there is nothing but primary vegetation, sometimes without even a road. There are no good harbors, and even the government has found it difficult to find places to build docks. Brief flashes of earlier prosperity, largely based on playing host to (or wrecking) sailing ships passing through the Crooked Island Passage, didn't last long.

Today, if you call in, you'll find a warm welcome. In the settlements there's always water, very basic food stores, and sometimes, if you're lucky, some fuel in drums or cans. The lack of safe anchorages probably dictates that you'll soon move on, and your ability to move around the islands, from one settlement to the other, is limited to the endurance of your dinghy or hitching a ride. The only bonus is that both Crooked and Acklins Islands are served by *Bahamasair* if you need to fly in our out, and of course there's always Batelco if you need to contact the outside world, and clinics in the larger settlements. There is no bank on either Crooked or Acklins, so make sure you have enough cash to cover your needs before you arrive.

For these reasons we don't cover the islands exhaustively, but have simply chosen to give a brief review of the places where you are most likely to make a landfall.

CROOKED ISLAND

BASRA in LANDRAIL POINT VHF 16

For the sailor, the Landrail Point area is the only settlement that can offer basic marine facilities where you can access Crooked Island. Some 2.5 miles north of Landrail Point, on a superb site, is the *Pittsdown Point Landings*, one of the best-kept secrets in the Bahamas. Private and charter aircraft can come in here on the *Landings'* own 2,300 foot landing strip. Landrail itself has a government dock, and all that you expect to find in one of the larger settlements.

However, the administrative heartland of Crooked Island is centered on the Colonel Hill–Cabbage Hill area, strung along its northern spine, which is virtually inaccessible from the ocean. It is here that *Bahamasair* flies in to the airport at Colonel Hill, about 15 miles from Landrail Point. There you will also find the *Crooked Island Beach Inn*, at Cabbage Hill. It offers basic accommodations, and meals that may be ordered in advance from the Evangelical minister/owner.

Outside these two areas there is little in Crooked Island to attract you, other than the anchorage at French Wells in the south (see our main account). This is accessible by boat only. There is no road between Landrail Point and French Wells.

SERVICES ON CROOKED ISLAND

Churches
Seventh Day Adventist Church in Landrail Point. Saturday service at 11 am.
Church of God Baptist in Cripple Hill. Sunday service at 11 am.
Clinic
There is a clinic at Landrail Point, but call Batelco if you have a medical emergency. They can get help for you.
Ferry
A government ferry runs between the southeast tip of Crooked Island and Lovely Bay on Acklins Island, 9 am to 4 pm. Trips cost $5.

ACCOMMODATIONS

Pittsdown Point Landings Tel: 242-344-2507 Rooms from $165. Full American plan $55 per day. This small resort, much dependent on its own airfield, is centered around a bar and restaurant in what is reputed to be the oldest stone building (of military origin) on the island. The detached, cottage-type, simple rooms, with their own verandas, face either one of the two beaches or the palm grove garden. Excellent homebaked bread and freshly caught seafood is their specialty; they are happy to cook your catch if you've had a successful day trolling the dropoff contour. Special dietary needs can be accommodated. Bonefishing available for $160 for a half day, $240 for a full day. Visa and MasterCard accepted.

Crooked Island Beach Inn Tel: 242-344-2321 Rooms from $50, no credit cards. Serves Bahamian meals on request.

THINGS TO DO ON CROOKED ISLAND

- Go to see French Wells. Maybe anchor there for two days or so and go gunkholing and fishing.
- Take your dinghy out to Bird Rock. If you have an interest in lighthouses, you'll be fascinated by *Bird Rock Lighthouse* (and saddened by its deterioration).
- Find someone to guide you across the lagoon to see ruins and the few old cannon at the *Marine Farm*, a onetime British fortification.

ACKLINS ISLAND

Acklins Island is, if anything, poorer than Crooked Island. It's hard to believe that until the cotton crops were wiped out by blight in the last century, large, working plantations covered this island. No longer heavily populated, Acklins has little to show for its former prosperity. The local tarpon and bonefishing is some of the best in the Bahamas, but there are few onshore facilities and the ones we list are throughout the island, rather than in the individual settlements.

The only places you can access Acklins is at Atwood Harbour in the north and anchoring off Jamaica Bay in the south. This gives you Chesters settlement for the first point of contact, and Salina for the second. Neither are in the front rank. The center of the island is Spring Point, which you can reach only by road, for the ocean side offers no viable anchorage and the bight side is accessible only by shoal-draft craft. Spring Point is a *Bahamasair* stop and offers most backup facilities, such as they are.

SERVICES IN SPRING POINT

Airport
Bahamasair flies to and from Nassau twice weekly.

Accommodations
Central Guest House at Mason's Bay
Tel: 344-3628 • VHF 16 "Central"   Contact Ethlyn Bain.

Nais Guest House at Spring Point
Tel: 344 3089 • VHF 16 "Nais Place." Four double rooms, call a month ahead for reservations. Contact Naomi Mackey, or call the Batelco office at Spring Point if you have problems getting in touch.

Bonefishing
Greys Point Bonefishing Inn at Pinefield Point   Tel: 1-800-99-FLATS
Joe Deleveaux   VHF 16 "Lovely Bay" or call Elijah Beneby at 344-3087 to pass a message.
Newton Williamson   Tel: 344-3210 • VHF "Holiday Inn"

Churches
Most settlements have Sunday morning gathering places. Services are mainly Baptist.

Clinics
Main Island Clinic at Spring Point   Tel: 344-3550   This is the Batelco number, but they will contact Dr. Kim during working hours. In an emergency or at weekends the number is transferred to his home phone. The clinic is open from 9 am to 5:30 pm, Monday to Friday.

Clinic at Mason's Bay   Tel: 344-3169, or 344-3628 after hours and on weekends. Nurse Ethlyn Bain is the nurse in charge.

Clinic at Chesters. This clinic is not staffed at the moment, but Dr. Kim visits twice a month.

Clinic at Salina Point, VHF 16 "Humming Bird." Contact is clinic aid Pandora Williams.

Med-Evac is handled through Spring Point Airport.

Contacts
These people can act as contacts in the various settlements:

Chesters	Edmund Johnson	344-3108
Hard Hill	Leonard Collie	344-3613
Lovely Bay	Elijah Beneby	344-3087
Mason Bay	Ethlyn Bain	344-3628 VHF 16 "Central"
Pinefield Point	Newton Williamson	344-3210 VHF 16 "Holiday Inn"
Delectable Bay	Leon Cooper	344-3543 VHF 16 "Highway Inn"
Salina Point	George Emmanuel	344-3671

Ferry
A government-owned ferry runs between Lovely Bay and Crooked Island from 9 am to 4 pm. Trips cost $5.

Fuel
Diesel and gasoline are available at the government dock. Call VHF 16 "Central", or contact Felix at Batelco at Spring Point. Fuel at the settlements has usually been trucked in.

Groceries
McKinney's Grocery and Meats in Spring Point   Tel: 344-3614
Open from 7 am to 9 pm, Monday to Saturday, and from 7 am to 10 am, and 2 pm to 9 pm on Sundays. Well stocked.

Edmund Johnson's General Store in Chesters   Tel: 344-3108
The only store in Chesters, no set opening hours.

Police
In Spring Point   Tel: 344-3666   Open 9–5:30, Monday to Friday. There is also a police office at the airport, same hours.

Post Office
Tel: 344-3169   In Mason's Bay, since a fire destroyed the main office in Spring Point.

Restaurants
Nais in Spring Point   Tel: 344-3089 • VHF 16 "Nais Place"   Call ahead for serving time and menu selection of Bahamian dishes. A bar, with satellite TV & pool table, has music most nights.

Bluebird Bar and Restaurant at Salina Point.   Serves drinks, can provide lunch and dinner. Reservations must be made.

Telephone
Batelco at Spring Point   Tel: 344-3550 and 344-3536 • VHF 16
Open from 9 am to 5 pm, Monday to Friday.

Water
In Spring Point. Contact Mr. Heastie in town, by the tamarind tree, on the corner of the main road and the road leading to Batelco. Or you can use the government well, near the beach.

THINGS TO DO ON ACKLINS ISLAND
- Go bonefishing.
- Visit the caves in Havel Hill. Contact Leonard Collie at 344-3613 to put you in touch with guides.

MAYAGUANA

As far as Yellow Page information is concerned, Mayaguana falls into the same category as the islands in the Crooked–Acklins–Long Cay archipelago. Mayaguana is large, 24 miles long by 6 miles wide, and as you pass along its coast it seems to go on forever. There are only two sensible access points, the first on the west coast where the small settlement of Betsy Bay offers a fair-weather anchorage and a new government dock, just two miles north of the settlement. The new dock is of no value to you unless you want to call in to take on fuel, which in most cases has to be achieved can by can because the surge tends to make coming alongside perilous. The other access point on Mayaguana is Abraham's Bay, which offers good anchorages behind its barrier reef, but no direct access to Abraham's Bay settlement, which lies a ten-minute walk inland from its public dock. Don't be misled by the apparent convenience of that dock. You can't get close to it other than in a dinghy, and at low water even that can be difficult. Getting around Mayaguana is difficult, too. There are no taxis or buses, so you'll have to hitch rides; it's too hot and too far to walk.

So what can Mayaguana do for you? Well, there are the Abraham's Bay anchorages, which are as close as you can get to all-weather anchorages (but not severe-weather havens). There is a clinic, Batelco, basic food stores, and a twice-weekly *Bahamasair* service to Nassau. There is fuel in drums if they have it in stock. So we'll cover the facilities briefly.

ABRAHAM'S BAY

The main settlement has a Batelco telephone, police, a clinic, two small stores, and two bar/restaurants. A dormant Customs and Immigration Office is there, in the Commissioners Building, and *if* the officers will fly from Inagua, they will clear you in. The Commissioner also has vested powers to act in their absence, and can clear boats in, as flying the officials in from Inagua is time consuming. It used to be done only for drug-running busts when an aircraft was impounded. Abraham's Bay airport is fifteen minutes away by car or truck.

BETSY BAY

This settlement lost its dock in a hurricane. There is a Batelco office and one store. The new government dock is two miles to the north and used by *Lady Mathilda*, the mail boat from Nassau. It is absolutely remote; there's nothing there but this one dock cut out of the coral and limestone.

THINGS TO DO IN MAYAGUANA

- Go fishing or snorkeling.
- Go fishing or snorkeling.
- Go fishing or snorkeling.
- Read a good book (or a bad one if you've run out of good ones).

GREAT INAGUA

Famous for its salt and flamingos, Great Inagua is one of the largest islands in the Bahamas. For the cruising visitor, it lies almost directly on the Windward Passage route between the Bahamas and the Caribbean. This said, no marina support facilities have ever been developed on the island. Great Inagua owes its prosperity and continuing settlement to the Morton Salt Company, which exports over a million tons of Great Inagua salt each year. Morton Salt has its own company houses, backup facilities, and dock here. Matthew Town is very much a satellite to this activity. In Matthew Town, which is a Port of Entry, you will find the normal facilities that are available at any Bahamian settlement, but no more than that. The commercial harbor was designed to accommodate the Royal Bahamas Defence Force and the United States Coast Guard, both based at Matthew Town Harbour. However, the USCG is there as a guest. The waters around the Inaguas are Bahamian territory, and distress calls must be directed to the RBDF.

Customs and Immigration
Open from 9 am to 5:30 pm, Monday to Friday.
Customs in Matthew Town
Tel: 339-1254, or 339-1605 at the airport.
Immigration in Matthew Town
Tel: 339-1234, or 339-1602 at the airport.
Immigration officials advise boats to call the Royal Bahamian Defence Force on VHF 16 to announce their arrival, and request entry. The RBDF monitors Channel 16 around the clock, and they will notify Customs and Immigration for you.

MATTHEW TOWN

Accommodations
Crystal Beach View Hotel Tel: 339-1550
North of town, with its own restaurant.
Morton Bahamas Ltd. "Main House" Tel: 339-1267 Six rooms from $55, four with a bathroom; reservations necessary.
Walkines Guest House Tel: 339-1612 Five double rooms from $50, in town, but call ahead for reservations.

Airport
Bahamasair Tel: 339-1415 Flights to Nassau.

Bank
Bank of the Bahamas Tel: 339-1264 Open 9 am to 2 pm on Monday, Tuesday, & Thursday; 10 am to 5:30 pm on Fridays. Closed Wednesdays.

Bicycles
Rentals through Mr. Bertram Ingrahams at one of his stores.

Churches
St. Philip's Anglican Church Built in 1885, it is the oldest church on the island.
Wesley Methodist Church
Zion Baptist Church
Greater Bethel Temple Mission Church

Commissioner's Office
Tel: 339-1271 Open from 9 am to 5:30 pm, Monday to Friday.

Fuel
Far East Enterprise Petroleum Tel: 339-1550 Contact Leon Turnquest about diesel or gasoline at the fuel shed in the harbor. Telephone rings at the *Crystal Beach View Hotel*.

Groceries
Inagua General Store Tel: 339-1460 Open from 9:30 am to 5:30 pm. This is a well-stocked and good-sized store.

Hospital
In Matthew Town   Tel: 339-1249   For emergencies out of hours, call 339-1226; clinics held 9–5:30 with Dr. Mukerjee & Nurse Patty Fox, who can be called at 339-1808 in emergency.

Library and Museum
Erickson's Public Library and Museum   Tel: 339-1683. Ask about opening hours.

Mail Boat
M/V Windward Express from Nassau.

Liquor Store
Ingrahams Liquor Store   Open from 8 am to 8 pm Monday to Saturday, after church on Sundays. This store is owned jointly with *Ingrahams Variety Store,* so check both if one is not open. The *Variety Store* carries food and household goods.

Photo Shop
Abby's Photo Shop   Tel: 339-1750   Film and developing.

Police
Emergency call 919 or Tel: 339-1263
In Matthew Town   Tel: 339-1444
At the Airport   Tel: 339-1604

Post Office
Tel: 339-1248   Open 9 am to 5:30 pm, Monday to Friday.

Repairs
In an emergency, the *Morton Salt Company* might be able to help from its machine shop. Call 339-1300 or 339-1849. You could also try them if you need propane.

Restaurants
Cozy Corner Restaurant and Bar   Tel: 339-1440   Opens at 10 am Monday to Saturday, and 1:30 pm on Sundays. Bahamian food, snacks, pool table, satellite TV, weekend DJ.

Topp's Restaurant and Bar   Tel: 339-1465 • VHF 16   Open from 9 am to 10 pm Monday to Saturday, and from 6 pm to 10 pm on Sundays. Bahamian dishes and fantastic cracked conch. Call ahead for reservations and to check menu availability.

Snake Pit Bar   Open from 10 am Monday to Saturday, and from 2 pm on Sundays. Weekend music, large, local crowd. Snacks.

Telephone
Batelco   Tel: 339-1000, 339-1007 or fax 339-1323   Office open 9 am to 5:30 pm, Monday to Friday, with phone cards for sale.

Tours
Great Inagua Tours   Tel: 339-1862   Larry Ingraham organizes tours to the *Inagua National Park*, where huge numbers of flamingos and many types of birds can be seen, as well as donkeys and ducks, and maybe even wild boar. He can also arrange Cave Tours, which take about three hours.

INAGUA NATIONAL PARK

The Bahamas National Trust, with help from the Audubon Society, maintains the *Inagua National Park*. It is home to more than 60,000 flamingos, the largest nesting colony of West Indian Flamingos in the western hemisphere, as well as many other birds such as roseate spoonbills, rare reddish egrets, hummingbirds, blue herons, tree ducks and Bahamian parrots. You can also visit the *Caves*, the *Bonsai Forest*, and the inland *Blue Hole*. The road leading to the park is open to the public but you will need a guide. Henry Nixon is a contact for tours once you get there.

THINGS TO DO IN GREAT INAGUA

- Go and see the massive salt piles awaiting further action. These huge crystalline mountains look like snow.
- Take a bicycle ride down to the lighthouse, which became necessary after 65 boats met their final destination on the reef in one year, 1859.
- Dive the *Great Inagua Wall*, north of Matthew Town, at the edge of the Great Bahama Wall. This pure sand dropoff is marked by giant coral heads tumbling toward a vast abyss.
- Take a tour through the *Inagua National Park.*
- Walk down to *Kiwanis Park* in Matthew Town on a Saturday morning to share freshly cooked meals, with money going to local charities.

Chapter 18
The Unexplored Bahamas
South Andros
The Jumentos Cays

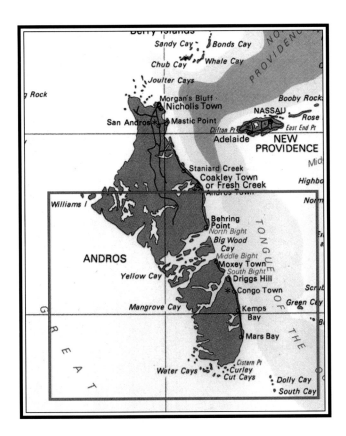

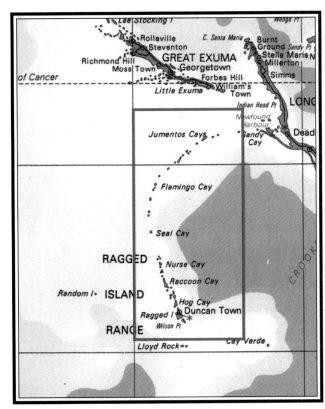

South Andros

TAKE an airline flight from Miami to George Town in the Exumas and look down all the way once you've crossed the Gulf Stream. The almost unbelievable maze of shallows, deeper-water channels, tidal inlets, coral heads, shoals, mangrove swamp, and land is the area we're talking about. South Andros. The land itself is almost totally devoid of settlement, for the most part tangled low-growth forest, scrub, sink holes, and shallow ponds. But winding through all this confusion there are channels that can offer you transits across Andros, and ways in which you can probe your way up and down, and part way inland, along both the west and the east coast.

Somehow we don't think we're likely to add this area to this Guide. But it's there, if you want to try it.

The Jumentos Cays

THE Jumentos Cays are the great 50-nm arc of cays that start just north of the Ragged Island range in Latitude 22° 30' N, and swing northeast toward Long Island, to end some 18 nm south of Little Exuma. They are bordered on the east by a pocket of deep water north of the Columbus Bank, and on the west by the southeast edge of the Great Bahama Bank. The Jumentos are an area for real exploration, shelling, fishing, and diving that remain largely untouched, although we've heard that the fishing there has been hard hit in recent years, given the mobility of a Bahamian skiff with an outboard.

Largely unvisited, except by fishermen, you are on your own there. There are no backups. Take note of your weather before you set out, and watch the sky while you're there.

Part VI

—

Reference Sections

Blue Pages:
Navigation, Seamanship, and Preparation

Green Pages:
History, Wildlife, and Fishing and Diving

Buff Pages:
Infrastructure and Government

Appendices

Reference Sections
Table of Contents

Chapter 19
Blue Pages
Navigation, Seamanship, and Preparation

Man-O-War schooner William H. Albury, *built 1963.*

The Ideal Boat for the Bahamas

WHAT are the qualities that go to make up the ideal boat for the Bahamas? For a start, the ability to cross the Gulf Stream safely, even if the weather turns against you. You'll want a draft that will take you safely over the Banks and into the anchorages and harbors. You need the endurance to take you from fueling point to refueling point, and the water-tank capacity to match your endurance. It goes without saying that you need a boat that's seaworthy, in prime condition, and well equipped. Nothing, you hope, will go wrong; but you need a measure of self-reliance. You'll want a reasonable stock of spares, and the tools to carry out your basic servicing.

Turn to the comfort side. Ventilation and shade from the sun come high on your list, particularly if you've not got air conditioning. Hopefully you'll have the capacity to accommodate everyone comfortably, for overcrowding and hot climates don't go well together. A swim platform is a plus, as is a dinghy you can use to get ashore, get provisions, and go gunkholing.

The boats that meet these parameters form a long list, covering both sail and power. We've cruised in the Islands happily in a sail catamaran that was just 22 feet on the waterline, to take the bottom of the scale, and in a 49-foot motor yacht with three double cabins with bathrooms (there's no other way to describe them) and every appliance you could find in a house, which is heading toward the top end. Did they have anything in common? Let's check the list:

- seaworthiness
- sound engines
- tankage to carry sufficient reserves of fuel and water
- draft under 6 feet (though you can get by with an 8-foot draft)
- good navigational equipment
- VHF radio, and, of course
- full safety equipment above the basic US Coast Guard requirements

One time when we were in West End someone was towed in by a Bahamian fishing boat shortly after dawn. The weather had been unsettled and the Gulf Stream had not quieted down, but it was by no means rough out there.

The boat being towed in was a 17-foot center-console open boat with just one man on board. He had set out from Palm Beach the evening before for a week in the Abacos. He'd run out of fuel during the night, was being thrown around a bit by the seas out there, and fired off the only two flares he had. He was lucky. A Coast Guard helicopter passing to the south saw the flares, and radioed West End to get help to him.

Despite his timely rescue, he wasn't altogether happy when his rescuer charged him $3,000 for the ride. Asked why he hadn't got enough fuel to cross the Stream, the reply was simple: "I didn't think it was that far."

Is there an ideal boat for the Bahamas? It's the boat that will take you safely there and back, and let you have all the fun you want while you're there. The rest (even the hull color!) is up to you.

Putting out to Sea

- Check diesel, outboard fuel, reserve oil and lubricants, water
- Check engine oil levels, coolant, hoses, belts, bilges
- Check navigation lights, spotlight, deck lights, all interior lights
- Check man overboard (MOB) equipment, flares and smoke signals, EPIRB, life raft, and survival equipment
- Check that dinghy and outboard are OK, scuba tanks filled, fishing rods and fishing gear on board

Complete Navigation Work

- Waypoints
- Courses, times, and distances—alternatives if bad weather
- Lights listed and tides known
- Weather forecast checked
- Set watch and ship's clock to USN Observatory time (call 900-410-8463)
- Set barometer
- Complete provisioning; list stores and spare parts
- Entertainment: videos, CDs, cassettes, and books
- Q flag and Bahamas courtesy flag
- Check that ship's papers are complete: documentation or State registration, FCC licence; insurance, passports, money
- Check that crew passports or proofs of citizenship are set for entry into the Bahamas; open log and list crew
- Complete float plan and leave with a relative or friend

- Prepare first day/night-on-passage food
- Stow for rough weather and clear decks. Secure open ports and hatches
- Garbage ashore
- Obtain marina or (if necessary) port authority departure clearances
- Turn on radios and navigation instruments
- Take a head count before sailing
- Hold a new crew safety briefing, including MOB drill, use of VHF, and abandoning ship

Float Plan

The person in whose hands this float plan is left is to keep it handy until *you* telephone and report your safe arrival. You should set a "fail safe" time, and if he or she has not heard from you by then, they are to call the US Coast Guard and report that you are missing at sea.

Coming into Port

- Have approach chart, coastal pilot, harbor chart on hand. Know location of reporting dock
- Check on any special timings: bridges or the like
- Know the state of tide and tidal stream, and the local wind pattern
- List navigation aids in order of likely utility: lights, marks, bottom contours and depths
- Have VHF, binoculars, hand bearing compass, loud hailer, and air horn on hand
- Have Q flag if it's your Port of Entry, courtesy flag ready to fly after clearance
- Prepare anchor, fenders, and lines
- Keep navigation instruments on until log data is recorded
- Arrival clearance if it's your Port of Entry—did you leave a float plan? If so, call and report your safe arrival.

After clearance

- Write up log
- Check bilges and engines
- Garbage ashore
- Fill water and fuel tanks
- Wash down decks
- Washing and laundry?

Clearing in to the US

Immediately on arrival the Captain must call US Customs at 800-432-1216 or 800-973-2867. No one should leave the boat until after US Customs clearance has been given.

Fly your Q flag, and keep it flying until you have clearance. Be prepared with the information listed below at hand.

Float Plan

Boat Name and Port _____

Year, Type, and Model _____

Radios _____ **Callsign** _____

LOA _____ **Color** _____

Registration # _____ **Flag (if not US)** _____

Engines _____ **Other Means of Propulsion** _____

Port and Date of Departure _____

Destination and Estimated Date and Time of Arrival _____

_____

Route Planned _____

_____

Persons on Board with addresses (note if young children) _____

_____

_____

_____ (continue list as necessary)

Safety Equipment (list flares, smoke, strobes, EPIRB (and type), life raft, dinghy)

_____

_____

_____ (continue list as necessary)

If a 406 MHz EPIRB   Model _____

         Category _____

         Unique Identifier # _____

Your name, Home Address, and Telephone Number

_____

_____

_____

Signature _____ **Date** _____

You may not be asked for anything more than the vessel name and registration number, and your US Customs decal number (if you have one), together with your port of departure. However in the event of a more detailed check on a US registered boat, you may be asked for more positive identification to prove that it is your vessel, and prove your own identity.

Details of the Vessel:
- Boat type, model, year
- US documentation number or state registration number with state decal number
- Registered name of vessel and the declared home port
- Your FCC callsign
- Your hull identification number
- LOA, LWL, beam, draft [for comparison with your registration]
- Your US Customs decal number [if you have one]

Details of the Owner/Captain:
- Nationality, passport number, date and place of issue
- Social security number (if a US citizen)

Details of the Crew:
- Total number and nationality
- Full names, dates of birth, social security numbers (US citizens), and passport details (US visas if applicable)

Passage Details:
- Date sailed from your US departure port
- Ports of call
- Last port of call before returning to the US

Firearms:
- Any firearms on board?
- Detailed list of ammunition on board

CLEARANCE NUMBER
When you have been given your clearance number, record it in your ship log. Everyone is now free to go ashore.
Welcome Back to the United States!

Bahamian Boating Regulations

POWER BOATS
- It is illegal to drive a power boat within 200 feet of the shore of every Bahamian island unless you are approaching or leaving a dock or marina.
- Within this 200-foot coastal zone speed is limited to 3 knots.
- It is illegal to drive a boat in a reckless manner, or while under the influence of alcohol or drugs.
- No one under 16 years of age may drive a boat with an engine greater than 10 hp, although 14- and 15-year olds may if they are under the supervision of someone over 16 years of age.

WATER SKIING
- Water skiing is forbidden within the 200-foot coastal zone, unless it is taking place in a lane clearly marked with buoys and lines.
- Water skiers are required to use flotation jackets.
- A lookout, in addition to the driver, is required in the tow boat. The lookout must be 16 years of age or older.
- Water skiing is forbidden at night.

Anchoring in the Bahamas
Ground Tackle
We all dream of idyllic, calm, isolated, and uncrowded anchorages. You'll find some in the Bahamas. But you don't win perfection all the time. Your Bahamian anchorage may well turn out to be swept by reversing tidal currents, open to squalls, or already crowded with other boats by the time you get there. We reckon you need to carry three anchors cruising in the Bahamas:

1. A plow type for rock and sea grass
2. A Danforth type for sand and mud
3. Maybe a second plow as a storm and reserve anchor

Fit your anchor to your boat length, and go oversize if in doubt. Go one anchor size heavier if you anticipate heavy weather, or your planned passage is going to take you to more open anchorages.

With a nylon rode we always have 50 feet of chain to prevent anchor rode abrasion and to get the optimum catenary curve so that the direct pull on the anchor is flattened to near-horizontal at the shank. In the Bahamas you can get by with 15–20 feet of chain, but don't go below that. Experienced skippers, especially those on larger and heavier boats, use an all-chain rode, and of course have the windlass for retrieving it. You should know the *safe working load* and the *breaking point* of your ground tackle.

Pull in Pounds:
Boat Length x Wind Velocity

LOA	Wind Speed (knots)			
(feet)	15	30	40	60
25	125	490	980	1960
30	175	700	1400	2800
35	225	900	1800	3600
40	300	1200	2400	4800
50	400	1600	3200	6400
60	500	2000	4000	8000

BAHAMIAN MOOR

The Bahamian Moor is designed to keep you secure against the reversal of a tidal stream and prevent you swinging into your neighbors in a crowded anchorage.

Set your first anchor upstream, motoring into the current, and then let the stream take you back (or motor back if the wind is blowing you off) to set your second anchor downstream from the first, ideally 180° apart. You can settle for a 90° separation if sea room is limited.

Once you have set the second anchor, pull yourself back on the first rode to get your desired scope on each rode and then make fast. Some skippers find it easier to set the first anchor normally, and then use their dinghy to take out and place the second anchor. You can add a third anchor, which will further reduce your radius of swing.

TIDAL RISE AND FALL

Work on a tidal rise and fall of 3 feet and you'll be about right. Remember you will get your highest tides with a full moon. If you have tide tables, check them.

SCOPE

Scope (the length of anchor rode you put out measured from the entry point of the rode into the water to the anchor) helps determine how well your anchor will hold under most conditions. Generally the greater the scope, the better. With an all-chain rode 3:1 (that's 3 feet of anchor chain for every foot of depth at high tide) may well be sufficient in sheltered water. With nylon and chain 5:1 scope is good. 7:1 is even better.

Both tidal current and crowding in an anchorage may dictate that you should use a Bahamian Moor and lie to two anchors, in which case you'll be unlikely to achieve anything like a 7:1 scope.

Anchoring: Depth and Scope

depth	3:1	4:1	5:1	6:1	7:1	8:1
15 ft	45	60	75	90	105	120
20 ft	60	80	100	120	140	160
25 ft	75	100	125	150	175	200
30 ft	90	120	150	180	210	240

Anchoring Advice: Local Wisdom, and Commonsense

- *Never* anchor in coral. You'll kill the reef.
- If other boats are already in your chosen anchorage, try to stand off as far from everyone else as possible. This isn't just for safety. They might not share your taste in music, or enjoy the shouts and screams during your midnight swims.

- If the shore is covered in vegetation, scrub, or mangroves, you'll be wise to anchor well out of insect range. Getting too close can spoil your night.
- Be prepared for 180° and 360° swings, and strong tidal flows, which are not uncommon in Bahamian anchorages. Do you need two anchors out? Don't wait until there's a crisis to decide you *did* need that second anchor.
- Always dive to check that your anchors have set, or check them using a dive mask or a glass-bottom bucket from your dinghy. Sometimes, if the bottom is hard-packed sand or rocky, you may have to dive and set an anchor by hand.
- Continue this checking daily, look at your anchors and the free run of your anchor rodes to ensure that all is OK, and that your two rodes (assuming you are lying to two anchors) are not twisted together, which could give you a nightmare situation if you wanted to get up and go in a hurry.
- Don't run your generator after sunset unless you're alone, or have a super-quiet generator. Sound carries at night. And it's antisocial to run your generator during the "cocktail hour" (unless it really is sound-proofed) for you'll spoil the magic of that special time of day for everyone else.
- Always set an anchor light. Your light warns latecomers to stay away from you. However remote you may be, however unlikely it is that another cruising boat will join you. In high-traffic areas you'll soon discover that local Bahamian boats go about their business at all hours of the night, often at high speed. We reckon the conventional mast head light is just too high to warn off someone racing along at sea level, who may have had one Goombay Smash too many. Consider mounting an anchor light not much more than 10 feet above the water, and see how that looks to you. It could be just the most sensible precaution you ever took.
- Take anchor bearings or your GPS fix and keep them displayed at your helm station so that you can check that you've not dragged. If the risk is high, make out a roster and keep checking throughout the night. Set an anchor alarm if you have one.

SEVERE STORM CONDITIONS

If you're unlucky and have to weather a severe storm at anchor, avoid exposed harbors and crowded anchorages. Try to find a hurricane hole, something like a channel in mangroves where you can secure lines to the mangroves. Use every line you have, making a spider web of lines allowing 10 feet of slack for tidal surge, and use all your anchors fanned out at 90°–120° to complement your spider's web.

Use chafe protectors on your lines where they come on board. Reduce your windage. Take down your canvas, your sails if you are a sailboat, your flybridge canvas and curtains if you are a power boat, lower your antennas, remove your davits if they are removable, and deflate and store your inflatable below deck. Lash down everything that must remain on deck. Make the hull watertight. You might even consider plugging your engine and generator exhaust ports: but don't forget that you have done this!

If you can't find a hurricane hole (and there are very few places that are ideal) you can anchor out to face the wind, setting three anchors in a 120° fan. Ideally lead the three rodes to a swivel, and then run line from the swivel to the boat. Try for a 10:1 scope. If you use all chain, put a nylon snubber (equal to 10 percent of the chain length) in the chain to absorb shock.

All of this is "last ditch" defensive measures in very severe conditions. You should never have to experience anything like this, and if you are caught out when hurricane or near-hurricane conditions are imminent, your boat is of secondary importance to your life and the lives of those with you. Your action should be to secure the boat if you can do so, but find a better place to take shelter ashore and leave the boat to take what comes.

How to prevent this kind of crisis situation? *Just listen to daily weather forecasts!*

Bahamas Tides and Currents

Tide is the vertical movement of water, while current is the horizontal movement of water. Both tides and currents will affect you in the Bahamas. As skipper and navigator, it's up to you to be aware of the state of the tide, particularly when entering and leaving harbors and negotiating passages. Even an inch can make the difference between being afloat and aground, but we try not to play it so close. If your boat draws more than 4.5–5 feet, you'll need to pay a lot of attention to tides in the Bahamas.

Now the Schoolwork

Bahamas tides are what's known as semi-diurnal, which means two high tides and two low tides in 24 hours, in other words two tides a day, with about six hours from high to low and low to high. You can easily chart the tide without a tide table. Just remember that at full moon and at new moon, high tide comes at 0800 and 2000 local time, and high tides then occur roughly an hour later each day, and use the Rule of Twelfths (see **Conversion Tables and Useful Measurements** on page 340) to plot the rise and fall.

The mean tidal range in the Bahamas is 2.6 feet. When the moon is full or new the range increases to around 3.1 feet. At the lowest range, the *neap* tides, which occur at the first and third quarters of the moon, you get your lowest levels, about six inches below the mean tidal range.

The time of high and low tides throughout the Bahamas varies only 40 minutes or less, except for the west coast of Eleuthera and the Banks side of the Grand Lucayan Waterway on Grand Bahama, both of which are about 2.5 hours behind Nassau. All Bahamian tides are based on Nassau. High winds can have a significant impact on tides, particularly in the Bahamas, sweeping water up much higher than normal in enclosed areas or, conversely, blowing away the water to produce what will appear to be much lower tides than normal.

If you tried to produce a "Tidal Atlas of the Bahamas," you might go insane. Perhaps that's why no one has done so. The Banks shed their water in every direction, and draw in ocean water from every direction when the flow reverses. How does this work? While this is a far from scientific explanation, here's a simplified view. Imagine the bank as a great shallow plate with an uneven rim, surrounded by ocean. The high bits of the rim are the islands. On a rising tide, ocean water rises up on to the bank over all the low bits of the rim and flows in trying to fill the plate from all directions. On a falling tide the plate sheds its water in all directions.

Figuring it out on the Banks

You can understand why that tidal atlas could be difficult to draw. When you're on the banks, what you need to know is where the nearest low part of that plate rim is, and of course where the "center" of the plate lies. A line between the two gives you an idea of the current you can expect, in one direction or the other depending on the state of the tide. In some places you'll find that the current is surprisingly strong and can take you well off course. If you make use of the XTE capability of your GPS you will see it, can correct it, and you'll have no problems.

What Else Should You Know?

Be aware that reef passages and cuts between the islands and cays can produce rip tides that will run from 2.5 to 4 knots, and can occasionally reach 6 knots in places. If the wind is against this current, this can produce a narrow mill race of water you're better off avoiding. Heavy offshore swells can compound the problem and produce the very dangerous seas known as a "Rage" (see page 66), which makes reef passages out into the ocean, like Whale Cay Passage in the Abacos, impassable. Make your transits through restricted waters and choke points only when wind and current are right.

Be cautious approaching an unfamiliar anchorage or harbor, and check the depth it carries and the state of tide before you commit yourself to an approach channel. If you are in doubt when you arrive, use your VHF and ask for local guidance. But if you're off the beaten track on your own, that's where eyeball navigation becomes vital. The best procedure, when you get in close, is to anchor where you're safe and then do your surveying in your dinghy.

Tide Tables

We've not published tide tables in this Guide because two years of coverage would take too much space and the information is readily at hand elsewhere. Tide tables covering the Bahamas are printed in *Reed's Nautical Almanac*, in *The Cruising Guide to Abaco* by Steve Dodge, and often reproduced privately. If you have a laptop computer, Nautical Software's *Tides and Currents* will serve you well. But at the end of the day, even with all this information, you still have to work it out on your own. Just remember why that tidal atlas was never written!

VHF Radio in the Bahamas

We've all been well trained and pay strict attention to the international rules governing the use of VHF radio. We use Channel 16 for distress and calling (and Channel 9 now, in the USA, for recreational boat calling). We keep a listening watch on Channel 16 the whole time we're at sea. When we make contact with someone on 16, we switch to a designated working channel immediately. On any channel we're conscious that other people are also out there, somewhere within range, and they too may want to use the radio. We keep our conversations brief, to the point, we don't use marine VHF radio as a telephone, and we never use VHF radios on land.

All this goes out of the window in the Bahamas. Bahamians, especially in the Out Islands, use VHF radios like party-line telephones, and take their pick of the channels in the recreational boating frequencies. Almost every house, certainly everyone in business in the Out Islands, makes use of VHF as a primary means of communication. You don't just stop at arranging a berth in a marina over the radio. You check menus at a restaurant, book a table, find a taxi to pick you up, ask for someone to do your laundry, or repair

your outboard. Even Channel 16 is no longer sacred and carries far more traffic than it should. Is any of this legal? Don't let the answer to this question disturb you, because that's the way it is in the Bahamas. Yes, there is cellular telephone service there, just as there is Batelco's (the Bahamas Telecommunications Company) conventional telephone service. But VHF radio is cheaper than paying Batelco bills.

Newcomers soon learn that in the main centers where visiting yachts concentrate (like Marsh Harbour and George Town) VHF radio has become something as close to stateside home commercial radio as you can get. The net comes to life sometime after dawn with morning news and weather updates, advertisements for future events and social get-togethers, offers of service from marine mechanics and the like, and from then on serves as a lifeline as vital as a chat show for the lonely and the compulsive talkers. Ride along with it. It can be useful. If you can't stand it, turn your radio off.

VHF Radio

['A' channels US waters only]

Distress and calling	16
Intership safety	06
Navigational (bridges & locks)	13
USCG	22A
VHF radio telephone stations	24-25-26-27-28
Ship-to-shore 26 & 28 primary	84-85-86-87-88
Recreational boats, ship-to-ship and ship-to-shore	68-69 & 71 & 78A
Recreational boats, general calling, ship to marinas	09
Ch. 9 is now used for bridges on the ICWE	
Recreational boats, ship to ship	72
Weather (receive only)	WX 1-2-3
Environmental (receive only)	15
Weather, sea conditions, notices to mariners	

Distress Calls

Even in the Bahamas Channel 16 is still the distress call frequency. We show the form a distress call should take for those not familiar with it. The codeword MAYDAY is the international alert signal of a life-threatening situation at sea. **After a MAYDAY message is broadcast Channel 16 must be kept free of all traffic, other than those directly involved in the rescue situation, until the rescue has been completed.** If you hear a Mayday message, if no one else is responding, it is **your** duty to step in to answer the call, relay it to BASRA (the Bahamas Air Sea Rescue Association) or any other agency, and get to the scene to help.

Remember a Mayday distress call can only be used when life is threatened. If you have run on the rocks but no one is going to lose their life, however grave the damage to your boat, that is not a Mayday situation.

Distress Call

Hello All Ships. MAYDAY! MAYDAY! MAYDAY!

This is [give your Vessel Name and Callsign].

Our position is [read it off the GPS, or give it as something like '2 miles SW of Royal Island.' Your rescuers **must** be able to find you!].

We are [then say what's happening: on fire? have hit a reef and are sinking?].

We have [say how many people there are on board].

At this time we are [say what you're doing about the crisis: abandoning ship?]

For identification we are [say what your boat is: type, length, color, so that your rescuers can identify you at a distance more easily].

We have [say what safety equipment you have on board: flares? smoke? ocean dye markers? an EPIRB?]

We will keep watch on Channel 16 as long as we can.

This is [repeat your vessel Name and Callsign]. *MAYDAY! MAYDAY! MAYDAY!*

Wait for an answer. If no one responds, keep repeating your distress call until you receive an answer.

Weather Broadcasts and VHF

In the Bahamas (apart from Grand Bahama and the Biminis) you are out of range of the US NOAA weather broadcasts. You may be able to access the Weather Channel on a dockside TV hookup or through a satellite antenna. Your principal sources of weather information will be Radio Bahamas (the ZNS stations), the broadcasts of the offshore stations of the High Seas Radio-Telephone Service, weather facsimile broadcasts, and a number of other miscellaneous sources. If you're unable to receive SSB broadcasts or do not have access to most of the sources we list, generally you'll always find someone on shore or another cruising boat willing to share weather information with you. For external (that is non-Bahamian) sources of weather information, such as SSB broadcasts and weatherfax, see **Appendix B**, pages 338–339.

Radio Bahamas

ZNS-1	Principal radio station (Nassau and South East Bahamas)	1540.0 kHz 107.1 MHz 107.9 MHz	24 hours
ZNS-FM	Contemporary music & sports	104.5 MHz	24 hours
ZNS-2	Religious & educational	1240.0 kHz	0600–2359
ZNS-3	Northern Bahamas (Grand Bahama, The Abacos, Berry Islands, and Biminis)	810.0 kHz	

Weather Broadcasts

The first weather reports of the day are at 0615 and 0645 on ZNS-1 and at 0700 on ZNS-3. Brief weather reports are normally scheduled either before or after the news at 1200 and 1800. The 0645 ZNS-1 broadcast is the best and often gives a three-day forecast, but be warned: the timings of the morning weather reports may slip from day to day, may occasionally be missed, and Sundays are always a blank. At times of intense interest in the weather, particularly if a tropical storm or a hurricane is threatening the Islands, full weather reports and warnings are virtually continuous.

WEATHER BY VHF RADIO

ABACOS—MARSH HARBOUR		
VHF 68	0815	Abaco Cruisers Net
EXUMAS		
Northern—Highborne Cay		
VHF 06	0730	*Weewatin* (Alison Albury) reports
Central—Over Yonder Cay		
VHF 12	0800	*Blue Yonder* (June Rosen) reports
Southern—George Town		
VHF 68	0800	George Town Cruisers Net
NASSAU AND NEW PROVIDENCE ISLAND		
VHF 72	0715	*Ranger* (Nick Wardle) reports
VHF 27	0800	C6N. Nassau Marine Operator (even hours on request)

A Pilot House Booklist

In addition to your charts, your shipboard library should contain the "standard" works most of us carry on a cruise:

- Manuals for all your equipment on board
- NOAA Chart No 1. Nautical Chart Symbols and Abbreviations
- *Reed's Nautical Almanac, North American East Coast Edition* edited by Catherine Degnon
- *Reed's Nautical Companion*
- Navigation Rules
- *Chapman Piloting, Seamanship & Small Boat Handling* by Elbert S. Maloney
- *Chapman Emergencies at Sea*

A cruising guide of this scope cannot, unless it is to run into more than one volume, cover the inshore waters in exhaustive detail, and we recommend that you carry in addition one of the excellent special-to-area guides now on the market. Under this heading we would list:

The Cruising Guide to Abaco by Steve Dodge.
The Exuma Guide by Stephen Pavlidis.
The Explorer Chartbook Exumas by Monty Lewis.

You might care to add, depending on your mechanical skills and knowledge, Miner Brotherton's *12V Bible for Boats* (International Marine, ISBN 0-915160-81-1), and Nigel Calder's excellent *Boatowner's Mechanical & Electrical Handbook* (International Marine, ISBN 0-07-009618X).

If your pharmacy didn't steer you to the right First Aid manuals, what about Dr. Paul Gill's *On-Board Midical Handbook* (International Marine, ISBN 0-07-024274-7) and, if you dive, *The DAN Emergency Handbook* (Aqua Quest, ISBN 0-9590306-1). If you are cruising into remote areas you might consider adding David Werner's *Where There Is No Doctor: A Village Health Care Handbook* to your bookshelf (The Hesperian Foundation). It is normally stocked by the larger maritime booksellers and marine stores such as West Marine.

Batelco Towers

Visual navigation in the Bahamas and identifying your landfall after a passage is not always easy, simply because the islands are relatively featureless and low lying. Cat Island is the only place in the Bahamas where the elevation of the land rises above 200 feet. Taking the 23 largest islands or island groups, Cat alone hits that 200 foot mark. Just three islands top 150 feet. Thirteen islands rise above 100 feet, but are less than 150 feet in height. The five remaining islands in our list of the 23 largest have elevations between 50 and 100 feet.

Your problems are eased considerably by the Bahamas Telecommunications Company. Batelco's radio towers are, more often than not, the greatest boon to your visual navigation, for where there is a tower, there is surely a settlement near it.

For a complete list of these towers, see **Appendix B** on page 338. Batelco, in providing us with this information, have made the point that they are not responsible for the accuracy of the positions given. We have not thought it necessary to take a hand-held GPS to double-check each one.

Day-to-Day Living in the Bahamas

In the Bahamas you can buy almost anything you can buy in the US. If it's not there, in stock, someone will order it for you. If you want, you can get it within 24 hours. But there is a *but* in all this. It will cost you. It will cost you more than you would pay in the states, both for what you buy off the

shelf in the islands, and whatever you might order specially.

Your special order import is going to be particularly expensive, for it can carry 6 percent import duty as well as freight and handling charges. Spare parts imported for installation on a foreign boat with a valid Bahamian cruising permit are supposed to be duty free (although we've been charged for them, as have others we've known). Perhaps much depends on your Customs Officer. See the **Buff Pages** on page 327 for the way in which to handle the importation of marine spares.

Other than fish, conch, and lobster tails, chicken, eggs, bread, beer, rum, soft drinks, Bahamian "spring" water, and a seasonal but slender stock of locally grown fruits and vegetables, the Bahamas produces almost nothing you require for your day-to-day living. Almost everything the Bahamians themselves need to sustain their daily lives has to be imported. Hardly surprisingly it carries prices way above stateside supermarket prices. Marine spares are high priced, and marine fuel is high priced.

The knock-on effect generally means that the cost of living in the Bahamas is high. Meals in a restaurant cost more than you would pay at home (with rare exceptions), the price of accommodations (if you need shoreside accommodations) is high in the winter season, taxis charge the earth for a short ride from an airport to a ferry dock, and refueling a power boat will make you wish your tanks had been larger at the start.

Above all this, fresh water is desperately scarce. In many places the water table has been so reduced by demand that salt water has permeated into the aquifers and turned all well water forever brackish. Islands rely on rain (each house having its own cistern), water brought in on a barge, or desalination. Water is expensive.

Before you set out for the Bahamas, the first and obvious conclusion is to take everything you can, leave with full fuel and water tanks, and take extra fuel if that is possible. In practice we're all limited by what we can take on board. There's another consideration which may not weigh much with you initially, but you become conscious of it in the islands. The Bahamians, in comparison to their visitors, have nothing. Tourists (and this includes cruising yachtsmen) underpin the Bahamian economy. If you never buy anything in the islands, you leave resentment in your wake. Buy some things there, put some money into their economy, for you are using their waters, their beaches, and their islands for your enjoyment. The price of a cruising permit is an entry ticket, not a pass for a free ride.

Locker and freezer space, and the length of your cruise, will dictate what you stow on board, but in drawing up your provisioning list, leave some things for that local store. Bahamas bread is delicious, fresh baked each day and free of artificial preservatives. The rum and the beer are good. Fresh produce is always worth getting. You pay the prices Bahamians pay themselves, and you'll get to know them as you do your marketing. Isn't that what cruising is all about?

MAJOR PROVISIONING STOPS

Freeport, Grand Bahama
Marsh Harbour, Abacos
Nassau, New Providence
Spanish Wells
George Town, Exumas

SOME PROVISIONS AVAILABLE

Alice Town, Biminis
Green Turtle Cay, Abacos
Man-O-War Cay, Abacos
Hope Town, Abacos
Highbourne Cay, Exumas
Sampson Cay, Exumas
Staniel Cay, Exumas
Cockburn Town, San Salvador
Fresh Creek, Andros

Priorities

The priority is to leave for the Bahamas with your fuel tanks and water tanks full, but there's nothing new in this. It's our standard drill, wherever we are, wherever we go. Let's turn to the broader field of general provisioning. A check list that you may find useful is on page 341, but it's still worthwhile running over the basic considerations you should have in mind before setting out for the Bahamas.

A reasonable quantity of oil and lubricants should go with you. Boat spares are vital, for quite apart from expense, a local dealer may not have them in stock, or you may be miles away from civilization when something breaks down. Bulbs, fuses, belts, impellers, filters, spare pumps, spark plugs, injectors, gaskets, and distilled water for your batteries. Go through your lists and ensure that you have a reasonable self-sufficiency, particularly in the line that everyone hopes will never malfunction, your marine sanitation system.

What then of foodstuffs? If you have a deep freeze, take ground beef, steaks, chicken breasts, chicken thighs, and the like. Don't take frozen seafood. You can buy it there, frozen if you wish, or fresh. But why not get a Fishing Permit and catch it yourself? Take frozen vegetables. Stock your refrigerator with a start-out quantity of eggs, cheeses, butter, margarine, fresh vegetables, and salad. Take as much fresh fruit as will last, for that can be hard to come by in the islands.

Some canned food is worth taking, like tuna, mushrooms, corned beef, beans, and maybe soups. Dry goods like rice, flour, pastas, and sugar make sense, and so do sauces and mustards, mayonnaise, salad dressings, spices, dried herbs, and cooking oils. Take tea and coffee, mixers for drinks, and all alcoholic beverages except beer and rum. If you're going to run short in the alcoholic drink line, the local prices are not exorbitant. Bottled water is not essential. You can buy it, and its bulk counts out taking any useful quantity.

The only other goods we would place on the priority list is drugstore stuff. Your own medication, if nothing else. Sunscreens, aftersun lotion, insect repellent, and the like. Even your own brand of toothpaste. It's easier to take your own stock. And while you're in the pharmacy don't forget to check your medical pack and build it up so that you have everything you might need for the length of your cruise, and a good book on first aid.

What Else Could You Take?

Otherwise what remains? The list of what you could take would be almost endless. Dry goods like paper towels, toilet paper, Kleenex, cleaners, and garbage sacks all come into it. Lemon Joy is popular for dishwashing because it lathers in salt water.

Perhaps if you are going cruising for the first time, the best answer is to walk round your house with a legal pad noting everything you need. For some time before your departure start recording the date you take a new bar of soap or tube of toothpaste into use. How long does a pack of five razor blades last? What about shampoo? Like Lemon Joy, Head & Shoulders lathers in salt water. But watch the quantities as you push your cart around the supermarket. It's so easy to overstock.

Just remember you can get everything you are likely to need in all the major centers of population, but if you're going off into the Out Islands, your provisioning at once takes on a different aspect. Then you should handle it rather as you would handle stocking up for a bluewater passage.

What Could You Take Them?

Don't arrive empty handed. In the islands both the libraries and the schools might welcome books. Maybe a child somewhere might welcome a toy. Have something, if you can, just to say "thank you," particularly if you plan to stay in one place for long.

Finally, Back to Water and Fuel

The price of fresh water in some islands runs as high as $1.25 a gallon. If you're considering extensive cruising in the Bahamas it might be worth thinking about reducing the size of your water tank(s), fitting a watermaker, and, if you've gained tank space, increasing the size of your fuel tankage. Work it out.

Chapter 20
Green Pages
History, Wildlife, and Fishing & Diving

Commemorating the Loyalist settlement of Green Turtle Cay in 1783.

The Story of the Bahamas

"*This island is very large and very flat. It is green, with many trees and several bodies of water. There is a very large lagoon in the middle of the island and there are no mountains.*"

"*I was alarmed at seeing that the entire island is surrounded by a large reef. Between the reef and the island it remained deep . . . there are a few shoal spots, to be sure, and the sea moves in it no more than the water in a well.*"

"*I have no desire to sail strange waters at night . . .*"

"*You must keep your eyes peeled where you wish to anchor and not anchor too near shore. The water is very clear and you can see the bottom during the daylight hours, but a couple of lombard shots offshore there is so much depth that you cannot find bottom.*"

You could say there you have it, in four bites. An introduction to cruising in the Bahamas, with all the vital lessons set out.

Don't expect any significant elevation in the land to guide you in. You can expect reefs around the islands, but you can find deep water inside the reefs and the reef itself will offer shelter. It's dangerous to sail Bahamian waters at night. Generally anchoring too close to a beach is a mistake, but you can choose exactly where you wish to drop your hook. The water is so clear. The dropoffs run closer to land than you'd expect, and are profound.

The author was Christopher Columbus and the date was 1492.

With 50 men you could subject everyone and make them do what you wished . . .

(Columbus, in the Bahamas.
Sunday, October 14, 1492).

His "handsome" islanders "as naked as their mothers bore them" are described as "very simple and honest, and exceedingly liberal with all they have; none of them refusing any thing he may possess when he is asked for it . . . they exhibit great love towards all others in preference to themselves; they also give objects of great value for trifles, and content themselves with little or nothing in return . . ." His simple people lived to regret the spotlight. The Arawak dividend from this first contact with European Man was extinction within a quarter of a century.

The Arawaks left no ruins in Bahamas in which you can imagine their presence, but the unspoiled landscape and the seascape, the deep blue, green, and turquoise waters, are just as they were when the Bahamas was their land. If you go quietly and gently you can assume an affinity with their life-style, for the daily concerns of their world were much the same as yours in the Bahamas. Theirs was a low-stress littoral life, in which boats and fishing were everything, with the freedom to move from island to island at will, even as far afield as Haiti and Cuba. Perhaps it's fitting that part of

A 17th-century Spanish galleon.

their language remains with us to this day, words that Columbus and his successors had to adopt, for there was no other way to name or describe the New World they had found. We have inherited avocado, barbecue, canoe, Carib, cannibal, cay, guava, hammock, hurricane, iguana, maize, manatee, potato, and tobacco, among others.

Once the terrible genocide of the Bahamian native population had been achieved through mass abductions into slavery, disease, and starvation, the Bahamas became a wasteland in Spanish eyes. A disappointment to Ponce de Leon in his search for the Fountain of Youth, and a trap for their treasure galleons lumbering north from Havana on their long haul back to Spain. Two hundred years passed. Then in 1648 the quaintly named Eleutheran Adventurers, seeking a Mayflower Pilgrim-type fresh start and religious freedom, literally hit Eleuthera. You could say their vessel was the first known victim of the Devil's Backbone. From then on, the Bahamas were on the map. By the end of the 17th century the slow re-population of the Bahamas had begun with over a thousand settlers divided between Eleuthera and its twin haven, New Providence Island. It was tough going. The new immigrants soon found that the Bahamas were no self-sustaining Garden of Eden, and their primary needs were imports, and vital imports needed hard cash. Happily the regular Spanish galleon run provided windfall jackpots, as did the wrecks of other ships unfortunate enough to be ill-set by wind and current in Bahamian waters. But there was a downside to this marauding. The sharks joined in.

My name was William Kidd, and so wickedly I did, when I sailed . . .

(The Ballad of William Kidd).

The sharks were not the ones with triangular dorsal fins, though undoubtedly the shipwrecks attracted them too, but two-legged ones with names like Henry Morgan (of Morgan's Bluff, in Andros), Edward Teach (the dreaded Blackbeard), Jack Calico Rackham, and a pair of terrifying Amazons, Anne Bonney and Mary Read, who, scuttlebutt had it, fought naked to the waist. Nassau paid host to enough real pirates and would-be pirates to fill the Bay Street waterfront bars every night and in consequence was hammered in retaliation by the Spanish four times in just a quarter of a century. The dreams of a simple, peaceful, agricultural God-fearing community had been totally eclipsed. It got so bad that eventually the British Government showed some interest in a territory it had arbitrarily claimed way back in 1629. An ex-privateer, Woodes Rogers, was given a clean Bill of Health and sent out to govern the islands and end piracy. By 1720 he was a long way down the road, yet another Spanish attack had been repulsed, life on shore became quieter, but was no easier. The wrecking went on.

Fort Montague, Nassau, captured by US Marines, 1776.

Edward Wilson

If this be treason, make the most of it . . .

(Patrick Henry, Williamsburg, Virginia.
May 29, 1765)

The foment of the watershed events of the end of the 18th century as the European Powers started to lose their hold on the New World rocked the Bahamas like a succession of tidal waves. In 1776 the new American Continental Navy attacked the Bahamas, captured Fort Montague, and occupied Nassau. Why? Because it was British. But there was little profit in it, and they left after two weeks. Two years later the Americans returned to raise their new flag over Nassau, but yet again had second thoughts, and left. There was a four-year gap. Then in 1782 the Spanish came back in strength, and that was it. The Bahamas became Spanish.

Meanwhile back in Europe at the Treaty of Versailles the British had conceded independence to the North American colonies, had hung on to Canada, traded a tenuous claim to Florida with the Spanish, and reclaimed the Bahamas. But an American Loyalist, Andrew Deveaux, unaware of the horse trading in France, set out from South Carolina to win the Bahamas back, and achieved it through a brilliant, simple, deceptive display of quite false overwhelming strength. His lead opened the doors to a rush of migration as Loyalists, unhappy at the prospect of living in a new United States, fled with all their worldly goods, their slaves, and sometimes even the bricks of their houses to start a new life, secure under the British flag. Deveaux himself took the southeast of Cat Island as his reward (you can still see the empty shell of his great house) and one by one all the larger islands were settled as plantation land. It

was a disaster. Within ten years crops had failed, the thin soil was exhausted, and many frustrated, ruined planters quit. Some, in leaving, set their slaves at liberty. They had no further use for them.

The fortunes of the Bahamas had been set in a cyclic pattern from the first ill-fated resettlement of the islands in the mid-17th century. Ignoring moral justification about good guys and bad guys, rights and wrongs, the first high spot was the success of piracy in the first part of the 18th century. That was a boom time. If you were a pirate. The second boom, short-lived, came with the migration of the American Loyalists. The plantation era, when it had seemed at first that Bahamian land was almost worth its weight in gold, barely lasted that decade. And then the Bahamas became a backwater. The only living that could be won came from the reefs and shoals of the shallow seas, and wrecking was the mainstay of survival.

Shall be thenceforward and forever free . . .

(Abraham Lincoln, Washington, DC.
September 22, 1862)

The character of the Bahamas had been formed. By the early 1830s permanent settlements existed on seventeen of the islands, and there was precious little land of agricultural value even in them. The black population outnumbered the white, but figures were hard to establish. A census of slaves in the 1820s, as the Abolitionist movement developed a ground swell, showed more than 10,000 in the Bahamas. By 1838

Illustrated London News, April 30, 1864. Confederate blockade runner unloading cotton in Nassau.

Courtesy Balmain Antiques, Nassau

slavery was ended, and the Royal Navy added to the Bahamas population the human cargo they had captured in slave ships. The newly-landed joined the newly-freed in scratching out a living somewhere near the survival line. As the hands of time moved closer to the 20th century the Bahamas, at grassroots level, was foundering.

The outbreak of the American Civil War was a wake-up call and a shot of adrenaline for the Bahamas. For five years it was like a Gold Rush boom or a return to the days of Bonney and Read as Nassau played host and haven to Confederate blockade runners. Strange it was that the emancipated slaves of the Bahamas should combine in commercial enterprise with the oppressors of the Deep South, but pragmatism wins over the contemplation of an empty bowl. When the guns fell silent it was curtains again over the Bahamas. Even the wrecking business was no longer a fail-safe. The rule of law was enforced, lighthouses were built, the islands at last were charted. A market for sponges kept the Bahamas alive, as did relatively productive, easy-to-grow crops such as pineapples. But the sponges became diseased and US import preferences along with the Hawaiian pineapple soon negated any regeneration through aquaculture or agriculture.

Prohibition comes into force.

US Headline. January 16, 1919

Another recession followed, not even alleviated by the First World War, when many Bahamians volunteered for service. Once again US internal politics were to catapult the Bahamian economy to another all-time high. In 1919 the Volstead Act was passed, prohibition was imposed, and the manufacture, sale, and consumption of alcohol in the United States became illegal. The Bahamian rum runners saved the day for those whose day was ruined without a martini, and Nassau and Bimini were back in a Civil War mode, this time with power boats. Nassau boomed, offering new hotel rooms, bars, and gambling, and PanAmerican, only too happy to print and sell the tickets, flew in regularly from Miami. In 1933 it all ended with the repeal of Prohibition. Nassau closed down, and Bimini went to sleep.

Roosevelt signs Lend-Lease Bill.

Headline. March 11, 1941

The Lend-Lease bases of the Second World War, the fame of the Duke of Windsor, the unusually high-ranking governor of the Bahamas (to say nothing of the Duchess, for whom a throne was surrendered), and the infamous Harry Oakes affair put the Bahamas on the map once again. There were hopes that with postwar affluence the benefits of tourism might come to the Bahamas, more so after the earlier spear-

The Duke and Duchess of Windsor on his arrival to assume the appointment of Governor of the Bahamas in 1940.

heading by PanAm, but the Bahamas relapsed again. The time was not ripe. The Bahamas had yet to work out a political *modus vivendi*, racial relations were as strained as the imbalance of domestic wealth, independence was clearly in the cards but worrisome, Florida was far from reaching capacity in attracting sun-seekers, Havana was more exciting than Nassau, and air tourism had yet to find its wings.

This is my island in the sun . . .

Calypso

By the mid-1950s it was time for another boom. Most of the ducks, other than independence, had come in line. With the development of Freeport, West End, Nassau Harbour, new air services, and the enactment of legislation deliberately designed to attract offshore investment, the Bahamas hit a boom period spurred by tourism, investors, and speculators. Private cays, once a dime a dozen, became premium property. It seemed there was no holding back. But the pace slackened. The builders stopped building. It had worked, but then the momentum failed. In place of the materialization of this new boom, drug running became an all-too-viable, and too visible, alternative route to riches.

A sudden demand for cigarette boats and used C-46s...

Market trends in the 1960s

The shades of piracy, blockade running, and rum running resurfaced. For the first time the remoter parts of the Bahamas became hot property, new airstrips spread like a rash over the Exumas and the Out Islands, and suddenly some people were becoming very rich. There was money to burn, and in an uneven distribution, the Bahamas enjoyed some kind of minor boom. It ended when the downside, not least of it the murder of anyone who happened to be in the wrong place at the wrong time, became intolerable.

A used C-46.

I simply do not know where to go next...

Columbus, in the Bahamas.
Friday, October 19, 1492

Why did the Freeport initiative stall? Perhaps three prerequisites had to come before the dreams of the 1950s initiatives were achieved. One was the resolution of the political future of the Bahamas. It was. The Bahamas became independent on July 10, 1973. The second was the halting of the drug trade, as far as traffic built on addiction can be halted, for it was debilitating the nation and distorting the economy. The third was the realization that wrecking, cotton, sisal, pineapples, and agriculture in general, as well as sponging, were

no ways to fortune. What the Bahamas had to offer were two immutable blessings that had come as a package deal with their environment. The first, the natural dividend of a multi-island people, was a maritime tradition dating back three hundred years. The second was also a natural dividend. It was the most brilliant waters in the Western Hemisphere.

Today the Bahamas is at the threshold of another boom period, which, unless there is a global catastrophe or catastrophic mismanagement, will eclipse and outlast any previous gold rush. It's a time of change, and you can see it in Nassau, on the docks and on Bay Street, and on Paradise Island. Grand Bahama is about to hit high stakes far beyond the expectations of the Freeport founders, with a totally reconstructed harbor and airport, vast new housing developments, the reconstruction of the Port Lucaya hotels, and the long overdue resurrection of West End.

Two private sky harbours for executive jets are being developed...

1997 Bahamas Business Report

Why has all this come about? We've suggested three reasons. What are the contributory factors? The 1997 change of government in the Bahamas. The upsurge and stability of the US economy. In tourism terms a growing disillusionment with the Caribbean. The continuance of the Castro regime, and the certainty that Cuba, even freed of communist dictatorship, will take years to find its feet. There are the motive pluses, the Bahamas is on the US doorstep, right there, just 50 miles across the Florida Strait. The language is English, and the law is English too. The banking laws are favorable and absolute. And Florida has now hit its zenith in constructing beach-obliterating shoulder-to-shoulder condominiums. There is no more coastline.

Is there any other factor? Yes, there is one. Not to be underrated. It lies in the lessons of another British colony founded on piracy, smuggling, and drug running, which turned to trading and tourism. Now after the handover of Hong Kong to the Chinese, the former colony may well continue as a potent commercial center, but it remains that the most successful self-regulating entrepot in the world has gone.

We may well see the Bahamas take the torch from Hong Kong, and make a bid to become the banking, shipping, and trading epicenter of the Western Maritime World with links to Europe, North America, South America, and, through the Caribbean and Panama, into the Pacific. The first indication lies in the Hong Kong money that even now has been, and is being, invested in Grand Bahama. The writing is on the wall. Let's hope that the wall itself is well-built, and maintained.

Meanwhile back on board . . .

Let's change the focus. What's in this for the cruising visitor? Better shoreside facilities. More marinas. Isn't this going to bring about the Floridization of the Bahamas, and spoil its attraction as a cruising ground? No. We think not. The total sea area is too great, there are so many islands, there will always be remote places. Those who want to hook up to shore power will be better served, and those who wish to drop a hook will still be able to find that magic anchorage.

As the words of the song go, 'Who Could Ask For Anything More'?

The Columbus Controversy

In November 1986 the National Geographic Society detonated a bomb under conventional theories about the track and landfalls of Columbus's First Voyage. In a well-researched, cogent analysis *Where Did Columbus Discover America?* a compelling argument was advanced that his first landfall was Semana Cay, not San Salvador. The first serious attempt to identify the site of Columbus's landfall in the Americas was published in 1625, and concluded that it was Cat Island. Since then there have been no less than nine different contenders for the honor of selection, of which the perennial frontrunner was Watling Island or San Salvador, as we call it today.

Guanahani

As for Columbus, his description of his landfall is hardly sufficiently explicit to identify one single island, but then try to write descriptions of each Bahamian island and cay as you come to them. The natives called his landfall *Guanahani*. Columbus renamed it San Salvador, for the standard operating procedure of the Spanish discoverers and *conquistadors* was an automatic assumption that the population of the places they found had no significance, other than as slave labor, and rechristening the land they found was tantamount to takeover. Guanahani, Columbus said, was surrounded by a large reef that had a narrow entrance, it was fairly large, very flat, green, covered in vegetation, and had several bodies of water (ponds? swamps?) as well as a large central lagoon. An inlet? Mangroves? The description could fit any number of the 723 islands and cays of the Bahamas. Out of the nine "possibles" the spotlight eventually rested on just two places, Watling Island, and Semana Cay.

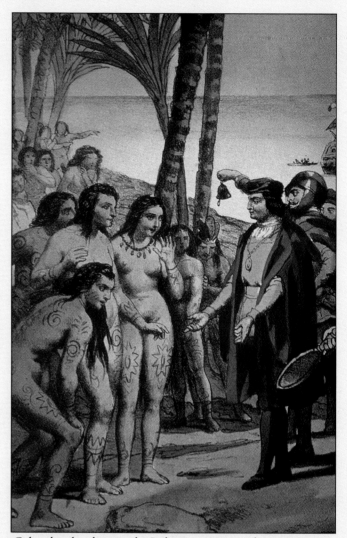

Columbus landing in the Bahamas. Artist unknown.

The Columbus Landfall Contenders

The list runs from Cat Island, Conception Island, East Caicos Island (Turks and Caicos Islands), Egg Island and/or Royal Island, Grand Turk Island (Turks and Caicos Islands), Mayaguana, the Plana Cays, Semana Cay, to Watling Island.

THE WATLING SCHOOL

You could say that the renaming of Watling Island as San Salvador in 1926 was the grant of *de facto* title as the proven landfall. One way or another, largely through the advocacy of early heavyweight naval historians, later joined by Samuel Eliot Morison, one of the premier authorities in this century on American maritime history, Watling Island was "it." Not everyone agreed. A small band of disbelievers said Columbus's recorded onward track didn't fit the geography of the Out Islands to the north of the

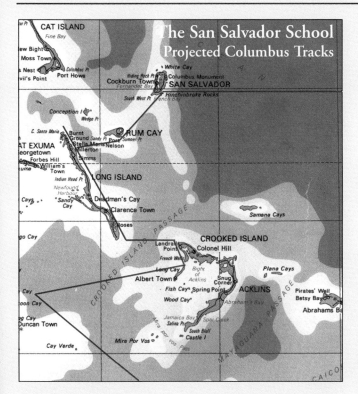

Tropic of Cancer. Everyone acknowledged that Columbus kept his log secret from his crew for fear of alarming them about their distance run from Spain, and everyone agreed that there were translation confusions, particularly about *leagues* run and *miles*. But it remained that however you projected his track after San Salvador, the Columbus log didn't fit. There were fundamental errors in distances and direction.

The Semana School

In 1880 Captain Gustavus Vasa Fox, President Lincoln's Assistant Secretary of the Navy from 1861 to 1866, published an article in which for the first time Semana Cay was proposed as the landing site. Despite the fact that suddenly the Columbus log fitted neatly into the Bahamian map like the long missing piece of a jigsaw puzzle, the Fox theory won little backing, even though in 1894 the National Geographic Society published a reinforcement of his argument. The debate continued with Conception Island, East Caicos, and the Plana Cays thrown in as confusion factors. In November 1975 the National Geographic Society threw in the towel and joined the San Salvador support group.

The Quincentennial Analysis

The advent of the Quincentennial of the Columbus Landing reawakened interest in the controversy, and the National Geographic Society took another long, hard look at Fox and Semana Cay. A highly skilled team was put

together to make the ultimate comparison between the San Salvador and Semana Cay theories using technology to advantage. The detailed study rested initially on a computer drawn analysis of the always suspect Columbus Atlantic Log with winds, currents, and leeway taken into account. Every projection run ended at Semana Cay.

A detailed analysis of his America log started. Columbus reported sending small boats to scout around his landfall. The boats returned in seven hours. Even a champion Eights crew couldn't make a round trip up the only part of San Salvador that half-fits his description (the 15-nm northwest coastline up to Grahams Harbour) in seven hours. But Semana (some 16 nm in total circumference) matches. And it fits in many other ways.

From Semana the recreation of Columbus's track led to North East Acklins, to Crooked Island (Pittstown Point, Landrail, and French Wells), on to the southeast coast of Long Island (Little Harbour and Clarence Town), and then back to Crooked Island (French Wells again) and Long Cay (Windsor Point). He tried the Bight of Acklins (it was too shallow), headed West, bumped the Jumentos Cays, turned south, and so "discovered" Cuba. In his three subsequent voyages he never returned to the Bahamas. Later Spanish expeditions were mounted to take Arawak males away to slavery in Española (Haiti and the Dominican Republic), which resulted in the total extinction of the Bahamian population within a generation. The islands that had marked, shared, but not enjoyed the First (European) Discovery of the New World were then ignored.

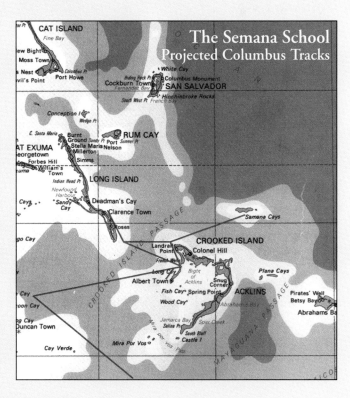

The Columbus Log

FOR those who venture into the Bahamas south of the Tropic of Cancer, we highlight and comment on some brief extracts from the log of Columbus's First Voyage.

Northeast Acklins Island (never named by Columbus)
The coast that faces San Salvador [the east coast facing his Guanahani landfall] *lies in a north-south line and extends for 15 miles. The other coast* [the north coast] *which I followed, runs east and west and is more than 30 miles long.*

Crooked Island (Santa María de la Concepción)
. . . the western cape. I anchored at sunset near the cape [Portland Harbour, probably just southeast of Bird Rock in the deep water inside the reef just off Pittstown Point] *in order to find out if there was gold there.*

Passage to Long Island (Fernandina)
Judged by the clouds and the signs made by the men from San Salvador [Guanahani men captured to serve as guides] *this large island to the west was about 27 miles distant.*

Long Island
It is very big and about 24 miles due west of Santa María de la Concepción [Crooked Island]. *This entire part where I am anchored runs NNW-SSE. It appears that this coast runs for 21 miles or more, and I saw 15 miles of it but it did not end there. It is very level without any mountains . . .*

Little Harbour
After I had sailed six miles from the island's cape [South Point] *where I had been anchored, I discovered a very wonderful harbor* [Little Harbour] *with one entrance, one may say two entrances, for there is an island in the middle. Both passages are very narrow, but once within, the harbor is wide enough for 100 ships. I did not think that either the entrance or the harbor was deep enough, however nor did I feel that the bottom was clear of rocks. It seemed reasonable to me to look it over well and take soundings, so I anchored outside and went in with the small boats. It was fortunate that I did, for there was no depth at all.*

Clarence Town. *After taking on water* [at Little Harbour] *I returned to the ship and sailed to the NW until I had explored all that part of the island as far as the coast that runs east-west* [from Booby Cay, just north of Strachan Cay, westward to Longitude 075° N].

The weather turned against Columbus and he was forced to put about and run before the wind. He retraced his track and eventually anchored off French Wells in Crooked Island.

Crooked Island—French Wells (Cabo del Iseo)
Before we had sailed three hours we saw an island to the east for which we steered, and before midday all three ships reach a small island [Rat Cay] *at the north point* [of Long Cay]. *There is a rocky reef at this island that runs to the north, and between the reef and the large island to the north* [Crooked Island] *there is another island* [Goat Cay]. *To the NE of this small island there is a great bay* [the northwest corner of the Bight of Acklins] *. . . I wanted to anchor in that bay . . . but the water is shallow and I could not anchor.*

Long Cay (Isabela)
The coast trends west for 12 miles from this small island to a cape [Windsor Point, named Cabo Hermoso]. *It is round, and the water is deep with no shoals offshore.*

The Bight of Acklins
I thought I might sail around the island [Long Cay] *to the NE and to the east, from the SE and the south . . . but the bottom is so shallow* [the Bight of Acklins] *that I cannot enter or sail . . .*

Columbus wanted to head for northern Acklins where *"the men from San Salvador tell me there is a king with a lot of gold . . ."* but was foiled by the shoal waters of the Bight of Acklins. He returned to French Wells, and this time tucked himself further in, probably just south of the French Wells Creek or the Turtle Sound Creek, off Gun Point, which he named the Cabo de la Laguna. They spent three days there, discovered the Bahamas boa constrictor, and killed two of them *"the people here eat them and the meat is white and tastes like chicken."* Then they sailed west-southwest for a large island they had been told was called Cuba, *"which I am told is magnificent with gold and pearls."* After bouncing off the southern Ragged Islands and adjusting their course to run almost due south, Columbus's small fleet made their Cuban landfall four days later. Perhaps by then Columbus was running out of names for his islands. Somehow Cuba escaped the ritual discovery rechristening.

Where does this leave us boating visitors some five hundred years after these events? If nothing else, with a fine project if you're intent on cruising in the Bahamas south of the Tropic of Cancer. Get a good, readable translation of Columbus's Log of his First Voyage. We'd recommend the Robert Fuson version published by International Marine—McGraw-Hill in 1987. Get a copy of that November 1986 National Geographic with its map. Then make like Columbus. Or not quite like him as far as today's inhabitants of the islands are concerned.

Wildlife in the Bahamas

Whales of the Bahamas

by Diane Claridge
Bahamas Marine Mammal Survey

THE Bahama Islands are home to at least twenty-one marine mammal species, including some of the world's most bizarre looking creatures. In 1991, Ken Balcomb and I founded the Bahamas Marine Mammal Survey to find out which leviathan species occur here, the seasonality and frequency of their occurrence, and to determine their population size and status, if possible. Today, with support from Earthwatch, we carry out surveys and photo-identification studies of marine mammals based from Hole in the Wall light station in Abaco.

Our survey efforts have been greatly enhanced by sighting reports and photographs that we receive from boaters traveling through the islands (see our sighting form on page 342). The following is information on whales and dolphins that are commonly seen in the Bahamas to aid and encourage boaters to continue to report sightings to us.

Sperm whales (*Physeter macrocephalus*) are the largest toothed whales in the world; adult males can grow up to 60 feet, although adult females are considerably smaller, reaching 35–40 feet in length. Sperm whales have a huge squarish head that is about one third the body length. With a single nostril on the left side and their wrinkled brown skin, these whales may have the appearance of a floating, occasionally breathing, log resting at the surface. However, if approached by a boat, a sperm whale will slowly move away and usually raise its tail in preparation for its dive, thus allowing researchers to take a photograph of the underside of the tail showing their individually distinctive

Sperm whale tail.

patterns of notches. Adult female sperm whales appear to be regulars to the Bahamas and are found here year-round in nursery pods. The mature males frequent the islands during the winter months in search of receptive females for breeding purposes, but spend the rest of the year feeding in higher latitudes in order to sustain their massive bulk of 60-plus tons.

Pilot whale underwater.

Short-finned pilot whales (*Globicephala macrorynchus*), also known as blackfish or potheads, usually grow to 18 feet long and weigh about 5,000 pounds. They are jet black and have a large, bulbous head with a faint white diagonal stripe behind each eye and a white or gray cape behind and below the dorsal fin. Their large, falcate dorsal fin is set quite far forward on their body. Pilot whales live in large matrilineal pods of 50–100 animals consisting of up to three generations of related females, which on calm days can be seen resting at the surface for hours in tight groups lying abreast. Pilot whales can be confused with three other blackfish species (melon-headed whales, pygmy killer whales, and false killer whales), but look sharply and note that these latter species have a relatively taller dorsal fin in the middle of their back and they lack the white eye stripes and cape of pilot whales. It is probable that many of the pilot whales seen in the Bahamas are year-round residents.

Dense-beaked whales (Blainville's beaked whale, *Mesoplodon densirostris*) are but one of at least three beaked whale species found in the Bahamas. Dense-beaked whales are a small (14–16 foot) brownish-tan cosmotropical whale with white, oval scars on the back from cookie cutter sharks, and longitudinal paired tooth scratches inflicted by congeners. Beaked whales in general have a small hooked dorsal fin that is located about two-thirds of the way back along their body. They have a pronounced beak or rostrum, which breaks the water first as the whale surfaces to breath. The rostrum of male dense-beaked whales consists of the densest bone known on earth. In the steeply arched lower jaw of this species there are only two teeth, and these only erupt above the gumline in sexually mature males. These hornlike teeth are apparently used in combat with other males, perhaps as part of a dominance display. Judging from the antiquity and layering of scars, the combat is typically sublethal, but often severe. The males have dense clusters of stalked barnacles growing on their jutting teeth, giving them the appearance of a strange sea monster. The females we studied remained year-round in the islands. On the other hand, although adult males can be seen during all months, it is still unknown whether or not the same individuals remain here year-round.

Dense-beaked whale.

Risso's dolphins (*Grampus griseus*) are generally gray in color but have a white head and extensive white scarring on the backs of adults and elders. These large dolphins have a rounded head with a deep crease down the center of the forehead. Individuals grow to 12+ feet and have a relatively tall dorsal fin. On the Atlantic side of the northern Bahamas, Risso's dolphins appear to move inshore toward the coast in the winter and spring, perhaps following prey. It is yet unknown where they range the rest of the year, but some individuals have been seen off the coast of Abaco repeatedly over the past five years. Risso's dolphins are often confused with pilot whales at a distance, but in the right lighting the white heads are very prominent.

Atlantic spotted dolphins (*Stenella frontalis*) grow to 8 feet, but are not always spotted! Newborns and juveniles do not have spots, but accumulate them as they mature, becoming quite mottled looking as adults. Generally found in groups of 30–50 animals, spotted dolphins will ride a boat's bow-wave and usually put on a spectacular aerial show. In some parts of the Bahamas, spotted dolphins can be quite

Risso dolphin surfacing.

friendly: but please, if you enter the water, do not attempt to touch them as it may provoke an aggressive response. Spotted dolphins occur on both the shallow banks and in the offshore waters, feeding on squid and flying fish along the "dropoff" at nighttime and resting on the shallow banks during the day.

As cruisers, you have a unique opportunity to observe these animals and other rarely seen marine mammal species. It is important to keep an accurate log, take photographs and/or video, and to be an ardent observer, while respecting the animals' needs for space. With the continued help of boaters cruising the islands, we hope to further our awareness of marine mammals and to gain a better understanding of their conservation needs in this part of the world, in order to provide protection for these species and their habitats.

Spotted dolphins.

Wildlife Preserves

The Northern Cruising Grounds

ABACO NATIONAL PARK
On Great Abaco Island between Cherokee Sound and Hole in the Wall. The preserve of the Bahama Parrot.

BLACK SOUND CAY NATIONAL RESERVE
A mangrove island in Black Sound, Green Turtle Cay, in the Abacos.

FOWL CAYS LAND AND SEA PRESERVE
An area of cays (the Fowl Cays and Fish Hawk Cay) just north of Man-O-War Cay in the Abacos.

PELICAN CAYS LAND AND SEA PARK
The area south of Tilloo Cay and north of Little Harbour, in the southern end of the Sea of Abaco.

TILLOO CAY NATIONAL PROTECTED AREA
North of Pelican Cay and south of Marsh Harbour in the Abacos.

LUCAYAN NATIONAL PARK
A 42-acre reserve with nature trails and boardwalks in Grand Bahama. The park area contains one of the world's largest chartered cave systems.

PETERSON CAY NATIONAL PARK
A small cay with a coral reef off the south coast of Grand Bahama, just east of Port Lucaya.

RAND NATURE CENTER
The headquarters of the Bahamas National Trust. A 100-acre preserve two miles outside Freeport, Grand Bahama. The site also contains a replica of a Lucayan village.

The Central Cruising Grounds

THE RETREAT
An 11-acre site in Nassau devoted essentially to palm trees.

The Southern Cruising Grounds

EXUMA CAYS LAND AND SEA PARK
A well-known and much-visited 160-square-mile nature reserve, primarily devoted to the sea, in the mid-Exumas.

CONCEPTION ISLAND LAND AND SEA PARK
The largest "whole island" reserve in the Bahamas. Conception is almost 3 miles long by 2 miles in width, rises to 60 feet in the center, and is surrounded by shoals and reefs that extend as far as 5 miles offshore. It is uninhabited, notable for its birds and nesting turtles, and a visit allegedly paid by Christopher Columbus in 1492.

INAGUA NATIONAL PARK
The largest colony of West Indian flamingos in the world.

UNION CREEK NATIONAL RESERVE
A seven-square-mile area of tidal creek in Great Inagua.

WILDLIFE PARK REGULATIONS

As you would expect, conservation rules in the park areas are strict. Essentially you are not allowed to fish, hunt, remove any living or dead animal, fish, vegetation, plant life, and coral, or in any way damage, alter, or leave a footprint on the environment. Most of the marine parks have moorings that you are required to take up. If you do anchor, you are required to anchor in sand well clear of any reef. You are not allowed to discharge any waste, nor to dump your garbage.

If you break the rules, not only are you in line for a $500 fine, but your boat may well be confiscated.

Insects

If you cruise in the Bahamas, sooner or later, somewhere, your dreams of an idyllic evening anchorage are going to be spoiled by ravaging insects, no-see-ums, sandflies, mosquitos, or whatever they may be, either invisible and soundless or near-invisible with the whine of an attacking dive bomber once they have you targeted. Most off-the-shelf insect repellents seem to have little effect as a chemical defense. It's hard to screen a boat without loosing all your free-moving ventilation. It's tough to screen yourself by pulling on long pants and long sleeves. What's the answer? Forget the scenic drink on the fly bridge or in the cockpit? Go for air conditioning?

We reckon not. You can't distance yourself from shore in a marina, but in an anchorage don't get too close. Try to keep out where there's wind, or beyond insect flight range. Otherwise just try your insect repellent. It might work. The best solution is to buy Mosquito Coils (slow burning coils, originally of Chinese origin, producing insect repellent incense), which you can usually find in almost all Bahamian general stores. They really work!

Fishing & Diving in the Bahamas

Fishing in the Bahamas

Sports fishing was the lure (we use the word *lure* deliberately!) that first brought recreational boaters to the Bahamas. When the word got around that the Biminis lay at the edge of one of the richest big game fishing grounds in the world, and that you could get there and back in a weekend, it hardly needed Ernest Hemingway to fire up the publicity. Fishing in the Bahamas took off.

Heading the list of the great gamefish are marlin. **Blue marlin** top the list with an average body weight of 250–300 lbs. The chance of catching a fish weighing 800 lbs. or more is always within the realm of possibility. **White marlin** follow with an average weight around 100 lbs, and make up for their lesser weight as a prize catch by a fighting stamina that outclasses the Blue. **Sailfish** rank with the marlin, matching the Blue Marlin in dramatic performance when hooked.

Tuna, and particularly migrating **bluefin tuna**, are the next on the list. The Bluefin, who pass through the Bahamas on the way north each year, can weigh anything up to nearly 1,000 lbs. and once hooked, you're in for a serious battle that can last hours. The other varieties of the tuna family, **blackfin**, **yellowfin**, and **bonito**, are Bahamian residents rather than visitors in transit, and not as spectacular nor indeed in the heavyweight class of the Bluefin.

Dolphin (not the Flipper variety but the fish the Spanish called *dorado*, whose name we adopted but got wrong) are next on the gamefish list. Around 10–15 lbs. in weight, tough fighters, with iridescent skin colors like a rainbow, the dolphin is prized both for its fighting qualities and its quality as an eating fish, reckoned by many to be better than swordfish or tuna.

The mackerel family is next with **wahoo**, the fastest fish in the ocean, and **King mackerel**, which can come close to 5 feet in length and are never taken without a fight. The fighting list also includes the marauders, **barracuda** and **sharks**. We see little point in shark fishing and we've found barracuda, only too ready to strike at any lure, more of a curse on a line than a blessing. **Tarpon**, who will often take a trolled line and fight fiercely, complete our gamefish list but, like the marauders, have no place on a food list.

Turning away from trolling to fishing the depths, **groupers** top the list of the prize fish for weight and for food value. After them come **snappers** and **amberjack**; the last respond to live bait and will take your line, when hooked, deep into a wreck or the holes of a reef if they have the chance.

The fish of the Bahamian shallows or flats, **bonefish** and the less widely known **permit**, are considered by many anglers to be the best prizes of all. You won't stock your larder with them, but once you get hooked by the lure of bonefishing, you'll spend hour after hour fishing the flats.

Fishing Licenses and Regulations

You must obtain a fishing permit (Permit to Engage in Foreign Fishing Conducted for Sporting Purposes Regulation 46 [4]), which allows you to fish in Bahamian waters, at the same time you apply for your cruising permit. The fishing permit costs $10. It is normally valid for four months.

Your fishing permit limits you to:

- The use of no more than six reels or six lines.
- Hook and line.
- A limit of six fish per person for kingfish, dolphin, and wahoo, and no more than 20 lbs. weight of fish at any one time.
- All migratory fish, unless to be used, are to be returned alive to the ocean.

Seasons and Sizes

- **Spiney Lobster** (Crayfish). Closed season is April 1–July 31. Carapace length is limited to 3⅜ inches with a tail length of at least 6 inches. No berried females (egg carrying) are allowed. The limit is six per person.
- **Conch**. Harvested conch must have a well-formed, flaring lip (*i.e.*, be adult). The limit is ten per person.
- **Stone Crab**. Closed season is June 1–October 15. The minimum harvestable claw length is 4 inches.
- **Turtles**. Are expressly forbidden.
- **Fish Sizes**

Blue Marlin	86 inches
White Marlin	62 inches
Sailfish	57 inches
Grouper	Over 3 lbs. in weight
Rockfish	Over 3 lbs. in weight

Prohibitions

- Scuba diving for fish is not allowed. Spear guns are illegal, and only Hawaiian slings or pole spears are allowed if you are diving to catch fish. Spearfishing is not allowed within 1 mile of the coast of New Providence Island (Nassau), the south coast of Grand Bahama Island (Freeport), and within 200 yards of all other islands.
- The use of bleach or similar stunning or poisoning chemicals is forbidden.
- The taking of any form of coral is forbidden under the Bahamian fishing regulations.
- Fishing is forbidden in all Bahamian marine park areas.

The Best Fishing Months

Blue Marlin	June–July
White Marlin	Winter–Spring
Sailfish	Summer–Fall
Allison Tuna	June–August
Bluefin Tuna	May–June
Blackfin Tuna	May–September
Yellowfin Tuna	June–August
Bonito	May–September
Dolphin	Winter–Spring
Wahoo	November–April
King Mackerel	Mostly winter months
Barracuda	Year round
Tarpon	Year round
Grouper	Year round
Amberjack	November–May
Bonefish	Year round

The Northern Cruising Grounds

The Abacos

OFFSHORE FISHING

The 100-fathom line from Walkers Cay down to Elbow Cay (Hope Town) and on to Southwest Point offers excellent fishing for blue marlin, white marlin, sailfish, bluefin tuna, blackfin tuna, dolphin, and wahoo. The sea area off Hope Town is particularly promising, for the "elbow" in the Abaco Cays produces an underwater shelf that extends some 10 miles out into the ocean with dropoffs on all sides.

BOTTOM FISHING

The entire area, rich with reefs, offers ideal fishing grounds for grouper, snapper, lobster, and all kinds of reef dwellers.

SHALLOW WATER FISHING

The Abacos has extensive flats. Grand Cays and Great Breasted Cays offer good fishing. South of Marsh Harbour the inlets into the Great Abaco coast are good, and the entire area of the Marls, the swamp-like water maze to the west of Great Abaco Island, is a bonefish paradise.

The Little Bahama Bank and Grand Bahama Island

OFFSHORE FISHING

As with the Abacos, the primary offshore fishing ground parallels the 100-fathom line, in this case the line running from West End northward to Matanilla Shoal. The edge of the Gulf Stream between West End and Memory Rock is the best fishing, with migrating bluefin tuna.

A secondary offshore fishing ground lies south of Freeport, along the run of the dropoff extending east–west from a point offshore of Bell Channel to the intersection of this line with the edge of the Gulf Stream. This fishing ground covers the intersection of the Northwest Providence Channel with the Gulf Stream, the confluence of these ocean highways producing the right conditions for a concentration of gamefish.

BOTTOM FISHING

The west edge of the Little Bahama Bank, for the most part north of Memory Rock, is a largely uncharted maze of innumerable runs and twists of reef with mini dropoffs, short cuts, holes, and shoals. For the most part it forms an ideal environment for grouper, snapper, and lobster, and is well worth attention.

SHALLOW WATER FISHING

The entire run of the north coast of Grand Bahama forms an ideal shallow-water fishing ground, and the east coast of Grand Bahama Island is reckoned to be particularly good for bonefish and permit.

The Central Cruising Grounds

The Bimini Islands

OFFSHORE FISHING

The main offshore fishing ground parallels the 100-fathom line from Great Isaac in the north to South Riding Rock in the south. The big game territory also continues, hooking around to the east and southeast from Great Isaac, running along the 10-fathom line bordering the southern edge of the Northwest Providence Channel.

BOTTOM FISHING

The best area for grouper and the medium-depth fish are the whole run of rock, reefs, and islands running from Great Isaac to the Gingerbread Ground along the southern edge of the Northwest Providence Channel. Immediately north of North Bimini the 3-fathom line running east from North Rock marks the edge of a good fishing area with a number of wrecks, such as the *Seminole*, which lies some 10 nm east of North Rock.

The wreck of the *Sapona* marks the best fishing grounds immediately south of the two Bimini Islands, but over the years both diving and fishing have overworked the area. Better alternatives lie further away down the line of reefs and rocks to the south of the Cat Cays.

SHALLOW WATER FISHING

The Great Bahama Bank side of the Bimini Islands is good for shallow-water fishing. A line drawn connecting the easternmost points of North Bimini and South Bimini defines the general run of the best grounds for bonefishing.

The Berry Islands

OFFSHORE FISHING

Predictably the offshore fishing grounds off the Berry Islands lie to the east of the island chain, along the 10-fathom line. The Berrys don't rate highly as a fishing destination with one exception, and that's southwest of Chub Cay in the southern Berrys. There the Tongue of the Ocean hooks toward the Northwest Channel, forming a deepwater dead-end that has the fish milling around with nowhere else to go. It's made even better when a southeast wind pushes water and fish that way.

BOTTOM FISHING

Bottom fishing in the Berrys is better in the north and central islands, with the best area from the Market Fish Cays down to Little Harbour Cay.

SHALLOW WATER FISHING

For shallow-water fishermen the whole "inside" arc of the Berry Islands offers almost unlimited fishing grounds, with the best areas in the south around the Cormorant and Fish Cays. These really are shallow waters. You're almost bound to get grounded sooner or later, and your problems may be compounded by isolated coral heads and rocks. If you're careful (or take a guide), you should be OK.

New Providence Island

OFFSHORE FISHING

The Tongue of the Ocean offers more miles of big-game water than you can cover adequately in a week. If you want a focal point, the ocean buoy 15 nm southwest off Clifton Point in New Providence Island is the Times Square for baitfish in the area. The gamefish, wise to this, use the buoy as a fast food stop. You can find them hanging out there much of the time.

BOTTOM FISHING

The best area for bottom fishing is the line of islands, reefs, and rocks running east from Paradise Island to Pimlico Island. You could also try around the isolated coral heads and small reefs on the White Bank and the Yellow Bank.

SHALLOW WATER FISHING

New Providence is not so good for shallow-water fishing. The southeast tip of the island may be worth trying.

Eleuthera

OFFSHORE FISHING

On the Atlantic side, the Eleuthera 100-fathom line should be a natural fishing ground, but it hasn't been greatly exploited, probably because it's a potentially hazardous shoreline. There the reef shielding the west coast of Eleuthera is near-continuous, and the prevailing weather, both wave and current, sets onshore. It's no place to be in bad weather.

To the north of Eleuthera, outside the reefs of the Devil's Backbone Passage area, there's a reasonable fishing ground, but once again the area is not easily accessible and it's weather dependent, a real no-no in wind or seas coming in from the northern quadrants. As for the south of Eleuthera, reports have it that the gap between Eleuthera Point and Little San Salvador is good. There's a shelf there with deep water on both the Atlantic and Exuma Sound.

BOTTOM FISHING

We've not found any particular area we'd recommend above all others for bottom fishing. Just as the geography of Eleuthera doesn't really fit the offshore fishing criteria, so there are few places that are a real setup for grouper and snapper. The fish are there, but you have to find your spot.

SHALLOW WATER FISHING

For bonefish and the like the best areas lie along the west coast of Eleuthera, particularly from Tarpum Bay down to Rock Point, and across the bight toward Powell Point.

Andros

OFFSHORE FISHING

Naturally the Tongue of the Ocean is the number one offshore fishing ground for Andros, easily accessible from either Chub Cay or Fresh Creek. You can run down to South Andros along the 100-fathom line, or try the 1,000-fathom contour off North Andros. One way or another you shouldn't miss.

BOTTOM FISHING

Bottom fishing is good either side of the Andros Barrier Reef, although the navigation inside the reef can be difficult. Bottom fishing is also good in the maze of shallows, reefs, and rocks running through the Joulter Cays to the north of Morgans Bluff.

SHALLOW WATER FISHING

Despite the premium usually placed on big game fishing, Andros should win its accolades for the best shallow-water fishing in the Bahamas. The bonefish grounds start with the Joulter Cays in the north, include just about every inlet and bight on the east coast of Andros, and the entire west coast. For the greater part these fishing grounds are rarely visited, largely uncharted, and you are on your own. If you don't want to go it alone, find a local guide in the nearest settlement and take him with you.

The Southern Cruising Grounds

The Exumas

OFFSHORE FISHING

The Exumas, spectacular cruising ground as they are, are not the top of the list when it comes to big game fishing. The place to try is along the lines of the 100- and 500-fathom contours running along the depths of Exuma Sound.

BOTTOM FISHING

For bottom fishing the reefs off great Exuma and south of Little Exuma are reputed to be good for grouper, and the reefs between Great Exuma and Long Island may be worth trying. If you want to venture further afield, try the reefs lying to the south and southeast of the Exuma chain.

SHALLOW WATER FISHING

The best bonefish areas in the Exumas are Norman's Cay Pond, in the shallow areas around Sampson and Staniel Cays, Compass Cay, Pipe Creek, Harvey Cay, in the central Exumas, and in the shallows off Great Exuma.

THE EXUMAS LAND AND SEA PARK

Don't forget that the entire sea area lying between the south of Norman's Cay to the north of Conch Cut is designated as the Exumas Land and Sea Park and is closed to all fishing.

The Out Islands North of the Tropic of Cancer

The Out Islands are remote cruising grounds and remote territory for the sports fisherman. The areas we mention are fishing spots that have come to our attention. There must be a thousand other places, rarely visited dropoffs, reefs, and shallows, in such a vast area, all of them worth attention. If you find somewhere that the fishing is great, and you don't care to keep it secret, will you let us know?

OFFSHORE FISHING

Cat Island. Off Garnsey Bank to the northeast of the island, and the deepwater contour off the south coast, the dropoff south of Northeast Point, and the southeast point, Columbus Point, around the 1,000-fathom line. Tartar Bank, to the west of this area may also prove productive.
Long Island. Try the deep water along the 500-fathom contour off the north tip of the island.
Rum Cay. The ocean dropoff to the east of the island.
San Salvador. The deep water contour to the north and west of the island.

BOTTOM FISHING

Cat Island. Try the south of the island, off Columbus Point and Tartar Bank.
Long Island. The inshore reefs, and the reefs between Long Island and Little Exuma.

Rum Cay. The reefs to the north of the island.
San Salvador. The close-in reefs, particularly to the north of the island.

SHALLOW WATER FISHING

Cat Island. The Moss Town bight.
San Salvador. The southeast coast of the island.

Far Horizons

The Out Islands South of the Tropic of Cancer

For most people this is really over the horizon and out of reach. You could say why go that way when there are many other productive fishing grounds all the way along your route south? The answer must be "because it's there" and maybe "because no one else goes there." Well, that's not entirely true, for generations of Bahamians have come to know and fish these waters, and the Cubans and the Haitians have come that way too. There's no virgin territory, and in each island the senior generation will tell you that the stock of fish, lobster, and conch has been significantly depleted in their lifetime. Even there, far from any center of population.

The area is too vast for specifics. In this brief review we'll just touch on some places we'd have on our list if we were going that way.

OFFSHORE FISHING

The Crooked Island Passage dropoff running south off Crooked Island from Bird Rock down to Long Cay.

BOTTOM FISHING

The Semana Cay reefs and the Mayaguana reefs.

SHALLOW WATER FISHING

The Bight of Acklins.

You'll note that we've left unmentioned the Jumentos Cays and the Ragged Island Range, Hogsty Reef, and the Inaguas. The last two are too remote to be considered accessible fishing grounds. As for the arc of the Raggeds and the Jumentos Cays, years back it was the place for reef fish and lobster. It's been hit hard now, we're told, but in truth we've yet to try it.

CIGUATERA

The possibility always exists of ciguatera poisoning from eating fish you have caught in the Bahamas. See our warning and advice that is given in detail in the **Buff Pages** under **Medical Facilities, Health, and Health Hazards** on page 325.

Diving in the Bahamas

The Bahamas are one of the best destinations for diving in the world. The islands offer everything from shallow reef dives to wall dives, with ocean dropoffs, blue holes, drift dives, and encounters with dolphins, rays, and sharks. The potential dive sites in the Bahamas are endless. Andros alone has the third largest barrier reef in the world. Above all, not only is the marine life everything you've always dreamed about, but the sea temperature is in the 80°s, and the visibility is beyond belief. One hundred feet is not uncommon.

Many cruising visitors may prefer to explore and find their own favorite areas for diving, rather than signing on with a dive operator for scheduled dive trips. However most of us need to touch base at a dive shop sometime to fill tanks, fix equipment if something goes wrong, or seek local advice. So we've listed the dive facilities in the islands to help your planning. For telephone numbers, addresses, and amplifying details see the **Yellow Pages** for each island. Liveaboard dive boats are not included in our listing.

We would have to write an encyclopedia to list every dive site in the Bahamas. With regret this is beyond our scope. What we have done is give an overview of the diving in each area and, to give a taste of the dive scene, list some of the more commonly visited sites. We suggest, particularly in cases of deep dives (over 80 feet) and specialist dives (such as wrecks) that you seek advice from the local dive operator, and join one of their dive trips to gain familiarization before setting off on your own.

The Northern Cruising Grounds

The Abacos

The 130-mile span of the Abacos has countless shallow reefs, caves, coral heads, shipwrecks, and blue holes. The diving is good, for the most part in comparatively shallow water (80 feet or less), and because the depths are not so great, probably better for photography than the deeper dive sites. The Abacos is also home to two marine parks, the Fowl Cay Land and Sea Preserve just north of Elbow Cay, and the Pelican Cays Park, on your way south to Little Harbour. Both are well worth visiting.

GREEN TURTLE CAY

Dive Operators
- Bluff House Club & Marina.
- Brendal's Dive Shop (CMAS, NAUI, SSI). Specializes in fish feeding and stingrays.

Dive Sites
- **The Catacombs** Shallow caverns. Fish and turtles.
- **Coral Caverns** Caverns.
- **Coral Condos** Coral heads in 60 feet of water.
- **San Jacinto** 1865 Civil War gunboat wreck at 40 feet.

MARSH HARBOUR

Dive Operators
- Dive Abaco. (Conch Inn Resort & Marina) (CMAS, NAUI, PADI).

Dive Sites
- **Grouper Alley** Coral head tunnels. 40 feet.
- **Towers** 60-foot dive. Coral pinnacles.

SPANISH CAY

Dive Operators
- Spanish Cay Watersports.

WALKERS CAY

Dive Operators
- Walkers Cay Undersea Adventures (Walkers Cay Hotel & Marina) (NAUI, PADI, SSI, YMCA). Specializes in shark dives.

Dive Sites
- **Pirate's Cathedral** Swim-through cavern at 40 feet.
- **Shark Rodeo** Shark feeding at 35 feet.

Grand Bahama

With 3,000 hotel rooms in the Freeport–Port Lucaya area and a throughput of a million visitors a year, diving in Grand Bahama is largely geared to shallow-water sites, fish feeding, and shark dives. The dedicated diver may well feel that it is better to find less frequented places to dive. If you are in Grand Bahama, you might consider diving the barrier reefs to the north of West End, or White Sand Ridge, a dolphin ground on the northwest of the Little Bahama Bank.

FREEPORT

- Grand Bahama Watersports (Taino Beach Hotel & Yacht Club). Specializes in fish feeding and shark dives.
- Xanadu Undersea Adventures (Xanadu Beach Resort) (NAUI, PADI, SSI). Specializes in shark dives.

PORT LUCAYA

- Underwater Explorers Society (UNEXSO) (NAUI, PADI, SSI). Specializes in dolphin and shark dives.

Dive Sites
- **Theo's Wreck** 230-foot freighter lying at 100 feet. Moray eels.

The Central Cruising Grounds

The Biminis

The Biminis profit from the Gulf Stream that sustains prolific marine life along the reefs running parallel to the Stream. Although North Bimini itself, and particularly the area around the wreck of the *Sapona*, has been overdived, especially at peak times such as spring break, diving in the Biminis is still good.

DIVE OPERATORS

North Bimini
- Bill and Nowdla Keefe's Bimini Undersea Adventures (NAUI, PADI).

South Bimini
- Bahama Island Adventures (Bimini Reef Club & Marina).
- Scuba Bimini (South Bimini Yacht Club). Specializes in shark dives.

DIVE SITES
- **Bimini Barge** Wreck close to Gulf Stream dropoff. 85–100 feet.
- **Bimini Road** The "Atlantis" site. 20 feet.
- **Victory Reef** Dropoff and caverns. 90 feet.

The Berry Islands

The 30-mile span of the Berry Islands with its thirty-two cays has enough reefs and rocks on the ocean side to offer countless dive sites, but scheduled diving has always concentrated on Chub Cay and the Tongue of the Ocean. In part this may be due to the high proportion of islands that are privately owned, which, as beaches are out of bounds, discourages casual diving and dive development. Much of the Berrys remain largely unexplored as diving grounds.

DIVE OPERATORS
- Bahama Island Adventures (Chub Cay Resort). Operated from South Bimini.

DIVE SITES
- **Chub Cay Wall** Tongue of the Ocean wall. 80–110 feet.
- **Mamma Rhoda Rock**   Bahamian National Trust marine coral preserve. 10–20 feet.

New Providence Island

Nassau and New Providence Island at large play host to some two million visitors a year and the dive attractions in the area reflect this. Hardly surprisingly shark dives feature high on most lists, and wreck dives, with artificial sites such as The Graveyard, created as a dive attraction, are well-frequented. This apart, the adjacent Tongue of the Ocean in the west produces superb diving, as do the shallow reefs lying to east of the island.

DIVE OPERATORS

Coral Harbour
- Custom Aquatics (PADI).
- Dive, Dive, Dive (NASDS, NAUI, PADI, SSI). Specializes in shark dives.
- Nassau Scuba Centre (NASDS, NAUI, PADI, SSI). Specializes in shark dives.

- Stuart Cove's Dive South Ocean (South Ocean Golf & Beach Resort) (NASDS, NAUI, PADI, SSI). Specializes in shark dives.
- Sunskiff Divers (IANTD, NAUI, PADI). Specializes in fish feeding and shark dives.

Nassau
- Bahama Divers (PADI). Specializes in fish feeding and stingrays.
- Divers Haven (PADI).
- Sun Divers (PADI). Specializes in fish feeding.

Paradise Island
- Bahama Divers (PADI). Specializes in fish feeding and stingrays.

DIVE SITES
- **The Graveyard** Four wrecks sunk in 45–60 feet as dive sites.
- **Hole in the Wall** Pierced coral pinnacle at 110 feet.
- **Lost Ocean Blue Hole** 100-foot wide, 200-feet deep blue hole in sand at 30 feet.
- **Mahoney** Steamship sunk in a 1929 hurricane lying at 30–100 feet.
- **Razorback** Tongue of the Ocean dropoff ridge. 45–130 feet.

Eleuthera

Harbour Island has the most "known" dive sites, followed by the North Eleuthera reefs in the Devil's Backbone area with the famous Train Wreck. Current Cut, the passage between North Eleuthera and Current Island, is arguably the best known drift dive in the Bahamas. For the rest, with 100 miles of reefs and rocks, Eleuthera is largely unexplored as far as the diving world is concerned.

DIVE OPERATORS

Harbour Island
- Romora Bay Dive Shop (Romora Bay Club) (PADI).
- Valentine's Dive Center (Valentine's Yacht Club Inn) (PADI, SSI).

DIVE SITES
- **The Arch** A 60-foot-wide natural arch at 65–110 feet.
- **Current Cut** 3–8-knot tidal drift dive in a 100-foot channel.
- **Train Wreck** 1865 train lost off a barge in a storm.

Andros

If Eleuthera is largely unexplored, Andros, with its 120-mile long barrier reef bordering the abysmal (over 6,000 feet) depths of the Tongue of the Ocean, is outer space in dive terms. Add blue holes to the wall dives of Andros and the only word you can use about diving in Andros is "awesome." Take care. Diving in Andros is not for the novice.

DIVE OPERATORS
Fresh Creek
- Small Hope Bay Lodge (NAUI, PADI).

DIVE SITES
- **The Barge** Artificial reef. Deliberate 1960s sinking in 70 feet.
- **Over the Wall** Tongue of the Ocean dropoff. 80 feet to abyss.
- **Potomac** 1929 wreck of a 345-foot tanker.

The Southern Cruising Grounds

The Exumas
With 95 miles of islands and offshore reefs, diving in the Exumas can hardly miss. Perhaps the best feature of the Exumas is the 177-square-mile Exuma Cays Land and Sea Park, an area of shallow reefs that have been protected (and benefited from that protection) since 1958. Don't miss it.

DIVE OPERATORS
George Town
- Exuma Fantasea (PADI).

DIVE SITES
- **Angelfish Blue Hole** Cavern at 30 feet running to 90 feet in depth.
- **Edwin Williams** Defence Force ship intentionally sunk in 55 feet.
- **Stingray Reef** 50-foot dive with good photo opportunities.

The Out Islands North of the Tropic of Cancer
Cat Island has hardly been touched. Some 50 miles of diving ground with dropoffs starting in 40 feet of water wait for exploration. Two operators are now in business there. Long Island with 90 miles of coast falls much in the same category, with the exception of the dive sites found by the Stella Maris Resort, which has been the sole dive operator in the area for some time. San Salvador's reputation as a dive destination comes with its wall dives, for the island is nothing other than the peak of a mountain, and on all sides falls 13,000 feet to the ocean floor. Its dive operators know the best sites.

Conception Island has three miles of wall falling from 40 to 6,000 feet, and elkhorn and staghorn corals in shallower waters together with 150 recorded wrecks. Rum Cay has coral pinnacles set against white sand, but this apart, Little San Salvador, Conception Island, and Rum Cay remain largely unexplored dive territory.

DIVE OPERATORS
Cat Island
- Cat Island Dive Center (Greenwood Beach Resort) (PADI, PDIC).
- Fernandez Bay Dive Shop (Fernandez Bay Village).

DIVE SITES
- **Elkhorn Gardens** Shallow-water elkhorn coral forest.
- **Tartar Bank** 30-foot shallows 5 miles out with 80–130-foot dropoffs.
- **Tiger Shark Spot** Swim-through tunnels and corals. 70 feet.

Long Island
- Stella Maris Resort Club (PADI, SSI). Specializes in shark dives.

DIVE SITES
- **Comberbach** Artificial reef. 125-foot freighter in 100 feet.
- **Shark Reef** The first Bahamian shark dive venture.

San Salvador
- Club Med Columbus Isle.
- Guanahani Divers (Riding Rock Inn) (PADI, SSI).

DIVE SITES
- **Great Cut** A 200-foot section of fallen wall forming a double dropoff.
- **Telephone Pole** Wall dive descent from 45 to 100 feet.

Far Horizons

The Bahamas South of the Tropic of Cancer
You are on your own here. There are no dive operators, and as far as we know, no places where you can get your tanks filled. This alone had a material affect on our diving plans, and largely for this reason we bought a Brownie's Third Lung system, which at least allows two people to dive to 60 feet on surface-supplied air. Forget about caves and wreck penetration, and you'll find it works fine. But for regular diving, if you really want to cover this area, a live-aboard dive boat is probably your best bet, or invest in a compressor.

Crooked Island has a dropoff at its northern point starting in 40 feet, and there are some 60 miles of wall running toward Acklins Island, which are largely unexplored. Hogsty Reef, an atoll to the south of Acklins Island over 30 nm from land in any direction, has legendary diving, allegedly hundreds of wrecks, and is visited occasionally by live-aboard dive boats. The Ragged Island Range, rarely visited, has 50 miles of fringing reefs. The other islands, the Plana Cays, Mayaguana, and the two Inaguas, Little Inagua and Great Inagua, are virgin ground, although Great Inagua is known to have an abysmal wall to the north of Matthew Town.

DRESS AND PROTECTION

In the winter months the ocean temperature will drop from the summer 80s (°F) to the 70s. A 2mm wetsuit is your best bet for the winter months. During the summer you hardly need a wetsuit for shallow dives (80 feet or less), but a wetskin is sensible to give you some protection in case you accidentally brush against fire coral or encounter sea lice.

DIVING EMERGENCIES

All dive operators in the islands have rescue-trained personnel and oxygen. Any island with an airfield or airstrip can provide air evacuation. There is a hyperbaric chamber in Port Lucaya, Grand Bahama.

If you are diving in the Bahamas you should first read our cautions and notes in the **Buff Pages** under **Medical Facilities, Health, and Health Hazards** on page 324 and the section on **The Bahamas Air-Sea Rescue Association** on page 329.

LIVE ENCOUNTER DIVING

This statement may not be politically correct in today's world, but we have strong reservations about live-encounter diving. We do not believe that live feeding should be carried out to produce a circus display and increase dive trip revenue.

Why do we take this stand? Let's deal with the shark dives first. The longer-term effects of this are unquantifiable, distort the pattern of nature, and bring predators into waters they did not frequent before. Inevitably the shark population will come to associate divers with food. The prognosis for such an automatic association is not good. Somewhere, sometime, quite possibly in a place not associated with feeding dives, a shark will turn on innocent divers who fail to provide a free meal. Beyond this, there are always mavericks, unstable and unpredictable creatures, just as the human race produces its psychotics. Is shark feeding wise? The only sensible, logical answer must be "No."

We also believe that playing with dolphins should not be encouraged, and that dolphin captivity, in any form, should be banned. Dolphins are highly intelligent, intuitive, tolerant, gentle, and playful creatures with a very strong sense of family and pod (clan) bonding. They are used to ranging far, born free and swimming free, over a vast range of water, where other than sharks, they have no enemies. They are dependent for their navigation and communication on a long-range sonar system that eclipses our best submarine sound ranging and communications. To pen a dolphin is cruelty, and to confine a dolphin within a tank, where its sonar reechoes on all sides like a scream in a prison cell, is torture. As divers we should enjoy random encounters with dolphins in the open ocean and bless our good fortune when these happen.

Let's ban the circus acts.

Books about the Bahamas

So many books have been written about the Bahamas, but one of the most delightful stories that at the same time gives you all the flavor of Bahamian history is Robert Wilder's *Wind From the Carolinas*, which has been republished by Bluewater Books & Charts (ISBN 1877838098). It's a classic. Bluewater has graciously prepared this list of books you may wish to add to your Bahamas bookshelf (some of them probably only obtainable in the Bahamas):

General Reading
Abaco, History of an Out Island and its Cays. Steve Dodge (White Sound Press. ISBN 0-932265-34-0).
The Bahamas, A Family of Islands. Gail Saunders (Caribbean Guides. ISBN 0-333-59212-3).
Bahamas: Out Island Odyssey. Nan Jeffrey (Avalon House. ISBN 0-9627562-3-7).
Bahamas Rediscovered. Nicholas Popov. (MacMillan Caribbean. ISBN 0-333-56603-3).
Gulf Stream: Encounters with the Blue God. William MacLeish (Florida Club. ISBN 0-395-40621-8).
My Castle in the Air. Evans W. Cottman (Rehor Publishing).
Out-Island Doctor. Evans W. Cottman (Landfall Press. ISBN 0-9134218-3).

Other Cruising Guides
Cruising Guide to Abaco. Steve Dodge (White Sound Press. ISBN 0-932265-41-3).
The Exuma Guide: A Cruising Guide to the Exuma Cays. Stephen Pavlidis (Seaworthy. ISBN 0-96395667-1).
Explorerer Chartbook Exumas. Rick Butler (Lewis Offshore).
Yachtman's Guide to the Bahamas. Meredith Fields (Tropic Isle. ISBN 0-937379-19-0).
Bahamas GPS and Loran Handbook. (Better Boating Assn.)

Marine Reference
Fishes of the Atlantic Coast. Gar Goodson. (Stanford University Press. ISBN 0-8047-1268-9).
Guide to Corals and Fishes of Florida, the Bahamas, and the Caribbean. Idaz & Jerry Greenberg. (Seahawk Press. ISBN 0-913-00807-9).
Reef Fish Identification Guide. Paul Human (New World Publishing. ISBN 1-878348078).

General Reference
Bahamas Handbook and Businessman's Annual. Etienne Dupuch (E. Dupuch. ISBN 0-914755-63-3).
Insight Guide to the Bahamas. Insight Guides (Houghton-Mifflin. ISBN 0-395-66175-7).
Frommers The Bahamas. (MacMillan. ISBN 0-02-861647-2).
Fodor's The Bahamas. (Random House. ISBN 0-679-03174X).
Pilot's Bahamas & Caribbean Aviation Guide. (Pilot Publishing).

Chapter 21
Buff Pages
Infrastructure and Government

The Bahamas National Flag.

Ministry of Tourism

Infrastructure

A Bahamian ABC

BANKING

The Bank of the Bahamas, Bank of Nova Scotia, Barclays Bank, Canadian Imperial Bank of Commerce, Chase Manhattan Bank, Citibank N.A, and the Royal Bank of Canada are all active in the Bahamas. All of them accept and change traveler's checks (you will need your passport for verification) and some have ATMs.

All currency transactions must take place through the banks, as there is no Bahamian equivalent of Western Union or any similar money handling system. However, as there is no restriction on the amount of money that you may bring into the Bahamas and the amount you may take out, it's prudent to overestimate your expenditures and carry traveler's checks in reserve.

Banking hours are normally Monday to Thursday from 9:30 am to 3 pm, and Fridays 9 am to 5 pm. We list banks and their specific hours in the **Yellow Pages** for each port of call.

BUSINESS HOURS

Government offices work Monday to Friday, from 9 am to 5 pm. There may be minor changes, and don't necessarily expect that these hours will be kept by a small customs office that may be a one-man or one-woman band, and the office holder, to complicate matters, may well be double-hatted, running a second office at the same time.

Generally the business hours set by the government offices set the pace for most businesses in most places, save where financial interests dictate more flexible, often extended, opening hours. We have tried to give precise times in our **Yellow Pages** but it's not always possible to tie people down to a declared schedule.

CREDIT CARDS

MasterCard and Visa are widely accepted, although a credit card surcharge (sometimes as much as 5 percent) can be added. You can always refuse and use your traveler's checks or cash. American Express and Diners Club are not so widely accepted. The smaller islands and cays may well not take credit cards, and you should be prepared for this. In general you could say that as you go down the scale in size and up the scale into remoteness, first of all the utility of credit cards fades out, then the utility of traveler's checks. Make sure you have adequate cash on hand, and if your destination is really remote, favor them with the currency of their own land, for US dollars may be rare currency there.

CURRENCY

The Bahamian currency is the Bahamas dollar, which rates on par with the US dollar. Both Bahamian and US currency are accepted universally in the Bahamas, although as we've said, in remote settlements the Bahamian may well be preferred. A curious anomaly is that many Batelco coin phones will only operate on a US quarter (25¢) and fail to work with a Bahamian quarter. Save your US quarters. You may need them.

DEPARTURE TAX

A $15 departure tax must be paid by every passenger leaving the Bahamas by air, which is collected at the airline desk on check-in. There is an additional $3 security fee at Freeport International Airport.

DRESS CODES

The Bahamas are informal and the jacket and tie of normal business attire is rarely required, although the upper strata of restaurants often prefer men to wear a blazer or a sports jacket in the evening. Check if you have doubt. In such places a shirt with a collar is invariably preferable to a tee shirt, and long trousers rather than shorts. Otherwise you may dress casually virtually wherever you are.

Remember that just because **you** are on vacation and wearing beach attire much of the time, it's not the way you should dress to tour Nassau or even an outlying settlement. The Bahamians are offended by nudity and near-nudity; bikini bras and short cut-offs do not go down well as street attire, and they have a deeply ingrained sense of propriety. Respect the life-style. You are a guest in their islands.

DRIVING

Visitors may drive in the Bahamas for up to three months on their own driver's licence. The Bahamas adheres to the British system of driving on the left side of the road. As most vehicles are imported from the US with the steering wheel on the left of the vehicle, a "co-pilot" is often useful to help the driver see the road ahead. It takes some concentration to get used to the "keep left" rule, and it's easy to forget which side of the road you should be on in remote stretches in a place like Eleuthera, when you meet no other traffic for quite a while.

Speed limits are 25 mph in built-up areas and 30 mph everywhere else, except for some specified sections of new road in Nassau and Freeport where a 45-mph limit has been set. There are no seat belt rules. Motorcyclists are required to wear helmets.

DRUGS

Drugs that are illegal in the US (marijuana, LSD, cocaine, morphine, opium, and the like) are also illegal in the Bahamas. If you are caught in possession, at the least you will face a fine of $100,000 and anything up to five years in prison. Under US rules, it may well be that the boat is confiscated with no appeal possible. There's only one way to go: *don't do drugs*.

DUTY FREE

Generally in the Bahamas china, crystal, fine jewelry, luxury leather goods, linens, tablecloths, liquor, perfume, cologne and toilet water, photographic equipment, sweaters, watches, and wine are classed as duty-free goods.

ELECTRICITY

Electricity supply is 1 phase 3 wire 120V 60 cycle AC, which is the same as in the US. Power in the small islands is provided by locally owned generators and you can expect inexplicable surges and occasional low voltage. If you're operating sensitive equipment like a computer, you would be wise to have a good surge protector in use when you're hooked up to shore power. Otherwise, generate your own power.

GARBAGE

We put garbage in our ABC with no apology. Garbage is always a problem for the cruising sailor, and the disposal of garbage is an ongoing and vexing problem for the Bahamas, who have no land mass to play with and cannot excavate landfills. For your part, *never* dump plastic at sea or anywhere else. Don't even think of burying your garbage on a deserted island. Anything that is truly biodegradable may be jettisoned at sea, well offshore, in deep water. If you must, glass bottles (broken first) may be disposed of in this way, and cans (cut open at both ends) other than aluminum cans. For the rest you must carry your garbage with you until you can dispose of it, bagged, wherever there is a recognized disposal site.

Walk the beaches of the Bahamas and you will see what the heedless disposal of garbage, particularly plastics, has already done to the environment. What you will not see are the seabirds and turtles who have died caught in six-pack rings, and the fish who have died ingesting the detritus of passing boaters.

LANGUAGE

Yes, of course they speak English. But you may take some time to get used to the lilt, catch phrases, and inflection.

LIQUOR LAWS

The drinking age is 18.

MAIL

You must use Bahamian stamps (which are pretty). For the US, a letter is 55¢ and a postcard is 40¢. For Europe a letter is 60¢ and a postcard is 40¢.

TAXES AND TIPPING

A tax of 8 percent is added to all hotel bills and villa rentals. A three-night minimum stay is not uncommon. Tipping? The standard rate is 15 percent.

TIME ZONE

The Bahamas are in the same time zone as the east coast of the US, which is Eastern Standard Time (EST), 5 hours behind UT or Greenwich Mean Time. When it's noon in the Bahamas, it's noon in Washington DC, 9 am on the west coast of the US (Pacific Time), and 5 pm in London, England.

The Bahamas change to Daylight Savings Time (EDT) on the first Sunday in April and revert to EST on the last Sunday in October (as does the US).

WEIGHTS AND MEASURES

Weights and measures for linear, dry, and liquid measurement used in the Bahamas are the same as in the US. Fuel is sold in US gallons. The Bahamas is likely to follow any moves made by the US Government toward adopting the metric system, but as yet this has amounted to no more than the requirement that consumer goods are labeled in both metric and US measurements.

Medical Facilities, Health, and Health Hazards

Medical Facilities

Hardly surprisingly the best medical facilities are found in the centers of population, Nassau and the Freeport–Lucaya area. In Nassau there are two main hospitals, the Princess Margaret Hospital and the Doctor's Hospital. There is also the Lyford Cay Hospital and Bahamas Heart Institute in the greater New Providence area at Lyford Cay. In Freeport there is the Rand Memorial Hospital.

Over the rest of the Bahamas medical facilities are available in a well-distributed spread of some thirteen health centers and thirty-six clinics. It remains that if you are not in either Nassau or the Freeport–Lucaya area and someone needs urgent attention in the event of a serious injury or condition, they will have to be flown to Nassau. This may not be the first step in their medical evacuation, for the casualty may have to be taken first by boat (it could be in your boat) to the nearest island or cay with a clinic, and from there (after stabilizing treatment), by boat once again to the nearest airfield or airport, and then moved by air to a hospital.

Two broad conclusions can be drawn from this:

- You should carry the fullest possible medical pack on board, together with first-aid manuals, so that you (or your crew) are able to respond with effective immediate first aid after any accident or medical crisis. As a preventive measure you should ensure that everyone on board has an adequate stock of prescription medication to last the voyage. Your aim, even before you set out on your cruise, must be to achieve the medical capability of being able to deliver someone, in an emergency, in a no-worse state to the nearest clinic or health center from wherever you might be, or to an airfield with a waiting air ambulance.

- If the casualty is in serious danger, rather than risk the trauma of repeated interisland moves, it may be better to seek direct air evacuation from the nearest airport (such as Marsh Harbour or Treasure Cay in the Abacos, George Town in the Exumas) straight to a hospital in Florida. To this end the Divers Alert Network (DAN) and other organizations offer insurance with emergency air evacuation included. It's well worth considering. Failing this cover, it would be sensible to travel with an air evacuation service contact number listed in your Log Book. Take care of this before you set out for the Bahamas.

National Air Ambulance in Fort Lauderdale, who fly out of Fort Lauderdale International Airport, are one of the best-placed air evacuation services for the Bahamas. Their telephone numbers are 800-327-3710 and 305-359-9900. There are a number of other operators offering similar services. Air ambulances apart, we list all the medical facilities in the Bahama Islands in our **Yellow Pages**. We also list dental facilities, of which there are few outside Nassau. Because this is so, we always carry a dental first-aid kit.

Health

You should have no particular health problems in the Bahamas. There are three health hazards, all marine related, which we'll deal with separately, but taken across the board the Bahama Islands are a healthy environment. Although Bahamas-piped water is not always good, and may well be brackish in many places, there are plentiful supplies of bottled drinking water. Food in the Bahamas is generally good and wholesome, and there are no problems there. Both daytime and nighttime temperatures, and humidity, are normally well within your comfort zone.

Are there any areas for concern? Yes, watch the sun. You wouldn't believe how many people get sunburned. Whatever sun lotion, cream, or gel you use, it should have a sun protection factor of at least 15. It should be waterproof. If your skin is sensitive or your complexion is fair, the chances are that you should use a high-rating PABA-free product to prevent blistering. In the evenings and at night, particularly if you fall into that "fair skin and attractive to insects" category, protect yourself against mosquitos and no-see-ums.

Is there anything else to watch? Yes, watch your drinking. We're not talking about counting your Goombay Smashes here (though it's not a bad idea to try) but your water intake. There have been periods when we've reckoned on and gone through one gallon of drinking water per person per day, just to keep normally hydrated.

Health Hazards

CIGUATERA

Top of our list, though mercifully we've escaped it so far, is ciguatera, poisoning by eating seafood. The name comes from the Spanish "cigua," a marine snail that the early Spanish settlers in Cuba tried to add to their diet and found poisonous. That particular snail is no longer a part of our diet, but fish carrying ciguatoxin may well be part of your catch. It's a naturally occurring toxin that passes along the food chain and, if it reaches you, will cause nausea, vomiting, and vertigo at best (after an initial tingling and numbness), and paralysis at worst.

The most suspect species are reef fish: barracuda, eels, red snapper, amberjack, sea bass, and grouper. Since grouper is a staple Bahamian food (every menu features fried grouper, grilled grouper, and grouper fingers) this sounds like bad news. The key is to go for the smaller fish (5 lbs. or less), and don't eat the internal organs. Fine, you might say, but who ever heard of anyone saying "small is beautiful" in the commercial fishing stakes and going for the 3-lb. groupers? Point taken, we'd say. The carry-on is this: listen to local advice. The Bahamians are not immune to ciguatera. If they catch a grouper and reckon it's OK for them, it's OK for you too.

Can you test for ciguatera? The answer is no. Not yet. People are working on it. Can cooking neutralize it? The answer, once again, is a no. Neither cooking, freezing, marinating, or pickling kills the ciguatera toxin.

Finally, if you do get ciguatera? What can you expect? Symptoms within 2–12 hours after eating the affected fish. Seek help at a clinic, or call the DAN Ciguatera Hotline in the States. You have two points of contact. Call 305-661-0774 or fax 305-667-2270 (Dr. Donna Blythe), or 305-361-4619 (Dr. Donald da Sylva). Rest assured, however bad it is, ciguatera is rarely fatal.

SEA LICE

Sea lice or jellyfish larvae can "bloom" in sea areas at times on a very local basis. Often the larvae come from seagrass that has been kicked up or disturbed, bringing the larvae to the surface. In contact with the human skin both sea lice and jellyfish larvae parasites burrow into the upper layers of the skin causing a rash, sometimes tenderness, sometimes small pimples, but always irritation and itching. This condition will last a week or so and then disappear. The only counter is to wash yourself thoroughly in fresh water.

DECOMPRESSION SICKNESS

The deep dives of places like the Abaco Barrier Reef (where regular dives to 185 feet are offered by local dive operators) can produce at best narcosis with all its dangers and at worst, decompression sickness. If you are not in training, and not experienced in deep diving, do *not* attempt it. If you do go along for the ride, pay particular attention to your safety stops on your ascent, and keep it *slow, slow, slow*. Don't neglect to have that extra tank with a regulator hooked up hanging on a line at your last stop, so that anyone low on air can stay there until your degassing is complete.

Just in case you need to think of it, the nearest decompression chamber is at Port Lucaya in Grand Bahama. See the **Buff Pages** entry on the **Bahamas Air-Sea Rescue Association (BASRA)** on page 329.

Cellular Telephone in the Bahamas

The Bahamas Telecommunications Corporation (Batelco) does not as a matter of routine provide roaming facilities for the cellular telephones that most cruising visitors may have on board. Batelco have a list of US, Canadian, and Mexican cellular companies with whom they have roaming agreements, which is available from their Roaming Department at 242-394-3685 or 242-394-4000. Most of these companies tend to be relatively small, local US cellular services rather than the giants, and as the list is changing constantly, we think it better that you check with your own cellular company and ask if they have a roaming agreement with Batelco, or check with Batelco directly.

Batelco offers the cruising visitor full roaming facilities in the islands through their own facilities. To arrange this you need to produce:

- A passport or valid ID such as a voter's card or driver's license.
- A credit reference letter from your bank.

And you are required to pay the following charges up front:

Security deposit	$500.00
Activation fee	50.00
Interisland roaming fee	20.00
Programming fee	50.00

Thereafter Batelco's charges are:

Monthly access charge	48.00
Rate per minute 7 am–7 pm	0.45
Rate per minute 7 pm–7 am	0.30

Your monthly charges are deducted from your initial deposit. When you choose to close your Batelco account, the balance remaining will be refunded to you.

These arrangements can be set up ahead of your visit by faxing the relevant identification and credit information to Batelco, but on your arrival it is necessary to call at Batelco to complete the process. We give the details of their Nassau office with whom you should first deal. If your landfall is planned for an island other than New Providence, Batelco will advise you where you should complete the formalities they require.

Their address is:

Bahamas Telecommunication Corporation
Wireless Department
PO Box N-3084, The Mall at Marathon
Nassau, Bahamas
Tel: 242-394-4000 and 242-394-5000
Roaming Department: 242-394-3685
Fax: 242-393-3516 and 242-393-4798

Coastal Radio Stations

There are only two specified Public Correspondence (Marine Operator) radio stations in the Bahamas. These are:

CALL SIGN	FREQUENCY	NAME
C6N2	2182 kHz	Nassau Public Correspondence
C6N3	VHF 27	Nassau Public Correspondence

Government

Entering the Bahamas

You are required by law to clear in with Customs and Immigration on entering the Bahamas. The geographic spread of Bahamian entry ports gives you options that allow you to approach the Bahamas from any direction. You may sail on past one entry port and clear in later at another as you wish, provided that no one in your crew lands until you have cleared in.

When you reach your chosen port of entry you'll be flying your yellow Q (quarantine) flag, which will have been flying from your starboard spreader (or the equivalent position on a power boat) ever since you entered Bahamian waters. You have 24-hours grace to clear in from your time of arrival at your entry port, and that Q flag stays flying until you've cleared in.

Only the captain of the vessel is allowed on shore to report for clearance. He or she should take the ship's papers, and the passports (or acceptable proof of ID) of all on board.

Passports or Proof of ID

US citizens: Valid passport, voter registration card, birth certificate
Canadians: valid passport
UK citizens: valid passport
If any member of your ship's company is planning to leave while you are still cruising in the Bahamas, they require a valid air ticket for the return journey. This should be taken by the ship's captain with the passport of the person concerned.

The Paperwork

One way or another, it takes some time to clear in, even if you're the first in line or the only person clearing in at that time. Be patient. There's a lot of paper to fill out and more carbons than you will ever remember seeing at one time. Let's start with the first form. We'll cover the main points. All of them are too lengthy to reproduce in this Guide.

Bahamas Customs Department—Inward Report, Pleasure Vessels

This is a straightforward declaration but requires a full crew and passenger list, with addresses and nationality, and the details of any arms and ammunition on board.

Bahamas Immigration—Inward Passenger and Crew Manifest, Pleasure Ship

This again requires a full crew and passenger list with addresses and nationality.

Bahamas Immigration Cards

You complete your immigration card. Each person has to complete and sign his or her own card, which has to be presented with their passport. For this reason this part of the proceedings may become a two-act serial (but see our later comment).

The passport is stamped, the card is stamped twice, and the main part of the card is retained by the immigration or customs officer. The passport is returned with the tear-off tab, which has to be surrendered on leaving the Bahamas.

Bahamas Customs—Maritime Declaration of Health

This is a question-and-answer form that requires you to account for the state of health of everyone on board. We feel that the form itself has been overtaken by time, but consider it an interesting insight into earlier days. Among the matters you're required to address or furnish are:

- A report on cholera, yellow fever, and small pox cases.
- A report on the unusual death of rats and mice during your voyage.
- How many people died on board (on the reverse of the form you are asked what you did with the bodies).

Application For a Permit to Engage in Foreign Fishing for Sporting Purposes

You may ignore this last form if you don't want a fishing permit.

At the end of all this you should emerge with:

(1) A cruising permit valid for 12 months.
(2) A fishing permit (if you wanted one).
(3) Your own stamped passport with your immigration card tear-off stub.

It will have cost you $10.00 for the cruising permit and $20.00 for the fishing permit.

If you're lucky, you may be able to have your passengers and crew at hand during this procedure so that you can get them to fill out their immigration cards while you are tackling your mountain of paperwork. So much depends on where you are. If the customs officer is clearing you on board, then that's fine. They're right there with you.

If you have to hike to an office further afield, much depends on the drill in that place. Some entry ports don't mind if your crew tag along and sit on a bench outside. Others play it straight. Check with others who've already cleared in to see how it works where you are. If you're unlucky, you have a second trip to make to the customs office with those passports and immigration cards.

Once you have your cruising permit, take down your Q flag and fly the Bahamas Ensign (*not* the National Flag) in its place. See **The Bahamas Flag and Flag Etiquette**, page 328.

What You May Bring In
ALCOHOL AND TOBACCO
You may import alcoholic drinks for your own use (nominally 1 quart of spirits and 1 quart of wine) and 1 lb. of tobacco, or 200 cigarettes, or 50 cigars.

BOATS
For your own boat, your cruising permit is obviously your authority to cruise in the Bahamas for up to one year without paying import duty on your vessel. Thereafter you would be liable for 7.5 percent (30–100 feet LOA) or 22.5 percent (less than 30 feet LOA) of its value if you import the boat. Alternatively you can extend your cruising permit for up to three years for a fee of $500 per year.

An important new change has been made in respect to the duty-free importation of boats for cruising in the Bahamas. In the past, to get your cruising permit, you had to bring the boat in under its own power and import it in person to qualify for a cruising permit. Now you, a non-Bahamian national, may have your boat shipped in by freighter and imported as cargo for temporary use, provided that it is going to be reshipped out of the Bahamas. This change applies to boats of not less than 23 feet LOA.

The Bahamian customs have put in effect a procedure in which the boat is unloaded from the freighter bringing it in at the port of entry and, for a flat fee of $50, is granted a cruising permit (under Duty Exemption Clause 23 listed in Part B of Schedule 4 of the Bahamas Tariff Act). Those who do not want to face a Gulf Stream crossing may now fly in to pick up their boat, use it in the Islands, and then ship it out.

BOAT SPARES
You may bring in boat spares for your own use. If you sell one of your boat spares to someone else, Bahamas law con-siders that a disposal on your part that should be reported to a customs officer, who will assess the import duty due on the sale. There's no import duty on the spares you carry that you take in to use on board your own boat.

DRUGS
You may bring in your own prescription drugs. Otherwise it's a big *no* to anything that is illegal in the US.

FIREARMS
You may import firearms (rifles, shotguns, and hand guns) and ammunition provided that they are declared, and kept on board under lock and key. Automatic weapons, such as assault rifles, are banned. If your cruise is to extend over three months, you must report to the police to obtain a firearms certificate. Firearms may not be used in Bahamian waters nor taken ashore.

FOOD
You are permitted to bring in food in bulk for your own cruising requirements. If you are inspected and have abnormal quantities of food, it might be suspected that you intend to barter or sell your surplus, and you may be asked to explain why you are so well stocked. Most people who cruise in the Bahamas buy as much as they can in the islands.

MOTORCYCLES AND BICYCLES
These are subject to import duty and must be licensed in the Bahamas and insured before you may use them on shore. If you do not wish to pay import duty, a bond in lieu (such as a cash deposit or a bank guarantee) may serve. We reckon it's not worth the trouble. Forget it and rent a local bicycle, golf cart, or car when you need wheels.

PETS
Dogs and cats over the age of six months may be admitted with you to the Bahamas. You will need to start work on the import papers required for a pet about two months ahead of your cruise. First you must apply to the Director, Department of Agriculture, PO Box N-3028, Nassau, Bahamas (242-325-7502/9 or fax 242-325-3960) for an application to import your pet. Return the form with a $10 fee (use an international money order). You should get your import permit.

You also need a certificate of health (issued within 48 hours of your embarkation for the Bahamas), and a rabies certificate. The rabies certificate, if issued with a one-year validity, should be valid from not less than one month and not more than ten months before your entry to the Bahamas. If the validity of your rabies certificate covers three years, the acceptability bracket is not less than one month prior to entry and not more than 34 months.

There have been changes in these rules, and you would be wise to check before starting any inoculation process. Nonetheless, it remains that if you get your paperwork in order *before* you declare yourself in to the Bahamas, your pet should be able to remain signed on as part of the crew while you're in the islands.

BARTERING—A WARNING

The Bahamian customs have become increasingly intolerant of bartering carried out by cruising boats in which otherwise dutiable goods, allowed in duty free with the issue of a cruising permit, are traded for local goods or services. If you are caught in this kind of activity, you'll be in trouble.

DUTY FREE SHIPMENT OF MARINE SPARES

If you have to order spare parts to be sent in from outside the Bahamas during your cruise, Bahamas customs regulations allow for duty-free importation. You must have the package clearly marked:

For Marine Use Only for Named Vessel in the Bahamas Under C-39
DUTY FREE
Under Item Subch. 4, Part B, Chapter 28 Tariff Act of May 26, 1993

Ensure that the shipper labels the package for you as the captain of your vessel and that your boat name, as well as your address, is clearly displayed.

Leaving the Bahamas

You don't have to report to Customs and Immigration to clear out of the Bahamas. If your last port is an entry port, you may hand in your cruising permit and the immigration card stubs of everyone who is with you just before you leave. However if you do this, and if you have to put back for any reason, you may have set yourself a problem with your premature surrender of these vital forms. Alternatively, you may mail your cruising permit and the immigration form stubs back to the Bahamas government from the US (or your next landfall). The address to use is on the reverse of the cruising permit.

THINKING ABOUT US CUSTOMS ON YOUR RETURN

See the **Blue Pages** under **Clearing In to the US** on page 294. While it's on our mind, may we remind you:

US CUSTOMS DECAL

If you've not already paid your annual customs user fee and got your decal, add it to your list. It will simplify your return entry into the US.

The Bahamas Flag and Flag Etiquette

The Bahamas flag was taken into use on Independence Day in 1973. Its design rests primarily on three equal bands of color. Two aquamarine stripes, one at the top and one at the bottom, represent the colors of Bahamian skies and waters, with a central yellow stripe representing sand and shore. The three bands have a black triangle superimposed on the left (the staff side), which represents unity. This is the national flag, which is not flown as a courtesy flag.

Courtesy Flag

The courtesy flag flown by visiting yachts is a variation of the ensigns flown by Bahamian craft. The civil ensign, which you will fly, is based on a white St. George's cross on a red background (a variation of the English national flag), with the Bahamas national flag superimposed in the upper left quarter.

Normal flag etiquette dictates that you fly a courtesy flag immediately after you are granted clearance to cruise in the Bahamas. You take down your Bahamian courtesy flag when you leave the Bahamas, normally when you are three miles out in international waters.

War Ensign

You may see a variation of this ensign on Bahamian warships. In the War Ensign the background is white (again taken from the British, this time the Royal Navy) with a red cross on it. The War Ensign also has a national flag superimposed in the upper left quarter.

Q Flag

Remember it is international law that you fly a yellow Q flag on entering territorial waters from another country. This applies to you entering the Bahamas, and returning to the United States, regardless of your nationality and registration. You take down your Q flag as soon as you are granted clearance.

The Bahamas Air-Sea Rescue Association (BASRA)

The Bahamas Air-Sea Rescue Association (BASRA) is the leading marine rescue organization in the Bahamas. It is a volunteer service, very similar in its conception to a Volunteer Fire Service. Its members contract to respond to emergency calls at any time of the day or night, and, very often, will use their own boats, and on occasion seaplanes, to effect a rescue. BASRA does not, however, operate in isolation and has close and constant links with the Royal Bahamas Defence Force and the US Coast Guard.

BASRA monitors Channel 16 on a 24-hour basis. Should you need BASRA the normal means of summoning help is by an emergency broadcast on Channel 16, but both Nassau and Freeport also monitor 2182 kHz. If you get no response, and there's no one in your area to relay your message or distress call, try Channel 22A, which the Royal Bahamas Defence Force monitors for BASRA on a 24-hour basis. You may also be able to contact a US Coast Guard ship or aircraft, if they are within range.

In addition to their rescue services, BASRA also maintains links with the Underwater Explorers Society (UNEXSO) in Port Lucaya, Grand Bahama, who maintain a decompression chamber that can be activated at any time in the event of a decompression diving accident. Contact Channel 16 or Channel 86 or by telephone at 242-352-2628. This is one of the very few decompression chambers available on an emergency basis outside the US. Scuba divers should take note.

Think you might never need BASRA? Their report for the past twelve months issued in May 1997 puts it plainly. BASRA answered 603 calls. 132 were vessels in distress, 54 were boats requiring towing, 84 were calls for help that were passed to third-party assistance, 19 were air searches, 157 were messages relayed, 16 were EPIRB alerts, 5 were downed aircraft, 19 were hoaxes, 68 resulted from reports of overdue vessels, 15 were boats that had run aground, 7 were for medical evacuation, 3 were boats on fire, and 5 were for crewmen missing, lost overboard.

BASRA would wish, we believe, to make plain that they are not a fallback service for those who run out of fuel, nor are they a towing service if you have mechanical failure. Your primary responsibility is to look after your own vessel and your crew, and solve your own problems. BASRA are there to step in when lives are in danger.

May we make a plea that all cruising visitors make a point of becoming members of BASRA? Life membership is $500. Sponsorship is $250 and above, each year. Individual membership is $30 per year. Other than its fundraising activities, BASRA has no source of income. Do you know the cost of running BASRA? An air search costs over $100 an hour. A rescue boat costs $60 an hour to operate. Do you think those rescued by BASRA ante up this kind of money to say

BASRA Emergency Stations in the Bahamas (24-Hour Monitoring)

LOCATION	VHF CHANNEL OR SSB FREQUENCY
Abacos	
BASRA Guana Cay	VHF 16
BASRA Hope Town	VHF 16
BASRA Little Harbour	VHF 16
BASRA Man-O-War Cay	VHF 16 & 2738 kHz
BASRA Marsh Harbour	VHF 16
Grand Bahama	
BASRA Freeport	VHF 16, VHF 84, & 2182 kHz
Berry Islands	
BASRA Great Harbour	VHF 16
Chub Cay	VHF 68
Nassau	
BASRA HQ Nassau	VHF 16 & 2182 kHz
Eleuthera	
BASRA Spanish Wells	VHF 16 & 2738 kHz
BASRA Governors Harbour	VHF 16
Exumas	
BASRA Black Point	VHF 16
BASRA Staniel Cay	VHF 16
BASRA George Town	VHF 16
Cat Island	
BASRA Hawks Nest	VHF 16
Crooked Island	
BASRA Landrail Point	VHF 16
Long Island	
BASRA Gemeni Deadmans Cay	VHF 16
BASRA Dockmaster Clarence Town	VHF 16
BASRA Hiseas	VHF 16
BASRA Sunseeker Salt Pond	VHF 16

"thank you" for their lives or their vessel? Sadly and regrettably not.

It just may happen that one day your contribution to BASRA may save a life. It could be your own.

If you join, you're not committed to playing an active part in BASRA if you don't wish to do so. If you are semi-permanent in the Bahamas in one area and willing to help, you may be welcome as a Boat Captain, Boat Crew, for the Air Wing, for help in fund-raising, or for some other activity. Contact:

The Bahamas Air-Sea Rescue Association
PO Box SS-6247
Nassau, Bahamas
242-322-3877 and 242-325-8864
fax 242-325-2737

The Royal Bahamas Defence Force

An armed force combining naval and air elements, the Royal Bahamas Defence Force is charged with the protection of the Bahamas, fishery protection, countering illegal immigration and drug smuggling, and search and rescue. It's a tall order for a small force faced with the operational responsibility for 100,000 square miles of Bahamian territorial water, with the complication of some 700 islands and well over 2,000 nm of coastline. Under a bilateral agreement with the US Government, joint patrols are conducted in the Biminis with the US Customs, and Royal Bahamian Defence Force personnel also serve on board US Coast Guard cutters, when required, to give the US Coast Guard jurisdiction in Bahamian waters.

The Royal Bahamas Defence Force has a fleet of 26 coastal and inshore patrol craft ranging from PO 1, HMBS Marlin, a 103-foot patrol boat, to 29-foot patrol boats and a handful of cigarette boats. All the patrol boats are painted naval grey, carry their pennant numbers (PO 1, etc.) on the sides, and bear that HMBS designation, standing for Her Britannic Majesty's Bahamian Ship. The honor goes to the Queen of the United Kingdom as the head of the British Commonwealth, to which the Bahamas belongs.

The Force also has two fixed-wing aircraft, a Cessna Golden Eagle 421C, and a Cessna Titan Ambassador 404, which are used for reconnaissance, patrols, search and rescue, and in a transport role.

All told the Royal Bahamian Defence Force numbers some 850 officers and other ranks, 71 of whom are women. Their working dress may be naval blue fatigues or tropical white full dress uniforms, or may be camouflaged combat dress. All personnel may be armed. The Force is based in Coral Harbour on the southwest coast of New Providence Island, where they have a sea firing range (see our section on **Nassau and New Providence Island** on page 157).

The Royal Bahamas Defence Force has the right to board and inspect any vessel in Bahamian waters. They will be armed during such inspections. If you are boarded, you'll be asked to sign a certificate at the end of the inspection to state that it was carried out politely, correctly, and that the captain of the vessel boarded (or his or her representative) was allowed to be present throughout the inspection.

The members of the Royal Bahamas Defence Force are well trained (often graduates of the Britannia Royal Naval College in Dartmouth, England, or the US Coast Guard Officer Candidate School in Yorktown, Virginia), are friendly, and approachable. All patrol boats monitor Channel 16. Channel 22A is their primary frequency. Coral Harbour has a 24-hour watch on 22A, and to broaden their range there are repeater stations in the Berry Islands (at Chub Cay), the Abacos (at Hole in the Wall), and in the Exumas (at Highborne Cay).

The Royal Bahamas Police Force

The maintenance of law and order in the Bahamas rests with the Royal Bahamas Police Force, whose current strength is 2,023 police officers, who are supported by a clerical staff of 220 civilians. While the main strength of the Force is based in the centers of population, with Nassau and New Providence Island hardly surprisingly rating the greatest police presence, isolated detachments are stationed in virtually all the settlements.

Royal Bahamas Police Force Band drummer.

Bahamas police normally are unarmed, but the carriage of weapons is not unknown. Violent crime, much of it drug related, has increased in recent years. The Bahamas Police Force Drug Enforcement Unit works closely with the Royal Bahamas Defence Force, the US DEA, and the US Customs Service. The Force was computerized for record keeping in 1990, maintains a forensic science laboratory, and on a more human note, also runs a canine section and believes strongly in community policing, which suits their island environment well. Outside the Bahamas the police force are generally better known for their ceremonial activities, especially in the form of the Royal Bahamas Police Force Band, which has won acclaim both on state duties in the Bahamas and abroad, at prestigious events such as the British Royal Tournament. If they are on parade while you are in the Bahamas, be sure to see them. Check with the Ministry of Tourism in Market Place, Bay Street, in Nassau. They have a program of forthcoming events.

Bahamian Holidays and Special Events

Public Holidays

New Years Day. January 1.
Easter. In March or April. **Good Friday**, **Easter Day** and **Easter Monday**
Labour Day. The first Friday in June.
Whit Monday. The first Monday seven weeks after Easter.
Independence Day. July 10.
Emancipation Day. The first Monday in August.
Discovery Day. October 12.
Christmas Day. December 25.
Boxing Day. December 26.
If a public holiday falls on a Saturday or a Sunday, it will be switched to the Friday before or the following Monday.

Special Events

FURTHER INFORMATION AND FIRM DATES

As this Guide is republished every second year and at the time of going to print for each edition the dates of many Bahamian annual fixtures have not been set, we show the events that normally fall in each calendar month, which gives guidance on the places where you may want to be, or perhaps, if you don't want the crowd scene, places you'll want to avoid! Detailed calendars covering the regattas, fishing tournaments, Summer Boating Flings, and holidays are obtainable from:

Bahamas Tourist Board
19495 Biscayne Boulevard, Suite 809
Aventura, Florida 33180
305-932-0051

Bahamas Out Islands Promotion Board
1100 Lee Wagener Boulevard, Suite 206
Fort Lauderdale, Florida 33315
954-359-8099

The Bahamas Sports and Aviation Center
255 Alhambra Circle, Suite 415
Coral Gables, Florida 33314
800-327-7678 or 305-932-0051

Bimini Big Game Fishing Club
866 Ponce de Leon Boulevard, 2nd Floor
Coral Gables, Florida 33134
800-737-1007 or 809-347-3391

JANUARY

New Years Day (January 1).
Junkanoo. Just before dawn on New Year's Day the Bahamian *Junkanoo Festival* kicks off. It's the party of the year over most of the islands. Nassau and Freeport-Lucaya, as the centers of population, stage the largest events, but you can be swept up into Junkanoo just about anywhere. It's a carnival time with extravagant costumes, parades, wild dancing, and all that goes with it, and has its roots in a mix of African drumming, Mardi Gras, Carnival in Rio, and Haitian frenzy, just about anything you care to name in that line, rolled into one wild celebration.

Biminis (Alice Town). Annual Mid-Winter Wahoo Tournament (normally late January–early February).
Exumas (Staniel Cay). New Year's Day Cruising Regatta.
Nassau (Paradise Island). New Year's Day Regatta.

FEBRUARY

Biminis (Alice Town). Annual Mid-Winter Wahoo Tournament.
Exumas (Farmers Cay). Annual Farmers Cay Festival.
Grand Bahama (Xanadu). Deep Sea Fishing Tournament.

SPRING BREAK

The spring break vacation, wherever it falls, sometime between February and April, has the Bahamas as a premier destination, at least for east coast colleges. The Bahamas in turn does much to attract this influx of visitors bent on celebration. Charter boats are a favored means of reaching the islands, but time and distance dictate that the Biminis, the Northern Abacos, Chub Cay in the Southern Berrys, and Nassau are about as far as this traffic will reach. Dock space along these routes, and popular anchorages such as Honeymoon Cove in the Biminis, may well be crowded.

MARCH

Easter. Could be in April. Date changes annually.
Biminis (Alice Town). Bacardi Billfish and Hemingway Fishing Tournaments. Also an Annual Regatta.
Exumas (George Town). Annual Cruising Regatta on Exuma.
Long Island (Stella Maris). Out Islands International Game Fish Tournament.

APRIL

Easter. Could be in March. Date changes annually.
Abacos (Marsh Harbour). Annual Boat Harbour All-Fish Tournament.
Abacos (Treasure Cay). Power Boat Week.
Andros (Morgans Bluff). North Andros Easter Mini-Regatta.
Biminis (Alice Town). The Bimini Break Blue Marlin Tournament. Also a Bimini Regatta.
Eleuthera. South Eleuthera Sailing Regatta.
Eleuthera (Gregory Town). Annual Fishing Tournament.
Exumas (George Town). Annual Bahamas Family Island Regatta.

MAY

Whit Monday. Date (linked to Easter) changes annually.
Abacos (Marsh Harbour). At Boat Harbour. Bertram-Hatteras Shoot Out and the Bahamas Billfish Championships.
Abacos (Treasure Cay). Billfish Tournament.
Abacos (Walkers Cay). Billfish Tournament.
Berrys (Great Harbour Cay). What's Out There Fishing Tournament.
Biminis (Alice Town). Annual Bimini Festival (fun fishing tournament).
Cat Cay. Billfish Tournament.
Long Island (Salt Pond). Long Island Regatta.

JUNE

Labour Day. First Friday in June.
Goombay Summer Festival. A kind of summertime Junkanoo, the Goombay Summer Festival starts in June but continues through the summer months generating parades, street festivals, and whatever may be decided to whet the appetite of the locals or tempt the tourists.
Abacos (Green Turtle Cay). Green Turtle Club Fishing Tournament.

Abacos (Marsh Harbour). At Boat Harbour. Bahamas Billfish Tournaments.

Andros. Big Yard Bonefishing & Bottom Fishing Tournament.

Andros (Morgans Bluff). Annual Regatta.

Biminis (Alice Town). Big Five Fishing Tournament. Also the Annual Ocean Harbour Marine Tournament, and the Annual Bimini Bash (some 50 small boats).

Eleuthera (Gregory Town). Eleuthera Pineapple Festival.

Grand Bahama. Annual Grand Bahama Sailing Regatta (could be held June–July or in July).

Bahamas Tourist Office Summer Boating Filings

In June, July, and August regular Summer Boating Flings take off from Florida for the Bahamas. These are flotillas of small boats (not less than 24 feet LOA or, for the Biminis, a 22-foot minimum is permitted) guided by a lead boat, which set out from the Radisson Bahia Mar Marina in Fort Lauderdale for either the Biminis, or Freeport-Port Lucaya in Grand Bahama, and may extend their range to include either the Abacos or the Southern Berry Islands. The purpose is to encourage those who might not otherwise dare to cross the Gulf Stream but have always wanted to cruise in the Bahamas.

Departures are scheduled virtually on a weekly basis through the summer. For information contact the Bahamas Sports and Aviation Center.

JULY

Independence Day (July 10). Celebrated by a week of events. Parades, fireworks, regattas, and partying above all, Kaliks and Goombay Smashes, mark the remembrance of the ending of 300 years of British rule.

Abacos (Green Turtle Cay). Bahamas Sailing Cup.

Abacos (Marsh Harbour). Regatta Time.

Andros (Mangrove Cay). Independence Day Regatta.

Biminis (Alice Town). South Florida Fishing Club Tournament. Also the Columbia Kendall Fishing Tournament and the Latin Builders Fishing Tournament.

Exumas. World Invitational Bonefishing Championship. (A new event in 1997. Might be held in July–August or in August in later years).

Exumas (Staniel Cay). Annual Bonefish Tournament.

AUGUST

Emancipation Day (the first Monday in August). Emancipation Day marks the setting free of all slaves in 1834.

Andros. Regatta.

Biminis (Alice Town). Annual Bimini Family Tournament and Native Fishing Tournament.

Cat Island. Regatta (held over the Emancipation Day weekend).

Eleuthera. All-Eleuthera Sailing Regatta.

Exumas (Black Point). Regatta.

SEPTEMBER

Abacos. Abaco Regatta.

Biminis (Alice Town). Bimini Big Game Fishing Club Small B.O.A.T Tournament (for boats under 27 feet LOA, held in three legs over three successive weeks.

Nassau (Paradise Island). Annual Bahamas Atlantis Superboat Challenge. (Power boat races. May be held September–October).

OCTOBER

Discovery Day (October 12). The date in 1492 when Christopher Columbus made his landfall in the Bahamas (it's still disputed which island was his initial landing) but San Salvador holds the official title at this time. We believe it was Samana Cay. Be that as it may, October 12 is a Public Holiday.

Eleuthera. North Eleuthera Sailing Regatta (held between Harbour Island and Three-Island Bay).

NOVEMBER

Guy Fawkes Day (November 5). As a curious link with their onetime British overlordship, the Bahamas celebrates Guy Fawkes Day, each year. Guy Fawkes, the leader of a "Gunpowder Plot" to blow up the British Houses of Parliament in 1605, failed and was cruelly executed. The anniversary is commemorated in a macabre but traditional form with firework displays and the burning of a Guy Fawkes effigy.

Biminis (Alice Town). Annual Ossie Brown Memorial Wahoo Tournament and the Bimini Big Game Fishing Club All Wahoo Tournament.

Exumas (George Town). Bahamas Bonefish Bonanza I and II Tournaments.

DECEMBER

Abacos (Green Turtle Cay). New Plymouth Historical Cultural Weekend.

Christmas Day (December 25).

Boxing Day (December 26). Another traditional British holiday, celebrated with a Rehearsal Junkanoo.

Those Strange Bahamian Names

JUNKANOO AND GOOMBAY

Have you ever wondered where those oddball names, Junkanoo and Goombay, came from? There are many theories, many explanations. Our preferences are these. The word *Junkanoo* came from Haiti. In French (which is the Haitian language) it was the festival of the *Gens Inconnus,* the "Unknown or Disguised People" from the masks the dancers wore and wear today. *Goombay* seems firmly African. It's a kind of drum, and we've been told, the Bantu word for rhythm.

Appendix A
Bahamas Waypoint Catalog

Part 1: Florida Departure/Arrival Ports

East Coast

Stuart (St. Lucie Entrance)	LUCIE	27° 10' 00 N	080° 08' 00 W
Jupiter Inlet (1.2 nm SE)	JUPTR	26° 56' 00 N	080° 03' 00 W
Palm Beach (1.5 nm E)	PPALM	26° 46' 00 N	080° 00' 00 W
Fort Lauderdale (1 nm due E)	LDALE	26° 05' 30 N	080° 05' 15 W
Miami (just off harbor entry)	MIAMI	25° 46' 00 N	080° 05' 00 W

Part II: The Northern Cruising Grounds

The Little Bahama Bank

WEST END–INDIAN CAY PASSAGE–MANGROVE CAY–GREAT SALE CAY

West End (1 nm W)	WESTW	26° 42' 00 N	079° 01' 00 W
Ocean side (just W)	INDCW	26° 43' 00 N	079° 01' 00 W
Pass between piles	INDCP	26° 43' 25 N	079° 00' 15 W
2nd mark (50 ft. N)	INDC2	26° 43' 45 N	078° 59' 50 W
3rd mark (50 ft. N)	INDC3	26° 44' 45 N	078° 59' 10 W
Barracuda Shoal Mark (SE)	INDCB	26° 45' 45 N	078° 58' 05 W
Mangrove Cay (1.5 nm N)	MANGR	26° 57' 00 N	078° 37' 00 W
Great Sale Cay (1 nm W)	GSALE	26° 59' 00 N	078° 14' 30 W
Great Sale Anchorage	GSANC	26° 59' 52 N	078° 12' 54 W

WEST END–SANDY CAY–MANGROVE CAY–GREAT SALE CAY

Sandy Cay (3 nm W)	SANDC	26° 49' 00 N	079° 07' 00 W
Mangrove Cay (1.5 nm N)	MANGR	26° 57' 00 N	078° 37' 00 W
Great Sale Cay (1 nm W)	GSALE	26° 59' 00 N	078° 14' 30 W
Great Sale Anchorage	GSANC	26° 59' 52 N	078° 12' 54 W

MEMORY ROCK–MANGROVE CAY–GREAT SALE CAY

Memory Rock Light	MEMRK	26° 57' 00 N	079° 07' 00 W
Memory Rock (2 nm S)	MEMRS	26° 55' 00 N	079° 07' 00 W
Memory Rock (3 nm N)	MEMRN	26° 59' 15 N	079° 08' 00 W
Mangrove Cay (1.5 nm N)	MANGR	26° 57' 00 N	078° 37' 00 W
Great Sale Cay (1 nm W)	GSALE	26° 59' 00 N	078° 14' 30 W
Great Sale Anchorage	GSANC	26° 59' 52 N	078° 12' 54 W

MEMORY ROCK–TRIANGLE ROCKS–WALKERS CAY

Memory Rock (3 nm N)	MEMRN	26° 59' 15 N	079° 08' 00 W
Triangle Rocks (0.75 nm N)	TRIRK	27° 11' 00 N	078° 25' 00 W
Walkers Cay (end of channel)	WLKRS	27° 14' 00 N	078° 24' 00 W

GREAT SALE CAY–CRAB CAY–GREEN TURTLE CAY

Great Sale Anchorage	GSANC	26° 59' 52 N	078° 12' 54 W
Great Sale Cay (1 nm W)	GSALE	26° 59' 00 N	078° 14' 30 W
South Sale Cay (3.5 nm S)	SSALE	26° 53' 00 N	078° 14' 00 W
Veteran Rock (0.5 nm S)	VETRK	26° 55' 30 N	077° 52' 30 W
Hawksbill Cays (0.75 nm NW)	HAWKB	26° 57' 00 N	077° 48' 00 W
Center of World Rock (0.5 nm S)	CENWD	26° 55' 30 N	077° 42' 00 W
Crab Cay (0.5 nm N)	CRABC	26° 56' 00 N	077° 36' 00 W
Angel Fish Point (0.5 nm NE)	ANGEL	26° 55' 30 N	077° 35' 00 W
Coopers Town (1 nm NE)	CPSTN	26° 53' 00 N	077° 30' 00 W
Green Turtle N (3.5 nm NW)	GTNTH	26° 47' 00 N	077° 23' 00 W
Green Turtle Cay (1 nm W)	GTRTL	26° 46' 00 M	077° 21' 00 W

GREAT SALE CAY–TRIANGLE ROCKS–WALKERS CAY

Great Sale Anchorage	GSANC	26° 59' 52 N	078° 12' 54 W
Great Sale Cay (1 nm W)	GSALE	26° 59' 00 N	078° 14' 30 W

Triangle Rocks (0.75 nm N)	TRIRK	27° 11' 00 N	078° 25' 00 W
Walkers Cay (end of channel)	WLKRS	27° 14' 00 N	078° 24' 00 W

The Abacos

WALKERS CAY TO THE GRAND CAYS

Walkers Cay (end of channel)	WLKRS	27° 14' 00 N	078° 24' 00 W
Triangle Rocks (0.75 nm N)	TRIRK	27° 11' 00 N	078° 25' 00 W
Grand Cays (1 nm S)	GRAND	27° 11' 00 N	078° 25' 00 W
Deep Water off Grand Cays	DWOGC	27° 12' 00 N	078° 19' 30 W
Grand Cays Anchorage	GCANC	27° 13' 10 N	078° 19' 18 W

GRAND CAYS TO THE DOUBLE BREASTED CAYS

Deep Water off Grand Cays	DWOGC	27° 12' 00 N	078° 19' 30 W
Double Breasted Cays	DBRST	27° 11' 00 N	078° 16' 45 W
Double Breasted Approach	DBAPP	27° 11' 17 N	078° 16' 35 W

DOUBLE BREASTED CAYS–LITTLE SALE CAY–CARTERS CAY

Double Breasted Cays	DBRST	27° 11' 00 N	078° 16' 45 W
Little Sale Cay	LSALE	27° 04' 00 N	078° 12' 00 W
Mid-Carters (1 nm off)	MCRTR	27° 03' 00 N	078° 01' 00 W
Carters Cay (just off)	CRTRS	27° 04' 00 N	078° 01' 00 W
Carters Anchorage	CTANC	27° 05' 03 N	078° 00' 07 W

CARTERS CAY TO HAWKSBILL CAY

Carters Cay (just off)	CRTRS	27° 04' 00 N	078° 01' 00 W
South Carters Cay (3 nm S)	SCRTR	27° 01' 00 N	078° 01' 00 W
Hawksbill Cay (3.75 nm NW)	HWKBL	26° 57' 00 N	077° 48' 00 W

HAWKSBILL CAY TO MORAINE CAY

Hawksbill Cay (3.75 nm NW)	HWKBL	26° 57' 00 N	077° 48' 00 W
Fish Cays (safely off)	FISHC	27° 01' 30 N	077° 48' 30 W
Moraine Cay Approach (1 nm S)	MORAP	27° 01' 30 N	077° 46' 15 W
Moraine Cay (0.5 nm S)	MORAI	27° 02' 15 N	077° 46' 15 W

CARTERS CAY–FISH CAYS–MORAINE CAY

Carters Cay (just off)	CRTRS	27° 04' 00 N	078° 01' 00 W
South Carters Cay (3 nm S)	SCRTR	27° 01' 00 N	078° 01' 00 W
Grouper Rocks (3 nm S)	GRPRR	27° 00' 00 N	077° 57' 15 W
Fish Cays (safely off)	FISHC	27° 01' 30 N	077° 48' 30 W
Moraine Cay Approach (1 nm S)	MORAP	27° 01' 30 N	077° 46' 15 W
Moraine Cay (0.5 nm S)	MORAI	27° 02' 15 N	077° 46' 15 W

MORAINE CAY TO ALLANS-PENSACOLA CAY

Moraine Cay (0.5 nm S)	MORAI	27° 02' 15 N	077° 46' 15 W
Allans-Pensacola (0.5 nm NW)	ALPEN	26° 59' 15 N	077° 42' 15 W

ALLANS-PENSACOLA CAY TO ANGEL FISH POINT

Allans-Pensacola (0.5 nm NW)	ALPEN	26° 59' 15 N	077° 42' 15 W
Crab Cay (0.5 nm N)	CRABC	26° 56' 00 N	077° 36' 00 W
Angel Fish Point (0.5 nm NE)	ANGEL	26° 55' 30 N	077° 35' 00 W

ANGEL FISH POINT TO GREEN TURTLE CAY

Angel Fish Point (0.5 nm NE)	ANGEL	26° 55' 30 N	077° 35' 00 W
Coopers Town (1 nm NE)	CPSTN	26° 53' 00 N	077° 30' 00 W
Green Turtle N (3.5 nm NW)	GTNTH	26° 47' 00 N	077° 23' 00 W
Green Turtle Cay (1 nm W)	GTRTL	26° 46' 00 M	077° 21' 00 W

ANGEL FISH POINT TO SPANISH CAY

Angel Fish Point (0.5 nm NE)	ANGEL	26° 55' 30 N	077° 35' 00 W
Spanish Cay (0.5 nm NW)	SPNSH	26° 56' 30 N	077° 32' 15 W

BETWEEN POWELL CAY AND GREEN TURTLE CAY

Powell Cay (off beaches)	PWELL	26° 54' 19 N	077° 29' 05 W
Ambergris Cay Warning Stake	AMSTK	26° 51' 35 N	077° 25' 50 W
Manjack–Crab Cay Anchorage	MANCR	26° 49' 03 N	077° 21' 47 W

GREEN TURTLE CAY TO GREAT GUANA CAY

Green Turtle SW (Settlement Pt.)	GTCSW	26° 45' 30 N	077° 20' 30 W
Whale Cay Passage 1 (2.8 nm SW)	WHLP1	26° 42' 00 N	077° 17' 00 W
Whale Cay Passage 2 (offshore N)	WHLP2	26° 43' 30 N	077° 14' 15 W
Whale Cay Passage 3 (offshore S)	WHLP3	26° 42' 30 N	077° 12' 25 W
Whale Cay Passage 4 (inshore S)	WHLP4	26° 42' 00 N	077° 12' 00 W
First Deep Channel Marker	DMKR1	26° 42' 15 N	077° 12' 10 W
Second Pair of Markers	DMKR2	26° 41' 52 N	077° 11' 53 W
Baker's Bay 1 (deepwater slot)	BKRS1	26° 41' 25 N	077° 10' 15 W
Baker's Bay 2 (deepwater slot)	BKRS2	26° 41' 05 N	077° 10' 05 W
Great Guana Cay (Delia's Cay Rk)	GGANA	26° 39' 45 N	077° 07' 00 W

THE TREASURE CAY TRIANGLE

Whale Cay Passage 4 (inshore S)	WHLP4	26° 42' 00 N	077° 12' 00 W
Fish Cays S (1 nm S)	FISHS	26° 40' 00 N	077° 08' 00 W
Treasure Cay Entrance (1 nm SE)	TREAS	26° 39' 30 N	077° 15' 45 W

GREAT GUANA CAY–MAN-O-WAR CAY–ELBOW CAY (HOPE TOWN)

Great Guana Cay (Delia's Cay Rk)	GGANA	26° 39' 45 N	077° 07' 00 W
Man-O-War Cay (NW of)	NWMOW	26° 36' 00 N	077° 02' 00 W
Man-O-War Cay (harbor ent.)	MOWAP	26° 35' 15 N	077° 00' 25 W
Point Set Rock (E of)	EPTST	26° 34' 00 N	076° 59' 45 W
Hope Town (approach)	HPTAP	26° 33' 00 N	076° 58' 30 W

ROUTES IN THE MARSH HARBOUR TRIANGLE

Man-O-War Cay (NW of)	NWMOW	26° 36' 00 N	077° 02' 00 W
Man-O-War Cay (harbor ent.)	MOWAP	26° 35' 15 N	077° 00' 25 W
Point Set Rock (E of)	EPTST	26° 34' 00 N	076° 59' 45 W
Point Set Rock (N of)	NPTST	26° 34' 20 N	077° 00' 30 W
Hope Town (approach)	HPTAP	26° 33' 00 N	076° 58' 30 W
Marsh Harbour (off entrance)	NMRSH	26° 33' 25 N	077° 04' 00 W
Marsh Boat Harbour Marina	SMRSH	26° 32' 30 N	077° 02' 15 W

HEADING NORTH TO TREASURE CAY

Marsh Harbour (off entrance)	NMRSH	26° 33' 25 N	077° 04' 00 W
Point Set Rock (N of)	NPTST	26° 34' 20 N	077° 00' 30 W
Man-O-War Cay (NW of)	NWMOW	26° 36' 00 N	077° 02' 00 W
Fish Cays S (1 nm S)	FISHS	26° 40' 00 N	077° 08' 00 W
Treasure Cay Entrance (1 nm SE)	TREAS	26° 39' 30 N	077° 15' 45 W

ELBOW CAY–TILLOO CAY–LYNYARD CAY–LITTLE HARBOUR

White Sound (just off)	WHSND	26° 31' 00 N	076° 59' 00 W
Lubbers Quarters N	LQNTH	26° 30' 20 N	076° 59' 05 W
Lubbers Quarters Mid Pt	LQMID	26° 29' 55 N	076° 59' 30 W
Lubbers Quarters S	LQSTH	26° 29' 05 N	076° 59' 45 W
Tilloo Bank W	WTILO	26° 25' 50 N	077° 01' 00 W
Tilloo Bank S	STILO	26° 25' 15 N	077° 00' 15 W
Tilloo Bank E	ETILO	26° 25' 15 N	076° 59' 15 W
North Bar E (0.75 nm SE)	NBARE	26° 23' 15 N	076° 58' 00 W
North Bar W	NBARW	26° 23' 40 N	076° 59' 15 W
Lynyard Mid Pt	LYNMD	26° 22' 00 N	076° 59' 40 W
Lynyard Anchorages	LYNAN	26° 21' 20 N	076° 59' 45 W
Little Harbour N	LHRBN	26° 20' 45 N	076° 59' 50 W
Little Harbour (just off)	LHRBO	26° 20' 00 N	076° 59' 45 W

MARSH HARBOUR–WITCH POINT–TILLOO BANK

Marsh Boat Harbour Marina	SMRSH	26° 32' 30 N	077° 02' 15 W
Long Cay (safely off)	LONGC	26° 31' 00 N	077° 02' 30 W

Witch Point (safely off)	WITCH	26° 29' 40 N	077° 01' 40 W
Tilloo Bank W	WTILO	26° 25' 50 N	077° 01' 00 W

CONTINUING ON SOUTH–LITTLE HARBOUR TO CHEROKEE SOUND

Little Harbour (just off)	LHRBO	26° 20' 00 N	076° 59' 45 W
Little Harbour N	LHRBN	26° 20' 45 N	076° 59' 50 W
Little Harbour Bar Pass	LHRBP	26° 19' 55 N	076° 59' 20 W
Little Harbour Bar E	LHRBE	26° 18' 55 N	076° 58' 50 W
Ocean Point (safely off)	OCNPT	26° 17' 45 N	076° 59' 20 W
Cherokee Point (off)	CHERP	26° 15' 40 N	077° 03' 15 W
Cherokee W	CHERW	26° 16' 00 N	077° 04' 15 W

Grand Bahama Island

GRAND BAHAMA

Freeport (3 nm offshore)	FRPRT	26° 28' 30 N	078° 46' 00 W
West End (1 nm W)	WESTW	26° 42' 00 N	079° 01' 00 W
Xanadu (2 nm off)	XANDU	26° 28' 24 N	078° 42' 22 W
Running Mon (2 nm off)	RNMON	26° 28' 56 N	078° 39' 22 W
Ocean Reef (2 nm off)	OCNRF	26° 29' 22 N	078° 39' 50 W
Bell Channel (2 nm off)	BELCH	26° 29' 53 N	078° 37' 46 W

THE GRAND LUCAYAN WATERWAY

Bell Channel (2 nm off)	BELCH	26° 29' 53 N	078° 37' 46 W
S Mark Lucayan Waterway	SLNWW	26° 31' 48 N	078° 33' 14 W
N Entry Posts Waterway	NLNWW	26° 36' 50 N	078° 38' 30 W
Waypoint off N Entry Posts	ONLNW	26° 37' 00 N	078° 38' 32 W
Cormorant Point (5 nm W)	CORPT	26° 41' 00 N	078° 42' 00 W
Mangrove Cay (1.5 nm N)	MANGR	26° 57' 00 N	078° 37' 00 W

Part III: The Central Cruising Grounds

The Bimini Island Group

HEADING FOR NORTH ROCK

Fort Lauderdale (1 nm due E)	LDALE	26° 05' 30 N	080° 05' 15 W
Miami (just off harbor entry)	MIAMI	25° 46' 00 N	080° 05' 00 W
N Rock (1 nm N of Bank)	NROCK	25° 51' 00 N	079° 16' 30 W

HEADING FOR BIMINI

Fort Lauderdale (1 nm due E)	LDALE	26° 05' 30 N	080° 05' 15 W
Miami (just off harbor entry)	MIAMI	25° 46' 00 N	080° 05' 00 W
Bimini (0.5 nm W offshore)	BMINI	25° 42' 30 N	079° 19' 00 W

HEADING FOR GUN CAY CUT

Fort Lauderdale (1 nm due E)	LDALE	26° 05' 30 N	080° 05' 15 W
Miami (just off harbor entry)	MIAMI	25° 46' 00 N	080° 05' 00 W
Gun Cay (1.5 nm NW Gun Cay Pt)	GUNCW	25° 34' 15 N	079° 19' 30 W

HEADING FOR SOUTH RIDING ROCK

Miami (just off harbor entry)	MIAMI	25° 46' 00 N	080° 05' 00 W
S R Rock W (2 nm SW Castle Rk)	SRDRW	25° 13' 30 N	079° 11' 00 W
S R Rock E (1 nm S Castle Rk)	SRDRE	25° 13' 30 N	079° 08' 30 W

NORTH BIMINI

Bimini (0.5 nm W offshore)	BMINI	25° 42' 30 N	079° 19' 00 W
Bimini Approach Range	BIMAP	25° 42' 05 N	079° 18' 54 W
The Atlantis Dive Site	ATLDS	25° 45' 44 N	079° 16' 44 W

GUN CAY CUT

Gun Cay (1.5 nm NW Gun Cay Pt)	GUNCW	25° 34' 15 N	079° 19' 30 W
Cat Cay (0.25 nm E of marina)	CATCE	25° 34' 00 N	079° 17' 00 W

CAT CAY

Cat Cay (0.25 nm E of marina)	CATCE	25° 34' 00 N	079° 17' 00 W

RETURNING TO FLORIDA

Stuart (St. Lucie Entrance)	LUCIE	27° 10' 00 N	080° 08' 00 W
Jupiter Inlet (1.2 nm SE)	JUPTR	26° 56' 00 N	080° 03' 00 W
Palm Beach (1.5 nm E)	PPALM	26° 46' 00 N	080° 00' 00 W
Fort Lauderdale (1 nm due E)	LDALE	26° 05' 30 N	080° 05' 15 W
Miami (just off harbor entry)	MIAMI	25° 46' 00 N	080° 05' 00 W

Crossing the Great Bahama Bank

NORTH ROCK TO THE NORTHWEST CHANNEL LIGHT

N Rock (1 nm N of Bank)	NROCK	25° 51' 00 N	079° 16' 30 W
Mackie Shoal (1 nm off Beacon)	MCKIE	25° 41' 30 N	078° 38' 30 W
NW Light Shoal	NWLSH	25° 29' 00 N	078° 14' 00 W
NW Channel Light (just NW)	NWCHL	25° 28' 45 N	078° 09' 45 W

CAT CAY TO THE NORTHWEST CHANNEL LIGHT (THROUGH GUN CAY CUT)

Gun Cay (1.5 nm NW Gun Cay Pt)	GUNCW	25° 34' 15 N	079° 19' 30 W
Cat Cay (0.25 nm E of marina)	CATCE	25° 34' 00 N	079° 17' 00 W
NW Channel Light (just NW)	NWCHL	25° 28' 45 N	078° 09' 45 W

SOUTH RIDING ROCK TO THE NORTHWEST CHANNEL LIGHT

S R Rock W (2 nm SW Castle Rk)	SRDRW	25° 13' 30 N	079° 11' 00 W
S R Rock E (1 nm S Castle Rk)	SRDRE	25° 13' 30 N	079° 08' 30 W
NW Channel Light (just NW)	NWCHL	25° 28' 45 N	078° 09' 45 W

OPTIONS AFTER THE NORTHWEST CHANNEL LIGHT

NW Channel Light (just NW)	NWCHL	25° 28' 45 N	078° 09' 45 W
Chub Cay Entry Waypoint	CHUBC	25° 24' 15 N	077° 54' 50 W
Chub Cay (1 nm S)	CHUBS	25° 23' 15 N	077° 54' 50 W
Nassau Harbour NW (2 nm off)	NASNW	25° 06' 30 N	077° 23' 00 W
Nassau Harbour W (0.25 nm off)	NASHW	25° 05' 30 N	077° 21' 30 W
Morgans Bluff (2 nm E)	MRGNE	25° 11' 00 N	077° 59' 00 W
Bethel Channel (1.5 nm E)	BTHEL	25° 08' 30 N	077° 57' 30 W
Fresh Creek (1 nm E)	FRESH	24° 44' 00 N	077° 45' 00 W

The Berry Islands

THE ROUTE FROM GRAND BAHAMA ISLAND

Bell Channel (2 nm off)	BELCH	26° 29' 53 N	078° 37' 46 W
Little Stirrup Cay (0.5 nm off)	LSTRP	25° 49' 30 N	077° 57' 00 W

GREAT HARBOUR CAY AND MARINA

Little Stirrup Cay (0.5 nm off)	LSTRP	25° 49' 30 N	077° 57' 00 W
West Marker Piling	WMARK	25° 46' 25 N	077° 57' 00 W
Great Harbour Approach	GHARB	25° 44' 45 N	077° 52' 30 W

MOVING ON SOUTH FROM THE STIRRUP CAYS

Market Fish Cay Inside Route	MFIRS	25° 40' 45 N	077° 45' 45 W
Little Harbour Cay Ocean Appr.	LHCOA	25° 33' 30 N	077° 42' 30 W
Guana Cay Shoal Passage	GCSHP	25° 34' 10 N	077° 44' 05 W
SW Comfort Cay Anchorage	SWCCA	25° 34' 30 N	077° 44' 05 W

THE SOUTHERN BERRY ISLANDS

Frozen Cay Anchorage	FRCAN	25° 32' 55 N	077° 43' 03 W
Bond Cay Reef	BREEF	25° 29' 12 N	077° 43' 04 W
Bond–Little Whale Gap	BLWGP	25° 27' 15 N	077° 44' 15 W
Bond–Little Whale Anchorage	BLWAN	25° 27' 45 N	077° 46' 30 W
Off Whale Cay Light	OWCLT	25° 23' 25 N	077° 48' 15 W
Bird Cay Anchorage	BRDAN	25° 23' 40 N	077° 50' 10 W
Off Texaco Point (Frazers Hog)	OTXPT	25° 24' 05 N	077° 50' 50 W
Chub Cay Entry Waypoint	CHUBC	25° 24' 15 N	077° 54' 50 W

THE CHUB CAY ENTRY ROUTE FROM FLORIDA

NW Channel Light (just NW)	NWCHL	25° 28' 45 N	078° 09' 45 W
Chub Cay Entry Waypoint	CHUBC	25° 24' 15 N	077° 54' 50 W
Chub Cay (1 nm S)	CHUBS	25° 23' 15 N	077° 54' 50 W

CHUB CAY TO NASSAU (NEW PROVIDENCE ISLAND)

Chub Cay Entry Waypoint	CHUBC	25° 24' 15 N	077° 54' 50 W
Chub Cay (1 nm S)	CHUBS	25° 23' 15 N	077° 54' 50 W
Nassau Harbour W (0.25 nm off)	NASHW	25° 05' 30 N	077° 21' 30 W

CHUB CAY TO ANDROS

Chub Cay Entry Waypoint	CHUBC	25° 24' 15 N	077° 54' 50 W
Chub Cay (1 nm S)	CHUBS	25° 23' 15 N	077° 54' 50 W
Morgans Bluff (2 nm E)	MRGNE	25° 11' 00 N	077° 59' 00 W
Bethel Channel (1.5 nm E)	BTHEL	25° 08' 30 N	077° 57' 30 W
Fresh Creek (1 nm E)	FRESH	24° 44' 00 N	077° 45' 00 W

THE WEST SIDE ROUTE, CHUB CAY TO GREAT HARBOUR CAY

Chub Cay Entry Waypoint	CHUBC	25° 24' 15 N	077° 54' 50 W
Chub Cay (1 nm S)	CHUBS	25° 23' 15 N	077° 54' 50 W
NW Channel Light (just NW)	NWCHL	25° 28' 45 N	078° 09' 45 W
SW Edge of the Berry Bank	SWEBB	25° 30' 15 N	078° 10' 30 W
NE Edge of the Bahama Bank	NWBAB	25° 40' 00 N	078° 10' 30 W
1 nm W of West Marker Piling	WMAW1	25° 46' 25 N	077° 58' 00 W
West Marker Piling	WMARK	25° 46' 25 N	077° 57' 00 W

Nassau and New Providence Island

NASSAU HARBOUR

Nassau Harbour NW (2 nm off)	NASNW	25° 06' 30 N	077° 23' 00 W
Nassau Harbour W (0.25 nm off)	NASHW	25° 05' 30 N	077° 21' 30 W
Nassau Harbour E (0.75 nm off)	NASHE	25° 04' 30 N	077° 17' 30 W
Porgee Rocks	PRGEE	25° 03' 45 N	077° 15' 00 W

MOVING TO ELEUTHERA AFTER NASSAU

Nassau Harbour E (0.75 nm off)	NASHE	25° 04' 30 N	077° 17' 30 W
Porgee Rocks	PRGEE	25° 03' 45 N	077° 15' 00 W
Porgee Rocks N	PRGEN	25° 04' 45 N	077° 15' 00 W
Hanover Sound S	HNVRS	25° 05' 15 N	077° 15' 40 W
Hanover Sound N	HNVRN	25° 05' 50 N	077° 15' 45 W
Chub Rock	CHBRK	25° 06' 45 N	077° 15' 00 W
Little Egg Island (0.5 nm S)	LEGGI	25° 28' 00 N	076° 53' 15 W
Royal Island (1 nm S)	ROYLI	25° 29' 50 N	076° 50' 30 W
Meeks Patch (1 nm NW)	MEEKP	25° 31' 45 N	076° 48' 00 W

MOVING TO THE EXUMAS AFTER NASSAU

Nassau Harbour E (0.75 nm off)	NASHE	25° 04' 30 N	077° 17' 30 W
Porgee Rocks	PRGEE	25° 03' 45 N	077° 15' 00 W

Eleuthera

THE WESTERN APPROACH TO SPANISH WELLS

Little Egg Island (0.5 nm S)	LEGGI	25° 28' 00 N	076° 53' 15 W
Royal Island (1 nm S)	ROYLI	25° 29' 50 N	076° 50' 30 W
Meeks Patch (1 nm NW)	MEEKP	25° 31' 45 N	076° 48' 00 W
Spanish Wells S entry (just off)	SPNWS	25° 32' 05 N	076° 48' 00 W
Spanish Wells E entry (just off)	SPNWE	25° 32' 38 N	076° 44' 20 W

SPANISH WELLS TO HARBOUR ISLAND

Spanish Wells E entry (just off)	SPNWE	25° 32' 38 N	076° 44' 20 W
Ridley Head stake	RIDHS	25° 33' 30 N	076° 44' 24 W
Bridge Point (just off)	BRPTO	25° 33' 55 N	076° 43' 20 W
The Monument (just off)	MONMT	25° 33' 33 N	076° 40' 52 W

MOVING ON TO CENTRAL AND SOUTH ELEUTHERA

Spanish Wells E entry (just off)	SPNWE	25° 32' 38 N	076° 44' 20 W
Spanish Wells S entry (just off)	SPNWS	25° 32' 05 N	076° 48' 00 W
Meeks Patch (1 nm NW)	MEEKP	25° 31' 45 N	076° 48' 00 W
Current Cut W (0.75 nm NW)	CURCW	25° 24' 30 N	076° 48' 00 W
Current Cut E (1 nm S)	CURCE	25° 23' 00 N	076° 47' 15 W
Hatchet Bay (just off to N)	HATBN	25° 20' 45 N	076° 30' 00 W

CENTRAL AND SOUTH ELEUTHERA

Hatchet Bay (just off to N)	HATBN	25° 20' 45 N	076° 30' 00 W
Hatchet Bay (just off to S)	HATBS	25° 20' 30 N	076° 29' 30 W
Governors Har. (1.5 nm NW)	GOVHN	25° 12' 24 N	076° 16' 45 W
Governors Harbour (just S)	GOVHS	25° 11' 00 N	076° 15' 30 W
Tarpum Bay (8 nm due W)	TAPMW	24° 59' 50 N	076° 17' 55 W
Davis Channel (just E)	DAVCE	24° 53' 05 N	076° 16' 05 W
Cape Eleuthera (0.5 nm W)	CAPEW	24° 50' 20 N	076° 21' 05 W
Davis Harbour (3 nm W))	DAVOF	24° 43' 49 N	076° 17' 50 W
Davis Harbour Entry Mark	DAVHM	24° 43' 49 N	076° 15' 05 W

SOUTH ELEUTHERA TO CAT ISLAND

Cape Eleuthera (0.5 nm W)	CAPEW	24° 50' 20 N	076° 21' 05 W
Davis Harbour (3 nm W))	DAVOF	24° 43' 49 N	076° 17' 50 W
South Eleuthera (3 nm W)	SELEU	24° 40' 00 N	076° 15' 05 W
Eleuthera Point (1.5 nm SW)	ELEUP	24° 35' 55 N	076° 10' 05 W
Little San Salvador (2 nm SW)	LSSAL	24° 33' 00 N	075° 59' 00 W
The Bight (7 nm W)	BIGHT	24° 15' 00 N	075° 33' 00 W
Hawk's Nest (3 nm W)	HWKN1	24° 08' 45 N	075° 35' 00 W

Andros

THE MID-EXUMAS TO FRESH CREEK

Staniel Cay (1.5 nm W)	STANW	24° 13' 00 N	076° 32' 00 W
Fresh Creek (1 nm E)	FRESH	24° 44' 00 N	077° 45' 00 W

NASSAU TO MORGANS BLUFF, BETHEL CHANNEL, OR FRESH CREEK

Nassau Harbour W (0.25 nm off)	NASHW	25° 05' 30 N	077° 21' 30 W
Nassau Harbour NW (2 nm off)	NASNW	25° 06' 30 N	077° 23' 00 W
Nassau Goulding Cay (1 nm W)	GLDNG	25° 01' 30 N	077° 35' 30 W
Morgans Bluff (2 nm E)	MRGNE	25° 11' 00 N	077° 59' 00 W
Morgans Bluff Entry Buoys	MRGNB	25° 11' 09 N	078° 01' 02 W
Bethel Channel (1.5 nm E)	BTHEL	25° 08' 30 N	077° 57' 30 W
Fresh Creek (1 nm E)	FRESH	24° 44' 00 N	077° 45' 00 W

CHUB CAY TO MORGANS BLUFF, BETHEL CHANNEL, OR FRESH CREEK

Chub Cay Entry Waypoint	CHUBC	25° 24' 15 N	077° 54' 50 W
Chub Cay (1 nm S)	CHUBS	25° 23' 15 N	077° 54' 50 W
Morgans Bluff (2 nm E)	MRGNE	25° 11' 00 N	077° 59' 00 W
Morgans Bluff Entry Buoys	MRGNB	25° 11' 09 N	078° 01' 02 W
Bethel Channel (1.5 nm E)	BTHEL	25° 08' 30 N	077° 57' 30 W
Fresh Creek (1 nm E)	FRESH	24° 44' 00 N	077° 45' 00 W

FRESH CREEK TO THE BETHEL CHANNEL AND MORGANS BLUFF

Fresh Creek (1 nm E)	FRESH	24° 44' 00 N	077° 45' 00 W
Bethel Channel (1.5 nm E)	BTHEL	25° 08' 30 N	077° 57' 30 W
Morgans Bluff (2 nm E)	MRGNE	25° 11' 00 N	077° 59' 00 W
Morgans Bluff Entry Buoys	MRGNB	25° 11' 09 N	078° 01' 02 W

Part IV: The Southern Cruising Grounds

The Exumas

FROM NASSAU

Nassau Harbour E (0.75 nm off)	NASHE	25° 04' 30 N	077° 17' 30 W
Porgee Rocks	PRGEE	25° 03' 45 N	077° 15' 00 W
Porgee Rocks SE	PRGSE	25° 03' 00 N	077° 12' 00 W
Junction White & Yellow Banks	WYBNK	24° 52' 00 N	077° 12' 00 W
Allan's Cay	ALLAN	24° 44' 45 N	076° 51' 00 W
Highborne W	HIGHW	24° 42' 30 N	076° 51' 00 W
Highborne E	HIGHE	24° 42' 00 N	076° 48' 00 W

FROM ANDROS

Fresh Creek (1 nm E)	FRESH	24° 44' 00 N	077° 45' 00 W
Edge of Bank	FDBNK	24° 27' 30 N	077° 04' 00 W
Conch Cut W (6.5 nm W)	CONCW	24° 17' 00 N	076° 39' 00 W
Conch Cut E (0.5 nm E)	CONCE	24° 17' 30 N	076° 31' 00 W

FROM ELEUTHERA

Cape Eleuthera (0.5 nm W)	CAPEW	24° 50' 20 N	076° 21' 05 W
Davis Harbour Entry Mark	DAVHM	24° 43' 49 N	076° 15' 05 W
Highborne E	HIGHE	24° 42' 00 N	076° 48' 00 W
Highborne W	HIGHW	24° 42' 30 N	076° 51' 00 W
Conch Cut E (0.5 nm E)	CONCE	24° 17' 30 N	076° 31' 00 W

FROM THE SOUTH

Cape Santa Maria (2 nm N)	SANTM	23° 43' 00 N	075° 20' 30 W
George Town Harbour (N entry)	GTHAR	23° 34' 30 N	075° 48' 00 W

THE ALLAN'S CAY GROUP

Allan's Cay	ALLAN	24° 44' 45 N	076° 51' 00 W
Highborne W	HIGHW	24° 42' 30 N	076° 51' 00 W
Highborne E	HIGHE	24° 42' 00 N	076° 48' 00 W

ALLAN'S CAY TO NORMANS CAY

Allan's Cay	ALLAN	24° 44' 45 N	076° 51' 00 W
Highborne W	HIGHW	24° 42' 30 N	076° 51' 00 W
Highborne E	HIGHE	24° 42' 00 N	076° 48' 00 W
Highborne Stake (0.5 nm due W)	HSTKW	24° 42' 30 N	076° 50' 00 W
Highborne (2 nm SW)	HIBSW	24° 42' 00 N	076° 52' 00 W
Norman Spit (W of)	NMSPT	24° 35' 30 N	076° 52' 30 W
Norman Cay (1 nm SW)	NRMNS	24° 34' 35 N	076° 49' 30 W

NORMANS CAY TO WARDERICK WELLS

Normans Cay (1 nm SW)	NRMNS	24° 34' 35 N	076° 49' 30 W
Elbow Cay (1.5 nm W)	ELBOW	24° 31' 00 N	076° 51' 00 W
Cistern Cay (4 nm W)	CSTRN	24° 25' 00 N	076° 47' 30 W
Warderick Wells (5 nm W)	WWOFF	24° 21' 00 N	076° 42' 00 W
Warderick Wells (2.5 nm SW)	WELLS	24° 22' 30 N	076° 40' 15 W

WARDERICK WELLS TO SAMPSON AND STANIEL CAYS

Warderick Wells (2.5 nm SW)	WELLS	24° 22' 30 N	076° 40' 15 W
Conch Cut W (6.5 nm W)	CONCW	24° 17' 00 N	076° 39' 00 W
Sampson Cay (off Twin Cays)	SAMSN	24° 12' 20 N	076° 31' 00 W
Sandy Cay (0.5 nm W)	SANDY	24° 11' 15 N	076° 30' 00 W
Staniel Cay (0.25 nm W)	STANL	24° 10' 15 N	076° 27' 15 W

CONCH CUT

Conch Cut W (6.5 nm W)	CONCW	24° 17' 00 N	076° 39' 00 W
Conch Cut E (0.5 nm E)	CONCE	24° 17' 30 N	076° 31' 00 W

CONCH CUT TO STANIEL CAY

Conch Cut E (0.5 nm E)	CONCE	24° 17' 30 N	076° 31' 00 W
Conch Cut W (6.5 nm W)	CONCW	24° 17' 00 N	076° 39' 00 W
Sampson Cay (off Twin Cays)	SAMSN	24° 12' 20 N	076° 31' 00 W
Sandy Cay (0.5 nm W)	SANDY	24° 11' 15 N	076° 30' 00 W
Staniel Cay (0.25 nm W)	STANL	24° 10' 15 N	076° 27' 15 W

STANIEL CAY TO THE FARMERS CAYS

Harvey Cay (0.75 nm W)	HARVY	24° 09' 15 N	076° 30' 00 W
Black Point (0.25 nm W)	BLKPT	24° 05' 25 N	076° 25' 00 W
White Point (0.4 nm SW)	WHTPT	24° 02' 00 N	076° 23' 00 W

DOTHAM CUT

Dotham Cut E	DTHME	24° 07' 00 N	076° 23' 00 W
Dotham Cut W	DTHMW	24° 06' 30 N	076° 25' 00 W

BLACK POINT TO LITTLE FARMERS CAY			
Black Point (0.25 nm W)	BLKPT	24° 05' 25 N	076° 25' 00 W
White Point (0.4 nm SW)	WHTPT	24° 02' 00 N	076° 23' 00 W
Farmers Cut W (0.75 nm NW)	FMRSW	23° 58' 05 N	076° 19' 40 W

FARMERS CAY CUT			
Farmers Cut E (0.25 nm E)	FMRSE	23° 57' 50 N	076° 18' 30 W
Farmers Cut W (0.75 nm NW)	FMRSW	23° 58' 05 N	076° 19' 40 W

GALLIOT CUT			
Galliot Cut E (0.4 nm NE)	GALLE	23° 55' 40 N	076° 16' 35 W
Galliot Cut W (0.25 nm W)	GALLW	23° 55' 10 N	076° 17' 15 W

CAVE CAY CUT			
Cave Cut E (0.25 nm E)	CAVEE	23° 54' 10 N	076° 15' 10 W
Cave Cut W (0.25 nm W)	CAVEW	23° 53' 55 N	076° 16' 05 W

RUDDER CUT			
Rudder Cut E (0.25 nm NE)	RUDRE	23° 52' 15 N	076° 13' 25 W
Rudder Cut W (0.1 nm SW)	RUDRW	23° 51' 50 N	076° 13' 40 W

ADDERLEY CUT			
Adderley Cut E (0.4 nm E)	ADDYE	23° 47' 25 N	076° 06' 25 W
Adderley Cut W (0.7 nm W)	ADDYW	23° 46' 45 N	076° 07' 25 W

RAT CAY CUT			
Rat Cay Cut N (0.25 nm NNW)	RATCN	23° 44' 05 N	076° 02' 05 W
Rat Cay Cut S (0.1 nm S)	RATCS	23° 43' 45 N	076° 01' 55 W

THE WEST ENTRANCE TO GEORGE TOWN HARBOUR			
George Town Harbour Ent. (W)	GTAW1	23° 34' 30 N	075° 48' 30 W
W approach Waypoint 2	GTAW2	23° 33' 40 N	075° 48' 40 W
W approach Waypoint 3	GTAW3	23° 33' 15 N	075° 48' 10 W
W approach Waypoint 4	GTAW4	23° 32' 45 N	075° 48' 00 W
W approach Waypoint 5	GTAW5	23° 32' 10 N	075° 47' 30 W
W approach Waypoint 6	GTAW6	23° 31' 55 N	075° 46' 30 W

THE EAST ENTRANCE TO GEORGE TOWN HARBOUR			
Black Rocks (1 nm S)	BLKRS	23° 27' 00 N	075° 32' 00 W
George Town Harbour Ent. (E)	GTAE1	23° 30' 00 N	075° 40' 00 W
E approach Waypoint 2	GTAE2	23° 29' 10 N	075° 40' 15 W
E approach Waypoint 3	GTAE3	23° 29' 25 N	075° 42' 00 W
E approach Waypoint 4	GTAE4	23° 29' 25 N	075° 42' 35 W
E approach Waypoint 5	GTAE5	23° 30' 25 N	075° 44' 40 W

The Out Islands North of the Tropic of Cancer

APPROACHES TO THE OUT ISLANDS FROM ELEUTHERA			
Davis Harbour (3 nm W))	DAVOF	24° 43' 49 N	076° 17' 50 W
South Eleuthera (3 nm W)	SELEU	24° 40' 00 N	076° 15' 05 W
Eleuthera Point (1.5 nm SW)	ELEUP	24° 35' 55 N	076° 10' 05 W
Little San Salvador (2 nm SW)	LSSAL	24° 33' 00 N	075° 59' 00 W
The Bight (7 nm W)	BIGHT	24° 15' 00 N	075° 33' 00 W
Hawk's Nest (3 nm W)	HWKN1	24° 08' 45 N	075° 35' 00 W

LITTLE SAN SALVADOR			
Little San Salvador (2 nm SW)	LSSAL	24° 33' 00 N	075° 59' 00 W

CAT ISLAND			
The Bight (7 nm W)	BIGHT	24° 15' 00 N	075° 33' 00 W
Hawk's Nest (3 nm W)	HWKN1	24° 08' 45 N	075° 35' 00 W
Hawk's Nest (at the dropoff)	HWKN2	24° 08' 45 N	075° 32' 00 W
Orange Creek (2 nm S)	ORNGS	24° 37' 00 N	075° 43' 00 W
Bennett's Harbour (2.5 nm NW)	BNTNW	24° 34' 00 N	075° 41' 00 W
Smith Bay (1 nm W)	SMTHW	24° 20' 00 N	075° 30' 00 W

Fernandez Bay (1.5 nm W)	FNDEZ	24° 19' 30 N	075° 30' 00 W
Hawk's Nest (marina entry)	HWKNM	24° 08' 46 N	075° 31' 36 W

CONCEPTION ISLAND			
Conception (NW anchorage)	CONNW	23° 50' 30 N	075° 07' 45 W
Conception (Wedge Point)	CONWG	23° 48' 00 N	075° 07' 00 W

RUM CAY			
Rum Cay (Sandy Point)	RUMSP	23° 38' 45 N	074° 57' 30 W
Rum Cay (SE)	RUMSE	23° 37' 15 N	074° 47' 30 W
Rum Cay (Port Nelson)	RUMPN	23° 37' 15 N	074° 51' 00 W
Rum Cay (marina outer buoy)	RUMOB	23° 38' 10 N	074° 51' 00 W

SAN SALVADOR ISLAND			
San Salvador (Cockburn)	SNSAL	24° 02' 45 N	074° 33' 45 W

THE NORTH OF LONG ISLAND			
Cape Santa Maria (2 nm N)	SANTM	23° 43' 00 N	075° 20' 30 W
Cape Santa Maria E (3 nm E)	SANTE	23° 43' 00 N	075° 17' 00 W
Calabash Bay (2 nm W)	CALAB	23° 39' 15 N	075° 22' 45 W
Stella Maris (off Dove Cay)	STELA	23° 33' 30 N	075° 21' 00 W

Part V: Far Horizons

EASTERN ROUTE SOUTH: GEORGE TOWN TO THE TURKS AND CAICOS			
George Town Harbour Ent. (E)	GTAE1	23° 30' 00 N	075° 40' 00 W
Cape Santa Maria (2 nm N)	SANTM	23° 43' 00 N	075° 20' 30 W
Cape Santa Maria E (3 nm E)	SANTE	23° 43' 00 N	075° 17' 00 W
Mid-Crooked Island Passage	MIDCP	23° 00' 00 N	074° 39' 30 W
Crooked Is. Bird Rk (2 nm NW)	BRDRK	22° 53' 00 N	074° 23' 00 W
Crooked Is. Landrail Pt (1 nm W)	LNDRL	22° 48' 30 N	074° 21' 15 W
Acklins Is. Atwood Har. (3 nm N)	ATWOD	22° 46' 00 N	073° 53' 00 W
Acklins Is. NE Point (4 nm NE)	ACKNE	22° 46' 00 N	073° 43' 00 W
Semana Cay (2 nm S)	SMANA	23° 02' 00 N	073° 46' 00 W
Plana Cays W (5 nm W)	PLNAW	22° 37' 00 N	073° 43' 00 W
Plana Cays S (7 nm SW)	PLNAS	22° 30' 00 N	073° 43' 00 W
Mayaguana SW (S of Low Pt)	MAYAW	22° 18' 30 N	073° 04' 00 W

TURKS AND CAICOS ISLANDS			
Providenciales N (7 nm NW)	PROVN	21° 55' 00 N	072° 15' 00 W
Sellars Cut (at the reef)	SLLRS	21° 48' 50 N	072° 12' 50 W
Sandbore Approach (2 nm NW)	SBORA	21° 46' 00 N	072° 28' 00 W
Sandbore Pass W (at the reef)	SBORW	21° 44' 55 N	072° 27' 30 W
Sapodilla Bay (1 nm SW)	SPDLA	21° 44' 00 N	072° 18' 00 W
Caicos Shipyard (1.75 nm S)	CAIYD	21° 43' 00 N	072° 10' 05 W

WESTERN ROUTE SOUTH: GEORGE TOWN TO THE WINDWARD PASSAGE			
George Town Harbour Ent. (E)	GTAE1	23° 30' 00 N	075° 40' 00 W
Exumas Black Rocks (1 nm S)	BLKRS	23° 27' 00 N	075° 32' 00 W
White Cay Bank N	WCB-N	23° 24' 55 N	075° 20' 30 W
Long Is. Salt Pond (2 nm W)	SALTP	23° 20' 20 N	075° 10' 00 W
White Cay Bank E	WCB-E	23° 19' 45 N	075° 18' 10 W
White Cay Bank W	WCB-W	23° 19' 55 N	075° 31' 05 W
Nuevitas Rocks (1 nm E)	NUEVR	23° 10' 00 N	075° 21' 30 W
Long Is. South Point (2 nm W)	STHPT	22° 52' 00 N	074° 54' 00 W
Long Cay (2 nm off Windsor Pt)	LONGC	22° 32' 30 N	074° 25' 00 W
Acklins Is. Salina Pt. (1 nm NW)	SLINA	22° 14' 00 N	074° 18' 00 W
Mira Por Vos Passage	MIRAP	22° 06' 30 N	074° 25' 00 W
Hogsty Reef (3 nm W)	HGSTY	21° 41' 00 N	073° 54' 00 W
Gt. Inagua (3 nm W Mtthw Twn)	INAGA	20° 57' 00 N	073° 44' 00 W
Sandbore Approach (2 nm NW)	SBORA	21° 46' 00 N	072° 28' 00 W
Windward Passage Approach N	WINDN	20° 30' 00 N	073° 50' 00 W

Appendix B
Blue Pages Supplement

Batelco Tower Locations

Batelco, in providing us with this information, have made the point that they are not responsible for the accuracy of the positions given. We have not thought it necessary to take a hand-held GPS to double-check each one.

LOCATION	HEIGHT IN FEET	POSITION
ABACOS		
Cherokee	250	26° 16' 48 N 077° 03' 12 W
Coopers Town	200	26° 52' 26 N 077° 30' 52 W
Fox Town	200	26° 55' 03 N 077° 47' 44 W
Grand Cay	275	27° 14' 20 N 078° 19' 30 W
Green Turtle Cay	100	26° 45' 25 N 077° 19' 32 W
Guana Cay	50	26° 41' 10 N 077° 08' 16 W
Hope Town	40	26° 32' 07 N 076° 57' 30 W
Man-O-War Cay	40	26° 25' 44 N 077° 00' 15 W
Marsh Harbour	250	26° 33' 35 N 077° 03' 25 W
Moores Island	200	26° 18' 51 N 077° 23' 53 W
Sandy Point	260	26° 01' 30 N 077° 23' 53 W
Treasure Cay	200	26° 40' 08 N 077° 17' 29 W
GRAND BAHAMA		
Basset Cove	400	26° 37' 15 N 078° 19' 21 W
Eight Mile Rock	200	26° 32' 51 N 078° 49' 17 W
Freeport	200	26° 31' 45 N 078° 41' 47 W
Mcleans	200	26° 39' 02 N 077° 57' 24 W
South Riding Point	225	26° 37' 44 N 078° 14' 21 W
West End	150	26° 41' 44 N 078° 58' 27 W
BERRY ISLANDS		
Bullocks	235	25° 49' 20 N 077° 53' 20 W
Chub Cay	200	25° 24' 39 N 077° 54' 03 W
NEW PROVIDENCE		
Coral Harbour	100	25° 00' 08 N 077° 28' 12 W
Delaporte	200	25° 04' 41 N 077° 31' 15 W
Lyford Cay	150	25° 01' 43 N 077° 31' 15 W
Paradise Island	150	25° 04' 50 N 077° 19' 10 W
Perpall's Tract	150	25° 04' 16 N 077° 21' 43 W
Poinciana Drive	200	25° 03' 37 N 077° 21' 15 W
Soldier Road	260 & 220	25° 02' 47 N 077° 19' 10 W
ELEUTHERA		
Current	50	25° 24' 28 N 076° 47' 00 W
Current Island	40	25° 22' 53 N 076° 47' 00 W
Governors Harbour	180	25° 11' 56 N 076° 14' 30 W
Green Castle	240	24° 46' 37 N 076° 12' 54 W
Harbour Island	60	25° 30' 01 N 076° 38' 11 W
Hatchet Bay	265	25° 21' 18 N 076° 28' 50 W
Lower Bog	200	25° 26' 56 N 076° 42' 56 W
Rock Sound	100	24° 52' 00 N 076° 09' 30 W
Savanah Sound	200	25° 05' 17 N 076° 07' 58 W
Spanish Wells	120	25° 32' 34 N 076° 44' 56 W
Tarpum Bay	200	24° 58' 51 N 076° 11' 02 W

LOCATION	HEIGHT IN FEET	POSITION
ANDROS		
Cargil Creek	100	24° 29' 32 N 077° 43' 30 W
Fresh Creek	225	24° 43' 44 N 077° 47' 13 W
Kemps Bay	180	24° 05' 28 N 077° 32' 58 W
Mars Bay	100	25° 52' 06 N 077° 31' 00 W
Nichols Town	255	25° 08' 42 N 078° 02' 40 W
Stanard Creek	200	24° 49' 35 N 077° 54' 07 W
EXUMA		
Barreterre	150	23° 41' 50 N 076° 02' 55 W
Black Point	100	24° 05' 45 N 075° 24' 05 W
Farmers Hill	40	23° 36' 56 N 075° 54' 33 W
George Town	180	23° 30' 07 N 075° 46' 15 W
Highbourne Cay	260	24° 42' 53 N 076° 49' 21 W
Little Farmers Cay	260	23° 57' 21 N 076° 19' 13 W
Rolle Town	40	23° 27' 54 N 075° 42' 25 W
Staniel Cay	260	24° 10' 20 N 076° 26' 30 W
Williams Town	200	23° 25' 22 N 075° 33' 36 W
CAT ISLAND		
Arthur's Town	200	24° 37' 23 N 075° 40' 31 W
Bight	230	24° 17' 26 N 075° 24' 53 W
LONG ISLAND		
Clarence Town	60	23° 05' 50 N 074° 48' 05 W
Deadman's	225	23° 09' 36 N 075° 05' 31 W
Simms	200	23° 29' 45 N 075° 14. 02 W
RUM CAY		
Port Nelson	200	23° 40'00 N 078° 48' 00 W
SAN SALVADOR		
Cockburn	200	24° 03' 07 N 074° 31' 57 W
MAYAGUANA		
Abraham's Bay	175	22° 22' 03 N 072° 58' 05 W
Betsy Bay	104	22° 24' 52 N 073° 08' 05 W

Non-Bahamian Weather Services
SSB Weather Broadcasts

EST	EDT	UT	STATION	FREQUENCY
0030	0130	0530	NMN	4426.0 kHz
			[USCG, Portsmouth, VA]	6501.0 kHz
				8764.0 kHz
0500	0600	1000	NMN	4426.0 kHz
			[USCG, Portsmouth, VA]	6501.0 kHz
				8764.0 kHz
0630	0730	1130	NMN	6501.0 kHz
			[USCG, Portsmouth, VA]	8764.0 kHz
				13089.0 kHz

EST	EDT	UT	STATION	FREQUENCY
0700	0800	1200	WOO	4387.0 kHz
			[AT&T, Manahawkin, NJ]	8749.0 kHz
0700	0800	1200	BASRA Nassau	4003.0 kHz
0720		1220	Bahamas Weather Net [winter]	7096.0 kHz
0720	0820	1220	Bahamas Weather Net [summer]	3696.0 kHz
0720	0820	1220	C6AGG (Carolyn Wardle)	3936.0 kHz
				4003.0 kHz
0730	0830	1230	NCF [USCG, Miami, FL]	VHF Ch 22A
0800	0900	1300	WOM [AT&T, Fort Lauderdale, FL]	4363.0 kHz
				8722.0 kHz
				13092.0 kHz
				17242.0 kHz
				22738.0 kHz
1000	1100	1500	NCF [USCG, Miami, FL]	2670.0 kHz
1100	1200	1600	NMN	6501.0 kHz
			[USCG, Portsmouth, VA]	8764.0 kHz
				13089.0 kHz
1230	1330	1730	NMN	8764.0 kHz
			[USCG, Portsmouth, VA]	13089.0 kHz
				17314.0 kHz
1700	1800	2200	NMN	6501.0 kHz
			[USCG, Portsmouth, VA]	8764.0 kHz
				13089.0 kHz
1700	1800	2200	WOO	4387.0 kHz
			[AT&T, Manahawkin, NJ]	8749.0 kHz
1730	1830	2230	NCF [USCG, Miami, FL]	VHF Ch 22A
1800	1900	2300	WOM	4363.0 kHz
			[AT&T, Fort Lauderdale, FL]	8722.0 kHz
				13092.0 kHz
				17242.0 kHz
				22738.0 kHz
1830	1930	2330	NMN	6501.0 kHz
			[USCG, Portsmouth, VA]	8764.0 kHz
				13089.0 kHz
2000	2100	0100	WOM	4363.0 kHz
			[AT&T, Fort Lauderdale, FL]	8722.0 kHz
				13092.0 kHz
				17242.0 kHz
				22738.0 kHz
2250	2350	0350	NCF [USCG, Miami, FL]	2670.0 kHz
2300	2359	0400	NMN [USCG, Portsmouth, VA]	4426.0 kHz
				6501.0 kHz
				8764.0 kHz

NOAA and Other Weather Services

Time Signal Radio

WWV	best at night	2500.0 kHz
[Fort Collins, CO]	best at night	5000.0 kHz
Storm warnings 8 min. after the hour	night or day	10000.0 kHz
	best by day	15000.0 kHz
	best by day	20000.0 kHz

NOAA Radio Stations

KEC-50	NOAA Weather Radio, West Palm Beach	WX-3	162.475 MHz
KHB-34	NOAA Weather Radio, Coral Gables	WX-1	162.55 MHz
WXJ-95	NOAA Weather Radio, Key West	WX-2	162.40 MHz

Gulf Stream data broadcasts:

Monday, Wednesday, and Friday	between 1600 and 2000
Tuesday, Thursday, and Saturday	between 0400 and 0800

SSB Radio Weather Nets

EST	EDT	UT	STATION	FREQUENCY
0600	0700	1200	Caribbean Weather Net	7240.0 kHz
0610	0710	1110	Puerto Rico Weather Net	3930.0 kHz
1810	1910	2310	Puerto Rico Weather Net	3930.0 kHz
0745	0845	1245	Waterway Net (Bahamas, SW N Atlantic, FL coastal)	3964.0 kHz
				7268.0 kHz
1900	2000	2400	Hurricane Net or as required	14325.0 kHz
				14275.0 kHz
1515	1615	2015	Southbound Two Herb Hilgenberg	12359.0 kHz

Weather by Telephone

Nassau Meteorological Service	242-377-7040	in Nassau dial 915
National Hurricane Center [Coral Gables]	305-229-4483 Fax 305-229-9901	also 305-229-4470
National Climatic Data Center	704-271-4800 Fax 704-271-4876	Gulf Stream data

Weather by Internet

National Hurricane Center	http://www.nhc.noaa.gov
NOAA Weather Service	http://www.nws.noaa.gov
The Weather Channel	http://www.weather.com
USA Weather	http://www.intellicast.com
WXP: The WeatherProcessor	http://www.atms.purdue.edu
Yahoo! Weather	http://www.yahoo.com

Weatherfax

NMF   6340.5, 9110.0, and 12750.0 kHz   [US Coast Guard, Marshfield, MA]

AREAS OF INTEREST

The Bahamas lie within the area 20° N to 30° N and 070° W to 080° W. In weatherfax terms your principal areas of interest are therefore:

Area 3	15° N to 65° N 40° W to 95° W
Area 5	20° N to 55° N 55° W to 95° W
Area 8	18° N to 38° N 62° W to 98° W
Area 10	18° N to 38° N 65° W to 82° W

Broadcasts are transmitted four times each 24 hours, starting with a test pattern and a schedule of broadcast. As these schedules may change, for details see Reed's Nautical Almanac for the North American East Coast for the current year. At press time the start of these broadcasts were:

NMF WEATHERFAX BROADCASTS

EST	EDT	UT
0300	0400	0800
0920	1020	1420
1400	1500	1900
2130	2230	0230

Conversion Tables and Useful Measurements

Tides: Rule of Twelfths

HOUR	RISE/FALL	SUM
1	1/12th	1/12
2	2/12th	3/12
3	3/12th	6/12
4	3/12th	9/12
5	2/12th	11/12
6	1/12th	12/12

Distance Equivalents

1 Degree of Latitude	60.00 nm	111.120 km
1 Minute of Latitude	1.00 nm	1.852 km
1 Second of Latitude	33.77 yds	30.880 m

Seconds to Thousands (Latitude)

SECONDS	THOUSANDS	IN TWO FIGURES	LOG COUNT
05	083.33	08	0.083
10	166.66	17	0.166
15	249.99	25	0.249
20	333.32	33	0.333
25	416.65	42	0.416
30	499.98	50	0.500
35	583.31	58	0.583
40	666.64	67	0.666
45	749.97	75	0.749
50	833.30	83	0.833
55	916.63	92	0.916
60	999.99	00	0.999

1 second = 101.33 feet = 33.77 yards = 30.88 meters

Nautical Miles to Miles

1 nm = 1.15 mile. 1 mile = 0.86 nm

NMS	MILES	MILES	NMS
1.0	1.15	1.0	0.86
5.0	5.75	5.0	4.30
10.0	11.50	10.0	8.60

Depth

1 fathom = 6 feet = 1.83 meters
1 foot = 0.305 meters
1 meter = 3.281 feet

Fathoms and Feet–Feet–Meters

FATHOMS AND FEET	FEET	METERS
0_3	3	1
1_1	7	2
1_4	10	3
2_1	13	4
2_4	16	5
3_2	20	6
3_5	23	7
4_2	26	8
5	30	9
5_3	33	10
6	36	11
6_3	39	12
7_1	43	13
7_4	46	14
8_1	49	15
8_4	52	16
9_2	56	17
9_5	59	18
10_2	62	19
11	66	20

Magnetic Variation

VARIATION WEST	VARIATION EAST
True to Mag: ADD VARIATION	True to Mag: SUBTRACT VARIATION
Mag to True: SUBTRACT VARIATION	Mag to True: ADD VARIATION
[Variation West Compass Best]	[Variation East Compass Least]

Weights

Diesel oil	1 US gallon	7.13 lbs
Fresh water	1 US gallon	8.33 lbs
Gasoline	1 US gallon	6.1 lbs
Salt water	1 US gallon	8.56 lbs

Provisioning Checklist

ABANDON SHIP PACK
pre-prepared Panic Bag or
pre-list items to take

BOAT SAFETY
flares and smoke
dye markers
distress flag
EPIRB
MOB equipment

COMMUNICATIONS
hand-held VHF
cellular telephone

FRESH FOOD ITEMS
milk
orange juice
butter or margarine
yogurt
sour cream
eggs
meats for sandwiches
hot dogs

CHEESE
cheese slices
grated cheese
Parmesan
Philadelphia

FRUIT & VEGETABLES
cabbages
carrots
cucumber
garlic
grapefruit
green bananas
green beans
green peppers
Iceberg lettuce
lemons
limes
melon
onions
oranges
potatoes
squash
sweet potatoes (yams)
unripe tomatoes
zucchini
fresh herbs in pots
flowers or pot plant(s)

FREEZER
bacon
best ground beef
chicken pieces
frozen vegetables
ice cream
frozen yogurt
sausages
shrimp

CANS
chick peas
chili beans
coconut milk
corn
corned beef
corned beef hash
ham
mushrooms
red kidney beans
tomatoes
tomato paste
pasta sauces
olives
salmon
spaghetti sauce
tuna
water chestnuts

SOUPS
variety of canned soups

DRY GOODS & PASTA
rice, plain, brown, and wild
Granola
flour
packet soups
instant mashed potato
dried lentils and beans
bouillon cubes
sugar
variety of pastas

SAUCES
chutney
Dijon mustard
hot dog mustard
jams and marmalade
Marmite
mayonnaise
soy sauce
Tabasco
tomato ketchup
variety of oils and vinegars
Worcestershire sauce

HERBS & SPICES
salt
black pepper
black peppercorns
chilli powder
curry powder
dried basil
dried chives
dried mint
dried parsley
Italian seasoning

COFFEE, TEAS
tea
coffee
sugar substitute
UHT milk

SNACKS
mixed nuts
nachos
potato chips
cheese balls

DRINKS
fruit juices
mixers
sodas
water
beer, wine, or liquor

PAPER GOODS
foil
garbage bags
paper towels
plastic wrap
plastic bags (quart & gallon)
tissues
toilet paper

CLEANERS etc.
ant and roach traps
air fresheners
cold water soap powder
cleaning cloths and handy wipes
Joy dishwashing liquid
matches and cigarette lighter
mosquito coils
Murphy's Oil Soap
nightlights
rubber gloves
scouring pads
white vinegar for the heads
window cleaner
wood polish

bilge cleaner
boat soap, Spray 9, fender cleaner
bucket with lanyard
clothes hangers
clothes pegs and clothes line
deck swab, squeegee, sponges
dust pan and brush, small wet/dry vacuum
holding tank biodegradable active agent
scrubbing brush, sponges, rags
sewing kit
toilet brush, toilet plunger

DRUGSTORE
after sun lotion
antiseptic cream
Band Aids
body lotion/hand cream
dental floss
deodorant
insect repellant
mouthwash
shampoo
soap
sunscreen
toothpaste and toothbrushes
vitamins
check ship's medical pack

BASIC GALLEY EQUIPMENT
nonstick cooking pans including fry pan, medium and small saucepan, kettle, baking tray, and pressure cooker
plastic bowls and plates, coffee mugs, glasses
knives, forks, spoons
kitchen knives, wooden spoons, ladle, grater, bottle opener, can opener, corkscrew, ice pick
sieve
mixing/serving bowls
plastic food and drink containers
measuring cup
chopping boards

kitchen timer
garbage pail
washing up brush

LINEN AND BEDDING
drying up cloths
pillows, blankets
sheets
towels, beach towels

PAPERWORK
Passports
Health certificates (only if going on)
Ship's Papers
FCC license
Log Book
credit cards
cash and traveler's checks
camera(s) and film
Polarized sunglasses
Bahamas courtesy flag
Q flag
US ensign

SWIMMING GEAR
masks, snorkels, fins, gloves
scuba gear
pole spears
spare rubber slings

FISHING GEAR
rods, reels, lures
handlines
spare leaders and hooks
gaff

MISCELLANEOUS
tool kit
flashlights
spare dry batteries
tender anchor and rode
inflatable repair kit
binoculars
hand-held compass

BOAT SPARES
oils and lubricants
bulbs, fuses
impellers
filters (fuel and oil)
spare pumps
spark plugs
spare belts
rebuild Heads kit
spare injector
gaskets, hose clamps
duct tape

CENTER FOR WHALE RESEARCH, INC.
a 501(c)(3) non-profit organization

BAHAMAS MARINE MAMMAL SURVEY

Help us to document the presence of marine mammal species in the Bahamas and adjacent waters. Please record the following information and take photographs of species encountered, if possible.

Observers Name(s) _____

Vessel Name _____

Location _____

Date _____ Time _____

# of Animals_____ Species _____

Size (in feet) _____ Color _____

Spots or Stripes? _____

Comments _____

_____

IDENTIFICATION GUIDE:

dolphin
7-14 ft.
grey

pilot whale
12-20 ft
black

beaked whale
16-25 ft.
brown/grey

sperm whale
40-60 ft.
brown

humpback whale
25-45 ft.
black

If near Marsh Harbour, Abaco, you may contact the survey team on VHF channel 65A or 16 (call sign **Widgeon**). Alternatively you can mail this form to:

Bahamas National Trust   or   **Center for Whale Research**
P.O. Box N-4105   P.O. Box 1577
Nassau   Friday Harbor, WA 98250

If you would like a summary of the results of this survey or more information about marine mammals in the Bahamas, please include the following information.

Street Address _____

City_____State_____Zip Code_____

Country_____Phone No._____

Afterword
The Dolphin Voyaging Guide Team

MATHEW WILSON

After a career in the British Army during which he traveled widely and served in every quarter of the globe, Mathew Wilson became the Executive Director of the Wilderness Foundation (UK) and pioneered camel and foot safaris in Kenya and wildlife tours in India concerned entirely with conservation and environmental education. Moving to live in the US, he turned to writing and lecturing. His current lecture series, developed over ten years, has as its theme the influence of early voyaging on the spread of civilization. His lectures have been given for five of the premier cruise lines on voyages in the Atlantic, Pacific, and Indian Oceans, and the Aegean, Mediterranean, and Caribbean Seas.

Mathew Wilson's first introduction to the Bahamas was in 1952. In 1990–92, pursuing a long-held ambition, he took a 26-foot Heavenly Twins catamaran, *Terrapin*, from England to Florida by way of the French rivers and canals, the Mediterranean, the Canary and Cape Verde Islands, Barbados, the Caribbean chain, the Turks and Caicos, and the full length of the Bahamas. His book about this voyage, *Taking Terrapin Home*, was published in 1994. Since 1992 he has returned to the Bahamas each year, and has cruised there under both sail and power.

In 1995 he established Dolphin Voyaging primarily to take on the writing of this new cruising guide to the Bahamas, with the secondary aim of setting a new standard in marine guides. This guide has been the first step in a development that will eventually embrace CD-ROMs and internet services. He and his wife Janet have a home in Jupiter, Florida, and spend the summer months restoring a once long-neglected small farm in Vermont. He is a certified Divemaster and a member of the Explorers Club.

JANET WILSON

Janet Wilson has traveled widely, both with her husband as well as independently, taking in both Russia and China. A talented gardener and garden designer she would tell you that her Vermont paradise carries a far higher rating in her heart than boats and cruising, but the long Vermont winters with five feet of snow on the ground have reinforced the appeal of the Bahamas, and the attraction holds until the first daffodils break through the last pockets of New England snow crust.

Janet provided the inspiration, the framework, and the targets for the Yellow Pages, the "shore" side of the Guidebook and, hardly surprisingly, the advice on commissioning and provisioning. Without her patient dedication, and hours spent locked in near-mortal combat with a cantankerous computer, this book might not have reached its final form. Under her direction a succession of volunteer researchers have added to our information bank, covering the islands from top to bottom, literally from Walkers Cay to Great Inagua. Somehow Janet found time to manage all our travel arrangements.

The Research Team

The book could not have been written in the time frame we set without the help of our volunteers, willing to talk to everyone they met in the Islands, see everything there was to see and do everything there was to do in every place, live life to the full, and then put it all down on paper. This team included **Sophie Bell**, a member of the Americas and Caribbean Team of PWS International Insurance Brokers in London and at Lloyds, who twice took time to join us, and covered most of the Abacos. Her highpoints? The island life in Green Turtle Cay, everything from looking for sand dollars to jumping up to the music of the Gully Roosters, and above all, being missed when we went away and greeted as a friend when we returned.

Delaying a post-university plunge into a business career, **Victoria Makepeace-Warne** saw the Bahamas from the remoteness of Cherokee Sound to the heart of Nassau. Somehow she survived. Her most telling images? Having milk coconuts cracked to go with the rum in Pete's Pub in Little Harbour, and running aground (no, not our boat, in an inflatable!) in mid-Bank in the Northern Berry Islands.

A trained diver and a veteran ex-member of the team that had laid the foundation for a new national maritime park in Tanzania, Africa, **Helen Platt** saw Eleuthera from top to bottom and the wilds of Andros, dived the barrier reef, and survived two memorable squalls and a run back to Florida just ahead of Hurricane Bertha in 1996.

Michael Sponable came to us from Falls Church, Virginia, during a gap in his teaching career. A graduate marine biologist and a diver, Mike saw more shallow-water work than he had bargained for, as time and again we found ourselves setting and resetting anchors as we made our way around the Out Islands in weather that was not so good.

Sadly, **Deborah Spanton** had her time curtailed when a lightning strike took out most of our electronics, but Cat Island was her territory until fate intervened in the Central Exumas.

A Look Forward to the Next Edition

In our next edition, the **Millennium Edition** of **The Bahamas Cruising Guide**, we intend to start bringing air photographs into our guide on a limited, highly selective basis. Up to this time our judgment has been that air photographs are of interest but of questionable naviga-tional value in a cruising guide. All too often the shot has been taken from the wrong angle, the field of view is too restrictive, and the photograph dates, for the land scene changes and sandbores change. This business of dating is a major concern, for magazine-standard air photography is expensive, and to stay right up to date with air coverage could significantly affect the produc-tion costs of the Guide. But we shall try (perhaps over the run of more than one edition) to see how far we can usefully go down this road.

We'll cover Nuevitas Rock, which we failed to cover at first hand in this Edition, and who knows, we may even dive Hogsty Reef. We will add new sections to our Green Pages on Baha-mian cuisine, and Bahamian trees and flowers. Above this, we plan to select one place we think special as a feature "Cruising Target" in each future edition. It'll be somewhere you might not have thought of including in your itinerary, and we'll package in one page all the information you need to get there. Finally, we hope that whatever may be improved in this Guide will be improved, and that where we have got it wrong, with your help we will get it right.

A Recruitment Notice

A guidebook covering an area the size of the Bahamas faces a dilemma in its updating. You need more time than you might guess to cover the area, and the weather factor is bound to cut in somewhere along the line. But start the process too soon, and inevitably you'll be out of date when you go to print. Leave it too late, and you'll never make your print date unless you have a small army of researchers. Of course there's a middle way. For "small army" read "small navy," and let the updating be continuous, for it is never-ending and our files are never closed. You, the readers of **The Bahamas Cruising Guide**, are that small navy. We welcome your notes and observations.

You've seen how we divided the Bahamas geographically into cruising grounds, each with its contiguous island groups. Most of you have, we're certain, your favorites, a particular affin-ity for a particular island group, or indeed an entire cruising ground. If you spend time there each year and might wish to consider a commitment to Dolphin Voyaging to help us update this guide, would you let us know? We are feeling our way forward into how we might best approach this commitment, and all our options are open.

Dolphin Voyaging, Inc.
1340 US Highway 1, Suite 102
Jupiter, FL 33469
561-745-0445
Fax 561-745-0650

Don't be disappointed if our response to contributions, suggestions, or inquiries is delayed. The laptop computer has given us the ability to spend more time away from base than tied to a desk, and we take advantage of it. But wherever we are, we stay in touch.